Barry Chant's exploration of the origins and developments of the Pentecostal movement in Australia breaks new ground and opens up avenues for further research. Dr Chant tells for the first time the fascinating history of the early movement in Australia and explodes some popular myths about Pentecostal beginnings. This is a book that should be read by scholars interested in a new historical perspective. It is also a book for anyone who just wants to sit down and enjoy a good read.
—*Walter J. Hollenweger,*
  Internationally acclaimed historian of Pentecostalism.
  Former Professor of Mission at the University of Birmingham,

Barry Chant, who has been well known for decades as a Charismatic educator and leader in Australia, will now be equally well known for his Ph.D. dissertation that is now published as *The Spirit of Pentecost*. This book is an excellent example of historical research and writing and is a valuable addition to the literature on worldwide Pentecostalism. In this book, which covers the years from 1870 to 1939, we learn in what ways Australian Pentecostalism was uniquely different from the movement in other parts of the world. His research on the Wesleyan roots of the Australian Pentecostal movement is a particularly valuable contribution to the literature. I highly recommend this book to everyone who wants to understand the roots of Australian Pentecostalism, one of the most dynamic, influential and expanding movements in the world.
—*Vinson Synan,*
  Professor of Church History,
  Dean Emeritus, Regent University, Virginia.

Premier Australian historian and theologian Barry Chant, in his monumental study *The Spirit of Pentecost*, challenges ecclesiastical presuppositions on the origins and development of the Australian Pentecostal movement. With lucidity and a prophetic-edge, Chant's careful research establishes the movement's beginnings firmly in the Australian cosmopolitan middle class, predominately in rural regions, and mainly run by women in full-orbed leadership roles.

This experiential religious phenomenon was founded under the British influences of the Wesleyan and Keswick movements and the ministry of John Alexander Dowie, and its outstanding growth coupled with a compulsory encounter with God in the baptism of the Holy Spirit and the practice of glossolalia. Chant's case clearly argues that if this Pentecostal movement is to continue its impetus into the twenty first century then an understanding of the historic origins and development together with a reflective reassessment on its potential is essential. And so is the reading of this fascinating historical analysis to all who follow the Spirit of Christ.
—*Robert L. Gallagher,*
  Associate Professor of Intercultural Studies,
  Wheaton College Graduate School, Wheaton, Illinois.

In his account of the first half-century of Australian Pentecostalism, its much-revered historian gives us here the fruit of more than three decades of research. This is authoritative history, more wonderful than myth, and full of surprises. The earliest Australian Pentecostal we learn was most likely to be born in Australia, humble, self-effacing, female, and middle-class, with a passion to serve the poor, the Indigenous people and the unsaved overseas. In the same painting are the colours we do love to see: extraordinary gifts, the Baptism of the Spirit with the sign of tongues, healing and revival. There are the saints, such as Sarah Jane Lancaster and Isabella Hetherington. And there are the squabbles, between those who believed that their interpretation of Scripture was fashioned by their own experience of God and could not therefore be denied. This would be more than enough, but there's more! Barry Chant has the gift of writing – so this is a great read.
—*Stuart Piggin*
Historian, Director of the Centre for Christian Thought and Experience, Macquarie University, Sydney, Australia.

This is the long awaited scholarly account of the rise of Pentecostal movements in Australia. With the whole world singing tunes from the far south, I welcome the fact that this, the authoritative account of Australian Pentecostalism by the author who invented the genre, should now be made available by Emeth Press. It will be of interest not only to academics and their students, but to anyone who wants to understand from a non-North American perspective how Pentecostalism percolated into the world and remade the global religious landscape.
—*Mark Hutchinson,*
Historian,
Associate Professor, Alphacrucis College, Sydney, Australia.

Barry Chant is a prolific writer and astute scholar. His history of the Pentecostal movement in Australia paints a rich and carefully nuanced account of "the South Land of the Spirit." Moreover, no one is better qualified to explore the unique contours of Pentecostalism "down under." This book helps us see the beauty and diversity in the global church.
—*Cheryl Bridges Johns*
Professor of Discipleship and Christian Formation,
Pentecostal Theological Seminary, Cleveland Tennessee.

What an inspiring story! I just could not put Barry Chant's book down as I felt I was actually there with Sarah Jane Lancaster, Fred Van Eyk, William Booth-Clibborn, William Cathcart, Ernest Kramer and all the other colourful characters. I found myself worshipping Jesus with both joy and tears as I reflected on the miraculous signs that followed these early pioneers and by their sheer dogged determination under great hardship to share the Good News about Jesus. Their selfless commitment and sacrificial servant-hood cannot help but awe those of us who are following in their footsteps.

The author's scholarly research, storytelling ability, sound analysis and sensitivity to our present 21st century needs offer invaluable lessons for all who are committed to an authentic Pentecostal ministry experience.

—*Bill Vasilakis*
   Senior Minister Christian Family Centre Association of Churches
   National Chairman, CRC Churches International

General Editor's Introduction

Asbury Theological Seminary Series in World Christian Revitalization Studies

This volume is published in collaboration with the Center for the Study of World Christian Revitalization Movements, a cooperative initiative of Asbury Theological Seminary faculty. Building on the work of the previous Wesleyan/Holiness Studies Center at the Seminary, the Center provides a focus for research in the Wesleyan Holiness and other related Christian renewal movements, including Pietism and Pentecostal movements, which have had a world impact. The research seeks to develop analytical models of these movements, including their biblical and theological assessment. Using an interdisciplinary approach, the Center bridges relevant discourses in several areas in order to gain insights for effective Christian mission globally. It recognizes the need for conducting research that combines insights from the history of evangelical renewal and revival movements with anthropological and religious studies literature on revitalization movements. It also networks with similar or related research and study centers around the world, in addition to sponsoring its own research projects.

Barry Chant's carefully researched interpretation of Australian Pentecostal Churches breaks new ground in engaging and assessing the impact of Pentecostal history and doctrine upon that Continent. It complements similar studies documenting the impact of Pentecostal work in other continents, thereby helping to document the amazing phenomenon of the rapid world Pentecostal ascendancy in the twentieth century and beyond. As such, it appropriately contributes to the research objectives of this Series and that of the Center for the Study of World Christian Revitalization Movements.

—J. Steven O'Malley, Director
  Center for the Study of World Christian Revitalization Movements
  Asbury Theological Seminary

Sub-Series Foreword

Pentecostal and Charismatic Studies

Of all the renewal traditions that have engaged the theological landscape, the Pentecostal Movement has undoubtedly made the most significant impact since it emerged at the turn of the twentieth century. Starting as a revival in a small African-American congregation on Azusa Street in Los Angeles, California, the movement soon swept the world, establishing itself in more than forty countries in the first three years. One hundred years later Pentecostalism has grown to an estimated 500 million global adherents or approximately twenty-five percent of all of Christendom. In the same manner that Wesleyanism burst beyond the bounds of Methodism to embrace an interdenominational holiness movement following the American Civil War in the nineteenth century, Pentecostalism transcended denominational lines in the form of the Charismatic Movement during the second half of the twentieth century.

This sub-series is designed to explore the historical, theological and intercultural dimensions of these twin twentieth-century restorationists' traditions from a global perspective. This volume presents the definitive interpretation of Pentecostalism during the first fifty years of the movement's history in Australia. This monograph is the culmination of over thirty years of research and reflection as the author grounds the movement roots in the nineteenth century soil of Australian culture and Wesleyan/Keswick theological heritage. Chant also breaks new ground by providing a detailed analysis of the early ministry of John Alexander Dowie who would later become so instrumental for the emergence of the Pentecostal Revival in the United States. The author then goes on to trace the development of Australian Pentecostalism and analyze some of its most salient features.

—D. William Faupel
   Sub-Series Editor, Pentecostal and Charismatic Studies

The Spirit of Pentecost

The Origins and Development of the Pentecostal Movement in Australia, 1870-1939

Barry Chant

The Asbury Theological Seminary Series in World Christian Revitalization Movements in Pentecostal/Charismatic Studies, No. 5

EMETH PRESS
www.emethpress.com

The Spirit of Pentecost:
The Origins and Development of the Pentecostal Movement in Australia, 1870-1939

Copyright © 2011 Barry Chant
Printed in the United States of America on acid-free paper

All rights reserved. No part of this book may be reproduced, or stored in a retrieval system or transmitted in any form or by any means, electronic, mechanical, photocopying, recording, scanning or otherwise, except as permitted by the 1976 United States Copyright Act, or with the prior written permission of Emeth Press. Requests for permission should be addressed to: Emeth Press, P. O. Box 23961, Lexington, KY 40523-3961. http://www.emethpress.com.

Library of Congress Cataloging-in-Publication Data

Chant, Barry.
 The Spirit of Pentecost: The origins and development of the Pentecostal Movement in Australia : 1870-1939 / Barry Chant.
   p. cm. -- (The Asbury Theological Seminary series in world Christian revitalization movements in Pentecostal/Charismatic studies ; no. 5)
 Includes bibliographical references and index.
 ISBN 978-1-60947-013-5 (alk. paper)
 1. Pentecostalism--Australia--History. I. Title.
 BR1644.5.A8C43 2011
 279.408--dc22
                              2010049719

Graphic on front cover is used by permission by Ain Vares,
"The Holy Spirit`s coming on the day of Pentecost" www.ainvaresart.com

Dedication

Thank God this now too tedious task is done
(Although the making of this story has been fun).
Thanks, too, to those who cheered me as I ran
or offered (in due time) a helping hand.
But chiefly to those early pioneers
who freely shared their laughter, love and tears.
Their trailblazing lives in word and deed
are captured here in print for Time to read.
In them the Spirit burned with holy flame.
Their world – and ours – will never be the same.

Invocation

"And now, adorable Spirit, proceeding from the Father and the Son, descend upon all the Churches, renew the Pentecost in this our age, and baptize Thy people generally—O, baptize them yet again with the tongues of fire! Crown this nineteenth century with a revival of 'pure and undefiled religion' greater than that of the last century, greater than that of the first, greater than any 'demonstration of the Spirit' ever yet vouchsafed to men!"
　—William Arthur, *The Tongue of Fire*
　　(London: Wesleyan Conference Office, 1856)

"When the day of Pentecost came, they were all together in one place. Suddenly a sound like the blowing of a violent wind came from heaven and filled the whole house where they were sitting. They saw what seemed to be tongues of fire that separated and came to rest on each of them. All of them were filled with the Holy Spirit and began to speak in other tongues as the Spirit enabled them." Acts 2:1-4

Contents

Tables..xv
Abbreviations...xvii
Foreword..xix
Preface..xxi
Acknowledgements..xxiii

1. The South Land of the Spirit...1
2. The Spirit of Wesleyanism (1870–1908)
   Christian Perfection and the Baptism in the Holy Spirit........................25
3. The Embryonic Spirit of Pentecost (1875–1920)
   John Alexander Dowie and the Ministry of Divine Healing...................59
4. The Spirit of Evangelicalism (1875–1920)
   The Quest for Holiness and the Fullness of the Holy Spirit....................83
5. Following the Spirit (1908–1934)
   Sarah Jane Lancaster and the First Australian Pentecostal Church............107
6. The Spirit of Love (1922–1934)
   Responding to Criticism and the Needs of the Poor 129
7. The Free Flowing Spirit (1926–1934)
   F.B. Van Eyk—Carrying the Message across the Land 153
8. The Spirit of Revival (1925-1939)
   The Pentecostal Church of Australia..189
9. The Spirit of Prophecy (1930-1939)
   The Apostolic Church—New Structures, New Controversies 219
10. Obeying the Spirit (1905-1939)
    Pentecostal Ministry to the Aborigines 239
11. Women of the Spirit
    The Role of Women in Evangelising and Church Planting 263
12. Preaching in the Spirit
    The Content and Focus of Pentecostal Preaching............................301

Appendix A: Bibliographical essay..321
Appendix B: Biographical background material..................................333
Appendix C: The Place of Experience—An Essay on the Significance
            in Early Australian Pentecostalism of an Experiential En-
            counter with God 361
Bibliography..387
Name Index..413
General Index...419

Tables

Table 1. Populations of selected Australian cities and towns 1854-1981...........8
Table 2. Pentecostal occupations 1910-1947..11
Table 3. Occupations in Australia 1933..12
Table 4. Nineteenth century religious groups...27
Table 5. Church membership 1891..29
Table 6. Views of baptism in the Holy Spirit..34
Table 7. Membership Richmond Temple 1928-1942..............................200
Table 8. Membership Richmond Temple 1928-1942..............................201
Table 9. Comparative table of recognition of spiritual gifts........................222
Table 10. Australian Pentecostal women in ministry prior to 1939...............291
Table 11. Topics of articles in Pentecostal journals 1913-1945...................307
Table 12. Comparison of topics in Pentecostal journals...........................307
Table 13. Summary of topics in 177 sermons of W.J.Enticknap 312

Abbreviations

AAA = Australian Aborigines' Advocate
ADB = Australian Dictionary of Biography
ADEB = Australian Dictionary of Evangelical Biography
AE = Australian Evangel
AFM = Apostolic Faith Mission
AH = Apostolic Herald
AN = Apostolic News
AO = Alpine Observer
APS = Australasian Pentecostal Studies
AV = Authorised Version of the Bible
BCM = South Australian Bible Christian Magazine
BSC = Bible Standard Call
CE = Cessnock Eagle
CM = Courier Mail
Cooee = Canvas Cathedral Cooee
CP = Cairns Post
EG = Echoes of Grace
FGE = Elim Foursquare Gospel Express GC = Gathering Call
GN = Good News
HG = Herald of Grace
JPT = Journal of Pentecostal Theology
JRH = Journal of Religious History KQ = Keswick Quarterly
KJV = King James Version of the Bible
LH = Leaves of Healing
MC = Maryborough Chronicle ND = New Day
NIV = New International Version of the Bible
PT = Pentecostal Times
RE = Revival Echoes
RTS = Richmond Temple Souvenir SC = Southern Cross
SE = Southern Evangel
SMH = Sydney Morning Herald
TLS = Times Literary Supplement
WC = Wesleyan Chronicle

Foreword

Barry Chant, Australian church historian and Senior Pastor of Wesley International Congregation in Sydney, has done the religious world a great service by researching and publishing the first history of the origins of Australian Pentecostalism. This new American edition of this history will introduce his groundbreaking work more widely to both religious historians and the Pentecostal community in the United States.

As most historians of religion know, Pentecostalism was the fastest growing branch of world Christianity during the latter part of the twentieth century, and that phenomenal growth has continued unabated into the twenty-first century. Australian Pentecostal churches have been a part of that growth, despite the fact that Australian Christianity in general has been stagnant during this period. However, Australian Pentecostalism, like many things in Australia, has exhibited distinctive characteristics that do not fit into the accepted historical and sociological theories. Chant lays bare these distinctive features in this book.

After discussing the three main sources of the Pentecostal Movement in Australia (Wesleyanism with its emphasis on entire sanctification and the baptism of the Holy Spirit, John Alexander Dowie and his stress on divine healing and separation from the world, and the Evangelical Movement and its desire to win the nation for Christ), Chant then unravels the dynamic, sometimes stormy, history of early Pentecostalism in his country. His narrative is honest and straightforward, revealing a fresh, innocent movement that is at the same time often embroiled in controversy, both internal and external. Early Australian Pentecostalism was not well received in many quarters, religious and secular, because of its enthusiasm, its emphasis on speaking in tongues, its habit of "dancing in the spirit," its stress on faith healing and its insistence that the end of the world was near.

He also notes the unique role played by women in they early days of the movement. Sarah Jane Lancaster, for example, established the first permanent Pentecostal assembly on Australian soil in 1909, and continued to work for the extension of the movement until her death in 1934. In fact, women founded over half of the first thirty Pentecostal congregations, and they continued to play an important and equal role with men in the further expansion of the movement from 1909 to 1939. Along with the surprising openness to women's ministry in the churches, Chant reveals that early Pentecostals also engaged in extensive evangelism and welfare work among the poor and among the Aboriginal people.

Chant is a scholarly insider, and his analysis of the movement is lovingly critical. This means that his view of the movement between 1909 and 1939 is both insightful and enlightened. American Evangelicals in general and Pentecostals in particular can learn much from Chant's account of the Australian experience.

—Robert D. Linder
University Distinguished Professor of History
Kansas State University

Preface

When a year or so before I planned to begin this work an arsonist set fire to my office and many valuable and unique documents perished – documents I had painstakingly collected for many years – it was a huge setback. Nevertheless, as with Micah, it was a time to rise again and continue the task. The result was a doctoral dissertation and now, at last, this publication.

In this monograph I hope to show that Australian Pentecostalism exhibits distinctive elements that do not fit accepted historical and sociological theories. Neither the deprivation theories of the 1970s and 80s nor more recent sociological and psychological explanations are adequate to explain its development.

I will also argue that the movement's major contribution to Australian Christianity lies in its rekindling of an openness to experiential religion, specifically through the baptism in the Holy Spirit accompanied by speaking in tongues, and that this has been both a strength and a weakness. Then it will be seen that the movement grew from three major nineteenth century tributaries. These were the Wesleyan movement with its emphasis on entire sanctification; the ministry of John Alexander Dowie with its focus on divine healing and separation from the world; and the Evangelical movement, with its fervent and growing desire for revival.

The early development will then be examined. This was mainly attributable to Sarah Jane Lancaster who was the outstanding pioneer of Australian Pentecostalism. She was responsible for the establishing of many local churches, she engaged in extensive welfare work during the Depression and there was a strong emphasis on experiencing the presence and power of God, especially through 'Tarry meetings.' Although certain unorthodox beliefs marginalised her from the Evangelical mainstream, her life and ministry were highly influential in the early development of the movement.

This study will then trace the origins and development of three extant Pentecostal denominations — the Assemblies of God, the International Church of the Foursquare Gospel and the Apostolic Church. It will be seen that while local leadership was indigenous, there was a strong multicultural element in these groups. Disputes over doctrine reflected the dilemma that arises when experience-based approaches to Scripture prove to be in conflict with each other.

Dedicated and determined efforts to take the gospel to the Aborigines will be considered. In spite of limited resources and the fragile state of the early movement, there was ongoing mission among the indigenous people.

Three aspects of the dynamics of the movement will then be discussed. First, the role of women. The Spirit was seen to be bestowed on both men and women equally and so, in the initial three decades, women had a unique freedom to preach, administer the sacraments and lead churches. Over half of the first thirty Pentecostal congregations were founded by women.

Secondly, for all its emphasis on the spontaneous work of the Spirit, Pentecostal preaching was not confined to this. An analysis of extant sermons reveals a range of topics and a primary focus on the Second Coming, Christian living and the work of the Holy Spirit.

Thirdly, it was their experience of God through the Holy Spirit that motivated the early Pentecostals. Historically, it will be seen that the movement's distinctiveness has rested in its enshrining of the practice of glossolalia in an experiential encounter with God.

The phrase 'spirit of Pentecost' is used in this work both in reference to the Holy Spirit and to the ethos and spirit of the movement. The context will usually indicate the intended meaning.

—Barry Chant
January 2011

Acknowledgements

Particular thanks go to my wife Vanessa who waited patiently and cheerfully for a long, long time, for the final word to be written, and then enacted justice by launching into a research program of her own. Also to Professor Jill Roe who guided me safely through the exciting and sometimes treacherous paths of historical research; and to Dr William Faupel for his incisive and kindly editorial skills and his enthusiasm to see this book in print.

And gratitude beyond measure to the host, too large to be named, of family members, supervisors, colleagues, associates, students and friends who encouraged me in what was at times a lonely task – especially to those kindly faithful saints who unveiled their memoires for me, offered me rare documents, produced treasured photos, fossicked for long-buried papers, made suggestions, introduced me to other pioneers and, in their own way, worked together with me to tell a story that would otherwise have remained untold.

CHAPTER ONE

THE SOUTH LAND OF THE SPIRIT

Distinctive Aspects of the Pentecostal Movement in Australia, Socio-economic Factors, the Practice of Glossolalia, and the Nature of Pentecostalism

Over a half-century ago, Herbert Butterfield related how frustrated he and other examiners were with a student who ascribed everything to God's direct intervention and saw no need to consider less supernatural factors. This is not to say that Christian historians must ignore divine providence or pretend it does not exist. But clearly the role of a historian of Christianity is to present it from the human perspective as well as the divine; not only to narrate history—as important as narrative is—but also to interpret it in the light of all the relevant material, both informative and critical.[1] As Keith Sewell has pointed out, writing Christian history is not engaging in uncritical hagiography: as far as humanly possible, the picture presented must be objective and fair.[2] This is not as easy as it sounds. Sewell notes the impossibility of constructing an accurate and comprehensive historical narrative—it is now seen, he says, to be a 'hopeless task.'[3]

First, there is the impossibility of gaining all the necessary information to make a definitive judgement. No matter how extensively we research, we will never be in possession of all the facts. In writing this book, I have been painfully aware of this difficulty. In many cases, I seem to have exhausted every line of inquiry, and yet still found frustrating clefts in the range of information.

Second, there is the problem of human fallibility: even with the best of intentions, complete freedom from bias is unattainable, not so much in the inclinations of which we are aware, but in those more dangerous and subtle bents which lie crocodile-like beneath the surface.[4] In my case, writing Pentecostal history as a Pentecostal inevitably blinds me to some of the faults and follies of the movement, and, no doubt, renders me less incisive in my exploratory surgery than I should be. I may well be too close to my subject to see it clearly enough in the larger scheme of things. On the other hand, my stance also offers me insights, subtleties of understanding and sympathies that another observer might lack. David Clines argues that historians cannot be 'objective observers' but that they are 'interested parties with some personal or institutional ideological investment in the business of reconstructing the past'.[5]

Interpreting history implies presenting critical perspectives that will add to the general understanding.[6] The history of Pentecostalism, for example, may be validly viewed from a number of vantage points—sociological, psychological, ideological, ecclesiastical and the like. But there is a need also for theological, the charismatic and the pastoral.[7] In this work, all these will be evident, with varying degrees of dominance.

We can go further and argue, as Piggin does, for the prophetic role of history 'to discern in all this human business the activity of God and to bring this home to our conscience'.[8] Historiography should not just set down what has happened in the past, but should also present the implications of this for the present and the future. To achieve these goals, there must be a strong interpretive and prophetic element. In a sense, writers of history do not just record it, they also determine it. Anne McLay puts this succinctly when she says, 'The goal is not so much INformation as TRANSformation.' She goes on to ask, 'Could a deeper understanding of the past be a channel of TRANSformation for the people of the present time?'[9] So while a study of Australian Pentecostalism may be viewed quite specifically as a representation of the perceived acts of God in the life of one part of the Christian Church, it is also an analysis of how those acts are to be seen in context and how people have responded to them, interpreted them and been influenced by them. Furthermore, such a study necessarily offers a sense of direction for the future. There is a subtle prophetic flavour. A historian is also a seer.

Because little serious research has yet been carried out on the early history of the Australian Pentecostal movement, this book necessarily contains a high and perhaps even disproportionate degree of narrative, with considerable detail about people, places and events. The dates 1870–1939 have been chosen because the former represents the first known Pentecostal meeting in Australia and the latter the commencement of World War II. Further, by 1939, the Apostolic Church had adopted its national constitution—the last Pentecostal body in Australia to be formally constituted in the pre-War period. This is a pioneering inquiry, and hence a kind of narrative cartography is essential. Without the guidance of this mapping, it is not possible either to explore fully or to appreciate the nature of the movement and the conclusions being drawn. In any case, no matter what we do with it, history is fundamentally *story*. Without the primary narrative, secondary analysis has no meaning.

It is also important that as much of the primary data as possible be made available for further reflection and analysis by others. If future scholars are to have a reliable and comprehensive source on which to draw, there are many important historical incidents which need to be incorporated. A strong structural narrative framework must therefore be established so that researchers and scholars have a rich and reliable lode to mine.

Two major theses emerge in this volume. First, from the beginning, Australian Pentecostalism differed from its overseas cousins in several significant ways. First, it was primarily a middle-class movement, not a movement of the disenfranchised, as has commonly been observed elsewhere. Whereas the popular understanding of Pentecostalism is that its origins were among the poor, in Australia, its origins were among people of relatively comfortable socio-economic status. A comparative study of occupations, for instance, shows that the percentage of Pentecostals involved in professional occupations in the 1930s was roughly double that of the community while the percentage of labourers was approximately half.

Second, in contrast to the beginnings in the United States and Great Britain, where Pentecostalism blossomed in the cities, its earliest expressions in this country were rural rather than urban. Twenty-three of the first 34 Pentecostal congregations in this country were in country towns and many of the pioneers were from farming communities.

Third, many of its earliest leaders were women, in distinction from other Western expressions where men generally took the lead. Over half the Pentecostal congregations functioning by 1930 were established and led by women. In the 1910s and 1920s, women travelled to faraway Perth in the south-west of the continent to Cairns in the distant north-east preaching the faith in the power of the Spirit, usually in the face of great difficulty, but often with striking results. From 1925, male leadership became more and more common, but in the first twenty years, the ministry of women was highly visible.

Fourth, Pentecostalism was both a cosmopolitan and an indigenous movement. Although it is commonly believed that Australian Pentecostalism was an American import, like Mormonism or the Jehovah's Witness movement, in fact, its roots were primarily European.[10] The one church that could be described as resulting from a direct overseas missionary outreach was the Apostolic Church—and this was based in Wales.

The three major tributaries were Wesleyanism, the Dowie movement and the Evangelical movement. Firstly, Wesleyanism. Most nineteenth century Methodist ministers were English-born and overseas connections were generally maintained with England. It was the Wesleyan emphasis on Christian perfection and baptism in the Holy Spirit that formed a fertile seed bed for Pentecostalism. In the latter part of the nineteenth century prominent Wesleyan leaders such as John Watsford and William Taylor were calling for a return to perfectionism and what they called a 'Pentecostal baptism of the Spirit' among Methodists. Some became Pentecostals through responding to that call.

The second tributary was the Dowie movement. Scottish-born John Alexander Dowie spent the first 16 years of his ministry in three States of Australia. When he finally migrated to the USA in 1888, he left a committed group of several hundred people who all held strongly to a belief in divine healing. It was this emphasis on divine healing and the gifts of the Holy Spirit that challenged thousands of people to open their hearts and minds to the possibility of further supernatural manifestations of the Spirit in their own lives. Some of the finest Pentecostal pioneers were formerly Dowieites.

The third tributary was Evangelicalism.[11] Around the turn of the century, the Evangelical movement provoked thousands of Christians to attend prayer meetings and conventions and to engage in widespread evangelism. The Simultaneous Mission of 1902 and the Chapman-Alexander visit in 1909 were widely-acknowledged public expressions of this. Here, there was more American input, with Torrey, Geil, Chapman and Alexander all speaking to large audiences in many places. But the English-inspired Keswick Conventions and locally-led prayer gatherings also touched many people. It was in some of these conventions and prayer gatherings that Pentecostal manifestations such as glossolalia and falling to the floor occurred. Evangelicalism as a whole rejected these, but those who experienced them usually did not. Here was another seed bed where the new movement could take root.

Although there was further American input over the next four decades (Aimee McPherson, A. C. Valdez, Kelso Glover, Mina Brawner), there were also strong and significant contributions from several other countries including England (Smith Wigglesworth, William Booth-Clibborn), India (the Ramabai Mission), Scotland (William Cathcart), South Africa (F. B. Van Eyk) and Wales (John Hewitt).

It is also important to note that the earliest Pentecostal leaders were Australian-born. The first assembly (Good News Hall) was founded and led by an Australian (Sarah Jane Lancaster). Of the first 25 congregations established before the beginning of the church planting work of F. B. Van Eyk from South Africa in 1927, 24 were started by people born in Australia. The ongoing leadership of the Pentecostal Church of Australia through men such as C. L. Greenwood, Philip Duncan and Charles and Will Enticknap, was Australian. The leaders in each of the capital cities in the 1920s were born or raised in this country—Sarah Jane Lancaster, Charles Greenwood and Robert Horne in Melbourne; Frederick and Philip Duncan in Sydney; Florrie Mortomore, Harold Martin and W. A. Buchanan in Brisbane; Edie Anstis and Ruby Wiles in Perth; Joy Heath in Adelaide.[12] In country areas, people like Will Jeffrey and Will Sloan were Australian-born.

Joy Heath.

The second major thesis is that Pentecostalism's primary contribution to Australian Christianity has been its understanding that religious experience is vital to authentic faith. 'The person with an experience,' Pentecostals have argued over and again, 'is never at the mercy of one who has only an argument.' One preacher, prominent in this study, regularly used to declare, 'It's better felt than telt'.[13] Of course, the stirring of the affections has often been part of wider Christian expression, but through Pentecostalism's teaching and practice of baptism and gifts of the Holy Spirit, such a personal perception and knowledge of God has been enshrined as an integral and ongoing element of Christian life.

Historically, this emphasis on an experience of God has been the movement's major drawing power. A study of its first few decades clearly demonstrates this. For most people, the perceived attraction of Pentecostal worship was its focus on an experiential and sensate encounter with God. In this regard, Pentecostalism has filled a gap both in society and the Church. This is likely to be the ongoing contribution of the movement for the future, given that Australians, like all human beings, demonstrate fundamentally religious aspirations, with hearts that, as Augustine would have put it, are restless till they find their rest in God.[14]

On the other hand, I will also attempt to show that, ironically, this focus on experientialism also proved to be a hindrance to the movement's growth. The disagreements over doctrine and practice that occurred amongst the various groups usually resulted from their own spiritual experiences and passionate convictions that they were being led by the Spirit and so could not shift ground. The conflicts between Good News Hall and the Pentecostal Church of Australia and later, between the Apostolic Church and all the other groups, provide ample evidence of this fact.

In recent years, sociological theories of both the Pentecostal movement and Pentecostal phenomena have abounded. These have sometimes been treated with disdain by Pentecostals, in the belief that it is impossible to subject the things of the Spirit to psychological or sociological analysis. However, given that the New Testament itself enjoins us to 'test everything' and to 'test the spirits' to see whether they are from God (1 Thessalonians 5:20–21; 1 John 4:1), there seems no biblical reason to fear in themselves attempts to understand, define or explain spiritual phenomena. From the earliest times, such phenomena have caused varied reactions. The second century charismatic Montanist movement, for example, was seen by the orthodox Church as a dangerous heresy, but by such a notable figure as Tertullian as a genuine work of God.[15]

Harvey Cox's *Fire From Heaven* is a sympathetic and in many ways perceptive analysis of the movement. Initially, Cox sees it as having many of the same qualities as city life—in both cities and Pentecostal meetings there is always a sense of the unpredictable that is attractive and at the same time disturbing. A generation ago, Max Weber also argued for the necessity of an urban environment for the development of a congregational faith.[16] A case in point is the growth of Brazilian Pentecostalism which has reflected the nation's growing urbanization since World War II.[17]

Cox sees a number of reasons for the success of Pentecostalism. In the United States, while liberal theologians 'tried to impart the latest ideas from Europe to their suspicious congregations, the Pentecostal revolution, a genuinely American spiritual revolution, if ever there was one, was bubbling up from underneath.'[18] At the small Pentecostal mission at Azusa Street, in April 1906, with its one-eyed, poorly educated black preacher William Seymour as its leader, its plank seating and its shoe box pulpit, people found acceptance. Racial barriers were broken down.[19] The power of God was experienced in unusual ways—healing, tongues, visions, prostrations and other wonders. Within a week of the revival beginning, the San Francisco earthquake added a note of eschatological urgency. It was a ripe climate for revival.[20]

Cox argues that the disillusionment of the early 1900s, the artificiality of life in Los Angeles and the traumatic effect of the San Francisco earthquake all conspired together to create an apocalyptic atmosphere in which the message of hope presented by Seymour, fell on receptive ears. All in all, argues Cox—

> The revival persuaded participants that the last Days were indeed approaching and that they were all pivotal actors in the grand new drama that God's Spirit was preparing to enact. The worm-eaten foundations of Babylon were tottering. The old world was passing away. The glorious city was about to descend. And they, the despised and rejected of the earth were both its beneficiaries and it heralds. No wonder people came, and no wonder they went forth to proclaim the message to the world.[21]

While all this may be true of Los Angeles, in Australia, the early movement was generally rural. The first known Pentecostal meetings were in country Victoria around 1870. Then, while the movement formally began in 1908 with Good News Hall in Melbourne, with another congregation in Ballarat (population around 35,000), it found its first most fertile growth in the farming communities of Queensland. In the 1920's, Ayr's population numbered less than 5000. Bowen's was about half that—a decade later only 2,619. Cairns, Mackay and Maryborough were all between 10,000 and 15,000,[22] while Toowoomba, Rockhampton and Townsville each numbered around 25,000. It was in these small towns that Pentecostalism was firmly planted (see Table One). Similarly, in New South Wales, the first purpose-built Pentecostal building was erected in 1919 near Parkes, a community approaching 5,000 people. By 1929, of the 34 congregations then in existence, two thirds of them (23) were in country

**First purpose built Pentecostal Church Building in Australia at Cleveden, NSW.
Pastor C. Enticknap, centre.**

towns.²³ In Australia, apart from a couple of churches such as Good News Hall, the early strength of Pentecostalism was clearly outside the cities. To see it as an urban phenomenon is to look through the wrong lens.

Deprivation Theories

Weber's distinction between congregational, salvation and rational-ethical religions suggests that Pentecostalism—as a salvation religion—ought to have flourished, like the fourth century African Donatists or the fifteenth century Bohemian Taborites, among the underprivileged.²⁴ Since the earliest days of the movement, it has been common to explain involvement in Pentecostal worship as a result of social or personal deprivation. Pentecostals and non-Pentecostals alike, subscribe to this thesis.²⁵ American religious sociologist Robert Anderson's *Vision of the Disinherited* (1979) is a recent strong attempt to argue this case. Anderson suggests that the original Pentecostals were basically economically deprived, socially mobile or people whose lifestyle was disrupted in some way. In Pentecostalism, they found acceptance and fulfilment. He alleges that Pentecostals are basically to be found in 'the working poor from whose ranks the… movement drew the overwhelming bulk of its recruits'.²⁶ Cox calls this 'a now well-established fact of historical scholarship'.²⁷

Thirty years ago, British sociologist Bryan Wilson argued that 'oppressive, frustrating and bewildering social circumstances' prompted people to join Pentecostal churches, that Pentecostalism 'thrives among dislocated populations' and that Pentecostals were 'relatively simple people with unsophisticated concepts of doctrine and church government'.²⁸ In 1986, Nathan Gerrard suggested that 'almost all' the Holiness churches in Southern Appalacia originated from the lower socio-economic levels of society.²⁹ David Martin, whose particular interest is Latin America, while questioning the prevailing academic dismissal of Pentecostals as 'alien' to the world of the erudite, notes that from the beginning 'Pentecostals were disproportionately poor, black and female'.³⁰ Other writers agree.³¹ Ofelia Ortega puts it plainly: 'I have visited Pentecostal churches in Chile, Peru, Nicaragua, and Brazil. In almost all of them, I have found the poorest and most excluded strata of society. Pentecostalism has become the "religion of the poor" in Latin America.'³² American Pentecostal historian Vinson Synan describes the Pentecostal movement as 'essentially a religion of the socially disinherited and the economically underprivileged'.³³

Roger Thompson describes Australian Pentecostalism, too, as 'a refuge for victims of economic recession and the vicissitudes of rapid social change'.³⁴ Australian sociologist Alan Black questions this hypothesis and suggests there are other possible considerations.³⁵ He points out that contemporary Australian Pentecostalism attracts people from a wide cross-section of the population and that 'theories such as that Pentecostalism attracts predominantly the socially or economically deprived, do not appear to apply in either Australia or the United States at the present time.'³⁶ Nonetheless, he states categorically that 'in its early stages' the Pentecostal movement in both countries attracted 'mainly people from lower social strata'.

Table 1 Populations of selected Australian cities and towns 1854–1981.[37]

	1854	1864	1880	1901	1911	1933	1981
Townsville		1140 (1871)		7860 (1886)		25876	86112
Adelaide	18303 (1861)			175641 (1906)		312619	882521
Ayr			70		1236	4792	8787
Bowen		717 (1871)		1130		2619	7663
Bright		551 (1871)			972	595	1545
Brisbane		12551		54434			942831
Cairns			278	3537		11993	46557
Geelong	20115	16613		17445 (1891)		39223	125271
Mackay		340 (1868)		3597 (1891)	6135		35361
Maryborough		2929 (1868)		10159	9410	14395 (1947)	20111
Melbourne	53235					991934	257875
Mossman					829		1614
Orange	28 (1851)		1456 (1871)		5263	13780 (1947)	27626
Parkes			1961 (1881)			5846	9047
Perth	1148 (1848)		8447 (1891)		31300	272528 (1947)	80903
Portland		2804 (1861)		2185		4759 (1954)	9353
Rockhampton		6906 (1871)		15461		34988 (1949)	50146
Sydney			99857 (1881)		636353	1235267	287650
Toowoomba	1183 (1861)			7007 (1891)		26423	63401
Townsville		1140 (1871)		7860 (1886)		25876	86112

Walter Hollenweger tends to agree, but points out that it is only when people *feel* deprived that they seek refuge in groups like Pentecostalism. He also alleges that through glossolalia 'power of expression' is restored to people 'without identity and powers of speech' and that they are healed from 'the terror of loss of speech'.[38] Cox follows a similar line. 'Pentecostals succeed,' he argues, 'because they respond with such effectiveness not only to the religious awakening but to a tidal change in what religion itself is and what it means to people.'[39] The expansion of megacities, the shrinking of provincial towns and the resulting dislocation of traditional frameworks, including those of religion, has left many people disillusioned with old ways and structures. Pentecostalism offers them 'new forms of community'—

> At first, this message appealed mainly to the most disenfranchised; those with little stake in the status quo, people with no reason to hope that things would improve. To these wretched of the earth the pentecostals held out the possibility of a radically new order that would come about not because of the patchwork efforts of mere mortals but by the action of a loving God.[40]

Clearly, there are many instances where socially deprived people have found refuge and expression in tongue-speaking communities. Calley's thesis on the West Indian sects in Britain is a case in point.[41] Among other things, Calley noted that people who were despised in the world could become leaders in the context of their congregation, on the basis of their charismatic gifts. On the other hand, as Mayers points out, there are others who like the authoritative and definitive leadership that commonly emerges in Pentecostal assemblies, in contrast to the often uncertain direction being given in the world.[42] During World War II, a Queensland pastor reported that the fear of invasion coupled with a bereavement in the church caused many young people to turn back to God.[43]

In recent times, questions have been raised about the validity of deprivation theories.[44] It now appears the proposition may have been flawed from the very beginning. A. Cerillo asks—

> Were most Pentecostals so economically disinherited, so out on the fringes of society, as suggested by historian Anderson, that they were people whose lives the concept of Progressivism fails to embrace or capture? Interestingly, as Goff makes clear, Parham himself came from a rather economically and socially secure home, studied for three years at Southwest Kansas College, was a talented speaker and obviously had leadership abilities.[45] Although his intellectual and spiritual orientations may have put him at odds with the prevailing religious and academic orthodoxies in late-nineteenth century America, at least socially and economically the young Parham hardly fits the mold [sic] of the marginalised.[46]

Virginia Hine asserts that even if deprivation theories were once acceptable, they are not now. Evidence is mounting that they are simply inadequate to explain the emergence of the Pentecostal movement.[47] The spread of the charismatic movement through the middle-class members of historic denominations since the 1960s is in itself evidence to the contrary. Cox agrees that by the mid-twentieth century, the tide had changed, and it was now among the young and rising affluent that Pentecostalism burgeoned. Here was a new form of disenchantment. The consumer culture had failed to meet the greatest needs—those of the heart and the soul.[48]

Weber distinguishes between the likely origins of congregational, prophetic, salvation and rational-ethical religions, but in many ways, Pentecostalism is a blend of all four. It is clearly congregational, a form of religious expression which Weber suggests can only develop in an urban environment. It is prophetic, with a deep sense of proclaiming the Word of God, and sometimes triumphalist, a trend which is usually seen among the privileged. It is salvation-oriented, which Weber argues would place its origins in the lower classes. It is strongly ethical, which suggests a bourgeois mentality.[49]

In the light of this, it is interesting to assess the accepted wisdom about Pentecostal origins in reference to Australia. In simple terms, deprivation theories just do not work here. The early Pentecostal pioneers did not stem from the disenfranchised. They were not the outcasts or neglected of society. Typical ground-breaking Pentecostal males were likely to be farmers, or small businessmen, or gainfully-employed workers in industry, solid members of the community with stable families, a reasonably secure economic position and a willingness to use their initiative. Pentecostal married women considered their families their primary responsibility but took a keen interest in church or community affairs. Single women may well have had little hesitation in giving themselves to itinerant evangelism or to active involvement, and even leadership, in the local church.

The socially and economically deprived were not strongly represented in these early congregations. From the earliest days of the movement, with the first Pentecostal meetings in Portland, Victoria, in 1870, attempts were made by detractors to dismiss the participants as ignorant, poor people, but the evidence was non-existent. Even during the Depression and early post-Depression years, there was little unemployment among the members.[50] Some of the younger, unmarried women carried out home duties. Otherwise, the majority were gainfully employed.

Given that nearly one third of the work force may have been unemployed in 1932,[51] it is clear that the membership of these churches was not typical of the community at large. Rather than being a congregation of the disenfranchised seeking help, the Pentecostals regularly gave themselves to help the disenfranchised. The Bernhardt home at Ovingham, South Australia, for example, was often open to the needy—whole families being accommodated at times.[52] Similarly, the Apostolic Mission House at Mile End had a steady flow of homeless and needy people living there. There was a small fund at the Mission for the help of the poor.[53] The Fabians, brother and sister, purchased a new Ford motor car between them in order to carry those who had no transport of their own.[54] 'People in the church had means,' recalled Iris Wahlquist. 'My father always had work. He wasn't a wealthy man but we weren't on the poverty line or anything like that. But there were some unemployed people... who came looking for help.'[55] At Good News Hall, in North Melbourne, for several years, there was a comprehensive program of ministry to the poor and needy, with hundreds of unemployed men being fed and clothed every day. Often, jobs were found for them as well.[56]

It is difficult to compare the occupations of Pentecostal people with those of the community at large, because it is impossible to obtain precise figures for any given year. In 1939, there were approximately 70 Pentecostal congregations. It is difficult to know how many people were involved. In the early 1990s, there were around 100 people per ordained minister.[57] It is probable, however, that the average was considerably lower in 1939. Records suggest that a figure of 50 or less per church would be more likely.[58] This would represent a total constituency of 3,500 at most. Given that most women were engaged in domestic duties and that a significant number of attendees were children, there may have been a maximum of 1,200 employed persons.[59] I have been able to analyse the occupations of 206 Pentecostal people over a 35-year period including the names and occupations of 72 pastors and preachers and of 134 active members, which represents around 15% of the total.[60] In the case of some pastors and evangelists, the occupations listed are those in which they were engaged prior to entering the ministry, or those which they continued to pursue, in order to underwrite their church work. It may be that there were other less involved people whose lifestyles might present a different profile, but there does not seem any sound reason to suspect this. Also, only 32 women are included because prior to World War II, few were employed outside the home. For many of those who are listed, the nominated occupation ceased when they married. In the cases where, over a period of years, there was more than one job, I have recorded the primary one.

On occasion, too, it is not clear whether the occupation was that of employer or employee (e.g. carpenter). In these cases, I have usually opted for 'employee'. It is also difficult to draw exact parallels with government figures, as sometimes the grouping of jobs is different. In the 1947 census, for instance, shop keepers were included with shop assistants, although the former were self-employed.[61]

Even allowing for these difficulties, a comparison of Pentecostal employment figures with those of the community at large is illuminating. For example, there was a significantly higher percentage of professional and business people in Pentecostal churches than in the community (see Tables 2 and 3). Whereas around one in ten Australians was engaged in professional employment, over one in five of the group surveyed was so employed. The majority of these were in the lower rather than the higher professional bracket, including several clergymen who transferred from other denominations, with few engaged in high level management. The percentage of small business people was dramatically higher than that for the community—one in five as against one in thirty. Of considerable interest is the fact that the number of workers in industry was about half the national figure. The pattern that emerges is not unlike that of the Victorian Wesleyans in the previous half-century who were 'predominantly petty-bourgeois' with most church attendees being either proprietors of small businesses or skilled tradesmen.[62]

Table 2 Pentecostal Occupation in Australia 1910-1947.

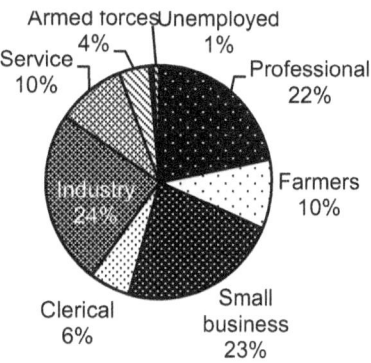

Table 3 Occupations in Australia 1933.

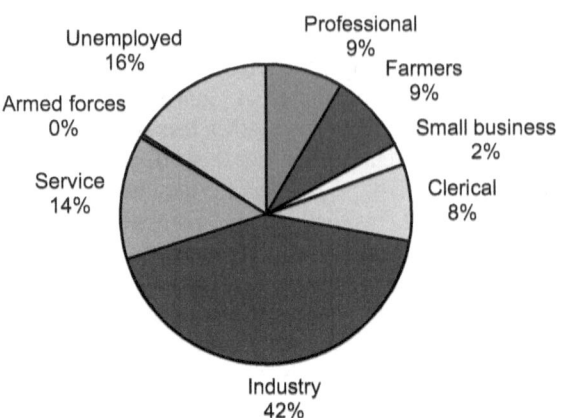

The suburbs from which people came may have reflected a similar picture but there is insufficient data to draw a firm conclusion. In South Australia, for example, while there was a couple from Bowden or Mile End, both inner suburbs in lower socio-economic areas, most members were scattered widely over a range of some 35 different suburbs. There were about ten from Prospect and half a dozen from Kensington-Norwood. Otherwise, no meaningful pattern of social origins emerges.[63] Similarly, in Sydney, while some of the earliest meetings were held in the older suburbs of Leichhardt and Balmain, others were conducted in comfortable, prestigious Northbridge.[64] In Melbourne, the first Pentecostal church was in the inner-city suburb of North Melbourne, but the second was established in Caulfield, and later more leafy Brighton.[65] And as we have already seen, many Pentecostals lived in country towns or on farms.

It is interesting to note the professions and/or occupations of some of the early leaders of the churches in Adelaide, South Australia. Annie Chamberlain served full-time as a captain in the Salvation Army for over ten years.[66] Later she was proprietor of a produce store and manager of a boarding house for blind people. In 1923, she moved to a large house in the inner middle class suburb of Hyde Park.[67] Her son-in-law, Norman Priest, had a small business in Prospect, where he was also the local Postmaster, before he left Adelaide in 1926 to enter full-time ministry.

Pauline Heath, the leader of the Apostolic Mission, had been in business for nearly five years at the time of her conversion as proprietress of the Lone Hand Cafe in Rundle Street, in the CBD.[68] Gustav Jansen was a school teacher of German descent who had spent about ten years teaching in South Australian country schools at remote Elliston and then at the Lower North towns of Terowie and Watervale. For a couple of years, he dabbled in land broking at Point Pass, and then returned to his home town of Eudunda where he tried his hand at running a motor garage. He became a Justice of the Peace, and moved between Adelaide and Eudunda, spending most of his time in Adelaide. He took up a retail agency and eventually bought a house at Mile End that was devoted to the work of the Mission.[69]

Hines Retchford was a commercial traveller. In 1927, he 'relinquished his secular occupation to devote all his time to gospel work' with the South African evangelist F. B. Van Eyk.[70] A. W. Allen had a painting and decorating business. H. Weber was an electrical engineer. L. B. Wheaton had a grocery store. Phil Lovell set up his own electrical business when he moved to Queensland, to pastor a small church there.[71] Norman Fabian, who became honorary pastor of the Apostolic Mission, worked as a clerk in the Treasury Department. In 1940, he resigned both his job and the church to join the Armed Forces.

Among the lay people in the Apostolic Church were young Laurie Wahlquist, who was later to be for many years a senior executive in the Motor Industry [72]; Ross McNeill who became a sharebroker, with his own company;[73] and Iris Bladon, who was a school head mistress.[74] F. C. Payne of the Apostolic Mission was an engineer who was responsible for a number of inventions, including a new fuse box.[75] Later, he established a scenic garden in the northern foothills of the Mount Lofty Range.

O. Chenoweth was a hairdresser and tobacconist at Norwood. Ernie Long owned Charming's Sports Depot, in the city's commercial centre. Francis Bernhardt was a blacksmith and moulder.[76] Among those in clerical jobs were Ruby Broadbent, who worked as a clerk in the Adelaide Town Hall, Marj Fabian, a typist and ledger machinist at Woodroofe's soft drink factory and John Kirwan, a shop assistant. Those in skilled trades were mainly dressmakers, in the case of the women, and mechanics, in the case of the men, including Perce Rogers, nick-named 'the screwdriver king' because of his ability to fix almost anything.[77]

In describing John Cavill, Charles Anstis and, some of the leaders at Good News Hall, North Melbourne, Jeannie Lancaster wrote that their reputation stood just as high in the commercial world as in the religious—a tribute to both their spirituality and their economic position. Cavill was a builder; Anstis was originally a blacksmith and then later a poultry farmer; Adams was a barrister.[78]

The overall picture that emerges of these early Australian Pentecostals is of an enterprising group of people, able to take initiative and often possessing leadership qualities. They were the kind of people who were willing to take risks, to try new ideas and to explore new concepts. It is interesting that Martin has made a similar observation about Pentecostals generally. Of South American Pentecostals, he notes that they are 'self-improving, self-confident and devout,' and even though found initially among the poor, they are not afraid to 'lay the axe to popular culture' and to set about introducing change.[79]

Some evidence for a deprivation theory may be found in the surge forward from 1930 to 1935 with the ongoing work of F. B. Van Eyk, the ministry of William Booth-Clibborn in Brisbane and the emergence of the Apostolic Church through William Cathcart and John Hewitt. The positive, joyful, celebratory approach of these men offered people in a depressed community something to hope for and something to be glad about. The result was three new church groups—the Elim Foursquare Church (1929), Glad Tidings Tabernacle (1929) and the Apostolic Church (1930). On the other hand, well before the effects of the Depression were being felt, there was similar expansion through the work of A. C. Valdez in Melbourne in 1925 and a year later with F. B. Van Eyk in Western Australia, South Australia, Victoria and Queensland and the resultant establishment of both the Pentecostal Church of Australia and the Apostolic Faith Mission.[80]

Tertiary education was not as common among the Pentecostals as in the community generally.[81] Of 87 pastors, for example, only a dozen had attended university (5) or seminary (7) and only eight had undertaken Bible school training. Two of the latter had also completed a post-secondary course.[82] In this respect, the contrast between Pentecostalism and the Brethren, in many ways a similar kind of church group, is striking. While both bodies eschewed traditional denominationalism and ecclesiastical structures and majored on congregational involvement and an experience of God, the Brethren were noteworthy for the level of education represented among their members.[83] Nevertheless, there were some Pentecostal people with university education. Dr Ruby Davy, the first woman in South Australia to earn a doctorate of music, led the choir for a short time at the Apostolic Church.[84] Mina Brawner and Robert Duguid, who was for many years an Apostolic elder, were both medical practitioners.[85] John Adams was a barrister from Dunedin, New Zealand.[86] Sarah Jane Lancaster was a school teacher, as were several other women in the movement.[87] B. Buley, who led the choir at Richmond Temple, had earned two academic music awards.[88] Miss Flett, a foundation member of the Apostolic Church in Perth held an M.A. degree.[89]

Although the value of a sound education was readily accepted, theological education was regarded with some suspicion. At Good News Hall, a small Bible school was established to give those who enrolled a 'thorough working knowledge' of the Scriptures in a course which would both improve their English and strengthen the memory. Practical experience in public meetings and open air work was also offered, together with part-time work in the print shop.[90] The approach was utilitarian and practical; the aim was to train men and women to evangelize.

In 1925, the Pentecostal Church of Australia also established a Bible Institute, which was short-lived, but later redeveloped into what is now known as the Alphacrusis College.[91] But there was a genuine hesitancy about the effect of formal theological studies on a student's faith and a conviction that the local church was God's preferred school of biblical training.

We are indebted to Lancaster for a clear statement of the Pentecostal position.[92] In a lucid and irenic article, she begins by lamenting the fact that, in spite of a spirited attack on Peake's *Commentary* by the Methodist patriarch W. H. Fitchett, who, she said, described it as 'deadly poison packed in beautiful phrases and reflections,' the Victorian Methodist Conference in March 1923 endorsed its use in the training of probationers. She asked why Christian teachers should upset in the minds of their pupils that faith which had already brought them out of the bondage of sin, and sent them forth as flaming evangelists to preach the Word. She herself knew of two 'fine young men' who were baptized in the Holy

Spirit in Melbourne around 1907 or 1908 who were 'on fire for God'. One had trained for the Methodist ministry and had now lost his zeal; the other trained as an Anglican and was now a 'High Church cigarette smoker'. She went on—

> Admittedly, a thorough knowledge of the Word of God is a necessity, and it is an advantage to be able to speak, read and write plain English, and have a working knowledge of the origin and history of the Holy Scriptures, but it is not necessary to go to a theological college to get these...
>
> No; a member of the true Church, which is Christ's body, should receive his training in that Church; wherein the Holy Spirit has set some as teachers. What for? That the saints may be *perfected for the work of the ministry* (1 Cor 12:28; Eph.4:11, 12).

She urges those teachers who 'mutilate the Word of God' to leave the Scriptures alone. Why, having eaten up all the good pasture, must they tread down the rest with their muddy feet? On the other hand, she commends the Presbyterian T. J. Smith, a leader writer for the *Argus*, and, according to Susan Emilsen, the 'fundamentalist' Professor of Old Testament Studies at the Presbyterian Theological Hall, for his endorsement of the Scriptures.[93] In spite of her distrust of theological seminaries, she might consider making an exception in his case. Ultimately, the spirit of Pentecost was the telling factor. The risk of losing the fire of God was just too great.

When the Pentecostal Church of Australia commenced, there was a similar suspicion of theological training. This was understandable given that neither C. L. Greenwood nor A. C. Valdez, the two founding evangelists, had completed their basic education and Bible teacher Kelso Glover turned his back on seminary studies in order to evangelise. In his advocacy of life in the Spirit, Glover related the old gibe about 'theological cemeteries'[94]—a gibe that would be often repeated in Pentecostal circles in the years to come.

Kelso R. Glover.
Photo, Richmond Temple Souvenir, 1939.

Other Factors

Cox sees a number of other factors which he suggests help to explain the emergence of Pentecostalism. He focuses on the extraordinary prominent place music has played in the movement, especially jazz. 'Jazz and Pentecostalism belong together,' he says. Each was once ridiculed. Each finds its origins in Black

America. Each majors on improvisation. In Latin America, the rise of Pentecostalism was more complex, including factors such as giving expression to those who had formerly been without it; the neglect of the traditional Catholic Church; or, the very opposite, a natural development from the spiritualistic foundations laid by that Church. In Italy, it was a kind of reincarnation of the mystic saints. In Korea, it reshaped some of the traditional characteristics of shamanism and flourished by the Korean genius for organization. In Africa, the movement responded to the free-flowing African style of corporate activity and, far from separating itself from the local culture, absorbed it and dignified it.[95]

What about Australia? It is difficult to identify any specific factors here which have been significant. Although there has been an upsurge in sociological research in the last decade, through agencies such as the Christian Research Association and the National Church Life Survey, there is virtually none for the early years of the Pentecostal movement's existence. Apart from his reference to deprivation theories, Alan Black suggests factors such as the charismatic style of leadership; the opportunities provided by Pentecostal churches for individual initiative, including those not formally qualified for traditional ordained ministry; and the clear-cut belief system.[96]

Fundamentally, all these suggestions still leave unanswered the basic question of why Pentecostalism has flourished and bloomed in so many different and varied seed-beds. As both Cox and Martin have made very clear, Pentecostalism's 'astonishing adaptability to local cultures and situations' has been one of the intriguing aspects of the movement.[97] Somewhere, if it is deemed a genuine work of God, it should meet a fundamental human need that transcends culture, economics and race. Cox hints at this when he suggests that an encounter with God is at the heart of Pentecostalism.[98] Cepeda *et al* point out that churches which cultivate the love of God and true Christianity will thrive 'because people need these things at all times, not just during crises'.[99]

Bernado Campos argues that Pentecostalism cannot be properly understood without an appreciation of the spiritual dimension—

> The failure to consider Pentecostal spirituality and its theological perspectives would deform any hermeneutic of Pentecostalism... Sociological interpretations usually fail to appreciate the meaning of a community's religious experience to the community itself. For instance, it is impossible to understand Pentecostal growth without exploring the doctrine of sanctification, which is the motor of its aggressive evangelism.[100]

Baptism in the Holy Spirit

From its inception, the distinctive feature of Pentecostalism has been the baptism in the Holy Spirit with the accompanying sign of *glossolalia* (Greek: *glossa* = 'tongue'; *laleo* = 'I speak'). Other features of the movement such as its commitment to the Scriptures, its emphasis on the second coming, its strong belief in healing, its concern for holiness, its focus on evangelism were all to be found in other churches and religious organizations—but not speaking in tongues. This was a unique phenomenon which resulted in a unique group. Frank Macchia writes—

Pentecostals regard tongues as a kind of primary sacrament or *kairos* event that signifies, while participating in, the empowerment of the Spirit in the Christian life. Tongues are the 'new sign of the Christian Church,' according to Thomas Barratt, the 'root and stem' out of which all other spiritual gifts grow, according to Edward Irving, and the 'spiritual rest of the new covenant,' according to the Oneness Pentecostal J.L. Hall.[101]

For Pentecostals, the process of Christian initiation includes three major aspects. The first is repentance and faith in Christ; the second is baptism in water by immersion, in which this new-found faith is demonstrated; the third is baptism or infilling with the Holy Spirit,[102] the initial sign of which is speaking in tongues (Acts 2:38–39). Such empowered tongue-speech means the ability to pray in a language which has never been learned. This language is seen as a gift of the Holy Spirit, an elevating, non-rational expression of worship, framed in words which originate in the human spirit, rather than the human mind (1 Corinthians 14:14f). New converts are encouraged to pray to God for the coming of the Holy Spirit, often on their knees. They normally pray aloud, asking God to fill them and then praising and thanking Him for doing so. Usually, during this time, they begin to utter non-rational sounds which soon become fluent. This phenomenon may be accompanied by emotional expressions such as tears or trembling or laughter, but such expressions are not always either expected or present. Those who are baptized in the Spirit usually report greater intimacy with God, a deeper commitment and a sense of joy and/or peace. The ability to pray in tongues is normally ongoing. The common idea that baptism in the Spirit always results from a trance-like state or is accompanied by feelings of ecstasy is erroneous. Those who speak in tongues are usually aware of what is happening around them and are able to stop or start speaking at will.[103]

Certainly, the early Pentecostals had no doubt that glossolalia was a supernatural gift from God. Richard Beauglehole, one of the first Australians ever to exercise glossolalia, clearly saw the phenomenon as entirely of God—

> For a time I was lost to everything and when I came to myself, my lips were trembling... and I heard the Spirit's voice, for He had taken possession of my throat and tongue, and *was speaking through me* in other tongues.[104]

Charles Enticknap, another of the Pentecostal pioneers, told he felt 'a marvellous sense of God taking hold of all my vocal organs... and then came a flood of other tongues'.[105]

There was also a belief in xenolalia—that, at least on some occasions, to speak in tongues was to speak an actual, human language. This view was common overseas. In Zion, Illinois, a new group of Pentecostal believers claimed that German, French, Italian, Russian, Spanish, Norwegian and Chinese had been spoken among them, prompting a local journalist to suggest that secondary students struggling with foreign language studies should 'get the Pentecostal Spirit' to improve their grades.[106] Parham taught that glossolalia was given to hasten the task of world evangelization by enabling believers to preach immediately to the heathen. He was not alone in this. Others shared this conviction. As attempts to put this hypothesis into practice soon proved ineffective, the idea did not survive very long.[107] There is little evidence that Australian Pentecostals believed they could preach in tongues, but the conviction that tongue-speaking could be understood if you happened to know the language was prevalent. On more than one occasion, there were anecdotes of people hearing an expression of tongues, claiming that their own language was being spoken and that they understood the message.[108]

Others dismiss such claims out of hand. Anderson, for instance, with a cavalier abandonment of the scientific spirit, argues that since it is plainly impossible for anyone to speak a language they have never learned, there must be some other explanation.[109]

In summary, the practice of glossolalia is a recognition of the validity and place of religious experience. To say that a pianist, for example, plays her instrument to give her a sense of accomplishment, significance and value may be quite true. If she is retiring and ignored in other respects, her playing may well fulfill a genuine and deeply-felt sense of deprivation and frustration. But this is not an explanation of her ability to make music in the first place. Her musical gifts can be perfected by practice and expressed by determination and skill. But these cannot bestow on her a talent for music if she does not already possess it. Similarly, psychological and sociological explanations of the reasons why people speak in tongues are clearly of value. But ultimately, they are incapable of a definitive explanation of the nature and origin of the practice itself.[110]

It is Pentecostalism's ability, not only to encourage people to experience the presence of God, but to enshrine that experience in an audible, visible, sacramental and sanctifying encounter called baptism in the Holy Spirit, which has been its unique drawing power. As glossolalia offers a tangible experience of God, it defies a purely cognitive or rationalistic approach to Christianity. Yet it satisfies the need for observable criteria, too. Being experienced by the speaker and observable by others, it is both subjective and objective. Psychologically, sociologically and historically, it resists satisfactory analysis. But as a historical phenomenon, glossolalia will not go away. Stubbornly, it remains the significant factor in the emergence of Pentecostalism. And the emergence of Pentecostalism remains the significant factor in the reawakening for the whole Church to the validity and indeed the necessity of an experiential encounter with God.

Notes

1. H. Butterfield, *Christianity and History* (London: George Bell and Sons, 1949), 20, 23.

2. K. Sewell, 'Christian Historiographical Methodology: Some Foundational Considerations,' *Lucas: an Evangelical History Review* (No.15, June 1993): 1ff. Butterfield (1949:134ff) also warns against the dangers of politic-ecclesiastical history, 'especially the kind in which churchmen seem concerned to establish or justify a kingdom of this world'.

3. K. Sewell, 'The Eclipse of History and the Crisis in the Humanities' (unpublished paper, 1996), 3.

4. See also S. Piggin, 'God in History: Some thoughts on the Recovery of a Useful Christian History' in *Lucas* (No.1, November, 1987): 10.

5. D. Clines, 'The Postmodern adventure in Biblical Studies,' in *Australasian Pentecostal Studies* (No. 1, March 1998): 48. Sewell also notes that it may not be necessary to write a comprehensive history—the Scriptures, for example, are clearly selective because the aim is not to provide a thorough narrative but a divine revelation of the matters which we ought to know. See Sewell, 1993: 11.

6. Compare S. Piggin's comments in his review of B. Dickey, 'Holy Trinity Adelaide, 1836–1988: the History of a City Church' in the *Journal of Religious History*, June, 1990, 105ff.

7. Sewell, 1996, 13.

8. Piggin, 1987, 13.

9. A. McLay, 'Writing Women's History: One Feminist Approach,' in M.Hutchinson and E. Campion (eds), *Long Patient Struggle: Studies in the Role of Women in Australian Christianity* (Sydney: Centre for the Study of Australian Christianity, 1994), 20.

10. Several times recently I have asked classes of adult students how many of them thought Pentecostalism had come to Australia from the United States. Without exception, they all said 'yes'.

11. While Methodists were, by and large, Evangelical, the Evangelical movement was broader in both its appeal and its scope, and did not, as a movement, necessarily embrace Methodist emphases. It is necessary, therefore to treat Methodism and other forms of Evangelicalism separately as antecedents of Pentecostalism. Faupel has pointed out that in the United States, there were two major 'wings' to Evangelicalism, the Wesleyan and the Reformed (W. Faupel, *The Everlasting Gospel* [Sheffield: Sheffield Academic Press, 1996], 60–69). In some ways the scene in Australia was similar except that the term 'Evangelical' generally transcended denominationalism, whereas 'Methodist' was a denominational term. Although some denominations (Baptists, for example) were consistently Evangelical, participants in the Evangelical movement could be found in all denominations. Methodism and derivative groups such as the Salvation Army were clearly Evangelical in doctrine, but differed in their emphasis on holiness. For 'Evangelicals' holiness was appropriated by faith; for Methodists it was also the result of an experience of 'Christian perfection' or 'entire sanctification'. Even so, when they came together, these differences were generally overlooked. Methodists and their kin clearly comprised what came to be known elsewhere as the Holiness Movement, but they were not openly identified by that name in Australia. No significant group used the term 'Holiness' in an official or denominational sense. In Australia, many of the Evangelical leaders were lay people.

12. Heath may have been born in India where she spent her childhood, but she lived most of her life in South Australia.

13. F. B. Van Eyk, 'The Baptism of the Holy Spirit,' GN, 17:9, September, 1926, 4.

14. Augustine, *Confessions* I: i: 1. The extraordinary reaction to the death of Princess Diana in 1997 was indicative of people's need for icons.

15. Tertullian, *Against Praxeas,* c. 200, in A. Roberts and J. Donaldson (eds), *The Anti-Nicene Fathers* Vol III (Grand Rapids: Eerdmans, 1978), 8f, 597.

16. M. Weber, *The Sociology of Religion* (London: Methuen, 1922, 1965), 84f — 'Christianity was an urban religion'.

17. B. F. Gutierrez and D. Smith, eds, *In the Power of the Spirit* (Drexel Hill: AIPRAL and CELEP with Skipjack Press, 1996), 72.

18. H. Cox, *Fire From Heaven* (Reading, Mass: Addison-Wesley, 1994), 30.

19. See Vinson Synan, *The Holiness-Pentecostal Movement in the United States* (Grand Rapids: Eerdmans, 1989), 178ff; F. Bartleman, *Azusa Street* (Plainfield: Logos International, 1925, 1980).

20. Cox oversimplifies the beginnings of the Pentecostal movement by seeing Azusa Street as the starting point. In fact, William Seymour first learned of glossolalia from Charles Parham in Texas, through whom there had been Pentecostal phenomena six years earlier. See S.M. Burgess and E. M. Van der Maas, (eds), *New International Dictionary of Pentecostal and Charismatic Movements* (Grand Rapids: Zondervan, 2002), 955–957; Faupel 1996, 182–183. Also, Cox is mistaken in his claim that the outpouring at Poona, India, took place after the girls there heard about Azusa Street. In fact, it took place a year earlier. See H. Dyer, *Revival in India* (London: Marshall, Morgan and Scott, 1907), 41ff.

21. Cox 1994, 60. Compare Butterfield's comments on the historical nature of Christianity and the way in which its most 'daring assertions' have been grounded in 'the ordinary realm of history.'—Butterfield, 1949, 3.

22. GN, 18:8, August, 1927, 11—'Maryborough is about the nicest little town I've seen in Australia as yet... The population is about 12 or 14,000.'

23. In 1933, just over half the Australian population (56%) lived in rural areas. See J. Caldwell in W. Vamplew (ed), *Australians: Historical Statistics* (Broadway, NSW: Fairfax, Syme and Weldon Associates, 1987), 24, 41. There may have been a mentality among Pentecostals that one church per city/town was enough and that having established a church in a capital city, it was then important to go to country towns where there was no Pentecostal presence. However, this does not seem to have been the case with Good News Hall, for example, who quite early set up suburban meetings. The evidence suggests that Pentecostals went anywhere they could gain a hearing and that rural areas offered greater opportunities.

24. Weber, 1965, 80ff, 95ff.

25. For example, the editors of the inaugural issue of the *Journal of Pentecostal Theology* declared, 'Beginning among the poor and marginalised, the movement's adherents may now be found in all socioeconomic strata ...' (No. 1, October, 1992, 3).

R.Anderson, *Vision of the Disinherited* (New York: Oxford, 1979), 225.

27. Cox, 1994, 261.

28. B. Wilson, *Religious Sects* (London: World University Library, 1970), 72, 89–90.

29. N. Gerrard, 'The Holiness Movement in Southern Appalachia,' in W. E. Mills, ed, *Speaking in Tongues: a Guide to Research in Glossolalia* (Grand Rapids: Eerdmans, 1986), 205.

30. D. Martin, 'Space for the expansive Spirit,' *Times Literary Supplement*, 28 March 1997, 8.

31. See Gutierrez and Smith, eds, 1996, 44f,

32. O. Ortega, 'Ecumenism of the Spirit,' in Gutierrez and Smith (eds), 1996, 172. Celia Loreto Mariz sees a number of contributory factors for Pentecostal growth in Brazil, all of which are centred around the ways in which Pentecostalism provides a haven for the poor and underprivileged. These include—

- the warm welcome received at the door
- the emphasis on spiritual rather than material riches
- the building of self esteem (e.g. by an emphasis on dressing well for church)
- mutual support networks through the church community
- compensation for social powerlessness by experiences of supernatural power
- giving meaning to irrational events through faith in the providence of God
- deliverance from spirits and spells
- protection by the power of faith from danger
- modernising elements such as encouragement to read and study
- an emphasis on rebirth

See C. L. Mariz, 'Pentecostalism and Confrontation with Poverty in Brazil,' in Gutierrez and Smith, eds, 135ff.

33. Synan, 1989, 177.
34. R. C. Thompson, *Religion in Australia* (Melbourne: Oxford University Press, 1994), 136.
35. Alan Black, 'Pentecostalism in Comparative Perspective' in A. W. Black, *Religion in Australia: Sociological Perspectives* (Sydney: Allen and Unwin, 1991), 112ff.
36. Black, 1991, 113.
37. Based on figures quoted in G. Aplin, S. Foster and M. McKernan, *Australians: Events and Places* (Broadway, NSW: Fairfax, Syme and Weldon Associates, 1987).
38. W. Hollenweger, *The Pentecostals* (Peabody: Henrickson, 1988), 459, 465. A similar point is made by David Martin—'Certain people hitherto dumb or tongue-tied found their tongue and felt they had a voice in the Church...'—D. Martin and P. Mullen, eds, *Strange Gifts? A Guide to Charismatic Renewal* (Oxford: Blackwell, 1984), 68.
39. Cox, 1994, 103f.
40. Cox, 1994, 105.
41. M.Calley, *God's People: West Indian Pentecostal Sects in England* (Oxford: Oxford, 1965).
42. Mills, ed, 1986, 414f,
43. AE, 8:4, March, 1942, 14.
44. It should be noted that when the despised and rejected find satisfaction and blessing through the Spirit, this is a fulfilment of the Christian gospel. Jesus placed great emphasis on preaching good news to the poor (Matthew 11:5; Luke 4:18).
45. Charles Parham (1873–1929), one of the earliest Pentecostal pioneers in the USA. See Burgess and Van der Maas, eds, 2002, 955–957.
46. A. Cerillo Jr., 'Interpretive Approaches to the History of American Pentecostal Origins' *Pneuma* 15:1 (Spring 1993): 81.
47. Mills, ed, 1986, pp.439ff. See also Williams in Martin and Mullen, eds, 1984, 76.
48. Cox, 1994, 105.
49. Weber, 1965, 80ff; 95ff.
50. Dorothy McKenzie, personal interview, 25 September 1991. In one family, the father spent most of his time in the country seeking work and so was not numbered among the members. Of course, it was not unusual for men to do this in the 1930s. See S.Gray and P. Hempenstall, `The Unemployed' in B. Gammage and P. Spearritt, eds, *Australians 1938* (Sydney: Fairfax, Syme and Weldon Associates, 1987), 327ff.
51. The unemployment rate during the height of the Great Depression was 28.99% in 1932 (Trade Union figures—Butlin estimates were 19.74%) and still almost ten per cent in 1939 (9.7%—Trade Union figures; 8.76%—Butlin estimates). See G. Withers, A. Endres and L. Perry, 'Labour' in Vamplew, ed, 1987, 52.
52. D. McKenzie, personal interview, 25 September, 1991.
53. N. Fabian, personal interview, 15 August, 1991; D. McKenzie, personal interview, 25 September, 1991.
54. N. Fabian, personal interview, 15 August, 1991.
55. I Wahlquist, personal interview, 19 November, 1991.
56. It cannot be argued that the number of unemployed people seeking help at Pentecostal churches validates deprivation theories as all missions and charitable organisations during the Depression experienced similar approaches from the needy.
57. Minutes of the Australian Pentecostal Ministers' Fellowship Steering Committee, 28 February 1995.
58. For example, the Apostolic Mission in Adelaide had around 30 people; in 1937 only a dozen people attended the members' meeting at Ballarat . See *Minutes of the Apostolic Mission* 31 December 1936; 24 October 1937; 16 April 1939. There were about 60

people in Perth in 1928—GN, 20:5, May, 1929, 16. On the other hand, there were 200 in Maryborough—GN, 19:6, June, 1928, 13.

59. Another variable is found in the fact that my list of Pentecostal occupations is spread over three decades. I have assumed that it is representative of given slices of years within that overall period.

60. This is not a high percentage but compares favourably with acceptable responses to surveys and questionnaires.

61. Although 1947 is technically outside the scope of the period of this thesis, the figures are the nearest available after 1939.

62. R. Howe, 'Social Composition of the Wesleyan Church in Victoria During the Nineteenth Century,' in JRH, June, 1967, 210.

63. Personal research.

64. N. Armstrong, personal interview, October, 1993; GN, 18:6, September, 1927, 19; 20:3 March, 1929, 5.

65. *Age*, 12 October, 1922; Minutes of the Southern Evangelical Mission, 1927.

66. L. Priest, interview, 17 September, 1991.

67. The term 'middle class' is commonly used in the context of contemporary Australian social structures, although the concept of 'class' is not obvious. While it would be oversimplifying matters to refer to a 'classless society', the lines of division are blurred. In the 1920s and 1930s, there was a plain differentiation between rich and poor, but no easily recognised 'middle class'. In the context of this discussion, the term refers primarily to economic levels and to those people whose earnings or assets were average or above average, but who would not be classified as 'rich'. See Stuart Macintyre, 'Class' in G. Davison, J. Hirst and S. Macintyre (eds), (*The Oxford Companion to Australian History* South Melbourne: Oxford, 1999), 1310ff; T. H. Irving, 'Class' in Aplin et al., eds, 1987, 78f.

68. *The News*, 30 November, 1927.

69. See the appropriate Trade Directories, 1912–1939. Also, N. Fabian, personal interview, 15 August, 1991; D. McKenzie, personal interview, 25 September, 1991; GN, March, 1927, 19; AN 1:1, September 1, 1929, 1.

70. *The News*, 5 October, 1927.

71. Phil Lovell, personal interview, 6 September,1991.

72. Laurie Wahlquist, personal interview, 19 November, 1991; M. Hurst, personal interview, 14 August, 1991; Phil Lovell, personal interview, 6 September, 1991.

73. N. Fabian, personal interview, 15 August, 1991.

74. Alan Geoffrey (Dick) Bain, personal interview, 20 August, 1990; M. Hurst, personal interview, 14 August, 1991.

75. N. Fabian, personal interview, 15 August, 1991.

76. D. McKenzie, personal interview, 25 September, 1991; 1930 Sands and McDougall *Trade Directory*; AN 6:3, March, 1935, 1.

77. Personal interviews, A. Bain, 20 August, 1990; M. Hurst, 14 August, 1991; Frank Elton, 11 September, 1991.

78. GN, 17:10, October, 1926, 10ff.

79. D. Martin, TLS, 28 March, 1997, 8.

80. Although it is not the subject of this volume, the explosive growth of the movement in the 1980s and 1990s raises yet a different set of questions.

81. Compare H. Mol, *The Faith of Australians* (North Sydney: George Allen and Unwin, 1985), 18f.

82. These figures represent the maximum possible numbers. It may be that less than seven actually attended seminary.

83. One hundred recognised Brethren pioneer leaders included at least 42 university graduates and a dozen doctors, several lawyers and high ranking army or navy officers. John Nelson Darby, the founder of the Brethren, was himself no mean scholar. A graduate of Trinity College, Dublin, he was called to the Irish Chancery Bar. Later he was ordained into the Church of Ireland. He was fluent in French, German, Greek, Latin and Hebrew. In the late nineteenth and early and mid-twentieth centuries, Brethren scholars included people like Samuel Tregelles, B. W. Newton, H. L. Ellison, W. E. Vine, Professor S. H. Hooke, G. H. Lang, W. J. Martin and the young F. F. Bruce. The Brethren publishing houses Pickering and Inglis and Paternoster produced substantial theological books. Henry Frowde, MA, became manager of the London office of the Oxford University Press. Conferences for biblical and theological exposition were popular. See H. Pickering, *Chief Men Among the Brethren* (London: Pickering and Inglis, 1961); J. D. Douglas, *The New International Dictionary of the Christian Church* (Grand Rapids: Regency 1978), 282f; F. F. Bruce, *In Retrospect: Remembrance of Things Past,* (London: Marshall Pickering, 1993), 20ff, 74ff, 110f, 112ff, 120, 150, 167, 315. It may also be of interest to note that among the one hundred leaders were ten of noble birth—including Lord Congelton, Sir Edward Denny, Lord Farnham and Sir Robert Anderson. See Pickering, 1961, 1, 35, 44, 46.

84. J. McCabe, personal interview, 18 September, 1991; K. Kirwan, personal interview, 11 September, 1991. Dr Davy was awarded a Doctorate in Music from Adelaide University in 1918. According to the inscription on her tombstone in the West Terrace Cemetery, Adelaide, she was a descendant of the Earl of Litchfield. She wrote the music to lyrics by Apostolic leader William Cathcart entitled 'Welcome to Australia,' written in tribute to visiting British pastors, but, according to Kath Kirwan, left the church before it could be performed.

85. GN, 19:12 December, 1928, p.10. I knew Robert Duguid personally.

86. J. Dowie, 'Satan the Defiler,' LH, 14 May 1904, 100.

87. F. Lancaster, interview, 18 December, 1993.

88. *Richmond Temple Souvenir*, 1939, 14, 15.

89. *Acts '89,* November, 1989, 14.

90. GN, 12:8, September, 1923, 21.

91. AE, July, 1926, 5.

92. GN, 12:8, September, 1923, 14f.

93. S. Emilsen, *A Whiff of Heresy* (Kensington, NSW: New South Wales University Press, 1991), 20, 133.

94. AE, September, 1926, 4, 5.

95. Cox, 1994, 143–259.

96. Black, 1991, 113ff.

97. Martin, TLS, 28 March, 1997, 8.

98. Cox, 1994, 304ff.

99. R. Cepeda, E. Carrillo, R. Gonzales and C. Ham in Gutierrez and Smith, eds, 1996, 108.

100. B. L. Campos, in Gutierrez and Smith, eds, 1996, 43. Williams agrees: 'Any study of glossolalia needs to take full cognisance of how glossolalics themselves understand the phenomenon.' See Martin and Mullen, eds, 1984, 72.

101. F. Macchia, 'Tongues as a Sign: Towards a Sacramental Understanding of Pentecostal Experience,' *Pneuma,* 15:1, Spring, 1993, 69.

102. Also described in the New Testament as receiving the Spirit, receiving the gift of the Spirit, having the Spirit fall upon you or being sealed with the Spirit (Acts 2:38; 8:15–17; 10:44–48; 11:15f).

103. These observations are based on my own extensive pastoral and professional experience over the last four decades. For a more detailed discussion of various psychological and sociological approaches to glossolalia, see B. Chant, 'Expressing the Inexpressible', www.barrychant.com.

104. R. Beauglehole, 'God Baptized in Portland, Victoria, Nearly Fifty Years Ago,' GN, 1:1, April, 1910, 4.

105. C. G. Enticknap, 'Address given at the Christian Revival Crusade, Rosewater, SA,' 17 October, 1965. Quoted in B. Chant, *Heart of Fire* (Unley Park: Tabor, 1984), 46. The idea of the Spirit speaking through a believer may have been seen in the light of the biblical statement that God did special miracles 'through the hands of Paul' (Acts 19:11). See Appendix B for more on Enticknap.

106. E. Blumhofer, 'Charles F. Parham's 1906 Invasion: a Pentecostal Branch Grows in Zion,' *Assemblies of God Heritage,* Fall, 1986, 4.

107. See Cerillo Jr, 'Origins,' *Pneuma,* 15:1, Spring, 1993, 83; Anderson, 1979, 90ff.

108. Joyce Whitburn, personal interview, 22 March, 1997; K. Chant, 1993, 117. I personally know two people who have understood an utterance in tongues and another three who have been told that they were speaking a known language—in every case, a language unknown to them personally. The languages concerned were, in the case of the first two, German and English, and in the others, Arabic, French and Hebrew. The veracity and integrity of these witnesses is unquestioned. See B. Chant, *Empowered by the Spirit* (Miranda: Tabor, 2008), 127f, 132f

109. Anderson, 1979, 19.

110. C. S. Lewis's concept of Transposition is relevant here. Lewis readily concedes that glossolalia may arise from natural, hysterical or even pathological causes, but argues that this is to over-simplify the matter. The realm of the emotion, he suggests, is far more complex than that of the senses and hence the same action may derive from very different emotional stimuli. To deny the possibility of a genuinely spiritual or divine origin for glossolalia is like someone who lives in a two dimensional world denying the reality of a further dimension; or like insisting that because an acute angle in a drawing represents a similar angle in real life it cannot also represent the concept of depth. So for Lewis, Transposition means viewing phenomena like tongue-speaking, as far as this is possible, 'from above'. So 'those who spoke with tongues, as St. Paul did, can well understand how that holy phenomenon differed from the hysterical phenomenon—although, be it remembered, they were in a sense exactly the same. phenomenon.' See C. S. Lewis, 'Transposition' in *Screwtape Proposes a Toast* (London: Collins/Fontana, 1965), 75ff.

CHAPTER TWO

THE SPIRIT OF WESLEYANISM

Christian Perfection and the Baptism in the Holy Spirit (1870–1908)

The Australian Pentecostal movement is essentially an indigenous movement, enriched by a variety of overseas influences, and its origins are divergent from those in other Western countries. They are to be found in three major tributaries—Wesleyan perfectionism, the Dowie/divine healing movement and evangelical revivalism.

Walter Hollenweger, whose studies on Pentecostalism were for years the benchmark for other historians, sees five general roots of Pentecostalism—
- the oral/black tradition
- Wesleyan catholicism, which he defines as a blend of Wesleyan perfectionism and love
- the Holiness movement
- evangelical ecumenism (that is, non-denominationalism)
- the critical tradition (reforming both traditional Christianity and society)[1]

The first of these does not apply to Australia. Nor was there any significant denominational Holiness movement here.[2] But, Wesleyanism and evangelicalism were, as in the United States, major tributaries. It was the Wesleyan emphasis on the need for a discrete experience of entire sanctification that, for many people, developed into the Pentecostal concept of baptism in the Holy Spirit. A significant number of the first Pentecostals were Methodists who diligently sought to be baptized with the Holy Spirit. The language they spoke was orthodox Wesleyan. The difference was a phenomenon that Methodists had not known—that of speaking in tongues.

Edith Blumhofer identifies a different set of origins for American Pentecostalism. These are restorationism, premillennialism, healing, Wesleyan Holiness teaching and various evangelical trends and movements such as the emphasis on the Holy Spirit of the Congregationalist Reuben Torrey (1856–1928), the stress on holiness by Presbyterian Charles Finney (1792–1875) and the Keswick movement's deeper life teaching.[3] The Australian background differs from these as well. While premillennialism, for example, was a prominent part of Pentecostal preaching and teaching in the first few decades, there is no evidence that the movement grew out of it in any significant way.

Augustus Cerillo Jr helpfully categorises four 'interpretive paths' of American Pentecostalism. These are the providential, which explains the movement's origins largely in terms of the sovereign purposes of God; the 'historical roots', which sees Pentecostalism as a natural development from the Wesleyan-Holiness-Evangelical tradition; the multicultural, which understands the movemet to have been initiated primarily by Black Christians; and the functional, which explains its origins in socio-economic or psychological terms.[4]

South African Pentecostalism admits to being an American import,[5] although this may be an oversimplification, as there were clearly local influences as well, such as the writings of Andrew Murray.[6] The Swedish movement stemmed largely from Baptist ecclesiology.[7] In Chile, the Methodist influence was paramount; in Brazil, the Baptist.[8] In England, the formative influences were a blend of Calvinistic Methodism, Congregationalism and Anglicanism. The Welsh Revival of 1904–05 was of considerable significance, and English Pentecostalism owes some of its ambience to the early leaders who were first introduced to the moving of the Spirit in Wales.[9] James Worsfold sees a connection between the Irvingite movement and modern Pentecostalism, especially the Apostolic Church.[10] Strachan and Allen, even though the latter calls Irving 'the Morning Star of Pentecost,' are more cautious, seeing similarities, rather than overt links.[11] Certainly, in Australia, there is no evidence of the Irvingite movement having any influence on the development of Pentecostalism. The Catholic Apostolic Church, established after Irving's death, has been in Australia since 1883 under the name Apostolic Church of Queensland. It recognises apostles and uses prophesying from time to time for direction, but does not practise glossolalia. As its initial constituency was largely German and the first services were German-speaking, it has tended to be isolationist.[12]

It is popularly believed among evangelicals today that Australia has never experienced a religious revival. While this may be valid in the nation-wide sense, it is not true of many local areas. The nineteenth century was a time of prolific religious revival in Australia, as it was around the world. Stuart Piggin has identified 71 specific Christian revivals between the years 1834 and 1891 (see Table Four).

Most of these, he points out, were among Methodists. However, there were also revival movements among Catholics—especially through Redemptorist missioners—Presbyterians and Baptists, who received added incentive from the ministry of Thomas Spurgeon, one of Charles Haddon Spurgeon's twin sons.[13]

Table 4 Nineteenth Century Religious Groups.

Name	Place	Date
Christian Israelites	Melbourne	1841
The New Church	Adelaide	1844
Churches of Christ	Adelaide	1846
Young Men's Christian Association	Adelaide	1850
Unitarianism	Sydney	1850
The Church of Jesus Christ of Latter Day Saints	Sydney	1844
Christian Brethren		Mid–1850's
Christadelphianism	Sydney	1866
Spiritualism	Melbourne	1870
The Salvation Army	Adelaide	1880
Young Women's Christian Association	Sydney	1880
The Theosophical Society	Brisbane	1881
The Apostolic Church of Queensland	Hatton Vale	1883
The Christian Catholic Church	Melbourne	1883
Seventh Day Adventism	Sydney	1885
Christian Science	Sydney	1890
The Keswick Movement	Geelong	1890
Student Christian Movement		1892
The Watchtower Bible and Tract Society	Melbourne	1904

During the nineteenth and early twentieth centuries, there was a plethora of visiting revivalists including William 'California' Taylor (1863–65), Gordon Forlong, Emilia Baeyertz (1878 onwards), Thomas Spurgeon (1878 and 1880), Margaret Hampson (1883), George Williams, William Noble, Matthew Burnett, Harry Grattan Guinness (1885, 1901), George Muller (1886), Henry Varley (1877), Alexander Sommerville (1877), George Grubb (1891), Thomas Cook and Gypsy Smith (1894), John R. Mott (1896), Reuben Torrey (1902), Wilbur Chapman and Charles Alexander (1909, 1912), and Herbert Booth.[14]

The nineteenth century was also a time of prolific religious growth in other ways. There was a flourishing of new religious movements, mission organisations and parachurch groups. Given that Australia was growing rapidly through immigration, it is not surprising that new religious groups should emerge and find fertile ground in this country. The groups listed in Table 4 all began in Australia in the 1800's, some of them within a decade of their founding overseas.[15]

For all that, and in spite of the fact that nearly all Australians claimed allegiance to a Christian denomination, the indications are that at no time during the nineteenth century did more than half the population attend church. In fact, if they had, the church buildings could not have contained them all. According to Broome, there were 70,000 Anglicans in Sydney in 1901, but only 9,000 seats in churches. Piggin argues that in South Australia in the same year, there were only enough seats in church buildings for 45% of the population. Phillips claims there were 623,148 nominal Anglicans in New South Wales but only 36,294 members.[16] Jackson estimates that in 1851, in Victoria, about 14% of people attended church, a figure which rose to 34% in 1881, allowing for variations between localities and denominations.[17] Bollen suggests that church attendance was 35% in 1870, 30% in 1880 and 28% in 1890.[18] One writer claims that generally, attendance was highest among Baptists, Methodists and Congregationalists and weakest among Anglicans, with Catholics and Presbyterians somewhere in between.[19] In 1891, in New South Wales, Victoria and South Australia, only six in every one hundred Anglicans were active church members. Methodists and Presbyterians fared better, with figures of around 13 and 11 per cent respectively, while Baptists (18.5%) and Catholics (41.5%) showed the highest rates. The figures in South Australia were slightly higher in most cases than in the other States (see Table 5).[20]

It was the Methodists, especially the Wesleyans, who pioneered Christian revival. From 1852 to 1867, affiliation with Methodist churches increased by 300%, a rate nearly double the population growth, which was itself significant (163.2% from 1851 to 1861), largely as a result of gold fever. At the conclusion of Daniel Draper's ministry at Wesley Church, Melbourne, in 1864, it was noted that in the 28 years since his arrival from England in 1836, the number of Wesleyan ministers had grown from nine to 129 and the number of members from 532 to 15,061. Draper, astonishingly capable in organisational skills, fundraising and administration, was described as 'an honoured instrument in securing this glorious result.'[21]

In New South Wales, Methodism grew from 10,008 people in 1861 to 23,682 in 1871. It did even better in Victoria where numbers rose from 4,988 to 46,511 in the same ten year period. Sunday School enrolments in Victoria also escalated—13,631 in 1861 to 30,653 in 1871. In the same decade, the population of both States grew by less than half.[22] Overall, Methodism grew from 6.7% of the Australian population in 1861 to 10.2% in 1901.[23] Actual recorded membership increases (excluding children) for 1861–1871 are not so dramatic—33.4% in New South Wales, 67.3% in South Australia and 95.3% in Victoria, but still promising enough.[24]

Table 5 Church attendance as a percentage of membership 1891.

	Anglican	Baptist	Catholic	Methodist	Presbyterian
NSW	4.6	14.0	35.0	9.3	8.6
Vic	6.1	19.3	70.4	12.5	8.6
SA	7.2	22.3	19.0	17.3	10.2
Average	5.9	18.5	41.5	13.0	10.7

George Eliot's Anglican Edward Casaubon may have devoted his days to unlocking the key to all mythologies while Jane Austen's sycophantic William Collins bowed and fawned to Lady Catherine de Bourgh, but the Methodist preachers of Australia were pounding the back tracks of their vast new country, penetrating new frontiers for the gospel. So Brian Dickey writes—

> They [the Methodists] were the evangelicals par excellence through the nineteenth century: they carried revival and their Bibles all over Australia and beyond to proclaim the cross as the way of salvation, to call men and women to repentance and conversion, and on to an active life of service. They were the Protestant light cavalry of Australia.[25]

D. B. Walker points out that 'the Methodist Church above all others sought revivals and taught their spiritual necessity.'[26]

Perfectionism

One distinctive feature of Wesleyan preaching was that of Christian perfection or, as it was otherwise called, entire sanctification. This was the concept that through a discrete, identifiable and possibly emotional experience of sanctification, similar to conversion, one could reach a stage of Christian perfection. At this point, one was cleansed from inbred sin and enabled to live without conscious or deliberate transgression.[27]

In John Wesley's own writings, the matter is not as clear-cut as this. In his *Sermons*, he seems to argue that perfection means avoiding deliberate sin[28], although this is difficult to nail down precisely.[29] In a letter written in 1771, he said—

> Entire sanctification or Christian perfection, is neither more nor less than pure love; love expelling sin, and governing both the heart and life of a child of God. The Refiner's fire purges out all that is contrary to love, and many times by a pleasing smart.[30]

The most lucid statement is in his *Plain Account of Christian Perfection,* a document which was revised several times during his lifetime and took its final form in 1777—

> To this day both my brother and I maintained, (1) That Christian perfection is that love of God and our neighbour, which implies deliverance from all sin. (2) That this is received merely by faith. (3) That it is given instantaneously, in one moment. (4) That we are to expect it, not at death, but every moment...[31]

John Wesley 1703 – 1791.

It was not sinless perfection; people might still sin unintentionally. It was not behavioural perfection. Being human, people might still make mistakes of judgement or emotion, even though they were in 'the highest state of grace.' The important thing was to act in love. 'Where every word and action springs from love, such a mistake is not properly a sin.' So a person filled with God's love might still commit 'involuntary transgressions', but these were not sins.[32]

Wesley claimed to have taught this doctrine from the beginning and stressed that in the Conferences of 1744–1747, there had not been one expression of disagreement. However, in the years to follow, there was to be more controversy over this than anything else. He found himself writing letters over and again to explain his position. In 1758, he wrote to Miss H—, who was 'much perplexed' over the doctrine of perfection. 'By "perfection",' he explained simply, 'I mean "perfect love".' This was something every believer could attain. Three years later, he wrote with some impatience to one Mr Hosmer, 'Shall we call them (mistakes) sins or no? I answer again and again, Call them just what you please.' The following year, he penned a short note to S. F., trying to clarify his terms. A few months later, he painstakingly explained to Mrs Maitland that Christian perfection was simply loving God and loving our neighbours. Those who did this were 'scripturally perfect'. But sinless perfection, he had never taught. In 1772, he expressed to his brother Charles his dismay that most Methodist preachers were no longing teaching Christian perfection.33 Five years later, he wrote—

> I have drawn a full picture of it (Christian perfection) at full length, without either disguise or covering... Whence is all this outcry, which, for these twenty years and upwards, has been made throughout the kingdom; as if all Christianity were destroyed, and all religion torn up by the roots? Why is it, that the very name of perfection has been cast out of the mouths of Christians; yea, exploded and abhorred, as if it contained the most pernicious heresy? Why have the Preachers been hooted at, like mad dogs, even by men that fear God;...? I pray you, what harm is there in it?... It is giving God all our heart... It is the devoting, not a part, but all our soul, body and substance to God... It is the loving God with all our heart, and our neighbour as ourselves... which I have believed and taught for these forty years, from the year 1725 to the year 1765.[34]

The following year, in a letter to Rev Plenderlieth, he refuted mis-statements of his position. Wesley could not understand the opposition. Who, in their right minds, could oppose the idea of giving all to God and being 'sanctified wholly through his Spirit'? A large part of his *Plain Account* was taken up with answering the many arguments and questions that had been raised.

Charles's hymns also spoke often of the eradication of sin and the perfection of love—

> From this inbred sin deliver;
> Let the yoke Now be broke;
> Make me thine forever.
>
> Saviour from sin, I wait to prove
> That Jesus is the healing name;
> To lose, when perfected in love,
> Whate'er I have, or can, or am.[35]

This perfecting in love was not the same as conversion. Wesley could recall no single instance where anyone received forgiveness of sins, the presence of the Spirit and 'a new clean heart' simultaneously. Christian perfection was received instantaneously by faith through grace, but it was discrete from conversion. In fact, while new converts could experience it, it was more likely to be the province of mature Christians.[36]

Wesley himself underwent a dual entry into an experiential knowledge of God. Initially there was the Aldersgate conversion on 24 May 1738, where his heart was 'strangely warmed' and he felt for the first time that he did trust in Christ. But he still felt he lacked the inward witness of the Spirit and was waiting patiently for it.[37] Then a few months later, in January 1739, at the Fetter Lane Society, there was a deep sense of God's power in the meeting and they continued in prayer till the small hours of the morning.[38] It was not the only time such events occurred. In May of the same year, a similar thing happened—

> The power of God (so I call it) came so mightily among us, that one, and another, and another, fell down as thunder-struck. In that hour many that were in deep anguish of spirit, were all filled with peace and joy. Ten persons, till then in sin, doubt, and fear, found such a change, that sin has no more dominion over them; and instead of the spirit of fear, they are now filled with that of love, and joy, and a sound mind.[39]

It was to Wesley that Bishop Butler made his famous allegation: 'Sir, the pretending to extraordinary revelations and gifts of the Holy Ghost is a horrid thing, a very horrid thing.'[40] Wesley did not, in fact, lay claim to such supernatural powers and disapproved of those who did.[41] But he did believe in a faith which touched the heart and transformed the life. Soon after his conversion, he told his brother Samuel he was convinced 'by the most infallible of all proofs, inward feeling'.[42] Henry Fielding's Mrs Whitefield may have been 'untainted by the pernicious principles of Methodism', and have discovered no evidence of 'the extraordinary emotions of the Spirit', but for true believers, a warm heart was the essence of faith.[43]

As time went on, Wesley became uneasy about extremism, but he never discouraged emotional expression. To Ronald Knox, this was a conundrum —

> That is the disconcerting fact about early Methodism—that its founder sympathised with enthusiasm... in its most violent forms, yet was never himself carried away by it. The two brothers, almost alone among the supporters of the movement, kept their heads.[44]

Knox seems to overstate Wesley's position here. On more than one occasion, Wesley spoke strongly against 'enthusiasm'. In his *Plain Account*, enthusiasm is the second of six dangers he sees to genuine faith. He does not mince matters—

> Beware of that daughter of pride, enthusiasm. O keep at the utmost distance from it! Give no place to the heated imagination. Do not hastily ascribe things to God. Do not easily suppose drams, voices, impressions, visions or revelations to be from God. They may be from him. They may be from nature. They may be from the devil... Try all things by the written word, and let all bow down before it. You are in danger of enthusiasm every hour, if you depart ever so little from Scripture; yea, or from the plain, literal meaning of any text, taken in connexion with the context. And so you are, if you despise or lightly esteem reason, knowledge, or human learning; every one of which is an excellent gift of God, and may serve the noblest purposes...

> I say yet again, beware of enthusiasm. Such is, the imagining you have the gift of prophesying, or of discerning of spirits, which I do not believe one of you has; no, nor ever had yet. Beware of judging people to be either right or wrong by your own feelings.[45]

When five or six 'honest enthusiasts' predicted the end of the world on 28 February 1759, he preached against them and in 1762, at the Beech-lane meeting, Wesley was dismayed to discover a few who mistook their own imaginations for the voice of God, and to observe 'horrid screaming, and unscriptural, enthusiastic expressions', which he promptly put an end to, an action which brought him further criticism from some quarters. To another Methodist, he said, 'Nothing under heaven is more catching than enthusiasm.' The danger was that when a faith was based only on inner sensations, when they dissolved, the faith might well go too.[46]

Did Wesley ever speak in tongues? Ronald Foulkes's attempt to build a case that he did, is less than convincing, although he does quote Thomas Walsh, a Methodist lay preacher, as saying, 'This morning the Lord gave me a language that I knew not of, raising my soul to him in a wonderful manner',[47] which may have been a reference to glossolalia.

Nevertheless, there was no questioning Wesley's major thrust. It was not enough to be converted. It was necessary to experience entire sanctification, too. And both were matters of the heart as well as the mind. Ultimately, the *Plain Account* became a kind of manifesto for Holiness groups. Wesley's dislike for enthusiasm notwithstanding, two separate phases of experience were identified for the believer—

- Conversion (justification)
- Christian perfection (sanctification)

Bishop Hedding, of the American Methodist Episcopal Church, writing in the Australian *Spectator* a century later, went even further than Wesley. Regeneration would keep the believer from deliberate sin, he said, but sanctification would also cleanse him from involuntary sins. He would be 'filled with the love of God' and 'feel none of those passions in his heart' which lead to sin. In a Christian, sin may be 'some time dying', but there would be an instant in which it did die—and 'that event is full sanctification'. Such a work could only be effected by the Holy Spirit. No other power could do it.[48] Jill Roe suggests that at least part of the reason why Methodists succeeded in nineteenth century Australia was that they 'had always preferred to appeal to the hearts rather than the heads of men'.[49]

Wesley did not particularly emphasise the work of the Holy Spirit in his teaching on Christian perfection. His view was that the Holy Spirit was received at the point of conversion. However, 'if they like to call this (Christian perfection) "receiving the Holy Ghost",' he wrote in a letter to Joseph Benson, 'they may.'[50] Laurence Wood has shown in recent Wesleyan studies that this connection between the baptism with the Spirit and Christian perfection is derived from John Fletcher whom Wesley personally designated as his successor and who drew from Wesley's own sermons to make this connection explicit, with Wesley's approval.[51] In America, in the late nineteenth century, it became common to call the sanctifying second blessing a 'baptism in the Holy Ghost.'[52] Evangelist Phoebe Palmer edited a journal called *Guide to Holiness* (from 1839). 'By the turn of the century, everything from camp meetings to choirs was described in the *Guide* as 'pentecostal'.[53] Every aspect of Pentecostalism except tongues was evident in the Holiness movement there.

Second Blessing

By 1900, the idea of a second blessing was being taught around the world by such esteemed evangelical leaders as A. J. Gordon, F. B. Meyer, A. B. Simpson, Andrew Murray and R. A. Torrey.[54] There was also a diverting of concentration from the love of God to holiness of life and power for service.[55] James Bowers sees this as a backward step, feeling that the Pentecostals have been the poorer for this shift of emphasis,[56] but it probably helped to give more focus to the nature of the experience and to bring it out of the somewhat amorphous realm of divine love into the more readily identifiable and distinctive arena of charismata.

As it happened, early American Pentecostals did not re-shape this second blessing teaching to include baptism in the Holy Spirit—they added the baptism in the Holy Spirit to it. William Seymour (1870–1922), the acknowledged leader of the Los Angeles 'Azusa Street revival' which began on 14 April 1906, was committed to the Holiness doctrine of entire sanctification and taught accordingly.[57] Earlier, he had been influenced by Charles Parham (1873–1929), a wandering evangelist who himself had come to believe in a baptism in the Holy Spirit accompanied by speaking in tongues in Topeka, Kansas in 1901.

Seymour adopted a three-stage theology of repentance for justification, second blessing for sanctification and baptism in the Spirit for power[58]—

> FIRST WORK—Justification is that act of God's free grace by which we receive remission of sins...
>
> SECOND WORK—Sanctification is [a] second work of grace and the last work of grace. Sanctification is that act of God's free grace by which he makes us holy. The Disciples were sanctified before the Day of Pentecost ... You know they could not receive the Spirit if they were not clean...
>
> The Baptism of the Holy Ghost is a gift of power upon a sanctified life; so when we get it we have the same evidence as the Disciples received on the Day of Pentecost (Acts 2:3,4), in speaking in new tongues.[59]

William Durham (1873–1912), a Baptist pastor from Chicago, received the Pentecostal blessing on 2 March, 1907. He was, said one of his associates, 'a pulpit prodigy'.[60] However, Durham did not accept Seymour's three-stage concept. He rejected the Holiness sanctification concept in favour of the 'finished work' teaching, that believers were justified and sanctified at the same time, with sanctification continuing progressively. The work of salvation, including sanctification, was 'finished' at Calvary. For him, the result of baptism in the Spirit was 'increased love and power' to equip for service (see Table 6). Parham and Seymour strongly opposed Durham's views, and when Durham later visited Los Angeles, he found many doors closed to him. Nevertheless, he still drew large crowds.[61]

Table 6 Views of baptism in the Holy Spirit.

Group	First stage	Second stage	Third stage
Wesleyan/Holiness	Regeneration	Sanctification	
Parham/Seymour	Regeneration	Sanctification	Baptism in Holy Spirit
Durham/'Finished work'	Regeneration; sanctification	Baptism in Holy Spirit	

As the revival continued, the general trend was to identify the experience of sanctification with conversion and to see the impartation of the Holy Spirit more in terms of empowering for service. In April 1914, about 300 leaders of the 'finished work' group called a general council at Hot Springs, Arkansas, and combined under the name Assemblies of God. It was basically white. The Holiness people continued under various names such as Apostolic Faith Mission or Church of God, some being primarily black fellowships. From that time on, the 'finished work' view was accepted by the majority.

In Australia, the 'three-stage' view was never popular, although it was taught here, as a leaflet printed in Portland, Oregon, and distributed in the 1920s by a Parramatta church illustrates—

> There are two works of grace—justification and sanctification—and there is the gift of the Holy Ghost that empowers for service ... When our sins are washed away, and we have been sanctified from all carnality, by the second definite work of grace, God pours out on the soul and on the flesh the mighty rivers of the Holy Spirit. Let no soul come and expect the baptism of the Holy Ghost until they have first been cleansed by the Blood of Jesus and sanctified wholly.[62]

Generally the trend in Australia was to identify the experience of sanctification with the impartation of the Holy Spirit. In the late nineteenth century, it became common to call this experience a 'baptism in the Holy Ghost'.

John Watsford

Several names stand out among the Methodist revivalists. John Watsford (1820–1907) is a distinguished example. Born in Parramatta on 5 December 1820, 'Father Watsford' as he was affectionately known, was the first Australian-born Methodist minister.[63] His autobiography *Glorious Gospel Triumphs as seen in My Life and Work*[64] is an old man's reminiscence of over half a century of ministry, but for all that, it was acknowledged by his contemporaries as a faithful record, just as he was recognised as 'a burning evangelist and a great soul winner in many districts' and his name was considered 'a household word' in all seven colonies.[65]

John Watsford 1820–1907.

The editor of the *Southern Cross* noted that Watsford was 'so good and so able a man' that he deserved to be heard on any subject he chose to address. 'Few men in Australia,' he went on to say, 'have worked with more energy and success in the service of Christ's Kingdom or have a larger experience in philanthropic enterprises.'[66]

Wherever he went, the indefatigable Watsford preached and taught the Wesleyan gospel of faith in Christ both for salvation and for sanctification. In Adelaide, in 1862, he ministered in the Pirie Street Methodist church—

> We had it crowded Sunday after Sunday, and the Lord heard prayer, and in a very remarkable manner poured out His Spirit. We had soon to carry on our meetings night after night for weeks together, and every night sinners were converted. Our midday prayer-meeting was continued for six months: sometimes as many as one hundred and fifty and two hundred were present, and each meeting was a time of great power. The local preachers, leaders, and Sabbath-school teachers were all baptized in the Holy Spirit and heartily entered into the work. It was delightful to see our local preachers going out in different directions on a Sunday morning, all full of love for souls, and longing to bring them to Jesus.[67]

In September 1877, Watsford's visit to South Australia resulted in 'crowded churches, delighted audiences and frequent acknowledgments of profits received.' If these were indications of popularity then 'our old friend was deservedly popular,' said a report in the *Spectator*.[68]

In 1879, in the Victorian Brunswick Street circuit, there was a time of awakening. There were 'showers of blessings' and 'signs and wonders'. Many were reported to have sought and found sanctification. Many others were converted. The local ministers were assisted by Watsford as services continued nightly for three weeks. At the Sunday School anniversary, there was 'an abundant outpouring of the Spirit' and many turned to the Lord. At a neighbouring congregation, forty young people expressed their desire to serve God. Some of the gatherings were 'bright' with the blessing of the Lord, the 'holiest influences' were evident and there was a growing consciousness of the presence of God.[69]

There are frequent references in Watsford's writings to the need to be baptized or filled with the Spirit or to 'Pentecostal power' or 'Pentecostal baptism'. In 1860, 'praying men' in Bourke St, Sydney, had been crying out to God for an outpouring of the Spirit. Watsford preached there on successive nights. The church was crowded and 'the mighty power of God' came upon people. Many fell to the floor in agony with loud cries for mercy. These phenomena were so unusual, 'the police came rushing in to see what they could do'! There were hundreds of penitents, many returning next morning, still in a state of spiritual distress.

In 1891, as a supernumerary minister of 71 years of age, Watsford became more convinced than ever that there was a great need of a revival of holiness in the Church, and was deeply persuaded that... his 'special work was to spread Scriptural holiness throughout the land.' In two months, Watsford travelled 2,400 miles by rail and visited thirteen circuits. As he travelled, 'at every place ... the word was in demonstration of the Spirit and in power.' Everywhere, he preached on being filled with the Spirit—

> The Churches need the Pentecostal baptism: then we shall have Pentecost, holy living, simplicity, power, success and, perhaps, persecution. May our day of Pentecost soon fully come on all Australasia!

Two years later, the retiring President Rev F. Neale noted how 'Father Watsford' had successfully presided over a holiness Convention and pointed out that if the Church was to experience a 'widespread revival,' it would be necessary to give themselves to 'earnest, importunate, prayer'.[70] That same year, Watsford held a fortnight's mission, where there was 'a blessed spirit of quiet fervour' and 'souls were athirst for such a baptism of the Holy Ghost as would fully prepare them to be co-workers with God.'

> Many came forward to seek the blessing of holiness, and not a few then and there found that Christ was able to save to the uttermost... The communion rail and sometimes two vestries were filled with weeping seekers and rejoicing workers. Many remarkable cases of conversion occurred.[71]

In Bermond, New South Wales, they had 'a Pentecostal season' and the whole congregation experienced a 'breaking down'. At Portland, Victoria, 'sinners were converted and believers baptized with the Holy Spirit.' On the Baptist Missionary Society Centenary, he reflected, 'We need the Pentecostal baptism of the Spirit on all our Churches. Then we shall have all the missionaries we require— missionaries full of the Holy Ghost, and fully equipped for their work.' Recalling a Holiness Convention at Prahran, he yearned, 'A full baptism of the Spirit, such as they received at Pentecost, would make us all of one heart and soul. May the good Lord speedily give us that Pentecostal baptism!'

In Hobart, Tasmania, it was thought that the people might be slow to respond, 'but with the power of the Holy Spirit on them there was no difficulty at all.' In 1895, in Footscray, Victoria, 'some fifty or sixty of God's people were in downright earnest seeking to be filled with the Spirit. It was a glorious time of emptying and filling.' Three years later, at the Central Mission in Sydney, such large numbers responded to his invitation to seek the fullness of the Spirit that there was standing room only in the committee room set aside for the purpose.'

William Taylor

William George Taylor (1845–1934), Superintendent of the Mission, was delighted.[72] Taylor had himself seen revival through his ministry and believed strongly in the Wesleyan two-stage initiation. In 1876, at the age of 31, he had been appointed to the Methodist Church at Toowoomba, Queensland. Here, in this community of 4,700 people,

William Taylor 1835 – 1934.

he found a 'contented' congregation of about 80 members, who were, in his opinion, 'too contented by far'. He managed to persuade them to shift to the local School of Arts hall for one Sunday and some 300 people turned up in the morning with about 500 at they continued in that hall. By 'a gracious and wonderful visitation of the Holy Spirit a blessed revival swept the town' and a new church building was erected. It was Toowoomba's 'first baptism of fire'.[73] Recalling the events, Taylor later wrote—

> The work began, where all genuine revivals should begin, within the church itself. At Pentecost the Holy Spirit came upon the infant Church, and then followed the gathering in... Would that, at this writing, I could reach the ear of every minister and every church member in Australia... It would be an earnest cry for the Church itself to awake and put on its strength...
>
> In each case it has been the same—a gracious spiritual revival, manifestly, in every case, the work of the Spirit of God, preparing the way for permanent material advancement such as could never have been but for this wonderful leading

of the Holy Ghost. When will our beloved Methodism, when will the church of God generally, awake to this paramount fact?[74]

Taylor spared no energy in his pursuit of spiritual revival. In Taree, NSW, in the three years from 1879–82, he preached 463 sermons, conducted 350 class meetings, baptized 130 children and travelled nearly 15,000 miles, mostly on horseback or by rowing boat. In one series of special services, he preached to full churches, sometimes with people standing outside. At times, he could hardly be heard because of 'suppressed sobs and cries of "Glory!"' There were 180 professions of faith. This was all, he said, 'absolutely... the result of the outpouring of the Holy Spirit.'[75]

In 1884, he was appointed to the languishing York Street church in Sydney. Here he used innovative means and an emphasis on prayer to revive the flagging fortunes of the church. Ultimately, it became the Central Methodist Mission and later Wesley Mission.

He himself experienced occasional evidences of the prophetic power of 'divine impulse' and was clearly convinced of the need for churches to emulate the methods of the apostles.

> Loyalty to the flag unfurled at Pentecost has ever been demonstrated as God's ordained plan for the creation of Churches that shall move and bless and save the people. Apostolic methods will still produce Apostolic results... I tremble as I think of the bare possibility of this work ever being shifted from its old moorings. Disaster would be bound to follow.[76]

Taylor's passion for revival was well expressed in a sermon he preached to the New South Wales Methodist Conference in 1912, on the one hundredth anniversary of the first class meeting in Australia. He urged his hearers to retain the class system because of its beneficial effects on the Church. Methodism's only safety lay in its spirituality, he continued. And he pleaded with them—

> Back to Wesley! Back to the upper room! Rekindle the waning fires of the Church's inner life! Give the Holy Ghost an opportunity, even yet, to make us the great soul-saving force of the twentieth century!

He urged the Conference itself to resolve to discover the power necessary to drive the Church's 'vast machinery'. It would pay them 'a thousandfold' to stop everything for a year and fall to their knees to ask God to 'alter the atmosphere of the Church.' He challenged the ministers. 'Put fire in the pulpit, and you will soon get fire in the pew.' He asked every member to 'fall into line'.

> Let the Church go to its knees and master the art of 'tarrying' there, and then, ere this year closes, there shall come to our great Church the one thing, the only thing, that can permanently settle this question—a Pentecost, which, bursting upon us with all its original power, shall give God the Holy Ghost His chance, and shall hand back to us our old influence. And then we shall no longer lament that our exchequers are half empty, our congregations are small, our fellowship a dead letter; but ... we shall enter upon the golden age of our Church, and there shall be added to our numbers daily such as are being saved.[77]

Methodists as a whole did not take seriously Taylor's call to 'tarry', but there were others who did. In the very year Taylor gave this address, 'tarry meetings' were being conducted regularly in the first Pentecostal church in Melbourne, Victoria, as they waited on God for an outpouring of the Spirit.[78]

One of the formative influences in Taylor's life was the English Methodist William Arthur's *Tongue of Fire* (1856) which went into eighteen printings in the first three years and in which Arthur urges his readers to pursue a baptism in the Holy Spirit.[79] The chapter headings say it all—The Promise of a Baptism of Fire, The Waiting for the Fulfilment, The Fulfilment of the Promise, Effects Which Immediately Followed the Baptism of Fire—Spiritual Effects, Miraculous Effects, Ministerial Effects, Effects Upon the World, Permanent Benefits Resulting to the Church. The book concludes with an impassioned prayer—

> And now, adorable Spirit, proceeding from the Father and the Son, descend upon all the Churches, renew the Pentecost in this our age, and baptize Thy people generally—O, baptize them yet again with tongues of fire! Crown this nineteenth century with a revival of 'pure and undefiled religion' greater than that of the last century, greater than that of the first, greater than any 'demonstration of the Spirit' ever yet vouchsafed to men!

While Arthur dismissed the Irvingite expression of 'unknown tongues', which he felt were fraudulent, he nevertheless spoke positively about the possibility of the biblical gift of tongues appearing again. He advocated the exercise of spiritual gifts but urged his readers primarily to be filled with the Holy Spirit so they could lead lives of holiness and grace.[80]

Arthur's exhortations influenced many believers in Australia as well as England and America, where his writings were also popular. In 1929, a 'Pentecostal' member of the Salvation Army told how he had been converted through reading *Tongue of Fire*.[81]

The Spectator, the weekly organ of Victorian and Tasmanian Methodism, carried frequent articles urging its readers to revival, holiness and the baptism of the Holy Spirit.[82] In 1879, J. F. Horsley asked outright, 'Have ye received the Holy Ghost?' He began—

> This question, which Paul put to the company of disciples which he found at Ephesus, allow me, Christian believer, to put to you. Have you received the Holy Ghost *since you believed?* Carefully ponder over the question. Have you received the Holy Ghost since you were converted? Has your Pentecost come?[83]

When the Spirit came, He would do so powerfully and the result would be more successful evangelism. 'To your tents, O Israel!' he wrote, 'Get before God...and let us not rest until our Pentecost has come.'

Clearly, for Methodists, revival meant holiness and soul-winning. And this was the result of an infusion of the Holy Spirit into the lives of believers. An editorial in the *Spectator* refers to being 'richly baptized with the Holy Ghost'.[84] In 1877, one I. J. Lansing urged people to ask God to baptize them 'with the Holy Ghost and fire'.[85] In June of the same year, the *Spectator* stated, 'Beyond all doubt, revivals are the methods of the Spirit's operations for saving men and building up Christ's kingdom.'[86] In June and July, there were reports of revival in Port Adelaide, South Australia, where the people became 'visibly affected' by the remarks of Rev J. Haslam, and cries of mercy were heard throughout the congregation, and in Eaglehawk, Victoria, where W. H. Fitchett reported the conversion of 100 people in five weeks and where the revival was marked by 'affecting scenes and incidents.' A 'mighty wave of power seemed to sweep suddenly over the whole congregation, and in an instant penitents were in all parts of the building crying aloud for mercy...' It was 'the happiest and most remarkable meeting' ever held at Eaglehawk.[87]

> At the 1893 Victorian Wesleyan Conference, one man cried, 'What we need...is not the organisation only, but above all, the gift of the Holy Ghost—the Pentecostal fire to consume our differences... what we want now is the Baptism of Fire.'[88]

Alexander Edgar (1850–1914), the founder of the Methodist Mission in Melbourne also saw the need for Christian revival.[89] As the last President of the Victorian Wesleyan Conference before Methodist Union took place, Edgar clearly influenced at least one of the resolutions passed that year at the Conference gathering—

> Recognising the great source and secret of spiritual success is the grace of our Father, God, in the mediatorship of Christ, and the gift of the Holy Ghost, we give up ourselves in renewed devotion to God's cause, praying and striving that a Pentecostal baptism of the Spirit may be granted to our churches in the year upon which we have entered, and the new century which has begun.[90]

Whatever the reaction of Australian Methodism as a movement to the theme of this,[91] many individual Methodists took it to heart.

The Bible Christians

While the Wesleyans seem to have been in the forefront of Methodist Revival movements, the field was not uniquely theirs. There were persistent and repeated reports of revival and the need for the power of the Holy Spirit among the Bible Christians, another of the four major nineteenth century Methodist groups.[92] In 1870, an article in the *South Australian Bible Christian Magazine* pointed out that it was usually just one single Christian filled with the Holy Spirit who touched off a revival. The Christian needed to pray, believe, confess until he felt his heart 'all subdued and melted by the Holy Spirit' and until his love for Christ was 'glowing, fervid and burning' and until, like Jesus, he was in an agony of prayer over the lost.[93]

Three years later, T. McNeil, a Bible Christian minister, stressed the need for believers to have the power of the Holy Ghost in their lives—

> The Spirit of God is the source of ministerial power and success... Can we in our enlightened age afford to forego the baptism that descended on the early church...? We also believe in the power of the Holy Ghost; we feel that we must have it... to reap a harvest of precious souls, we must have the power of the Holy Ghost...
>
> Let us secure the divine presence how we may—by prayer, by faith, by humiliation, by self-sacrifice, by any way or every; but let us never rest till we get the baptism of the Holy Ghost.'[94]

The following year, Rev R. Kelley reported an influx of 30 converts at a small church near Kadina, in South Australia's mid-north. At Bowden, an Adelaide suburb, some 50 or 60 were added to the Bible Christian church—and even more to the Wesleyans. 'There is nothing we so much want as a *revival*,' Kelley concluded.[95] Within a few months, his prayer was granted. He was personally instrumental in what a contemporary witness described as a revival 'unparalleled in the history of the colony.'[96] In a period of six weeks, in a community of some 12,000, an estimated 1,250 were converted. No doubt there was fertile ground for such a harvest. There were some 14 Methodist churches in the district, including the huge 1200-seat Wesleyan chapel at Moonta Mines[97] where the awakening began on Sunday 4 April 1875 with a funeral address by Kelley, who was the minister at the neighbouring town of Kadina, for a popular and well-loved girl named Kate Morecombe whose death had been sudden and unexpected. Fifteen young people professed conversion. By the end of the week, through the efforts of the local ministers, the number had grown to 45. The following Sunday, a report in a local magazine said—

> O! What a mighty display of the saving power of God! Throughout all the services of the day, God was present among us. Crowds of people came to the chapel to hear the word of life... At the close of the evening meeting... what a glorious sight we were favoured to behold. Cries of mercy were heard from all parts of the chapel... Forty persons were added to the church.

The revival touched both believers and unbelievers. James Stephens was delighted that all the members of the church choir and a number of Sunday School teachers were converted! But there were also conversions from the world. During the following week, a circus arrived in town, but nobody attended—'all the people went to the prayer meeting.' Next morning, the circus left.

The revival spread from the Mines to the township. A notable feature was the way that ministers and members of Baptist, Wesleyan, Independent, Primitive Methodist and Bible Christian churches all cooperated. As a result, church attendances increased—the Wesleyans by 20 per cent, and the Bible Christians and Primitive Methodists by 40 per cent each. The combined total increase was around 500. This was less than the number of converts, but some of those converted were already church attenders.[98]

The Simultaneous Mission

Methodists were much to the fore in the interdenominational Simultaneous Mission of 1902–03. Sponsored by the Evangelical Council of New South Wales and largely financed by the Methodist 'merchant, manufacturer and philanthropist' Ebenezer Vickery, the managing director of the Mount Kembla Coal and Oil Company,[99] the Mission conducted fourteen-day outreaches in 50 centres simultaneously, with aggregate attendances of some 30,000 people. Twelve fully-equipped tents were used in country areas. Some 25,000 conversions were recorded and social manners reportedly improved, including the prompt payment of debts.[100] One fascinating result of the tent meetings in Mount Kembla, was that pit ponies no longer understood their orders, phrased as they now were, without swearing.[101]

Joseph Marshall

In 1870, a farmer named Joseph Marshall, formerly of Yorkshire, who had taken up land west of Portland, Victoria, was conducting cottage meetings in the area.[102] As far as is known, these were the first Pentecostal meetings held in Australia and among the first conducted anywhere in the world.[103] Marshall probably had a Wesleyan upbringing, had professed conversion a few years previously, and been baptized by immersion by 'a fellow convert' in the First River, 15 kilometres from Portland. He had also come to believe that the infilling of the Holy Spirit was accompanied by speaking in tongues with the result that several people experienced glossolalia. At least some of those who attended were Methodists. Unusual work of the Spirit was not unknown in the area. In 1858, the Portland circuit had enjoyed 'seasons of refreshing' when in answer to fervent prayer, God had 'poured... His Spirit from on high'.[104]

For all this, the church continued to urge those in other circuits to join with them in praying for the Lord to revive His work. Capacity attendances were reported in subsequent years for visits by the renowned D. J. Draper, the District Chairman, and Rev J. S. Waugh[105] and new churches being established. In one of these, in 1868, the Spirit was again poured out and some 20 converts received into fellowship.[106]

In 1873, special services were held daily for a period of four weeks. During this time, there were an estimated 40 converts, as well as a number of others who were 'made perfect in love,' restored from backsliding or deepened in their spiritual lives. As a result, they were now holding special meetings for the outpouring of the Spirit upon the church and indeed upon the whole circuit.[107]

In such an environment, it was not surprising that Pentecostal phenomena should appear. The intensity of desire and the determination to be Spirit-filled is indicated by the testimony of Richard Beauglehole (1846–1920).[108] Born in Cornwall, he emigrated with his stonemason father to Australia in 1854 where he took up farming.[109] At the age of 22, he sat under the ministry of the English Wesleyan layman Matthew Burnett,[110] and on the fourth night, found himself at the penitent form.[111]

In 1869, Beauglehole married Joseph and Ann Marshall's daughter, Sarah (c.1851–1923). There were to be twelve children from the union. He continued in his newfound faith for two years, but he was still not satisfied. Although he had responded as a 'true penitent,' he felt he had received nothing from God. With 13 others, he attended early morning prayer meetings at an old farm house and at the church. Finally, one night, he did have an experience of God's love, when he felt a light shine all around him and a 'well of life' within him. Then he attended a meeting conducted by his 43-year-old father-in-law.

Because of their speaking in tongues, local people began to refer to the group as either 'Marshallites' or 'Sounders.' It was the Anglican Bishop of Ballarat who first drew public attention to them in a speech made in England in 1883. He claimed they believed 'the way to get to Heaven was to make a peculiar sound with the voice, this belief being based on a text of Scripture, 'Blessed are the people who know the joyful "sound".' In reporting this 'grotesque' idea, the *Southern Cross* could not resist either sarcasm or scepticism—

> If any individual of the curious ecclesiastical species Dr. Thornton has discovered can be caught alive, it should certainly be placed in the Zoological Gardens, and would, as a curiosity, outshine the new elephant. Perhaps, with still more useful results, it might be exported to England and shown throughout the country to awaken compassion for Victorian darkness. Has Dr. Thornton fallen a victim to those sinners, the reporters? The old Cornish name for a Methodist itinerating minister was 'a rounder.' Has the unhappy Bishop heard this word and invented a new sect to suit?[112]

The Rev James Watson of South Yarra was able to set the record straight. There was indeed a group known as 'Sounders' in the Portland area.[113] In raising funds for a new building, an Anglican priest had used them as an example of the urgent need for 'such religious enlightenment as the Church alone can give.' The Portland correspondent for the *Warrnambool Independent* was inclined to think that no matter what churches were built, the Sounders were not likely to be affected by them, as there were already Methodist chapels within easy distance, which they did attend on occasion. He saw Marshall as having an excessive and dangerous faith in his own ability to interpret the Scriptures and felt that although the group as a whole were 'not ignorant of the doctrines taught by the churches' they were, on the other hand, mostly ignorant and illiterate, and 'unable to read the Bible for themselves'—a claim certainly not applicable to Beauglehole.[114]

The reporter himself had not attended the meetings, but had heard tales of people engaging in vigorous dancing, cooing like doves, bleating like sheep and pursuing other extravagances to 'a very late hour', which he compared to 'the vagaries of the Salvation Army'. This latter comment suggests he was not particularly well-informed about the behaviour of either group. However, he did concede that he had never heard any charges of immorality being laid against them. They were basically 'hard-working honest fellows' and 'upright in all their dealings' and 'not at all the kind of people to be taken in'. In any case, the numbers were evidently very small, only about 20 people being involved.[115]

Other reports give a different impression. Beauglehole's description seems not unlike that of many another Methodist revival meeting, except for the occurrences of glossolalia. The same ingredients of earnest wrestling with God and anguish of soul are evident—

> After three weeks' seeking, we were all on our knees praying when God took a wonderful hold of me. It was like being in an electrical machine. Although I was kneeling on the ground with my elbows on a stretcher, my knees knocked together, and my belly trembled and I saw a light shining round me brighter than the noonday sun, and One in that light.

> It overcame me and my breath was leaving me, but I said, 'Here goes, Lord; sink, live or die, I must have the Holy Spirit.' And, glory to God, He did answer me. For a time I was lost to everything and when I came to myself, my lips were

trembling... and I heard the Spirit's voice, for He had taken possession of my throat and tongue and was speaking through me in other tongues. My mate got through the next morning at nine o'clock. And, oh, the heights and depths of the glory of God![116]

At times, people fell prostrate to the floor, too overcome to remain standing. This was too much for two Wesleyan ministers' sons who fled one meeting. Forty years later, Beauglehole's fervour was still too much for others in the district. 'If we get into a conversation with them,' he lamented, 'they do not want to meet us again.'

Nevertheless, Beauglehole helped erect the Methodist church at Bridgewater, adjacent to his farm and continued to be involved in Methodism for the rest of his life, a charcoal inscription on the wall of the disused Mount Richmond chapel making reference to both 'old Dick Beauglehole' and 'Marshall' as being among those who worshipped there. 'These courageous pion(eer) names are indelibly stamped in the minds of (a) (f)ew remaining old (members),' it reads. 'May they never be forgot'.[117]

Others to accept Marshall's teaching were young Tom Francis and Margaret McCuspie, nee Morrison (1826–1917).[118] Margaret wrote to her sisters Rachel, who lived in Nairne, South Australia, and Jessie, from Farina, in the Far North, and told them of the blessings she was experiencing at Marshall's meetings. Rachel was weak and ill and basically bedfast, but made the journey in the hope of finding some help. Jessie was sceptical, but when she found Rachel after a prayer meeting 'dancing in the Spirit and speaking in tongues', she, too, believed. Not long after this, Tom Francis married her daughter.

Rachel's 13-year-old daughter Martha (Mattie) accompanied her to Portland. Years later, married to Benjamin Pillifeant, she and her husband conducted Pentecostal meetings in their home, some of the earliest in Adelaide. The family continued in the Pentecostal movement, their daughter Dorothy, her husband Thomas Reekie and their grandson David Reekie all being ordained as pastors in the Assemblies of God.[119]

Many Pentecostal pioneers had a Methodist background. Sarah Jane (Jeannie) Lancaster (1858–1934), founder in 1908 of the Pentecostal Mission (more commonly known as Good News Hall), the first Pentecostal congregation to be formally established in Australia, had been a member of the York St Methodist Mission in Ballarat, a city frequently stirred by Wesleyan revivalists.[120] Robert Horne, founder of the Southern Evangelical Mission in 1911, the second Australian Pentecostal congregation, was a Methodist missioner in South Melbourne.[121] J. M. Roberts, another early Pentecostal pastor, was previously a Methodist lay preacher for 40 years.[122] The Enticknap family of North Queensland were also Methodists.[123]

William Cunningham Sloan (1870–1922) was a 'staunch Methodist' who for a time joined the Salvation Army in Bright, Victoria. He visited Good News Hall, in Melbourne, 1908, and after five weeks of praying, in October of that year, he and his wife Eliza were both baptized in the Spirit and spoke in tongues.[124] For over ten years, the Sloans conducted Pentecostal meetings in their home in the Ovens Valley.[125]

A cluster of Methodist preachers joined the Pentecostal ranks. In Melbourne, in the 1930s, a minister named Egan-Lee left his church within five years of retirement, forfeiting his pension and alienating his wife and family, in order to join the Pentecostals.[126] During the First World War, as a soldier on leave in London, Arch Newton visited a Pentecostal church and was baptized in the Holy Spirit.[127] Around 1929, he was the Methodist minister in Wynyard in Tasmania. During his first twelve months, 248 young people were converted to Christ. Newton constantly preached on the need to be baptized in the Holy Spirit.[128] South Australian Methodist minister, Richard Marks,[129] and Queenslander Pastor Ralph Read[130] also became Pentecostals.

Two sisters, Elizabeth Sutton and Claire Buley, who had been life-long Methodists, used to pray together in Melbourne. In 1906, Sutton found herself speaking in tongues. Shocked and concerned, Buley began to pray for her so that God would not allow her to do anything wrong and she, too, experienced glossolalia. Buley's family later became Pentecostals, with her daughter and three of her grand-daughters marrying Pentecostal pastors.[131]

Other former Methodists to join the Pentecostal movement included musician Edith Buley, youth worker Annie Sandlant, women's leader 'Sister' Reinhardt (a cripple who was healed through the ministry of A. C. Valdez), Pastor H. S. Slade and Pastor C. B. Swensen.[132]

The Salvation Army

Given its Methodist origins, it was not surprising that an emphasis on the fullness of the Spirit was always present in the Salvation Army.[133] In 1884, when Colonel Booth addressed a gathering of soldiers in Sydney—

> The altar was soon crowded on both sides with willing seekers after holiness, and after being dealt with... they rose and testified to the joy and peace which now possessed them. Shouts of praise all the while burst forth from the soldiers... The power of God ran through the place and loosed every tongue and melted every heart. It was glory to be there!

Later in the meeting—

> Then came the wave offerings, and the volleys, with the clapping of hands, and the shouts of praise—a real hallelujah gallop—until the Colonel was obliged at last to pull them up sharp to take a breath.[134]

Another report in 1884 described 'peculiar visitations upon many of our soldiers.' Several had unexpectedly 'fallen down insensible' and had remained unconscious for up to 36 hours. But during this time, their faces were lit up with ecstasy and they were acknowledged to have been in communion with the Lord. Some later tried to prophesy, but this was strongly rejected.[135] The previous year, John Singleton described how in six different towns and cities the Army was experiencing 'a steady revival' and that in Collingwood, Victoria, over one thousand people had claimed to be converted.[136] The emphasis on the baptism and gifts of the Holy Spirit was an ongoing one. In 1896, Major Graham wrote—

> Now this baptism (in the Holy Spirit) is strictly essential in order to be of service to God and humanity, and whatever ability or talent a person may possess naturally is of little or no use for eternal work until quickened and energised by the indwelling Spirit of God.[137]

In the same year, a symposium on 'How to Bring About a Revival' was held at Norwood, South Australia.[138] While many factors were mentioned, including Bible study, holiness, praise and dedication, several of the speakers pointed out the need for the power of the Holy Spirit. Mrs Colonel Bailey declared how she loved the apostle Peter because even though he denied his Lord, 'when he got baptized with the Holy Ghost, he became a man of resolute purpose.' If they also were baptized in the Spirit, she argued, God would honour them and revival would be sure to come. Captain Gardiner agreed that they needed to honour the Holy Spirit and Captain Mary Moreton reminded the gathering of their need to abandon all unclean habits before they could be Spirit-filled. Colonel Bailey spoke at some length on prayer and their need to pray in faith, with perseverance and purpose, for revival to follow. A report on the next page reminded readers that 'God the Holy Ghost' was the life of the Army.

William Booth was a believer in spiritual gifts. After describing the various gifts of the Holy Spirit, he went on to say that—

> There is not a word in the Bible which proves that we may not have them at the present time, and there is nothing in experience to show they would not be as useful today as in any previous period of the Church's history. No man therefore can be condemned for desiring them...

> Far be it from me to say one word that would stay the longing of any heart for the extraordinary gifts already mentioned. I long for them myself. I believe in their necessity, and I believe they are already amongst us. By all means let us have the perfection of the Divine method of working...

> Let us covet, let us seek earnestly—nay, let us never rest until we possess in all its fullness [sic] this celestial passion.[139]

The Army's *Field Officers' Orders and Regulations* contained a long section on divine healing, which was defined as 'the recovery of persons afflicted with various diseases by the power of God, in answer to faith and prayer, without the use of ordinary means, such as doctors, medicines, and the like.' That God should heal in this way was 'in perfect harmony' with the teachings of the Army.[140]

An article by Catherine Booth published in the *War Cry* in 1915 lamented the great want of power in the lives of Christians. The early Christians had it because they needed it. Was not our need just as great? And if we needed it, was it not likely that God would bestow it? The baptism of the Holy Spirit would transform us just it did them. 'Will you come and let Him baptize you?' she pleaded.[141]

W. F. South, an English Pentecostal pastor, claimed that Catherine Booth longed for the power of God to be demonstrated and defended manifestations such as people falling prostrate under the impulse of the Spirit. He argued that her book *Aggressive Christianity* was widely circulated in the early days of the

Army and was 'no doubt used by God to bring many into the Pentecostal experience.'[142]

Bramwell Booth, a decade later, spoke approvingly of the displays of emotion often seen in the early days of the Army. There was shouting, weeping, clapping, dancing and groaning aloud. Many received visions and revelations. Many sick people were healed. Even speaking in tongues had been experienced, although usually suppressed.[143] A Salvation Army Bandmaster wrote of his conviction that it was the power of the Holy Spirit that enabled the early Christians to fulfil Christ's commission. The disciples had to wait for ten days for divine enduement. They were expectant, so they received. 'Without Pentecost,' he wrote, 'the story of the Gospels would have been simply classed with the legendary narratives of other religions.' Facts of history had no power to convert, but Pentecost had set those facts alight. The Holy Spirit filled men and women with boldness. Jesus' final words urged us to tarry for power from on high.[144]

The first of the Booth family to have a Pentecostal experience was William Booth-Clibborn, grandson of William Booth.[145] In 1930, Booth-Clibborn and his family arrived in Australia where he was to spend the next two years engaged in effective Pentecostal evangelism.

Jeannie Lancaster, although a Methodist, attended Salvation Army meetings many years before she became Pentecostal. In later years she noted that many Salvation Army people had testified to divine healing through the pages of *Good News* and told how Mrs Catherine Booth had affirmed her strong belief in divine healing and how her son Herbert had looked in vain for someone to pray for her in her time of need.[146]

One of those whose story appeared in *Good News* was Dolly Cridge. In 1910, she related how as an 'Army lassie' she had tried for years to live the Christian life in her own strength, but had failed. But on 16 January that year, she had been baptized in the Holy Spirit. Not long after this, she was praying in tongues and was told she had been speaking in Italian, praising God for saving her and filling her with the Spirit and offering to spend her life in God's service. She also gave several interpretations of glossolalia. She later gained a reputation as a prophetess.[147]

M. A. Alway and her father had joined the Salvation Army around 1885 because of their teaching on holiness and their use of women in ministry. In 1907, she asked the Staff Captain to pray for her for healing from a varicose vein in her leg—with positive results within two days. She now marched and sang with more energy than any woman in the corps. Within a few months, however, she suffered a slight stroke and had to retire. She read some Pentecostal literature and attended prayer meetings in an upstairs room in Collins Street. When she was baptized in the Spirit, she spoke in tongues and was healed of the effects of the stroke.[148]

There were many testimonies among early Pentecostals who had formerly been members of the Salvation Army. In South Australia, Mrs Annie Chamberlain had served full-time as a captain in the Army for a decade or so before being baptized in the Spirit and commencing Pentecostal meetings in her home. J. L. H. Wilson of Maryborough, Queensland, had been 'seeking the Holy Spirit for years' as a member of the Army. Finally, under the ministry of F. B. Van Eyk, his prayer was answered. A member of the Salvation Army testified to the good work done in Brisbane. Harold Hultgren and his family were in the Army before attending Good News Hall. C. Cousins was invited to a tarrying meeting by three young women from the Salvation Army Corps she was attending. When South African evangelist Van Eyk first preached in Adelaide in 1926, a Salvation Army officer said, 'Van Eyk is lovely; full of fire, and charged with divine power.' A 74-year-old Salvation Army woman was immersed in water at Maryborough after Van Eyk's visit there. Several members of one Salvation Army family group in Queensland were baptized in the Spirit after hearing of Pentecostalism through a young man in the Army in Ballarat.[149]

H. S. Kilpatrick, who became secretary of the Apostolic Faith Mission in Perth, had been a Salvation Army officer for 25 years. He had many 'glorious experiences' and had claimed the baptism in the Spirit by faith, but ultimately realised he did not have it in reality. In December 1926, he spoke in tongues. Captain Rose was baptized in the Spirit in Rockhampton in late 1927. A year later, another Salvationist told the Good News Hall congregation how he had been baptized in the Spirit and spoken in tongues, and was determined to enjoy other gifts of the Spirit as well, and another testified that he 'wanted all the Lord had' for him, so he 'tarried' (at Good News Hall), and God filled him with the Holy Spirit. 'Daddy' Clarkson, who pastored for a time in the Pentecostal church in Bendigo, had formerly been a Salvation Army officer. J. E. Ellis, a Pentecostal elder and pastor for many years, was converted in 1888 in the Salvation Army at Hawthorn, Victoria, as was Reg Price, a deacon in Richmond Temple, in Bendigo in 1917. Queensland pastor L. Barnes was converted in the Salvation Army in Rockhampton, Queensland, and Pastor D. Scott had been an Army Officer for ten years before she became a Pentecostal.[150]

Conclusion

From their earliest days, both Methodism and the Salvation Army taught believers that the Christian faith was not just a creed to be understood but a faith to be experienced. Conversion was not a realignment of one's thinking; it was a life-changing encounter with God. And it was through being baptized in the Holy Spirit that believers became holy and fully equipped for victorious living.

Whether their failure to accept Pentecostal phenomena like speaking in tongues was a conscious rejection or lack of fervour or general disinterest is not clear; there seems more evidence for the latter view.[151] For most Methodists, tongue-speaking and associated gifts were seen as neither necessary nor beneficial. This may well have been a reflection of John Wesley's own opinion. He saw little place for the gifts of the Spirit, believing that they had generally been withdrawn from the Church, and that those who imagined they used them, were deceiving themselves.[152] The overwhelming evidence is that evangelical Methodists basically saw revival in terms of two things—the saving of souls and holiness of living. Although there were glimpses of recognition of the gifts of the Spirit, these do not seem to have been of particular interest. There is scarcely a mention of them anywhere in nineteenth century Methodist writings while references to conversion and holiness are widespread.[153]

It is also of interest to note that the 1923 Conference, in response to the 'advance' of Christian Science, denied its 'sophistries' but reaffirmed the Church's understanding of biblical healing, pointing out that Methodists believed firmly in prayer for the sick, that ministers should be encouraged to pray for the sick and that the bounds of healing might be wider than they thought. On the other hand, spiritual healing should always take precedence over physical healing and that there should be a close relationship between medical and spiritual practice. No one should expect a clergyman to be a physician as well.[154]

By the twentieth century, there was another reason for Methodist disinterest in charismata, namely the rise of theological liberalism. With a gradual shift by many Methodists from belief in a literal approach to the Bible came a concomitant drift away from an experiential and expressive faith. The celebrated controversy over the use of Peake's *Commentary* was simply one indicator of this.[155]

It may be argued that Wesley did leave the door open to the possibility of charismata. In his published sermon, 'The More Excellent Way,' he wrote—

> It does not appear that these extraordinary gifts of the Holy Ghost were common in the church for more than two or three centuries. We seldom hear of them after that fatal period when the Emperor Constantine called himself a Christian... The cause of this was not (as has been vulgarly supposed) 'because there was no more occasion for them,' because all the world was become Christian. This is a miserable mistake; not a twentieth part of it was then nominally Christian. The real cause was, 'the love of many,' almost of all Christians, so called, was 'waxed cold'... This was the real cause why the extraordinary gifts of the Holy Ghost were no longer to be found in the Christian Church; because Christians were turned heathen again, and had only a dead form left.[156]

In spite of his reservations about those who claimed such gifts, Wesley may have welcomed their reintroduction, as, for him, it would have marked a return also to vital Christianity. Many Methodists in nineteenth century and early twentieth century Australia did have a fervent passion for an outpouring of the Holy Spirit that would result in revival and holy living. What Pentecostals did was to take this one step further. Not only was it possible to experience the power of the Spirit of God, but there was a clearly recognisable and very specific sign of its coming—namely, glossolalia. In this way, religious experience became not just a desirable option, but rather an essential ingredient of authentic faith. It was this insistence on people bearing tangible witness to God's power that was the essential spirit of Pentecost.

Notes

1. W. Hollenweger, 'The Five Roots of Pentecostalism,' a paper presented at the Conference on Pentecostal and Charismatic Research in Europe, Kappel, Switzerland, 3 July, 1991; *Journal of Pentecostal Theology* No. 1, October, 1992, 8.

2. While Methodism was a 'holiness movement' it was not labelled in this way in Australia.

3. Blumhofer, 1989, 17ff.

4. A. Cerillo Jr, 'Interpretive Approaches to the History of American Pentecostal Origins,' *Pneuma* 19:1 Spring, 1997, 29ff. As has been noted earlier, these categories do not readily apply to the Australian scene.

5. `Relevant Pentecostal Witness,' pamphlet, Chatsglen, n. d. but c.1991, 9.

6. A. Murray, *Waiting on God* (London: Oliphants, 1961); Hollenweger, 1988, 111ff.

7.L. Pethrus, *A Spiritual Memoir* (Plainfield: Logos, 1973); S. Burgess, G. McGee. P. Alexander eds, *Dictionary of Pentecostal and Charismatic Movements* (Grand Rapids: Zondervn Regency, 1988), 711; S. Frodsham, *With Signs Following* (Springfield: Gospel Publishing House, 1946), 77ff; D. Gee, *Upon All Flesh* (Springfield: Gospel Publishing House, 1947); M. Harper, *As at the Beginning* (London: Hodder and Stoughton, 1966).

8. B. Gutierrez and D. Smith, eds, 1996, 53; Burgess et al, eds, 1988, 54f.

9. J. Worsfold, *The Origins of the Apostolic Church in Great Britain* (Wellington, N.Z., Julian Literature Trust, 1991), 1–52; Hollenweger, 1988, 176ff; Burgess et al, eds, 1988, 268ff; Gee, 1947; Harper, 1966.

10. Worsfold, 1991, 19. Edward Irving (1792–1834) was a Scottish Presbyterian who was dismissed from the Church because of a dispute over the deity of Christ. He established the Catholic Apostolic Church in London, where he encouraged gifts of the Spirit, especially speaking in tongues. See Burgess et al, 1988, 470f; D. Allen, *The Unfailing Stream* (Tonbridge: Sovereign World, 1994); A. Dallimore, *The Life of Edward Irving* (Edinburgh: Banner of Truth, 1983); G. Strachan, *The Pentecostal Theology of Edward* (Peabody, Massachusetts: Hendrickson, 1973); B. Warfield, *Counterfeit Miracles* (Edinburgh: Banner of Truth, 1918, 1983); T. G. Grass, 'Edward Irving: Eschatology, Ecclesiology and Spiritual Gifts,' in *Christianity and History Newsletter* , No. 15, June, 1995, 16ff.

11. Strachan, 1973, 19; Allen, 1994, 80ff.

12. *The Apostolic Church of Queensland and Hatton Vale Community Centenary*, n. d., 2ff; Humphreys and Ward, 1986, 100ff.

13. S. Piggin, 'The History of and Prospects for Religious Revival in Australia,' Heads of Churches Seminar paper, 23 March, 1993; Piggin, 1996, 40ff.

14. See H. R. Jackson, *Churches and People in Australia and New Zealand 1860–1930* (Wellington: Allen and Unwin, 1987), 48ff; Piggin, 1996, 57ff; I. Breward, *A History of the Australian Churches* (St Leonards: Allen and Unwin, 1993), 63f.

15. Sources: Humphreys and Ward, 1986; R. Brown (ed) *Collins Milestones in Australian History, 1788 to the Present* (Sydney: Collins, 1986); Gillman, 1988; K. Newton, *A History of the Brethren in Australia,* unpublished thesis, 1990; J. Roe, *Beyond Belief: Theosophy in Australia 1879–1939* (Kensington: New South Wales University Press, 1986); Chant, 1984; B. Bolton, *Booth's Drum* (Lane Cove: Hodder and Stoughton, 1980).

16. R. Broome, *Treasure in Earthen Vessels* (Brisbane: University of Queensland Press, 1980), 37; S. Piggin, 'Revivalism: the Holiness Movement and Millennialism, 1875–1899,' unpublished paper, 1993, 16; W. Phillips, 'Religion,' in Vamplew, ed, 1987, 421, 428.

17. Jackson, 1987, 104f.

18. J. D. Bollen, *Protestantism and Social Reform in NSW, 1890–1910* (Melbourne: Melbourne University Press, 1972), 185.

19. Broome, 1980, 33ff.

20. The percentages were calculated from statistics provided by Walter Phillips' entry entitled, 'Religion,' in Vamplew, 1987, 421, 428. Note that Catholic figures are at best only an indication, as they are based on records in NSW for 1803, in Victoria for 1881 and in SA for 1931.

21. E. K. Ditterich, 'Daniel James Draper—Master Builder,' *Heritage* (Melbourne: The Methodist Historical Society of Victoria and Tasmania, No. 26, October, 1874), 13.
22. See J. C. Caldwell, 'Population' and W. W. Phillips, 'Religion' in Vamplew, ed, 1987, 26, 30, 421ff. See also Chant, 1984, 29.
23. Piggin, 1993, 16.
24. Note that Methodists, at least, happily recognised the discrepancy between members and adherents. In 1901, they claimed over six and a half million members worldwide with about 30 million adherents. See W. J. Palamountain, *A.R. Edgar: A Methodist Greatheart* (Melbourne: Spectator, 1933), 160
25. B. Dickey, ed, *The Australian Dictionary of Evangelical Biography* (Sydney: Evangelical History Association, 1994), ix.
26. R. B. Walker, 'The Growth and Typology of the Wesleyan Methodist Church in New South Wales 1812–1901,' JRH, December, 1971, 334.
27. Dougas, ed, 1978, 474.
28. John Wesley, *The Works of John Wesley* (Nashville: Abingdon, 1985), Vol I, *Sermons 1–33*, 332f; Vol II, *Sermons 34–70*, 97–124.
29. H. Lederle agrees. See H. Lederle, *Treasures Old and New* (Peabody, Mass: Hendrickson, 1988), 9. C. T. Symons' explanation of sanctification and Christian perfection does not line up easily with eighteenth and nineteenth century approaches; it seems to be an attempt to rephrase Wesley's teaching in a manner palatable to current thought. See C. T. Symons, *Our Fathers' Faith and Ours* (Adelaide: Young People's Department, Methodist Church of Australasia, South Australia Conference, n. d.), 84–86.
30. J. Wesley, *Works* (Grand Rapids: Baker, 1996, Vol 12), 432.
31. J. Wesley, *A Plain Account of Christian Perfection,* in *Works,* Volume 11, 1996, 393.
32. Wesley, *Works,* Vol 12, 1996, 395f; Dr Moulton, 'John Wesley's Doctrine of Christian Perfection,' *Spectator,* 20 May, 1925, 471.
33. Wesley, *Works* Vol 12, 1996, 131,138, 227, 239, 241f, 246, 257.
34. Wesley, *Works* Vol 11, 1996, 445.
35. Wesley, *Works* Vol 11, 1996, 385, 392.
36. Wesley, *Plain Account* in *Works* Vol 11, 1996, 374, 380.
37. Wesley. *Works* Vol 12, 1996, 34.
38. J. Pollock, *John Wesley 1703–1791* (London: Hodder and Stoughton, 1989), 95,106; John Capon, *John and Charles Wesley: the Preacher and the Poet* (London: Hodder and Stoughton, 1988), 99f, 108.
39. Wesley, letter to Samuel Wesley, 10 May, 1739, *Works* Vol 12, 1996, 36.
40. Wesley, *Works* (Vol 13, Albany: Sage Digital Library, 1996), 595.
41. Wesley, *Works,* Vol 12, 1996, .408, 430; Vol 10, Sage, 1996, 77. In his reply to Conyers Middleton, Wesley argues strongly for the genuineness of spiritual gifts such as exorcism, divine healing, prophesying and speaking in tongues, in the first three centuries. Although he also refers to tongues being exercised in France among the 'French prophets,' he makes no attempt to argue that such gifts ought to have been used in his own day. See Wesley, *Works,* Vol 10, Sage, 1996, 11ff, NB 71f.
42. Wesley, letter to Samuel Wesley, *Works* Volume 12, 1996, 33.
43. H. Fielding, *Tom Jones* (Ware: Wordsworth, 1994), 295f.
44. R. Knox, *Enthusiasm* (London: Collins, 1950, 1987), 450.
45. Wesley, *Plain Account*, in Works Vol 11, 1996, 430.
46. Wesley *Works* Vol 11, 1996, 406ff; Vol 12, 1996, 125, 281.
47. R. Foulkes, *The Flame Shall Not Be Quenched* (Devonport: Methodist Charismatic Fellowship, n. d.), 65. The quotation is from Walsh's *Journal* 8 March, 1750.

48. 'What is Christian Perfection?' *The Spectator and Methodist Chronicle*, Vol 5, No 223, 8 August, 1879, 175f. Hedding seems to be going further than Wesley himself went here.
49. J. Roe, 'Challenge and Response: Religious Life in Melbourne, 1876–86,' JRH December, 1968, 155.
50. Wesley, *Works* Vol 11, 1996, 416.
51. Cf. Laurence W. Wood, *The Meaning of Pentecost in Early American Methodism* (Lanham, Maryland: Scarecrow Press, 2002).
52. K. Latourette, *Christianity in a Revolutionary Age* Vol 3, 1969, 16ff; Burgess et al, eds, 1988, 406ff.
53. Dayton and Synan in Synan, ed, 1975, 47.
54. See R. A. Torrey, *How to Receive the Holy Ghost* (Melbourne: Church Missionary Association, 1904); *The Baptism with the Holy Spirit* (Belfast: Revival Movement Association, n. d.).; Murray, *Waiting* , 1961.
55. R. Wessels, 'The Spirit Baptism, Nineteenth Century Roots,' *Pneuma* 14:2, Fall, 1992, 127ff.
56. J. Bowers, 'A Wesleyan-Pentecostal Approach to Christian Formation,' JPT, No. 6, April, 1995, 66.
57. See Burgess et al, eds, 1988, 31ff, 778ff; Bartleman, 1980.
58. This view was not uncommon among nineteenth century Holiness groups. See Burgess and Van Der Maas, eds, 2002, 358.
59. W. Seymour, 'The Apostolic Faith Movement,' in C. Robeck, Jr., ed, *Readings in Pentecostal History* (Pasadena: Fuller Theological Seminary, 1987), 47. The heading, 'Third Work' which would be expected at the beginning of the third paragraph does not appear. The whole document shows signs of amateurish and poorly organised presentation.
60. F. Ewart, *The Phenomenon of Pentecost (a history of the 'Latter Rain')*, (St Louis: Pentecostal Publishing House, 1947), 72.
61. W. Durham, 'A Testimony of the Power of God,' reprinted from *Pentecostal Testimony*, Adelaide: ABC printing Works, n. d.; Burgess et al, 1988, 255f; Ewart, 1947, 71ff.
62. 'The Baptism of the Holy Ghost,' a four-page leaflet. Although it is undated, it seems to have been in circulation in the 1920s. It carries the stamp of the Apostolic Faith Mission, Albert Street, North Parramatta. I can find no other information about this church nor any evidence that it was related to the Apostolic Faith Mission whose headquarters were at Good News Hall, North Melbourne, of whom there is no evidence that they ever taught the three-stage approach to baptism in the Holy Spirit.
63. C. I. Benson, *A Century of Victorian Methodism* (Melbourne: Spectator Publishing Co, 1935), 393.
64. J. Watsford, *Glorious Gospel Triumphs as seen in My Life and Work* (London: Charles H. Kelly, 1900), 123.
65. *Spectator, Vol* LI, 21 Feb 1925, p.173; see also W. H. Fitchett's 'Introductory Sketch' to Watsford's *Glorious Gospel Triumphs*, ix–xiii. Benson calls Watsford's autobiography 'a book of singular spiritual power' (1935, 394). It is interesting that John Dowie spoke highly of Watsford. On 20 March 1904, preaching in Adelaide, he said, 'A very distinguished and beloved Methodist minister for whom I have always had, and have today, the utmost respect and veneration, came to me one day. You all know him here. He is known throughout the colonies—dear old Father Watsford.'—LH, 28 May, 1904, 166.
66. SC, II: 16, 21 April, 1883, 8. Not that the editor always agreed with him. In 1883, he was roundly criticised for his intransigent and impractical stance on voluntary reli-

gious education in Victorian schools and for claiming that the minority who voted with him were the true representatives of Methodism. SC, II: 33, 18 August, 1883, 5; SC, II: 36, 8 September, 1883, 9.

67. Watsford, 1900, p.128. Following quotations and references are from pages 271, 274, 279ff, 286, 287f, 298, 313.

68. *Spectator,* 8 September, 1877, 221.

69. *Spectator,* 5:223, 8 August, 1879, 176.

70. *Spectator*, 10 March, 1893, 185.

71. *Spectator*, 10 March, 1893, 198.

72. Watsford, 1900, 314

73. W. G. Taylor, *The Life-story of an Australian Evangelist* (London: Epworth, 1920), 107f.

74. Taylor, 1920, 108.

75. Taylor, 1920, 116f.

76. Taylor, 1920, 142f, 175ff.

77. Taylor, 1920, 342f

78. See various issues of GN, e.g. 1:1, April, 1910; GN, 9:1, 1 February, 1923, 23f.

79. Taylor, 1920, 298; William Arthur, *Tongue of Fire* (London: Wesleyan Conference Office, 1859), 63, 146, 148, 162, 164, 343; in December 1927, J. L. H. Wilson testified that reading this book helped him in his quest to be baptized in the Holy Spirit: 'At the same time, I was reading a book by W. Arthur, *The Tongue of Fire*, which proved a great blessing to me.' GN, 18:12, December, 1927, 10f.

80. J. E. Carruthers was another who saw the need for revival. Recalling his early days in the Methodist church at Kiama, New South Wales, under the instigation of the saintly Thomas Angwin, where there was a vital awakening, Carruthers wrote—

Nearly all the congregation remained to the prayer-meeting, but although many were pricked in their hearts they did not openly yield. The next night there was almost equally as large a congregation at the prayer-meeting. Then began what the good old people called a 'breaking down.' The communion rail was crowded with seekers. Some hoar-headed men were amongst them; a storekeeper in the town, notorious for his fearful temper and furious conduct when under its influence; some gentle-spirited women; a number of senior lads and girls from the Sunday school... Night after night... the meetings continued... It was a revival that gave workers to the Church, teachers to the Sunday School, local preachers to the circuit plan, and ultimately several ministers to the Australasian Methodist Church. Nor did the work cease with the close of the revival services...

Years later, Carruthers himself was instrumental in initiating a revival in the New South Wales country centre of Wagga Wagga. Within a few days, fifty converts were added to the church. 'And the debt?' Curruthers asks. 'Well, that disappeared.' See J. E. Carruthers, *Memories of an Australian Ministry, 1868–1921* (London: The Epworth Press, n. d.), 30f, 86f.

81. 'A Red Hot Salvationist's Story, as Told in Good News Hall,' GN, 20:12, December, 1929, 8.

82. *Spectator,* 5:209, 2 May, 1879, 7; 5:210, 9 May, 1879, 19.

83. J. F. Horsley, 'Have Ye Received the Holy Ghost?' *Spectator* 5:242, 19 December, 1879, 403.

84. *Spectator* 5:216, 20 June, 1879, 90.

85. I .J. Lansing, *Spectator,* No. 109, 2 June, 1877, 53.

86. *Spectator,* No. 111, 16 June, 1877, 81.

87. *Spectator* , No. 113, 30 June, 1877; No 115, 14 July, 1877, 125.

88. *Spectator,* 10 March, 1883, 193.

89. As a young man of nineteen, kneeling beside a great log on the outskirts of Stawell, Victoria, 'in full and unreserved surrender to God,' Edgar had set himself to seek the baptism in the Holy Spirit. Six years later, he was still pleading with God for the ongoing power of the Holy Spirit in his own life. Palamountain, 1933, 32.

90. Palamountain, 1933, 155.

91. Class meetings, regarded by many as the life of Methodism, declined towards the end of the century. See D. Hilliard, 'The City of Churches: Some Aspects of Religion in Adelaide About 1900', in *Journal of the Historical Society of South Australia,* No. 8, 1980, 9.

92. These were the Wesleyans, the Bible Christians, the Primitive Methodists and the Methodist New Connection. See Hunt, 1985, for details.

93. *South Australian Bible Christian Magazine* (BCM) May, 1870, 183.

94. BCM, November, 1873, 320.

95. BCM, August, 1874, 2.

96. James Stephens in 'The Moonta Revival' BCM, August, 1875, 99. Further details are from this source unless otherwise stated.

97. Aplin et al, eds, 1987, 348.

98. Hunt, 1985, 126f. By way of contrast, R. B. Walker claims that a year later, overall membership was actually slightly less than it had been in 1875—R. B. Walker, JRH, December 1971, 338.

99. G. P. Walsh, 'Vickery, Ebenezer (1827–1906),' in ADB, Vol 6, 1851–1906, 333f; Taylor, 1920, 261ff. Vickery's name is preserved today in a stained glass window in the Wesley Mission Church, 220 Pitt Street, Sydney.

100. Taylor, 1920, 263ff; Broome, 1980, 56ff; S. Piggin, *Faith of Steel* (Wollongong: University of Wollongong, 1984), 135ff. Broome notes that many of the converts may already have been churchgoers, as Methodist attendances, for example, rose by only 1000 more than usual. Piggin quotes twelve tents; Taylor says 'there must have been ten or twelve'; Broome suggests there were only seven. Similar phenomena were to occur in Wales three years later.

101. Piggin, 1984, 137.

102. With their two daughters Mary, 3, and Sarah, 1, Joseph Marshall (c.1827–1889) and his wife Ann (c.1829–1882) emigrated from Yorkshire to Moreton Bay, Queensland in 1853, where two sons were born, and then, around 1859, moved to Portland, Victoria. Their third son was born there. Sources: Anne Grant, Portland Family History Advisory Group Inc., 1993; Register of Immigrant Arrivals, Mitchell Library. Note that the relevant section is a copy of an original register damaged in a flood in Brisbane in 1893 and later destroyed. The name 'Joseph' is given as 'Joshua.' It is possible that Marshall had learned about glossolalia from the Irvingite movement in England, but I can find no evidence to this effect nor any suggestion that he was affiliated with the Church of Scotland, Irving's original denomination. The popular opinion in the Portland area was that he had come to his understanding of baptism in the Spirit on his own.

103. *Christian Weekly and Methodist Journal,* 20 July 1883; Bohan Johnstone, 'A biography of Joseph Marshall', unpublished essay, Tabor College, NSW, 2007.

104. *Wesleyan Chronicle,* August 1, 1858, 259.

105. WC, May 3, 1862, 68; December 20, 1864, 209.

106. WC, July 20, 1868, 107.

107. WC, May 20, 1873, 83.

108. R. G. Beauglehole, 'God Baptized in Portland, Victoria, Nearly Fifty Years Ago!' GN, 1: 1, April, 1910, 3, 5. This is a testimony by Richard George Beauglehole (1846–1920), whose name is incorrectly given as R. S. Beanglehole in the article. See

also R. Hope, personal interview, 1990; Dorothy Reekie, personal interview, 14 August, 1991.

109. Anne Grant, Portland Family History Advisory Group Inc., 1993; compare: 'I came from Cornwall to Portland fifty-five years ago,' GN, 1:1, April, 1910, 4.

110. *Spectator,* 15 April, 1925, 363; Hunt, 1985, 127. Converted in May 1857, after several years of alcoholism, Burnett had emigrated to Victoria in 1863, and was employed by the Home Mission committee as an evangelist and temperance crusader. He visited Portland intending to hold a fortnight's evangelistic services; but the mission was extended to 13 weeks. 'Very many are with the Missioner in Heaven,' reported the *Portland Circuit History* years later, ' but there are some remaining...' Burnett visited nearby Warrnambool in 1869, with striking effect. Billed as the 'famous Yorkshire evangelist,' he showed 'amazing fervour and determination' and drew large crowds. Many people could not gain admission. 'The power of the Holy Ghost came down' and many people, old and young, devoted themselves to fervent prayer. It was a revival that they prayed would spread in every direction and affects all the churches of the area. See WC, April 20, 1869, 62; *Portland Circuit History,* Vol 2, 3; Vol 4, 6.

111. R. Gribben, *The Portland Bay Methodists* (Portland: Wesley, 1972), 6; GN, 1:1, April, 1901, 4. Further details of Beauglehole's testimony are from this source unless otherwise stated.

112. SC, II:19, 12 May, 1883, 5.

113. SC, II:20, 19 May, 1883, 9.

114. 'By reading the Scriptures... I believed there were greater things to be received,' GN, 1:1, April, 1910, 4.

115. *The Warrnambool Independent,* 2 July, 1883; *Christian Weekly and Methodist Journal,* 20 July 1883; Beauglehole, GN, 1:1, April 1910—'I can only find two others with this precious gift. There used to be five, but death has removed them.'

116. Beauglehole, GN, 1:1, April, 1910, 3, 5. Given that this testimony was written forty years after the event, it is possible that there was some reinterpretation of what happened in the light of the Pentecostal manifestations then occurring in Melbourne, but there is no evidence to suggest that this was the case.

117. Gribben, 1972, 42–43.

118. Dorothy Reekie, personal interview, 14 August, 1991.

119. Personal knowledge; D. Reekie, personal interview, 14 August, 1991; AE, 13:5, April, 1947, 12; *Richmond Temple Souvenir,* Melbourne, 1939, 50.

120. GN, October, 1926, 10, 11; Chant, 1984, 34f.

121. Chant, 1984, 80ff

122. Chant, 1984, 94.

123. C. Enticknap, 'Address,' 17 October, 1965. See also GN, 15:4, April 1, 1924, 13; GN, 15:9, September, 1924, 9f; Agnes Davidson (nee Enticknap), personal interview, 20 November, 1990. For further details on the Enticknap family see Appendix B.

124. GN, 1:1, April, 1910, 3; GN, 9:1, February, 1923, 16; E. Rayner, personal interview; P. Sheather, personal communication, 1992; C.Evans, personal communication, 1992; E. Faulkner, personal interview, 10 April, 1992; M. Jackson, personal communication, 8 May, 1992. Further details are from these sources unless otherwise stated.

125. For further on the Sloans see Appendix B.

126. J. Heath, letter to the congregation at the Apostolic Mission, Adelaide, 29 December, 1936.

127. G. Chilcott, personal interview; RE, 2:12, May, 1935, 230.

128. For more on Newton see Appendix B.

129. M. Hancock and F. Liebelt, *A Tangled Web* (Adelaide: Hancock and Martin Family Reunion Committee, 1986), 238ff.

130. R. Read, personal interview, 19 November, 1990.

131. S and M. Douglas, personal interview, 21 November, 1989. Edith Buley married Harold Akehurst. Ruth Akehurst married Stan Douglas; Elsa married Eric Wilson; Joyce married Kevin Conner.

132. *Richmond Temple Souvenir,* 1939, 15, 19, 21, 42, 48

133. See J. Pentecost, *William Booth and the Doctrine of Holiness* (Sydney: Department of Studies in Religion, University of Sydney), 1997.

134. 'Grand Council of the Sydney Troops' in *War Cry*, 2:74, Sydney, October 11, 1884, reprinted in *War Cry*, 19 March 1983, 2. See also Bolton, 1980, 54ff.

135. *War Cry*, 19 March, 1983, .3, a reprint from 2 August, 1884

136. SC, II: 26, 30 June, 1883, 9.

137. 'The Gift and Gifts of the Holy Spirit,' *Full Salvation,* 1 February, 1896, 51f

138. 'How to Bring About a Revival,' *Full Salvation,* 2 March, 1896, 78ff

139. *War Cry,* 21 November, 1914, quoted in GN, 17:6, June, 1926, 2 and in AE, 7:7, June, 1941, 5.

140. Quoted in GN, 21:1, January, 1920, 5.

141. C. Booth, 'By the Power of the Holy Ghost,' *War Cry,* 27 November, 1915, quoted in GN, 20:11, November, 1929, 7.

142. W. F. South, 'Mrs William Booth and the Baptism of the Holy Ghost,' *Elim Evangel* quoted in GN, 21:2, February, 1930, 17.

143. GN, 17:6, June, 1926, 2.

144. 'Have the Holy Spirit?' by a Salvation Army Bandmaster, GN, 20:12, December, 1929, 8.

145. W. Booth-Clibborn, *The Baptism in the Holy Spirit* (Dallas: the Voice of Healing, 1962), 10; W. Booth-Clibborn, 'How "The rest and the Refreshing" Came to Me,' GN, 20:7, July 1929, 5ff; P. W. Wilson, *General Evangeline Booth* (New York: Scribners, 1948), 139.

146. GN, 17:9, September 1926, 11; J. Lancaster, 'The Army Mother and Divine Healing,' GN, 18:11, November 1927, 16. As will become obvious in later chapters, divine healing was an important part of Pentecostal teaching.

147. See Appendix B.

148. M. A. Alway, 'Jesus Christ the Same, Yesterday, Today and Forever,' GN, 1:1, April, 1910, 14f.

149. L. Priest, personal interview, 17 September, 1991; Salvation Army records, Melbourne; for further details see Appendix B; GN, 18:12, December, 1927, 10f ; GN, 9:1, February 1923, 19; H. Hultgren, 'What God Has Done for Others He Can Do for Me,' GN, 17:2, February 1926, 7; C. Cousins, 'Ask and Ye Shall Receive,' GN, 17:2, February, 1926, 11; GN, 17:5, May, 1926, 18; G. Burns, 'God's work in Maryborough, Qu.,' GN, 19:2, February 1928, 17; GN, 19:5, May 1928, 12.

150. GN, 19:8, August, 1928, 7; GN, 19:3, March 1928, supplement, p.1; 'A Red Hot Salvationist's Story, as Told in Good News Hall,' 20:12, December, 1929, 8; GN, 24:9, September, 1933, 9; S. Douglas, personal interview, 21 November, 1989; RTS, 1939, 13, 25; 27.

151. In 1926, Jeannie Lancaster warned of the dangers facing the Pentecostal movement— 'The early days of the Salvation Army were so like these days of Pentecostal Manifestations that... we must conclude that God would have given the Salvation Army the ministry of the Holy Spirit, if they had retained the humility and faith which characterised the early disciples and apostles... and were not moved from their position by all the ignominy and derision which the peculiar manifestations of this wonderful gift evoked. Let the leaders of Pentecost take warning and keep humble lest... the Lord call yet another people for His Name.' GN, 17:6, June 1926, 2.

152. Wesley, *Plain Account* in *Works,* Vol 11, 1996, 406f, 430; 'The More Excellent Way,' *Works,* 8, 26f.

153. One exception is J. F. Horsley's article, 'Faith-work—Healing the Sick,' in which he asks, 'Has God promised us anything specifically upon the subject?' and answers— 'Yes, emphatically yes. "...the prayer of faith shall save the sick and the Lord shall raise him up..." Blessed promise! ... God will honour faith in the healing of the sick in our own day.' See *Spectator,* 5:240, 5 December, 1879, 377.

154. *Minutes of the Seventh General Conference of the Methodist Church of Australasia,* (Adelaide, 1923), 140.

155. Breward, 1993, 120f; *Minutes of the Eighth General Conference of the Methodist Church of Australasia,* 1925, 62; GN, 12:8, September 1923, 14.

156. Wesley, *Works,* Vol 8, 1996, 26f.

CHAPTER THREE

THE EMBRYONIC SPIRIT OF PENTECOST

John Alexander Dowie and the Ministry of Divine Healing (1875–1907)

Although he was never a Pentecostal, a significant number of pioneer Pentecostal leaders trace their spiritual heritage to John Alexander Dowie (1847-1907). Dowie spent only eight and half years of his astonishing career in Australia. Yet during this time, he developed a philosophy of ministry and leadership that would catapult him into international fame as a religious leader. John Dowie was an enigma, a figure of contrasts. He was a major contributor to the early development of Pentecostalism, yet he was also in some ways a major hindrance to its acceptance. Dowie was so admired by many Australians that hundreds of them left their homes to live in Zion City in Illinois, the theocratic city he planned, conceived and brought to birth. Yet when he returned to Australia in 1904, he was vilified, scorned and abused by angry mobs in Sydney, Melbourne and Adelaide and had to flee for safety. Dowie's preaching and teaching indicate a fervent love for Jesus and a longing for holiness and godliness, yet at the end of his life, he was demanding allegiance as Elijah the Restorer and the First Apostle of the Lord Jesus the Christ in the Catholic Apostolic Church in Zion. For all that, the movement he established was a womb in which the embryonic spirit of Pentecost was nurtured.

Ministry in Sydney

Early in 1873, Dowie moved to Sydney from his home State of South Australia, to take up the Congregational pastorate at Manly.[1] According to Dowie, although there had been just 25 or so worshipers when he first arrived, the church was soon 'filled to overflowing with a most earnestly attentive audience every Sabbath, especially in the evening.' This evidently represented about a hundred people. The new Sabbath School which he commenced had 70 scholars within three weeks of its opening. Indeed, everything seemed 'bright and prosperous' for the new minister.[2]

Dowie was a passionate pastor. His love for his Saviour and his earnest desire to see his people unreservedly committed to him is indicated in the following letter he wrote to a young convert—

Dowie as a Young Man.

> It rejoices me to know that you are growing in grace. Oh, keep very near to Jesus always. Get down very often in prayer, and you will rise in power to do and bear His will in all things. O that we loved Him more, and looked to Him more steadfastly![3]

At the same time, from the earliest days of his ministry, Dowie displayed a continuing longing for bigger and better things. He was never satisfied with his achievements. The church may have been full, but it was not enough. He wanted 'more room, more population, to work on.'

Dowie was also becoming increasingly concerned over social problems, especially alcoholism. He perceived what he called a 'terrible flood of moral evil.' Unhappily, the churches were not addressing the real need. They were not preaching the gospel of mercy and pardoning love that would rescue men and women from evil. This could only be done through a baptism of the Holy Spirit. Yet at the same time, he himself felt terribly inadequate for the task. 'Oh, how miserably weak and empty of goodness and power do I feel!' he lamented. 'God give me more strength and fill me with grace!'

The Manly church continued to grow and by the end of 1874, the building was enlarged and improved. But Dowie became increasingly critical of the established churches and began to denounce them more openly. There was some talk of Dowie's returning to his native Scotland, but this did not eventuate. So he began to look elsewhere in Sydney and was soon considering the Newtown congregation. This was seen as being 'next to Pitt Street in importance' and stood in the midst of a rapidly rising population. Dowie saw it as a challenge, especially as it would require a 'high order of preaching'. In February 1875, he began at

Newtown. It was a large building, with seating for nearly 1000 people, but only about 120 members.[4] There were some 350 to 450 on the Sabbath school rolls.

It was during this year, when Dowie was 28 years of age, that he fell in love with his uncle Alexander's daughter Jeanie. This was clearly a relationship which pleased the daughter more than the father. Alexander was concerned that the marriage of cousins might be detrimental. He was also worried about his nephew's ability to provide for his daughter. The wedding went ahead on 26 May, the following year, at the prestigious Brougham Place Congregational Church in Adelaide, with its esteemed pastor, the Rev Dr James Jefferis officiating. But for the next few years, there was to be ongoing antagonism between Alexander and his new son-in-law. The successful businessman continued to be concerned about Dowie's apparently impecunious state. As for Jeanie, in years to come, she was to be a valuable partner in the ministry, especially to the sick.[5]

Divine Healing

Eighteen seventy-five was a hard year, although the congregation continued to grow. Dowie recorded that he conducted some 25 funerals, 20 of them for members of his own church. There was a terrible time of sickness, with 'fevers of every sort'.[6] Years later, he claimed he had buried some 30 of his flock, and conducted 40 funerals altogether. The nature of the illness was not specified. It was possibly measles or scarlet fever, or perhaps a combination of both, as there were major epidemics of each along the east coast of Australia in 1875–76.[7] The large number of deaths caused Dowie great concern. Why were the sick not healed in 1875 as they had been in AD 75?

> There I sat with sorrow-bowed head for my afflicted people, until the bitter tears came to relieve my burning heart... How my heart longed to hear some words from Him who wept and sorrowed for the suffering long ago, the Man of Sorrows and Sympathies. And then the words of the Holy Ghost inspired in Acts 10:38 stood before me all radiant with light revealing Satan as the Defiler and Christ as the Healer. My tears were wiped away, my heart was strong, I saw the way of healing, and the door thereto was opened wide, and so I said, 'God help me now to preach that word to all the dying round.'[8]

At that very time, he was urgently summoned to the home of a young lady who was dying.

> The doctor, a good Christian man... said, 'Sir, are not God's ways mysterious?' ...'God's way!' I said..., 'How dare you, Dr. K—, call that God's way...? No, sir, that is the devil's work, and it is time we called on him who came to "destroy the work of the devil," to slay that deadly and foul destroyer, and to save the child. Can you pray, Doctor, can you pray the prayer of faith to save the sick?' At once, offended at my words, my friend was changed, saying, 'You are too much excited, sir, 'tis best to say, "God's will be done."' ... Excited! The word was quite inadequate for I was almost frenzied with Divinely imparted anger and hatred of that foul destroyer.

Dowie prayed for the girl and she fell into a deep sleep. Later she awoke, completely recovered. Lindsay records that there were no further deaths in the

Newtown congregation from that time.⁹ Years later, Dowie claimed that he 'went about laying on hands and saved thousands from dying' and that in the next twelve years, he was called upon to bury only five people. In October 1877, however, he was still lamenting the fact that there was much sickness among the people in Newtown, just as there had been in 1875. The Newtown death rate was higher than elsewhere and he feared another 'dread time of fever'. Then, early on the first Sunday morning in November, 1885, he and his wife faced the death of their own little daughter, Jeanie. Before she died, Dowie realised there was 'no hope of recovery'. He preached that morning on 2 Samuel 12:23—'But now she is dead, wherefore should I fast? Can I bring her back again? I shall go to her; but she shall not return to me'. And Dowie himself, suffered from persistent nausea, probably a result of stress.[10]

The next year, he wrote to a friend describing himself as 'one whom the Lord has used for four years in the Ministry of Healing, and for nearly twenty years in the Ministry of Salvation through faith in Jesus'. This marks his healing ministry as beginning in 1882.[11] Clearly, his ventures into the practice of divine healing were initially spasmodic, with uneven results, and his own recollections were not always accurate.

Dowie was not the first in recent times to promote the ministry of healing. German evangelical leader Johann Blumhardt (1805–1880) began to do so in 1843 in the small village of Mottlingen, in Germany, and in 1852 established a healing centre.[12] About the same time, in 1851, Dorothea Trudel acted on James 5:14f and anointed with oil some of her co-workers in the Swiss village of Mannedorf, on Lake Zurich. Their recovery projected her into a healing ministry, and she, too, opened several healing homes. In 1867, Otto Stockmayer launched a healing ministry in Switzerland and later wrote on the subject. It may also be noted that Charles Spurgeon regularly prayed for the sick, with evident success.

In America, in 1846, Ethan O. Allen began to teach a correlation between Christian perfection and physical healing. He was followed by Charles Cullis, 'the single most important figure in the development of the divine healing movement in America.' After reading the life of Dorothea Trudel, he embarked on a ministry to the sick in 1870. The early 1880s saw a blossoming of books on divine healing. Carrie Judd Montgomery wrote *The Prayer of Faith* (1880), which was widely distributed. In 1881, Cullis published *More Faith Cures; or, Answers to Prayer in the Healing of the Sick*. In the same year, William Boardman issued *'The Lord That Healeth Thee'* and A. B. Simpson, founder of the Christian and Missionary Alliance, experienced divine healing. In 1882, the year Dowie began his public healing ministry, South African pastor and writer Andrew Murray became convinced of the veracity of divine healing and A. J. Gordon published his first treatise on this subject, *The Ministry of Healing*. This was soon followed by R. L. Stanton's *Gospel Parallelisms: Illustrated in the Healing of Body and Soul* (1883) and *The Atonement of Sin and Sickness* by R. Kelso Carter (1884). In 1885, the American revivalist Maria Woodworth Etter began to pray for the sick publicly. Books by Blumhardt, Trudel, Boardman and Cullis were all available in Australia very soon after publication.[13]

If 1875 marked the beginning of his belief in divine healing, it seems improbable that Dowie was seriously influenced by this movement. Even in 1882, when he began his public healing ministry, there is little likelihood that he would have yet been aware of it. However, it was not long before this situation changed. In 1885, he was invited by William Boardman to attend the London International Conference on Divine Healing, to which he responded with a letter affirming his desire to preach the message of divine healing around the world within three years.[14] Later, in 1888, after crossing the United States, he intended to visit England, 'where he planned to meet others who had come to know the truth that the Lord Jesus Christ is the Healer as well as the Savior (sic) of men.'[15] Ultimately, he was to take a more radical stance, by opposing the use of medicinal care completely, whereas most of the other advocates of healing saw any valid form of care for the sick as appropriate.[16]

Social Issues

In his Newtown days, Dowie was clearly more stirred by other problems. The liquor industry continued to arouse his ire. So, too, did gambling and smoking. He also found himself at frequent odds with Roman Catholicism and Spiritualism. He was regularly critical of the press. He was also still much concerned over the 'languid state' of the churches, including his own. He soon began to realise that to be outspoken on these issues might endear him to many people, but it would not win him friends among the leaders of either community or church.[17]

By October 1877, Dowie was planning to found his own Free Christian Church. In a long letter to his wife, he explained how he would never again accept a denominational church. He would be truly independent, something which the Congregational Union, for all its proclaimed liberty of creed, did not allow. Indeed, the spirit of popery was to be found even there.[18] Moreover, over the previous five years, only 535 new members had been added to the 43 churches in the Union, which Dowie saw as a cause for 'humiliation and shame,' especially since he believed that at least 100 of these had been the result of his own ministry.[19]

Again, it is interesting to reflect on Dowie's motives for such change. One has already been mentioned—the desire for freedom to minister as he saw fit. The other was 'a holy passion for the misguided, ignorant, uncared for, and perishing thousands who are in the bondage of Satan in our cities'. The third was what might be called a constant sense of destiny. Dowie clearly believed he was made for greater things. Constantly through his letters and comments in the Newtown years, there are hints of dreams of greatness.[20]

The Free Christian Church

Dowie resigned from the Congregational Union at the end of 1877 and began independent meetings in Sydney's Theatre Royal. Within four weeks, over 1000 people were in attendance. But the venue was costly, and they were forced to move to the Protestant Hall, and then to the Masonic Hall where Dowie was surrounded by a group of several hundred 'loyal and devoted people', most of whom had been converted through his ministry. However, the winter weather did not help attendances here, the place proved unsuitable for their purposes and money was in short supply. Dowie's father had to come to the rescue to save their furniture from being sold. Gradually Dowie was able to assemble a committee who took responsibility for the financial affairs and the position improved.[21]

For the first time, members of the new church found themselves being called 'Dowieites'—a factor which annoyed Dowie, who only wanted his name 'hidden behind the One Great Name of Christian, which alone God's people should bear.'

By 1879, he was preaching in the large Victoria Theatre, in Pitt Street, Sydney. Here again, crowds of 1,000 people regularly attended his Sunday services. A large number of these were men between twenty and fifty and many free thinkers were drifting into his meetings, some to stay.[22] Not only were Dowie's preaching gifts 'extraordinary',[23] he was also a prolific writer and pamphleteer. In addition to his voluminous letters, in 1877, he wrote *Rome's Polluted Springs*, a reply to statements by Catholic Archbishop Vaughan. In 1879, he published *The Drama, the Press and the Pulpit*. There were 2,000 copies printed of each.[24] In the main, these were the substance of lectures he had delivered in the Victoria Theatre in mid-1879.[25] In 1882, *Spiritualism Unmasked* was issued.[26]

Dowie told his father that he had written twenty tracts and distributed some 210,750 copies by late 1879 and to an anonymous critic, he replied that there

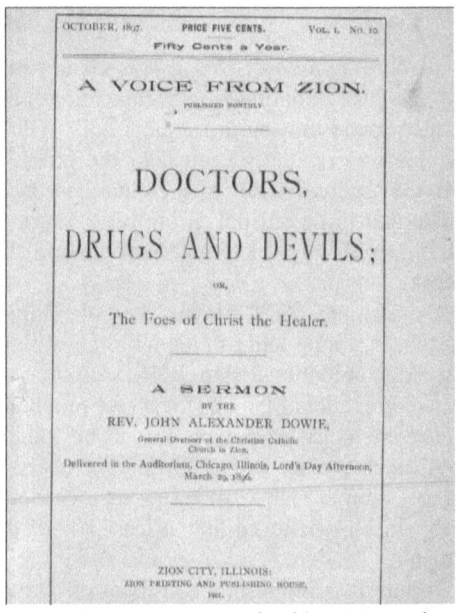

A Dowie sermon, preached in 1896 and published 1901.

was a weekly average of 6,000 leaflets given away, of which 89,500 were 'direct appeals to the heart and conscience to accept God's gift of pardon, peace and life in Christ', 79,250 dealt with social evils and 42,000 were addressed to Roman Catholics, setting out the errors of their faith.[27]

During his three years of independent ministry in Sydney, Dowie made two major errors. The first was to offer himself as a candidate at a by-election for the seat of East Sydney in the New South Wales Parliament. There were four candidates— Arthur Renwick, Robert Tooth, T. D. Dalveen and John Dowie.[28] Renwick and Dowie were seen as Temperance campaigners. Tooth, on the other hand, was both a Catholic and a supporter of the liquor industry. Dowie had been a late entrant into the election. His supporters saw a seat in Parliament as a short cut to prominence in the community and possibly to the success of the new church.[29] Dowie campaigned enthusiastically on several issues. He defended the national system of education against denominational (mainly Catholic) schools; he advocated land reform, to make ownership more equitable; he argued for limiting liquor licences; he declared he had no pecuniary interest in standing for parliament; he saw the need for better public services, especially of water and gas; he wanted Chinese immigration restricted; he saw the need for taxation reform; he felt that his habits of life qualified him as a worthy candidate.[30]

But Dowie was unpopular with the community at large, a fact acknowledged by his church secretary and prime supporter, Thomas Hutchinson, who in proposing him as a candidate, admitted that Dowie 'had made himself obnoxious to a certain section of the community, because he had rebuked iniquity in high places, and therefore... was not liked'.[31] Dowie himself felt he was betrayed. He had been assured of support from both the Temperance Platform and the Protestant League, but they both abandoned him. He felt he was not defeated, but sacrificed. Furthermore, he was scurrilously attacked by his opponents who used his personal financial position against him.[32]

In the final analysis, Dowie was never in the race. The votes were—Renwick, 4,663; Tooth, 2,748; Dowie, 147; Dalveen, 28.[33] Dowie admitted that this loss seriously affected attendances at his services. Even faithful supporters like Hutchinson fell away for a time. Meetings were now being held in the International Hall, which was too small and cramped, but which was apparently all they could afford. They were hopeful of soon acquiring a property of their own.[34]

Money Matters

The second problem Dowie faced involved money. A friend named Holding promised him a sum of 21,000 pounds for the establishment of the work in Sydney. In spite of the improbability of this happening, Dowie believed Holding to be honest and trusted him to provide the money. Dowie's dreams of a tabernacle where they could establish a true church and share the Lord's table blinded him to reality. Also, there was, in Dowie's mind at least, a strong bond of affection between the two men, whom he addressed in one letter as his 'best beloved'. Holding went to England, ostensibly to get the money. Meanwhile, malicious rumours were being circulated that Dowie had already received (and misused?) it. So he left Sydney, in an attempt to visit England himself, but stayed in Adelaide, where letters from Holding continually delayed him. Finally, news arrived of Holding's death. It was with great surprise and considerable outrage that Dowie later met him in Melbourne, posing as a Salvation Army officer. The whole episode undermined Dowie's credibility and was a factor in the closing of the Sydney work. It was no wonder that Dowie later described Holding as 'a clever scoundrel, with forged credentials, a smooth tongue, great simplicity of manners, and most accomplished hypocrisy'.[35] But the matter was to hang over him for a long time. Some fifteen years later, a correspondent to *The Bulletin* gleefully retold the tale.[36]

For a short time, Dowie was associated with the Salvation Army in Adelaide.[37] Then, in Melbourne, in 1882, he sought employment with a Temperance organisation but was unsuccessful. 'Once more,' he wrote to his wife, 'I have to write the discouraging word "failed"'.[38] Then he was invited to take over the pastorate of the Collingwood Tabernacle, an independent church in Melbourne, Vic, while the minister, C. M. Cherbury, was taking leave of absence. Dowie gladly accepted. Although himself a strong advocate of temperance, he became concerned that unconverted temperance speakers were being allowed the use of the church. Again, this brought the church into conflict. By the time Cherbury returned at the end of the year, Dowie had attracted a measure of support, so much so, that he was accused of being unwilling to hand the church back again. He did leave, but again, took to the pen, this time writing a whole book defending his actions at the Tabernacle.[39]

Ministry in Melbourne

In February 1883, Dowie launched the Free Christian Church, in Fitzroy, an inner suburb of Melbourne, with services in the Town Hall. Probably, some of Cherbury's congregation followed him. About 100 people attended the first meetings. By the end of 1884, Dowie finally saw the realisation of a dream—the Free Christian Tabernacle was built, a large building in Johnston St, with seating for some 3,000 people.[40] Dowie later claimed that thousands were turned away daily.[41]

Central Zion Tabernacle, Melbourne, Australia c.1904.

The attendances were impressive, although not exceptional for Christian gatherings with skilled preachers. During this same period, Anglican Bishop James Moorhouse preached regularly to crowds of four thousand people at the Town Hall.[42] The difference lay in the fact that Moorhouse had an existing constituency to draw on: Dowie had to create his. He was not unsuccessful. Lindsay claims that at least once, as many as 20,000 people attended an open air rally.[43]

Services were an interesting blend of non-conformism and traditional liturgy.[44] It was now that Dowie began to preach more consistently on the subject of divine healing. Health has always been a common concern and there have always been those willing to profit by it. In times of uncertain medical care, in particular, people may be more open to experimentation in alternative treatment. Certainly, in the press of the day, health remedies were prominently advertised.[45] Dowie's preaching about healing began to attract people, and as a result, several notable cures were recorded. A young pregnant married woman named Lucy Parker was blind in one eye, the result of cancer. After healing prayer at the Free Christian Tabernacle, sight was restored to her eye and later, her baby was born normal and healthy. A sixteen year-old boy, crippled from tuberculosis in the bones, recovered.[46] In December 1887, 3,500 copies of a *Record of the Fifth Annual Commemoration* were published which included these and over 70 further testimonies of healing.[47]

John Alexander Dowie and seven members of his church who suffered imprisonment in Melbourne jail, 1885, rather than pay a fine imposed for alleged violation of ordinance prohibiting street preaching; they were freed by an unconditional release from the Governor. Reading from left to right: H. Martin, J. S. Wallington, H. G. Mence, John Alexander Dowie, W. Foxcraft, J. L. Morrish, R. Hood, J. Ray.

Dowie in Melbourne, 1885.

Soon Dowie formed the International Divine Healing Association with branches in various parts of the world.[48] Dowie was careful to insist that divine healing was very different from spiritist or occult healing.[49] His own understanding of it is clearly outlined in the following extracts from an address to a ministers' conference in the US—

> First: That Jesus Christ is the same yesterday, today and forever, and being so, is unchanged in power.
>
> Second: That disease like sin, is God's enemy, and the devil's work, and can never be God's will (Act 10:38).
>
> We do not present our theories. Jesus did three things. He taught, he preached, he healed. This is the divine order, and the kingdom can only be extended by that three-fold ministry.

Divine healing points to a still more beautiful thing—holiness of life (Is[aiah] 35). If you defile your body by any nicotine poison ... then you sin against God and your own soul. To pollute the body with alcohol is a sin. The doctrine of divine healing comes with great force to them that are sick, causing them to quit sin.

That Christ is the healer does not depend on any human testimony; it rests upon the word of God ... We need to get back to the old church lines, as laid down in the New Testament.

We teach what is recorded in the 12th chapter of First Corinthians, that the Gifts of Healing are in the Holy Spirit, like all other Gifts of God.[50]

Polemic and Controversy

Not only did Dowie teach the efficacy of divine healing, but he rejected any other kind. Doctors, drugs and devils were all denounced as 'foes of Christ the Healer.'[51] Dowie also continued to attack the liquor interests. There is little doubt that he enjoyed polemic and controversy. The temptation to arraign and pour scorn on the views of those with whom he disagreed seemed irresistible.[52] Because of his outspoken opposition to the use of alcohol, there was some lobbying resulting in a by-law forbidding street meetings. Dowie saw this as preventing him from obeying God's commands to go into the 'highways and byways' to preach the Gospel, and said so publicly. He promptly advertised and organised a street procession. He was duly prosecuted. He attended a meeting of the Council and unsuccessfully endeavoured to persuade them that the charge was *ultra vires*. On 20 April, 1885, the case was tried before four magistrates who found him guilty.[53]

He refused to pay the fine and was imprisoned for 30 days. He promptly took to the streets again and was again imprisoned. Seven of the church members joined him there and hundreds of others expressed a willingness to be incarcerated if necessary. After two days, there was such public concern that the Governor of Victoria, Sir Henry Brougham Loch, ordered his release.[54] More trouble was to come. In September 1885, Dowie arrived at the Tabernacle to find his office demolished as the result of an explosion.[55]

In spite of the problems, things were still going well over all for Dowie. He had founded his own church; hundreds of people were attending his meetings; his preaching was growing in effect; there were significant results in the healing ministry. Yet there was still a restlessness in his spirit. Part of this was a growing conviction that the time for preaching the gospel was short. Earthquakes, international tensions, a Tory government and resultant warfare were all signs of the near return of Christ.[56] But there was also a sense of compulsion in his heart that he had not yet arrived at the place of true calling. In 1886, he told his wife of a strange encounter with God where he was sleeping only four hours a night and experiencing 'a fresh baptism of Power from on High' for witness and service.

Wave after wave of Holy Power has come upon me, and it remains. All else seems trivial compared to this. Christ is unspeakably dearer, clearer, and nearer to me in all things... If you are like Sarah of old, we shall have a glorious future here and hereafter.[57]

Then there was a growing concern for humanity. His faith in Christ, he wrote to a friend in 1888, forbade him from being narrowed down to a denomination or sect. He believed there was a score of places open to him at the time (he was being pressed to go to England).[58] Looking back on these days, he later wrote—

> Then suddenly, the earth seemed to be vocal. I could hear the wail of pain and the cries of the dying from all continents, swelling up from all the cities and hamlets and villages and solitudes. I could hear the cry of suffering coming up from all the earth... and I knew it was right to leave the lovely Australian land, and go forth on a pilgrimage carrying leaves of healing from the Tree of Life to every nation I could reach.[59]

America

Dowie's home in Zion, now a museum.

Finally, he decided to resign from the Free Christian Tabernacle and sail for America. There were long meetings for prayer, both with office-bearers and people, and amidst many tears, his resignation was accepted, to take effect from 19 February 1888. Meanwhile, the Fifth Annual Commemoration of Dowie's ministry of healing took place in December 1887, during which over 70 people presented convincing testimonials of healing.[60] After an 'All-night of Prayer and Teaching' in January 1888, Elders Joseph Grierson and John S. Wallington were ordained to lead the work[61].

A few days after his last meetings, the church presented him with a cheque for 100 pounds and an 'address' to mark the occasion of his departure to America and Europe to engage in 'the Divine Healing Mission' to which the Holy Spirit had called him. Part of the address read—

John Dowie preaching at Central Zion Tabernacle, Chicago, Illinois.

> We ... beg to present this testimonial as a very small token of the love and appreciation borne toward you for your untiring and devoted zeal in bringing very many in these lands from darkness into God's marvellous light, and for the promotion of Divine Healing. You have been made the Divine Agent in doing many mighty works. The Lord has, in a most manifest manner, heard your prayer of faith, and raised up many, in some cases more than ten thousand miles distant. Truly the Lord has made you a chosen vessel, in leading hundreds, by your teaching from His Holy Word, to the sanctification of spirit, soul and body. We cannot even estimate the

number blessed under your ministry—eternity alone will reveal them—but we know that hundreds, who have been both saved and healed, regret, as we do, your departure from these shores. The loss of your spiritual exhortations, your kindly counsels, and your faithful prayers, will be deeply felt throughout Australasia; but your Church and people have felt, from the date of your letter of the 16th April 1885, to the London International Conference on Divine Healing... till now, that the Holy Spirit was leading you to visit America and Europe, to preach Christ as the Saviour and Sanctifier of the spirit, soul, and body, and we submit to the will of the heavenly Father, and pray that you may be used to a far greater extent than you have been, and that, if it be His will, you shall return again to this land.[62]

An elderly man who had been healed of a cancer in the face, presented Dowie with a new Bible.

At midnight, on Saturday 3 March, 1888, the family boarded the *Maranoa*, and hundreds of friends sang and prayed with them before they sailed. They journeyed via New Zealand, where successful meetings were held in Auckland and the groundwork laid for the later formation of a branch of the Christian Catholic Church.[63]

Sixteen years later, John Alexander Dowie returned to Australia. In the intervening period, he had become an international figure.[64] The Christian Catholic Church which he founded in Chicago in February 1896, with 500 members[65] had rocketed to an estimated 40,000 members world-wide.[66] Not only had he established a new church, he had built Zion city as well—a theocratic community where there were no taverns, no vaudeville theatres, no doctors, no chemist shops, no places of gambling and certainly no smoking or drinking. The new Tabernacle seated some 8,000 people. Citizens came from all over the United States and from overseas as well—including a large contingent from Australia.[67] During this period, Dowie adopted the practice of baptism by triune immersion. He also became an American citizen.[68]

On 14 May, 1902, he and his wife suffered the horrific tragedy of the death of their 21-year-old daughter Esther, who was burned to death in a fire caused by an upturned lamp fuelled by alcohol, the very thing he had so often denounced.[69] Notwithstanding this tragic event, the healing ministry continued with great effect, with dozens of crutches and braces and the like being mounted on display as 'trophies captured from the enemy'.[70] Land was available on an eleven hundred year lease—on the assumption that the return of Christ would occur within one hundred years to be followed by a 1000 year millennium.[71] There had also been a shift in Dowie's perception of himself. Somewhere he acquired the title 'Dr', although he does not seem to have earned it in an academic sense.[72] He was later to add more controversial designations. In 1896, when one of his associates suggested he was a modern apostle, Dowie replied—

> I say to you from my heart, I do not think that I have reached a deep enough depth of true humility; I do not think that I have reached a deep enough depth of true abasement and self-effacement, for the high office of an apostle... In becoming an apostle, it is not a question of rising high, it is a question of becoming low enough ... Power in the church is shown in this, that a man gets lower and lower, and lower and lower, until he can put his very spirit, soul and body underneath the miseries and at the feet of a sin-cursed and a disease-smitten humanity and

live and die for it and for Him who lived and died for it. That is what I understand by the Apostolic Office.[73]

'The Elijah Declaration'

Yet in 1901, Dowie declared that he was Elijah the Restorer and in 1904 that he was the First Apostle of the Lord Jesus the Christ in the Catholic Apostolic Church in Zion. He had special robes prepared, which reputedly took 40 women three months to make. Part of the 'Elijah Declaration', written in his own hand, reads—

> As Elijah the Restorer, God has sent me to you and to all the World, with Authority to advise
>
> First, A Message of Purity (Malachi 3)
>
> Second, A Message of Peace (Malachi 2:6)
>
> Third, A Message of Power (Matthew 17:11)
>
> More than two thousand of Zion's [illegible] will carry these words to every Continent saying, PEACE BE TO THIS HOUSE![74]

John Alexander, First Apostle of the Lord Jesus, the Christ, in the Catholic Apostolic Church in Zion.

Wilbur Voliva, his American associate who had come to Melbourne in 1901 to take over the leadership of the church, was an efficient organizer. Although, in Dowie's absence, the work had declined, under Voliva's supervision it soon regained its strength. By 1904, the year of Dowie's 'visitation' in Australia, there were some 1300 members in the Melbourne congregation.[75] Voliva promoted the visitation well. Furthermore, news of Dowie's new roles had also preceded him to this country. When he arrived in Sydney in February 1904, however, there was a mixed reaction. From the moment he set foot on the wharf he was greeted by a crowd both of his own followers and of those who came to jeer.[76]

Australia

By this time, Dowie was a balding, portly 57-year old, with a kindly face and clear, warm eyes over a long, bushy, white beard. He began his visit with two meetings on Sunday 14 February in the newly completed and imposing Town Hall. Week night meetings were also proposed, together with early morning prayer meetings, 10.30 am teaching meetings on divine healing and healing services at noon each day when 'those who are seeking the Lord for Healing will pass into the Prayer room and the General Overseer and Ordained Officers of the Christian Catholic Church in Zion will conduct a Prayer service of one hour, laying hands upon as many as are prepared for that ministration.'[77] A contemporary report noted that when Dowie announced the offering, there was a significant element who objected either by interjecting or leaving.[78] There were continued interruptions to the meetings in Sydney and the final service had to be closed early.[79] American newspapers carried reports—

> 'Dowie forced to flee from mob...'; '...Meeting in Sydney, New South Wales, is Broken up by a Crowd of 5,000 men...'; '...howling multitude...'; '...Dowie flees...'[80]

Dowie, by contrast, sent the following cable home—

> Enthusiastic receptions at Auckland and Sydney. Ten thousand attendance today at City Hall and Sydney deeply stirred. Australia awake everywhere. All glory to God alone. Overseer Jane Dowie is well. I am informed that she addressed crowded intelligent audiences in Adelaide in city hall this afternoon. Many are coming to Zion City from Australia this year. See Zechariah 10. Love to all. Zion, pray for us. Dowie.

Hooliganism also occurred in Melbourne, Victoria, where rallies were held in the Exhibition Building. Again, the press reported that meetings were broken up by a mob and that Dowie asked the US Consul for protection. Dowie cabled from Adelaide—

> Read Psalms 124th and 125th. We continued the visitation in Melbourne until Friday 4th. The authorities surrendered to riotous rabble, and the commissioner of police and the secretary of State declared their inability to preserve order, and refused adequate protection at the Exhibition Building today. We held ten meetings in Zion Tabernacle during the week and God blessed them. A brutal mob surrounded us Monday afternoon, grossly insulted Mrs Dowie, seized the horses' heads, and tried to cut the traces and overturn the carriage... Their newspapers— *The Southern Cross*, *The Argus* and *The Age*—were full of lies, which encouraged the disorder. The powers of hell united in church, in State, in press, secret empire and criminal populace. The Masons were especially mad because of our exposures. The lawless one will soon be revealed. We will begin the visitations here March 29. Mizpah. Pray for us. Love to Zion. Dowie.[81]

The Bulletin, cynical about religious matters in general, found in Dowie a continuing source of fun. A front cover cartoon on 10 March shows him teaching Abraham how to raise money. In the same issue, he is seen flying 'Zionwards', accompanied by angels singing, 'We want Dowie!' A week later, he is portrayed ejecting a Methodist clergyman from his meetings. Signs outside the building proclaim, 'Millionaires relieved of everything immediately' and, 'Diseases cured while you wait [No limit to the time you may wait].' The following week, Dowie goes *down* in a chariot of fire. A couple of weeks later, he arrives in heaven, only to see Peter smoking.[82]

Adelaide

Ironically, it was in Adelaide, his old home town, and one of Australia's most conservative cities, still today known as the 'City of Churches', that Dowie's reception was the most violent. Some 25,000 tickets were issued for his meetings. Six thousand people thronged to the Jubilee Exhibition Building for the first meeting on Sunday 21 March. The crowd was basically orderly, being partly composed of 'prominent business men, stock-brokers and other hard-headed citizens' who 'desired to hear what Elijah had to say.'[83] A newspaper reporter described him as attired in a long, flowing black gown, with a white surplice and a beautiful purple stole while 'his high, round, shining forehead, his flowing hair, and his streaming grey beard gave him a patriarchal aspect,' and 'looking as much like the conventional idea of Elijah as possible.'[84]

On the platform with Dowie were W. G. Voliva, C. Hawkins, who was in charge of the work in Adelaide, J. S. McCullagh, Voliva's assistant, and leader of the Sydney branch, and their wives. Both Hawkins and McCullagh were later to turn against Dowie and publish a booklet exposing what they called the 'Zion City Mockery.'[85] Dowie's wife, Overseer Jane Dowie and his son, Gladstone were also on the platform. So was Colonel Carl Stern, in his uniform of black and gold, as leader of the First Regiment of the Zion Guard. The reporter noted that the service was 'of a purely evangelical character' and that Dowie responded to occasional interjections by pointing out that he regularly preached to 7000 people in Chicago without interruption and that in one service some 6000 affirmed that they had been healed by faith.

At this point, there was an interruption as a policeman tried to remove an interjector, and Dowie pleaded for respect and courtesy from the people of Adelaide, his wife's birth-place. Finally, he closed with 'the solemn assertion that he preached no other gospel than that of salvation by the healing and cleansing power of God through Jesus Christ.' After the meeting, a sizeable crowd paraded through the streets seeking to make fun of Dowie, but he eluded them.

There was continued disorder in the meetings. At the Adelaide Town Hall, on Monday 22 March, the meeting had to be abandoned. The newspaper headlines, modest by modern standards, but bold for the time, summarise succinctly what happened—

DOWIE IN ADELAIDE

RIOT IN TOWN HALL

A WILD RABBLE STOPS THE MEETING

GREAT DISORDER IN THE STREETS

POLICE INJURED AND WINDOWS BROKEN

YORK HOTEL BESIEGED BY A VAST CROWD

MR J.DARLING'S HOUSE DAMAGED

NIGHT MEETINGS ABANDONED[86]

A huge crowd had gathered for the meeting, until finally, the attendants closed the doors. Many with tickets could not gain entry, and thousands of others thronged outside. Taking their cue from Dowie's frequent description of smokers and drinkers as 'stinkpots', someone smashed a bottle of 'sulphurated hydrogen' which resulted in a repulsive odour spreading through the building. Another 'stinkpot' soon followed. After the meeting got under way, some of the congregation broke into an offensive song.[87] Outside a crowd estimated at between 10,000 and 15,000 had gathered, mostly of boys and youths. All the city's police force assembled in an attempt to control the mob, using mounted policemen to hold the crowd back from the entrance. There was some scuffling, with police suffering minor injuries. By nine o'clock, things were growing nasty. Two Town Hall windows were broken. Then a tram car passed, and several windows in the tram were smashed by a youth from the crowd. The lad was arrested.

Meanwhile, inside, seats were being overturned and people were running about the hall. There were constant interjections and heckling. Dowie appealed for the right to speak, but without success. There were cries of, 'Dowie is a fraud!' and, 'Flap your wings, Elijah!' and, 'You call us all stinkpots!' and, 'We'll hang old Dowie on a sour apple tree'. Finally Dowie closed the meeting. While the police diverted attention, he slipped out unobserved.

The crowd then moved to the York Hotel, assuming Dowie had returned there, and there was more violence. Windows were broken, and more 'stinkpots' smashed. A knife was thrown at a policeman who was trying to remove a disorderly youth. Fortunately no harm resulted. When there was no sign of Dowie, some of the crowd went to the home of his brother-in-law, Mr J. Darling, JP. Again, windows were smashed, but Darling courageously addressed and dismissed the mob. Dowie returned to the hotel late that night, when most of the crowd had dispersed.

As a result of these events, Dowie announced that there would be no more night meetings, but that afternoon services would continue. The press reported this under the heading 'Message from Elijah'. Dowie continued to denounce the use of alcohol (which he called 'liquid fire and distilled damnation') and the smoking of tobacco. He fulminated against the eating of pork. He lamented the coldness of the churches.[88] He attacked Freemasonry and other lodges. And he proclaimed the validity and efficacy of Divine Healing.

Two of the men arrested were fined and Dowie publicly announced that he would pay for the damage to both the Town Hall and the York Hotel, which he did. The next day, the afternoon meeting was quiet and orderly. Several hundred people attended, and there were no major problems. Letters began to appear in the press both attacking and defending Dowie. Even some who disagreed with Dowie's teaching and beliefs, nevertheless deplored the refusal to allow him freedom of speech. The editor of *The Advertiser* was particularly outspoken, arguing that there was 'no valid excuse' for the disorder and that mob rule constituted 'the most terrible kind of tyranny'.[89]

Methodists lamented his attacks on the church, and complained that Sabbath-school classes and regular church services had been abandoned on the first Sunday of Dowie's visit by people 'prompted by nothing higher than vulgar curiosity'.[90]

Dowie's Adelaide meetings came to a sudden end. On Friday 25 March, he commented that not only was King Edward of England subject to the King of Kings but that everybody knew he had 'no religion to spare'.[91] This was ill-taken by the good citizens of Adelaide. The Mayor, Mr L. Cohen, wrote to Dowie warning him against repeating such statements and informed him that he could no longer use the Town Hall because of his 'disloyal utterances concerning his Majesty the King.' A similar letter from the Superintendent of Public Buildings forbade him the use of any building under Government control.[92]

A columnist in *The Bulletin* was not slow in pointing out the hypocrisy behind these actions. A large cartoon showed Dowie running before King Edward's chariot, as 'in a previous state of existence' he had done before King Ahab. So Dowie was forced to leave his old home-city, and, according to one report, still fleeing the mob, had to hide in a small boat before boarding his vessel the *Mongolia*.[93] He was never to visit these shores again.

In 1905, Dowie was partly paralysed as the result of a stroke. In April, 1906, his own associates in Zion felt they could no longer accommodate his increasingly irrational behaviour, and deposed him as General Overseer. Just twelve months later, on 9 March 1907, after a time of illness, he passed away.[94] The Melbourne branch of the Free Christian Church, now the Christian Catholic Church continued and at the turn of the century a small congregation still existed in that city.[95]

As a pioneer of the ministry of healing, Dowie was possibly without equal. One writer says—

> A. B. Simpson's lifelong associate Kenneth Mackenzie identified Dowie as 'unquestionably the apostle of healing in his day.' At the peak of his ministry from 1894 to 1905 he was known by more people throughout America than any other propagator of the message of divine healing in the nation's history. His periodical *Leaves of Healing* enjoyed the largest circulation of any publication of the movement....No individual within the healing movement has ever reached so many people worldwide with the message of divine healing as John Dowie.[96]

Influence on Pentecostalism

Some of the pioneers of the Pentecostal movement had their interest in the things of the Spirit awakened by Dowie. Although Dowie was never himself a Pentecostal, he expressed strong belief, not only in divine healing, but in all the gifts of the Holy Spirit. In his charge to the Christian Catholic church at its founding on 22 February, 1896, he declared—

> We shall teach and preach, and practice (sic) a Full Gospel... May this Church be endowed with the nine gifts of the Holy Spirit, with the word of Wisdom, the word of Knowledge, Faith, Gifts of healing, Workings of Miracles, Prophecy, Discernings of Spirits, Divers kinds of Tongues and Interpretation of Tongues, and with the gift of Love which is the crown of all...[97]

Dowie was recognised not only as being a prophet in the general sense, but also as exercising gifts of prophecy. He foresaw the link between smoking and cancer, for example and he foretold the preaching of the gospel through radio and television.[98] Moreover, Dowie saw the need for being baptized in the Holy Spirit and hence, empowered for service. He spoke of his own experience of a baptism of 'Power from on High', which he believed was given to him for witness and for service. 'If the Holy Spirit does not witness for us and back up our Witness [sic],' he once wrote, 'where shall we be?'[99]

A significant number of Dowie's followers took seriously what he said about spiritual gifts and, when the new Pentecostal movement started, they found a congenial spiritual home there.[100] Australian Earl Mintern was a member of the Zion Headquarters staff. The third General Overseer of the Christian Catholic Church from 1942 to 1959 was the 'greatly loved' Michael Mintern, who migrated to Zion in 1905.[101] Twenty years later, another member of the Mintern family, R. A. Mintern, a farm implement merchant from Horsham, Victoria, joined the recently founded Pentecostal Church of Australia. The following article appeared in the pages of the newly-published *Australian Evangel* in 1926—

JOHN ALEXANDER DOWIE
Founder, under God, of the Christian Catholic Church and of the City of Zion

MEMBERS OF THE ZION MOVEMENT HEALED AND BAPTIZED.

The Lord worked mightily in the great Zion movement introducing the miraculous powers of God in the healing of multitudes everywhere it went, preparing the way for further steps of faith, which steps many are now taking into the fullness of the Baptism of the Holy Spirit

Then followed the Mintern's testimony of being baptized in the Spirit.[102] J. Ellis, a seed merchant, had been a deacon in the Zion movement for 23 years. He was grateful for what he had received, but felt impelled to go further—

I shall always thank God for Zion and the experiences and blessings received in it. I believe it was right and taught the truths of the Scriptures, with the one exception of the Baptism of the Holy Spirit with speaking in tongues. They were also wrong in teaching that everyone else was in error... So I set out to investigate a new move that had come to Australia, which taught the Baptism of the Holy Ghost according to Acts 2: 4...

I had to ask the Lord to enlarge my heart to receive it all. Our church could not receive our message because of the speaking in tongues so we reluctantly left, but many have followed and received their baptism and we are trusting and believing that they will all come, for we know how earnestly they wish to serve the Lord Jesus.[103]

Booth-Clibborn family.

Another significant Pentecostal leader was John A. D. Adams, a New Zealand barrister. In 1887, Adams, a Grand Master in Freemasonry, was wasting away with palsy and the medical prognosis offered no hope. Dowie 'knocked all the Masonic devilry out of him,' prayed for him and his wife Maggie, who was also seriously ill, and they both recovered.[104] In 1926, Maggie died at the age of 85 and Adams was still active in ministry in Good News Hall, North Melbourne, Australia's first Pentecostal church.[105] C. L. Greenwood, one of Australia's best-known Pentecostal preachers, was first interested in the Pentecostal message as a result of a testimony that owed its origin to John Dowie.[106] Evangelist William Booth-Clibborn's family made the transition from the Salvation Army to the Pentecostal movement through Zion.[107] Many early Pentecostals recognised their debt to Dowie. As the *Australian Evangel* put it, he 'prepared the way for further steps of faith.'

The Zion movement was not the only parent of the new-born Pentecostal movement, and Pentecostalism was not its only child. But through it the family was certainly started, at least in part. It was Evangelicalism which was to provide, unintentionally, another source of gestation.

Notes

1. Dowie was born in Scotland and at the age of 13 migrated with his family to South Australia, where he was ordained as a Congregational minister. For further on Dowie's background see H. J. Gibbney, 'Dowie, John Alexander (1847–1907),' in ADB, Vol 4, 1851–1890; see also Appendix B.

78 The Origins and Development of the Pentecostal Movement in Australia

2. E. Sheldrake, ed, *The Personal Letters of John Alexander Dowie* (Zion, Ill: Wilbur Glenn Voliva, publisher, 1912), .30, 42, 50.

3. Following details are from Sheldrake, 1912, 35–58.

4. The *Jubilee Souvenir of the Municipality of Newtown,* c.1912, 75, notes that the building 'seats easily 800 people.' The building still stands in King St, Newtown. Today it is the Church of St Helen and St Constantine, a Greek Orthodox church.

5. Sheldrake, 1912, 339, 96.

6. Sheldrake, 1912, 96.

7. See J. H. L. Cumpston, *The History of Diphtheria, Scarlet Fever, Measles and Whooping Cough in Australia* (Canberra: Commonwealth of Australia Department of Health, 1927), 513. In 1875, there were 1,541 deaths from measles in Victoria, 752 in New South Wales and 178 in Queensland. In the following year, there were 1,097 deaths from scarlet fever in New South Wales and 2,240 in Victoria.

8. G. Lindsay, ed, *The Sermons of John Alexander Dowie* (Dallas: The Voice of Healing, 1951), .28.

9. G. Lindsay, *The Life of John Alexander Dowie* (Dallas: The Voice of Healing Publishing Co, 1951), 26; *Leaves of Healing,* Vol XCVI, No 4, April, 1959, 30.

10. Lindsay, *Sermons*, 1951, 28; Sheldrake, 1912, 160, 218, 320.

11. Sheldrake, 1912, 328. Carl Lee, Overseer in 1951, claimed that it was in 1884 that Dowie entered 'fully upon that enlarged ministry.' See LH, Vol LXXXVIII, October, 1951, 77.

12. P. G. Chappell, 'Healing Movements' in Burgess et al, 1988, .353ff. Following details on the healing movement are mainly from this source. See also Blumhofer, Vol 1, 1989, 26ff.

13. SC, II:26, 30 June, 1883.

14. Hollenweger, 1988, 116.

15. C. Lee, 'God's Messenger', LH, Vol LXXXVIII, No 10, October, 1981, 77.

16. Blumhofer, 1989, 32; M. Mintern, 'The Founding of the Christian Catholic Church', LH, Vol XCVI, No.4, April, 1959, 27—'I took my last medicine in 1902.'

17. Sheldrake, 1912, 98–106, 134—'I was never popular anywhere with our ministers as a whole.'

18. Sheldrake, 1912, 138, 188ff. Clearly this was the kind of decision that caused his father-in-law constant concern. Much of Dowie's correspondence to his wife at this time is actually defending himself against charges of irresponsibility from his uncle Alexander. Dowie's approach was simple—the Lord would provide.

19. Sheldrake, 1912, 217. The source of Dowie's figures is not known. Recorded statistics for the decade suggest an average growth over the decade of just over 500 members per annum. Congregational membership in NSW rose from 9,253 in 1871 to 14,328. See W. W. Phillips, 'Religion' in Vamplew, ed, 1987, 421. In South Australia, Congregationalism declined from 5.3% of the population in 1861 to 3.7% in 1901. See Hilliard, 1980, 6.

20. E.g. Sheldrake, 1912, 111, 112, 139, 175.

21. Sheldrake, 1912, 206ff, 237ff. Following details are also from this source. Financial embarrassment was to prove an ongoing problem to Dowie. When Wilbur Voliva came from the USA to lead the Zion work in Australia, he found a few people in Sydney, Melbourne and Adelaide who claimed Dowie owed them money and the debts were settled. See J. Taylor, *Wilbur Glenn Voliva* (Zion, Ill: Zion Historical Society, n.d), 6.

22. See I. Breward, *Australia: The Most Godless Place Under Heaven?* (Mitcham, Vic; Beacon Hill Books, 1988), 34; Clark, Vol IV, 1978, 366f, 385, 399; Roe, 1986, 40ff. Dowie would have seen rationalists joining his church as a significant achievement.

23. E. S. Kiek, *An Apostle in Australia* (London: Independent Press, 1927), 297.

24. Sheldrake, 1912, 253.
25. See the relevant title pages.
26. *Spiritualism Unmasked* contained correspondence between Dowie and Thomas Walker, a lecturer for the Victorian Association of Spiritualists, with an introduction by Dowie. Walker had threatened Dowie with the publishing this material himself, but then prevaricated, so, with the assistance of friends, Dowie became the publisher. All profits went to charity.
27. Sheldrake, 1912, 224, 253.
28. SMH, 16 December, 1879, 3.
29. A letter which Sheldrake dates 3 September, 1880, refers to Dowie standing for the seat of South Sydney for an election due to take place in November of that year. It is not clear whether this is referring to another by-election after the East Sydney loss, which seems unlikely, or to an earlier attempt to gain a seat in Parliament, in which case, the date of the letter is wrong. See Sheldrake, 1912, 257ff.
30. SMH, 13 December, 1879, 3.
31. SMH, 16 December, 1879, 3.
32. Sheldrake, 1912, 266, 270f; .SMH, 16 December, 1879, 3.
33. SMH, 18 December, 1879, 5.
34 .Sheldrake, 1912, 283; SMH, 31 January, 1880, 1.
35. Sheldrake, 1912, 258, 303ff; .J. A . Dowie, *Sin in the Camp* (Melbourne, Vic: Henry Cooke, 1883), 8.
36. *The Bulletin*, 3 March, 1904, 15.
37. Sheldrake, 1912, 302f.
38. Sheldrake, 1912, 397.
39. Dowie, *Sin in the Camp*, 1883.
40. This building no longer exists, but in 1885 it occupied numbers 52–80 of Johnston Street, which gives an indication of its size. See *Sands and McDougall's Melbourne and Suburban Directory* for 1885 and 1888. When Wilbur Voliva came to take over the work in October 1901, the numbers had dwindled, but rose again under his leadership. The Free Christian Tabernacle building was disposed of, and in May 1904, the building containing the Atheneum and Hibernian Halls was purchased for $165,000 and became the Central Zion Tabernacle, seating some 1,600 people. The sign 'Zion' was said to be readable from a mile away. See Taylor, *Voliva*, 5f.
41. *The Register*, 11 March, 1907.
42. Roe, 'Challenge and Response,' JRH, 5:2, December, 1968, 159.
43. Lindsay, 1951, 76.
44. LH XV: 3, 7 May, 1904, 58.
45. In the 3 May 1906 edition of *The Bulletin's* 44 pages, for example, some 35 health remedies were advertised—ranging from Hudson's Eumenthol Jujubes to Carter's Little Liver Pills to Dr Ricord's Essence of Life to Dr Williams' Pink Pills.
46. Lindsay, 1951, 75.
47. *Record of the Fifth Annual Commemoration of the Rev John Alexander Dowie and Mrs Dowie's Ministry of Healing through Faith in Jesus held in the Free Christian Tabernacle, Fitzroy, Melbourne, on Lord's Day, December, 4th & Monday December 5th 1887. Containing Testimonies from those healed and Ebenezer Addresses.* (Melbourne: M. L. Hutchinson, 1887); Sheldrake, 343; *Age*, 17 December, 1887, 9.
48. E. Mintern (ed),*This We Believe!* Zion, Ill: Christian Catholic Church, n. d., 5.
49. Sheldrake, 1912, 329.
50. Lindsay, *Sermons*, 1951, 98–104.
51. J. A. Dowie, *Doctors, Drugs and Devils* (Zion: Zion Printing and Publishing House, 1901).

52. See for example his 'First Reply to Robert Ingersoll' and his 'Reply to Ingersoll's Lecture on Truth' in Lindsay, *Sermons*, 1951, 79–97.

53. Sheldrake, 1912, 322ff. Dowie conducted his own defence claiming that he had only been exercising common rights to the use of highways; that the procession had been orderly and in accordance with the distinct commands of Scripture in Luke 4:21 and Mark 16:16; that he had already held street meetings for two years in Melbourne without let or hindrance; that there was no such restriction in other States; and that the new law was *ultra vires*. His arguments were all overruled.

54. According to a statement attributed to Dowie in *The Register*, 11 March, 1907, these two periods were 25 days and five days respectively. See also *The Age*, 4 May, 1885, 5; 20 June 1885, 12; 24 June 1885, 7.

55. In a letter written at the time, Dowie noted that he had felt a premonition of death on him during that day, and that he had gone home early, although there were four people waiting to see him, which was 'an unprecedented thing'. Years later, he claimed that there were some 20 or 30 people waiting to see him, and that he had actually heard a voice saying, 'Rise! Go!' Sheldrake, 1912, 325f; Lindsay, 1951, 79ff.

56. Sheldrake, 1912, 332f.

57. Sheldrake, 1912, 334–335.

58. Sheldrake, 1912, 338, 340.

59. Quoted in Lindsay, 1951, 86.

60. This also indicates that Dowie's healing ministry only began in earnest in 1882.

61. Sheldrake, 1912, 342ff.

62. Sheldrake, 1912, 345f.

63. J. Worsfold, *A History of the Charismatic Movements in New Zealand* (Julian Literature Trust, 1974), 86.

64. American journalist, Fred Leroy, in a syndicated report, wrote of Dowie, 'As a preacher, Dowie is a failure to all except those who believe in him. He has a rasping voice, a pompous air, delivers a disconnected sermon, becomes extremely radical, at times offensively so, and yet withal he is at the present time a wonderful success and one of the world's prominent men'— *The Independent Times*, January, 1904 in one of the Dowie *Srapbooks* held by the Zion Historical Society in Shiloh House, 1300 Shiloh Boulevard, Zion, Dowie's former residence which is now a museum.

65. C. Lee, 'God's Messenger' in LH, October, 1951, 77.

66. J. Taylor, *The Development of the City of Zion* (Zion, Ill; Christian Catholic Church, n. d.), 4; J. A. Dowie, *The Love of God in the Salvation of Man* (Chicago: Zion Publishing House, 1900), 38.

67. Taylor, *Voliva*, 5, 6. There seems to be little general knowledge of this migration. Marjorie Newton, for example, is clearly unaware of it. See M. Newton, *Southern Cross Saints* (Laie: Hawaii: Institute for Polynesian Studies, 1991), 157.

68. A. Darms, *Life and Work of John Alexander Dowie 1847–1907* (Zion: Christian Catholic Church, n. d.), 9, 13.

69. Lindsay, *Life*, 1951, 214ff. Lindsay argues that Esther's death was a factor in the aberrations in Dowie's thinking in the following years, especially his rising fury against alcohol.

70. Lindsay, *Life*, 1951; Darms, *Dowie*, 7ff; P. Cook, *Zion City, Illinois: John Alexander's Democracy* (Zion: Zion Historical Society, 1970); Mintern, ed, *This We Believe*; Taylor, *Development*, 4; LH, Vol XCVI, No 4, April, 1959; Vol CXXII, No 1, 2, January–February, 1986; R. Ottersen, *Peace to Thee!* (Zion: Christian Catholic Church, 1986), 9.

71. M. J. Mintern, 'Fifty Years Nearer the Rapture' in LH, October, 1951, 74. In a Christmas sermon in December 1903, in Shiloh Tabernacle, Zion, Dowie was reported as

saying, 'Within 100 years Christ will return again to this very spot to reign for ten centuries. I, whom you know to be the prophet Elijah, will come back with Him, and that is why I have made all leases in Zion City run for 1,100 years. At the end of Christ's reign the world will smash up, the bad will be burned in hell fire and the good will be called to their reward... All Zion knew I was a prophet before I announced it and I had hard work keeping them from exploiting the fact before I was ready.' See a cutting from the *Chicago Record-Herald*, 26 December, 1903, in one of the Dowie *Scrapbooks*. It should be noted that it is unlikely that Dowie would have used some of the terminology contained in this statement. So its authenticity as a direct quotation is probably questionable. However, see also *Australian Christian Commonwealth*, 13 May, 1904, 4; Darms, 13.

72. Dowie was not poorly educated. His treatise on drama, for instance, indicates an extensive knowledge of the Greek playwrights. Schools were established in Zion City with solid curricula which included church history and systematic theology. Similarly, as an Evangelical, Dowie took the opportunity to attack liberal theology. Hollenweger,1988, 117, 123.

73. Lindsay, 1951, 155f.
74. A copy of the Declaration was printed in *Quiz*, 23 October, 1901, 14.
75. Taylor, *Voliva*, 5.
76. Chant, 1984, 20.
77. From newspaper advertisements of the Sydney meetings.
78. From an unidentified news clipping c. Feb 1904. Part of the report reads—'Rev J. A. Dowie... wore a surplice of blue, white, yellow and purple. He was accompanied on the platform by his son (Mr Gladstone Dowie), several officers from Zion City, and two personal attendants, members of Zion Guards, wearing the uniform of police. Mr Dowie delivered short addresses. Some amusement was caused when he made an appeal for offerings to pay the cost of the meetings in Sydney. He questioned the audience as to whether such a thing was fair or not, and there were loud cries of 'Yes, yes,' and 'No, no.' He was perfectly surprised at anybody answering in the negative, and said he would keep them in fine order—he meant the element that had answered 'No.' He then called upon those who would like to retire before free-will offerings were taken up to do so, and there was a ready response from a large number, especially in the rear of the hall.'

79. Chant, 1984, 20.
80. These and the following reports are quoted from the Dowie *Scrapbooks*.
81. Cutting from the *Chicago Tribune*, 13 March, 1904, in one of the Dowie *Scrapbooks*.
82. *Bulletin*, 10 March, 1904, 7, 18; 17 March, 1904, 22; 24 March, 1904, 15; 14 April, 1904, 20.
83. *Advertiser*, 21 March ,1904. Following details are also from this source.
84. *Advertiser*, 21 March, 1904.
85. *The Downfall of Dowie!* (Hawthorn, Vic: J. H. Edmonson, n. d.)
86. *Advertiser*, 23 March, 1904, 5. Following details from this source.
87. *Bulletin*, 10 March, 1904, 13.
88. Dowie claimed that Victorian Methodists, for instance, had only increased by one member in the previous year— *Advertiser*, 22 March 1904, 5. In this, he may well have been right as the number of Methodists in Victoria declined from 180,272 in 1901 to 176,662 in 1911—W. W. Phillips, 'Religion' in Vamplew, ed, 1987, 422.
89. *Advertiser*, 23 March, 1904, 4; 24 March, 1904, 6; 25 March, 1904.
90. *Australian Christian Commonwealth*, quoted in the *Advertiser*, 25 March, 1904, 4.
91. Dowie reaffirmed these sentiments after his return to America—'I said that the King of England had no piety to spare... that if he was saved it would be by the skin of

his teeth... Call him defender of the faith? What faith has he to defend?'— Unidentified news clipping, June 1904.

92. The Town Clerk's letter read as follows: 'I have the honor [sic], by direction of the Mayor of Adelaide, to inform you that he has cancelled the remainder of your engagements at the Adelaide Town Hall. This action has been taken in consequence of your disloyal utterances concerning his Majesty the King, as reported in the press yesterday afternoon and morning. The balance of the hire paid will be refunded to you on application to the city treasurer's office.' See *Advertiser*, 28 March, 1904, 5.

93. *Bulletin*, 21 April, 1904, 12, 18; see also *Quiz*, 1 April, 1904.

94. Chant, 1984, 22.

95. At Dowie' s death, there was a group of about 100 of his followers in Sydney and a sizeable congregation of over 800 in Melbourne meeting in the imposing Central Zion Tabernacle (formerly the Hibernian Hall) in Swanston Street. The rear wall of this building was decorated with crutches, boots, plaster casts, surgical appliances, aprons and regalia from orders such as Freemasonry. By now, a Zion liturgy had been developed which included strong preaching but also a processional and a robed choir singing the *Te Deum*. Also, from Kangaroo Island, a few miles south of Adelaide, there were some who migrated to Zion City. See M. Sollit, 'Australian Dictator In Zion,' *People* 10 August, 1966, 50; LH, XV:3, 7 May, 1904, 57f; Kiek, 1927, 299.

96. Chappell in Burgess et al, eds, 1988, 366f. *Leaves of Healing* was a weekly publication which contained sermons by Dowie and reports of his ministry, together with testimonies, news items and photographs.

97. Ottersen, 1986, 14, 16.

98. 'The Five Porches of Bethesda' quoted in Chant, 1984, 281; I came across references to these predictions in the Dowie papers in Zion, but unfortunately did not record the sources.

99. Sheldrake, 1912, 334; Ottersen, 1986, 13.

100. Chant, 1984, 23f. It is interesting to note that many of the early Pentecostals in America, South Africa and Sweden can also trace their origins back to Dowie. These include such well-known figures as F. F. Bosworth, John G. Lake, Raymond Richey and Gordon Lindsay. See relevant articles in Burgess et al, 1988; Hollenweger, 1988.

101. Mintern, ed, *This We Believe,* 1f ; Taylor, *Voliva*, 40f.

102. AE, July, 1926, 10.

103. AE, July, 1926, 10.

104. J. Dowie, 'Satan the Defiler,' LH, 14 May, 1904, 99.

105. J. Adams, 'God Hath Spoken,' GN 17:7, July, 1926, 3f.

106. Greenwood, *Life Story,* 1965, 10ff.

107. See Appendix B.

CHAPTER FOUR

THE SPIRIT OF EVANGELICALISM

The Quest for Holiness and the Fullness of the Holy Spirit (1875–1920)

'Oh that a preacher might arise and expound from the Book of books a religion with a God, a religion with a heart in it,' lamented Sybylla Melvyn in *My Brilliant Career,* Miles Franklin's ground-breaking 1890s depiction of Australian country life. In the closing years of the nineteenth century, there were many who shared her sentiments.

As has been noted, the previous decades had seen the emergence of a number of new religious groups in Australia. It was also a time of intellectual challenge for the churches. The publishing of Charles Darwin's *The Origin of Species* in 1859 had radically changed many people's attitudes to the Bible. Secular rationalism was not new—since the days of the Enlightenment it had been gaining favour—but in nineteenth century Australia, it took on an almost evangelistic fervour. Rationalist speakers held regular meetings, more often than not, on Sundays, with musical programs to attract clientele and with vigorous arguments against faith in a higher power.[1] Testimonies were given of 'conversion' from religion to rationalism. Books were sold. Debates were invited. Reason was proclaimed as the final arbiter of truth. The Australasian Secular Association, founded in Melbourne in 1882, soon spread interstate. Rationalist associations were formed in New South Wales (1910), Queensland (1914), Western Australia, Victoria and South Australia (1918).[2]

On the other hand, during the two and a half decades from 1890 to the beginning of World War I, there was also an increasing level of evangelical Christian fervour. The pervasive influence of Wesleyan revivalism and the extraordinary career of John Dowie have already been noted as has the succession of overseas evangelists who toured Australia in the late 19th century. The early years of the twentieth century were equally punctuated with evangelistic campaigns.³

There was increasingly animated debate over traditional moral or social issues such as Sunday observance, temperance, and mixed bathing.⁴ Gradually, the restrictions of sabbatarianism gave way as Sunday newspapers were introduced and public buildings such as art galleries opened on the Lord's Day. On the beaches, thousands of people began to defy the laws which in some places forbade sea-bathing during the daylight hours, and in other places forbade mixed bathing at any time. By the mid 1890s, Sunday amusements were becoming more acceptable with concerts, picnics excursions and sporting events taking place with increasing frequency.⁵

The 1890s were also difficult economically. The withdrawal of overseas investments in Australia had a domino effect, resulting in the cessation of public works and the closure of some banks—some fifteen in the Eastern States by 1892. Prices of farm produce fell and there was industrial unrest. For many, the rising Labor Party offered a heaven on earth which had more immediate appeal than the less tangible after-life proclaimed by the churches. For others, it was the promise of a foretaste of heaven now, through the presence of the Holy Spirit, that sent them to their knees in prayer.

In 1899 the Boer War broke out in South Africa, and thousands of young Australians rushed to enlist. At home, senior politicians and statesmen were working painstakingly towards the final shape of Federation of Australian States, which took place in 1901. And those most popular inventions of the 20th century, the moving picture, the motor car and the aeroplane were making their first hesitant beginnings. Like the 1990s, the 1890s were a time of rapid change, the questioning of traditional values, the struggle for economic betterment, the search for identity and rigorous debate over the future direction of the nation. In all this, there was a significant number of people who believed that only an evangelical gospel which stressed a vital relationship with Christ through the power of the Spirit would satisfy human need and resolve social ills.

The Keswick Movement

Keswick Convention at Upwey, Victoria, December.

In the early 1870's, Robert Pearsall Smith from Philadelphia initiated a series of conferences in England, where several other Americans, including Smith's wife, Hannah, were involved. Humbled through an act of indiscretion, Smith withdrew from the convention scene but Dundas Harford-Battersby, Vicar of St. John's, Keswick, took over.[6] He had been praying earnestly for a more meaningful experience of Christ. As a result, he explained, 'I got a revelation of Christ to my soul so extraordinary, so glorious and so precious that from that day it illuminated my life. I found HE was ALL I wanted.'[7]

In 1875, he organised a convention in Keswick, for worship, prayer and teaching, where he shared something of his own new experience in Christ. He told how he had learned the difference between a seeking faith and a resting faith. Seeking faith came to Christ bearing a burden, but resting faith had found Christ—and the burden was gone. Soon Keswick Conventions were being held regularly. The message was simple—

> Keswick stands distinctively for this: Christ our righteousness, upon Calvary, received by faith, is also Christ our holiness, in the heart that submits to Him and relies upon Him.[8]

This concept was presented with such conviction that it struck responsive chords in many hearts. There was also a focus on the need to be filled with the Holy Spirit. Years later, H. P. Smith summarised the Keswick emphases from the beginning as having been—

1. The exceeding sinfulness of sin
2. The way of cleansing and renewal
3. The life of full surrender
4. The fullness of the Holy Spirit
5. The path of service and sacrifice[9]

Keswick theologians rejected the perfectionist emphasis of the Wesleyan-Holiness tradition, but stressed that the fullness of the Spirit was normative for Christian living.[10] To be filled with the Spirit, it was necessary to yield your will completely to Christ and to 'surrender' to Him. At one of the early Conventions, Andrew Murray (1828–1917), Keswick leader and pastor of the Dutch Reformed Church at Wellington, South Africa, set down eight steps to the fullness of the Spirit—

1. I know and believe there is a Pentecostal Blessing still to be enjoyed by God's people.
2. I have not got it.
3. It is for me; and it is my own fault that I have not got it.
4. I cannot grasp it. God must give it.
5. I long and desire, at any cost, to become possessed of this Blessing.
6. I am going to surrender all to obtain it.
7. I believe that He accepts me, and I claim the Blessing now— this very moment.
8. I reckon that He now fulfils His promise; and I go forth to obey.[11]

In 1876, Hussey Burgh Macartney, the Irish-born Vicar of St Mary's Anglican church in Caulfield, Victoria, and son of the Dean of Melbourne, presided over a small convention in Melbourne.[12] Two years later, he visited Keswick and was so impressed he began similar conventions in Melbourne when he returned. These were the beginning of what was to become a series of annual gatherings in Victoria for decades to come.

Waiting on God, a book of short readings on prayer by Andrew Murray, was being circulated and hungrily read. It culminated with an exhortation to pray earnestly for the fullness of the Holy Spirit.[13] The popularity of books like this was another indicator of the desire among Evangelicals for a more meaningful spirituality.

George Carleton Grubb

In 1890, George Carleton Grubb arrived in Australia with an evangelistic party. Hailing from Tipperary, he was a vigorous man of 33 years, although his balding head made him look older. If Harford-Battersby was a typical Anglican clergyman, Grubb was the opposite—a boisterous Irish rover. Pollock describes him like this—

> Everything about him had a rip-roaring wild Irishness. He would have an audience cringing in fear of judgement one moment and bursting their sides with guffaws the next... Grubb was a man of emotions, not happy unless in strong measure he could feel the presence of God, but a man of sheer faith who fully expected and often saw the most improbable occurrences in answer to prayer.[14]

It did not take long for Macartney and Grubb to meet.[15] For two weeks the two Irishmen conducted a mission before Grubb travelled on to New Zealand. A year later, in 1891, with a tour group including E.C. Millard and his wife and V.D. David, a Tamil evangelist, he returned to Australia, and again held meetings in New South Wales, Victoria and Tasmania.[16] His topics were varied but generally focused on commitment to Christ.[17]

He was met by an enthusiastic response. Six hundred people were turned away from one gathering he held. Most of his financial needs were provided by the local people, and many were led to commit their lives to Christ. A number of these later entered full-time Christian work. The impact of his athletic preaching was such that 'amazing scenes' were witnessed at his services.'[18] Anglicans, like Methodists, were enthused by Grubb's fervent approach and his emphasis on the revitalising, experiential power of the Spirit and congregations often responded with spontaneous shouts of praise. His emphasis on holiness and separation from the world was attractive to people looking for more effective Christian living. Judd and Cable credit Grubb with originating the ongoing distinctive Sydney Anglican emphasis on evangelism, emotional consecration hymns, invitations to follow Christ, the signing of decision cards, holy life-style and stirring up greater involvement in foreign missions.[19] But Sydney Anglicanism has been shaped by other influences as well. Nathaniel Jones, Principal of the Anglican Moore College in Sydney, although initially happy to cooperate with Grubb, began to develop misgivings. What Jones saw as Grubb's emphasis on 'imparted righteousness' and his own teaching of 'imputed righteousness' were not comfortable bed-fellows.[20] Grubb emphasised the power of the Spirit for service; Jones the power of the Gospel for salvation through the all-sufficient work of the Cross. Grubb advocated the Holiness idea of ongoing sanctification; Jones held to the Reformed position of completed redemption in Christ which would be realised eschatologically at the Second Coming.[21]

Consequently, Sydney Anglicanism never embraced revivalism in the way that Grubb expressed it and today still reflects the direction set by Jones, with a strong, almost bibliolatrous adherence to the text of Scripture and a stern scepticism about emotional expressions of faith. The Keswick movement, on the other hand, pursued its emphasis on an experience of Christ and, in its early days at least, its participants were encouraged to continue to cry out to God for a Pentecostal outpouring.[22]

It is interesting that Millard's record of Grubb's visit begins with a complete quotation of 1 Cor. 12:1–11, the one New Testament passage that lists in detail the special gifts of the Spirit such as prophesying, healing and tongue-speaking. Wherever Grubb went there was an emphasis on the need to be filled with the Spirit.[23] One congregational minister had such an experience with God that he left his church to himself become a revivalist.[24] After one meeting, the team members had an enlivening experience of the Spirit—

> I went back to the hotel, where I heard a tremendous shouting of Hallelujah in our private room. The others were literally jumping around the room, and David was shouting, 'Glory to God! Glory to God! Glory to God!'

On the other hand, their joy was tempered by Mrs Millard enduring a painful swelling in the face, which nothing would alleviate. Finally, they decided to put aside all medical treatment and ask God to heal her. Within a few minutes she declared she was quite free of all pain. The shouting began again.[25] It was not uncommon for Grubb to encourage people to give voice to their praises. He poured scorn on those who would grow excited over football but not about the safety of their souls. The question asked (about the preachers) was not, 'What Church does he belong to?' but, 'Is he up to shouting pitch yet?'[26]

When teaching and preaching about the baptism in the Holy Spirit, the emphasis was consistent—the need to yield to God in total obedience and then to take the blessing of the Spirit by faith.[27]

Preparation in Prayer

Around 1890, a small group of men, led by John MacNeil (1854–1896), began praying together for revival in Australia.[28] MacNeil, born into a Presbyterian family in Scotland, was brought up in Ballarat, Victoria, and worked as a 'railway contractor.'[29] After studying theology at New College, Edinburgh, he was ordained in 1879 and shortly after introduced to the Keswick movement. He experienced 'an anointing of the Holy Spirit' and in 1881 began evangelistic ministry. A battle with health hindered his itinerant work until he recovered after laying on of hands by an Anglican minister. He was no mean evangelist, drawing crowds in many places—he saw as many as 1200 professions of faith in six weeks in 1894 in Queensland.[30]

In 1890, together with Allan Webb, John Watsford and a handful of others, he formed a prayer group which came to be known as 'The Band' which met regularly to pray for revival, even if it was to be years coming. They also focused strongly on the need for an infilling of the Holy Spirit as part of the 'higher Christian life' espoused by Keswick and were praying for 'the full Baptism of the Holy Spirit for themselves and for all ministers, officers and members of the Churches.'[31] MacNeil wrote a popular booklet called *The Spirit-filled Life*.[32] The devotion of these men to prayer was internationally acknowledged.[33] Out of their intercessions came the decision to mount a Keswick-style convention in Geelong, a Victorian provincial city, some 80 kilometres from Melbourne, with George Grubb—who had addressed Keswick Conventions in England—as the primary speaker, along with MacNeil, Webb and others.[34] The large Mechanics Institute was used and people came from all over Victoria and even from 'neighbouring Colonies.' There were overflow meetings in the Presbyterian church next door. For four days, there were four meetings a day and they could not accommodate all those who came, 'not to hear eloquent addresses or exquisite music, but to hear of Pentecostal Christianity, and how it may be ours.'

The theme was 'Apostolic Christianity' and the focus from the beginning was on Christ. 'We want to write up over this Mechanics hall,' said Grubb, in his opening address, '"For Jesus Only": for we are met here for the glory of our Saviour, and to learn His holy will.'[35]

There were frequent calls to holiness, to love and to the fullness of the Spirit, Grubb did not mince matters—

> Ah! my friends, the baptism of the Holy Ghost means the identification of ourselves with the common herd of sinners around us. No one will obtain the baptism without this. Come down from your ecclesiastical perches, oh! reverend teachers of men, for power and unction of the Spirit can only come to you if you be identified with the baptism of sinners. May the Lord deliver us from the pride of reputation.

and,

> The effect of the baptism of the Holy Ghost is to set our tongues free. First the heart free, then the tongue free; that is the Holy Ghost's order. He sets the heart free and our heart begins to bubble and swell, and it comes out at our mouth. We should get ill if we could not shout and sing. If you have the Holy Ghost in you you will not need a spiritual force-pump to get up a shout or a sermon either... Oh Lord! Give us the Spirit of Pentecost for Thy name's sake.[36]

When MacNeil spoke, he was equally direct. He had not got ten lines into his message when he said, 'Look here, man! Are you born again? You need not begin to think about Apostolic service until you can say "yes" to that.' He concluded with a strong challenge to his hearers to be sure they had the power of the Holy Spirit in their lives—

> What then was the secret of the Apostolic Power? God—God the Holy Ghost, within them, around them, that was their equipment. The same equipment may be

ours today. Have you got it? ...If you had asked Peter, or Thomas, or John... they would have said, 'Yes.' They knew they had it. Some of you are living on the wrong side of Pentecost...[37]

Edward Harris, of West Melbourne Baptist church,[38] raised the issue that some people felt the need to distinguish between being baptized with the Spirit and being filled with the Spirit. In that case, he said, 'go in for both of them.'[39] There was a strong emphasis of the centrality of Christ, on prayer, on holiness, on entire sanctification, on absolute surrender to God. Allan Webb declared, 'Apostolic Christianity meant complete surrender... You want to be useful? ... There is only one way. It is to be surrendered to God.'[40] At one rally, after a woman sent up a gift of two pounds for the China Inland Mission, people streamed to the platform to present a missionary offering. 'There was no excitement, no hysterics, no rushing from seats and clapping of hands. The Holy Spirit just laid on the people's hearts an intense yearning for the heathen, and gave the world a practical illustration of Apostolic Christianity.' They brought silver, gold, rings, chains, watches, jewellery, cheques, notes and laid them on the table. The value was estimated at over a thousand pounds. An archdeacon gave his archidiaconal ring; one man gave a cottage and nine acres of land; a couple offered 120 pounds per year to support a missionary. Ultimately, after Grubb's Victorian mission, fifty people offered themselves for mission work.[41]

In New South Wales, the story was similar. At St. Peter's, Woolloomooloo, after Grubb had ministered, 'as the people moved out they seemed to walk on tiptoe, as if it were holy ground... no talking... an unmistakable solemnity...'[42] At the Sydney Convention, (5–7 January, 1892), Christians of all denominations met and 'the Lord was present in Holy Ghost power', while the expectation of the people was so great that all the seats in the Centenary Hall, York Street, were occupied at least two hours before the advertised hour.[43]

In Launceston, Tasmania, 'the blessing... without doubt surpassed the previous ones held at Geelong and Sydney...' There was 'clear teaching' that it was pointless to ask for the fullness of the Holy Spirit without first being cleansed of all sin. Over two thousand people packed the auditorium and forty or fifty ministers sought to be filled with the Spirit.[44]

Another convention was held in Geelong in September 1892—it had already become an annual event—and again crowds attended. Again, there was plenty of excitement as 'from all parts of the building came shouts of "Hallelujah!", "Glory be to God!" and a wave of glory seemed to roll over the audience.'

Grubb did not stay in Victoria. He travelled through England, South America and even Russia, as well as various parts of Australia. His popularity waned when it was reported that he held the view known as conditional immortality or annihilation,[45] and his associations with the Keswick movement were for a time broken. Nevertheless, the Geelong conventions which George Grubb started formed the background to the convention movement that was to continue in Victoria into the twentieth century.[46]

Reuben Torrey

In 1899, the popular American evangelist D.L. Moody (1837–1899) received a petition from 15,831 people in Australia and New Zealand inviting him to preach.[47] Moody's death prevented his coming. But two years later, Yale graduate and Congregationalist minister Dr. Reuben Torrey (1856–1928) did, together with his song leader, Presbyterian layman Charles Alexander (1867–1920). Torrey is still well-known because of the books he wrote, many of which continue in print—including those on the ministry of the Holy Spirit.[48] And Alexander's hymns are still widely sung.

R.A.Torrey.

Torrey's visit was part of a well orchestrated Simultaneous Mission which involved thousands of people and hundreds of churches and Christian workers. There was a committee of 70 with sub committees handling specific areas such as finance and venues. Thirty large tents were secured for regional meetings. Missioners were drawn from seven denominations. Extensive door-to-door visitation took place.[49] In Melbourne, main meetings were conducted in the Town Hall and later in the vast Exhibition Building; in Sydney the venue was the Town Hall—where 10,000 people tried to gain admittance, and William Taylor declared, 'We have never known Sydney so moved.'[50] Regional rallies were conducted in the suburbs and in provincial cities such as Ballarat, Bendigo and Geelong. Some 214 churches were involved in the Melbourne mission, with 50 missioners, 2000 'personal workers,' 16,800 home meetings attended by 117,600 people, 2500 choir members and 700 men on local committees. Lunch time meetings at the Town Hall resulted in hundreds being turned away.[51] Torrey was accompanied by the more outgoing Walter Geil, whose preaching also drew large crowds and was received with good effect. In Footscray, for example, in one service, some 700 people signed cards as an expression of their confession of Christ. By May, press reports referred to what was happening as a 'religious revival'. The Mission also raised some 3000 pounds for the YMCA.[52] Overall, the visit was so successful that 20,000 conversions were reported throughout the country.

Not every church was involved. Roman Catholics neither participated in it nor opposed it, until Geil made some harsh comments on the activities of Catholic friars in the Philippines. And the Melbourne branch of Dowie's Christian Catholic Church in Zion publicly challenged Torrey on his statements about Dowie and his alleged inconsistency in denouncing 'secret societies' while 'worshiping with their members.'[53] Torrey was not 'revivalistic' in methodology. He dressed immaculately, he preached clearly and consistently, he attempted to persuade by force of reason rather than through stirred emotions. Among his sermon topics were—

- Is the Bible the Word of God (several addresses)
- The Power of Prayer
- Hell and Who Are Going There
- Every Man's Need of a Hiding Place
- Causes of Infidelity
- The Most Important Question
- What Shall I Do to be Saved?
- What does it Cost not to be a Christian?
- Hindrances to Prayer
- Proofs of the Resurrection
- The Holy Spirit and His Work
- A Manufacturing Business Which Does Not Pay
- The Baptism of the Holy Spirit[54]

His constituency was largely middle class Protestantism.[55] Although his primary aim was conversions, he repeatedly stressed the need to be baptized in the Holy Spirit. Both in Melbourne and Sydney he concluded his meetings with a strong challenge in this area. His theology was straight Wesleyan. He himself had experienced a personal encounter with the Spirit—

> One day as I sat in my study, something fell on me, and I literally fell to the floor, and I just lay there and shouted. I had never shouted before... but I lay there shouting 'Glory to God! Glory to God! Glory to God!' ...The Spirit had put something in me that was not there before.[56]

He taught others that their experience could be the same—that just as it was possible to know the certainty of salvation, it was possible to know the reality of being baptized in the Spirit. It was a work additional to the Spirit's regular work of salvation. It was not to make us happy, but to make us useful. The results would be joy, boldness, clear knowledge and appropriate spiritual gifts. The promise of the Spirit was for people of all ages and in every church. If we were to be soul-winners, we must be baptized in the Holy Spirit. To receive the Spirit we needed to repent, to confess Christ openly, to be obedient to God— which meant absolute surrender to him—to thirst for the Spirit like a dying man for water, to ask specifically for the Holy Spirit and then to believe.[57]

It is noteworthy that this has been classical Pentecostal teaching on this subject since its inception—the significant difference being Torrey's lack of reference to tongues. A few years earlier, Torrey had often pondered the question, 'If one is baptized with the Holy Spirit will he not speak in tongues?' He also believed that the gifts of the Holy Spirit listed in 1 Corinthians 12:8–10 would be expressed through Spirit-filled people.[58] But he felt it was 'a mistake to suppose that everyone should speak in tongues'. In practice, this seems to have meant that none should.[59] In later years, he rejected 'the Tongues Movement' altogether.[60] Nevertheless, there is no doubt that Torrey's emphasis on the need for an experiential encounter with the Holy Spirit fostered the growing spiritual hunger in the evangelical churches and that it was indirectly responsible for the nascence of the infant Pentecostal assemblies that emerged struggling and crying into the twentieth century world.

Hervey Perceval Smith

One of Torrey's most significant converts was Hervey Perceval Smith (1869–1947). In 1893, Smith, a former journalist, succeeded his father as manager of the Federal Palace Hotel, 'the greatest and most exotic hotel Australia has seen,'[61] in Collins Street West, Melbourne, Victoria,[62] where Torrey and his party were accommodated. Walking home one night after a Torrey meeting, he decided to believe the gospel and the realisation transformed him.[63]

He became leader of what was known as the Melbourne Gospel Crusade with its emphasis on the 'three R's' of ruin by the Fall, redemption by the blood and regeneration by the Holy Spirit,[64] and devoted himself to evangelism, welfare work, hospital visitation and the like. He spent much time in prayer. His board of directors later challenged him to license the establishment, but he refused, believing that with God's help, he would make it prosper without a licence.[65] Room 7, on the second floor, a large sitting room, became the venue for many Melbourne believers who met together to study, to pray and to hear visiting speakers. Later, Smith founded the Keswick Tea Rooms and Book Depot at 315 Collins Street, Melbourne.[66]

Federal Hotel, Melbourne.

Smith found himself strongly in the Keswick tradition and recounted how the early Keswick meetings in England had resulted from a hunger for a closer walk with God, a life of 'unbroken fellowship with Christ', victory over all known sin and a conscious sense of need for the anointing of the Holy Spirit and the resultant power for service.[67]

Pandita Ramabai.

After nearly twenty years, the Geelong Conventions had dwindled. So in 1909, under Smith's leadership, several small conventions were organised elsewhere. The first was at Eltham, a pastoral spot on the outskirts of Melbourne, which was attended by about 50 people. In 1918–19, another was held at Upwey, in the Dandenongs, east of Melbourne, where annual conventions continued for the next 30 years. An undated general guideline for speakers at Upwey, based on those for the English Keswick conventions, lists the topics for Day Five as, 'The Fullness of the Spirit', with subheadings 'A command', 'A birthright', 'A promise', 'A need', and, 'The way to receive'.

Indian Revival

In 1898, Pandita Ramabai (1858–1922), of Mukti (i.e. Salvation) Mission, the celebrated Indian Christian reformer,[68] visited a Keswick Convention in England, where she urged the 4000 delegates to 'pray for an outpouring of the Holy Spirit on all Indian Christians'.[69] News of 'the Revival in Australia', the result of evangelical initiatives such as the Simultaneous Mission, prompted Ramabai to send her daughter Manoramabai and American missionary Minnie Abrams (1859–1912) there 'to catch the inspiration of the Revival fire' and to form groups to pray for Mukti.[70] Later, reports of the Welsh revival of 1904–05[71] stirred them to organise daily prayer meetings at Mukti, which were attended by over 500 girls. There, Minnie Abrams began to teach on the baptism of the Holy Spirit for effective service.

Minnie Abrams 1859-1912.

At 3.30 am, on 29 June, 1905, she was woken by a girl who had seen flames over one of her companions and had run to get a bucket of water. But there was no fire: it was a new Pentecost (c.f. Acts 2:3). Soon all the girls in that compound were weeping, praying and confessing their sins.[72]

On June 30, while Ramabai was expounding the Scriptures 'in her usual quiet way', she had to stop because 'the Holy Spirit descended in power' and the girls began to cry out aloud to God. Some saw visions; two little girls had 'heavenly light shining on their faces' as they prayed for hours. After times of strong conviction and much weeping, the girls had a clear understanding of Christ's work on the Cross and there was a sense of peace, followed by joy.

Pandita Ramabai and girls.

Normal meals were missed; the regular program was abandoned. There were waves of prayer over the meetings as hundreds cried audibly to God. There were similar manifestations as Mukti workers visited other missions nearby—visions of Jesus, shining faces, weeping for sin, dancing, overflowing love and joy, shaking, falling to the floor, casting out of demons, all nights of prayer. Missionaries, too, had to humble themselves, repent before God and put things right. On 7 November, 1905, Ramabai closed the school and announced ten days of prayer. Most of the 700 girls gathered together, while about 60 each day went to the villages in evangelism. In March, at the general assembly for churches in the area, thousands gathered. There were 'Pentecostal scenes'— people testified to the miraculous supply of food, to visions of angels, even to the building shaking.

During the first twelve months, five thousand conversions were recorded. People claimed miraculous healing. Others were freed from addiction to tobacco. Stolen property was returned. Many were called to the ministry. Most remarkable was the occurrence of glossolalia. Speaking in tongues was widespread at Mukti and at other nearby missions, to which girls from Mukti went to testify. On several occasions, there were well-authenticated reports that Indian girls had spoken clear, idiomatic English under the influence of the Spirit.[73] Shortly after this, 'a bright, intelligent lady' named Joan McGregor came to Melbourne from Mukti mission, attended meetings in the Federal Hotel and told of these remarkable events.[74] Furthermore, reports also came to hand of the Welsh Revival, with its widespread conversions, and its emphasis on the fullness of the Spirit.[75] These stories were greedily absorbed by Christians in Melbourne.

Wilbur Chapman

In 1909, another American, the Presbyterian Wilbur Chapman (1859–1918), visited Australia, accompanied by Charles Alexander. As with Torrey, there was an astonishing response by Australians to his evangelistic approach. The meetings extended over a period of four months and drew huge crowds.[76] Chapman's preaching covered similar themes to those addressed by Torrey— the authority of Scripture, the need for repentance, salvation by faith in Christ and the Spirit-filled life. He made no bones about the need to be Spirit-filled—

Chapman-Alexander Mission Book, South Australia, 1909.

> If you will allow me to choose between the man who has had a definite experience in conversion , and knows little of the Holy Ghost, and the man who may be uncertain as to the time of his conversion, but who knows about the third person of the Trinity, I will choose the latter every time, for I am certain that I may be a Christian and not know when I crossed the line, but I cannot be a Christian with an experience of power until I know something definite about the Holy Ghost.[77]

The party travelled through four States with campaigns in Sydney, Melbourne, Brisbane, Adelaide, Ballarat and Bendigo and single rallies in several other regional centres. In Adelaide, a city of 140,000, there was an aggregate attendance of 144,000. In Melbourne, some 400 churches contributed to a choir of 1,500 voices. As with Torrey's campaign, people spoke of it as a revival. Alexander's wife and biographer later described these events as a time of Pentecost for the whole Commonwealth.[78] In 1912, Chapman and Alexander returned for an even larger evangelistic mission. Although press reports spoke inevitably of emotionalistic fervour, much of the support for the reasonably conservative

Chapman came from equally conservative middle class Evangelicals. Chapman's ongoing emphasis on the fullness of the Spirit was a significant factor in the emergence of Pentecostalism.

The Eltham Convention

While most of the impact of the prayer movement, the Simultaneous Mission, and the visits of overseas evangelists was felt in the Evangelical world, with 'a revived spirit' in the churches and 'the reinspiration of flagging church institutions,' there was also another result—namely, the emergence of new movements.[79] One of these was Pentecostalism. The cry for revival, for the infilling of the Holy Spirit, for a closer experience of God's presence, for holiness and power for service found expression in an identifiable baptism in the Holy Spirit marked by speaking in tongues.

When the 1910 Eltham Convention was conducted, it had behind it a rich and varied series of influences—Wesleyanism, Dowie, Keswick, Grubb, Torrey, Chapman, Alexander, Murray, Ramabai, H. P. Smith. While Wesleyanism was the dominant factor in all this, it is interesting to note that both Anglicanism and Congregationalism were also strongly represented, with some Baptist and Salvation Army elements evident as well.

Jessie Ferguson, 1927.

It would be an exaggeration to suggest that all these developments affected all members of the small group of people present at Eltham. But there was an atmosphere of hunger for God and an eager expectation of revival. At one of the prayer meetings, a young woman named Fraser, was praying for the fullness of the Spirit when she spoke in tongues. Others began to have the same experience, including Ada Painter and well-known Pentecostal identity, Maudy Rabley. Jessie Ferguson, who was to become a missionary, received the Spirit later.[80] One woman was laid in a bed in the meeting tent through serious sickness. Prayer was offered for her and that evening she played the organ for the singing. Another woman suffering with eczema collapsed at the door of the tent. When they picked her up the eczema had gone.[81]

These manifestations caused a furore. While some saw them as answers to their prayers for the fullness of the Spirit, others rejected them. Although it is said George Grubb practised healing,[82] most of the leaders, saw these phenomena as extremist. When one person spoke in tongues on emerging from baptism in water, somebody tried to stop her, but without success.[83]

After this, Smith continued to conduct meetings in the Federal Coffee Palace, and to allow reference and testimony to baptism in the Holy Spirit. Meetings were also held in the Assembly Hall in Collins Street. Ultimately, however,

Keswick officially rejected the new manifestations, and refused to allow people to speak about them publicly. The emphasis on the fullness of the Spirit was sustained, but emotions, feelings and outward expressions of the Spirit's presence were plainly discouraged. The esteemed British evangelist and convention speaker F. B. Meyer (1847–1929) told how when, as an old man, he received the baptism of the Holy Spirit, 'there was nothing emotional ... nothing ecstatic, nothing sensational about the experience'. Yet this made him 'a spiritual power that was literally Pentecostal'.[84] The fullness of the Holy Spirit was a free gift. It was important to 'dismiss from our minds forever the idea that we must struggle and agonise' to receive it. Just as salvation was accepted by simple faith, so was baptism in the Holy Spirit.[85] H.P. Smith adopted this approach, abandoned the emphasis on Pentecostal phenomena and continued to work in Keswick meetings and conventions until his death in 1948.[86] Two of his sisters went to India as missionaries. One of them, Rosa, accepted Spirit-baptism and spent the rest of her life at Mukti.[87]

John Henry Coombe and John Barclay

One man who exemplified the blend of the old evangelicalism and the new Pentecostalism was John Henry Coombe (1883–1957). On 28 February 1907, Coombe was the first person in Melbourne, Victoria, to speak in tongues.[88] He was, for a time, a Pentecostal leader, known for his excellence in biblical exposition. 'John Coombe taught deep things from the Word of God,' recalled Elizabeth Barclay. 'The folk came to hear him because he was so earnest and so hungry for the things of God. His teaching was so rich.'[89]

Born in Drouin, Victoria, and brought up in New Zealand, with a Methodist father and a Presbyterian mother, Jack, as he was known to his family, was an accomplished cyclist and cricketer and skilled with the rifle.[90] At one point, he planned to take up cycle racing, but felt called by God to a ride a different race.[91]

In September 1906, he attended the first Pentecostal meetings held in Melbourne in the North Carlton home of an elderly woman named Mrs J. H. Nickson.[92] How these meetings began and to what extent they were a product of the various conventions and campaigns of the previous two decades is not known. But it is a fair assumption that they did not emerge in isolation but grew out of that well-cultivated Evangelical soil. Only three people attended the first gathering, but the numbers grew and on 28 February 1907, this 'earnest young brother' spoke in tongues. Mrs Nickson described the incident with wonderment—

> I had not heard anyone speak in unknown tongues before, and a great awe came over the meeting. Some fell down under the mighty power of God. This brother spoke and sang, and gave some of us sweet messages from the Lord, in the unknown tongue which he also interpreted. It was a wonderful time and we were full of praises to our God, for condescending to come among us in such a marvellous manner. All glory to Jesus be given.[93]

Around June 1907, as some of the group planned to attend a meeting at the local Church of England, they decided to meet for prayer first. They never did arrive. 'The Lord came down in great power' and four more people spoke and sang in tongues. Over the next few weeks, similar phenomena occurred and soon there was a sizeable company who had experienced charismata.

Another woman told how she had attended meetings at Canning Street, Carlton, in May 1907, 'in deadly earnest' to receive the fullness of God's blessing. In October of the same year, she 'received Pentecost.' Again, it was a vivid encounter with God—

> The blessing was so wonderful, I was prostrate, trembling and shaking from head to foot. I did know that the blessed Holy Spirit was poured out upon me as in the days of Pentecost. Words fail to express what I felt and know of Jesus. I do praise Him, He has given me such love for everyone... People said when I first received the blessing it was excitement and would soon pass away; but glory to Jesus, it is Jesus only, He is still the same wonder working Jesus.[94]

Another to be immersed in the Spirit was policeman John Barclay. Born in Northern Ireland on 26 October 1881, Barclay had come to Australia at the turn of the century. In late 1906 or early 1907, he began to attend the meetings at the Nickson home. At Easter 1907, he attended a Holiness Camp at Ferntree Gully, now a Melbourne suburb.[95] He was soon numbered among those who experienced the power of the Holy Spirit—

> I saw the heavens opened and my precious Jesus sitting on the throne. Oh, the joy and beauty and glory! It is unspeakable. Then Jesus came right down into the room and I saw Him smile all around. But he looked so sadly at me, and His look condemned me for refusing before to yield myself fully up to Him. His loving but sad look broke my heart, and I burst into tears, and cried: `Lord, I yield my all up to you to do with me as Thou wilt.' I just cried from my heart that verse, "I'll go where you want me to go, dear Lord..." It was simply celestial; no beauty on earth like it! No words on earth can describe what it was like.[96]

Barclay was for about an hour and a half unconscious to everything except the Lord's presence. When he 'returned to earth again', one of the women present began to entreat God for blessing on the believers and for the conversion of unbelievers, after which she began to pray and sing in a strange tongue which sounded to Barclay like Chinese. He was entranced—

> What heavenly music! It sounded very much like an angel's voice coming rolling over the balconies of heaven. Of all the grand singers I have heard, I have never heard anything so sweet. She gave messages from God to several. Our meeting lasted till four o'clock in the morning.

As a result of this experience, Barclay had an earnest desire for a more intimate knowledge of God and began 'seeking in real deep earnest for the baptism of the Holy Ghost and fire'. He was beset with doubts for a time, but after praying about this, he felt an encouraging peace of mind. Indeed 'a beautiful calm and peace' permeated his being and he 'saw a light shine from heaven far brighter than the noonday Sun' and so intense that he had to cover his eyes with his hands.

That night he went to another house meeting but was again troubled with doubts. Nevertheless, he persisted in prayer until about 10.30 pm with some others, some of whom were speaking in tongues. Finally, about one o'clock the next morning, one of the men laid hands on him and he was baptized in the Spirit. For him it was a powerful encounter—

> My hands, arms, and whole body trembled greatly and I was thrown to the floor. All the others were praising the Lord... He is the same yesterday, today and forever. He baptizes with the Holy Ghost the same today as nineteen centuries ago. On that night the Lord gave me the tongues, and since then I have spoken in four or five different languages. All glory to His Name!

He soon ran into criticism and opposition, with Christian friends telling him it was 'all of the devil'. But his experience was so meaningful, he was convinced it was from God. How could Satan give the peace, joy, and happiness that he was experiencing?

The leadership of the home group was early put into the hands of John Coombe, although the meetings were equally recognised as Mrs Nickson's. They were marked by extraordinary phenomena—

> I might say many have seen Jesus... Many have also seen Fire. I think all interpret. The interpretations seem to show the near coming of Jesus... and following Jesus all the way... The precious Blood is always exalted in our midst. I think all who have received the gift of tongues have seen the Fire of God as well as felt it... Sometimes our meetings are all praise to Jesus and adoration with this heavenly singing.[97]

The sense of wonder that permeates this report was matched by a reflective sense of humility. Those who had received the gift were 'very lowly' and of little account in the world's eyes. Hence, they were often criticised. But they did not mind for the Lord filled them with 'so much joy.'

Following his baptism in the Holy Spirit Coombe and his fiancee Lillian Carroll were helpers at the Chapman-Alexander Mission of 1909. That same year, Coombe married Lillian and moved to Essendon. In 1910, with the assistance of A. S. Joyce, who provided the money, Coombe established a Mission in Palmer Street, Fitzroy and asked Barclay to join him there.[98] This small church of about 100 people, was never known as 'Pentecostal,' although Pentecostal manifestations did occur at times. One story is still recalled today of how one Ben Gibson spoke in tongues and a Chinese person alleged he had used textbook Chinese.[99] Around 1920, Gibson was involved in a business partnership with C. L. Greenwood, at Sunshine. Greenwood, who attended meetings at Palmer Street on occasion,[100] later became one of Australia's most effective Pentecostal evangelists and a leader in the Assemblies of God.[101] Overall, however, their practices were more Evangelical than Pentecostal. People like the movement's matriarch Jeannie Lancaster were seen as 'extreme' with too great an emphasis on the gifts and manifestations of the Holy Spirit.

Tarrying meetings, where people prayed to be filled with the Holy Spirit, were held regularly on Saturday evenings. 'We had wonderful times there,' recalled one woman. 'People came from all over Melbourne.'[102] A single sheet ascribed to Coombe for conducting these 'Waiting Meetings' outlines guidelines for the evaluation and control of physical expressions of emotion and worship.[103]

The emphasis at Palmer Street was on witnessing and evangelism. Often, people were brought from the streets to the meetings. Sunday morning services were devoted to prayer, the sacrament of communion and testimonies. There was an afternoon Sunday School and in the evenings, the services were again given over to worship and prayer. There was 'a lovely spirit of love and unity.' Basically, Coombe was the teacher, Barclay the evangelist. During May, June and July, 1913, at the Esperanto Hall, Coombe preached a series of sermons on the Second Coming of Christ.[104] In one of these, commenting on international trends, the Welsh Revival and the Pentecostal effusion at Azusa Street, he makes an oblique, but pointed reference to his own experience of the Holy Spirit—

> The Holy Flame of Fire burned not only in the East— the Western Hemisphere is also lit up by its beacon light; Wales bursts into flame; but Wales alone could not contain it; soon it burns with intense heat in Los Angeles, and America is aglow, and, Bless God, the Fire has reached us here.[105]

Around this time, Coombe also visited the small group of Pentecostal people led by William Sloan at Freeburgh, near Bright, Victoria

From the beginning, the fresh outpouring of the Holy Spirit was seen as a commission to engage in world-wide evangelistic outreach.[106] Taking Acts 1:8 literally, they sought to go to the ends of the earth. So in 1910, as a result of these experiences, at a meeting in Coombe's home addressed by Miss J. C. Cole, the Nepalese Mission Band was formed. This was subsequently to become the Australian Nepalese Mission and ultimately to be merged with the Regions Beyond Missionary Union. William Jarvie, who was later to lead the Palmer Street Mission, became chairman of the Board and Coombe's brother Alfred was secretary.[107]

Overseas Influence

In spite of the significant number of overseas evangelists and missioners who visited Australia between 1890 and World War I, there is little evidence that Pentecostalism was imported. Like Evangelicalism, early Pentecostalism benefited from the cosmopolitan flavours being added to the local Christian fare, but the leadership and the major work was carried out by Australians.[108] Certainly, both news and ministry from other countries had an effect. The Pentecostal phenomena in Keswick circles were inspired both by visits of overseas speakers and news of overseas revivals. Yet it is equally clear that the first Pentecostal meetings were not started as planned outreaches from overseas organisations. They were basically indigenous movements. It is not known where Joseph Marshall first heard of glossolalia. If his detractors are to be believed, he discovered the idea for himself.[109] Sarah Jane Lancaster, for her part, resolutely denied any external influence on her thinking.[110] Other pioneer leaders such as Florrie Mortomore, Ellen Mather, C. L. Greenwood, Robert Horne, W. A. Buchanan, Philip Duncan, Maxwell Armstrong, Charles Enticknap were Australian-born.

Once the movement was under way, there were further visitors from America, India, England, South Africa, New Zealand and other lands. These helped to shape the movement, but not to make it. The first Pentecostal believers may have been influenced from overseas, but their experience was their own. They were very clear about it. No one formulated a three-stage initiation as Seymour had done. The approach was simple. Regeneration was for salvation; baptism in the Spirit was for service—and this was evidenced by speaking in tongues. That glossolalia was the initial sign of the coming of the Spirit was plainly expressed in the writings of early Pentecostal preachers.

'In all of these outpourings of the Spirit,' claims a Parramatta leaflet, 'the same evidence was manifested, the speaking in tongues. The Holy Ghost gave us the three incidents of companies receiving the Holy Ghost to establish the fact that the Spirit always speaks in tongues through a baptized believer.' The Statement of Faith for Good News Hall declared, 'We believe that a definite physical manifestation accompanies the reception of the Holy Spirit.' The Assemblies of God Statement of Faith was even more plain—

> (We believe) in the Baptism of the Holy Spirit for all believers with the initial evidence of speaking in other tongues as the Spirit gives utterance.

An examination of the available evidence shows that the Pentecostal movement in Australia did not begin in a vacuum. It was germinated in a bed of revivalism that drew its life both from Methodist perfectionism and Dowie's focus on divine healing and was cultivated in the wider evangelical garden of those who simply wanted 'more of God'. From the earliest-known meetings in the home of Joseph Marshall (1870) to the establishing of Good News Hall in 1908, all three played a significant part in its development. The forces that shaped the movement were rich and varied—both religiously and internationally.

Notes

1. W. W. Phillips, *'Defending a Christian Country': Churchmen and Society in New South Wales in the 1880's and After* (Brisbane: St Lucia, 1981), 114f
2. Brown, 1986, 229
3. George Bernard Shaw commented that in England there was such a reawakening of religion 'that not the Church of England itself could keep it out.' See G. B. Shaw, *Plays Pleasant and Unpleasant: Volume II, Pleasant Plays* (London: Constable: 1898, 1947), vi.
4. Jackson, 1987, 108ff, 114; Brown, 1986: 336, 361; M. Hogan, *The Sectarian Strand* Ringwood: Penguin, 1987, 134; Hunt, 1985, 170; F. B. Smith, 'Sunday Matters' in Gammage and Spearritt, eds, 1987, 391; O'Farrell, 1985, 282.
5. Jackson, 1987, 114.
6. Burgess et al, eds, 1988, 518; Jackson, 1987, 63; A. Deane, *The Contribution of the New Evangelical Movements of the Late Nineteenth Century to Evangelical Enterprise in Australia 1870–1920* (unpublished MA thesis, University of Sydney, 1983), 47.
7. J. C. Pollock, *The Keswick Story* (London: Hodder and Stoughton, 1964), 12.
8. Pollock, 1964, 74.
9. *Keswick Quarterly,* November, 1947.
10. Burgess et al, eds, 1988, 518.

11. J. S. Holden, ed, *The Keswick Convention 1929: Notes of the Addresses Revised by the Speakers* (London: Paternoster, 1929), 157.

12. Piggin, 1996, 72; Jackson 1987, 63ff.

13. Greenwood, 'Address given at Australian Pentecostal Fellowship Convention,' Beulah Heights, Victoria, 1964; D. Cragg in Douglas (ed), 1978, 685 ('Murray was the most influential leader of his own church in the nineteenth century, and an evangelical Christian of international stature'); Murray, 1961, 101–103.

14. Pollock, 1964, 90

15. Millard who accompanied Grubb, refers to Macartney and his wife as 'our kind of friends.' See E. C. Millard, *The Same Lord: An account of the Mission Tour of the Rev. George C. Grubb M.A. in Australia, Tasmania and New Zealand from April 3rd 1891, to July 7th 1892* (London: Marlborough, 1893), 39.

16. Millard, 1893, Frontispiece and 46.

17. Subjects were—The Cities of Refuge; God's Dealings in Distress; Learn of Jesus, Lean on Jesus, Live for Jesus; What the Daily Life of a Christian Ought To Be; Walking with God; Tests of Discipleship; Wash and be Clean; 'Nothing' (1 Tim 6:7); The Silence of Christ. See G. Grubb, *Notes of Sermons and Bible Readings* (Hobart: Mercury, 1893).

18. Pollock, 1964, 92.

19. S. Judd and K. Cable, *Sydney* Anglicans Sydney: Anglican Information Office, 1987, 150f.

20. 'Imparted righteousness' implied a sense of *feeling* forgiven and hence justified (i.e. made righteous); 'imputed righteousness' meant believing you were forgiven and justified whether you felt anything or not.

21. W. Lawton, *The Better Time To Be* (Kensington: NSW University Press, 1990), 94f, 99, 101; Judd and Cable, 1987, 152. Jones's position on sanctification was similar to that held by the 'finished work' believers who established the Assemblies of God in the United States.

22. Keswick Conventions as such are no longer held in Australia. In New South Wales, Evangelical conferences like the annual Katoomba Conventions now cater for Evangelical believers and are dominated by Sydney Anglicanism.

23. For example, 'At the invitation of the minister of the Baptist Chapel, about four miles away, we went to a prayer-meeting of all denominations—to ask the Lord for blessing on the mission—and after two hours' waiting upon God, we sought for a special baptism of the Spirit for our own souls, and followed the apostolic example of "laying on of hands" (Acts 8:18). It was a solemn scene, when clergy, ministers and laymen alike, took their turn in being thus prayed over.'— Millard, 1893, 61f.

24. Millard, 1893, 84n.

25. Millard, 1893, 108f.

26. Millard, 1893, 161.

27. When Mrs Millard talked with one clergyman, he showed particular grace by being 'willing to humble himself and be dealt with by a woman'— Millard, 1893, 140, 149.

28. See M. Prentice, 'John MacNeil,' in ADEB, 243f, for an outline of MacNeil's life.

29. John MacNeil in *Reports of Addresses at the Christian Convention September 15th, 16th, 17th, 1891* Ballarat: E. E. Campbell; Melbourne: Bible and Tract Depot; Melbourne: M. L. Hutchinson and Co.; Adelaide: Wesleyan Book Depot, 1891, 8.

30. 'The Rev John McNeil [sic], B.A., is continuing his evangelistic services in Warrnambool with a large amount of success... Large audiences are attracted, and it is believed that he is effecting a large amount of good' (*The Warrnambool Independent* Wed July 11 1883); 'The people of Portarlington have just been favoured with the valuable services of the Rev John MacNeil... At all these meetings, there were large congrega-

tions, in some cases many had to go away, or be content to stand outside... Many responded to his earnest pressing invitations to accept of a present salvation, while others have been much encouraged and strengthened in the faith' (SC II:25, 23 June, 1883, 7); 'Colac has just been favoured with a second visit from the Rev. John McNeil [sic] the well-known evangelist' (SC II:26, 30 June, 1883, 6). In 1896, MacNeil toured Queensland again. At the end of the tour he collapsed and died in a city shop. American missionary Minnie Abrams, with a touch of the dramatic, told a congregation in Chicago in 1909 how John MacNeil and Allen [sic] Webb had devoted themselves to prayer for revival and how the 'DeLong' Convention and the visits of Torrey and Alexander had grown out of this. She noted that MacNeil, she thought, had died in the pulpit 'the very night of the first meeting of that great revival' and that Webb 'so poured out his soul to God in prayer that he fell dead praying.' See *The Latter Rain Evangel* July, 1909, (Chicago: The Evangel Publishing House), 8.

31. Watsford, 1900, 272.

32. D. Paproth, 'Revivalism in Melbourne from Federation to World War I: the Torrey-Alexander-Chapman Campaigns,' in Hutchinson et al, eds, 1994, 147,165.

33. *Latter Rain Evangel* July, 1909, 8.

34. Watsford, 1900, 272–293. Following details are also from this source, unless otherwise stated.

35. George Grubb, 'Apostolic Christianity—Is it Ours?' in *Reports*, 1891.

36. Grubb, *Reports*, 1891, 17, 24.

37. MacNeil, *Reports* 1891, 28.

38. *The Torrey-Alexander Souvenir, Special Mission Number of the Southern Cross*, Melbourne, 10 September, 1902, 10.

39. Harris, *Reports*, 1891, 74.

40. Webb, *Reports*, 1891,.48.

41. From a letter to clergy and leading layman quoted by Millard, 1893, 167.

42. Millard, 1893, 215f.

43. Millard, 1893, 261f.

44. Millard, 1893, 269.

45. That is, that the wicked do not suffer eternally in hell but are annihilated. This was a view also held by Sarah Jane Lancaster.

46. In later years, Keswick Conventions were conducted at Belgrave Heights, whose auditorium seated nearly 2000 people.

47. Piggin, 1996, 59.

48. Torrey, *How to Receive,* 1904; *Baptism,* n. d.

49. Paproth, in Hutchinson et al, eds, 1994, 150.

50. W. Taylor in *Souvenir*, 1902, 84f.

51. *Age*, 19 April, 1902, 6; 22 April, 1902, 4; Torrey, *Baptism*, 3.

52. *Souvenir*, 1902, 26; *Age,* 14 May, 1902, 6; 27 May, 1902, 4.

53. *Age*, 19 May, 1902, 6; 26 April, 1902, 15.

54. *Souvenir,* 1902.

55. Paproth, in Hutchinson et al, eds, 1994, 151

56. *Souvenir*, 1902, 77.

57. *Souvenir*, 1902, 78ff.

58. Torrey, *Baptism*, n. d., 6.

59. Torrey, *Baptism*, 16, quoted in J. Wimber, *Power Evangelism* (London: Hodder and Stoughton, 1985), 137; *The City Was Moved: Special Daily Edition of the Australian Christian World,* 29 August,1902, 2ff.

60. Ewart, 1947, 7; L .Jones, letter to C .H. Nash, 20 May, 1925.

61. D. Beer, 'Keswick Book Shop: its beginnings and now.'

62. *Age*, 25 June 1902, 10.
63. A. Pocklington, personal interview, n. d.; *Rivers of His Grace* (Melbourne: Belgrave Heights Convention, 1959); J. Wright, 'Hervey Perceval Smith,' Sydney: Tabor College, unpublished essay, 1993. Further information about Smith is from these sources, unless otherwise stated.
64. Piggin, 1996, 99.
65. A licence was finally granted in 1924 and Smith resigned. See W. Renshaw, 'Hervey Perceval Smith' in ADEB, 1994, 344.
66. Renshaw, ADEB, 1994, 344.
67. KQ May 1929.
68. For brief biographical details see Douglas, ed, 1978, 823; Burgess et al, 1988, 755f.
69. Dyer, 1907, 41. Following details are from this source unless otherwise stated. See also H. Dyer, *Pandita Ramabai: The Story of her Life* (London: Marshall, Morgan and Scott, 1914), 101ff; Frodsham, 1946.
70. Minnie Abrams was an Episcopalian missionary to India from Minneapolis, Minnesota, who joined Pandita Ramabai in 1898. She was baptized in the Spirit and spoke in tongues in 1905 at Mukti. She later wrote a booklet entitled *The Baptism of the Holy Ghost and Fire* (Kedgaon: Mukti Mission Press, 1906), in which she described the revival there, some copies of which reached Australia. See Burgess et al, eds, 1988, p.7; Frodsham, 1946, 105ff.
71. For further detail on the Welsh Revival, see E. Evans, *The Welsh Revival of 1904* (Bryntirion, Wales: Evangelical Press of Wales), 1969; B. P. Jones, *An Instrument of Revival: The Complete Life of Evan Roberts 1878–1951 (*South Plainfield: Bridge, 1995); Frodsham, 1946, 101f; J.E. Orr, *The Light of the Nations* (London: Paternoster, 1965), 230–235.
72. M. Abrams, *The Baptism of the Holy Ghost and Fire* (Kedgaon: Mukti Press, 1906), 5ff.
73. Dyer, *Ramabai*, 1914, 101ff. Frodsham records incidents where one woman who knew no English prayed, 'O Lord, open the mouth; O Lord, open the heart; O Lord, open the eyes!' and another, equally ignorant of the language, said, 'Oh, the love of Jesus! Oh, my precious Lord! My precious Lord!' See Frodsham, 1946, 107ff.
74. Greenwood, Address, 1964; M. Hurst, personal interview, 14 August 1991. Joan McGregor, who was possibly a New Zealander, worked with the Pandita Ramabai Mukti Mission for over 30 years. Around 1906, she visited Australia and New Zealand seeking support for the work, and distributing 'mite boxes' for people to save their spare coins for the Mission. She spoke Marathi fluently and spent at least 30 years supervising the printing and publishing of Scripture booklets, farming, sewing and evangelism. Ultimately, she was to become one of the leaders of the Mission. One photo, taken in the 1930s shows her as an elderly lady. C. Hood, personal correspondence, 20 August 1996; E. R. Bruerton, correspondence to C. Hood, 13 December, 1995; H. Johnstone, correspondence to C. Hood, 22 January, 1996; *Prayer Bell* July–August, 1929, 11ff; September–October, 1932, 25ff; September–October, 1933, 4f; September–October, 1935, 26ff; September–October, 1936, 22ff; RE 3:2 July 1935, 25.
75. See Evans, 1987; Jones, 1995.
76. Piggin,1996, 60; Deane, 1983, 65; Paproth, 153ff. Following details are from these sources unless otherwise stated.
77. W. Chapman, *Power and Its Secret* (Melbourne: T. Shaw Fitchett, n. d.), 78. Although this book was published after Chapman's visit, it was a reprint of an earlier volume, *Received Ye the Holy Ghost*.

78. Helen Alexander, *Charles M. Alexander* London: n. d., 153, quoted in Deane, 1983, 65 and Piggin, 1996, 60.
79. *The Missionary Review of the World*, December, 1909, 882, quoted in Paproth, 155.
80. Ada Painter, her three sons Alan, Robert and Reginald Wilson and her daughter and their families all became lay leaders in Pentecostal churches. Her grandson Ron Wilson is an Assemblies of God pastor. Wilson family, personal interviews; Jessie Ferguson, personal interview.
81. Greenwood, Address, 1964. To this point, I have only been able to confirm the story of Ada Painter.
82. Broome, 1980, 65; see also Millard, 1893, 108f.
83. Greenwood, Address, 1964.
84. Holden, ed, 1929, p.43. One Keswick hymn said, 'I ask no dream, no prophet ecstasies; no sudden rending of the veil of clay; no angel visitant, no opening skies; but take the dimness of my soul away.' At the 1929 Keswick Convention in England, J. Russell Howden declared, 'You may not feel anything. Well, I hope you don't, and I hope you won't, because your filling, as your saving, does not in the least depend upon what you feel. It depends upon God's fact, not upon your faith. And when you dare, in the absence of all feeling and all emotion to believe what God says, He fulfils His word.' Holden, ed, 1929, 43, 157.
85. R. Wallis, 'The Fullness of the Spirit,' in W. H. Aldis, ed *The Keswick Convention 1938: Notes of the Addresses Revised by the Speakers* (London: Paternoster, 1938), 216f. Although this address was given in 1938, it is fair to assume it reflected a long-standing Keswick approach. Ian Randall points out that 'unlike Keswick, Pentecostal insisted that they taught a baptism which was not a "faith" baptism—believe you have received—but rather a "power" baptism.' See I. M. Randall, 'Old Time Power: Relationships between Pentecostalism and Evangelical Spirituality in England,' in *Pneuma*, 19:1, Spring, 1997, 62.
86. *New Life*, Vol.35, No.66, 21 September, 1972, 1; Renshaw, ADEB, 1994, 344.
87. Ferguson, interview.
88. J. H. Nickson, 'Pentecost in Melbourne, Australia,' in M. W. Moorhead, *A Cloud of Witnesses to Pentecost in India*, Pamphlet No. 4, (Bombay, 1908), 28.
89. S. Muirhead, 'John Barclay,' unpublished essay, (Tabor College, Adelaide, 1988), research notes.
90. B. Coombe, 'A Tribute to Dad,' handwritten note, n. d.
91. 'Our Pioneer Missionary: An appreciation of the late Rev J. H. Coombe by a Council Member,' R.M.B.U. News Bulletin cutting, n. d. but probably around 1957. A. Coombe, 'Notes on the Coombe Family,' 1 February, 1982; J. A. Coombe, 'Notes on the Coombe Family,' n. d.; Gwenda Cowell, personal interview, 22 March, 1997; Joyce Whitburn, personal interview, 22 March, 1997; S. Muirhead, essay, 1988; Beryl Coombe, 'Rev John Henry Coombe,' n. d.. Family details are generally from these sources unless otherwise stated. For a general summary of Coombe's family background see my unpublished paper, 'John Henry Coombe (1887–1957): a Dream Fulfilled.'
92. Muirhead, 1988, 2; J. H. Nickson, 'Pentecost in Melbourne, Australia' in Moorhead, ed, 1908, 28. More research is still to be done about Mrs Nickson as virtually nothing is currently known about her background. .
93. Nickson, in Moorhead, ed, 1908, 28; Ninety years later, Coombe's nephew could recall being aware that Coombe had received a 'rich experience' at this time—S. Coombe, personal interview, 21 March, 1997.
94. M. McDonald, 'Pentecost in Melbourne,' in Moorhead, ed, 1908, 30.

95. E. Barclay, personal interview, 30 December, 1987. Eighty years after the event, Elizabeth Barclay, John Barclay's widow, affirmed the camp was held at Ferntree Gully. There is no reason to doubt this. See also Muirhead, 1988, 2; 'A Policeman Receives Pentecost', *The Apostolic Faith,* Los Angeles, Vol. II, No. 12, May, 1908, 1. In his testimony here, Barclay refers to a camp 'about twenty-seven miles from Melbourne' (i.e. 48 kilometres). Ferntree Gully is 35 kilometres from Melbourne. It is possible the camp was in the Ferntree Gully district. It is unlikely to have been at Eltham, which was closer to the city.

96. John Barclay, `A Victorian Policeman's Witness' in Moorhead, ed, 1908, 31. Subsequent quotations are also from this source.

97. J. H. Nickson, 'Pentecost in Melbourne' in Moorhead, ed, 1908, 29.

98. Mrs Ridge, personal interview, n. d.

99. Muirhead, 1988, 3; Whitburn, personal interview, 22 March, 1997.

100. Ridge, personal interview.

101. Greenwood, *Life Story*, 1965, 48ff.

102. Ridge, personal interview.

103. J. Coombe (?), 'Waiting Meetings,' typed sheet, n. d. Original supplied by E. Barclay.

104. Muirhead, 1988, p.2; J. Coombe, 'The Second Coming of Our Lord,' typed transcripts of sermons in possession of Gwenda Cowell, Melbourne, Vic.

105. J. Coombe, 'The Vision of Nebuchadnezzar and its Interpretation,' sermon transcript, 19 June, 1913, in possession of Gwenda Cowell, Melbourne, Vic..

106. 'The Australian Nepalese Mission,' typed transcript, no author, n. d.

107. Coombe personally felt called by God to reach Nepal with the gospel. As Nepal was one of the few countries closed to missionaries at that time, this was an unlikely commission. The members of the new Mission prayed for several years for Nepal and finally, in March 1917, with their two children, Beryl, 6, and Keith, 3, the Coombes journeyed to India on the *Mongolia* and settled at Ghorasahan, a railway settlement near the border of Nepal. Before leaving Melbourne, Coombe organised some thirty monthly prayer meetings in several cities to undergird the work. Coombe lived in India, on the border of Nepal, for the next 25 years, engaged in a wide range of missionary activities. After his wife's death, he returned to Australia and spent the next three years recuperating in the home of his son Keith and daughter-in-law Grace. In 1947 he married Jean Clezy. The couple settled in Naracoorte, South Australia, where he continued to serve God and to encourage support for the Mission. Ten years later, in 1957, he died, but not before hearing that Nepal was at last open to Christian missions. Barclay took over leadership at Palmer Street and two years later resigned from the police force to give himself to the work full-time. He and Elizabeth never did go to China: he continued at the Fitzroy Mission until his death in 1946. Jarvie was 'not Pentecostal' and discouraged Pentecostal practices, See 'Australian Nepalese Mission'; Ridge, personal interview.

108. Paproth points out the local flavour of Evangelicalism in Melbourne during this period and suggests that Chapman, for example, may well have learned from the cooperative approach taken here as he seems to have duplicated the concept of a simultaneous mission elsewhere. See Hutchinson et al, 1994, 147ff.

109. *Christian Weekly and Methodist Journal*, 20 July, 1883.

110. S. J. Lancaster, 'From Our Letter Box', GN 19:11, Nov 1, 1928, 4f. It is interesting to compare the introduction of Mormonism which was substantially the work of foreign missionaries. See Newton, *Saints,* 1991. Compare also movements such as Theosophy, which seem to have owed considerably more to overseas input. See Roe, *Beyond Belief,* 1986.

CHAPTER FIVE

FOLLOWING THE SPIRIT

Sarah Jane Lancaster and the First Australian Pentecostal Assembly, 1908–1934[1]

Wherever we look in the first twenty years of Australian Pentecostal history, the imprint of Sarah Jane (Jeannie) Lancaster (1858–1934) can be found.[2] It is not, at first glance, obvious. Her ministry was humble and unobtrusive. No published photo of her appears in over 25 years of printing and distributing magazines, books and tracts. Articles written by her were rarely signed. Yet she did publish the photos of others and always gave credit to other writers when she published their works. She was not ambitious for position or human acclaim. Much of what she did was deliberately kept discreet. Yet her influence extended from east to west, from north to south. There are many members and pastors of Pentecostal churches today whose forebears were won by Jeannie Lancaster. From Perth in the deep south-west to Cairns in the far north 'Top End', she was involved in evangelism, church planting, preaching and prayer. She proclaimed the Word on street corners. She handed out tracts. She talked with strangers. She conducted meetings in halls and houses. She communicated with people of all ages. She edited a magazine. She published thousands of tracts. She engaged in welfare work with the poor. She prayed for the sick. She encouraged people to be filled with the Spirit. She eschewed the things of the world for the things of God. Perhaps most significant of all, she was a woman of integrity, prizing love, sacrifice, unity and honesty above all else.[3] Australian Pentecostalism is her enduring legacy.

(Front) Sarah Jane Lancaster (Bible in hand) with Mina Brawner (Rear) Ray Lancaster, Winnie Andrews.

In 1909, after decades of rivalry between Victoria and NSW, Canberra was finally chosen as the site for the nation's new capital city. That same year, the first 'picture palaces' were being built, introducing what was to become a favoured means of entertainment for millions of people. And it was in 1909 that a North Melbourne Temperance Hall was purchased by Jeannie Lancaster and some friends and renamed Good News Hall, the meeting place of the 'Pentecostal Mission.'[4]

Lancaster had been baptised in the Holy Spirit on 2 April 1908, having already come to a strong conviction that she was to practise divine healing. She now needed a meeting place for her new-discovered ministry. The Hall was opened on New Year's Eve, 1909, with an all-night prayer meeting. Then 'for six weeks such a glorious revival continued night and day,' wrote Lancaster, 'that we never entered our home again. Our furniture was sent for and willing hands soon adapted various rooms to living purposes.' There were extraordinary reports of healing and Lancaster claimed in later years that even the dead were raised to life again. Soon a fully operating assembly was established.[5]

Lancaster was not at first glance the sort of person to lead a congregation. Of medium height and buxom build, she normally wore a full-length dress and kept her hair tied in a bun. She was motherly in her appearance, so much so that, though like the other women at the Hall, she was often referred to as 'Sister,' many people referred to her as 'Mother' or 'Mummy' Lancaster.[6] Towards the end of her life, Baptist minister Gordon Bennett said—

> I have known our Sister, who is affectionately known to many as 'Mother,' for over twenty five years: during that time, she has been a gracious, loving and helpful 'Mother' to many of God's children and to many who did not know God.[7]

Ivor Warburton, one of her most devoted adherents, described her as looking like a washerwoman.[8] She clearly won people's hearts—

> She was a woman of God. She could only talk of the Spirit-filled life. She was a wonderful woman. I can hardly express it. I suppose she had faults, but we could never see them.
>
> She was a lovely old darling, a sweet old dear. She was shortish and plump, motherly and sweet. Everyone loved her.

Mummy Lancaster, as they used to call her, was... a woman of God. She was not a forceful preacher, but a good one. She knew the Word of God.

She preached the word in quiet style. She was gracious and compassionate. She did not make an issue of doctrines. Getting Christ into the hearts of people was what she was about.[9]

Lancaster was strong-minded and strong-willed. One man described her as a martinet.[10] But she had a deep and sincere affection for those who worked with her. Her habit of calling people 'dear ones' became universal in the work.[11] She was humble—she rarely reported on her own activities, preferring to speak of the works of others.

Good News Hall seated about 300 people, and was usually attended by about 100 on Sundays. Across the front of the building, above the platform, was boldly painted the text, 'The Lord God Omnipotent Reigneth.' During the week there was plenty of activity.[12] The Hall was always open for prayer and prayer meetings were held regularly. The building had a number of smaller rooms including a living apartment for the Lancasters. Consequently, people would often go there to stay for a few days or even a few weeks. During this time they prayed and studied the Bible, seeking deeper spiritual experience. There was a Bible, Book and Tract Room.

Good News

During 1910, Lancaster visited every State of Australia. Evangelists were sent out, many of them women.[13] That same year, she began to publish a free periodical called *Good News*.[14] For 25 years this magazine was circulated throughout Australia. Before long, a printing plant was set up and it was produced at the Hall. Although only six issues were published in the first three years, in 1923 it became a monthly publication, with a subscription price.[15]

There was a four-page loose supplement for young people. Few photographs appeared in its pages and few of the features were written by Lancaster or her assistants. In most cases, articles were reprinted from overseas Pentecostal magazines. The doctrines expressed were generally sound and, from a Pentecostal point of view, orthodox. Its circulation reached 3,000 copies per month—a high rate for a religious magazine of this kind.[16] James Self, who worked at the Hall as the printer of the magazine for many years, described it as containing 'the cream of other Pentecostal papers'.[17]

One pastor recalled—

I suppose there was never up to that time such a challenging evangelical organ edited and published in Australia. It was taken from all the leading Pentecostal papers of the day but it was new to Australia. It caught the imagination. The message proclaiming the full gospel was one that was so true, so Scriptural and backed by such zeal and energy and appeal that it was a voice crying in the Australian wilderness.[18]

Good News was sent interstate and even overseas. Its correspondence columns regularly included letters from every Australian State and occasionally from New Zealand, India, Africa, England and the United States.[19] Its influence was largely responsible for the early spreading of the Pentecostal message throughout Australia. Over and again, there were reports of people coming to Christ or being baptised in the Spirit through reading the magazine. Often people made special visits to the Hall to find out more—many times travelling from country areas.[20]

Apart from regular editorials, few of Lancaster's own articles appeared and when they did, they were often unsigned and hard to identify. In spite of a disclaimer that writers were 'allowed latitude to express their own thoughts,' the editor accepted responsibility for the overall content and general character of what was printed.[21] The magazine tended to cover topics such as the baptism in the Holy Spirit, divine healing, Christian living and—most commonly of all—the second coming.

Lancaster's editorials show evidence of wide reading and well-informed opinion. She kept close watch on events around her, both locally and internationally, and was not afraid to interpret them biblically. A fascinating piece published in March 1924, argued persuasively that a kind of madness had settled on the world. For a start, people were ignoring God, stubbornly refusing to recognise that 'storm, sword, drought, or pestilence (were) marks of His displeasure.' Then, Japan had to be seen as a serious threat to Australia, a sadly prophetic thought.

How is it that politicians everywhere—while ardently desiring peace—commit their countries to policies which must engender strife? There is only one answer: 'They are mad.'[22]

A doctor had recently diagnosed Russia's leaders as all being of unsound mind. And while Singapore was clearly a strategic Far East base for both America and England, the British Government had decided to abandon it. Was this common sense or madness? An American editor had pointed out that Italy's bombing of a Greek town was 'insane.' So, concluded Lancaster, 'we may expect to meet little but madness in the world from now on until our King comes.' As Jeremiah prophesied, the nations would drink the cup of God's fury and 'be mad' (Jeremiah 25:15f).

In October 1928, newspaper reports of a hurricane in Bavaria, a devastating flood in China, a collapsed dam in India and a terrifying storm in Haiti were all seen as warnings of God's judgement. Similarly, a burst dam in Los Angeles was a parable of the need to sound the warning of God's wrath. It was time to 'get on the solid foundation, Christ Jesus,' before it was too late.[23]

In March, 1929, she commented on a report from Germany that people there were going to be invited to renounce Christianity; on a visit by a 'modernist' Anglican to Melbourne, who denied many basic biblical teachings; on the creation of a sovereign papal state in Italy; on the suggestion that the locusts of Revelation chapter nine were a prophetic depiction of aeroplanes; and on the upsurge of lawlessness in American cities.[24]

There is no doubt that the theme of the Second Coming of Christ was dear to Lancaster's heart. In one of her few signed articles, entitled 'Behold He Cometh,' she describes a kind of dream in which she saw many signs around the world heralding Christ's return.[25] Another signed piece was entitled, 'Anti-

Christ: That Wicked One,' in which again world events were evaluated according to biblical prophecies and which concluded with the question, 'Will you be ready when the Bridegroom comes?'[26]

Baptism in the Holy Spirit

Lancaster's other great theme was the baptism in the Holy Spirit. She strongly believed in the need to be filled with the Holy Spirit with the sign of speaking in tongues. It was important to pray earnestly for this, and not to give up until the Spirit came. Picking up a number of reported comments from Melbourne pulpits on Pentecost Sunday 1930, characteristically, she took the positive aspects and used them as springboards to encourage people to believe God for an outpouring of the Holy Spirit—

> What if there came to a waiting, praying, united Church today another Pentecost! What changes would result! Fear and timidity would yield to confidence and holy boldness. The sense of weakness would be replaced by the consciousness of power. Outside the Church society would feel the impact of new spiritual forces, and no longer would the awakened Church be despised and ignored.[27]

While baptism in the Spirit was a gift, sincerity and obedience were still necessary in order to receive.[28]

It was a feature of Lancaster's style, that she often engaged the reader in dialogue. In an article on speaking in tongues, she proposes a hypothetical objection that it was sufficient to praise God in one's own language, and then responds, 'Sufficient for you perhaps, but not sufficient for God... You don't want tongues anyhow? Well, Paul the apostle did.' And then, 'Must it be written of you, dear friend,' she asks, 'that you cannot receive God's Spirit? Do you refuse to speak in Tongues [sic] as the Spirit gives utterance?'[29] In an article commenting on the views of a correspondent about eternal hellfire, she writes, 'Fair and softly, friend... Why do *you* suggest that God IS [sic] going to be eternally punishing? He does not hint at such a monstrous thing Himself.'[30]

Lancaster's influence was expansive. By 1925, there were congregations to be found in five Australian States in Adelaide, Ballarat, Brisbane, Cairns, Mackay, Melbourne, Nambour, Parkes, Perth, Rockdale and Rockhampton together with numerous home groups in places like Burnie, Freeburgh, Heidelberg, Lilydale, Springvale and Wonthaggi. She personally visited virtually all of these at some point, teaching, encouraging, praying and exhorting, as she did.

Divine Healing

From the beginning, there were numerous reports of healing, visions and supernatural experiences through Lancaster's ministry. Whatever interpretation is to be placed on these reports, there is no doubt that Lancaster herself believed them to be true, which lends favour to their credibility. Adherence to the truth was a quality of her life. She doggedly stood by her conscience and refused to be diverted from it: integrity was one of her characteristics.

When praying for the sick, she would usually practise laying on of hands or anointing with oil.[31] Her son-in-law, W. A. Buchanan told how his mother was healed of a long-standing and serious illness after visiting Good News Hall and being anointed with oil. He himself was delivered from a swelling in his throat. His sister Kate was healed of rheumatism and persistent headaches.[32]

An Oakleigh woman reported that her little son, who was born with deformed fingers, was now normal. Another told of release from a nervous disorder and another from kidney stones. A baby whose life was threatened was, four months after healing prayer, healthy and putting on weight. Ruby Lewis, a little girl with a nasal growth, was 'quite delivered'. Jessie Smart was so weak she could not get to the Hall on her own for anointing, but friends took her and after prayer the pain left her. A. Hultgren was at the point of death with pneumonia, but refused to take medication. After a visit from one of the women at Good News Hall, he showed dramatic improvement. A man who had been 'stone deaf' for 85 years, declared that he could now hear a clock ticking. Another suffered with severe heart trouble and could not climb two steps without pain, but after being anointed with oil, could 'run up and down two or three flights of stairs without noticing them.' A thirteen-year-old girl contracted appendicitis. After laying on of hands she felt relief. Five months later she was still free from pain. 'God sent dear Mother (Lancaster)' to a woman who had not been able to kneel in prayer for many years, and she was healed. Ruby Anstis had a badly broken arm which remained swollen and bent for months. After Lancaster prayed for her, the arm became normal.[33]

H. McLennan told how a specialist had advised that her little daughter needed ten weeks' complete rest. She took her to Good News Hall for anointing and prayer. Within a week she was back at school and 18 months later was brighter than ever. M. G. Parker reported that the Lord had given her surprising strength and energy when she was weak and down to 48 kilograms in weight. In 1929, Margaret Clapp testified to having been healed from cancer four years' previously in Ballarat, Victoria. George Christian thanked God for healing him from cancer ten years previously. A mother brought her six-year-old son who had been in an iron frame for twelve months. After anointing with oil and prayer in the name of Jesus, he began to walk and was soon running and jumping without support. As a result, his older brother and sister were baptised in water and his mother was baptised in the Spirit. Emily Huston, 62 years of age, reported how she had suffered from rheumatoid arthritis for five years, spending many weeks in hospital and being forced to use a wheelchair to get about. On 12 May 1930, she was brought by ambulance and wheeled into Good News Hall. That same night she walked out on her own. A mother related how her daughter's arm had been broken in two places but had healed perfectly. There was no shortening of the limb and there was now normal freedom of movement.[34]

The testimonies continued to pour in month after month—healing from ulcers, rheumatics, pneumonia, injury, bronchitis, abscesses, epilepsy, cancer, curvature of the spine, deafness, a perforated ear drum, leukemia, inflammation of the bladder, constipation, insomnia, asthma, failing eye sight, depression, a septic throat.[35]

Sometimes, healing occurred at a distance. Nellie Robson from Queensland suffered from dengue fever and neuralgia and became blind in one eye. Encouraged by correspondence from Good News Hall, she prayed for healing and her health was restored. A young man admitted to hospital with bronchial pneumonia recovered dramatically— 'At the time prayer was offered (at Good News Hall) he was made instantly whole.' May Wilson was suffering unusual pain in her third pregnancy. Although doctors had administered chloroform on the two previous occasions, this time, 'her little one was delivered painlessly.' M. Hart was crying with pain from an abscess on the tooth. She wrote a brief request for prayer and before she could send it, the pain diminished.[36]

Sometimes, this healing was the result of 'anointed handkerchiefs' being sent to the sufferer. Taking a cue from Paul's experience (Acts 19:11–12), people often asked for handkerchiefs to be anointed and prayed over to take to sick friends.[37] Even a copy of *Good News* magazine could be an instrument of healing. Before the magazines were posted out, hands were laid on them and prayer was made to God that when they touched the bodies of sick people, they would be made whole.[38] There were frequent testimonies to this effect. Lillian Jarrett told how after laying the magazine on her body there had been no recurrence of an illness she had endured for a year. A mother told how she laid the magazine on her daughter's throat while she slept and how next morning painful ulcers had gone. On another occasion she brought healing to her swollen knee by the same method. A woman who feared she had cancer laid the 'little paper' on the area of pain and suffered no more while another woman with a bad back found relief through sleeping on the magazine! A reader in Eagle Creek, Oregon, USA, wrote, 'I could tell you of many wonderful healings in our family through this precious paper,' and went on to report relief with various family members from colds, earache, toothache, headache, influenza and physical deformity.[39]

Year after year, the reports continued. One woman wrote—

> You will remember anointing for paralysis the young girl whose mother and father sought the Lord? This morning she prepared lunch for her mother and myself with her own hand and is now using her foot to work the sewing machine. Glory to Jesus.[40]

Another testified that a fibroid tumour of ten years' standing had gone instantly when she prayed. Her ticket of admission to hospital was no longer needed. Another told of a young man who had been in a plaster cast for five weeks in 1921 because of tuberculosis in the spine. In faith, he had removed the cast and for the previous three months had been picking and lumping potatoes. In 1924, Lancaster reported that the man was still 'well, strong, and happy, and seeking God's best'. Another man with heart trouble and catarrh who had been told he might drop dead at any time and rarely rose before 10.30 am was now, after anointing, rising at 6.30 am and coping with hard work.[41]

Any need was considered a fair subject for prayer and faith. 'Grandma' Abrahams knelt in a barren, stunted field and prayed for a crop to grow in the midst of a drought and saw an unprecedented harvest. A young man cutting thistles at Echuca and a farm hand in Rochester reported how God kept them from being attacked by a bull or troubled by snakes. Several people testified to being cured of smoking. A woman named Rosie told how, after 18 years of addiction to opium, she had not touched it for over a year. She had now been baptised and filled with the Spirit and was speaking regularly at open air meetings. Often, there were reports of financial needs being met. One man who wanted to travel around preaching the gospel prayed successfully for a horse.[42]

Sometimes, complaints were seen as demonic. For example—

> I would like to tell you what the dear Lord has done for me. I came to Good News Hall with bad nerves and I asked the Lord to heal me and He did! Glory to His name. I also had evil spirits in me and I asked God to cast them out in Jesu's name and He did...'[43]

A frail little two-year-old who weighed only ten kilograms and whose flesh was wasting away from marasmus began to improve steadily and within three weeks was running about and playing. The cure was the result of exorcism— 'We anointed him with oil in the Name of the Lord and he soon began to vomit. We realised the evil spirits were coming out... '[44]

After a particularly graphic letter from Charles Mortomore, in which he described seeing demon spirits like bluish, wriggling creatures, Jeannie Lancaster commented—

> This statement concerning evil spirits may seem strange to Western ears, but to the dwellers in the East is nothing new... The demi gods of Heathen mythology are not 'myths' but actual beings, half god—half man, the impious offspring of the sons of God (Gen 6: 4)... but through all the bitter conflict Jesus IS Conqueror... Jesus commanded the unclean spirits and they came out of the man... 'In my name they shall cast out demons.'[45]

Having been prayed for, people were often encouraged to demonstrate their faith by acting as if they were already healed. A woman with diabetes was told to thank God for her healing, to eat anything as though she was well and to leave the rest to God. Later she told excitedly how her diet was back to normal without ill effect.[46]

The Use of Medicine

Although she herself seems to have given little direct instruction in the matter, it was evidently Lancaster's belief that taking medicine was incompatible with faith in God. While not everyone agreed with this and many people did seek medical aid, others refused to do so.[47] Fred Lancaster, Jeannie Lancaster's grand-son, tells how he had a migraine attack once and a friend wanted to suggest he take an aspirin but was tentative about doing so—

> We never went to doctors until I cut myself and was bleeding. I suppose Mum prayed but she also got the doctor. They were strong on divine healing. It was almost a sin to go the doctor. But their attitude was that if you took a pill you had failed God. I respect that high profile my mother taught us as kids.[48]

This attitude to medicine comes out again and again in the testimonies of healing published in *Good News*. John Russell told how he had contracted rheumatic fever and pneumonia with pain 'like toothache' all over his body. After a week, his wife finally sent for a doctor who prescribed some medication. He refused to take it. After three days, the doctor gave up on him and told him that without treatment he would die. A few weeks later, Russell was preaching in an open air meeting when to his great delight the doctor drove past. 'He is the doctor who attended me and said I could not live without taking his medicines,' he told his hearers, 'yet here I am, perfectly healed by God.' Another man even threw out his 'cough lollies' and affirmed, 'I have not touched medicine of any description since.'[49]

Harry Hultgren was drifting in and out of consciousness with pneumonia. An elder prayed for him and he claimed to be healed but was still very weak. Furthermore, his family had been told that a spiritualist medium had predicted his death. They urged him to see a doctor. He yielded to their urgings and was examined both by a general practitioner and a specialist. Neither found evidence of any infection or illness. In 1920, he severely burned one hand at his place of work. Again, he refused medication, anointed his hand with oil and prayed for healing. The next day there was no trace of any injury. In 1922, he was suffering with tuberculosis but refused to take any medicine. Again, he submitted to family pressure and on 11 February, finished up in a hospital for incurable cases. Here, he had 'another great battle for refusing remedies,' but the first Sunday after Easter was discharged from hospital, evidently recovered. Four years later, there had been no recurrence. On another occasion, when he was 65 years old, he had two of his fingers crushed in a factory accident. He refused to allow his fingers to be washed in water with disinfectant in it. Within two weeks, he was back at work.[50]

Often, this attitude required enormous faith and determination. In April 1918, one woman accidentally chopped off the top of her thumb just beneath the nail. Six years later she told the astonishing story of how initially she had simply put it back on and bandaged it. After a few days, it turned completely black. Then part of the severed bone worked its way out through the skin, new flesh started to grow from the bottom part upwards, and 'in a short time, nothing could be (seen) of the accident.' Another man was dying with pneumonia. His family finally called a doctor who told him his lungs and heart were affected and he would never leave his bed alive. 'God had no... help when He created man,' came the reply, 'and He doesn't need... help to mend man.' Fourteen years later, he was still testifying to his medicine-free healing.[51]

At times, refusal to use medical help seemed foolhardy. On 5 January 1925, three-year-old Joshua Rowston of Orange, NSW, was bitten on the foot by a black snake. Both parents laid hands on him and 'commanded satan [sic] to leave in the name of Jesus.' The next day, Joshua's foot was swollen and very painful. That night, on the basis of Mark 16:18 they prayed again, he slept well and next morning the foot was almost normal. Three months later the whole family testified to his healing, pointing out that 'no doctor was called, neither was any ligature used.' May Mansell told how she had brought her little daughter home from hospital, with a leg infected by tuberculosis, removed the plaster cast and watched an abscess drain for twelve months with no medical application other than bathing. This was a severe test of her faith, but now two and a half years later, little Joan was fully recovered, except that her leg was bent. But Jesus would fix that, too. Nothing was too big or too small to bring to the Lord. When one woman had a broken needle impaled in her hand, her friend prayed and the needle came out.[52]

Even when healing did not seem to come, people refused to give in. One lass told how the Lord had healed her of a cough, the result of a nervous condition. The next Sunday at church she wanted to cough, but remembered she was healed and stuffed her handkerchief into her mouth to prevent it. It was 'only Satan' trying to make her cough, she said. The reason people were not healed, wrote Florence Holman, was that their faith wavered. Only firm faith would be effective. And healing did not always come as readily as it might. R. Close was travelling with his wife Emmy through outback New South Wales in missionary work among Aboriginal people when he became very ill with rheumatics. Although they prayed much, he suffered for days, while they remained trapped in the wagon by rain, living only on water and bread and butter until a kindly neighbour gave them some milk. Edwin Ridgway's daughter suffered polio as a child but was never given medical treatment. It was only when she became an adult that she underwent surgery. Tom Henderson was another who was not healed. After months of suffering from 'a grievous complaint' he 'fell asleep' as did 'Brother' Purvis, following 'a sharp battle with the enemy.' The well-loved 'Blind Dolly' did not receive her sight. Nor was Ada Boaler released from her wheelchair. Lancaster's nine-year-old grand daughter Esther May ('Blossom') died in April 1933 at the age of eleven after ten weeks of illness. And death was the only relief 'Sister' Adams, wife of Philip Adams, found after 'a protracted painful illness of several months.'[53]

Opponents were quick to pounce on these apparent failures as proof of the errors of Pentecostalism. Alan Price, a detractor of the Pentecostal work in Maryborough, Queensland, in 1927, claimed that wherever Pentecostalism was to be found, there would be 'quite a formidable list of premature and avoidable deaths.'[54] In a little booklet sold in Queensland in the 1920's, A. E. Bishop pointed out that many 'of the choicest of saints' had not been healed, because it was clearly not God's will that they should be.[55] Yet, while Lancaster freely acknowledged that some did not receive healing, there are no recorded significant cases of misadventure.

There were two fundamental reasons behind Lancaster's healing ministry. One was a conviction that divine healing was clearly taught in Scripture. *Good News* frequently carried teaching articles on the subject of divine healing. Lancaster clearly approved of the Anglican James Moore Hickson's healing missions and there are frequent references to him in the pages of *Good News*.[56] In an article published by Lancaster, Hickson simply pointed out that Jesus healed the sick when on earth, because God was in Him and with Him, and that the only hindrance to the 'outflow of Divine healing' was human unbelief. When Christ suffered for us, it was not only for our sins but also for our sicknesses—

> Christianity has accepted Jesus as the Saviour of the soul, and to a great extent forgotten Him as the Saviour of the body.

But 'is it nothing to you, all ye that pass by,' that Jesus Himself took our infirmities and bare our diseases? That He made atonement for us, and by the new covenant has made a way to 'the Lord that healeth thee'—even Himself?[57]

Lancaster could not have put it more simply. In the same issue, she also published a sermon which English evangelist Smith Wigglesworth (1859–1847) preached in Good News Hall in 1922 on the subject of faith. Taking the story of Abraham and Sarah, Wigglesworth argued that just as Abraham believed the word of God above all other evidences, so regardless of how we feel, we must believe.[58]

In a short piece evidently written by Lancaster, there are listed six practical aspects of receiving healing. These are—

1. Healing is a free gift from God (Matthew 8:9)
2. Healing is secured through Christ's atonement (Job 33:24; Isaiah 53:4; Matthew 8:17)
3. We need to obey the Scriptures and call for the elders (James 5:14). If a wrong attitude prevents us, we must deal with it as wrong attitudes can prevent healing (1 Cor 11:30–32)
4. Our faith must not be in people's prayers, but in the Lord Himself.
5. Our aim must be God's glory rather than our comfort (Philippians 2:13; Romans 14:8)
6. Rejoicing and praising the Lord precedes healing (Psalm 40:11).[59]

But it was not only a conviction of the truth of Scripture that motivated Lancaster. It was also a genuine concern for those in need. 'Our hearts have yearned with compassion,' she wrote, 'over the many who knew not that Jesus could heal them, and our prayers and tears have gone up to our Almighty Father that He would work His mighty works here as He has done in other lands.'[60]

Nevertheless, physical health was always secondary to spiritual health. Lancaster told a homely tale of a teenager who scoffed at the idea that God could heal his broken arm. But they prayed and God did heal it. As a result, the lad began to read his Bible. So Lancaster concluded, not with an exhortation to believe God for healing, but with a challenge to encourage others to start reading the Scriptures.[61]

In an anonymous article entitled, 'The Healing of Disease,' the writer argued that many people continued to be sick because they persisted in 'wrong methods of living.' To receive healing, it was important to discover, if possible, what caused the affliction in the first place. The original cause of all diseases was sin, so it was of primary importance, when seeking healing, to deal with this first.[62]

Doctrinal Issues

In spite of Lancaster's effectiveness as a pastor, there were still some who had grievances. In particular, there was criticism of her leadership, many feeling it was not work for a woman. Some attempt was made to overcome this in 1923 by the appointment of three elders—John Cavill, Charles Anstis and Philip Adams.

A nine-member Council was set up for the Good News Pentecostal Alliance of which John Cavill was president, Winnie Andrews secretary and Jeannie Lancaster treasurer. Lancaster accepted the new arrangements with equanimity and grace. As treasurer and editor of the magazine she was, in practice, the leader. Years later, she was still referred to as the pastor.[63] In 1926, under the influence of South Africans Isaac Hugo and F. B. Van Eyk[64], she could see the growing need for the various assemblies to develop closer relationships through a 'fellowship tie,' so she published profiles of each of the three elders. There was no division in their homes. They were all men of the Spirit. And although 'the winds of persecution' had blown from all sides, they simply 'blew them into one'. The greater the hatred and scorn flung at them, the more they stood together 'for God and His Son'.[65]

This latter comment was clearly a reference to another aspect of Lancaster's work which was to prove a stone of stumbling for the rest of her life. This was her doctrinal stance. Although later editions of *Good News* were Pentecostally orthodox, early editions were more controversial. In the formative years of Pentecostal development in the United States, two major schools of thought were represented, namely, the trinitarian and the unitarian (or, Oneness) which resulted in the movement being irreversibly divided within a decade of Azusa Street.[66] Lancaster presented yet another view. In simple terms, what she taught was that God the Father and the Holy Spirit were one, and that Jesus Christ was God's Son. In January 1913, an article by 'A.W.' made the issues plain—

> Here is the key to the mystery. God the Father and God the Holy Spirit are One and the Same Person...
>
> We acknowledge and worship One God, Jehovah, the Holy Spirit who spake by the prophets, the Father who dwelt in Jesus Christ and who is pouring out His Spirit today (His substance is spirit) 'upon all flesh'.
>
> We can say with the apostle Paul, 'To us there is but ONE GOD, the Father, and One Lord Jesus Christ' 1 Cor 8: 6.[67]

Other articles point out the same concept, and go to some length to discount trinitarian teaching. The obvious question that other Pentecostals—and other Christians generally—wanted to ask, of course, was, 'Who, then, is Jesus Christ? Is He also God? Or is He less than God?'

In an accompanying article by 'A. S.', *Good News* goes on—

> Many held various opinions about Christ, so He asked His disciples, 'But whom say ye that I am?' And Simon Peter answered and said, 'Thou are [sic] the Christ' (that is in Hebrew, the Messiah), 'The Son of the Living GOD.' Matt 16: 13–17.
>
> This is the only Apostles' Creed that Jesus ever commended. There is nothing in the Bible about an equal and co-eternal, 'God the Son'.
>
> The Son (is) inferior both in Dignity and in Time to the Father. Jesus said—'My Father is greater than I.' John 14: 28 . . . The term 'God' is applied to our Lord as Son of God in a lower degree, as it is also used of men. Ps 82:6...[68]

The article points out that Christ was pre-existent and that God 'used the instrumentality of His divine Son' in making the world. God put everything except

Himself under the authority of His Son and He must reign until even death is subject to Him. Then the Son Himself will submit to the Father 'that God may be all in all' (1 Cor 15: 24–28). Furthermore, in a realistic sense, Jesus did not become the Christ, that is, the anointed One, until the Spirit came upon Him at the time of His baptism. This in no way took away from His pre-existence. Just as He had always been the Saviour, but did not actually bear our sins until He died on the cross; so He had always been the anointed One, but was not actually anointed until the Jordan.[69] In evangelical eyes, all this amounted to a denial of the deity of Christ. It was not enough to call him the Son of God; He must clearly be called 'God the Son'.

In the next issue of *Good News*, the textual authority of the trinitarian statement in 1 John 5:7 was challenged and Pope Leo XIII blamed for endorsing it. An editorial comment, no doubt from Lancaster, noted that the previous issue had been sent out with the prayer that the Father would keep them true to Scripture and that the Spirit would 'move our pen' so that they would print nothing contrary to God's will. They had expected a 'gale of criticism from those trained in the traditions of men' in response to their statements about the godhead. But instead of a gale, only 'the gentlest breezes' were felt.[70] This judgement was, unfortunately, both premature and ill-formed. The gales might not yet have touched them, but they would certainly be stirred up. Although Lancaster did not seem to realise it, her isolation from the Pentecostal mainstream was thereafter ensured.

However, she and her fellow-believers were not of such mettle as to change for the sake of expediency. Ten years later, an article in the magazine pointed out—

> If we desire to be overcomers we must, according to 1 John 5: 5, believe that Jesus is the Son of God; and when church dignitaries make such confusing statements as, 'I believe that the little Babe of Bethlehem was God Himself, the infinite God Who took on human flesh…' etc., worshippers who desire to approach God become perplexed…
>
> Why are the people not told that there is one God, the Father, and one Lord, Jesus Christ?[71]

A statement of faith published in the same issue seems, however, to allow for variety of belief—

> Jesus Christ is the Son of God, Who was with Him and in Him before the world was; begotten by the Father—through the Holy Spirit—of the Virgin Mary. He became flesh and dwelt among us. Through Him, God has revealed himself to mankind—Luke 1: 35; Mark 14: 61–62; Rom 1: 3–4; Col 1: 15–16; Phil 2: 6; John 1: 1, 18 and 17: 5; Heb 1:10

The next clause speaks of the Holy Spirit as proceeding from the Father and the Son and says that he is 'of one substance, majesty and glory with the Father and the Son, eternal God.'[72] The coming of F. B. Van Eyk in 1926 and the decision to adopt the name Apostolic Faith Mission had no doubt required further conciliation. Van Eyk was evangelically orthodox and preached accordingly. To accommodate him, the Mission had to modify its earlier stand. There is no doubt that Lancaster maintained her own personal views, but they were no longer expressed publicly. By 1935, a year after Lancaster's death, the new editor, H. Martin, for many years an AFM pastor, could publish an article entitled, 'The Deity of Christ,' in which the writer clearly said, 'The Bible proves conclusively that Jesus is not only the Son of God but God the Son.'[73] Whatever convictions Lancaster may have had, the retreat to orthodoxy was by then complete.

Another teaching concerned the fate of the wicked after death. The traditional, evangelical view has been the eternal punishment and torment of the unrepentant wicked. Lancaster did not agree. She believed in eternal punishment and eternal destruction for sin, but she did not believe that God would be eternally judging. Rather, God's judgement would be eternal in its effects.[74] Any thought of the immortality of the soul or of eternal, ongoing torment was unacceptable. The wages of sin were simply death. Allied to this was the concept that believers sleep until the resurrection. In other words, the common idea that the soul goes immediately either to heaven or hell at death was rejected.[75]

It is interesting to note that Lancaster's view, commonly known as 'conditional immortality' or 'annihilation,' was held by Charles Parham, the initiator of Pentecostal teaching in the United States.[76] It was also the belief of the Irish evangelist George Grubb and of Harold Begbie, whose writings were popular with *Good News* readers.[77] T. J. Ames, whose small church in Adelaide was loosely affiliated with Good News Hall wrote a tract entitled *Concerning the Punishment of the Wicked* in which he argued that the Scriptures very clearly taught that the wicked would be punished with destruction at the return of Christ. How then could the Church teach that sinners go to hell as soon as they die and even worse, that they suffer eternally? To Ames, the idea of an eternity of suffering was 'monstrous' and he wondered that 'Pentecostal believers, with the love of the Spirit,' had not cultivated 'a better understanding of the Word'. As there was regular communication between Ames and Lancaster, there may well have been an exchange of ideas. In 1926, Lancaster spoke of his views with approval. It is also likely that Lancaster was influenced by Seventh Day Adventist teaching. They had befriended her in her initial search for help in the realm of healing and in later years she occasionally published material by Adventism's founder, Ellen White. Nevertheless, Lancaster strongly rejected any suggestion that she believed in 'annihilation,' although making little attempt to explain why.[78]

There was a third distinctive area of teaching which does not seem to have been greatly challenged. This was the view that only certain believers constituted the Body and Bride of Christ and hence would take part in the rapture of the saints prior to His return.[79] This was not a matter of salvation. The Christian Church embraced all who confessed their sins and were 'cleansed in the precious Blood of the Lamb of God.' And you could not be a true believer without 'a measure of the Spirit.'[80] But being in the *Body* of Christ was different. 'A place in the Body is not ours or mine to give,' wrote Lancaster in 1913. 'It is "reserved" (1 Pet.1:4) for those for whom it is prepared by our Father; those baptised in the Spirit of God.' She went on to argue that just as God took Eve from the living body of her spouse, so 'Immanuel's Bride' would be taken from the living members of Christ's Body—'The Bride! She has none within her ranks but members of the Body; those who have been baptised in that 'one spirit' [sic].'[81] Ten years later, she repeated the same viewpoint in clear and plain terms, but added, 'The manifestation of the Body and Bride, however, is as yet unfulfilled prophecy, about which we cannot afford to be dogmatic.' Nevertheless there were many who were consecrated and who wanted to be in the Bride, but they were partly overcome by the lures of the world, the lusts of the flesh or the enticements of the devil. 'If they are in this condition,' wrote Lancaster, 'when our Lord comes for His Bride, they will not be in the Bride, but will have to go through the tribulations, which are coming upon the world when the Bride is taken away.' If, however, during the tribulations they were to get right with God, they would still 'serve God in His temple.'[82]

A believer was justified by faith and trusting in Christ for salvation. But only those who were willing to present their bodies as living sacrifices, forgoing not only sin, but even good things which needed to be abandoned for the sake of the gospel (Romans 12:1–2) would form the Bride of Christ. Only those who suffered with Him would reign with Him (2 Timothy 2:12). Under the heading, 'The Bride of Christ,' an unsigned article in *Good News* used Wesleyan terminology when it said—

> It is impossible to get to the mark of the prize without the Holy Spirit which God will give to everyone who asks and obeys. Luke 11:13; Acts 5:32; and impossible, also, without much prayer. Having got to the mark—which is perfection in love—the command is to stand firm. As we yield to the Lord moment by moment, so the Holy Spirit will overcome us; and all our fleshly desires will disappear.[83]

Florrie Mortomore, whose evangelistic endeavours penetrated as far as North Queensland, taught a similar view. So, too, did John Coombe and F. B. Van Eyk.[84]

In one of a series of sermons preached in 1913 on the return of Christ, John Coombe argued very strongly for a pre-Tribulation Rapture only of those who were sincerely and wholeheartedly serving Christ. The 'faithful,' he argued, will be caught away to meet the Lord; the 'greater part' of the Church will be left behind to face a time of Tribulation. Would it be fair or reasonable that 'triflers' with the faith should share the glory of the Rapture with faithful believers?[85]

William Booth-Clibborn agreed. Just as the Pharisees, although Jews, rejected Christ's first coming, so those who hardened their hearts against the Pentecostal message would not be ready when Jesus came the second time. 'There is no other means provided,' he declared, 'whereby we may be prepared except by the fullness of the Holy Spirit.'[86]

Such beliefs were widespread in the USA in the formative days of the Pentecostal movement there. Indeed, according to Faupel, 'virtually all the early Pentecostal adherents' held this view.[87] To what extent these American believers influenced their counterparts in Australia is unclear.

It is evident that this was a significant development of the Wesleyan view of perfectionism. Now, through the coming of the Spirit, not only would believers be made more holy, but they would precede other believers to heaven at the end of the age.

Interestingly, this view was not accepted by Pentecostalism generally. As early as 1933, C. L. Greenwood, of the Pentecostal Church of Australia, vigorously refuted it.[88] Nor did John Adams refer to it in his careful study on the work of the Spirit. For him, to be filled with the Spirit was the norm for everyone.[89] Lancaster's view would be rejected today by all major Pentecostal denominations. Except for occasional expressions of a similar exclusivism by minority groups, contemporary Pentecostals universally see baptism in the Spirit as giving power for more effective Christian service, but not in any way forming a spiritual elite.[90]

A Spirit of Tolerance

Lancaster was not afraid to challenge the status quo—

> The North Melbourne Pentecostal Mission has never sailed under the flag of orthodoxy i.e. it does not accept the creeds... of any established denomination, but stands solely on the Word of God, requiring a 'Thus saith the Lord' for every article of belief.[91]

On the other hand, there was never any intention to be needlessly controversial or antagonistic—

> We have no quarrel with any of God's dear children who differ from us in doctrine, believing that the Father permits these differences that we may receive practice in that greatest thing of all, 'Love'. Therefore, praising Him that by His grace our love is greater than our knowledge, we gladly fellowship all who comply with the essentials of salvation as given in Rom.10:9, recognising that if the Body of Christ are ever to be of one mind (and they are), the unity can only be achieved by meeting together and enjoying liberty of the spirit (2 Cor 3: 17), and that means liberty for my brother as well as for me.[92]

The profundity and depth of this sentiment is outweighed only by its idealism. Nevertheless, recalled one of her associates, 'Mummy was always the same. She preferred freedom of fellowship.[93] She argued that people were free to believe just the Scriptures. Getting Christ into the hearts of people was what she was after, not doctrines.'[94] In the statement of faith which was frequently published over the years, there was a continued expression of this spirit of tolerance—

> PUNISHMENT OF THE WICKED. We believe in the punishment of the wicked, who wilfully reject and despise the Love of God... And whereas believers are not of the same mind as to what shall be the manner or form of punishment given to the wicked, it is considered advisable that scriptural language only shall be employed where this doctrine is concerned, all argument being thereby avoided— Matt. 25: 46; Matt. 13: 49–50; Luke 12: 47–48; Rom. 2: 6–9; 2 Thess. 2: 8–9; Rom. 6: 23; Rev. 20: 11–15.[95]

In 1927, Lancaster printed an article by F. B. Van Eyk in which he roundly asserted his belief in a literal hell and literal fire and expressed amazement at any alternative view.[96] Lancaster's open attitude should have allowed sufficient freedom of thought and the Scripture references given are a combination of those used for either point of view. For evangelicals and other Pentecostals, however, nothing less than an unswerving commitment to a belief in everlasting punishment for the wicked would do. Questions were raised continually. So Lancaster began to publish a series of Bible studies which were largely composed of quotations from Scripture, covering major aspects of doctrine. The first one was practical, concentrating on conversion, holy living and prayer. The next few covered topics such as baptism in water and in the Spirit, the Lord's Supper, divine healing and the second coming.[97] But after this, there were no more.

In early 1925, someone asked, 'Should Pentecostal people divide from one another because they do not agree on every point of doctrine?' Not unless people make it their business to make it so, was the reply. Well, was there any way in which doctrinal finality could be reached? Lancaster took up the suggestion of 'a Pentecostal leader' that the Apostles' Creed might be a useful basis. Later, she suggested the Athanasian Creed.[98] Nevertheless, we still only saw through a glass darkly (1 Cor 13:8), and it was more important to be built up than to be puffed up! It was astonishing that people who had 'the unction of the Holy Ghost' should allow 'musty, fusty interpretations' of Scripture to blind their eyes to what it really said.[99]

This was the dilemma of Pentecostalism. On the one hand, a dynamic experience of the Spirit spoke with a unique authority. On the other, the rule of Scripture was still paramount. How could the two be reconciled? Where did tolerance end and compromise begin? Was it possible for people equally endowed with the Spirit to remain in fellowship even though holding different views of biblical doctrine? To Lancaster, the answer was clearly 'yes.' To others, as she was to learn yet again to her own deep and lasting hurt, such a response was untenable. This dilemma was to emerge more than once over the next two decades. Divine unction could be liberating and unifying. But it could also endow one's position with a sense of unshakeable authority. The wind of the Spirit might surge like a wild Australian willy-willy through neighbouring properties, but at the end of the day, the fences would all still stand.

Notes

1. Note that the term 'assembly' was commonly used to describe a congregation or local church.

2. For details of Lancaster's early life see Appendix B. In my earlier volume, I refer to her as 'Janet' Lancaster. There now seems to be no evidence that she or others used this name. She regularly signed letters as 'Jeannie Lancaster'. See *Confidence* October 1908, 18; also personal correspondence to Leila Mullin, 2 March, 1931.

3. A small example of her integrity lies in the publishing of a letter in February 1928 pointing out that a healing testimony printed two months previously, although largely true, had been exaggerated. See GN, 19:2, February, 1928, 32.

4. GN, 17:0, September, 1926, 10; GN, 19:3, March, 1928, 9.

5. GN, 17:9, September, 1926, 10.

6. GN, 17:3, March, 1926, 12 ('the next day, mother came down...'); GN, 18:2, February, 1927, 11; GN, 18:8, August, 1927, 16f ('With love to Mummy ...'); GN, 19:3, March, 1928, 12 ('Mummie, dear...'); GN, 22:6, June 1931, 5; GN, 23:1, July, 1932, 11f; GN, 23:4, April, 1932, 11 ('Now, dear Mother, ...'); GN, 23:12, December, 1932, 5 ('Please remember me to dear Mother ...'); GN, 24:2, February, 1933, 9; GN, 24:3, March, 1933, 7 (Here she is referred to both as 'Mother' and 'Sister'). Other women at Good News Hall were consistently referred to as 'Sister.'

7. GN, 23:7, July, 1932, 18.

8. Ivor Warburton, personal interview..

9. Warburton, Mrs Henderson, Robert Davis and Jim Mullin, personal interviews.

10. P. Duncan, 'Lecture to Students at Crusade Bible College,' Fullarton, SA, 1965.

11. At the death of one of the faithful women in the church she wrote, 'A highway shall be there... and thou, dear heart, with joy shalt walk thereon ... Good night, dear heart, 'twill not be long.'—GN, 24:3, March, 1933, 16; see also GN, 17:3, March, 1926, 12; GN, 17:4, April, 1926, 9; GN, 19:5, May, 1928, 13; GN, 19:9, September, 1928, 11,13; GN, 21:10, October, 1920, 10; GN, 22:2, February, 1931, 13.

12. See GN, 18:9, September 1927, 10 for a summary of activities.

13. For the role of women such as Florrie Mortomore, Edie Anstis and Ruby Wiles and the establishing of additional assemblies see Chapter Eleven..

14. GN, 1:1, April, 1910.

15. Compare 1:1, April, 1910, with 1:6, October, 1913. See also 15:1, February 1923, 20; 18:1, January, 1927, 10. By 1923 the cover featured a converntional drawing of Christ with a halo and light emanating from him. The title of the magazine was embellished with subheadings such as, 'Behold I come quickly!' and, 'The fields are white unto harvest.' In later issues (1924 onwards) further decorative devices were added—a harvest field, bunches of grapes and various scroll effects surrounding a table of contents.

16. GN, 19:6, June, 1928, 12.

17. James Self, personal interview, n. d. recorded.

18. Duncan, 'Lecture,' 1965.

19. GN, 16:5, May 1925, 10; GN, 17:8, August 1926, 19; GN, 19:11, November 1928,.11;
GN, 25:12, December 1934, 19; GN, 22:3, March 1931, 13; GN, 24:1, January 1933, 7; GN, 24:6, June 1933, 9.

20. GN, 22:8, August, 1931, 11.

21. GN 19:8, August, 1928, 10.

22. 'Retribution,' GN, 15:3, March 1924, 3–4.

23. GN, 19:10, October, 1928, 11.

24. GN, 30:3, March, 1929, 6f.

25. GN, 30:1, January, 1929, 7f.

26. GN, 23:4, April, 1932, 12f.

27. 'With the Churches,' GN, 21:8, August 1930, 10ff.

28. 'The condition for receiving the Holy Spirit was to keep the commandments of Jesus,' E. Ridgway, *'Ask for the Old Paths;' or Back to the Bible Way* (Foster, Victoria: published by the author, n. d.), 20. See also pages 8ff. Ridgway places a greater stress on the need to keep God's commandments before receiving the Spirit than Lancaster was wont to do.

29. Lancaster, 'What's the Use of Tongues?' GN, 1:6, October, 1913, 8ff; GN, 24:7, July, 1933, 5.

30. GN, 1:6, October 1913, 16.

31. Usually ordinary olive oil was used. Those praying would apply it to the forehead of the sick and then pray for them. No healing power was attributed to the oil: it was viewed sacramentally as a symbol of the Holy Spirit.

32. GN, 1:5, January 1913, 19ff.

33. GN, 1:6, October 1913, 5ff; GN, 16:4, April, 1925, 20.

34. GN, 16:8, August, 1925, 12; GN, 17:1, January, 1926, 5f.; M. Clapp, 'Can My Heavenly Father Remove Cancer?' GN, 20:12, December 1929, 14; GN, 22:6, June 1931,.7; GN, 22:6, June, 1931,.7; GN, 21:6, June 1930, 10; 'A Miracle of Healing', GN, 21:7, July 1930, 4; GN, 21:10, October, 1930, 13.

35. GN, 16:9, September, 1925, 14; GN, 16:12, December, 1925, 4; GN, 17:2, February, 1926, 7,12; GN, 17:6, June, 1926, 7f; GN, 17:12, December, 1926, 15; GN, 18:1, January, 1927, 12; GN, 24:8, August, 1933, 8; GN, 24:9, September, 1933, 9; GN, 25:1, January 1934, 7.

36. N. Robson, 'Showing Mercy unto Thousands of Them that Love Me,' GN, 1:5, January, 1913, 23ff; GN, 1:6, October, 1913, 5ff.

37. GN, 19:6, June, 1928, 6; GN, 24:6, June, 1933, 2; GN, 24:8, August, 1933, 8. This practice was also adopted in Richmond Temple and Glad Tidings Tabernacle. See G. and I. George, personal interview, 12 June, 1990.

38. GN, 17:8, August 1926, 19; GN, 19:6, June, 1928,.6.

39. GN, 17:8, August, 1926, 19; GN, 18:10, October, 1927, 11; GN, 19:6, June, 1928, 6; GN, 19:12, December, 1928, 14; GN, 20:3, March, 1929, 15; GN, 22:2, February, 1931, 7; GN, 24:1, January, 1933, 7.

40. GN, 9:1, February, 1923, 15.

41. GN, 9:1, February, 1923, 6–7; GN, 15:6, June, 1924, 7; GN, 9:1, February, 1923, 8.

42. GN, 20:12, December, 1929, 14f; GN, 22:2, February, 1931, 13; GN, 22:6, June 1931, 15; GN, 22:9, September, 1931, 7; 'Rosie's testimony,' GN, 23:12, December, 1932, 5; GN, 24:2, February 1933, 10; GN, 24:6, June, 1933, 8.

43. GN, 1:6, October 1913, 5.

44. GN 1:6, October 1913, 5.

45. GN, 1:6 October, 1913, 10.

46. GN, 18:6 June, 1927, 17.

47. Charles Greenwood shared this view, although he dissented from Lancaster on several other issues. Greenwood, *Life Story,* 1965, 45

48. F. Lancaster, personal interview, 18 December, 1993.

49. GN, 15:5, May, 1924, 7f; GN, 18:7, July, 1927, 7.

50. H. Hultgren, 'Did the Medium Know,' GN, 17:5, May, 1926, 7; H. Hultgren, 'God Heals Burns,' GN, 17:7, July, 1926, 5f.; H. Hultgren, 'An Incurable Consumptive Healed,' GN, 17:9, September, 1926, 6; H. Hultgren, 'It Pays,' GN, 17:6, June 1926, 6. Members of the Hultgren family are still involved in Pentecostal work.

51. 'The Great Physician,' GN, 15:5, May 1924, 6f; 'A Derelict Rescued,' . Hultgren, 'God Heals Burns,' GN, 17:7, July, 1926, 5f.; H. Hultgren, 'An Incurable Consumptive Healed,' GN, 17:9, September, 1926, 6; H. Hultgren, 'It Pays,' GN, 17:6, June 1926, 6. Members of the Hultgren family are still involved in Pentecostal work.GN, 17:1, January, 1926, 6ff.

52. L. Rowston, A. T. Rowston and John Rowston, 'Taking up Serpents,' GN, 16:5, May, 1925, 9; GN, 23:9, September, 1932, 5; GN, 16:9, September, 1925, 14.

53. GN, 15:7, July 1924, 4; GN, 23:9, September, 1932, 6; GN, 16:7, July, 1925, 11; I. Ridgway, personal communication, 4 June, 1998; GN, 16:8, August, 1925, 13; GN, 17:6, June, 1926, 15; GN, 16:9, September, 1925, 17; GN, 21:10, October, 1930, 16; S. J.

Lancaster, 'Waiting for the Trumpet Sound,' GN, 24:4, 5 April–May, 1933, 16; GN, 24:3, March 1933, 16.

54. A. Price, 'Pentecostalism,' leaflet, (Melbourne: Austral Printing and Publishing Co, n. d.), 6.

55. A. E. Bishop, *Tongues, Signs and Visions, not God's Order for Today* (Chicago: The Bible Institute Colportage Association, 1920), 17.

56. GN, 12:8, September 1923, 8 quotes a report from the *Brisbane Courier* [sic] headed, 'Wonderful Cures' and reporting healing from a twisted leg, infantile paralysis, cataracts, partial blindness, rheumatism, deafness, eczema, cardiac problems, violent headaches, muteness and other complaints—GN, 16:11, November 1925, 15f. An English layman, Hickson visited Australia in 1923 and conducted healing missions all over the country. Thousands of people thronged cathedral altar rails seeking healing and many claims were published of positive results. The Australian bishops approved and in 1924 issued a pastoral letter endorsing both Hickson's ministry and divine healing. While some were sceptical of the healing claims, it was generally agreed that a great deal of good was done. Stephen Judd writes, 'Virtually every parish [in the Sydney diocese] received spiritual reinforcement and revitalisation by the mission. Even the most sceptical and nervous were challenged to deepen their understanding of the merciful and healing power of the Creator. Hickson, who earnestly believed in God's willingness to intervene for a faithful people, encouraged Anglicans to incorporate healing into their pastoral ministry... Hickson's mission did not immediately produce a large home-grown healing ministry. But it did undoubtedly result in a renewed spirit of sympathy and prayer for the sick and suffering... It also gave a new and bold confidence to those few clergymen in the diocese who saw the healing ministry as an integral pastoral function'—Judd and Cable, 1987, 199; Jackson, 1987, 60; Breward, 1993, 119.

57. J. M. Hickson, 'The Healing Saviour,' GN, 9:1, February 1923, 2ff.

58. S. Wigglesworth, 'Faith,' GN, 9:1, Februar,y 1923, 8ff. Wigglesworth was an itinerant English evangelist who twice visited Australia. See Chant, 1984, 66ff; S. Frodsham, *Smith Wigglesworth: Apostle of Faith* (Elim, 1949); A.Hibbert, *Smith Wigglesworth— the Secret of His Power* (Chichester: Sovereign World, 1982); J. Hywel-Davies, *Baptised by Fire—the Story of Smith Wigglesworth* (London: Hodder and Stoughton, 1987).

59. 'Why am I Not Healed?' GN, 22:4, April 1931, 7.

60. J. Lancaster, 'Open Letter,' GN, 9:1, February, 1923, 17.

61. GN, 18:12, December, 1927, Supplement, 4.

62. 'The Healing of Disease,' GN, 15:2, February 1924, 17.

63. GN, 9:1,February, 1923, 20; GN, 12:8, September, 1923, 21; GN, 17:10, October, 1926, 10–12; GN, 16:4, April, 1925, 19; GN, 23:2, February, 1932, 19..

64. See Chapter Seven for more on Van Eyk.

65. GN, 17:10, October 1926, 10ff.

66. It is interesting to note that Frank Ewart, an Australian Baptist pastor who had become a Pentecostal while ministering in Canada, was one of the strongest advocates of the Oneness teaching. See Ewart, 1947, 50ff; Burgess, et al, 1988, 644f. William Booth-Clibborn, William Booth's grandson, who was later to minister effectively in Australia, also held the Oneness position, although there is no evidence that he taught it there. See Faupel, 1996, 299.

67. GN, 1:5, January, 1913, 15.

68. GN, 1:5, January, 1913, 17. I have not been able to discover who A.W. and A.S. were. No one with those initials figures prominently in the work of Good News Hall. It is tempting to speculate that they were pen names used by Lancaster— that 'A.W.' could

simply mean 'A Woman' and 'A.S.' could be 'A Sister.' However, as there seems no evidence of the use of pen names in subsequent issues, this may be going too far.

69. W. Andrews, 'Mrs McPherson's "Open Letter" Answered,' 24 October, 1922, 3; GN, 15:12, December, 1924, 19.

70. GN, 1:6, October 1913, 15, 25ff.

71. Chant, 1984, 52f.

72. GN, 9:1, February, 1923, 22.

73. H. Proctor, 'The Deity of Christ,' GN, 26:6, June, 1935, 11.

74. GN, 1:5, January, 1913, 6.

75. In describing the passing of his wife, missionary H. N. Todd wrote, 'My dear one has fallen asleep until the resurrection morn. (Hail, blessed day!)'—GN, 1:5, January, 1913, 6. Also, an obituary for the widow of Philip Adams bids her, 'Sleep well, sleep well, until His Kingdom comes...'—GN, 24:3, March 1933, 16.

76. Anderson, 1979, 89; Cerillo, 1993, 82; Burgess et al, eds, 1988, 19; Faupel, 1996,165. Note that Lancaster denied any belief in 'annihilation' but only on the grounds that the word does not appear in Scripture. In reality she side-stepped the real issue by making it a matter of semantics—GN, 9:1, February, 1923, 23.

77. 'Religion and the Crisis,' GN, 1:6, October, 1913, 4,

78. T. J. Ames, *Concerning the Punishment of the Wicked* (Elim Pentecostal Assembly Tract, No.23, Adelaide: ABC Printing Works, n. d.), 4, 5, 11, 12; J. Lancaster, 'First Impressions,' GN, 17:5, May, 1926, 18; F. Lancaster, personal interview, 18 December, 1993; GN, 22:9, September, 1931, 12f; GN, 9:1, February, 1923, .23.

79. From the late nineteenth century, premillennialism was popular among Evangelicals and Pentecostals. Largely popularised through the teachings of the Brethren leader J. N. Darby and the *Scofield Reference Bible*, dispensational premillennialism taught that there would be a 'rapture of the saints' in which they would be taken up to heaven out of the Great Tribulation either three and a half years or seven years prior to the Second Coming of Christ, which would in turn be followed by a thousand year millennium. For an overview of various millennial views see my *The Return* Chichester: Sovereign World, 1991. For a thorough discussion of the premillennial view, see D. Pentecost, *Things to Come* (Grand Rapids: Zondervan, 1981); for a more popular, sensationalist view, see H. Lindsey, *The Late Great Planet Earth* (New York: Bantam, 1974).

80. GN, 16:5, May, 1925, 10; J. Lancaster, 'Diversities of Operations,' GN, 20:5, May, 1929, 17.

81. 'The Body of the Christ,' GN. 1:6. October. 1913, 12f. Note that although this article is unsigned, its language and style is that of Jeannie Lancaster.

82. GN, 15:5, May, 1924, 5; GN, 16:11, November, 1925, 20.

83. GN, 17:9, September, 1926, 14f.

84. GN, Nov, 1923, 3; GN, 17:12, December, 1926, 5f; J. Coombe, 'The Rapture of the Saints,' transcript of sermon, 31 July, 1913.

85. J. Coombe, 'The Rapture of the Saints,' sermon transcript, 31 July, 1913.

86. W. Booth-Clibborn, 'Who Will be Translated?' GN, 19:8, August, 1928, 13.

87. Faupel, 1996, 304.

88. C. L. Greenwood, 'The Ten Virgins,' AE, 6:11, April, 1933, 2ff.

89. J. A. D. Adams, *The Scriptural Statement concerning the baptism of (or with or in) the Holy Spirit,* North Melbourne: Victory Press, n. d.; the contents of this book appeared as a series in *Good News* from February to May, 1928.

90. In the 1960s there was some teaching that there was a distinction between these two and that 'ordinary' Christians were in the Body, while only a select group formed the Bride. Again, mainstream Pentecostalism rejected this concept. See Chant, 1984, 203.

91. GN, 1:5 January 1913, 6; Lancaster's independence of thought is indicated also by her conviction that Christ was crucified on a Wednesday, not a Friday. See GN, 19:4, April, 1928, 10f; GN, 25:3, March, 1934, 2.

92. GN, 1:5, January, 1913, 7. See also GN, 15:5, May 1924, 5: '...prophecy, about which we cannot afford to be dogmatic.'

93. This attitude was demonstrated in 1925, when she lamented the death of her 'beloved brother' 74-year-old G. H. Cargeeg, a Western Australian Baptist who had given himself unstintingly to ministry to the sick, but was not Pentecostal—GN, 16:5, May, 1925, 9, 16.

94. Self, interview, n. d.; Mullin, interview, n. d.

95. GN, 9:1, February, 1923, 23. According to a *Notebook* (now destroyed by fire) compiled by a Mrs Hughes there were '210 positive Scriptures that the wicked shall die, perish, be destroyed, not see life, be consumed root and branch, cease to be etc.'

96. F. B. Van Eyk, 'Second Coming of Jesus Christ to this Earth,' GN, 18:10, October, 1927, 3ff.

97. GN, 15:9, September, 1924, 11: 'So many friends are asking questions on doctrine...'; GN, 15:9, September 1924, 20 to 15: GN, 12 December, 1924, 23. The October issue is missing.

98. GN, 20:9, September, 1929, 10—'If believers must have a creed in addition to the Bible, why do they not adopt that of Athanasius? It should be ample ground of fellowship for all believers and, at the same time, give plenty of scope for individual research.'

99. GN, 16:4, April, 1925, 12.

CHAPTER SIX

THE SPIRIT OF LOVE

Responding to Criticism and the Needs of the Poor (1922–1934)

Lancaster steadfastly refused to admit that her alienation was caused by her distinctive beliefs. For her, the real reason for Good News Hall's isolation was the fact that they were Pentecostal. This is illustrated by the events surrounding the visit of the American Pentecostal evangelist Aimee Semple McPherson (1890–1944) to Australia in 1922.[1]

When she arrived, she claimed to be shocked at Lancaster's views and did everything possible to avoid being identified with them. Although Good News Hall people had invited her to come, paid her fares and underwritten the campaign, and although she did have some meetings with them, she had not been in Melbourne long before she issued a public statement dissociating herself from Lancaster and her associates. Secretary Winnie Andrews responded to this statement[2] and sent a copy of her comments to Stanley Frodsham (1882–1969) at the Assemblies of God headquarters in Springfield, Missouri, to clarify the position.[3]

McPherson claimed that there were 'grave doctrinal differences' between her and Good News Hall, that these differences had been pointed out repeatedly, but that 'all evidences and proofs were denied' and that Good News Hall had continued to claim they believed the same doctrines as McPherson. Andrews responded that both an Anglican and a Baptist minister had seen no serious problems with Lancaster's teaching. Furthermore, there had been no direct conferring with McPherson at all on the subject. And as for 'evidences and proofs,' what was the evangelist talking about? None had been given. Furthermore, what was the problem with being identified with Good News Hall?—

She ought to have been proud to have been associated with Good News Hall. She would never have been heard of (to any extent) in Australia if Good News Hall had not made her name known. No statement was ever made broadcast by any representative of G. N. H. that they believed doctrinally 'exactly' the same as the Evangelist. How could they? We do not suppose that any two ministers on Mrs McPherson's platform believed doctrinally 'exactly' the same as the Evangelist.[4]

McPherson also claimed that the degree of support for the campaign had been exaggerated and misrepresented. She had expected ministers of all denominations to be cooperating with her. Andrews pointed out that her invitation had only ever been from 'a united Pentecost' which, with the exception of a couple of small assemblies in Melbourne and suburbs, had all issued the invitation.[5] There were several other trivial points raised, including that of being faced with unexpected expenses—a particularly nasty charge since Good News Hall had underwritten the visit and was left in debt.

The major question raised by McPherson continued to be that of doctrine. She averred that Lancaster had represented herself to be of the same faith as the Evangelist, and had sent her statements of their beliefs, but that she now had 'positive proof, both verbal and documentary,' that these statements were misleading.

Andrews argued that the boot was on the other foot. It was the Evangelist who had shifted ground. When she had first arrived she had spoken of the 'beautiful spirit' at Good News Hall and had declared that the atmosphere was 'as clear as heaven.' What had gone wrong? McPherson argued that she believed that God was 'Triune in His Being' and that the Son was 'Co-existent with the Father from Eternity.'

'We believe and teach,' replied Andrews, 'that the Godhead [sic] is manifested by the Father, Son and Holy Spirit; that the Son was in the Father and of one substance with Him in the beginning.' But they could not endorse the practice of triune baptism or the use of the word 'Trinity,' preferring the biblical word 'Godhead.' In view of the fact that the Godhead was a mystery, they would not be controversial on the matter, but would simply use the language of Scripture. She wished the Evangelist would 'content herself by doing the same.'

McPherson affirmed that she believed in the Baptism of the Holy Spirit and that none of the gifts of the Spirit had been withdrawn from the Church. 'True,' said Winnie Andrews. 'But Sister McPherson believes more than this.' And this was, in her opinion, the real problem. Those who now supported her had done so on the condition that she goes quiet on speaking in tongues—which she had agreed to do.

Moreover, even though 'dying people' came thousands of miles, they were kept waiting for days, and then were left disappointed as McPherson failed to lay hands on them. So since Good News Hall still retained their Pentecostal stance, it was true that their doctrines were not the same as the Evangelist's— which was actually an occasion for rejoicing. Finally, Andrews added, 'at the very time the letter (by Mrs McPherson) was being written and even after it was distributed the Good News Hall Friends were labouring for her.'

Success

Meanwhile, McPherson campaigned with great success. Newspaper reporters were unusually complimentary—

> Tall and finely proportioned, with soft brown eyes that melt to a smile, flash in authority and fervour, or snap in a merry twinkle, Mrs. Semple McPherson possesses a magnificent platform appearance.
>
> Her clear fine complexion is warmed to a golden glow suggestive of open air living and radiant health. Her personality is magnetic, with a joyous vitality that is mental, as well as physical; and her smile is a wholesome, hearty beam that calls 'Cheerio' to the world in general.[6]

So enthused a reporter from the *Sun News-Pictorial*. Moreover, she quickly won over the ministers of Melbourne. They were dazzled and charmed by her. At the conclusion of her meetings, 22 of them, including the President of the Conference of the Churches of Christ in Victoria, who was also the secretary of the Council of Churches, issued a statement which said among other things —

> We, the undersigned Ministers of various denominations in Melbourne and suburbs, have great pleasure in testifying to the splendid work which has been done here by Mrs. Aimee Semple McPherson. Personally, we have received a great spiritual uplift and quickening. We have had the joy of seeing hundreds profess decisions for Christ, and it has been to our great satisfaction to find that Mrs. McPherson's preaching here has been strictly orthodox and that her methods were extremely wise and effective. She possesses great natural ability, but the outstanding feature is spiritual power and her intense love for souls.[7]

By the end of her visit, she was preaching to crowds of 4000 in Wirth's Olympia. Although she did not major on healing, there was some ministry to the sick after the main meetings with claims that ninety per cent of those prayed for were healed.[8]

Towards Lancaster, McPherson was intransigent. On her return to America, she wrote a damning indictment for her constituency of the Pentecostal matriarch and the folks at Good News Hall.[9] If the best evidence of the Spirit-filled life is a loving, Christ-like spirit, Lancaster's response indicated the genuineness of her experience. In an Open Letter of her own, she responded to McPherson's charges with charity and grace. Even though McPherson did not openly pray for the sick, she said, it was clear that God had sent her and she had given a Gospel message which was 'far fuller' than people would hear in many churches. It was disappointing that she had not honoured her commitment, but no doubt God was in it all—

> Here let us say that we are sorry Sister McPherson did not keep faith with the public of Australia by filling the appointments made by us at her request, and ratified by her in her own periodical. The disappointment was keen, for in various places choirs had been practising, and many came hundreds of miles only to find closed buildings. However, we must take it as one of the 'all things' that are working together for good to those who love God and are 'the called' according to His purpose.[10]

And then, prophetically, she added—

Mrs McPherson has returned to the USA to face the heavy trials which must be hers if she is to gain a place low down in the foot of the Christ Body, as her dream showed.

McPherson's subsequent history was to prove the truth of these words.[11]

This 'Open Letter' reveals a lot about Jeannie Lancaster's character. No matter how many slings and arrows assailed her, she always responded positively, with love and forgiveness. Even when hurt and pain was evident, she did not waver from her commitment to the integrity of the gospel. She ever spoke courteously of people and honoured any who were faithfully serving God. In this letter, for instance, she writes favourably of the ministry of Smith Wigglesworth, who had been at the Hall a few months previously. She also commends longtime associate, William Sloan, who was killed that year in an accident; Florrie Mortomore, who took on herself the task of standing in for Aimee McPherson in Brisbane, when the evangelist withdrew; Ernest Kramer, who undertook missionary work with the Aborigines; Nathan Todd, missionary to Japan; and Edie Anstis and Ruby Wiles, leaders of the church in Perth. All this was to be expected, of course, as these were associates of hers. But she also commends the Anglican James Moore Hickson for his preaching and practice of divine healing and Herbert Booth who 'with his large-hearted love, drew the people very near to the God whose highest name is "LOVE"'.[12] In the pages of *Good News* she regularly published extracts from evangelical journals or articles by evangelical writers such as F. B .Meyer, D. M. Panton, A. B. Simpson, J. N. Darby, Campbell Morgan, Wilbur Chapman and Charles Spurgeon, who would not all have agreed with her views on the gifts of the Spirit, but who were clearly one with her on the authority of Scripture and the centrality of Christ.[13] In December 1924, Lancaster printed a long testimony of a woman who was healed from a spinal deterioration in Aimee McPherson's meetings at the Olympia.[14]

Ernest Kramer
(Photo courtesy M.Kramer).

In 1931, Lancaster argued that there were good reasons why God allowed differences of understanding of His Word. These were to test our faith, our sincerity, our industry, our openness to all truth, our willingness to suffer for it and above all, our love.[15] Her love was tested more than once. In 1922, Robert Horne (d.1950), who pastored the Southern Evangelical Mission, Melbourne's second Pentecostal congregation (1912), found it necessary to advertise in the press his dissociation with her doctrines and practices.[16] Then, when the American evangelist A. C. Valdez (1896–1988) came to Melbourne, he quickly abandoned Good News Hall because of its doctrinal position and finished up working with Charles Greenwood (1891–1969) at the Sunshine Gospel Mission (est. 1916) and then establishing the Pentecostal Church of Australia.

It is not without significance that Lancaster's first 'Unity Conference' planned for April 1925 addressed itself to 'the business of considering how to form a common working basis with a view to mutual help and encouragement, and to prevent depredations of wolves amongst the Good Shepherd's flock'.[17] There was some suggestion that for the sake of harmony, 'truth should be compromised'. But it was finally agreed that as the Scriptures affirmed that the nature of godliness was a great mystery, to deny one another fellowship on the basis of our understanding of the godhead was 'obviously an attempt at priestcraft'. By refusing to work for unity, they would make the Heart of Jesus bleed. Unity was 'all a matter of humility and love'.[18]

Lancaster's grace was superb. In July 1925 she reported that in three months some 209 people had been baptized in the Spirit through Valdez's ministry and hoped that this would be 'the beginning of a mighty wave of Pentecostal blessing throughout Australia'.[19] And two years later again, she could report 'a delightful time of refreshing' through the visit of George Clarke, an elder of the Pentecostal Church of Australia who gave them 'soul-stirring addresses'.[20]

The Apostolic Faith Mission

In May 1926, South Africans Isaac Hugo and F. B. Van Eyk persuaded Lancaster that it would be advisable for Good News Hall and its fifteen or so associate churches across Australia to combine under the name 'Apostolic Faith Mission of Australasia' (AFM). As the Melbourne church was already officially called the Apostolic Mission, the change of name was not difficult. Surprisingly, Lancaster was reluctant. Her reason is interesting. Although, in 1910, she had been 'the first to carry the "Latter Rain" message to Adelaide,'[21] and had been 'in loving fellowship' with the leaders there ever since, to forge a recognised link with them would require solving 'some difficult problems' and to do this would mean neglecting her 'direct ministry'.[22] Clearly, for Lancaster, preaching, evangelising and caring for people took precedence over administration. Her focus was pastoral rather than managerial. Nevertheless, in this instance, the two South Africans were so persuasive, she ultimately agreed to the proposal. Van Eyk was invited to Good News Hall for a series of meetings and the AFM was formed. The word 'Australasia' was used because Lancaster's ministry was already touching the Pacific islands through printed materials.

It was not easy. In the veiled terms common to public statements, Lancaster wrote a record of anguish, near-despair, relinquishment and ultimate resolution—

At the very outset... the committee met with unparalleled difficulties. Never did the devil contend with such ferocity, collectively and individually, and by many subtle means he fought every unit of the committee and every helper, down to the apparently most insignificant... Many desperate battles were fought, and the only way of safety was found to be lying low in the dust at the Saviour's feet, resolutely stamping out the self life, and reckoning it dead, that He might be exalted who has said: 'I, if I be lifted up, will draw all men unto Me.' At all hazards, He must indeed be lifted up, and to that end bodies must be presented as living sacrifices. None but God Himself will ever know the struggle endured by those going deeper, deeper yet, into the crimson flood... ; but victory is of the Lord, and so the Gethsemane soul travailing, culminated in a glorious victory. Floods of spiritual blessing were outpoured until the workers present could not stand before the glory of the Lord, but fell prostrate at His feet.[23]

Just what lay behind all this will probably never be known. Clearly, there were very strong differences of opinion and equally clearly, there was some extremely painful giving of ground for the sake of unity, perhaps most of all by Lancaster herself. It seems, for example, that Hugo and Van Eyk were able to encourage the Good News Hall people to regularise their doctrinal stance, an achievement that must have cost Lancaster dearly.[24] A new Statement of Faith regarding the Godhead read simply—

The Godhead, consisting of the Father, Son, and Holy Spirit, and the Deity as manifested as Father, the Son, and the Holy Spirit is eternal and uncreated (Mal. 2:10; John 8:42; John 15:26.)

And regarding the fate of the wicked, they believed in 'salvation from sin and death through faith in the atonement made by the blood of Jesus Christ'. A final clause on the 'lake of fire' used only the words of Scripture.[25]

Nevertheless, the criticisms continued. In late 1926, Lancaster found it necessary to warn New Zealand readers of *Good News* that people were circulating false statements that the editors did not believe in the deity of Christ or the personality of the Holy Spirit.[26] In February 1927, she made reference to 'a revival of divisionary activity' by people who desired position and were lying about God's servants. She listed seven simple statements of doctrine to which she adhered—the almighty God, Jesus the pre-existent Son of God, the person of the Holy Spirit, the three Persons in the Godhead, the death and burial of Jesus, the resurrection of Jesus, the presence of Jesus among His people—and which she had believed, she said, from the days of her youth.[27]

On Monday 18 April, 1927, the annual conference passed a four-clause resolution under the heading, 'The Spirit of Conciliation' again affirming their 'entire lack of any ill-feeling' towards those who persisted in laying charges of wrong doctrine against them. It pointed out that they might have made mistakes in the past by using words which lent themselves to misunderstanding or misinterpretation but that 'whatsoever had been written, printed or spoken, that had not assisted the unity of our work for God' they desired 'forever to put aside'.[28]

Evidently, this resolution was publicised immediately but treated with scepticism and suspicion by others. Less than a week later, the Executive Council met again and issued another memorandum regretting that there was a 'disinclination to accept the (original) statement in the spirit in which it was passed' and noting that the Council endorsed it 'most emphatically' and called upon all who had previously disagreed with them to accept their regret for 'certain expressions' which had appeared in early issues of *Good News*. In future, the doctrinal statement would be 'rigidly adhered to'.[29] It is probably no coincidence that the next issue of *Good News* contained both an article and a poem under the heading, 'On Being Misunderstood'.[30]

Although 68 years old, Lancaster continued her strenuous ministry. She journeyed north to Brisbane, Goombungee, Meringandan and Toowoomba to visit the churches there, gladly suffering exposure to tropical rain in her joy at seeing the breaking of a drought, even for the sake of the cattle, for the story of the sparing of Nineveh showed plainly that God cared for them, too.

In spite of all, the work continued to grow. The First General Conference of the Apostolic Faith Mission of Australasia at Easter 1927 was promoted with excitement and confidence. There would be delegates from India and New Zealand as well as Australia. There would be a ten days' united campaign 'unique in the history of Pentecostal Australia'. Speakers would include Cyrus Fockler from Milwaukee, USA; F. B. Van Eyk from South Africa; Evangelist Clark from New Zealand; H. N. Todd, missionary from India; together with local speakers E. Jarvis from Perth, Harold Martin from Brisbane and John Adams from Melbourne. It was an enriching time. There were several family reconciliations, many were healed and over the next two months, three baptismal services were held.[31] At the conference, in a development from the 1923 resolution, John A. D. Adams was elected president of the Mission. Lancaster continued as editor of *Good News*, vice-president and treasurer.[32]

Later that year, Lancaster expressed some thoughts on the Body of Christ which are worth reproducing, as they convey the heart of the matter from her perspective—

> It is quite a common thing for members of a denomination to take offence over some doctrine or some trifling difference in administering an ordinance, and—leaving one denomination—join up with another...
>
> Many of those accustomed to such methods of procedure have now received the Baptism of the Holy Spirit, but they still think division is a matter of little moment, an easy way to escape from difficulty; not realising that, though receiving 'the anointing that abideth' (1 John 2:27), they have been constituted members of Christ's Body... from which not one member may separate himself without injury both to the Body and to himself...
>
> In the natural we do not cut off the feebler members of our bodies, but cherish them. If there be something in the Body (Eph. 1:22, 23) which does not please us, we must not follow the natural impulse to fly from trial, or we cannot knit into the Body; we should rather bring into operation the contents of God's medicine chest (the 13th chapter of 1 Corinthians) which provides the panacea for every ill...

She then goes on to quote from an open letter 'to division makers' which pointed out that disputes over finance or management could all be remedied by prayer and discussion. The fact of disagreeing with the way things were done was no reason to 'break God's Word' or break down what God had built up. It was better to face the sacred duty of staying, helping and praying. Division in fact did more harm to the work of God than any opposition by the world or by other churches.[33] In practical terms, it was more Christian and more spiritual to face the hard task of resolving issues than to take the easy way of separation.

In 1928, the Secretary's conference report noted that services were not as well attended as they would have liked, 'the reason being well-known to most'—probably a reference to continued and ongoing criticism of Lancaster's beliefs.[34] A sad notice appeared in *Good News* in June of that year—

> It is our reluctant duty of give a word of warning and exhortation to every Assembly... Both our Saviour and St Paul found it necessary to warn the sheep against wolves.
>
> We love every member of the Body of Christ, and it is hard even to suggest that any of them could answer the above description, but it is true that, as we have gone forth weeping, bearing precious seed, others have seized every opportunity to follow in our tracks, endeavouring to make void the prayer of our Saviour, 'Father, that they may be ONE... that the world may believe that Thou hast sent Me...'
>
> To cover their real reasons, which are 'Envy and jealousy,' doctrinal reasons are advanced and wicked lies are freely circulated. All we ask is that any dear ones who are perplexed by the enemy's falsehoods should keep by them a copy of our doctrinal basis... and, if puzzled, write to the General Secretary for information, which will gladly be supplied.[35]

A few years later, Mina Brawner, a medical doctor turned evangelist, was to advise people not to 'stoop to the position of a religious detective.' It was important to stand on the fundamentals, but not to attack those of different views. 'Give sin no quarter,' she said, 'but love the brethren.'[36]

Mina Brawner (centre).

Wider Activities

During 1927 and 1928, Lancaster continued her itinerant evangelistic ministry. She journeyed to Portland, Victoria, where, together with 'Sister' Rooke and 'Sister' Casey, she ministered for two weeks. Here, with characteristic creativity, they used all manner of publicity, including writing invitations in chalk on the pavements. Lancaster commented that she knew no one who spent more time on her knees than Casey, but she supposed that the latter never thought she would be doing it in public streets!³⁷ Four people were baptized in water as a result. She also visited her old home town of Ballarat, as well as Geelong and Kilkunda. But the years of ministry and the ongoing criticism were beginning to take their toll. Now sixty nine years of age, she suffered nearly three months of severe illness during the year.

Nevertheless, over all, there was still an enormous output from Good News Hall. Seven services were conducted there weekly plus three open air meetings. There were two evangelistic campaigns and a Christmas Convention. Sunday school teachers were supplied to the City Mission and in January 1928 a Sunday School was commenced at the Hall. Six Bible instruction classes were given weekly at State schools. Twice weekly, workers distributed tracts and copies of *Good News* door to door. Welfare work was commenced among the unemployed. A stall was set up at the Agricultural Show in Melbourne, with between two and four workers daily. All told some 80,000 tracts and 900 copies of *Good News* were distributed. Tent missions were begun at Werribee, Victoria, under the supervision of former policeman Harold Sharman, his wife, H. Weimer, 'Sister' Casey and 'Sister' M. Parker. As a result a church was established at Werribee and the tent moved on to Portland. During that year, some 150,000 tracts were printed at the Hall, together with 36,000 copies of *Good News*. In addition to this was the ongoing evangelism of Van Eyk in Queensland and there were now congregations and home groups in at least 25 other places throughout Australia.³⁸

There were to be ongoing disappointments. In late 1928, Van Eyk was adjudged guilty of indiscretion and asked to return to South Africa. This must have been a shattering blow to Lancaster who had been so delighted with his ministry. After disappointments from Aimee McPherson and A. C. Valdez, she had finally found in Van Eyk someone who was prepared to work with her. Now he, too, had let her down. To rub salt into the wound, at Easter 1929, he spoke at Richmond Temple, the headquarters of the newly-formed Pentecostal Church of Australia in Melbourne (1925), when he would normally have been present at the AFM conference. With exceptional but characteristic grace, the AFM conference unanimously approved a motion by John Cavill that they send a fraternal greeting to Richmond Temple for their Easter gatherings.³⁹

This had further repercussions. The churches in Queensland dropped the name Apostolic Faith Mission and united under the new name of Assemblies of God with a new doctrinal statement and a new constitution.⁴⁰ Initially, they retained their fellowship with Good News Hall but it was a delicate arrangement. The Queensland Council brought some proposals to the 1929 conference for modifications to the national constitution, which were 'freely and lovingly discussed'. George Burns, however, sensing that the proposals would foster further disunity, withdrew them, with the agreement of the other Queensland delegates.⁴¹ It was a sign of imminent attrition. Subsequent history was to show that one by one many of them would dissociate themselves from the AFM.

George Joseph Clarke, who had been supported financially by the assembly at Ballarat for twelve months, resigned and joined the Pentecostal Church of Australia, taking half the AFM people with him. Charlie Anstis could still report blessing with thirteen people being empowered by the Spirit in two months. There was an average of 50 people attending on Sunday nights, with 25 to 30 participating in open air services and in Sunday morning gatherings. Nevertheless, he noted how they were praying that God would 'smash down such a devilish thing as division, so that this glorious work may go right ahead throughout the whole of Australia and the world.'[42] In Geelong, also, there was a split in the ranks. By the middle of 1929, they had fully recovered and were doing better than ever, with some 50 people attending regularly. But it was a traumatic time.[43] Dr Mina Brawner, on the other hand, wrote—

> For myself, I wish to say that I have thoroughly enjoyed my three months' labors [sic] under the Apostolic Faith Mission of Australasia. I have found it a sane, safe, and spiritual organisation, soundly orthodox from the Pentecostal viewpoint, with the same doctrinal basis as the best established Full Gospel organisations in America. It is with thrilling enthusiasm and buoyant expectancy that I return to my labors in this sunny south land, realising—yea, hoping—that my Lord will not long delay His coming.[44]

This statement, and the earlier affirmation by Van Eyk, would suggest that the AFM had now clearly placed itself in the evangelical mainstream in its non-Pentecostal doctrines and that the charges being laid were indeed ill-founded. However, dark suspicions are hard to kill, and they continued to skulk in the shadows. At the 1929 conference, reference was made to the defamatory statements still being circulated, and a suggestion put that all AFM credential holders—and in particular the vice-president—should sign a statement re-affirming their stance on certain doctrines. A committee appointed to review this idea concluded that the existing doctrinal statement, to which all credential holders were required to subscribe, was adequate. There was no doubt, however, that there were still questions in people's minds about Lancaster's personal views, and it was her own position which was the real issue.[45]

In spite of the efforts to institute male leadership in 1923, Lancaster was again elected president of the AFM in 1930 after John Adams and his wife transferred to Perth. 'The love between us was so deeply rooted,' wrote Lancaster, 'that parting was a wrench.'[46] In a sense, it simply regularised what really had not changed. The leadership had always been hers. And so was the burden. During that same year, Lancaster, now 72 years old, again suffered a time of ill health. She was so downcast that, like Elijah, she prayed that God would take her life. 'I was here and saw it,' said Council member Edwin Ridgway, 'and she looked like dying.' But in answer to prayer, she was raised up again.[47] By the time of the 1931 conference, she could say that the Lord was 'working gloriously' and that the Good News Hall congregation had greatly increased. However, there were still potential tensions. In her secretarial report, Winnie Andrews, noted—

> We are sorry to say that some who have been officers of the Mission have been working in a way detrimental to the work of the Mission; and the Pledge of Loyalty passed at last Easter Conference has proved of inestimable value in showing who are loyal and who are not.[48]

The Pledge was simple enough. It included the new, simplified statement of faith, and required delegates to 'solemnly promise by God's grace'—

* to accept the Doctrinal Basis of the AFM
* to be loyal to the AFM
* to work for the upbuilding of the AFM
* to make the AFM their place of worship
* to refuse to listen or take part in attacks on the work
* to voluntarily withdraw if they ever ceased to be 'in harmony or sympathy with the AFM'[49]

New applicants for ordination also agreed to submit to a six months' probationary period.[50] All the delegates at the 1931 conference willingly subscribed to the Pledge. In the reports from various assemblies, several talked of 'dry times' when few new people were added to their numbers. Philip Adams commented that God allowed them to wander in the dry places so he could teach them and that often the greatest victories came out of times in the desert.[51]

Davey Jack, a Scotsman who was baptized in the Spirit at Good News Hall in 1924, and was now leading a group at Korumburra, affirmed his loyalty to the AFM, but still reserved the right to ask questions and to disagree with decisions made by the Executive Council. He was freely offered access to all information and given 'perfect freedom in criticising everybody and everything he desired,' but the President and the Council were finally answerable to God and God alone. Jack was invited to close the conference in prayer and was later elected Chairman of the Advisory Council. But three years after this, he joined the newly-founded Apostolic Church and was sent to Flowerdale, Tasmania, and thence to Hobart, where he ministered faithfully for the new denomination.[52]

On 22 August 1930, Alfred Lancaster passed away. As far as is known, the first mention of him in the pages of *Good News* was an expression of thanks from 'Mrs Alfred Lancaster' and family for the condolences of their friends. The note also goes to some pains to affirm that Alfred Lancaster was indeed a Christian. It seems plain that over the years he had shared little in his wife's manifold activities. According to his grandson, he was 'a quiet, dear old gentleman' who used to enjoy playing bowls and, towards the end of his life, did the stapling for the magazine.[53] He attended the meetings at the Hall. Lancaster's note of grief at her loss was real enough—

> We sometimes drive him (death) away for a time with the prayer of faith, but back he comes and renews his attack until finally he carries his victim off in triumph.
>
> His, however, is but a brief victory, and those kind friends, whose loving words have so helped us... will be glad to know our loved one's end was peace...
>
> A few hours before he closed his eyes to earth, in answer to his daughter's remark, 'Safe in the arms of Jesus, Daddy,' he answered, 'Yes, and no one can take me out.'[54]

The end of 1930 marked the 21st anniversary for Good News Hall. Lancaster was in a celebratory mood. She felt something like 'the exultation which rises in the breast of a maiden who has been arbitrarily repressed and wronged during her minority.' The previous 21 years had seen much hardship and opposition. But they had come through successfully—

> Truly the Spirit of Glory and of God rests upon us today after twenty one long years of being reproached for the Name of Christ our Beloved Redeemer—the Son who shared the glory of the Father before ever the world was; and Who—because He loved Righteousness and hated iniquity—has received an everlasting throne and a sceptre of righteousness. We bow the knee before Him and cry with Thomas, 'My Lord and my God...'
>
> Whilst the enemy is still pulling down and destroying with cruel falsehoods the Work of the Lord... we are still praising God and praying that He will enlighten the eyes of those who are being overthrown in the race for the Prize of the High Calling.[55]

There is a mixture of gain and pain here. On the one hand, the blessing of God was continuing upon them; on the other, the work of the enemy was relentless. The statement also reflects Lancaster's ongoing, but evidently ineffective, battle to prove herself orthodox and her unwavering and unflinching commitment both to her Saviour and to the Scriptures.

Welfare Work

One of the outstanding features of Lancaster's work was her care and concern for the poor and needy. From the beginning, there was always an open door at Good News Hall for those in distress. On Christmas Day 1924, over one hundred men partook of a free Christmas dinner at the Hall, and 'in no millionaire's home,' reported the *Sun News-Pictorial*, 'was a Christmas dinner enjoyed more.'[56] Such work was never allowed to supplant the primary task of evangelism. After the meal, there was a concert and then Thomas Lennon, Florrie Mortomore and John Cavill all gave 'breezy addresses' which were well received. That night, there was an evening meal and another address by Lennon, as a result of which seven men professed conversion. It was not all celebration. Some of the men were so dirty that afterwards the Sisters had to scrub the Hall in preparation for ensuing services.[57]

The real social work began at the beginning of the next decade with the onset of the Great Depression. Unemployment rose to 19 per cent in 1930 and by 1932 had scaled to well over 30 per cent. As husbands and fathers were commonly the only wage-earners, the loss of work savagely affected family well-being. Dole queues lined the city streets; beggars drifted along the footpaths. People hawked home-made products from door to door. Others tried to earn a few pence by chopping wood or gardening. Sometimes women or children could get work as salary rates were considerably lower for them. Some older children's education was curtailed as a result. Thousands of unemployed dwelt in jerry-built encampments. Thousands of others wrapped a few essentials in a swag and, in a desperate search for jobs, took to the roads—where stock often wandered as well, set loose by farmers who could not afford to tend them. Politicians, both federal and State, seemed helpless. Hopelessness gripped many people. And those who were employed were often apprehensive about the threat of losing their jobs. In other cases, their working hours were reduced through labour rationing schemes. There were some food distribution programs, but they were inadequate for families. And they did not provide clothing or blankets and nor did they pay mortgage or servicing costs. Later money was offered but it was only a few shillings a week and too little for survival.[58] Avoiding landlords and bailiffs became a terrible game of hide and seek for many people. To lose could mean forfeiting house and home. On the other hand, some landlords were themselves in need. Unable to collect rent or evict tenants, they, too, slid into debt. Owning property did not necessarily mean prosperity. Some marriages and child-births were postponed. Many people relied on charitable organisations for their survival.

'Few can realise the mental strain to which these men are subjected,' wrote Lancaster. For some, suicide was their only resort. Others became so desperate they deliberately broke the law in order to get a bed in gaol. Others turned to Communism. Some became mentally unbalanced.[59]

From 1931 to 1933, Good News Hall undertook a regular and ongoing program of providing food, clothing and basic needs for the poor. People from as far away as New Zealand sent clothing and goods. Members walked through the city parks and streets offering to help the unemployed. Mothers brought their children to Queensberry Street and there found clothing and compassion. Vegetables and food were also made available. In 1931, between 140 and 180 unemployed men were coming daily to the Hall where they received 'both material and spiritual food'. An average of 700 free lunches were given weekly, and clothing was made available where possible. At times, men were given overnight accommodation, one young man being so urgently in need he was given the best of the staff bedrooms.[60]

Several of the women managed to provide meals from vegetable scraps scrounged from the market and from donated bread and other food. They even made a palatable coffee from boiled wheat. They always prayed before each meal. They spent long hours repairing damaged and worn clothing or making new singlets, shirts and socks. At times, women's clothing was restyled for men. On more than one occasion, members of the congregation gave their own clothes away. One man was left only with the trousers he stood up in. Sister' Alice MacCleary and 'Sister' Celia Casey were the mainstays of this work, but 'Sister' McLennan, 'Sister' Mary Self, 'Sister' Jones, 'Sister' Le Suers, 'Sister' Moysey and others were also involved. After a few months, 'Brother' Cornell supervised activities. To lonely and needy men, it was a comfort to have someone they could call 'Sister' and another who was a Mother to them all.[61]

Often, there was no money to pay for food or clothing. One of the workers sold some books so she could buy flannel to make singlets. On other occasions, somehow or other, God provided. 'The secret will be found,' said Lancaster, 'in the household's prayers.' Often, workers slipped away to some quiet place to cry out to God for some urgent need. On one occasion, Casey had no money to buy food at the market. They prayed and that night a man felt impressed to pay a printing debt and so the food was obtained.[62] By April 1931, Lancaster could report that their deficit was 'less than when we started to feed the men' and that the congregation had grown significantly. By mid 1931, however, the Father had 'seen fit' that they should be over 100 pounds in debt. Nevertheless, they still offered to guarantee 25 pounds bail for a young family man, trusting God to meet the need if it arose. On Christmas Day, they could not do much because of escalating printing and other bills. But they did make a huge Christmas pudding and each man was given a handkerchief and a Christmas card inviting them to receive Christ as Saviour. New Year's Eve was, as usual, marked by a short celebration followed by an open air rally and an all night prayer meeting. Enough cake was left over to give 200 men a piece each on New Year's Day.[63]

Heart rending tales appeared regularly in *Good News*. Early in 1931, a young mother whose baby had died, came once to the Hall. She was dying of starvation, but her young husband was too proud to beg for help. Finally, when her need was discovered and food was taken to her, it was too late.[64] Footwear was in particular demand. There were stories of men in desperate need who could not be adequately fitted—

> One man came in for a pair of shoes and said, 'My size ought to be easy to fix up, I only take fives.' But there is no need to search; we know there are no fives or sixes. He also is on the needy list, still unsupplied; so he is unfortunate...
>
> Another decent-looking young man called in one afternoon, asking for a pair of boots. He said he had just walked from Sydney. He was hungry-looking, and going by his boots one would think he had walked from Queensland, so old and broken were they. As we were unable to supply the need we promised him the first pair of sevens and prayed that a bundle of boots would soon arrive.[65]

Occasionally, there was a lighter note. One man wore two pairs of trousers because although both were holed, together they covered him. A young man's coat was in urgent need of repair. One of the brothers offered his own until it could be fixed. Two days later, when the young man was expected to return for his own coat, now looking almost new, he failed to show. 'He finds brother's coat more to his liking,' noted Lancaster, 'and is no more honest than old mother Eve who stole what belonged to someone else.'[66] On another occasion, one man left his old hat and took a better one. Later another man took the first man's hat and left his. Then a third man did the same. 'So one hat serves three men,' said Lancaster, 'and we are glad.'[67] Other men were too embarrassed to remove their outer garments because their ragged trousers were too revealing.[68]

In late 1931, an unbeliever argued outside the Hall for hours with three men against the existence of God. The Sisters invited him in. Shortly afterwards, they prayed for a young man with a throbbing headache and a woman with severe toothache. In both cases there was instant relief. Then during the meeting, several people fell to the floor under 'the mighty power of God' and lay prostrate for some time. Lancaster suggested to the sceptic that this was just 'Nature'. But he was a changed man. His experience outweighed his scepticism. That very night he was baptized and expressed his determination to seek out men whose faith he had previously shaken and win them back to God.[69] Another man, whose home was a disused railway carriage, needed to visit his mother 20 miles away but could not walk because of an infected leg caused by wearing shoes that were too small. They prayed for him and provided new shoes. Within hours he was well. A few days later the other leg was infected. This, too, was healed. Soon he testified publicly to his healing and found several weeks' work.[70]

The stories were multiplied. A young man collapsed at the door after seeking work for two weeks. Another fainted from weakness inside the Hall. Another's case and clothing had been stolen. Another needed ninepence to send a telegram to apply for a job in the country. Even a piece of soap was prized by many. So the workers prayed for it. Next day, two hundred weight of reject soap was offered to them. They boiled it down, cut it up into cakes and proudly gave it to all who were in need. There were also regular requests for such simple items as wool, cotton, needles, boot-laces, razors, socks, tea, sugar and the like.[71]

The Judgment of God

Lancaster and her helpers saw the Depression as an expression of the judgment of God. It was at such a time that men learned righteousness and it was exciting to see the Holy Spirit softening men's hearts and to observe those who once blasphemed God now responding to His love. They also interpreted their own activity in the light of the parable of the Good Samaritan. These needy people were their neighbours. They counted it a privilege to help them. They knew very well there were some who preferred to live on handouts and had no intention of seeking work, but those who worked among the poor soon learned to identify them.[72] In answer to those who saw many of these people to be imposing on the work of evangelism, Lancaster wrote—

> Improvident! Perhaps some were, but our Lord never stipulated that only the frugal and careful should be fed. It was enough for Him that they were hungry... Perhaps a percentage of them may deserve it, but if we see a drowning man we do not wait to ask how he got into the water, but hasten to get him out...
>
> It is when the judgments of the Lord are in the earth that men will learn righteousness, and the bright spot in the midst of this misery is to watch the wondrous Holy Spirit at work softening men's hearts, melting away their prejudices, and revealing to them as the God of love that great, noble, merciful, and gracious Being whom they formerly reviled and cursed as the tyrannical Author of their misery...
>
> Those of our readers who have a little of the love of God for lost humanity shed abroad in their hearts will keep on praying for a mighty harvest of souls to be the outcome of the present commercial depression.[73]

According to an article by an American writer published in *Good News*, the remedy for business depression was found in the words of 2 Chronicles 7:14—in humility, prayer and repentance.[74]

As at St Barnabas church in Sydney, where Arthur Stace ('Mr Eternity') turned to the Lord in 1930,[75] every opportunity was taken to preach Christ to those who were being helped. After each midday meal, there was an address or two, and people were invited to receive Christ. Many were the testimonies of those converted and baptized. It must have been a glad day, for instance, when one man demanded to be baptized that very afternoon, and then a few days later gave his testimony to the other unemployed men at the midday meal. One young man who was converted and baptized in the Spirit had found work in the country and was conducting regular Sunday services there; another, who six months previously had cared only for gambling, was now witnessing for Christ, even to the point of conducting prayer meetings in the gardens in the mornings with other men who had slept out for the night. Another spoke to the men at lunchtime and said, 'I hear some of you men are saying we converts only came here for what we could get. That is quite true, and so did you! But I got what I came here for, and more; for I got Jesus. I'm glad I came!' He went on to say how he had just had a job offer in the country at four pounds a week. Another was preaching regularly on Sunday mornings in rural Victoria; another was distributing tracts near Ballarat.[76] Frank Bryan, a confessed Communist, expressed his amazement that such a change could occur in a human life. Formerly repelled by what he saw as hypocrisy in the church, he was won over by contact with 'Mother,' what he described as her 'sympathetic and broad-minded interest in my ideals and aims' and the evidence he saw of a church not interested in material profit but in acting as Jesus would have done. Now, weeks later, he was healthier than he had been for a long time and determined to stand for Christ. He himself became a worker at the Hall.[77] The physical needs were serious enough, but the spirit of Pentecost was still the final answer.

In answer to the challenge, 'Do all the converts stand?' the response was simple. 'Of what Mission could it ever be said that the converts all stood?' True, there had been two or three 'disastrous failures', but there were many who were going joyfully on in their new-found faith.[78] One letter must have touched Lancaster's heart. It came from a young man who had now found work on a farm and signed it, 'From your son in Christ'.[79] Indeed, at the end of 1931, Lancaster could claim that men who had found Christ through the relief program were planting the seed of the Gospel around the State of Victoria in Sale, Lindenow, Tallangatta, Lake Tarral, Camperdown, Bunyip, Wandin, Noble Park, Byrneside, Warburton, Mirboo, Cockatoo, Avenel, Pakenham, King Island as well as several suburbs of Melbourne. Not only was the Gospel talked about, but so was Good News Hall. Men came there from hundreds of miles' distance seeking help.[80]

In spite of these reports, not all the people at the Hall approved of the welfare work. Some felt the assembly itself was being neglected and that it was suffering financially. But Lancaster's answer was simple: 'It's what the Lord would do.'[81] On one occasion she wrote—

> Is it worthwhile? If you could see the changed and happy faces of many of these dear men who accepted Jesus as their Saviour, followed Him through the waters of baptism, and see others filled with the Holy Spirit, you would say: 'yes, a hundred times.'
>
> They come in sad and weary, sometimes despairing of life, but as they listen to the Gospel message, hope rises within their hearts...[82]

It was not enough. At a 1931 AFM Council meeting, one of the members expressed the view that the funds being spent on the unemployed would be better applied to evangelising Victoria and thus building up the AFM, and, incidentally, bringing in more money.[83] Everyone else present agreed. Given the membership of the Executive Council, this vote of no confidence seems strange. At that time, it included Philip Adams, Winnie Andrews, Charles Anstis, J. Anstis, Edith Anstis, Mina Brawner, Harold Martin, Jotham Metcalfe, Charlie Kajewski, Edwin Ridgway, Ernest Tooth, Ivor Warburton and Tom Warburton. Most of these people were utterly loyal to Lancaster and continued to work with her till the day she died.[84] Perhaps some—Martin from Brisbane, for example, or Edie Anstis from Perth—were not present at the meeting. It is also possible that Lancaster was referring to the local Victorian Advisory Council. These were M. Anstis, John Cavill, J. Deacon, G. Holroyd, Davey Jack, Jim Mullins [sic] and 'Brother' Johnson.[85] Jack had already expressed some criticism of proceedings. But here, too, there were loyal souls such as John Cavill and George Holroyd. Whatever the explanation, this unanimous expression of disagreement with Lancaster's work with the poor was the last straw. She had suffered criticism for over 20 years from outside the movement. Now, this attack from inside proved terminal. From the beginning, she said, she had never wanted to build an organisation. Her reluctance to do so initially was no secret. She believed that to abandon the needy would in fact be hindering the work of evangelisation. So she took the only course of action that seemed honourable to her. On 23 January 1932, she called a meeting of the Good News Hall Assembly to discuss 'the relationship of the Assembly to the A. F. M.' Individuals were free to make their own choice, but with the vastly increased activities of the church together with the editing of *Good News*, occupying her fully, she would be resigning her position with the A. F. M. of Australasia. She felt she could serve God better outside of its activities—

> We have been impelled to obtain liberty for ourselves to follow the guidance of the Holy Spirit by sending in our resignation... This has not been done in any spirit of controversy... therefore, by God's grace, we have not (and shall not) ask a single person to resign from the 'A. F. M.', neither will we annex any 'A. F. M.' worker or evangelist, or try to hinder by word or deed the activities of the A. F. M., though the same loving fellowship will be shown to all as in the past, and we will still gladly extend a helping hand to both assemblies and individuals. The only difference so far as we are concerned will be a clerical one.[86]

For the rest of that year, *Good News* continued to include a listing of the same churches. Instead of an Easter Conference, however, there was a Prayer Convention at Good News Hall, with the usual Memorial Supper.[87] There were blessings in profusion; three people received the Spirit, including an 80-year-old woman, and there were many visions and revelations.[88]

As the bleak Melbourne winter of 1932 approached, the situation of many became worse. There were 70 men requiring boots, 80 needing shirts, more than 30 in need of trousers with many others waiting for socks or underwear. Moreover, women and children were now suffering hunger and privation. Mothers starved themselves to feed their families. Children had no clothes for school.

Often, they were cold and sick.[89] As the demands were growing so the debts were mounting. The Hall was closed for three days of prayer and fasting. No meals were served to anyone, members or mendicants. In her original style, Lancaster explained to an enquirer—

> Sufficient help to feed these needy men is not forthcoming, and as we are getting more deeply into debt each month, and the men keep increasing in numbers, it has become needful to lay siege to the courts of heaven for a cheque on the Bank of Philippi (Phil 4:19), and so, as a mission, we have decided to wait upon God, camping, as it were, at His gate...[90]

If only Spirit-filled Christians around Australia had been more generous, there would have been plenty for all. Or, if only those they had helped who were now employed gave ten per cent of their earnings. Meanwhile, *Good News* would only be printed as funds were available.[91]

Remarriage

In the midst of all this, on 15 June 1932, at the age of 74, Jeannie Lancaster re-married. Her new husband, Richard Hocking, seems to have appeared unexpectedly at the Hall: there is no extant reference to him being involved prior to this time, although he was evidently known as an active helper in other mission centres. Baptist minister Gordon Bennett, an old friend of Lancaster's, expressed some surprise at being asked to officiate. However, he was reassured by the fact that 'the whole matter had been planned in the atmosphere of prayer and in the interests of the Lord's work.' It was plain that the burden of the work at the Hall was too much for Lancaster and this union would enable the two to devote their united efforts to the ministry.

Hocking quickly made his presence felt. On three occasions he wrote the lead article for *Good News*; and a few rather pretentious poems of his were printed. He had a lucid, but grandiose style, but his writings lacked the warmth and affection for Jesus that characterised Lancaster's approach.[92]

The work was taking its toll in more ways than one. Weekend meetings were 'rich in blessing,' but the numbers had dropped and there were now few in attendance. Nevertheless, the welfare work and the open air meetings continued.[93] The thriving Pentecostal Church of Australia congregation at Richmond Temple was a probable lure for those who wanted a more regular kind of church with orthodox evangelical doctrines.

Jeannie Lancaster died suddenly on 6 March 1934 at the age of 75. Until a few hours before her death she was working 'in the service for others.' Some of her loyal supporters feared there had been foul play. Hocking had mistakenly believed, they alleged, that she had accumulated considerable wealth over the years.[94] The official reason for death was given as diabetes-mellitus and high blood pressure.

Harold Martin, pastor of one of the Brisbane assemblies, paid tribute at her funeral to 'the consecrated life and service of dear "Mother".' Baptist pastor Gordon Bennett, who had stood by her faithfully for many years, spoke at the grave of her Christian character and selfless devotion to her calling.[95] Given the extent of her ministry and its widespread effects, it is surprising that a relatively small item in *Good News* reports her death. But then, perhaps, that is how she would have liked it. On 7 March, she was buried as she had lived, self-effacing, uncelebrated and without acclamation, in the Fawkner Cemetery, Victoria, in an unmarked grave.

Lancaster's death clearly caused considerable trauma and disruption to the ministry. There was no *Good News* in April and in May, the August 1928 issue was re-issued with a new cover. There was evidently a mortgage on the Hall—perhaps Lancaster herself had financed its original purchase and the estate demanded settlement—and there was possibly still money owing from the heavy financial drain during the height of the Depression. Although an attempt was made to raise the necessary funds, the Hall had to be sold. John Cavill and Harold Martin were able to rent it back from its new owners and to regain all the furnishings.[96] So they resolved to continue the ministry, including the publishing of *Good News*. At Lancaster's death, Martin left Queensland for Melbourne, where he became secretary of the work and editor of the magazine.[97] There were many grateful letters from readers for the continuance of the magazine.[98]

The reprieve was not for long. The following year, the congregation was given notice to quit the Hall as it was to be turned into 'a place of amusement.'[99] Meetings were relocated in the Forester's Hall, Richmond, under the name Good News Mission.[100] The numbers were evidently small, the annual memorial supper in 1936 being held at Cavill's home.[101] The Mission continued as a small group into the 40s under the leadership of William Salisbury when it finally closed.[102]

With Lancaster's withdrawal and subsequent death, the Apostolic Faith Mission ceased to function and the few churches that had remained in fellowship with Good News Hall forged new alliances with the Pentecostal Church of Australia or the Apostolic or Foursquare Churches. Many well-known families in today's Pentecostal movement trace their origins to Good News Hall.[103]

Perhaps the best example of how Lancaster was seen by her associates is found in the words of Gordon Bennett at her wedding day—

> During all the years I have known her she has distinguished herself by her devoted, self-sacrificing work for her Lord and Master. This has called for much faith, and spiritual heroism, which has often been put to the test by the changing circumstances and the many disappointments that one meets with, even in the Lord's work.
>
> Being misunderstood, misrepresented and even opposed by those who have professed friendship and love, certainly means the testing of one's faith in God... Our Sister... has been subjected to these things; yet the work God has entrusted to her, to pioneer Pentecost in Australia and establish a centre, has continued to grow, souls have been saved, hearts cheered and the spiritual life of many a child of God has been nourished and strengthened by the Lord through the sanctified services of our dear Sister.[104]

Through all the criticism and conflict Lancaster endured, a spirit of love was evident. To quote Lloyd Averill, 'They weathered many storms and their opponents admit that they showed real Christian love despite any alleged errors.'[105]

148   *The Origins and Development of the Pentecostal Movement in Australia*

In her 26 years of ministry, Lancaster remained true to her own understanding of the Scriptures. Some of her views were unorthodox and unpopular, but she was not the kind of person who would change for the sake of expediency. Yet she was neither judgmental nor aggressive; for her, love was more important than doctrine. Her faith was expressed in actions as well as words. In many ways, this was the intrinsic spirit of Pentecost.

Regrettably, others who claimed to be filled with the same Holy Spirit were less charitable. The first fruit of the Spirit might be love (Galatians 5:22), but this was insufficient reason to overlook heretical beliefs. The same Spirit was also given to lead us into truth (John 16:13). Reconciling these two perspectives has been a challenge for the Christian Church since its inception. It was a particular challenge for a movement that derived its *raison d'etre* from the ministry of the Spirit.

Notes

1. See Appendix B for background material on McPherson.

2. See Appendix D for the text of another statement issued by McPherson after her return to the US and for more on Andrews.

3. In 1921, English-born Frodsham became editor of the American journal *Pentecostal Evangel,* a position he was to hold for 15 years and became well known as a Pentecostal leader and the author of some 15 books. Frodsham had previously questioned McPherson's commitment to the Pentecostal view of baptism in the Spirit and speaking in tongues, and Andrews felt her behaviour in Australia proved his point. See Burgess and Van Der Maas, eds, 2002, 647; Frodsham, *Smith Wigglesworth: Apostle of Faith,* 1971 and *With Signs Following,* 19 46.

4. W. Andrews, 'Mrs McPherson's "Open Letter" Answered,' 24 October, 1922, 1. Further details on McPherson's visit are from this source unless otherwise stated.

5. In 1922, there were three recognised assemblies in Melbourne—Good News Hall (1908), the Southern Evangelical Mission (1911) and the Sunshine Gospel Mission (1916). Perhaps the Palmer Street Mission was also seen as Pentecostal. The invitation may have come from all of them. But as we shall see, by 1922 there was little fellowship between them, and it seems more likely that the other Missions were the 'small assemblies' referred to by Andrews. There were also some suburban house meetings such as those conducted by Mrs Hickson. There was only one established provincial congregation at this time, in Ballarat but there were some gatherings in other capital cities and, as Andrews points out, people did come 'hundreds of miles' to McPherson's meetings.

6. *Sun News-Pictorial* 21 September, 1922.

7. A. McPherson, *This is That* (Los Angeles: Echo Park Evangelistic Association, 1923), 505f.

8. E. Jordan, *The Supreme Incentive* (East Brunswick, Vic: pub. by the author, 1970), 41; Duncan, Lecture, 1965.

9. See Appendix D.

10. Lancaster, 'Open Letter,' 17.

11. McPherson mysteriously disappeared in 1926, claimed she had been kidnapped and was subsequently subject to allegations of impropriety. See Burgess and Van Der Mass, eds, 2002, 856ff; Edith Blumhofer, *Aimee Semple McPherson: Everybody's Sister* (Grand Rapids: Eerdmans, 1993); Wilson, 1970.

12. See also GN, 15:8, August, 1924, 20.
13. GN, 14:9, September, 1923, 2ff; GN, 14:11, November, 1923, 2; GN, 16:6, June, 1925, 3; GN, 16:8, August, 1925, 15; GN, 16:11, November, 1925, 8; GN, 17:5, May, 1926, 3, 17; GN, 17:7, July, 1926, 8; GN, 17:8, August, 1926, 20; GN, 19:2, February, 1928, 30.
14. Nellie Mather, 'His Thrilling Touch,' GN, 15:12, December, 1924, 12ff; see also Jordan, 1970, 39ff.
15. J. Lancaster, 'Truth and Love,' GN, 22:4, April, 1931, 10.
16. *Age*, 12, October, 1922.
17. GN, 16:4, April 1925, 18.
18. GN, 16:5, May 1925, 10, 11.
19. 'Pentecostal Church of Australia,' GN, 16:7, July, 1925, 20.
20. GN, 18:10, October, 1927, 10.
21. The term 'Latter Rain' used here was not a reference to the 'Latter Rain' movement that emerged some years later. It was based on the Old Testament prophecy of Joel (2:23) that God would pour out both 'former rain' (i.e. autumn) and 'latter rain' (i.e. spring). The former rain was seen to have fallen at Pentecost; the latter rain was falling now, through the new Pentecostal movement.
22. GN, 18:6, June, 1927, 10.
23. GN, 17:8, August, 1926, 10.
24. GN, 17:9, September, 1926, 11; GN, 18:6, June, 1927, 10.
25. GN, 18:7, July, 1927, 18.
26. GN, 17:10, October, 1926, 19.
27. J. Lancaster, 'Being Defamed—we Intreat,' GN, 18:2, February, 1927, 20.
28. GN, 18:6, June, 1927, 12.
29. GN, 18:6, June 1927, 12.
30. GN, 18:7, July, 1927, 14. When Van Eyk first arrived in 1926, he had been aware of the doctrinal difficulties. Lancaster claimed that he was 'beset behind, and before' by those who opposed them both doctrinally and governmentally—the latter no doubt a reference to her leadership as a woman. But she went on to say that he had gone into both questions 'to his entire satisfaction' and could not be shaken. However, it is interesting to note that when he later established the Elim Foursquare Gospel Mission, he very clearly spelled out his beliefs concerning the deity of Christ and the fate of the wicked. The three persons of the Godhead were 'equal in every divine perfection' and the wicked would suffer 'eternal conscious punishment.' See GC, 3:2, August, 1934, 32.
31. GN, 18:7, July, 1927, 10.
32. GN, 18:6, June, 1927, 10f; GN, 19:6, June, 1928, 10.
33. J. Lancaster, 'The Body of Christ Jesus,' GN, 18:12, December, 1927, 16f.
34. GN, 19:6, June 1928, 10.
35. GN, 19:6, June 1928, 15.
36. M. Brawner, 'Shibboleth,' GN, 21:7, July, 1930, 11.
37. GN, 18:8, August, 1927, 10.
38. GN, 19:6, June, 1928, 10ff, 19f.
39. GN, 20:5, May, 1929, 16.
40. AE, June, 1984, 23. There was no connection at that time with the American denomination of the same name.
41. GN, 20:5, May, 1929, 16.
42. GN, 19:6, June, 1928, 12; GN, 20:5, May, 1929, 13.
43. GN, 20:5, May, 1929, 13.
44. GN, 20:5, May, 1929, 10. (Note: this page number is actually out of order in the magazine. It should be 15).

45. GN, 20:5, May, 1929, 16.
46. GN, 20:5, May, 1929, 24; GN, 21:6, June, 1930, 10.
47. GN, 22:5, May, 1931, 10, 14.
48. GN, 22:5, May, 1931, 12.
49. GN, 21:9, September, 1930, 11.
50. I am not aware of any extant records of the exact nature of ordination services in the 1920s and 1930s. Based on Lancaster's publicised attitude to theological training and my own personal experience in Pentecostal churches from 1958, it is probably fair to assume that no formal qualifications were needed for ordination. The recognised call of God was sufficient. Ordination itself probably took the form of laying on of hands by a group of elders, praying extemporaneously for the persons concerned and then commissioning them for the work of the ministry. This would normally have been done in a public service.
51. GN, 22:5, May, 1931, 14.
52. GN, 22:5, May, 1931, 14; GN, 22:6, June, 1931, 10f; RE, 2, 6–7 November–December, 1934, 133.
53. Lancaster, interview, 18 December, 1993.
54. GN, 21:10, October, 1930, 15.
55. GN, 22:2, February, 1931, 10.
56. *Sun News-Pictorial,* 26 December, 1923, quoted in GN, 15:2, February, 1924, 20.
57. GN, 16:2, February, 1925, 9.
58. GN, 22:8, August, 1931, 12.
59. GN, 22:9, September, 1931, 10f; GN, 22:10, October, 1931, 10; GN, 23:6, June, 1932, 10.
60. GN, 24:4–5, April–May, 1933, 8f; GN, 22:2, February, 1931, 10; GN, 22:5, May, 1931, 11; GN, 22:10, October, 1931, 10.
61. GN, 23:9, September, 1932, 8; GN, 22:2, February, 1931, 10; GN, 22:5, May, 1931, 11; GN, 22:8, August, 1931, 12; GN, 22:9, September, 1931, 10; GN, 22:12, December, 1931, 10f; GN, 25:3, March, 1934, 20; GN, 23:3, March, 1932, 10 ('Yes, and I have to thank you, Mother, for all your love and kindness'); Mullin, interview, n. d.
62. GN, 22:8, August, 1931, 12; GN, 22:3, March, 1931, 11; GN, 23:7, July, 1931, 10.
63. GN, 22:5, May, 1931, 10; GN, 22:10, October, 1931, 11; GN, 23:2, February 1932, 10.
64. GN, 22:3, March, 1931, 10.
65. GN, 22:12, December, 1931, 10.
66. GN, 23:3, March, 1932, 10.
67. GN, 22:10, October, 1931, 10.
68. GN, 22:11, November, 1931, 10; GN, 23:1, January, 1932, 10.
69. GN, 22:12, December, 1931, 11. This man was probably Frank Bryan, a former Communist. See GN, 23:7, July, 1932, 11.
70. GN, 23:1, January, 1932, 10f.
71. GN, 22:8, August, 1931, 12f; GN, 22:12, December, 1931, 10; GN, 22:4, April, 1931, 11; GN, 22:11, November, 1931, 10.
72. GN, 24:4– 5, April–May, 1933, 8.
73. GN, 22:2, February, 1931, 10.
74. W .E. Henson, 'God's remedy for business depression,' GN, 23:5, May 1932, 12f.
75. G. Rees, 'Eternity: the Unknown Man Who Wrote It,' pamphlet, n. d.; Lawrence Johnston, *Eternity,* documentary film; *Telegraph,* 3 May, 1995, 10; *Bulletin,* 9 May 1995, 88. It should be noted that the ministry at St Barnabas was on a larger scale than that at

Good News Hall, but in terms of the gospel, was similar in spirit and aim. See Breward, 1993, 125; Judd, and Cable, 1987, 196ff; Piggin, 1996, 88f.

76. GN, 22:7, July, 1931, 10; GN, 22:8, August, 1931, 12; GN, 22:9, September, 1931, 10; GN, 22:5, May, 1931, 11; GN, 23:8, August, 1932, 8; GN, 23:4, April, 1932, 11f.

77. GN, 23:7, July, 1932, 11; GN, 23:8, August, 1932, 8.

78. GN, 23:2, February, 1932, 10.

79. GN, 23:5, May, 1932, 11.

80. GN, 23:3, March, 1932, 11.

81. Mullin, interview, n. d.

82. GN, 22:9, September, 1931, 10.

83. GN, 23:2, February, 1932, 11.

84. Ridgway was one of the early members at the Hall. He was baptized in the Holy Spirit probably before 1920. In his *'Ask for the Old Paths'*, c.1946, he refers to having been baptized in the Spirit some 30 years previously.

85. GN, 22:5, May, 1931, 15. Jim Mullin told me forty years later that he felt the welfare work had become a distraction from the real mission of evangelism.

86. GN, 23:2, February, 1932, 11,19.

87. GN, 23:3, March, 1932, 20.

88.. GN, 23:5, May, 1932, 11.

89. GN, 23:6, June, 1932, 10f; GN, 23:7, July, 1932, 13; GN, 24:4–5, April–May, 1933, 8.

90. GN, 23:3, March, 1932, 11.

91. GN, 23:4, April, 1932, 11; GN, 23:11, November, 1932, 8;GN, 23:8, August, 1932, III.

92. GN, 23:8, August, 1932, 1f; GN, 23:9, September, 1832, 1f; GN, 23:10, October 1932, 6f, 12.

93. GN, 24:9, September 1933, 8.

94. 'Sister' Ethel Wordsworth claimed to have heard strange noises as of someone being strangled as she passed the Hockings' door that day and another suspected poison at the hands of her husband—Lancaster, interview, 18 December 1993; Warburton, interview, n. d. These stories were conveyed to me by several other interviewees as well.

95. GN, 25:3, March 1934, 19.

96. H. Martin and J. Cavill, 'An Open Letter,' GN, 25:4, May 1934, 19.

97. H. Martin, 'It Came to Pass,' GN, 25:11, November, 1934, 10. Months later he told how eight years previously he had seen himself in a vision cutting paper to wrap meat, and realised it was for the 'meat of the Word.' When he entered the Good News Hall printing room, he recognised it as the place he had seen in the vision. Now, as editor, he was literally cutting paper in the print room.

98. GN, 25:12, December, 1934, 19; GN, 26:5, May 1935, 19f; GN, 27:4, April, 1936, 19.

99. The following year, the Hall was once again used as a Pentecostal meeting place under the leadership of Mina Brawner.

100. GN, 26:6, June, 1935, 19f.

101. GN, 27:4, April, 1936, 9.

102. William Salisbury was a wood machinist by trade and an 'exhorter rather than a preacher.' Meetings were held above a shoe store in Albert Street, Brunswick. Some Good News Hall identities continued to attend including Jim Cavill, Jim Self, Tom and Ivor Warburton, Charles Mortomore and Irene Loutit. There was an annual foot washing service where, on one occasion, the Warburton brothers were reconciled after an argu-

ment through washing one another's feet. See Averill, 1992, 21f and L. Averill, personal interview, 20 November, 1990 and personal communication, 28 March, 1992

103. For example, the following families—Lancaster, Buchanan, Douglas, Mortomore, Peters, Swensen, Enticknap, Conwell, Deacon, Sharman, Priest.

104. A. G. Bennett, 'A Wedding,' GN, 23:7, July, 1932, 18.

105. Lloyd Averill, personal communication, n. d.

CHAPTER SEVEN

THE FREE FLOWING SPIRIT

F. B. Van Eyk—Carrying the Message across the Land, 1926–1934

In 1926, there came to Australia a South African evangelist named Frederick Bernadas Van Eyk (1895–1939).[1] Having formerly been both a 'notorious character in the wilds of Transvaal,' poorly educated, his life characterised by gambling, drinking, smoking, profanity and the like,[2] and later a mounted policeman,[3] he was converted in Durban and joined the Apostolic Faith Mission. Around 1916 he became an evangelist.[4] He was a vigorous preacher and an inspiring singer[5], and another of the significant international visitors who contributed to the development of the Pentecostal movement in Australia.

Van Eyk was not a tall man, but he was very strong.[6] Photographs display a determined, confident face, softened by fleshy lips. His personality was such that he won both fierce loyalty and fierce antagonism.

F.B.Van Eyk (R) and his only younger brother C.J.Van Eyk.

While some saw him as a powerful preacher 'sent by God',[7] others regarded him as a brazen charlatan.[8] As we shall see, opinions about him are still divided today. Given that he started two Pentecostal denominations and established some 17 Pentecostal congregations in Australia, his significance cannot be ignored.

Van Eyk was invited to Australia by a group of three men in the fledgling Pentecostal movement there—J. E. ('Grandpa') Rieschiek, Hines Retchford and 'Brother' Stevens. These men had been conducting regular open air meetings at the Kingston Statue on Victoria Square, in the centre of Adelaide, South Australia's quiet and sunny capital city. Later they were to form the Adelaide Council of the Apostolic Faith Mission. With them was another South African, Isaac Hugo, a lithographer, who had been engaged in Mission work for some twelve years since his baptism in the Spirit and was now coming to work for an Adelaide printer. On his first Saturday night, he had came across the open air meeting and soon joined the Pentecostal group. By 1926, he was pastor of the Adelaide assembly. The fifth in the leadership group was the secretary, Gus Jansen, a former school teacher.[9]

When Van Eyk arrived in Australia, he was accompanied by his wife Cecilia Isabel and four children, Neilsie, Dick, Freddie and Faith.[10] He arrived in Perth, Western Australia in March, 1926, where he held some meetings. An excited report noted how a man with an arm so painful and weak he could not even lift a teaspoon to his lips was dramatically healed.[11] He then sailed on to Adelaide. Meetings were arranged there with Van Eyk, Hugo and Jansen as the speakers. They were advertised with a strange blend of humility and hubris. Neither names nor photos of the evangelists were included in the advertising, so that 'Jesus Christ alone' was lifted up. Yet the meetings were featured as the 'greatest effort ever made to cope with the suffering and need of our fellow man.' The campaign was to be strictly non-sectarian and all Christians were invited to participate. There was a special invitation to the sick and suffering, and divine healing would be both preached and demonstrated. There would be no offering and seats were free. No closing date was set, so the Holy Spirit was 'being permitted to lead.'

Cecilia Van Eyk and her children Neilsie, Dick, Freddie and Faith, c.1928.

The invitation was anything but subtle—

COMPLETE DELIVERANCE FOR ALL CAPTIVES

Are you a sinner? Come and be saved
Are you a drunkard? Come and be delivered
Are you a sceptic? Come and be convinced
Are you a christian? [sic]. Come and be baptized in the Holy Ghost.[12]

Van Eyk's usual method of praying for the sick was to lay hands on their head and to command the sickness to go. Sometimes, people were given printed instructions on how to prepare themselves for healing.[13] The Protestant Hall in Hindmarsh Square was crowded and many professed to be converted and baptized in the Holy Spirit, with the 'evidence' of glossolalia. 'Many mighty miracles' were claimed. Among those who were declared cured were a blind girl, a hunch-back, a deaf woman, a dwarfed baby and a child with a growth in his throat. When Van Eyk invited those who had been healed to come to the front of the hall, there was insufficient room. On 9 May, over one thousand people attended a service of baptism by immersion at the River Torrens.[14] Rieschiek, described as a 'veteran Pentecostal elder', paid enthusiastic tribute to the evangelist—

> When on the platform or praying, he enters into the very presence of God, and is a changed man, full of fire; his whole being is in it.
>
> He is fond of music and singing, his delivery powerful, eloquent, and accompanied by action, his address—dictated by the Holy Spirit—flowing like rivers of living water. When he unfolds the mysteries of God's Holy Word, you are lost in wonder and adoration, and are just carried away on a higher plane into the presence of God. It is beautiful how he can bring a subject before us; explain, illustrate, and demonstrate it by the Word of God.[15]

Soon they were in Melbourne where 31 people claimed to be healed from complaints such as deafness, partial blindness, alcoholism, goitre, eczema, gastritis, catarrh, bad nerves, blood pressure, rheumatoid arthritis, back pain, asthma (of 25 years' standing), influenza, kidney trouble, curvature of the spine, insomnia and nervous tension.[16] Van Eyk also visited some country areas in Victoria. In Korumburra, his visit overlapped with that of Chief Stoker Stephens, a Methodist evangelist. The local press acknowledged Ste-

Report of Mrs E. Johnson, healed of rheumatoid arthritis after 18 years, the last three in a wheel chair.

phens's rallies but ignored Van Eyk's.[17] Similarly, although Van Eyk had been told that Geelong was 'the city of revivals,' a reference, no doubt, to the activities of people like George Grubb forty years previously, it proved difficult to find any churches willing to cooperate with him and attendances at the Eastern Hall initially were small. The evangelist lamented that there were 'walls of prejudice and barriers of denominationalism to be broken down,' apart from the 'usual' ignorance and fears. He preached on the theme of divine healing and soon people began to testify of recovery. Nevertheless, the sight of so many sick and suffering people was deeply challenging. He later said—

> As we looked with pity upon them, we saw only too plainly the meaning of our travailing in the Spirit, our groans and tears for God's mercy upon the people as we agonized before Him those long days and longer nights preceding these meetings. Those times when our souls were so burdened by God that they abhorred both meats and sleep, so engrossed were they in intercession on behalf of this awful condition of things. As we moved from one to another of these poor, afflicted ones, each bending low under the burden of one or another of the following:—Cancer, gallstones, arthritis, neuritis, nervous debility, defective eyesight, lameness or deafness—we cry from our innermost souls, 'Father, in the name of Jesus, and by the power of the Holy Ghost, we ask you to blast this cursed disease, and grant now a full and free deliverance from pain and suffering.' One after another we saw the finger of God touch, removing from their bodies the last vestige of pain.[18]

He admitted there were some who were apparently not healed, but claimed that 'the large majority' were set free, and that many testimonials of healing were received. Moreover, people began to come to his lodgings either to report a healing or to urge him to go with them to minister to someone in need. The *Geelong Advertiser* was warm in its appraisal of the meetings—

> In praying for the sick, Mr Van Eyk's axiom is, 'Remove the cause, and the patient is healed'; therefore, it is necessary for hatred, envy, jealousy, covetousness, and, in fact, all sin to be forsaken. On Wednesday night 14 persons rose to declare they had been wholly or partially delivered from various sicknesses or disabilities; a man suffering in feet and legs for eight months walked and jumped to demonstrate that he was completely healed. A young woman removed her powerful glasses, and claimed the complete restoration of eyesight, which had been partially destroyed through concussion of the brain caused by an accident... Deaf people said their hearing was restored. One deaf-mute spoke for the first time since babyhood.[19]

Van Eyk's audacity and daring faith was demonstrated when a woman of Christian Science persuasion came for healing. 'I want to demonstrate to you tonight the difference between 'Divine Healing' and Christian Science so-called,' pronounced the evangelist. Pointing to the woman, he said, 'This woman... has been under the treatment of Christian Science for the last six years, and here she is tonight with excruciating pains in body and head. I am now going to pray for her, and prove to you by her immediate healing that C.S. is a fake.' He anointed her with oil and prayed for her. She testified then and there that the pain had vanished.[20]

Good News reported a couple of dramatic incidents which took place at this time. Before Van Eyk's arrival in Adelaide, South Australia, a woman saw a vision of a man 'in apostolic garb' and heard a voice say, 'This man will teach you the way of righteousness.' A few weeks later, she saw a photo of Van Eyk in a newspaper advertisement and recognized him as the one she had seen. A woman in Melbourne had a similar experience. Another claimed that when Van Eyk was preaching in Good News Hall, his figure faded and Jesus was seen standing in his place. Others said they saw the figure of Jesus standing behind him while he spoke. Jeannie Lancaster was awestruck. She had witnessed the ministry of Aimee McPherson and Smith Wigglesworth and A. C. Valdez, but never, she whispered, had she seen 'such wonderful anointings of the Spirit' as had been granted to Van Eyk. 'Our God,' she continued, 'is exercising a peculiarly jealous care over him.'[21] The tragedy is that within three years a dark shadow would attach itself to him so closely that it would frustrate even this divine mantle.

The Apostolic Faith Mission

After a brief visit to New Zealand, Van Eyk proposed to Lancaster that Good News Hall, together with its handful of satellite churches, should adopt the name of his South African home church, namely Apostolic Faith Mission.[22] At their first annual conference, held at Easter, April 15–24, 1927, Van Eyk was appointed as their 'first evangelist.'[23] Lancaster was impressed with Van Eyk's 'sweet spirit of humility and conciliation.' She believed he would be used by God to bring unity and love, to those whose hearts were not already given over to bitterness, and that although he was a fearless man of God, he was so filled with love, even his words of rebuke would be 'shorn of offense'.[24] Soon his pioneering work began to open up new assemblies. Accompanied by Lancaster's son-in-law, W.A. (Alex) Buchanan, he travelled an estimated 27,000 kilometres through every State of the Commonwealth preaching the gospel.[25]

During this time, his methods became legendary. He was vigorous and athletic. He

F B Van Eyk c.1927. (Source, GN 18.8).

rarely stood still when he preached. He would leap, jump, walk, run across the platform. On one occasion, to make a point, he stood on the piano.[26] He would wave his handkerchief, shout, sing, weep. He sometimes tackled unruly interjectors himself, leaving the platform if necessary to evict them personally. 'The Lord prohibits me from hitting people,' he said, 'but he does not say that I cannot put them out.'[27] In street meetings, he drew large crowds and virile abuse. On at least one occasion, raw eggs were thrown at him. He loved repartee and used it to his advantage. When one man shouted, 'I believe in evolution,' he responded, 'Looking at you, I'm inclined to believe in it myself! But what do you say when you pray? "Our Father who art up a tree"?'[28] His son recalled—

> He was a vital person. He could eject interjectors, yet at the same time, he could be very gentle. People would turn and look at him as he walked down the street. He did not call attention to himself, but people were just attracted to him. He was always interested in people and wherever he went he drew a crowd. It didn't matter to him if he was preaching to five people or to a thousand. He did it with the same enthusiasm. He used to tell us never to run away from a fight—but never to go looking for one either![29]

His second wife described him as a 'strong, vital, energetic live-wire.'[30] An early supporter of his ministry wrote—

> He was an outstanding preacher of the Word on all subjects. People were gripped by the power of the Spirit as he spoke. He was fearless of persecution... He sang and played the piano with as much power as he did in preaching.[31]

Another man said—

> You couldn't help liking him. He was a man's man. He could lift a bag of wheat, wrestle, shoot better than anybody. He put on wrestling bouts for the boys in Parkes. He was musical, He had personality. He once boasted—my father and Uncle Ben Michalk and old Brother Marsh and I were sitting at the table when I was a boy—'I can fill any hall in Australia.' He could, too.[32]

George Burns noted that after Van Eyk's visit at least half his workers were men. Pentecost had solved the problem of catching men for Jesus Christ, he said, and made them realise that witnessing for Jesus Christ was 'a man's job.'[33] In February 1927, Van Eyk and Buchanan visited Maryborough, some 260 kilometres north of Brisbane, on the Queensland coast. Here as a result of Mortomore's ministry, George Burns, former journalist with the *Maryborough Chronicle*[34] and pastor of the local Church of Christ, had with about 40 of his original members, formed a new congregation named the Christian Mission. There was some scepticism in the community about the beginning of what they saw as a new sect and some predicted their early demise. At the first meal together, Burns felt 'a foregleam of heaven'—

> When our dear brother rose to speak the first dozen words were sufficient to satisfy my heart that we were in the presence of a prophet of the risen Christ... our Mission ran on for three weeks and three days, and during that time our eyes beheld the glory of God and majesty and power of God as we had never seen it before.[35]

Meetings began in the Orange Hall, with seating for about 250 people. Van Eyk also held consultations each morning. By the end of the week, the campaign was transferred to the much larger Naval Hall, which could handle some two thousand.[36] There were neither seats nor platform, but the small congregation worked hard and by Tuesday 2 April, it was ready. According to Burns, it was full for the first meeting. Some had clearly come to question and criticise, but a testimony of healing from diabetes and the evident recovery of sight to a blind woman were hard to refute. Burns reported healings from goitre, asthma, gout, rheumatism, diabetes, lumbago, ulcers, internal troubles, incipient cancer, paralysis, deafness and blindness. He was impressed with the way Van Eyk prayed with authority, telling sickness to go in Jesus' name. 'Whole families were swept into the Kingdom,' Burns claimed, usually as the result of at least one member being healed. He expected the church numbers to increase by one hundred as a result.[37] Van Eyk later claimed that on one occasion there had been a sound of rushing wind like that recorded on the day of Pentecost which swept through the building and resulted in about 15 people being converted.[38]

The campaign was not without competition. On weekdays, the local cinemas were making the most of the newest films. On Sunday 13 March, the International Bible Students Association hosted a rally in the Town Hall. And the churches, of course, all had their regular services.[39] Nevertheless, the crowds continued to flock to hear, and see, Van Eyk.

On Sunday 20 March, the final day of the campaign, 42 persons were baptized by immersion in the local river, a service witnessed by huge crowds.[40] By May of that year, some 300 people attended a church picnic, and within a few months, there were 200 members and 100 Sunday School children in regular fellowship. Between 30 and 50 people attended week night tarrying meetings with nearly 100 receiving the Spirit in the first year. Crowds of up to one thousand attended their open air meetings.[41] Like those before him, Burns was captivated by the two evangelists. 'Oh! How our hearts have grown to love these two dear servants of God as they have poured themselves out in service day by day in our midst,' he enthused. 'Of our dear Brother Van Eyk as a preacher of the glorious truths of the gospel one cannot speak too highly. He is, indeed, a ministry in demonstration of the Spirit and power.'[42]

Soon after the campaign, letters began to appear in the local press, disputing the claims to healing. A correspondent using the name 'Bible Student' argued that the recoveries were largely the result of suggestion.[43] Burns's response was to provide details of people who had been healed of such complaints as kidney trouble, heart trouble, gall stones, deafness, ulcers and paralysis.[44] Others soon joined in the debate with 'Old Timer' referring to Pentecostal orgies and the current Churches of Christ pastor Alan Price detailing cases of people who had not been healed.[45] Burns continued a steady stream of letters attempting to answer these charges. Then members of the church began to contribute, addressing letters to the editor containing their own experiences of healing.[46]

The debate continued until Van Eyk's return in September. He thrived on the challenge. Newspaper advertisements declared, 'Van Eyk is coming! You must hear this Fearless Preacher of the Living Christ' and the evangelist himself was quoted as saying, 'I have returned to Maryborough as a challenge to my critics on their own ground, not merely a challenge by argument... but by producing facts, substantiating my claims when here earlier in the year.' He went on to describe many cases of healing attributed to his ministry and to engage in a discussion of basic biblical textual criticism—a reflection of a sophistication not normally associated with his kind of evangelism.[47] 'Bible Student' took to his pen again, claiming that the dispute was not over the fact of the cures, but the cause of them, reaffirming his position that they were basically the result of suggestion.[48] Again, Christians responded with testimonials of healing and strong expressions of their faith both in God and Scripture.[49] Meanwhile, the meetings continued with 'exceedingly good audiences.'[50]

Controversial

These meetings in Maryborough demonstrated the controversial nature of the evangelist's ministry. People were either enthusiastic or antagonistic. It was difficult to take the middle ground. They also illustrate Van Eyk's strong conviction that Christianity was a faith to be experienced: and the most telling experience was to be found through the Pentecostal blessing.

Between his two visits to Maryborough, Van Eyk, accompanied by W. A. Buchanan, visited Perth, Western Australia and Brisbane, Queensland. In Perth, although interest was initially outweighed by the visit of the Duke and Duchess of York where over 30,000 people gathered for the opening of the new Parliament House in Canberra, the campaign 'eclipsed all his other Australian meetings'.[51] An enthusiastic report read—

> The trenchant truths of the full gospel were poured forth like a mighty burning lava stream that consumed criticism, withered opposition, exposed and demolished the subtle fingers of the devil, and lifted God's people up to heights where they beheld in the light of Calvary the stupendous possibilities of a church baptized in the Holy Ghost.[52]

There were testimonies of healing, many of a compelling nature. Stories came in of people being healed from paralysis, gall stones, partial blindness, deafness, arthritis, heart trouble, floating kidney, chronic dyspepsia, cancer, consumption, rheumatism, catarrh, gastric ulcers, diabetes, sciatica, gout, varicose ulcers and various complaints such as 'internal troubles' and bodily pain. Some of these afflictions were of many years' standing.[53] James Bell, 68 years of age, waited five months before declaring his healing of a chest complaint of seven years, the result of a bout of pneumonia.[54] Cecil Harris, who founded the National Revival Crusade,[55] told how he had been delivered from 17 years' addiction to nicotine. He never smoked again.[56] Young seven-year-old Leo, one of his two sons, was prayed for by Van Eyk for healing from tonsillitis. Years later he recalled how Van Eyk and Buchanan arrived at their home in a late model Chevrolet. Buchanan walked sedately up the steps, but the athletic Van Eyk vaulted the front fence, mounted the stairs two at a time, picked up the boy, threw him over his shoulder, talked and prayed with him, and left the way he had come.[57]

At the conclusion of the Perth meetings, 48 people were immersed in two separate baptismal services at the Crawley Baths. A Perth layman claimed he had been involved in every evangelistic campaign in Western Australia for the previous 30 years, but had never seen anything to compare with Van Eyk's ministry. 'Behind this man's message there is a spiritual power,' he declared.[58]

Florrie Mortomore had already started small meetings in Brisbane's West End. In August and September, 1927, the Bohemia, a disused theatre, in Stanley Street, South Brisbane, previously used for boxing and vaudeville events, and garishly decorated accordingly, was secured for Van Eyk's visit, and in spite of some criticism, night after night, people responded to the preacher's challenge. Van Eyk mainly addressed four themes—conversion, divine healing, the second coming and the baptism in the Holy Spirit. On one Sunday night, 35 people responded to the invitation to follow Christ.[59] The gatherings were so successful that Van Eyk wrote to his wife that the previous night had seen 'the most wonderful meeting we have yet had in Australia.' He went on—

> When I gave the altar call there was a rush for the penitent form. Many of the large audience just fell down in the dust, and began to pray and cry out to God... In about an hour and a half, nine came through to the baptism [i.e. spoke in tongues]... I must tell you of a miraculous healing. A young girl with a terrible hunch back was prayed for... The raised shoulder has dropped four inches, the hunch is diminishing, and the power of God is wonderfully straightening her out. Glory to the living Lamb![60]

For three weeks, this young lady, Ethel Everett, experienced 'invisible operations' during which these changes took place. Two months later, Van Eyk could claim that she was completely whole.[61] There were other reports of healing. A woman whose disease had mystified doctors for sixteen years was free of pain. A man with a dislocated neck was healed. Others testified to healing from catarrh, goitre, dropsy, deafness, blindness, rheumatism, longstanding damage to the vertebrae and numerous other complaints.[62] There were seventy reported conversions in three weeks and then followed a 'memorable mammoth baptismal service' in which 61 people were baptized by immersion in the baths at Wickham Street, Valley, and 31 were baptized in the Spirit. The evangelist exulted that this campaign had 'eclipsed everything yet experienced in Australasia.'[63]

Baptism

Whatever the Pentecostals thought about these events, as far as the Christian public was concerned, the campaign was just one of several options. In the Lyceum Theatre, one A. W. Anderson was preaching on biblical prophecy and the mainline denominations were all strongly advertising their own services. The Monday after the 'mammoth baptismal service,' the *Courier Mail* displayed prominent photos of a procession of Children of Mary, the laying of the foundation stone at St Margaret's School, the anniversary services at St Paul's Church of England and the Bishop-elect of Rockhampton. It also carried news of a Baptist Garden Party, St Andrew's fete and a Church of England fete, but there was no reference to the baptisms.[64]

Nevertheless, there were possibly more people immersed that day than in any previous single Christian service in Australia's history. The result was a congregation of about 200 enthusiastic people, engaged in a regular program of services at the Druid's Hall, open air meetings, magazine distribution and Sunday School work.[65] The spirit of Pentecost was very much in evidence. Langley Simmons, a converted Jew, was so enthused he thought these meetings might induce 'a mighty revival in Queensland which nothing can stem.'[66]

F B Van Eyk baptizing people in Toowoomba Baths, Qld, March 1928. (Source, GN, 19.7).

In Rockhampton, the story was the same. There were evangelistic rallies for nearly two months, the last three weeks of meetings being held in the Congregational church. Van Eyk reported—

> ...the healings supersede those of any previous campaign, both in percentage and greatness. One young girl, terribly deformed was prayed for...; her left shoulder blade has now dropped nearly six inches, and whereas, owing to the large hump and deformity on her back, the ridge of the spine could never be seen, yet now it is clearly discernible... It is her grandmother who has been healed from 47 years of paralysis. And there are more mighty healings from deafness, blindness etc... I have not in all my ministry seen such mighty baptisms [in the Spirit]... The hunger of these seekers is unique; some of them remain six or seven hours on their knees seeking... One can hardly describe the solemnity and grandeur of the presence of God in some of these meetings. The power of God would surge through us and sweep over the meeting like a mighty gale, while people would just sit in their seats not wanting to go...'[67]

J. H. Smith, the Congregational minister was equally enthused—

> I have worked with many ministers and preachers, but never have I worked with a man such as Mr Van Eyk. From the commencement of the campaign to its close, there have been manifest his unswerving loyalty to his Lord, his utter consecration to the work, his faithful and fearless presentation of the Gospel of salvation, and his earnest desire to win men and women for the Lord. His Scriptural basis is sound. His is the powerful preaching of a man filled with the Holy Ghost, proclaiming a risen Lord... A noticeable feature of his preaching is the exultation of Jesus Christ, and he demonstrates the fact that men and women can walk with the risen Lord without splitting hairs over obscure doctrines.[68]

At the conclusion of the campaign, 45 people were baptized in water in the Corporation Baths 'in the presence of the Mayor and Mayoress of the city and other interested members of the public.'[69] Within six months, Smith had left the

Congregational church and was pastor of the new AFM congregation in Rockhampton.[70]

Cairns

That same year, Carl Lewis (Charlie) Kajewski, the leader of a small Pentecostal group associated with Good News Hall, and his wife Bessie, having 'faithfully tithed their money,'[71] invited Van Eyk to visit Cairns, in Far North Queensland. Van Eyk arrived, together with Hines Retchford, of Adelaide, as his song leader.[72] On the opening night, 8 January 1928, in the Palace Theatre, in Lake Street, 1000 people turned up![73] Van Eyk preached on 'The Continuous Progressive Revelation of God to Man' or the 'Evolution of Divine Healing.' The 15 cm, two column notice in the *Cairns Post* announced, 'This is your opportunity, come and hear the message, and be Healed [sic], why suffer longer?'[74] The local newspaper described the evangelist's methods as 'original' and his exposition 'unorthodox', but the outline of his message indicates a systematic and consistent approach to Scripture. Perhaps the 'originality' lay in the fact that Van Eyk boldly informed his large congregation that he had come to Cairns to demonstrate that 'God was still the living God' and that before a week was out, there would be verifiable cases of divine healing in Cairns.

The evangelist's commitment to the Scripture was made clear. It was God's Word and he believed it. Those nations which had cast it aside, like France and Russia, had plunged into dissipation and depravity. Britain, on the other hand, by honoring the Scripture, was 'the highest amongst the respected countries of the world'. Yet Scripture was not only to be believed: it was also to be experienced. Divine healing was revealed in the Bible from the days of the Exodus through to the New Testament. The healing covenant was 'perfected in the vicarious death of Jesus Christ on Calvary's Cross and subsequently placed in the church as a perpetual gift by the Holy Spirit'. He challenged any minister to prove from the Scriptures that healing gifts had been withdrawn. Why wasn't the Church still ministering healing to the sick and needy? A girl in Adelaide had been healed of 'apoplectic fits.' A Brisbane girl being treated by two physicians had recovered. People in Maryborough and Rockhampton had experienced God's healing power.[75] The Word of God was foundational, but it was being presented in the spirit of Pentecost.

F.B.Van Eyk baptismal service, Freshwater Creek, Cairns, 1928.

The Mission continued over subsequent weeks. Van Eyk preached mostly on the Second Coming, world events and divine healing. On Friday night 13 January the message was again devoted to healing. During the address, Van Eyk declared, 'I will prove that the Word of God is true.' He asked who in the audience was suffering pain, and began to pray for them. According to the press report, the first person was 'instantly healed' and 'a wave of enthusiasm swept over the audience.'[76] Soon others were claiming relief from pain and distress. The result was that testimonies of healing were reported daily.[77]

His theme on Sunday 22 January was a denunciation of Roman Catholicism as the scarlet-clad mother of harlots; on another night, it was 'Jubilee'. 'Surely we heard the bells ringing,' said Bessie.[78] Instead of the usual listing among the churches in *Good News,* the Cairns entry now read, 'GREAT REVIVAL at CAIRNS, Hundreds saved—many healed.'[79] People in the streets were now friendly and cordial and whole families were coming to God.

Van Eyk continued to preach on the Second Coming.[80] On 29 January, the 'Cleansing Power of the Blood' was 'chemically demonstrated' and the newspaper editor was 'awestruck' at the way business men and prominent citizens respected Van Eyk.[81] Later Bessie Kajewski wrote—

> At times I could hardly believe that our brother was facing a Cairns audience; surely these keenly-interested people who sat forward in their seats couldn't be our indifferent citizens...
>
> The people are positively gripped. It is a joy to see the rapt expression as they listen to the blessed message. They have never heard anything like it before, and they come night after night, hungry for more.[82]

Finally, on 30 January, it was announced that the most important stage of the campaign had been reached. Now Van Eyk was going to address the theme of the baptism in the Holy Spirit. There were meetings from Tuesday to Friday night in the Hibernian Hall, with the daily consultations continuing. On Sunday 5 February, the evangelist chose the unusual topic of 'The Great Pyramid' which, he claimed, foretold 'the date of every event in English History since 1840... with amazing accuracy' including the start of the Great War.[83] After six weeks, the campaign came to an end on 12 February, with dozens testifying to conversion or restoration to health or baptism in the Holy Spirit. The campaign concluded with a baptismal service at Freshwater Creek, four miles north of the city, a farewell social and a closing Sunday night rally on one of the evangelist's 'greatest themes'—'Decision.'[84] For the baptisms, a special train was provided from the Central Station and according to Jesse Deacon, they had the foresight to engage two local police who were 'urgently needed to control the immense crowd.' He noted that the interest of hundreds of people had evidently been sufficiently aroused for them to want to witness 'such an old-time Gospel scene enacted in public view.' Thirty-seven believers were immersed. Others had apparently thought about joining them, but at the last minute, held back.[85] Bessie Kajewski was deeply moved—

> I'll never forget that scene; it was grand to see the ever-increasing courage of those who obeyed [the Lord], and their obedience made a great impression upon many of those around... The people of Cairns do not realize how deeply they have been stirred.'[86]

A subsequent report claimed—

> In many respects more wonderful things were witnessed than in any preceding Mission, and Brother Van Eyk declared it to be the high-water mark of his labors [sic] up till that time.[87]

The home meetings now became a church. Sunday services were conducted in the Oddfellows' Hall and the Sunday School at the Deacon house increased significantly. Further campaign meetings were planned for the Atherton tableland and Townsville. Van Eyk's preaching on the imminence of the Second Coming was so effective that Jesse Deacon wondered whether there would be sufficient time before the Lord's return for the Atherton and Townsville meetings to be held!

The local meetings continued in Cairns. Over the next two months, another 45 people were baptized in water. Regular 'instruction meetings' and 'waiting meetings' were held and one by one people received the Spirit and spoke in tongues. Sunday morning and evening services and mid-week Bible studies were conducted weekly.[88]

From Cairns, the party went to Toowoomba where meetings were held in the Princess Theatre. Again, the testimonies rolled in. People reported healing from tumors, gallstones, poor eyesight, catarrh, kidney trouble, headaches, rheumatism, bronchial problems, neuritis, deafness, rupture and heart trouble. Some 80 people were baptized in water in the Toowoomba baths, over 70 spoke in tongues, including eight out of ten in one family, and there were 300 reported conversions. Not everyone was impressed. Rowdy elements interrupted the meetings and rocks were thrown on the roof. Some of these people were stirred up, claimed P. B. Swenson, by 'a devil's agent and false shepherds.' But whether the local clergy were supportive or no, 'the side of Jesus won all the way.' Swenson was full of enthusiasm. 'Glory to God!' he wrote. 'Such blessed times are the outcome.'[89]

Difficulties

The evangelist himself found it a strain on his health and had to terminate his meetings for a time so he could rest. Nevertheless, a fully-fledged church was established and 'glorious open-air services' were conducted.[90] Van Eyk moved on to Ipswich and then Townsville and Mackay.[91] He was faced with some daunting requests. A returned soldier removed his glass eye and asked the evangelist to pray for a new one. A man with no teeth asked for a third set. In both cases, he prayed 'not even flinching'.[92] In Townsville, on 15 July, some 60 people were baptized at Picnic Bay, Magnetic Island. By September 1928, the Apostolic Faith Mission had grown sufficiently in Queensland for a State Advisory Committee to be set up and a conference to be held. Thirty eight delegates were present.[93]

Van Eyk's public notoriety may have been increasing, but there were difficulties in his personal life. When he and his family had first arrived in Australia, they had been received with love and admiration. Tributes were paid not only to the evangelist, but also to his wife Cecilia. Lancaster wrote—

In her are combined all the qualities required in the wife of an evangelist. Quiet, unassuming, affable, and accomplished, she stands unflinchingly with her husband, always on hand when wanted, and never too tired for service for her King.[94]

Cecilia was also appointed an evangelist with the Apostolic Faith Mission and sometimes assisted Van Eyk in his preaching ministry,[95] People came to her for counsel and healing. One lady told how Cecilia had laid her hands on her head and 'the power of God went surging and tingling through her body, encircling the affected part', resulting in her immediate healing.[96] Another had a vision of being prayed for by 'Sister Van Eyk,' a vision that was fulfilled.[97] Cecilia was also a soloist. After his return to India in 1927, and still grieving over the death of his wife, missionary H. N. Todd wrote—

All the time Sister Van Eyk's solo which she sang so sweetly is ringing in my ears: 'I will never leave thee, I will not forsake thee.' I praise God for it—and ask her to send me the words and music. They are a complete strength to me.[98]

Cecilia joined the evangelist in Maryborough in 1927 and preached there.[99] 'Undoubtedly our sister is a tower of strength and help to her husband,' wrote George Burns, 'and her consecrated talents will be much used of God for His glory in the future.'[100] On New Year's Eve, 1927, with her little daughter Faith in her arms, Cecilia led a band of women into the streets singing Christian songs before the reveling crowds.[101] But then she experienced a break down in health. Incompatible as it seems with other people's impressions, Bert Banton, who later worked closely with Van Eyk, claimed that she displayed 'signs of hereditary insanity'.[102] In late 1928, she returned, with her children, to South Africa. Five years later, Lancaster published a brief notice that 'friends of Sister Van Eyk will be glad to know that she is well again,' together with an address for correspondence. Eventually, however, she was to be confined to an institution.[103]

A year before her breakdown, Lancaster had published an unusually frank and serious appeal for prayer—

We believe the man in Australia who is most in need of your prayers today is the popular Evangelist, F. B. Van Eyk...

The change from being an insignificant unit in a community to the role of an eagerly and widely sought after evangelist, approved by God by the mighty signs and wonders wrought by him in the midst of the people, is one which places him in a precarious position; for the plaudits of the people are likely to become a dangerous asset; many of God's favored [sic] and gifted messengers have fallen through pride. So, beloved, do not fail to surround him with such a wall of prayer that satan [sic] and all his hosts shall find it impossible to break through.[104]

This was an extraordinary thing to put in print. It almost amounted to an accusation of arrogance on the part of Van Eyk. Had Lancaster observed warning signs? Did she see Cecilia's return as leaving Van Eyk vulnerable? Were there already indications of reckless behaviour? Was it womanly perception or an intuitive premonition? Or was it a telling example of the kind of spiritual insight that she herself prized so highly? Whatever the explanation, her words sounded a prophetic warning that was to be tragically fulfilled.

When Van Eyk and Buchanan left Maryborough, some 500 people had come to farewell them. There was 'a mass of weeping people thronging the evangelists and kissing their hands when they could not get close enough to kiss their faces.' Later, one disenchanted pastor claimed that Van Eyk gave special attention to the touches of the girls.[105] During his convalescence in Toowoomba Van Eyk was nursed by Hilda Kajewski, whose family were all involved in the work there, and who had been among the first to receive the Spirit.[106] The two became close friends. Soon rumours began to spread that the relationship was more than platonic. The newly established church in Toowoomba was split in two. Later, when Van Eyk attempted to conduct tent meetings in Bell Street, the tent was burnt down. Crowds continued to flock to his meetings, now transferred to various halls, including the Princess Theatre. But again there was a rising tide of discontent. Rotten eggs were thrown, people tried to break up the meetings. Banton was later to describe what happened as 'the fiercest physical opposition and persecution' he had ever witnessed. In the views of others, the meetings were marked by such extreme emotionalism, the reaction was predictable.[107]

The Assemblies of God

The Queensland pastors were forced to intervene. On 25 October 1928 and 8 January 1929, the Queensland Advisory Council of the AFM met with Van Eyk 'to strongly advise him to alter his ways in a certain direction.' However, the evangelist 'disregarded the advice.'[108] They reported this to the Executive Council who decided that Van Eyk should no longer be allowed to minister under the auspices of the AFM, unless he arranged for his wife and family to return to Australia and for her to accompany him in his campaigns. Finally, the 1929 Conference of the Mission in Melbourne was forced to erase Van Eyk's name from membership of the Council and of the AFM. The printed report of these resolutions is dispassionate, but it is not hard to imagine the blend of anger, disappointment, betrayal, grief and sorrow that lay behind them. The way Van Eyk was going, he could have left scores of churches all over Australia. Now the work was seemingly struck a devastating blow from which it might never recover. *Good News* would never again print a report of a Van Eyk crusade.

Gleefully, and with unusual piety, Sydney's *Truth* proclaimed—

> Van Eyk has been hounded out of Queensland by irate and respectable citizens... The [Apostolic Faith] Mission was... forced to listen to the reports that this missioner, this 'Shepherd of God,' a married man, was driving around in a motor car with an attractive young girl, the daughter of one of his parishioners with whom he stayed.[109]

On 5 July 1929, seventeen Queensland pastors met together in Brisbane. Charles Enticknap, whose assembly in Mackay had only been accepted into the AFM the previous October, moved that they adopt the name Assemblies of God, a motion carried by 15 votes to two. A doctrinal statement and constitution were approved.[110]

Charles Enticknap baptizing in the Johnston River, Innisfail, Qld, 1937.

Members of Van Eyk's family affirm the evangelist's innocence. His eldest son, though only a child of ten at the time, said, 'Many things have been said about him, but I don't believe them. He was a tremendous man and I am proud to be his son.'[111] The evangelist's brother was unflinching—

There is no truth whatsoever in the charges laid against him. Nothing unseemly happened at all. His wife's condition was such that the marriage was impossible. He tried as long and as hard as he could, but it just couldn't work. These are the facts I'm telling you. This is the truth.'[112]

Van Eyk himself continued to protest his integrity. Five years later, a Pentecostal journal reported that the Executive Council [of the Apostolic Faith Mission?] in South Africa had 'thoroughly investigated' the affair and that 'after negotiating with him for a few hours, the Council unanimously agreed that our brother has suffered much wrong...'[113] Van Eyk had put it to them that after his wife and children had returned to South Africa, the newspapers had taken advantage of the situation to attack him.[114] He would have had a harder time of it persuading the newly formed Assemblies of God in Queensland.

Van Eyk did finally agree to bring his family back to Australia and set out from Melbourne on the *S. S. Bendigo* for South Africa. When he reached Adelaide, South Australia, however, in response to what he saw as divine guidance, he disembarked.[115] There he teamed up with Albert Banton, and they held a few meetings. C. L. Greenwood of the newly formed Pentecostal Church of Australia (PCA), at Richmond Temple in Melbourne, invited them to attend an Easter Convention there. Given that earlier criticism of Good News Hall's distinctive doctrines and female leadership had come from Greenwood, and that Van Eyk had chosen to identify with them from the beginning, there seems to be a degree of opportunism in this decision—especially at Easter, the time of the AFM's annual conference.[116]

Cessnock

From here, Van Eyk and Banton continued to Parkes, NSW,[117] and thence to the coal mining town of Cessnock, bearing a letter of introduction to the Mayor of Cessnock from the Mayor of Parkes. In 1929, Cessnock was in the throes of unrest. On 15 February, miners were locked out when they refused to accept a reduction in the hewing rate. The dispute was not resolved until June of the following year.[118] Sydney newspapers carried almost daily reports of demonstrations by miners, of unemployment, of picketing, of employer-employee confrontation.[119]

When Van Eyk arrived, he sought and obtained the cooperation of both the local Methodist minister and the Salvation Army captain.[120] Plans were made for publicity and the hiring of the Strand Picture Theatre. One morning, Banton and Van Eyk found an angry meeting of miners in progress in the Theatre. There was some talk of violence and one man declared, 'We don't need any Father, Son and Holy Ghost—the union is our Father, Son and Holy Ghost.' With characteristic audacity, Van Eyk asked to address the meeting from his experience of mining disputes in South Africa. At the conclusion he sang them a gospel song! It was well chosen—lyrics by William Booth's grandson, William Booth-Clibborn ('Down from His Glory') and a well-known melody with whom people would readily identify ('O Sole Mio'). Banton recalled—

Cessnock welcome to F B Van Eyk on his return from South Africa. Photo, Gathering Call.

> The crowd were completely captivated and swept by the tide of God's love released in the song. They clamoured for more. He sang another verse and chorus; again, thunderous applause. More than that, the whole purpose of the meeting was defeated and as... we departed ... we heard one of the speakers frantically trying to get the meeting back to order saying, 'We don't want any of this Utopian dope! We don't want pie in the sky!' But it was of no avail. A crisis had passed.[121]

There was a meeting at the Salvation Army Hall on Tuesday 4 June for interested parties to meet the evangelist. The opening public rally was held in the Strand Picture Theatre on Sunday 9 June, with Alderman Hunter, the mayor of Cessnock in the chair and Van Eyk preaching on the theme, 'The Present Industrial Crisis (World Wide); Its Solution and Biblical Parallel, and Prophetic Significance.'[122] One hundred men stood to their feet in response to a challenge to consecrate their lives to God in the fight against sin.

People crowded to the meetings and there were notable conversions. Within a week the theatre was comfortably full with some 600 attending a healing meeting. On Sunday 16 June, the *Cessnock Eagle* reported that 'as the appeal was made, the whole audience as one man leaped to their feet expressing their desire to be ready when Jesus comes again.'[123] Some miners confessed to having made bombs which they had intended to use against the mine owners, but had now dismantled. People began to claim healing from various physical complaints.

For six weeks, Van Eyk's campaign continued in the Methodist Hall or the Strand Theatre. People arrived at 5 pm queuing up night after night with blankets and rugs, waiting for the doors to open. The *Cessnock Eagle* was enthusiastic—

> During the last week, scenes which defy description have been witnessed in Cessnock by many hundreds. Hundreds revived and saved from a life of indifference and sin, whilst many have been healed from all kinds of maladies. The city is in the grip of a religious fervour and enthusiasm which has no parallel in its history. Every night many can be seen at the altar seeking salvation and healing for their bodies.[124]

One meeting at the Methodist Hall lasted from 7 pm to 11.30 pm. Several claimed to have their sight restored. One woman was able to walk for the first time in seven years. A girl who had never taken a step unaided did so freely after a steel frame was removed from her leg. People responded to these events with singing, dancing, waving handkerchiefs in the air and shouts of joy. 'Cessnock is now in the throes of a religious revival,' wrote a local reporter. He described the 'most extraordinary scenes' and meetings which were 'growing in power, wonder and intensity'. There was a stream of testimonials to divine healing from various afflictions including deafness, goitre, poor eyesight, lameness and asthma. Overall, some 700 people made commitments to Christ. Crowds of between two and three thousand people were gathering for each rally.[125] In a community of around 14,000 people,[126] this represented at least 15% of the population. Towards the end of the series, on 4 July, a baptismal service was held in which 73 people were baptized.[127] This event aroused a great deal of interest. The Theatre was crowded and the service had to be cut short because of people crowding around the orchestra pit (which had been modified for the inclusion of a baptismal tank) for a better view. Later an offering was taken to pay for damages to the seating.[128] Banton recalls how some opponents of the campaign secreted Condy's crystals into the water, resulting in reports to the effect that Van Eyk baptized in red water while he, Banton, led the congregation in 'Wash me in the blood of the Lamb'.[129] Years later, a journalist named Frank Mattocks admitted to being responsible. 'It was worth it,' he recalled.[130]

There seems no reason to doubt these reports, although it is of interest that the newspapers made no mention of the incident. Sydney's irreverent *Truth* contained almost a full page feature headed, 'Drowning the Devil in a Two-foot tub!' with sub-headings which continued, 'Stop Van Eyk's balderdash! How cheeky quack, Duck-pond expert, has pulled Cessnock's leg. Uproarious assault on Old Nick.'[131] Accompanying photos showed people being baptized. The article went on with a brief report of the evangelist's work in Queensland, including a claim that residents of Mackay had ducked him before evicting him from town and that he was 'specially gentle' in baptizing girls.

The Melbourne *Argus* was scathing—

> A few women showed signs of hysteria… Others shouted and screamed… The proceedings got out of hand at one stage, and the ceremony had to be suspended until order was restored… One of the men fainted when he was baptized.[132]

Although some reporters came looking for things to criticize, one who, like Goldsmith's fool, came to scoff, remained to pray. Later he became a Foursquare pastor.[133]

By this stage, the early euphoria began to wane in some quarters. The reports in the *Cessnock Eagle* became less supportive and a touch of scepticism began to emerge. Young men invaded the meetings and let off fireworks during the proceedings. There were regular interjections. Van Eyk himself spoke of increasing persecution.[134] It seems likely that it was the first occurrences of glossolalia that alienated some people. Rev Evans, the Methodist minister, certainly found this phenomenon difficult to accept and offered to pay the hospital ten pounds if Van Eyk could produce one convert with genuine spiritual gifts; otherwise, the evangelist should pay. Van Eyk gladly accepted the challenge.[135] Letters now began to appear in the press denouncing glossolalia as 'gibbering foolishly' and 'blasphemy'.[136]

Although Van Eyk had begun his crusade by seeking the cooperation of existing churches, the baptismal service created a further difficulty for them as Methodists were not in the habit of practising adult baptism and the Salvation Army did not baptize at all. The Rev L. Ayescough, of the Church of England,[137] was affronted by the goings on. 'Sensationalism in religion,' he said, 'is a danger to the community.' He pitied those in whom sensationalism aroused a temporary enthusiasm which they confused with the Holy Spirit. And those who practiced re-baptism should consider whether they were not leading souls straight into the mouth of hell.[138]

When Van Eyk announced that he intended to establish a church, the rift was complete. Captain Franks of the Salvation Army took the stage at one of the rallies and alleged that Van Eyk had broken his word. They had supported him on the understanding that he did not intend to establish a church but now he was doing just that. Van Eyk replied, 'This man has gone around town saying things about me that I could put him behind prison bars for. He has withdrawn from the campaign without any intimation to me, and therefore it is my duty to look after the spiritual welfare of my converts myself.'[139] According to Banton's loyal report—

> The Salvation Army officers and the Methodist Minister got stirred up because we told the people God's plan of salvation... and the Truth of God's word cut across their traditions.[140]

This was clearly an oversimplification. As a gesture of good will, Van Eyk raised over fifteen pounds for the local hospital at a second baptismal service and later another thirty pounds for poor and distressed families. Meanwhile, the crowds continued to throng to the rallies, the ministers continued to distance themselves from the evangelist, and *The Cessnock Eagle* continued to publish letters by both supporters and detractors.

Now reports began to surface of the incident in Toowoomba, with the Methodist minister stating that Van Eyk had been dismissed from the Apostolic Faith Mission for not altering his ways 'in a certain direction'.[141] Van Eyk replied to the allegations by affirming that the Brisbane congregation of the AFM had stood by him and were convinced that the matter was a 'domestic' one which should not have been made public. As Van Eyk fell short of stating outright that he was innocent of the charges laid against him, Evans, reasonably enough, found this less than satisfactory.[142]

Elim Foursquare Church

On Sunday, 25 August 1929, the Cessnock Foursquare Temple was opened. Formerly 'Ezzy's Reliance Motor Works' in North Avenue, it was now dedicated as a place of worship. Hundreds of people were present and another 36 were immersed.[143] The building seated about 500 with provision for a choir of 60 and an orchestra of 10. Pastor E. Hooker was appointed as minister and a full program of meetings launched—

Sunday 10.30 am Breaking of Bread
3.00 pm Sunday School (300 children)
6.00 pm Open Air Meeting
7.00 pm Gospel Meeting

Monday Open Air Meeting at Bellbird
Cottage Prayer Meeting at the home of Brother and Sister Harris

Tuesday Teaching on Baptism in Water and Baptism in the Spirit

Wednesday Prayer and Tarrying Meeting for Baptism in the Spirit

Thursday Teaching on Divine Healing and Prayer for the sick

Friday Open Air Meeting in Vincent Street

Saturday Choir Practice.[144]

Office Bearers and Choir of Four Square Gospel Church, Brisbane, c. 1929.

There was some suggestion that Van Eyk's meetings had turned the tide of unrest in Cessnock and prevented an outbreak of violence.[145] But by the end of the year, the lockout continued, culminating in the Rothbury confrontation in the Hunter Valley in December, where one man was shot and others wounded. Socially and politically, the situation worsened.[146]

Van Eyk continued to campaign in other places. Soon there

Foursquare congregation at Newcastle, NSW, 1934. Photo, Gathering Call.

were Foursquare churches in many parts of New South Wales including Newtown, Orange, Molong, Parkes, Newcastle, Peakhurst, Auburn and Hurstville.[147] A magazine was launched in May 1932 called the *Elim Foursquare Gospel Express*. In September of the same year it was renamed *The Gathering Call*. The initial conference of the Foursquare Churches was held that year at Easter. Van Eyk wrote that 'never in all life's experiences had he witnessed such marvellous scenes as on that occasion.' The following year, Van Eyk was to describe himself as 'head of the greatest Pentecostal work in Australia.'[148] However, stories about the evangelist's past continued to circulate and he returned to South Africa on 9 August 1933 to bring back his family. When they arrived in Australia in July, 1934, they were given a glowing reception. *The Gathering Call* declared in bold print, 'Welcome to our Principal, To his dear Wife and Family.'[149]

By 1935, additional meetings had commenced in the provincial towns of Gympie, Lithgow, Armidale, Brisbane and Toowoomba where '70 Pentecostal saints' who had 'remained true to their first love, despite the difficulties' met with Van Eyk.[150] In Gympie, many people were converted; there was also persecution, with rotten fruit being thrown at the Pentecostals while they met together.[151] The Lithgow meetings were exceptional. In February, 1935, after four weeks of discouraging response, and 'many days spent in prayer and fasting,' there was a change in attitudes and 'a mighty break came'. Within a few days, one thousand people attended a special rally. There was an influx of converts and some remarkable healings claimed—from tuberculosis, paralysis, severe burns, blindness, ulcers, heart disease, influenza, visual impairment and appendicitis. A week later, 55 people were baptized by immersion in the town hall, which was 'packed to suffocation'. Some of these, so impressed by what they saw, came after the official service and requested baptism there and then. Van Eyk could not bring things to a close till after one o'clock the next morning.[152]

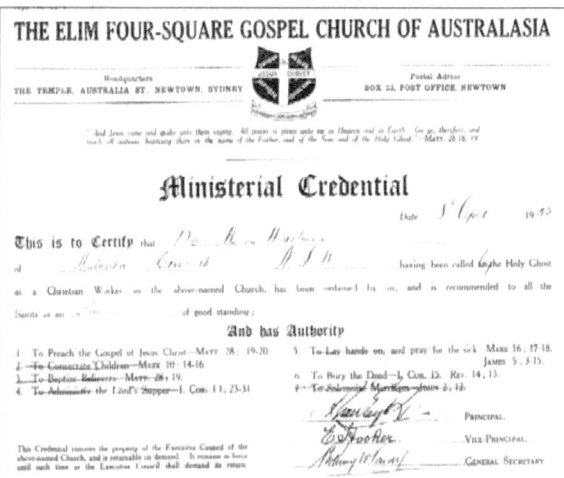

Copy of Foursquare Worker's credential issued to Stan Wheatman and signed by F.B.Van Eyk.

The evangelists were kept busy night and day, as people called on them for counsel and instruction. Within two months they had purchased and renovated a building for the new church and on 6 April 1935, it was opened 'amid scenes of delight and joy'.[153] Again, the spirit of Pentecost had proved to have exceptional drawing power.

The 1927 campaign in Perth had resulted in a more established assembly with a partner church at Fremantle. Ten years later, however, there was potential division. The State Administrator, Lieutenant-colonel T. J. Bentley (1899–1937), asked the pastor, Frederick Hammond, to move to Bunbury and he refused. Ever the innovator, Van Eyk flew from Sydney. The squabble became public, and the *Western Australian* described Van Eyk as pouring 'oil on troubled waters.'[154] Meanwhile Van Eyk began yet another campaign. The newspaper tribute was lavish, to say the least—

> Known throughout several countries as 'The Prince of Preachers,' Evangelist Van Eyk... is acknowledged to be one of the mightiest Men of God this age has produced and whenever he appears some of the largest halls have proved incapable of holding the thousands who flock to hear him.
>
> Brilliant and accomplished, his unique African songs, his magnetic personality, his incomparable command of Prophetic Scripture, his melody from the latest 'electric guitar' producing pure pipe organ effect, his indisputable 'Gift' of Healing, and his definite determination to give God Alone the glory, has [sic] endeared him to all.[155]

Then followed a strong, but carefully worded invitation to people to bring their sick friends and relatives to the meetings, to witness miracles of divine healing and to hear Van Eyk present 'amazing lectures.' Those who were 'in earnest' would be healed.[156]

Not everyone was convinced. L. G. Burgin, a Churches of Christ pastor challenged Van Eyk to a debate on the subject of healing.[157] According to Bentley's son, Burgin resorted to sarcasm and personal ridicule and Van Eyk presented a biblical approach in an unruffled manner.[158] At least one other person found deficiencies on both sides. The following week Pastor W. Rhodes Scragg 'reviewed' the event and offered 'a scriptural reply to both debaters.'[159]

Death

On the home front, matters were deteriorating. Van Eyk's marriage slid further into decline and he returned to South Africa where he obtained a divorce, leaving his children in Australia. His own health broke down and Hilda Kajewski went to join him. Within a year they were married. Five months later, in July 1939, Van Eyk and his brother were hunting when they were both bitten by a tse-tse fly and contracted trypanosomiasis. Van Eyk persistently refused medication, believing that as he had encouraged others to trust God, he should do the same. It was to prove a costly stand. His new bride recalled—

> The doctors came every week and tried to persuade him to take treatment, they impressed the seriousness of the disease upon us, and said that it was impossible to live, unless he had injections, but he firmly refused. He said that for over twenty years he had preached divine healing, telling others how they must trust the Lord and that now the test had come to him and he would trust God ... If anyone ever suggested treatment to him he used to say, 'Never! Never! If God doesn't want to heal me, then I'm prepared to answer His call...[160]

He recovered sufficiently to preach again in a four-weeks campaign in Pretoria,[161] but on 21 December, at the age of 44, he died.[162]

Opinions about Van Eyk still vary greatly. Although acknowledging the large crowds that attended his Cessnock meetings and the public baptisms, Alan Walker describes the phenomenon as 'mass-revivalism' and Van Eyk as a 'charlatan in religion'.[163] Bob James strongly agrees.[164]

Given that the essence of charlatanism is an intention to deceive, this charge is hardly plausible. There is nothing about Van Eyk's ministry which suggests that he deliberately set about to trick or mislead people. Clearly, he himself firmly believed what he taught. The fact that he was willing to die rather than go against his own preaching is the most telling witness to his sincerity. Further testimony of his genuineness was his practice of intense and earnest prayer. Van Eyk would spend hours at night on his knees or prostrate on the floor of his room crying out in an agony of desperation for the salvation of souls.[165] Not that he was without fault. As we have already noted, he was plainly prone to exaggeration. While this may be a weakness, it does not mark him as a deceiver.

F.B. Van Eyk's eldest son Neil at his father's grave in Benoni, South Africa.

Methodology

He was also extravagant in his methodology. Like Jonathan Edwards, he believed that a religion that does not touch the affections is no true religion.[166] He expected people to *experience* God. In Lithgow—

> Everywhere people were experiencing the outpouring of the Spirit: in their private homes, away from the meeting places, wondering, marvelling, amazed at what was happening...
>
> Amidst scenes of the wildest enthusiasm, doubts, misgivings, fears, joys and other mingled emotions on the part of many interested, the Evangelist cried with stentorian voice: 'This is that.' Shouts of 'Glory' met his declarations, during which time many decided for Christ...
>
> Never in the history of the Elim Foursquare Gospel Church, with probably Cessnock as an exception, have we witnessed such scenes of wonder, glory, awe and mighty salvation and baptisms in the Holy Spirit with rejoicings as at Lithgow.[167]

As in Cessnock, there was opposition from some Church leaders and criticism of the extravagant expressions of emotion. But for Van Eyk it was the spirit of Pentecost at its best.

People had very different responses to his ministry. The *Truth* had this to say about one of the Cessnock meetings—

> Van Eyk, when saying a prayer, works himself up into a veritable frenzy. Dramatic gasps, sob stuff, and all the well-known artifices of humbugs of this kind are exploited in his appeal to the congregation to turn away from sin.
>
> With arms outstretched, and loud Hallelujahs, the evangelist has kept the bulk of the large crowds highly amused with his acrobatics. Dancing in a circle, and at the conclusion of some of his hymns, during which the converts at his signal, frantically wave their handkerchiefs in a circle over their heads, Van Eyk jumps four feet into the air...
>
> It was all hallelujahs, with a few amens thrown in, but the choir clapped hands and banged tambourines and put it over well.
>
> They got an encore. There was a hankie-waving finale. There was no spare time, the moments being filled in with 'hallelujahs' full of fervour from the converts.[168]

It is helpful to compare this with a report of the Newcastle campaign, written by a sympathetic reporter—

> As one after another was healed, the beloved Evangelist lifted his hand and cried, 'Friends, haven't we got a wonderful Jesus?' Oh, what a storm of applause met this exclamation! Pent up feelings broke loose with fervent Amens, Hallelujahs and hand clapping and, yes, tears not of sorrow but of joy and thankfulness... After two weeks' ministry on the Baptism of the Holy Spirit, with evidence of a flowing intensity in each succeeding meeting, a culminating point was reached on Friday last when, at the first initiation, nearly one hundred people literally rushed to the altar, and falling on their knees cried out to God to baptize them with the Holy Spirit. He truly opened the window of heaven and poured out mighty blessings on all.[169]

Van Eyk was an exciting, vigorous, demonstrative, controversial preacher who believed in an experiential faith. The people who attended his rallies were enthusiastic and fervent. If the emotive language is removed from both reports, especially the first one, there is little to object to—and perhaps much to be thankful for.[170] To suggest that Van Eyk was knowingly manipulative is to read too much into the available evidence. On the other hand, he

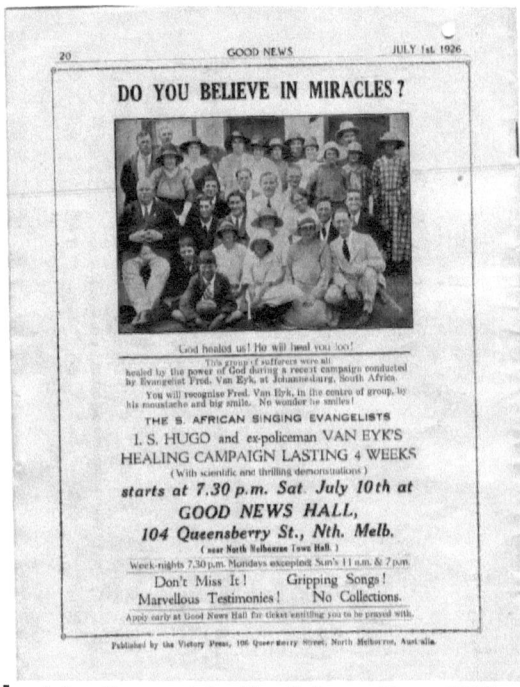

Advertisement for Van Eyk meetings, 1926.

was not afraid of emotion—it is clear that he saw it as a valid part of religious experience.[171]

Flamboyant he may have been, but there is no evidence of the unseemly or dehumanising behaviour that has occurred in other revivalist meetings. Among the 'French Prophets', in some 18th Century American camp meetings, and in come recent extremist charismatic gatherings, phenomena such as jerking, falling to the floor, making animal noises, laughing uncontrollably, groaning, going into trances and in at least one case, snake handling, have all occurred.[172] There is no record of such phenomena in the Van Eyk meetings.[173]

Theology and Epistemology

It is illuminating to read Van Eyk's sermons. They clearly illustrate his knowledge of Scripture, his understanding of Christian doctrine and his fervent love for Christ. The following extract from a message given at Maryborough on 7 October 1927 makes this clear—

> There are thousands of earnest Christians in denominational churches who live an exemplary life but have not yet experienced the fullness of the Pentecostal Blessing; neither do they enjoy the blessing of Divine Healing for the body. Why? Is it because there IS no Baptism of the Holy Ghost? Is it because there IS no healing in the Blessed Name of Jesus? No! A thousand times no! What then is the matter? The simple fact is that these folks have not, as yet, seen that the Word of God promises them healing for their bodies as well as the baptism in the Holy Spirit, and that one receives it exactly in the same way as salvation is received or any other blessing promised in the Word... they do not read the Word sufficiently to understand and appropriate by faith the other glorious promises contained therein...
>
> So, there on that cruel cross of Calvary, in the open eye of the angel-crowded heavens, whilst men trembled and demons howled, rang out the clear, triumphant voice of Jesus Christ, in those immortal words which have echoed and re-echoed in the lives of countless multitudes, 'IT IS FINISHED.' There he took his stand between the dead and the living, there the plague of death was stopped for every true believer. God so loved the dying world, that He gave His only begotten Son, that whosoever believeth on Him should not perish, but have everlasting life (John 3:16).[174]

James, apparently without reference to any of Van Eyk's own writings, seems to have seriously misunderstood the evangelist when he says, 'Van Eyk comes very close to claiming he *is* Jesus Christ in a second coming and he certainly claims he can work miracles.'[175] Even a casual reading of Van Eyk's own words quoted above show this to be absurd. The evangelist plainly proclaimed the Second Coming of Christ as a world-changing future event— indeed this was one of his great themes and he preached on it often.[176] In regard to healing, he was always careful to acknowledge that Christ is the Healer, as the passage just quoted makes plain. It is worth recalling the comments on the evangelist's preaching by the Congregational minister at Rockhampton.[177] He might have been talking about that great evangelist of half a century later, Dr Billy Graham.[178]

Van Eyk placed strong emphasis on the need to be baptized in the Holy Spirit with the initial evidence of speaking with tongues. In 1926, at the beginning of his ministry in Good News Hall, he preached on, 'The Far Reaching Results of the Baptism in the Holy Spirit'.[179] It was an uncompromising message in which he argued that there was a difference between being in the kingdom of Christ and being in the body of Christ. Those who were in the kingdom were redeemed but only those in the 'body' would take part in the first resurrection. It was through baptism in the Spirit that one became part of Christ's body (1 Corinthians 12:13). This required consecration and dedication to the Lord. In 1932, Van Eyk wrote a series of articles on the baptism in the Holy Spirit. He began in startling fashion—

> The Baptism of the Holy Spirit is the greatest event in Christian history; greater than the crucifixion; of greater import than the resurrection; greater than the Ascension; and mightier than the Glorification... The reason? Without it, all the other work would have been in vain.[180]

This statement is significant. It was not enough for Van Eyk that people experience the excitement of crowded rallies, of exuberant singing, of fiery preaching, of enthusiastic testimonies and of loving fellowship. The one experience *par excellence* was baptism in the Holy Spirit. In this matter, Van Eyk reflected the distinctive drawing power of the Pentecostal movement. By enshrining spiritual experience in a mandatory encounter with God, the movement ensured that it was neither optional nor ephemeral. It was insisted on: and there was a readily identifiable sign of it, namely, glossolalia. Subsequent articles by Van Eyk plainly outlined the Pentecostal position in this regard.

Personal Morality

The biggest question mark over Van Eyk lies in the area of his moral conduct. In this regard he was rejected by both sinner and saint alike. Reference has already been made to the actions of the Queensland Advisory Council of the AFM and his subsequent dismissal at the annual conference of the AFM in Melbourne in April 1929.[181]

For Philip Duncan, who for over fifty years served as a Pentecostal pastor, Van Eyk's behaviour was a tragedy—

> The Evangelist was a man of exceptional gifts, and at times displayed feats of audacity in faith. Numbers were saved and miraculously healed as he preached the true full Gospel message. Assemblies sprang up after his campaigns.
>
> I must draw a curtain over his sad history that finished even more sadly. As Samson he evidenced inspired courage and power, as Samson his end was dismal, but we are not his judge...[182]

However, there is little doubt that overall Van Eyk has been adjudged guilty in the affair of 1929. And as a minister of Christ Jesus, there is no doubt that he was. But to what extent? Had there been adultery, he would have been dismissed without question. From its inception, arising as it did partly from the Wesleyan tradition, Pentecostalism strongly emphasised holiness.[183] The fact that Van Eyk was asked only to get his family together again before continuing in ministry indicates that it was a case of indiscretion rather than of immorality. There is some evidence that Buchanan, who was as close to Van Eyk as anyone, did not believe that adultery had taken place, although he strongly urged Van Eyk to change his ways.[184]

It is significant that Hilda Van Eyk, the alleged partner in the offence, seems to have believed he was innocent. Describing his last days, she wrote—

> It is hard for me to realise that my darling has gone. We had such a short time of happiness, only five months,[185] and then he went away on that dreadful shooting trip with his brother...
>
> He lived in the presence of God. Night and day you could hear his voice in prayer or praises to God. Sometimes I'd find him weeping and when I'd ask why he wept, he'd say, 'Oh, Darling, God is so good. His Presence is so wonderful. I'm weeping because I love Him so.' And that's the way he was all through his illness. The last week he was unconscious most of the time, but whenever he came to, his first words were, 'Glory to God'...
>
> He died a hero, being faithful unto death and now he has gone to his reward ... Over a thousand mourners attended his funeral.[186]

In other respects, there were no questions about Van Eyk's moral and ethical values. In all the criticism leveled at him, he was never charged with financial mismanagement, using his position to make money, manipulating people to give to his work or misappropriation of funds.

Outcomes

For Van Eyk, his ultimate justification was the fruit of his ministry—in Cessnock, the ongoing church spoke for itself.[187] How convincing this was as a justification may be queried, on the basis of both logic and fact. According to his detractors, in Cessnock there was actually little continuing support. Reporter Frank Mattocks claimed that 'those who took him seriously were a very small section of the community, a hundred or so.'[188]

Walker indicates that the numbers who remained with the Foursquare Temple were small.[189] Yet according to the 1933 Census figures which he quotes, there were 383 people who belonged to churches other than the major denominations. As Seventh Day Adventists, Christian Scientists and Brethren were already listed separately, and it may be that the majority of these were Foursquare people. It is also possible that some Foursquare adherents were still putting the name of their original denomination in the census return. Walker points out that in 1942, 1,055 attended the various Protestant Sunday services. About half of these were involved in the major Protestant denominations. So the number at the Foursquare Temple may have been significant. Walker points out that 'three of the smaller churches' held regular open air services. One of these would almost certainly have been the Foursquare church.

In September 1930, William Kay became pastor and the next year locked horns with Van Eyk. There was some dispute over 'certain methods of ministry' and the occupancy of the building.[190] Kay, with some of the people, joined the newly founded Apostolic Church (1929). The original pastor (E. Hooker) was reinstated and in May 1932, reported that there had been serious attempts by 'religious charlatans and parasites' to destroy the work, but they had continued to make satisfactory progress. In July, he could say that hundreds stood for hours listening at open air meetings. The regular services were 'wonderfully blessed' and attendances had 'increased considerably'.[191] Van Eyk used to visit the church regularly during 1932. The results were healthy but there was little of the excitement and fervour of the original campaign.

Len Jones, formerly with the Pentecostal Church of Australia, conducted a crusade in January 1933. Over the three weeks period, 'the Temple was filled to capacity on many occasions.' There was great excitement—

Len Jones, c.1900-1974.

> It is almost impossible to describe the scenes which followed. Like a mighty gale the Spirit of God swept over the audience. So gloriously present was the Spirit of God that each one, as hands were laid on them, was smitten down, until scores were prostrated all over the floor under God's Almighty Spirit.[192]

Even Van Eyk could rarely report such a demonstration of power. In August 1934, Don Harris, one of the converts from the 1929 campaign, wrote that the church had never been in 'such a good spiritual way' and that despite cold weather they were experiencing 'wonderful attendances.' When Van Eyk returned from South Africa for a special celebration in 1934, he was greeted with a 'huge crowd'. Some 200 people attended a welcome tea.[193]

What of the long term? Walker offers the dismissive but flimsy assessment that—

> The final result [of Van Eyk's ministry in Cessnock] was that discredit was brought on all religion, and, by adding further division to the already broken ranks of practising Christians within the town, all were weakened.[194]

On the other hand, there are many long-standing Christians today who met Christ through those meetings. Bert Banton's wife Edith was one of the first to be baptized in Cessnock. Over 50 years later she was still serving the Lord.[195] The Foursquare pastor in Orange, NSW, in 1995 was the grandson of a couple converted at Cessnock. In 1979, George Muir could tell of 50 years service in the church since his conversion there in 1929.[196]

To what extent Van Eyk was culpable will no doubt always remain an open question. In reality, it has little bearing on the issue of his integrity as an evangelist. The best preachers are but sinners saved by grace, who minister, not because they have earned the right, but because they believe in the truth of the message they proclaim.

Notes

1. Actual dates are 6 June 1895 to 23 December 1939. See J. K. Wallis, *The Beginnings: an Account of the 1929 Cessnock Revival* (Aberdare: 1989), 58; there is also a photo of his grave in my possession.
2. GN, 17:9, September, 1926, 5; GN, 17:10, October, 1926, 12.
3. GN, June, 1926, 18; Duncan, 'Lecture,' 1965.
4. FGE, 1:3, July, 1932, 14.
5. GN, 17:9, September, 1926, 5; GN, 17:10, October, 1926, 12; GN, June, 1926, 18; Duncan, 'Lecture,' 1965; FGE, 1:3, July, 1932, 14; Isak Burger, personal interview, 14 July, 1997 ('He could sing you into heaven'.).
6. L. Harris, personal interview; GN, December, 1927, 10 ('You are a little man but you have big faith.').
7. Chant, 1984, 103.
8. E.g. 'Drowning the devil in a two-foot tub! Stop Van Eyk's balderdash!' in *Truth*, 7 July, 1929.
9. GN, 18:2, February, 1927, 11. For more on Jansen see Appendix B.
10. GN, April, 1928, 11; Wallis, 1989, 58.
11. GN, 17:4, April, 1926, 20.
12. GN, 17:4, April, 1926, 20; GN, 17:5, May, 1926, 18, 20. Within two months, Van Eyk's and Hugo's names were being used in advertising—GN, 17:7, July, 1926, 20.
13. GN, 18:12, December, 1927, 14.
14. GN, 17:6, June, 1926, 20.
15. J. Lancaster, 'First Impressions,' GN, 17:5, May, 1926, 18.
16. GN, 17:9, September, 1926, 12
17. *The Korumburra Times* 21 August, 1926.
18. F. B. Van Eyk, 'Evangelist Van Eyk's Report of the Geelong Campaign,' GN, 17:9, October, 1926, 14.
19. *Geelong Advertiser,* 4 September, 1926, quoted in GN, 17:10, October, 1926, 13.
20. *Geelong Advertiser,* 4 September, 1926, quoted in GN, 17:10, October, 1926, 13.
21. GN, 17:10, October, 1926, 15.
22. GN, 17:9, September, 1926, 11; GN, 18:6, June, 1927, 10.
23. GN, June, 1927, 10f.
24. GN, 17:9, September, 1926, 11; GN, 18:6, June, 1927, 10.
25. W. A. Buchanan, 'Know Your Minister,' AE, 20:12, December, 1963, 17.
26. F. Lancaster, personal interview, 18 December 1993. Other interviewees also referred to this.
27. CE, 12 July, 1929.
28. 'Van Eyk's Mission', SMH, 8 July, 1929, 11; *Cessnock Eagle*, 12 July, 1929; N. Armstrong, personal communication; *Truth,* 7 July, 1929; GC, November–December, 1932.
29. G. East, 'The failure of F. B. Van Eyk to establish a continuing movement in Australia,' unpublished essay, Tabor College, 1984.
30. Hilda Van Eyk in a letter to Marie Allsopp, 14 February 1940. Original in the possession of Marie Fraser.
31. G. Muir, personal communication.
32. N. L. Armstrong, personal interview, October 1993.
33. G. Burns, 'God's work in Maryborough, Qu.,' GN, 19:2, February 1928,.17.
34. *The Canvas Cathedral Cooee* Toowoomba, No. 1, 17 October, 1931.

35. G. Burns (?), 'The Land of Promise,' GN, 19:8, August, 1928, 10.
36. Note that Burns seems to have jumbled his reports in places. He claims that the meetings began on Wednesday 27 March. In fact, they commenced on Wednesday 23rd February. Furthermore, a press report claims there were one thousand people present. See GN, 18:5, May, 1927, 12; MC, 5 February, 1927, 22 February, 1927, 4.
37. GN, 18:5, May, 1927, 10f.
38. FGE, 1:3, July, 1932, 13.
39. MC, 12 March, 1927
40. MC, 21 March, 1927, 4. GN, 18:7, May, 1927, 11.
41. GN, 18:7, July, 1927, 12; GN, 18:8, August, 1927, 15; GN, 19:6, June, 1928, 13f; GN, 19:8, August, 1928, 10f; Duncan, *Pentecost in Australia,* 12f.
42. GN, 18:5, May, 1927, 11.
43. He was apparently an elder in one of the Maryborough churches. See GN, 19:1, February, 1928, 10.
44. MC, 19 March, 1927, 8.
45. MC, 8 April, 1927, 2; MC, 16 July, 1927, 2; MC, 30 July, 1927, 16; MC, 4 October, 1927, 2.
46. MC, 9 July, 1927, 8; MC, 14 July, 1927, 8; MC, 16 July, 1927, 14; MC, October, 1927, 2; GN, 19:2, February, 1928, 10f.
47. MC, 10 September, 1927; 24 September, 1927, 8.
48. MC, 1 October, 1927, 8.
49. MC, 5 October, 1927, p.14; 7 October, 1927, 2.
50. MC 27 September, 1927, 4.
51. GN 18:8 August, 1927, 10.
52. GN, 18:8, August, 1927, 11.
53. GN, 18:9, September, 1927, 12ff.
54. GN, 18:12, December, 1927, 13f.
55. Founded in 1942, the National Revival Crusade, soon led by Cecil Harris's son, Leo, later became known as the Christian Revival Crusade and then the CRC Churches International. At the turn of the century, it was the third largest Pentecostal denomination in Australia. See Cooper, 1995 for the story of the first fifty years.
56. GN, 18:9, September, 1927, 14. I personally heard Harris give this testimony thirty years later in Adelaide.
57. Leo Harris, personal interview, n. d.
58. GN, 18:9, September 1927, 11.
59. CM, 3 September, 1927, 3; CM, 10 September, 1927, 3; GN, 18:10, October, 1927, 12f; GN, 18:11, November, 1927, 11.
60. GN, October, 1927, 12.
61. GN, 18:11, November, 1927, 11; GN, 18:12, December, 1927, 3. Note that in late 1927 or early 1928, Phyllis Hobbs wrote to *Good News* pointing out that Ethel Everett was not yet completely healed, although her spine was much straighter and her hunch greatly diminished. GN, 19:2, February 1928, 32.
62. GN, November, 1927, 13.
63. GN, 18:10, October, 1927, 14; GN, 18:11, November, 1927, 10f. There were 75 immersed in water altogether during the campaign.
64. CM, 3, September, 1927, 3; 10 September, 1927, 3; CM, 19 September, 1927, 18f.
65. GN, 19:1, January, 1928, 31; GN, 19:8, August 1928, 10; Church notices, CM, 24 September, 1927, 3.
66. GN, 18:11, November, 1927, 12.
67. 'Rockhampton Campaign Special', Supplement to GN, 19:3, March, 1928, 1ff.

68. GN, 19:3, March, 1928, Supplement, 2.
69. GN, 19:3, March, 1928, Supplement, 1.
70. GN, 19:6, June, 1928, 14; GN, 19:11, November, 1928, 19.
71. Henry Freudenberg, personal communication, 15 April, 1993. Tithing is the practice of giving one tenth (a tithe) of one's income to God (Malachi 3:10) Although not usually compulsory, it is generally practised by Pentecostal people.
72. *The News*, 5 October, 1927—'Farewell to Bro. Hines Retchford, who is relinquishing his secular occupation to devote all his time to gospel work in conjunction with Evang. Van Eyk.'
73. CP, 9 January, 1928. See also GN, 19:3, March, 1928, 14; GN, 19:5, May, 1928, 5; GN May, 1928, 13. Following details are from these sources unless otherwise stated.
74. CP, 7 January, 1928.
75. CP, 9 January, 1928.
76. CP, 14 January, 1928.
77. B. Kajewski, 'The Angels Rejoicing', GN, 19:3, March 1928, 12; see also GN, 19:5, May 1929. Because of numerous requests, the evangelist was also available for consultation at Kelburn House, from Mondays to Thursdays, 10 a.m. to 2 p.m.
78. GN, 19:3, March, 1928, 12; GN, 19:5, May, 1928, 13. Following details are from this source unless otherwise stated.
79. GN, 19:1, January, 1928, 31; see also GN, 19:3, March, 1928, 12.
80. GN, 19:3, March, 1928, 14; GN, 19:5, May, 1929, 13. The report in GN says this message was preached on 8 January 1928, but this is clearly a mistake as press reports show plainly that Van Eyk preached on divine healing on that date.
81. GN, 19:3, March 1928, 12.
82. GN, 19:5, May, 1928, 13.
83. CP, 4 February, 1928. It is interesting that an article about this appears in GN, 19:3, March, 1928, 10.
84. One report says the campaign lasted only two weeks but this is obviously incorrect. The program started on 8 January and concluded on 12 February, five weeks in total. See GN, 19:3, March, 1928, 12, 14; GN, 19:5, May, 1928, 13; CP, 10 February, 1928) although George Burns of Maryborough described it as being of six weeks' duration which he averred was 'an undreamed of thing' in Cairns. See GN, 19:8, August, 1928, 11.
85. GN, 19:3, March, 1928, 13.
86. GN, 19:5, May, 1928, 13.
87. GN, 19:8, August, 1928, 11.
88. GN, 19:6, June, 1928, 19,
89. GN, 19:7, July, 1928, 12.
90. GN, 19:6, June, 1928, 16; GN, 19:7, July, 1928, Supplement, 5ff, 12.
91. GN, 19:6, June, 1928, 14; GN, 19:8, August, 1928, 11; GN, 19:10, GN, October, 1928, 5; GN, 19:12, December, 1928, 11f.
92. GN, 18:5, May, 1927, 10. There is no extant record of the outcome of these prayers.
93. GN, 19:11, November, 1928, 10.
94. GN, 17:10, October, 1926, 15.
95. GN, 19:6, June, 1928, 15; MC, 15 October, 1927, 7; MC, 19 October 1927.
96. 'These Signs Shall Follow,' GN, 18:8, August, 1927, 7.
97. GN, 18:6, June, 1927, 17.
98. GN, 18:8, August, 1927, 16.
99. MC, 15 October, 1927, 7; MC, 19 October, 1927.
100. G. Burns, 'God's Work in Maryborough, Qu.,' GN, 19:2, February, 1928, 17.

101. GN, 18:2, February, 1928, 16.

102. A. E. Banton, *Pentecostal Pioneering with the Foursquare Gospel in Australia* (Westmead: Essington Christian Academy, 1984), 4. See also C. J. Van Eyk, interview. Some others were of the opinion that it was Van Eyk who drove her to the point of collapse. See Lancaster, interview, 18 December 1993.

103. GN, 24:1, January, 1933, 16; GC, July, 1934, 3f; G. East essay; C. J. Van Eyk, interview.

104. GN, 18:5, May, 1927, 10.

105. GN, 18:5, May, 1927, 10; C. G. Enticknap, personal interview. n. d.

106. GN, 19:7, July, 1928, 12.

107. Banton, 1984, 9; see also Lenore Grey, personal communication, 13 November, 1983; T. Hallop, personal interviews, 15 April and 30 April, 1993.

108. GN, 20:5, May, 1929, 12. Following details are from this source unless otherwise stated.

109. 'Drowning the Devil in a Two-foot Tub,' *Truth*, 7 July, 1929.

110. AE, June, 1984, 23; a copy of *Good News* for September, 1924 has the name 'Assembly of God,' stamped on it.

111. C.J. (Neilsie) Van Eyk, personal interview with G. East, 10 April, 1984. Quoted in East essay, 1984.

112. C. J. Van Eyk, personal interview, March, 1984.

113. *The Comforter* quoted in GC, July, 1934, 4.

114. There is some evidence that reporters did hound him. See C. J. (Neilsie) Van Eyk interview.

115. Banton, 1984, 5; Chant, 1984, 150.

116. GN, 17:10, October, 1926, 15.

117. Banton, 1984, 5. Further details are from this source unless otherwise stated.

118. Aplin et al, 1987, 141.

119. E.g. SMH, 7–13 June, 1929.

120. *Truth*, 7 July, 1929; CE, 16 July, 1929 and following issues.

121. A. Banton, personal communication. Van Eyk was plainly uncomfortable with union activism—'The Unions are like the slimy paw of an octopus; stealthily but surely gaining hold of the working man, and one of these days the world will find itself hopelessly bound in their clutches'—GN, 18:10, October, 1927, 6.

122. CE, 4 June, 1929.

123. CE, 18 June, 1929.

124. CE, 25 June, 1929

125. CE, 25 June, 1929; CE, 5, 12 July 1929; A Walker, *Coaltown* (Melbourne: MUP, 1945), 59.

126. 1933 Census, quoted in Walker, 1945, 61.

127. Walker claims there were 73 men and 31 women, but this seems to be a mistake. According to CE 5 July, there were 42 men and 31 women. The Melbourne *Argus* reports that '70 converts' were baptized (*Argus* 6 July, 1929, 25). Note that the figures quoted in my *Heart of Fire,* 1984, 153, are also incorrect. See also Banton, 1984, 8.

128. CE, 5 July, 1929; 12 July, 1929.

129. Banton, 1984, 8. Banton's claim that newspaper headlines reported this story seems to be exaggerated.

130. CE, 19 February, 1946.

131. *Truth*, 7 July, 1929.

132. *Argus,* 6 July, 1929.

133. This was T. Lafsky. See Wallis, 1989, 63; C. J. (Neilsie) Van Eyk, interview, 10 April 1984, quoted in East, essay, 1984.

134. CE, 12 July, 1929.
135. As it turned out, neither would concede defeat, so the money was never paid.
136. CE, 12 July, 1929.
137. On 24 August 1981, the Church of England in Australia became the Anglican Church of Australia when Western Australia became the final State to legislate the change of name.
138. *Argus,* 6 July, 1929; CE, 5 July, 1929.
139. CE 18 July, 1929; *Truth* 7 July, 1929
140. Banton, 1984, 8.
141. CE, 30 July, 1929; GN, 20:5, May, 1929, 12.
142. CE, July, 1929.
143. CE, 27 August, 1929; G. and E. Muir, *Jubilee: a brief account of the Cessnock Evangelistic Campaign of 1929* (Cessnock, n. d. but c.1979), 7.
144. Muir, 1979, 7.
145. E.g. T. A. Bentley, 'Van Eyk did not realise he was saving Australia from revolution,' personal communication, August, 1994.
146. For brief details see Davison et al, eds, 1998, 563.
147. GC October, 1932, 32; February, 1933, 79; August–September, 1933, 136..
148. FGE, May, 1932, 6; GC, July, 1934, 4.
149. GC, July, 1934, 3.
150. GC, August–September, 1935, 88.
151. M. Nugent, personal interview, November, 1990.
152. GC, 3:5, June, 1935, 72ff.
153. GC, 3:5 June, 1935, 72.
154. WA, Saturday 20 November, 1927, 24; John Bentley, a talented musician, was said to be the first Pentecostal minister to use radio, with a monthly broadcast on 6PR— T. A. Bentley, personal communication, August, 1994; personal interview, April, 1997; WA, 20 November, 1937, 12, 25.
155. WA, 20 November, 1937, 12; according to T. A. Bentley, personal communication, August, 1994, this was the first electric guitar to be played in Perth.
156. WA, 20 November, 1937, 12.
157. This took place under the chairmanship of the Rev George Tulloch, of St Stephen's Presbyterian Church on Monday 13 December at the Unity Theatre. A week beforehand, 610 of the 1000 seats had already been taken—WA , 11 December, 1937, 26; T. Bentley, personal interview, n. d. recorded; Orr, 1936, 105.
158. T. Bentley, personal interview, n. d. Bentley's memory may have been inaccurate. He referred to Burgin as 'Burden' and claimed the debate was held in the Trades Hall.
159. WA, 18 December, 1937, 27.
160. Hilda Van Eyk letter, 1940.
161. Hilda Van Eyk letter, 1940.
162. C. J. Van Eyk, interview in East essay, 1984.
163. Walker, 1945, 59.
164. B. James, "Lots of Religion and Freemasonry": The Politics of Revivalism during the 1930s Depression on the Northern Coalfields,' in Hutchinson et al, 1994, 235. James appears to have come to his conclusion without any reference to Van Eyk's ministry in other places.
165. GC, 3:5 June, 1935, 72; S. Dougas, quoting W. A. Buchanan, personal interview, 21 November, 1989.
166. J. Edwards, *The Religious Affections* (Edinburgh: Banner of Truth, 1746, 1986), 27ff.

167. 'Mighty Foursquare Revival Scenes,' GC, 3:5 June, 1935, 72.
168. *Truth*, 7 July, 1929.
169. GC, November–December, 1932, 41.
170. One grateful parent took the trouble to write to the *Cessnock Eagle* pointing out that when Van Eyk visited her dying child, it was not with 'a series of antics' in which he 'deluded the grief-stricken parents into believing that being gifted with divine power, he would raise the child,' as a *Truth* reporter claimed, but that at his own invitation the evangelist simply 'held a little service at her bedside' and that 'as far as antics were concerned, there were none'—CE, July, 1929.
171. This is not to deny that abuses do occur in this area. I have personally gone on record as alleging that some evangelists do use emotional manipulation. See SMH, 25 February 1995, 1, although I am reluctant to suggest they do so intentionally.
172. See Knox 1987; I. Murray, *Jonathan Edwards: A New Biography* (Edinburgh: Banner of Truth, 1987); I. Murray, *Revival and* Revivalism (Edinburgh: Banner of Truth, 1994); G. Chevreau, *Catch the Fire* (London: Marshall and Pickering, 1994); Dixon, 1994; D. Roberts, *The Toronto Blessing* (Eastbourne: Kingsway, 1994).
173. Van Eyk's approach to the statement of Christ that believers would 'take up serpents' is indicative of a common-sense approach to charismata— 'It was suggested in one of our local papers, that I should drink a dose of *Rough on Rats*... to prove Mark 16:17... God did not intend us to go about the country as a side show to entertain brainless idiots, but He placed these blessed truths in our possession to be used in time of need. We might as well say: 'Let one of your leading physicians inoculate you with a deadly disease germ, and then come and have yourself anointed and prayed for, and see if you will be healed.'—GN, 18:12, December, 1927, 5. The allegation about the rat poison was made in Maryborough—see MC, 4 October, 1927, 2.
174. 'The Curse Removed or The Divine Antidote for Sin, Sickness, Snakebite, and Sorrow' in GN, 18:12, December, 1927, 3ff.
175. James, 1994, 236. There is no reason to doubt that Van Eyk claimed, as James alleges, that before he left Cessnock, people would know that Jesus Christ was alive. But this is not the same thing as claiming that he himself was Christ.
176. E.g. F. B. Van Eyk, 'A Telling Address on the Second Coming of Jesus Christ,' GN, 18:2, February, 1927, 3ff; 'Second Coming of Jesus Christ to this Earth' in GN, 18:10, October, 1927, 3ff; 'The Times of the Gentiles or the Time of the End,' GN, 18:3, March, 1927, 3ff; See also the various sermon titles mentioned above. Van Eyk clearly misinterpreted some aspects of biblical eschatology. In one message, he suggested strongly that Mussolini would prove to be the Antichrist and affirmed on more than one occasion that 1934 would mark the end of the age. But he never deviated from a strong belief in the Lordship of Christ.
177. 'A noticeable feature of his preaching is the exultation of Jesus Christ'—GN, March, 1928, 2.
178. It may be noted that I was personally acquainted with Van Eyk's associate Bert Banton until his death in 1995. The genuineness of his faith and the sincerity of his love for Christ were obvious.
179. GN, 17:12, December, 1926, 3–7.
180. FGE, 1:1, May, 1932, 3.
181. GN, 20:5, May, 1929, 12.
182. Duncan, *Pentecost,* 13
183. See Statements of Faith for the Apostolic Faith Mission, clause 8, the Assemblies of God and the Christian Revival Crusade, clause 8, in Chant, 1984, 354, 358, 361.
184. F. Lancaster, personal interview, 18 December, 1993.

185. Does this comment confirm there had been no sexual relationship prior to the marriage?

186. Hilda Van Eyk letter to Marie Allsopp, 14 February 1940. One ambiguous aspect of his public ministry was his conflict with the churches in Cessnock. There seems sufficient evidence to suggest that the ministers concerned may have had just grounds for believing that Van Eyk had misled them by not announcing his intention of starting a new church from the outset of his ministry. In every other town where he had ministered, if there was no existing Pentecostal church, he had initiated one. It seems unlikely that he did not have the same plan in mind for Cessnock. On the other hand, he claimed that he only began a church because the existing congregations were not looking after the converts.

187. CE, 27 August, 1929.

188. CE, 19 February, 1946.

189. Walker, 1945, 60.

190. George Muir, personal communication; CE, 8 July, 1931.

191. FGE, July, 1932, 9.

192. GC, March, 1933, 91; GC, February, 1933, 71.

193. GC, August, 1934, 29; GC, October, 1932, 26; GC, January 1933, 59; GC, September–October 1934, 38, 44. Given that there was significant communist activity in Cessnock during the Depression, it is interesting to note that there were now possibly more people in this small church than there were card-carrying communists in the whole of Australia.

194. Walker, 1945, 60.

195. Banton, 1984, 12.

196. Muir, 12f. I have personally met other people whose parents and grand-parents were converted under Van Eyk's ministry. I did not always record the details.

CHAPTER EIGHT

THE SPIRIT OF REVIVAL

The Pentecostal Church of Australia, 1925–1937

The spirit of Pentecost is the spirit of revival. From the first, there was a cry for renewal and revival, to be part of an age-ending spiritual regeneration that would touch the whole world prior to the return of Christ.

The first half of the twentieth century was a time of radical social and political change in Australia. They were also years of religious ferment which, although relatively insignificant at the time, were to have a long-lasting effect on the Australian church scene. On the broad canvas of Australian Church life, early Pentecostalism was a minor detail. At the time, its existence seemed irrelevant. However, that small detail has now proven to be vital to the balance of the whole picture. To outsiders, the pre-War Pentecostal revival movements were insignificant; for insiders, everything else *but* revival was insignificant. Just as post-war immigration softened traditional Anglo-Saxon reserve and encouraged Australians to be more expressive and less conservative in their ways, so the emergence of Pentecostalism had a leavening effect on Australian Church life. By and large, today's Church is less conservative and more informal in its style. This is partly, at least, the result of the growth of the Pentecostal movement. Even those who would not accept one iota of Pentecostal doctrine cheerfully adopt Pentecostal practices, especially in the realm of music.

In early 1912, a young man named Charles Lewis Greenwood (1891–1969) attended the Footscray Church of Christ in Melbourne, Victoria, under duress from his fiancee. Greenwood had grown up in a dysfunctional family of 12 children, with a disrupted education.[1] His earliest years were spent in the home of an uncle and aunt. He experienced poverty and bullying, undertaking part-time work even as a child to help his mother make ends meet. He was an enthusiastic sportsman, playing both cricket and football. By the age of 16, he was smoking, drinking, swearing, fighting, gambling and living a godless life. He had no significant experience of Christianity. His determined spirit was demonstrated by his practice of spending hours learning how to box and play quoits so that he would not be beaten at either pursuit.

Pastor C. L. Greenwood
Chairman of the Assemblies of God in Australia
and Pastor of Richmond Temple

Charles Greenwood, c.1935.

Somehow, Greenwood made a profession of faith and was baptized, but for all his diligent efforts, nothing changed. Eighteen months later, he knew in his heart that he was no different. Into that church came a man named Lisle Braun (later Brown) who told how his wife had been saved and baptized in the Holy Spirit in South Africa under John G. Lake's ministry and how he himself had been healed of cancer.[2] There was a mixed reaction to this story, some rejecting it and others delighted by it. The result was that 17 people were baptized in the Spirit, including Greenwood himself (20 November 1913).[3] After church, Greenwood, the girl and her mother visited Braun, who greeted him with, 'Young man, you are a great smoker.' Braun laid hands on him and prayed for him. Greenwood never smoked again.[4]

He now felt challenged in other areas. He told his fiancee that he wanted to sever the relationship until they were both filled with the Holy Spirit. In fact, the engagement was never resumed. He began an earnest quest for the Spirit. He began to attend Pentecostal meetings in Albert Park, a Melbourne suburb, probably conducted by Robert Horne.[5]

For three years, Greenwood struggled with his new faith, most of the time seeking earnestly to be filled with the Holy Spirit, at times regretting his decision to break off his engagement, at others drifting back into worldly ways. It was a young lady named Ada Painter, who had received the Spirit at Eltham, who warned him that he was 'grasping a bubble that would crumble in his hands' and urged him to take a stand for God.[6]

Since 1905, Greenwood had been working at the McKay Harvester Company at Sunshine, an outer western suburb of Melbourne. Once when there was industrial unrest Greenwood, now fervent in faith, refused to go on strike. As a result, he was ostracised by his work mates. It was all part of the making of him. 'I made a companion of the Lord,' he said later. 'I started to walk with Him.'

Finally, on 20 November 1913, at the age of 23, he attended a meeting where in earnest desperation he poured out passionate praise to God and in the process spoke briefly in tongues. Convinced he had made it up himself, he did not continue. By now, he had fallen in love again, this time with Frances Ella Reed, who was to become his wife. She had already experienced glossolalia and prayed for him in tongues. Later, on the Carnegie railway station platform, his patient longing was rewarded and there, waiting for the train, surrounded by other passengers, his inhibitions now finally broken, he burst out speaking in tongues! He later recalled—

> I was baptized with the Holy Ghost and with fire and I will never forget that wonderful experience... I was filled with the Holy Ghost as much as my little frame could take in at that time. In His loving kindness and tender mercy He has seen me from above. Thank God for the mighty baptism in the Holy Ghost.[7]

On 19 August 1915. Greenwood and Frances were married, and settled in Sunshine. One by one, Greenwood began to lead people to Christ and soon started a small Bible Study group in his home. There were some dramatic cases of healing and exorcism including that of Albert Lowe, an alcoholic.[8] For nearly a decade, the meetings continued. Some people were baptized in water in the Greenwoods' bath. Others were baptized in the Spirit.

Greenwood was small in stature, but lively, energetic and vigorous. Although acutely aware of his own lack of education, and uncertain of his speaking ability, he found himself able to hold people's attention when he preached and he proved particularly gifted in bringing people to a point of commitment. He spoke the language of the working man and pulled no punches. To his family, Greenwood's effectiveness was simply explained. Others relied on their knowledge and talents; Greenwood could only depend on the power of the Holy Spirit.[9] Leo Harris, who was converted under Greenwood's ministry in Perth in 1928, recalled, 'He spoke so vividly of judgement that he scared me out of my seat.'[10] He was not alone in his respect for Greenwood's preaching. Another man said—

> As a Gospel preacher I do believe that Charles Lewis Greenwood was not surpassed by any I have heard, with his clarity, sincerity and urgent yet generous appeal.[11]

The small group banked their tithes, purchased an acre of land in Martin Street and set about building the Sunshine Gospel Hall, a weatherboard structure seating 220 people with a small brick room at the rear, which was completed in February 1925.[12]

Alfred Valdez

In that same year, the inaugural flight from Europe to Australia was made by the Italian the Marchesse de Pinedo, the first moving pictures with sound were introduced to Australia and Sydney's population exceeded one million for the first time. And *Good News* announced with great excitement that A. C. Valdez (1896–1988), another American evangelist, would commence his Melbourne campaign on Sunday 8 March at Good News Hall.[13] Other congregations who wished to invite him to preach for them were urged to contact the secretary Winnie Andrews. After six months in New Zealand, Valdez arrived in Melbourne in 1925, at the age of 29, accompanied by his mother, his wife and small child, with little money and little idea of what he would do next.[14] At the beginning of March, he found himself at Good News Hall where he was generously received. At his first two meetings, as they began to pray, people were baptized in the Holy Spirit.[15] The initial newspaper advertisements promised 'a New Testament Revival' during a 'protracted campaign' at Good News Hall.[16] A late news item in *Good News* was full of hope—

> Evangelist Valdez and his mother have captured all hearts. His impassioned addresses, with their mingled pathos and humor [sic], reach right home to the hearers, and create a resolution to go clean through with Jesus.[17]

Within a week, however, the 'protracted campaign' was over. 'The Lord did not permit us to stay there,' Valdez recalled years later.[18] The following advertisement appeared in the press—

> SPECIAL NOTICE—The Evangelist has cancelled his engagement to conduct services at Good News Hall, Queensberry-street [sic], North Melbourne, and has severed all connection with that mission on account of doctrinal differences. The Evangelist hereby publicly states that he believes in the TRIUNE GOD, the UNCREATED DEITY of the LORD JESUS CHRIST and the PERSONALITY and DEITY of the HOLY SPIRIT; and that he holds and teaches all the fundamental doctrines of the Christian Faith.[19]

Plainly, Lancaster's unorthodox beliefs had again proven a barrier too large to surmount. After a couple of days, Valdez left the Hall and began to preach for Robert Horne's Southern Evangelical Mission.[20] It was there he heard a voice say clearly that he should go to Sunshine. He had no idea what this meant, but later discovered there was a Melbourne suburb of that name and took the train there. He called at the Sunshine Gospel Hall and there met Greenwood who was working on the new building. 'As he (Greenwood) got closer,' Valdez recalled, 'I could see that he was speaking in tongues. Then he stopped and said, "Come inside, brother; I knew you were coming."' Greenwood told him that he and his small group had been praying all night that Valdez would come to them.[21]

Not everyone agrees with this version of the story. Elviss Greenwood, C. L. Greenwood's son, believed that his father had gone to Good News Hall and invited Valdez to Sunshine.[22] Several former members of the Hall claim that Greenwood 'took Valdez out'.[23] In an address given in September 1965, Greenwood himself admitted he had invited Valdez, but after he left the Hall.. He told how he had heard Valdez at Good News Hall and how before Valdez spoke a young man, probably Alex Buchanan, made a statement about their belief in the Godhead, noting that 'whispers' had got to the ear of the evangelist. According to Greenwood, Valdez had insisted on their being open about their beliefs, or he would not take the platform. The result was that many people left the meeting.[24]

Sunshine

Greenwood later gained Horne's permission to talk with the evangelist, and invited him to Sunshine.[25] Valdez visited the new church, thoroughly quizzed Greenwood on his doctrines and agreed to preach for him. By the beginning of April, a full program of meetings was under way. There were tarrying meetings on Mondays, Tuesdays, Wednesdays and Saturdays, evangelistic services on Thursday and Saturday nights and two services on Sundays.[26] Within a few nights, capacity crowds began to attend. People stood outside, unable to gain admittance. Greenwood recalled—

> During this campaign the power of God was manifested in a wonderful way: sinners were converted, many believers were baptized in the Holy Spirit, and the power of God fell at every meeting. Soon the news spread that the Lord was pouring out His Spirit in Sunshine, and people came from near and far. Night after night the church was packed, the altar lined, and christians [sic] from all denominations were baptized in the Holy Spirit.[27]

Trains from Melbourne to Sunshine were crowded. As they travelled, the people sang favourite hymns such as 'Joy Unspeakable,' 'Love Lifted Me' and, a favourite of Valdez, 'I've Anchored in Jesus'. Some were reportedly converted on the trains.[28] Valdez claimed that people were woken up in the middle of the night and told to go to Sunshine.[29]

Others were so overcome by their experience they lay on the floor for hours at a time. Visions and revelations were reported. On occasion, there were demonic manifestations as people were liberated from oppression. The most common testimony was that of speaking in other tongues. It was assumed that people might spend hours on their knees or their faces before the Spirit came. Some people were so emotionally drained after these episodes they had difficulty standing and had to be assisted to the railway station. Others had lingered so long in prayer they missed the last train and either walked home or were driven by the few people who owned motor vehicles. Fortunately, the brick room at the rear of the hall was relatively sound-proof, for there was plenty of shouting, crying, tongue-speaking and singing.[30] Alan Wilson remembered the Sunshine meetings as being characterised by 'noise and fervour,' but not so much that he as a child could not sleep under the seats.[31]

Meanwhile Saturday tarrying meetings continued at Sunshine, with eighteen receiving the Spirit on one occasion. In the twelve months after the campaign commenced, some 400 people claimed to have been baptized in the Holy Spirit. Meetings also continued in the Town Hall each Tuesday and Thursday with three services on Sundays.[32]

Compared with the huge crowds that had flocked to hear Reuben Torrey in 1902 or Wilbur Chapman in 1909 and 1912, the Sunshine/Prahran gatherings were almost minuscule. The local community newspaper, the *Prahran Telegraph* did not consider them worth a mention. The visits of earlier Pentecostal evangelists Smith Wigglesworth and Aimee Semple McPherson had also drawn larger numbers, both needing the 4,500 seat Wirth's Olympia to accommodate them.[33] Within a few months, Gypsy Smith (1860–1947) was to visit Melbourne. He, too, would pack Wirth's Olympia where the choir alone numbered 1000 voices and where his messages were relayed by radio to suburban and country areas.[34] Around the same time, the Anglican James Hickson was attracting large crowds to his healing services and the Churches of Christ evangelist Ernest Hinrichsen was founding new congregations all over Australia.[35] And in terms of numbers, the Catholic Eucharistic Congress in Sydney in August 1928 far eclipsed all the evangelical activities, let alone the small gatherings led by Valdez.[36] Yet for those concerned, the 'Sunshine Revival' was highly significant. It marked the beginning of formal Pentecostal denominationalism and the emergence of an identifiable Pentecostal movement.[37] It relocated Pentecostal revival in the mainstream of evangelical theology. Historically, it was the legitimate child of the marriage of Evangelicalism and enthusiasm.

Among those who were baptized in the Holy Spirit was a 22-year-old Methodist named Len Jones (c.1900–1974), a student from the newly established (1920) Melbourne Bible Institute, also located in Prahran.[38] Jones was interested but not convinced of the validity of what he saw at Sunshine until challenged by Greenwood to measure it by the Bible. The next day, the principal of the College, Canon C. H. Nash, spoke on Luke 11:13 and James 4:2. Spurred by this unwitting guidance, Jones decided to return to Sunshine. J. M. Roberts, a former Methodist lay preacher, prayed with him and, with a wisdom not always characteristic of the new movement, did not coerce him. The next Sunday, 3 May 1925, Jones and a fellow student received the Pentecostal experience. Soon another eight students were baptized in the Spirit.[39] Ultimately, Nash, whose

J.M.Roberts (L) and C.L.Greenwood (Photo courtesy C.Manley-Breen).

genuine ecumenism enabled him to fellowship with Christians of many persuasions, but whose evangelicalism compelled him to set biblical boundaries, as he understood them,[40] became concerned about potential disunity. After talking with several of the students concerned, on 13 May 1925, he issued the following injunction—

> In view of the unsettlement already caused, and possible division threatened, by the present (so-called) Pentecostal movement, all students of the Institute are asked—
>
> To refrain from common action which might reasonably be regarded as taken in the interests of that movement
>
> To avoid as far as possible all discussion of the subject one with another
>
> To abstain from attendance at any meeting connected with that movement.[41]

This created a problem for Jones who was the Principal's secretary. On 20 May, 1925, Jones wrote a gracious but plain letter to Nash, resigning as a student from the Institute.[42]

Nash was evidently concerned that Jones might be going to Good News Hall, because he loaned him a couple of volumes on the theme of eternal punishment. Jones wrote back to assure him that in every respect he was orthodox in evangelical doctrine, and had simply added to his previous beliefs the baptism in the Holy Spirit and divine healing.[43] Subsequent correspondence reveals an ongoing love and respect between the two men, with Nash adhering to his longstanding conviction that he had seen the Holy Spirit 'working wondrously both in the formation of Christian character and in empowerment for service in quiet... normal ways' and reaffirming his prayer that God would continue to use Jones 'as an instrument of righteousness and holiness.'[44] His prayer was answered. Within a decade, Jones was conducting revival campaigns throughout Australia and New Zealand.[45] Jones was later to attribute his life-long passion for missions to his time at the Institute.[46]

Although Valdez's original instruction to Christians who were baptized in the Holy Spirit was to remain faithful members of their home churches, the hostile reaction many received from their denominations compelled him to rethink his stance.[47] Ultimately, accepting the need to consolidate the new work, Valdez proposed to establish a local church. The Prahran Town Hall was engaged and meetings were held nightly for the purpose of instruction on 'the truth of church government.' At these services, people continued to be saved and healed and baptized in the Spirit. People fell to the floor because of a sense of God's presence; one woman saw a ball of fire resting on the top of her head and then coursing through her whole frame, resulting in her being healed from a longstanding affliction and speaking in tongues; a Churches of Christ pastor was healed of a growth. At the end of the week, Valdez appointed elders, including Greenwood, and deacons. The Pentecostal Church of Australia was established.[48]

Identical advertisements placed in the Church Notices columns of both the *Age* and the *Argus* clearly and without subtlety described the function and ethos of the new body—

> THE PENTECOSTAL CHURCH OF AUSTRALIA is a newly organised Church in Melbourne, and it is founded on straight and clean orthodox teaching. Our object in organising this church in central Melbourne is to further propagate the fourfold truth of the New Testament, SALVATION, HOLY GHOST BAPTISM, DIVINE HEALING and the SECOND COMING OF CHRIST. This church will be in fellowship with the recognised PENTECOSTAL CHURCHES OF THE WORLD, and will have the expectation of a chain of Evangelists of international fame. We desire the prayers of all God's children. Pray with us for a nation-wide HOLY GHOST, REGENERATING, DEVIL REBUKING, REJUVENATING GLORIOUS REVIVAL. Until we locate in central Melbourne, our meetings will continue in the PRAHRAN TOWN HALL...[49]

There was no doubt about the distinctive emphasis of the new church—

> The revival continues. THE LATTER RAIN IS FALLING. ASK YE OF THE LORD RAIN IN THE TIME OF THE LATTER RAIN. JESUS HIMSELF is the Baptizer, many hungry souls are being filled with the Spirit, and have a real Bible experience. Come and be blessed.[50]

It is unlikely these Pentecostal meetings would have attracted much attention from the mainline churches, had Valdez kept them as revivalistic rallies. Divine healing, for instance, was not an issue. At the very time Valdez was ministering in Prahran, a conference on spiritual healing was being conducted as part of the 1925 Anglican Church Congress in which there was enthusiastic support for the healing missions being conducted by James Hickson.[51]

The moment Valdez decided to establish a church there was a predictable reaction. Naturally, some clergy were concerned at the prospect of losing people to the new movement. Evangelical leaders, Dr D. Stewart MacColl (Baptist) and Dr John James Kitchen (Brethren), who had been instrumental in the establishment of the Melbourne Bible Institute,[52] and were already disturbed by the Jones incident, called a meeting attended by several hundred clergy to discuss the matter.[53] In response, Valdez himself arranged a rally at the Collins Street Assembly Hall. A large crowd turned out for the occasion, including some civic leaders, and, according to Valdez, it was a '100% victory.'[54]

Overall, however, there is little evidence of the denominations being overly concerned about what was happening. Melbourne's Methodist *Spectator*, for example, includes a brief and relatively irenic half-page item noting that speaking in tongues is generally discouraged by Paul and that there is no biblical evidence to suggest that it should accompany baptism in the Holy Spirit, but there is no specific mention of Valdez or the Pentecostal Church. A further article on 'counterfeit Christianity' names Christian Science, Spiritism, Millennial Dawn, Theosophy, Mormonism, Seventh Day Adventism and Catholicism but not Pentecostalism.[55] There were almost certainly many unofficial comments, however. 'The leading churches of the day,' wrote Edwin Ridgway of Good News Hall, 'ascribe all "speaking in tongues" to the devil.'[56]

Late in 1925, the Richmond Theatre at 343 Bridge Road, Richmond, was offered to Valdez on a three months lease with an option to purchase. There was accommodation for some 1200 people and the purchase price was 6000 pounds—all of which was raised at one service.[57] Renamed Richmond Temple, the new building included shops across the front, which were used as a Bible and tract Department, and a large platform which accommodated the church's burgeoning choir and orchestra. Above the platform was a text: 'The blood of Jesus Christ His Son cleanseth us from all sin.' Rooms at the rear were used for counselling and prayer.

Kelso Glover

Within months, an invitation was extended to Kelso R. Glover, another young American, to visit Melbourne.[58] He and his wife arrived in 1926. For three weeks, there was a series of special meetings in which people continued to be converted, healed and baptized in the Spirit. Not long after his arrival, Valdez returned to America and the assembly unanimously invited Glover to be the new pastor. He was seen as 'a gifted teacher' whose steadying hand kept them founded on God's Word and whose wisdom steered them from needless error.[59]

Early in the piece, Glover began a popular ten-week series on the Second Coming of Christ.[60] Surviving transcripts of his lectures indicate a lively, genial but polemic style in which he readily took opposing views to task. He dismantled the increasingly popular pre-tribulation premillennialism of the Brethren leader John Nelson Darby (1800–1882).[61] Glover also refuted the common Pentecostal idea that only those baptized in the Holy Spirit would constitute the raptured Bride of Christ. The 'tribulation saints,' far from being inferior, would be those who had suffered tribulation and come through victoriously.[62]

Holiness was a strong theme for Glover. He eschewed the 'once saved always saved' teaching, which he attributed specifically to the Brethren movement, and taught plainly that those who did not continue in the faith would be lost—

> Pentecost is too expensive a religion to fool with. I want to tell you… you have to overcome or you will go into the lake [of fire]… I am here for serious business. We have to draw the line in Richmond Temple. You can stop on which side you like. I am a preacher of the Gospel of the Lord Jesus Christ. This is too serious a thing. One of the saints there was helping a poor drunkard along the street endeavouring to get him settled somewhere and another man comes along and says, 'Remember, brother, you were once saved, you can never be lost.' We have to stop that kind of stuff…
>
> Richmond Temple stands for holiness. You have got to believe in holiness or the other. This is a sobering thing. I am intensely in earnest, this is not a matter of doctrines, it is a matter of life and death for souls… A man can have differences of opinion on things, but friends, this point of once saved… is too dangerous a thing to tolerate for one second in Pentecost… Pentecost has a vision to sweep the world. I am a Pentecostal preacher, still preaching without holiness we are going to be lost… We are building a church that believes in holiness.[63]

It was not uncommon for Glover to punctuate his preaching with a statement in tongues followed by an interpretation, a practice which was continued by Greenwood throughout his ministry.[64]

Prior to his departure, Valdez had established the Victorian Bible Institute. Its name was imposing and, in fact, with its 30 students, it had a more encouraging start than the Melbourne Bible Institute, whose initial 1920 class numbered only one.[65] On the other hand, unlike its Evangelical counterpart, it was short-lived, lasting only for two years. Its purpose was to provide 'anointed preachers' and to counteract 'erroneous teachings'—an ill-disguised reference to Good News Hall.

Glover soon became the main teacher in the Institute and gave it a stability and balance it needed. The school was productive. Among those who emerged as ministers from the Institute were W. Jones, who went to Parkes, Norman Priest, to Orange, and Nellie Mather to Bendigo and Ballarat.[66]

The *Australian Evangel* appeared in July 1926. It was a house magazine, carrying sermons preached at the Temple and news reports from assemblies.

In the year 1927, Charles Kingsford Smith and Charles Ulm set a new record for circumnavigating Australia by air, Federal Parliament House was opened in Canberra and moves were made to establish the Australian Council of Trade Unions (ACTU). In that same year, Kelso Glover returned to the USA and Charles Greenwood became the new pastor at Richmond Temple. The position was initially offered to him for six months with a salary of eight pounds a week; he was to hold it for the next 41 years. Messrs Nokes, Ellis, Roberts, Ruffell, Beruldsen and Tuck were elected elders. It was also agreed to purchase the Sunshine Hall from its trustees.[67] The English Pentecostal evangelist Smith Wigglesworth visited Melbourne in March of that year and laid hands on both Charles Greenwood and Philip Duncan of Sydney commissioning them for the work of the Lord.[68]

It was not long before other assemblies around Australia began to request affiliation with the new movement. Although little explanation is given for the reasons for this, there seems no doubt that, in contrast with Good News Hall, it was the orthodox evangelical teaching and the stronger organisational structure of the Pentecostal Church that attracted people. So the original congregation in Parkes soon sought affiliation as did a small group of people in Perth, W.A.[69]

Spiritual blessings were not restricted to public services. At a deacons' meeting in February 1932, when the members knelt to pray, reported the secretary, the praises that resulted were reminiscent of a time at Sunshine when 'the very place seemed to be shaking with the power that was in there.' He had never seen the power of God so manifest at a deacons' meeting before.[70]

Richmond Temple

By 1928, there were 240 members at Richmond Temple. One hundred and twenty three of the 133 members present at a members' meeting voted for Greenwood to be called for a further six months. The Sunshine property was subdivided and some of the land sold, the building itself finally being purchased by the Scouts for 450 pounds in 1929. Greenwood was re-elected each year, but not without some demurring. In 1933, the elders decided on a three-months call with the option of further terms; the deacons wanted a more reasonable twelve-month appointment. The members unanimously endorsed the deacons' recommendation.[71]

Greenwood was now being called a pastor-evangelist and in 1934, 'after weeks of praying and seeking the mind of the Lord,' Greenwood suggested the assembly recall Glover as pastor and that he himself engage in evangelistic work throughout Victoria.[72] There was another reason as well—there had been a suggestion of Greenwood misappropriating funds and he felt the need of someone to assist in resolving the matter. Glover returned to Australia in 1935 and ministered in Melbourne and Adelaide. Greenwood was totally exonerated and shortly afterwards the Church Secretary resigned, being replaced by J. M. Roberts, who later became a pastor.[73]

There was a positive response to Glover's ministry and 'almost every meeting' saw 'an overflow to the altar of people seeking the Saviour'. A Thursday night teaching series on Hebrews provided 'a rich feast for the saints'.[74] Greenwood took the opportunity to visit other congregations. From January to March, he campaigned at Oakleigh where 23 'found salvation' and 13 were baptized in the Holy Spirit. As a result, a full time pastor was appointed. At Easter, he was in Adelaide where eleven people received the Spirit and several were converted. In May he travelled to Queensland. Meanwhile, a growing fellowship of churches was developing with congregations in Ballarat, Bendigo, Oakleigh and Williamstown in Victoria; Sydney, Parkes and Woy Woy in New South Wales; and Adelaide, Wallaroo and Kadina in South Australia.[75] However, Glover did not stay and Greenwood continued as pastor at Richmond Temple, being reappointed annually. In 1936, a Board of Pastors replaced the Board of Elders as the governing body of the church.[76] Greenwood had decided he would no longer work under an eldership.[77] He was a risk-taker and often found administrative procedures frustrating. Although he could be very tender with the needy and would drop everything to answer a pastoral call, when he was convinced something was right, nobody could swerve him from it.[78] 'He was a conundrum,' said one pastor. On the one hand, he was clearly a man of God; yet on the other he was insecure and threatened by other ministries. When new movements like the Apostolic Church started, he strongly opposed them.[79] People were often offended by his implacability.[80] He was stern with discipline in the church. Any office-holder who failed in some area of their Christian living would be firmly brought into line.[81] Yet for all that, he was very much aware of his own deficiencies—

> There was nobody in Richmond Temple more unqualified to do this work that God had given me to do... How the people put up with me I do not know. They were very, very gracious to me because remember I had no Bible School training, I had no education. It was pretty hard for me to read my Bible and understand it... It was hard going to learn by candle light but God in His loving kindness and tender mercy in a marvellous way helped me.[82]

From its inception, there were enthusiastic reports of the work. A 1928 news item described one Sunday morning as 'never to be forgotten.' The singing in the Spirit (i.e. in tongues) was like 'a heavenly choir'. It was like standing in God's presence. Greenwood's preaching was 'thrilling and heart-searching' and many were being converted. Six people had been baptized in the Holy Spirit, the congregation was increasing and they were 'on the tiptoe of expectation for a mighty revival'.[83]

In April 1931, twenty people were baptized in water and the next month, 1200 children attended a children's rally.[84] Four years later, the enthusiasm had not diminished. A report in the *Australian Evangel* spoke of God's 'continued blessing' and of 'deep ministry in the Spirit.' They rejoiced to see 'the unction and power' resting on Greenwood. Many had been baptized in water and there was an 'overflow' of both 'sinners and backsliders weeping their way to the cross'.[85]

Table 7 Membership Richmond Temple 1928–1942.

Year	Members
1928	240
1932	285
1933	220
1935	210
1936	202
1937	184
1942	135

Source: Minutes, Richmond Temple, various dates.

Nevertheless, after an initial surge, over the fifteen years following Greenwood's appointment, the membership declined significantly from 240 to 135 (see Tables 7 and 8).

A heavy blow was struck early in the piece with a loss of 65 members in 1932 to the Apostolic Church.[86] It also evident that Greenwood's strength lay in his evangelistic, rather than his pastoral gifts. 'He had a uniquely anointed ministry,' said one of his peers at his funeral, many years later. 'I have yet to meet his equal when it comes to an appeal for souls at the conclusion of a service.'[87] Was he less successful in shepherding the sheep he gained?

He was a lively, effervescent preacher. He was never still, ranging all over the platform, and jumping up and down 'like a jack-in-the-box'—he was even known to stand on the balustrade![88] He punctuated his preaching with utterances in tongues. He had a great concern for missions and promoted mission giving at

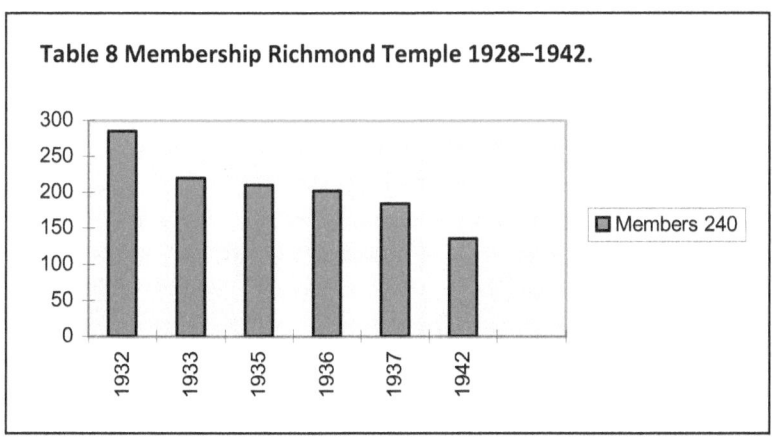

Table 8 Membership Richmond Temple 1928–1942.

every opportunity.[89] He prayed for the sick. When he prophesied, he did so, not with eyes closed, as Pentecostals usually do, but with eyes open, looking straight at the people concerned. Sometimes, he would step down from the platform and approach people individually, challenging them about secret sins or hidden practices in their lives.[90] He was fearless in his presentation of the gospel. His simple, direct style allowed no room for misunderstanding. The following extract is illustrative of his preaching—his passion to preach Christ; his enthusiasm for being baptized in the Holy Spirit; his commitment to holiness; his plain, forthright approach; his practice of interspersing his preaching with an utterance in tongues and an interpretation, with its mingling of Scripture quotations, pseudo-Elizabethan English and suggestions of divine inspiration and authority.

> Can any man add or take away from the efficacy of the sacrifice of Calvary? A thousand times, 'No.' So, brother and sister, if you teach that the Baptism of the Holy Spirit is necessary to qualify you for translation [to heaven], then that moment you magnify the baptism above the work of Christ wrought out on Calvary. . .
>
> Interpretation of tongues—Awake thou that sleepest. Arise from the dead and Christ will give thee light. For understandest thou that thou needest light for the darkness? Yea, and if thou shalt follow Me who continually is in the light, thou shalt not walk in darkness. But hearken thou diligently. He that walketh in the light as He is in the light hath fellowship with one another and the blood of the Lord Jesus Christ His Son cleanseth thee from all sin. And if thou wilt allow the Lord thy God by the power of the Holy Spirit to operate upon thy heart, and thou wilt be in subjection and obedient to His Spirit, know thee not that He will gird thee and clothe thee so that thou wilt be able to stand in His presence and not be ashamed when He cometh.
>
> God pity the day when in our hearts there is something that becomes greater than Calvary. There is nothing greater…
>
> But remember this, there is a mighty baptism in the Holy Ghost that takes the soul into a place of ecstasy, power and glory that there is nothing on earth can touch it. It is something more than doctrine. It is something more than speaking

in tongues. The baptism of the Holy Ghost is a mighty filling that reveals Jesus in His majesty and glory; that magnifies Him and makes Him to be the mightiest, the truest, the best, and most wonderful Saviour . . .[91]

C.G.Enticknap.
Photo, Richmond Temple Souvenir.

Greenwood continued to travel, visiting India and Queensland in early 1937.[92] In Queensland, discussions were held with Charles Enticknap and Henry Wiggins with a view to securing a closer unity of Pentecostal churches in Australia. Since Van Eyk's departure, most of the congregations in Queensland had regrouped under the name Assemblies of God and had already been accepted in co-operative fellowship with the Assemblies of God in Great Britain and the USA.[93] That year, at Easter, an 'all Australian Conference' was held in Sydney 'for the purpose of uniting all the Australian assemblies in a common loyalty to an approved Constitution.'[94] Some 150 delegates gathered for three days of worship and inspiration followed by another three of hammering out the new basis of union. They discussed methodology and structure, but strove to adhere to 'the faith which was once delivered to the saints.' At times, they wondered if they were trying to achieve the impossible, but with prayer, perseverance and 'every other means' in their power, an agreement was reached. They believed they had achieved a blend of autocracy and democracy, creating no 'mere organisation, but a blessed organism, impregnated with Divine life and power.' After several suggestions were put forward, the common name Assemblies of God in Australia was adopted by all. Charles Greenwood was elected chairman with Charles Enticknap vice-chairman and Henry Wiggins, newly arrived from England, as secretary.[95] The *Glad Tidings Messenger* of Queensland and Victoria's *Australian Evangel* were merged. There were 39 assemblies in the new movement.[96] When the proposal was put to the Richmond Temple congregation for endorsement, there were no dissenting votes.[97] In practice, Enticknap, Duncan and Greenwood were the leaders of the new movement, often working in concert, but always careful to maintain their own individuality and autonomy.[98]

Sydney

As in Melbourne, several small Pentecostal groups started spontaneously in the 1920s. Jotham and Kate Metcalfe, who had been baptized in the Spirit through the agency of Good News Hall, held gatherings in their home in Northbridge.[99] Irish preacher Thomas Bingham Lennon, a former Catholic, ran meetings in the Elim Mission Hall, Marrickville.[100] Langley Symmonds, an elderly converted Jew, conducted Friday night open air meetings and Sunday services at Rockdale under the name Assembly of God.[101] Maxwell Armstrong and his wife May conducted Pentecostal meetings in their home in Leichhardt. After fifteen months in Cleveden, near Parkes, they pastored an assembly at Rozelle.[102]

Interior of Assemblies of God church building, Parkes, NSW.

In 1922, the Duncan family joined the movement. Frederick Duncan (1865–1937), the proprietor of the Duncan and Sons Railway Overalls factory in Alexandria, was an enthusiastic lay evangelist who was a deacon at the evangelical Burton Street Baptist Tabernacle and well regarded as a lay Christian leader in Sydney.[103] During the dedication service for his son Philip Brandon (1899–1990), the minister declared that like his biblical namesake, the child would be an evangelist who would ultimately father four daughters who would prophesy, a statement which itself proved startlingly prophetic. In the early 1920s, Philip was converted under the ministry of John Ridley (1896–1976), the renowned Baptist evangelist, who had himself been converted in the Burton Street Tabernacle through the preaching of William Lamb, renowned for his teaching on the second coming of Christ.[104] Immediately, Duncan threw himself into evangelism and by 1923 had started a Sunday School in the then remote suburb of Oyster Bay. The following year, he and Mollie Jarvis were married at Burton Street. By 1926, there was a small church with its own building.[105]

Meanwhile, Dr R. H. Fallon, a member of Burton Street, had invited Smith Wigglesworth, to speak at the church.[106] Wigglesworth's Pentecostal approach and vigorous methods of ministering to the sick were legendary.[107] He was certainly ill-suited to a Baptist congregation and his ministry there was short-lived. With characteristic bluntness, he warned them they had missed the day of God's visitation, then moved to the Australia Hall and conducted services there for six weeks. His major emphasis was always faith. Fallon later wrote—

> 'Only believe.' That is the perpetual teaching of Brother Wigglesworth. This is his text for all time and everywhere, and everything he says illustrates and enforces it.[108]

Wigglesworth had a major impact on Duncan's life. He and his father were also asked to leave Burton Street. The spirit of Pentecost had again proven too unruly for an Evangelical sanctuary. The Duncan family began to attend Pentecostal meetings around Sydney. By 1924, Frederick Duncan was pastoring the assembly at the Elim Mission Hall.[109] The next year, they heard about what was happening at Sunshine and it was there Philip Duncan was baptized in the Spirit. He was praying in Greenwood's house, beset with doubts, when Greenwood's five-year-old daughter Hazel came to him and laid hands on him singing a chorus about the blood of Jesus. He saw a vision of approaching light and began to speak fluently in tongues.[110]

There was strong opposition to the fledgling Pentecostals from the Baptists and others, including allegations of immorality and fanaticism, a situation which was to make life difficult for Duncan's four daughters in their school years. There was clearly a need to gather the various Pentecostal groups together and moves were made to establish an organised assembly. In August 1925, a building was secured and renovated in Australia Street, Newtown, not far from where Dowie had begun to teach about divine healing fifty years earlier. Initially, they used the name Newtown Full Gospel Assembly, but by the end of the year it was known as the Sydney assembly of the Pentecostal Church of Australia. Greenwood and Roberts visited the new work, appointed deacons and elders and saw 27 people baptized in the Holy Spirit. Frederick Duncan led the work until Len Jones came from Melbourne. Wigglesworth returned in 1927, and during his visit, laid hands on Philip Duncan, declaring that God had called him into His service.[111] The next year, Duncan became pastor.[112]

The emergence of the Apostolic Church together with the impact of the Depression resulted in a loss of members and in 1931, they moved to Jubilee Temple, 470 Elizabeth Street, Surry Hills, the building being provided rent-free by F. Penfold, of W. C. Penfold and Co Pty Ltd, stationers. It was a rough area and some cutting-edge evangelism took place among prostitutes, criminals and outcasts. In 1934, Duncan took over Langley Symmonds' work at Rockdale. Meanwhile, the original church moved to Redfern and then to Petersham. By this time, the Duncan and Sons clothing business was doing very well, especially through making uniforms for the armed services, and Philip Duncan became manager.[113] Nevertheless, he turned his back on the business world to enter full-time ministry. After working in several country areas for a time, he became pastor of the work at Petersham where he stayed till his retirement. In 1945, he became chairman of the Assemblies of God in Australia.

William Booth-Clibborn

William Booth-Clibborn (b.1893), grandson of General William Booth, founder of the Salvation Army, was another who indirectly owed his Pentecostal experience to John Alexander Dowie. He was a man of unique talents. Duncan's description of him is revealing—

> He was a man who was quite eccentric—he had no compunction whatever. Nevertheless, he did a grand work in Queensland and they still talk of his sermons. No one ever preached like him. He was genius if ever there was one. I can remember some of his sermons. He'd preach for a couple of hours and he would put so much into his sermons it would seem like four hours. He was prodigious in his knowledge. He was a linguist—he spoke seven languages. A prodigy! He was a mighty violinist, and often he would preach with his violin tucked under his chin. He'd preach with it there for an hour and all of a sudden he would play it—and could he play![114]

Booth-Clibborn's whole family was musically endowed and his own musical talents were obvious. His uncle Herbert Booth was the 'musician of the Booth family' and his sister Evelyn was an accomplished pianist.[115] He published a song book called *Wings of Praise* containing 160 hymns including several of his mother's and father's compositions and some 38 of his own. Several of these were set to well-known secular tunes ('Ah, sweet mystery of life,' 'O Sole Mio') or to hymn tunes ('Count Your Blessings,') and even to 'God Save the King'. Some of the lyrics, such as 'Mule Religion' were creative, imaginative and provocative.[116] Tall and handsome, with a film star physique, Booth-Clibborn charmed his way into the hearts of many people. An obviously sympathetic review described him as a—

> Pastor, Worker, Lecturer, Teacher and Evangelist all in One. An Author, and editor and a finished musician whose original compositions are sung all over the world. The most unique man of God in evangelism today, some have said... Evangelist Booth-Clibborn is Heaven-born and Heaven-sent.[117]

Booth-Clibborn believed that while the message of the gospel should be unchanged, the methodology of presenting it needed constant updating. He pulled no punches—

> THE MESSAGE MUST NEVER BE CHANGED but the style and service should suit the century... My Grandfather General William Booth created a furore by striking out in novel fashion and procedure to reach the godless of England... 60 years have passed since that date and things have changed with a vengeance ... We must make the most of the moment... Modern preaching must be pointed, powerful and impertinent. The whole counsel of God must now be declared and in the power of the Holy Spirit... Fifteen minute sermons, pretty texts, vestments and ritual, lazy littanies [sic], antiquated anthems and all servile ceremonialism will attract fashionable pharisees, but our cry is back to the acts of the Apostles, the simplicity of true spirituality, means and methods for our times,

with a message superior to any, and a willingness to be made 'all things to all men.'[118]

So Booth-Clibborn used music, the printed page, radio, drama and even a 'moving picture' to proclaim the Word. His slogan was, 'Master music, Modern methods and Matchless messages'.[119] His unconventional yet not unsophisticated style of ministry proved to be highly successful in Australia.

After a brief visit to Melbourne, both he and his wife Genevieve ministered in the Railway Institute in Sydney, with some success. Around August, he proceeded to Brisbane, Queensland, while Genevieve continued the Sydney meetings. Finally, in October, she joined him in Queensland.[120] Successful meetings were conducted in Mackay, where numbers grew to around 700 on the final night, Townsville and Rockhampton, where there were some 60 converts, many of whom were baptized in the City Baths, and a number of cases of divine healing.[121]

Booth-Clibborn in Brisbane, 1931.

Like his grandfather, Booth-Clibborn was quick to use innovative methods to attract a hearing. In Rockhampton, he walked a chair upside down through the street, crying, 'Look! Look! This is how sinners are walking today—their heads dragging in the dirt and their minds grovelling on earthly things; their feet meanwhile trampling the treasures of God and Heaven underfoot!' There was 'no lack of a crowd that night,' wryly comments the reporter.[122]

Something of the strong Booth spirit was also evident in his attitude to the existing Pentecostal churches. In both Melbourne and Sydney, he tried to unite the churches under one banner but although they agreed with him in principle, they objected to his forceful manner of trying to accomplish his purpose.[123] He was more successful in Brisbane, where although he was clearly and unequivocally the leader, his charismatic gifts and his winning personality drew people's support.[124] In Brisbane, Booth-Clibborn was sponsored by the Christian Covenanters' Confederacy, an interdenominational organisation founded by his uncle Herbert ('Ambassador') Booth, who had toured Australia in 1922.[125] He hired a tent seating 800 people and erected it in Barry Parade, Valley. On 22 November 1930, 500 people attended the opening service and soon the numbers grew to 1000. Some 200 conversions were recorded.[126]

Booth-Clibborn tent, Brisbane c.19 (Photo courtesy P.Hobbs).

In 1930 and 1931 the Great Depression was at its height. Although Queensland was the only State to have an unemployment benefits scheme, available resources were soon exhausted and a means test was introduced. Voluntary and charitable agencies found their work increasingly in demand. Cinema proprietors urged people to escape their woes by losing themselves in the world of fantasy. Booth-Clibborn encouraged people to forget their hardships by celebrating the joys of faith—

People at Boot-Clibborn tent, 1932. Note orchestra at front. Booth-Clibborn, second row, centre; Len Chamberlain with trombone (Photo courtesy P.Hobbs).

> Preaching a gospel of gladness, Evangelist William Booth-Clibborn, a grandson of the late General William Booth, continued his mission in a large marquee at Barry Parade last evening... Louder and more joyously the song of challenge and encouragement rose until not only the flimsy walls of the big marquee, but roof and all threatened to fall. 'Good evening, everybody,' the young evangelist greeted the large congregation, 'let everybody shake hands with everybody else around them.' The leader of the mission himself set the fashion and it was vigorously followed.
>
> 'Get rid of that old Presbyterian starch,' he continued. 'Put a smile on your faces; toss off your troubles. Get the oil of gladness in your hearts.'
>
> The smiles came and unemployment and other troubles were forgotten as the audience lost themselves in the spiritual uplift of the sacred songs.
>
> 'Put up your hands,' called out the evangelist, and a forest of arms were upheld, as the choral procession of faith proceeded. Seizing a violin, he played an obligato which shrilled above the loud tones of the piano and the singing of the crowd.[127]

There seems little doubt that the privations of the Depression years were sufficient motivation for many people to attend these Pentecostal meetings. Yet there is also evidence that many of those who attended were employed or at least had adequate means. In December, the evangelist launched the Love and Loyalty League, for 'the maintenance of its programme' of 'a full gospel with signs and wonders following... arousing the masses from their lethargy and professors (of Christianity) from their formality.'[128] Membership cost one pound per annum. Funds raised in this way enabled the purchase in 1931 of their own tent—the Canvas Cathedral—which seated 2000 people. Not that everyone who signed up paid promptly. At the end of the year, there were clear reminders for delinquent payers to honour their commitment.[129] And there were other appeals for funds as well—for a grand piano, for a flag, for a collapsible organ for outreach work, for clothing for the needy, for a radio program, for a truck for country work, for foreign missions, for 168 pounds for repairs to the tent when it was damaged by a storm and for ten thousand pounds for a permanent building for the new church. The congregation was clearly not without means. Deprivation theories are inadequate to explain Booth-Clibborn's success.

By May 1931, there had been almost 600 recorded conversions—the target was 1000. By the end of the year, over 100 had been baptized in the Holy Spirit.[130] On 31 May, Booth-Clibborn began a series of radio broadcasts. His penchant for alliteration had already been demonstrated with sermon topics such as 'Reason or Revelation—Which?', 'Will the Trade Tide Turn?', 'In Training for Reigning,' and in slogans like 'The Great Sunday Night Super-Service', and 'Back to the Bible with Booth-Clibborn'. But in announcing the radio programs he excelled himself—

> At last! Your prayers are answered! We Broadcast Brisbane's Brightest Boon! On the Wings of the Wind, Wafted on the Waves of the air comes to every Queensland home the thrill and throb of the Revival over Radio Station 4BC (made to measure = Booth-Clibborn) another proof that the C.C.C. methods are modern.
>
> Two twenty pm. Tuesdays tune into CCC Trio 4bc Brisbane's brightest boon on Barry Parade broadcasting Booth-Clibborn's Canvas Cathedral Campaign Chorus Choir proclaiming, publishing, presenting, preaching, praising Christ crucified, crowned and coming King!

Crowd at Booth-Clibborn Tent campaign in Brisbane 1932–33. Photo courtesy Phyllis Hobbs (with violin).

By July 1931, 2,500 copies of the weekly *Canvas Cathedral Cooee* were being printed. The number soon rose to 3,000 and on one occasion 10,000 were published. There were open air meetings, youth functions, hospital visitation bands, camp meetings and special interest groups.

1932 began with a rush. Twenty three professed conversion in the second week of the month. By March, the total number since the tent meetings were launched was 900. In one two-week period in March, there were 57 'decisions for Christ.' Around a dozen baptismal services were conducted over 16 months. People talked of 'the Canvas Cathedral revival.'

Booth-Clibborn tried every possible means of attracting people. His sermon topics were provocative—

- How to drown
- Is sickness caused by sin?
- The Prodigal that Stayed at Home
- The Pulse of a Dying World
- Noise in the Cemetery
- A New View-point on the Problem of Evil
- Who Killed Jesus?
- Mule Religion
- The Worst Woman in Town

He used a blackboard to illustrate his preaching. There was a motion picture of his ministry in various countries around the world. Books and badges were on sale at the tent. On Saturday 31 October he preached 'the longest sermon in the history of Brisbane'—a four-hour marathon with a 'song intermission.' Hundreds came to hear it. This message was repeated 'by popular request' the following February. On the first anniversary of the tent campaign, 500 people attended a Sunday morning communion service and ten thousand flowers adorned the platform—symbolic of the launching of the fund for ten thousand pounds needed to erect a permanent building. Music was a crucial part of the ministry. In addition to the evangelist's own contribution there was a 150 voice choir and every week the choir items were announced in advance. Members were required to practise regularly and to dress appropriately. There was a meeting every night of the week so no one would ever come and find the tent empty.

It was not all glitz and glamour. The fact that Booth-Clibborn could preach several times a week for sixteen months as he did indicates a significant depth of intellectual and spiritual resources.[131] There were weekly Bible Studies and missionary meetings and regular gatherings for days of fasting and prayer. And Booth-Clibborn's preaching, although dramatic, was lucid, reasoned, biblical and clear.[132] On one occasion the tent was severely damaged by a tropical storm and a temporary tent was provided by a local business. There were also struggles with sickness. After his 'Chrysler car conquered floods, storms, running rivers (and) logs,' en route to Toowoomba, Booth-Clibborn returned to Brisbane by train 'grievously sick' and called for the church leaders to come and pray with him. Within a week, he was fully recovered. There was also criticism and opposition. 'Those who stand on their dignity are disturbed at our freedom,' wrote Booth-Clibborn—

> We are altogether too lively! We lift our hands in singing and laugh! We are too lavish, too loud. We stay too long and too late at it! Such extremes, such extravagances! Such abandonment to emotion! ...We are furiously assaulted as fakers, false teachers and fanatics by a class of religious zealots who having lost the power cling to a form or godliness. These crystalized Christians imagine the body may be kept healthy not by giving it food but by minding and mending the raiment only! THEY REST IN A FORM and are dead whilst the corpse remains well dressed. They have lost the spirit in the letter, they have left the substance and followed the shadow.[133]

Booth-Clibborn was not the only preacher. George Burns and Alex Buchanan[134] often ministered in the tent. George Burns, disillusioned after his experience with Van Eyk, was now engaged in itinerant work around Queensland. In July 1931, he reported twenty decisions for Christ in Nanango, 140 kilometres north-west of Brisbane, and a month later there were 44 potential new members for a church there. In September, he was in Rockhampton, where there was a 'full house' and the 'beginnings of a big blaze' and a local preacher in the Church of Christ was healed of defective eye sight. In November 1931, in nearby Toowoomba there were services every night of the week in 'Canvas Cathedral Number Two,' which was dedicated by Mrs Booth-Clibborn who preached there in early December. Here the work originally consolidated by Van Eyk was now represented by two Pentecostal congregations—the larger one now calling itself an Assembly of God; the smaller a remnant of the Apostolic Faith Mission. Burns became 'dangerously ill' and in January, 1932, the young Sydney evangelist Heather Burrows joined him in Toowoomba where she was soon followed by Genevieve Booth-Clibborn.

Leila Buchanan, Cecilia Van Eyk, W.A.Buchanan, F.B.Van Eyk.

Mrs Booth-Clibborn exercised a prominent role in the Brisbane ministry, as did Leila Buchanan, Heather Burrows and Mary Ayers, and visiting missionaries such as Jessie Ferguson and Isabella Hetherington. In August 1930, she arrived in Brisbane and after two weeks' rest, preached five times in one week. A month later she returned and preached regularly in the Canvas Cathedral until moving to Toowoomba. There, the tent was 'taxed to capacity' with enthusiastic people, many of whom were unchurched. *Cooee* reported that Mrs Booth-Clibborn had 'taken well' in Toowoomba. By the time she left, there were 40 recorded commitments to Christ. It was widely seen as revival.

At the first anniversary of the Tent ministry, a fund was launched for a permanent building. Three months later, the Executive Council 'with Evangelist William Booth-Clibborn's authority' sought to have the Canvas Cathedral Congregation incorporated as the Covenant Christian Church and on 28 February 1932, the new church was formally commenced. At the same time, the Booth-Clibborns announced their intention to journey on to the United States. Special farewell services were held in which the evangelist was 'supported by Mr and Mrs Buchanan.'

But it was to neither W. A. Buchanan nor George Burns that Booth-Clibborn turned when seeking a successor. The new pastor was a Welshman named John Hewitt. He had visited Queensland previously but had returned to England a year before. 'I am delighted to know I am still remembered,' he wrote.[135] Another evangelist, he was well able to sustain the momentum of the Canvas Cathedral—in his first six months there were 66 baptisms—and to see the laying of the foundation stone for Glad Tidings Tabernacle on 13 August 1932.[136] The new building was opened on 10 December. Hewitt's ministry there was brief and after ten months, he left to join F. B. Van Eyk in evangelism[137] and subsequently the Apostolic Church. By 1937, Buchanan was pastor of the Tabernacle.[138] 'There is much that could be said concerning the good hand of God upon us,' he wrote later, 'but at best we are unprofitable servants—graciously His for Time and Eternity.'[139] Ten years after this he opened a Christian book ministry which still bore his name half a century later.

By 1939, there were 39 Assemblies of God churches in Australia, mostly in Queensland.[140]

Much of the practice of the Pentecostal evangelists of the 1920s and early 1930s was common to evangelists of all denominations. The American J. Edwin Orr, visited Australia in 1936 and conducted rallies in major city churches where men stood to their feet to publicly confess their sins and there were extended times of prayer and penitent weeping before God and people knelt 'to seek the gracious infilling of God's Spirit'. At the final gathering in Melbourne, there were some 5000 people present.[141] He was particularly struck by the weekly gatherings for prayer initiated by William 'Cairo' Bradley in the basement of the Sydney Town Hall, where hundreds gathered for intercession and thousands of prayer requests were dealt with.[142] It was the Pentecostals' innovative style, daring claims and distinctive doctrine that set them apart. But for them, it was not just a matter of boldness or innovation or non-conformity. The distinctive feature was the infilling of the Holy Spirit. Revival was impossible without it. And successful Christianity was impossible without revival. For these 1920s preachers, the spirit of Pentecost was the essential and crucial element in all they did.

Notes

1. Greenwood, *Life Story,* 1965, 1ff. Unless otherwise stated, details of Greenwood's life are from this source.

2. In 1898, the wife of John Graham Lake (1870–1935), an American publisher, real estate and insurance businessman, instantaneously recovered from tuberculosis through Dowie's ministrations in Zion, Illinois. Lake became an elder in the Catholic Apostolic Church. In 1907, after Dowie's death, he was baptized in the Holy Spirit, turned his back on a lucrative career, and the following year, went to South Africa with his wife and seven children, where he began his ministry among Zion people. Within months, his wife died. However, he continued preaching for five years and by the time he left, there were some 600 new congregations in South Africa under the name Apostolic Faith Mission (AFM). The AFM is today one of the leading Pentecostal denominations in South Africa. Their practice of baptism by triple immersion is a reflection of their Zion origins. See Burgess et al, 1988, 531; John G. Lake, *Sermons* (Dallas: The Voice of Healing, 1949), 44, 130; G. Lindsay, *John G. Lake: Apostle to Africa* (Dallas: Christ for the Nations, 1980), 3, 17, 24, 27, 53; Lindsay, *Dowie* 1951, 271.

3. There are some discrepancies between different versions of Greenwood's story. In 1964, he claimed that 33 people received the Spirit and that he was baptized in the Spirit on 25 November, 1913. See APF address transcript, 1964.

4. The Brauns were also instrumental in leading the Armstrong family into Pentecostalism. See M. Brett, 'Maxwell Armstrong,' unpublished essay, Tabor College, 1996.

5. For more on Horne, see Appendix B. Further research is yet to be done on Horne. The details given here are based on personal interviews with L. Brabham, D. Brabham, I. Martin and H. Broadley, from comments by C. L. Greenwood and from an address given at the opening of the Southern Evangelical Mission's new building in Brighton in 1961, possibly by E. Holland, who succeeded Horne as pastor. Where there are discrepancies, I have taken the latter source as the more reliable. Unfortunately, some other printed materials were lost in the 1987 fire.

6. Ada Painter later became a close friend of Frances Greenwood. See L. and H. Dwight, personal interview, 12 June, 1990; L. Manley-Breen, personal interview, July, 1990.

7. Greenwood, *Life Story*, 1965, 25.

8. Some 50 years later, Greenwood described Lowe's exorcism in this way—'He came inside and knelt at the table. He had not been kneeling very long when the spirit that had controlled him all his life started to manifest itself. You have never seen anything like it in your life... That spirit lifted him up off his knees as high as the table and had him hanging in mid-air... That held him there and when he did that and started to make awful noises... I rushed behind the door... I was scared and as I put my face to the ground I cried to God and the power of God fell on me. I got up off my face, ran across to him (by this time he was flat on his back) and put my two knees on his chest. (I would never do it again.) I commanded the unclean demon to come out of him and... the demons gave way. That spirit was gone immediately. He burst out speaking in other tongues as the Spirit gave him utterance. He was delivered that night from demon power and baptized in the Holy Ghost.' Lowe was to become one of Greenwood's most loyal and devoted partners in ministry. At one point, when damaging rumours were being spread about the meetings at Sunshine and the Greenwoods in particular, Lowe's loyalty and encouragement were invaluable. See Greenwood, *Life Story*, 1965, 35f.

9. H. Dwight, personal interview, 12 June, 1990.

10. Leo Harris, personal interview, c.1970.

11. A. Wilson, personal communication, n. d. but late 1994. See also S. Douglas, personal interview, 21 November, 1989.

12. Ethel King and Jessie Ferguson, missionaries from India, were present at the opening. See C. L. Greenwood, 'The Melbourne Revival,' AE, July, 1926, 20.

13. For background on Valdez, see Appendix B.

14. Years later (in the 1960s?), Valdez, his memory less than reliable, said he was 26 at this time. See A. C. Valdez, 'The Call and Circumstances of A. C. Valdez coming to Australia and New Zealand in 1925,' transcript of taped address, Richmond Temple, Melbourne, n. d. but c.1964. Other details of Valdez' ministry are from this source unless otherwise stated.

15. C. Gadge, personal interview, 2 March, 1992.

16. *Age*, 7 March, 1925, p.11.

17. GN, 16:3, March, 1925, 17, 24; May, 1926, 9.

18. See Valdez, Address, c.1964.

19. *Age*, 14 March, 1925, 11.

20. *Age,* 14 March, 1925, 11; 21 March, 1925.

21. Valdez, Address, c.1964.

22. E. Greenwood, personal interview, n. d.; C. Gadge, personal interview, 2 March, 1992.

23. I. Warburton, personal interview, n. d.; Jessie Ferguson, personal interview, n. d.

24. There are several inconsistencies in the recollections of both Valdez and Greenwood. Greenwood, for example, incorrectly claimed that everyone walked out of Good News Hall when Buchanan spoke. He noted that Valdez was 23 (not 29) when he came to Melbourne. On the other hand, Valdez's story of his call to Sunshine is incomplete. He omitted significant facts, such as Greenwood's visit to the SEM. Valdez also claimed that 'scores' of students at the Melbourne Bible Institute were baptized in the Spirit, which was plainly an exaggeration.

25. Greenwood, *Life Story*, p.42. The young man mentioned her in the *Story* was possibly W. A. Buchanan.

26. *Age,* 4 April, 1925.

27. *Richmond Temple Souvenir,* 1939, 6f; c.f. AE, July, 1926, 20; GN, July, 1925, 20.

28. G. and I. George, personal interview, 12 June, 1990; C. Gadge, personal interview, 2 March, 1992.

29. Valdez, address, c.1964. No other reports of this are extant.

30. On Easter Monday, 1926, W. J. Nankervois penned the following lines about these tarry meetings which are handwritten on the inside cover of a bound volume of the *Australian Evangel 1926–1927,* owned by the Wilson family—

> There's a little brick room in Sunshine Hall
> Whose walls give forth no sound,
> You can shout as you will with never a fear
> Of troubling the folks around.
>
> The seekers flocked to the little brick room
> 'Till scores and hundreds there,
> Baptized in the mighty Spirit's power,
> The works of God declare.
>
> All hail to the great Baptizer,
> 'Twas there He set me free,
> 'Twas in a little room at the back,
> The blessing fell on me.

31. A. Wilson, personal interview.

32. *Argus,* 23 May, 1925, 18; RTS, 1939, 7; *Age,* 6 June, 1925, 10. Note that other figures have been quoted by different people (eg G. Gadge:500) including, years later, Greenwood himself, but 400 is probably nearest.

33. Chant, 1984, 66ff.

34. W. Phillips, 'Gypsy Smith in Australia in the 1920s,' in M. Hutchinson et al, 1994, 185ff.

35. Breward, 1993, 119; Dickey, ed, 1994, 168f.

36. O'Farrell, 1985, 373. Neither the 1928 Congress in Sydney nor the 1934 Congress in Melbourne seems to have attracted any interest or reaction from the Pentecostals. I have not found any reference to either in any of the Pentecostal journals of the day.

37. Although Good News Hall was the first Pentecostal congregation, Lancaster persistently resisted attempts to establish a denominational structure.

38. L. Jones, *Confess It!* (Hong Kong: World Outreach, 1974), Introduction, 13ff; Greenwood, *Life Story,* 1965, 52; GN, August, 1932, 10f. Further details are from these sources unless otherwise stated. The Melbourne Bible Institute is now called the Bible College of Victoria. For the background and origins of MBI see D. Paproth, 'The Mel-

bourne Bible Institute: its Genesis, Ethos and Purpose,' in G. Treloar, ed, *The Furtherance of Religious Beliefs: Essays on the History of Theological Education in Australia* (Sydney: Centre for the Study of Australian Christianity for the Evangelical History Association, 1997), 124ff ; 'Nash, Clifford Harris' in Dickey, ed, ADEB, 1994, 276ff and B. B. Darling, 'Nash, Clifford Harris (1866–1891) in ADB, Vol 10, 1891–1931.

39. Note that Jones gives the date as 1 May, but in 1925, this was a Friday.

40. Paproth, in Treloar, ed, 1997, 137ff. In his short (117 pp) study on hermeneutics, *The Fourfold Interpretation of Jesus Christ in the New Testament* (Melbourne: S. John Bacon, n. d.), Nash indicates his attitude to glossolalia, not by what he says about it, but by what he does not say. In reference to the conversion of Cornelius, for instance, Nash concedes that 'the sudden intervention of the Holy Spirit' made it impossible to argue against the admission of Gentiles to the Church, but makes no attempt to develop this (p.35).

41. *Minutes of the Executive Committee,* Melbourne Bible Institute, 2 June, 1925. The Committee, chaired by Dr J. J. Kitchen, unanimously endorsed Nash's action and a hand written note to this effect was added to the notice.

42. L. Jones, letter to C. H. Nash, 20 May, 1925, held in Bible College of Victoria archives. The following is part of Jones' letter—'As far as I can see at present I shall have to leave the Institute in view of the notice that has been put up. If I were to stay I would be responsible not only to you as Principal, but to God, to follow absolutely what has been set down... This is not a hasty conclusion but is the step after prayerful consideration, and I find I cannot stay under those conditions.

'It is very hard for anyone else to realise what this step has caused me, and if I were to follow my inclinations and desires (if any) instead of His leading, it would not be the way I am going... I have to leave my friends and go amongst strangers. I am misunderstood and thought to going into error... Man has not influenced me one way or the other in this matter, as I have held solidly to God's Word and I don't think He will lead me into error when I am endeavouring to follow His Word faithfully.

'My dear Mr Nash, I know you have been praying that I will be guided aright, and God knows... the influence your life has meant to me, which I shall never forget and thank Him for. I love you as I never have before, and I know that your love for me is still the same...'

43. L. Jones, letter to C. H. Nash, 8 January, 1926.

44. C. H. Nash, letter to L. Jones, 21 June, 1932.

45. GN, 24:1, January, 1933, 8. A feature of Jones's early ministry was what is currently termed being 'slain in the Spirit' i.e. collapsing to the floor under the laying on of hands or healing prayer. For nearly fifty years, Jones served as a Pentecostal pastor both in Australia and overseas, founding the Slavic and Oriental Mission (later World Outreach) in 1932 and editing the *Evidence* magazine. During World War II, he directed YMCA activities with the Australian Army in the Middle East. See Jones, 1974, Introduction, 8ff. Jones was not the only Pentecostal minister encouraged by Nash. Assemblies of God pastor Lloyd Averill also recalled how it was Nash who urged him to enter the ministry. See Averill, 1992, p.23.

46. Jones, 1974, 8.

47. C. Gadge, personal interview, 2 March, 1992.

48. P. Duncan, *Pentecost* n. d., 8; C. L. Greenwood, 'The Melbourne Revival', AE, July, 1926, 20.

49. *Age,* 9 May, 1925; *Argus,* 9 May, 1925, 16.

50. *Argus,* 12 May, 1925, 6.

51. *Argus,* 12 May, 1925, 6; see also Breward, 1993, 119.

52. Piggin, 1996, 99.

53. Jones later wrote, 'The first person I ever heard speak clearly in tongues was myself; it was very real and wonderful... Dr S. MacColl and others were greatly concerned about me and I spent time with them all during which they endeavoured to show me the wrongness of it all, bringing 40 years ago the same arguments against the experience that we still hear today.'— L. Jones, personal interview. According to one of those present at the public meeting, the Pentecostal cause was not helped by someone interrupting with a loud and prolonged utterance in tongues and ultimately being ejected. See C. Gadge, personal interview, 2 March, 1992.

54. D. Dawson, personal interview; Valdez, address, c.1964. Duncan claims that Valdez actually attended the Evangelical meeting and addressed those present with 'convincing power and dignity.' See Duncan, 1978, 17. This is confirmed by Gadge who recalls MacColl speaking of Pentecostal excesses rather than quoting Scripture and Valdez handling the debate in a gentlemanly manner (Gadge, personal interview, 2 March, 1992). As both Dawson and Gadge claim to have attended the meeting of which they speak, their comments cannot be easily dismissed but as, to this point I have been unable to locate any relevant newspaper advertising or other documentation, it is difficult to ascertain the correct version.

55. *Spectator*, Vol LI , No. 39, 30 September, 1925, 936; *Spectator*, Vol LI , No. 44, 4 November, 1925.

56. Ridgway, *Paths,* c.1946, 66. Ridgway wrote this around 1946, but it reflected a view he had heard many times in the previous two decades. In fact, this charge was still being laid in the 1950s and 1960s and was addressed to me personally on more than one occasion.

57. Duncan, *Pentecost,* 8.

58. For additional information on Glover see Appendix B.

59. Duncan, *Pentecost,* 8.

60. C. L. Greenwood, 'The Melbourne Revival,' AE, July, 1926, 20; RTS, 1939, 7.

61. Premillennialism was also taught by the charismatic Edward Irving (1792–1834), from whom Darby may have learned it. But it was Darby through the Brethren movement and the *Scofield Reference Bible* who popularised the theory. See Dallimore, 1983, 47ff; I. Murray, *The Puritan Hope* (Edinburgh: Banner of Truth, 1984). It is interesting that although Glover's teaching was well appreciated at the time, the Assemblies of God today have rejected his stance and generally embrace pre-tribulationism.

62. K. Glover, 'The Bride,' lecture given at Richmond Temple, n. d. Transcript in my possession.

63. K. Glover, 'The Overcomer,' 16ff.

64. Glover, 'The Overcomer,' 10.

65. A number which grew to four by the end of the year. In 1926, there was a total of 59 enrolments at MBI, which accepted new enrolments each term. Source: *Students of the Bible College of Victoria (inc.Melbourne Bible Institute)* 1989, 1.

66. AE, December, 1930, 10.

67. Minutes of General Assembly Meetings, Richmond Temple, 2 October 1927.

68. Duncan, *Pentecost,* .9.

69. *Minutes* Richmond Temple, 3 April, 1927.

70. *Minutes of Deacons' Meeting,* Richmond Temple, 24 February, 1932. From the outset, leadership in Pentecostal churches was usually in the hands of a pastor or pastors and elders, with deacons being responsible for the management of the finances, maintenance of buildings and the like. Both the term 'elder' and the term 'deacon' were derived from passages such as 1 Timothy 3:1ff which refers to the qualifications expected of both.

71. *Minutes*, Richmond Temple, 4 November, 1928; 22 December, 1929; 5 November, 1933.
72. *Minutes*, Richmond Temple, 20 October, 1934.
73. Greenwood, *Life Story*, 67; *Minutes*, Richmond Temple, 8 July, 1935; 13 October, 1935; *Minutes, Deacons' Meeting*, 6 October, 1934.
74. AE, 8:2, May, 1935, 8.
75. AE, 8:3 July, 1935, 3, 8; AE, 8:2, May 1935, 3, 8f.
76. *Minutes*, Richmond Temple, 28 October, 1936.
77. Greenwood, *Life Story*, 1965, 68. Greenwood was well-known for his reluctance to share authority. He opposed the establishment of new congregations in Melbourne, for example, unless with his prior agreement. See S. Douglas, personal interview, 21 November, 1989; personal knowledge.
78. M. Laurens, personal interview, 12 June, 1990; K. Lowe, personal interview, 12 June, 1990; G. and I. George, personal interview, 12 June, 1990. This comment was also made by members of Greenwood's family – H. Dwight, personal interview, 12 June, 1990; L. Manley-Green, personal interview, July, 1990.
79. K. Conner, personal interview, 6 June, 1991; comments made by several Apostolic pastors in interviews.
80. This opinion was expressed by several interviewees although they usually preferred not to be quoted.
81. G. and I. George, personal interview, 12 June 1990.
82. Greenwood, *Life Story*, 1965, 65, 77.
83. AE, December, 1928, 7.
84. AE, May, 1931, 10; AE, June, 1931, 10.
85. AE, 8:3, July, 1935, 8.
86. Greenwood, *Life Story*, 1965, 65.
87. A. C. Davidson; AE, February, 1969, 12; K. A. Lowe, personal interview, 12 June, 1990.
88. G. and I. George, personal interview, 12 June, 1990; W. Nugent, personal interview, November, 1990.
89. G. and I. George, personal interview, 12 June, 1990.
90. Greenwood, *Life Story*, 1965, 65; S. Douglas, personal interview, 21 November, 1989; H. Dwight, personal interview, 12 June, 1990; G.and I. George, personal interview, 12 June, 1990; K. A. Lowe, personal interview, 12 June, 1990.
91. C. L. Greenwood, 'The Ten Virgins,' AE, 6:11, April, 1933, 2ff. Note that the practice of using Elizabethan English for interpretations and prophecies was widespread amongst Pentecostals until the 1980s.
92. *Minutes*, Richmond Temple, 23 November, 1936.
93. *Minutes*, Richmond Temple, 23 November, 1936.
94. Duncan, *Pentecost*, 16; AE August 1937, 4.
95. AE, August, 1937, 4f; D and G. Smith, 1987, 35ff.
96. D and G. Smith, 1987, 36.
97. *Minutes*, Richmond Temple, 8 July, 1937.
98. S. Douglas, personal interview, 21 November, 1989; D. Armstrong, personal interview, 30 April, 1990.
99. GN, 1:6, October, 1913, 11.
100. GN, 15:3, March, 1924, 18.
101. Duncan, *Pentecost*, 71; P. Gossling, personal communication, 16 December, 1974; H. Hoskin, personal interview, 21 November, 1997.
102. N. L. Armstrong, personal interview, 30 April, 1990. See further on Armstrong in Appendix B.

103. J. Pittman, 'Frederick Duncan: his Significance and Contribution to the Pentecostal Movement,' unpublished essay, Tabor College, 1994; R. Woodham, *Philip B. Duncan Pentecostal Pioneer,* published by the author, 1997, 5ff; R. Woodham, personal interview, 29 October, 1993; M. Duncan, personal interview, 29 October, 1993. Further details of the Duncan family are from these sources unless otherwise stated.

104. J. Ridley, *A Soldier's Testimony* (Melbourne: S. John Bacon, n. d.), 7f. It is of interest that around 1950, Ridley was baptized in the Holy Spirit through the testimony of a converted actress named Janet Allen and a tract written by Duncan, and joined the Pentecostal movement for a time. G. Bowling, personal interview; my own personal knowledge.

105. AE, August, 1926, 6; Duncan, *Pentecost,* 70f.

106. Duncan, 1978, 5.

107. Frodsham, 1949; Hibbert, 1982; Hywel-Davies, 1987.

108. AE, April, 1927, 5.

109. GN, 15:7, July, 1924, 18.

110. Woodham, 1997, 12; H. Dwight, personal interview, 12 June, 1990.

111. SMH, 19 February 1927, 7.

112. AE, July, 1926, 6; Duncan, 1978 .7.

113. Duncan was a quick-thinker and when accused of militarism by manufacturing uniforms, he answered, 'Would you rather the men went to war naked?'

114. P. Duncan, 'Address,' 1965.

115. E. Booth-Clibborn, *50 Years for Jesus* (Chichester: New Wine, 1989), 27ff.

116. W. Booth-Clibborn (ed), *Wings of Praise*, published by the author, Sydney, n. d. Opinions varied about the quality of the songs—'He made up such wonderful hymns. Some of them were rubbish, but some were beautiful'—R. Woodham, personal interview, 29 October 1993.

117. *Cooee*, Toowoomba, No. 5, 22 November, 1931.

118. *Cooee*, Toowoomba, No. 5, 22 November, 1931.

119. *Cooee*, 1:19, 19 July, 1931.

120. AE, August, 1930, 9; H. Hoskin interview, 1997.

121. AE, December, 1930, 13f; January–February 1931, 7.

122. AE, January–February, 1931, 7. On another occasion he is reported to have set his hat on the ground and jumped around it pointing to it and shouting, 'It's alive! It's alive!' When sufficient people had gathered, he picked up his hat, revealing his Bible which he then grasped, held high and proclaimed, 'The Word of God which lives and abides forever!'

123. P. Duncan, Address, 1965; M. Duncan, personal interview, 29 October, 1993. Both Philip Duncan and his wife Mollie spoke of Booth-Clibborn as being strong-willed and domineering in asserting his own ideas—even on one occasion to the point of using physical force.

124. 'Our beloved leader ...,' *Cooee*, 2:16, 20 December, 1931.

125. Herbert Booth's ministry was appreciated by some of the early Pentecostals e.g. GN, 9:1, February 1923, 17; GN, 15:8, August, 1924, 20.

126. AE, March, 1931, 2.

127. A *Daily Telegraph* report quoted in AE, March, 1931, 2.

128. AE, March, 1931, 3.

129. *Cooee*, 2:15, 13 December, 1931.

130. These and further details of Booth-Clibborn's Brisbane ministry are taken from *Cooee*, 3 May, 1931 to 18 September, 1932, unless otherwise stated. *Cooee* was a one-page type-written newsletter published weekly and widely distributed.

131. One disillusioned lay leader wrote, 'Van Eyk would not have been able to hold an Evangelistic Crusade for over twelve months—he did not probe deeply into Scripture like Booth-Clibborn did.' In the light of Van Eyk's extant printed sermons this seems an unjust claim. See T. Hallop, personal correspondence, 30 April, 1993.

132. For a sample of Booth-Clibborn's preaching see GN, 5:10, October, 1924, 3f; Chant, 1984, 330ff.

133. *Cooee*, Toowoomba, No. 5, 22 November, 1931.

134. See Appendix B for background on Buchanan.

135. *Cooee*, 2:24, 21 February, 1932.

136. See the foundation stone of the church building in Valley, Brisbane.

137. GC, 2:1, March 1933, 89f.

138. Glad Tidings Tabernacle records; Alan and Jean Conwell, personal interview, c.1992.

139. W. A. Buchanan, 'Know Your Ministers,' in AE, 20:12, December, 1963, 16f. Buchanan's disposition was reflected in advice given to young Lloyd Averill who was concerned about taking on an Assemblies of God church when he had a Good News Hall background. Buchanan's opinion was, 'Just use biblical phraseology—don't try to interpret it.' This was a reflection of Mrs Lancaster's own approach. Lloyd Averill, personal interview, 20 November, 1990.

140. That there were twice as many congregations in Queensland as in all the other States combined possibly reflects the fact that Australian Pentecostalism flourished in provincial, country towns. Roe suggests that the relatively successful growth of theosophy in Queensland in the late nineteenth and early twentieth centuries was assisted by its congenial climate and that 'Queensland at this time presented a milieu in which theosophy might be expected to flourish—muddled, tense, volatile, futuristic.' She notes that the world's first Labour government was in Queensland; that it was from Queensland that William Lane migrated to Paraguay to establish his ideal colony; that assisted immigration and its resultant fermentation of new ideas and ideals continued longer in Queensland than anywhere else in Australia; that 'labour followed capital' from the southern States; and that after 1860, mining booms spurred development in the Far North. She argues that this proliferation of new and radical ideas and of progressive industry possibly provided a congenial climate for theosophy. See Roe, 1986, 115f. To what extent this argument applies to the development of Pentecostalism, which took place two decades after the establishing of theosophy, and during both a World War and a Great Depression, is not immediately evident. However, Queenslanders, with their more casual lifestyle and less conventional manners, may well have found in Pentecostalism an acceptable and comfortable form of religion suited to their less urban society.

141. J. E. Orr, *All Your Need* (London: Marshall, Morgan and Scott, 1936), 66ff, 89. It is of interest that Booth-Clibborn's mother was in correspondence with Edwin Orr (p.99).

142. ADEB, 1994, 48.

CHAPTER NINE

THE SPIRIT OF PROPHECY

The Apostolic Church—New structures, New Controversies (1930–1939)

The emergence of the Apostolic Church in Australia provides a clear example of how Pentecostal groups could be divided over differing doctrines held with equal passion and conviction. When a movement majors on personal spiritual experience, it enters the realm of the subjective where individual encounters with God have an authority of their own and where the validity of religious belief may be assessed by the degree to which it touches the heart. Truth then becomes contingent on testimony and certitude on satisfaction. Couple this with a conviction that the Scriptures are the final authority on matters of faith and practice, and that every believer has the right to interpret them personally, and controversy is inevitable. The spirit of Pentecost was vibrant and dynamic, but like the wind, difficult to restrain.[1]

Centre front, William Cathcart.

It was the arrival in 1930 of Scotsman William Cathcart which opened up the new area of dispute—the role of apostles and prophets in the church. For people in mainline denominations, this was a non-issue. For them, apostles and prophets were safely enshrined in the biblical records and to resurrect them in today's world was as anachronistic as equipping paratroops with swords and spears. For Pentecostals, however, strongly committed as they were to the conviction that the supernatural gifts and ministries of biblical times were still valid, the issue was very much alive.

William Cathcart (1893–1989) was tall, dignified and commanding in presence. 'He was a man who appealed to men,' recalled one of his associates, 'a godly man who preached the word with power and dignity.' People spoke of him as being of military bearing, distant yet compassionate. 'He had a presence,' recalled Kath Kirwan, who was in her late teens when she first met him. 'I was scared of him. You never called him by his first name and he didn't socialise.' He was awesome, agreed Lawrie Wahlquist, remembering his teenage response to Cathcart's presence. He was known as a 'good, solid teacher' and as a quiet, upright man.[2] Born of Scottish parents in Northern Ireland, he was converted at the age of 16. Five years later he fought in France in World War I, from which he was repatriated to a convalescent home for many months. 'He was shell-shocked,' recalled Joshua McCabe. 'I never saw a more miserable looking devil than he was.'[3] During this time, he was given a New Testament and while holding it in his hands, heard God say, 'I am going to heal you. I will give you a shepherd's heart and you will go to the uttermost parts of the earth for me.' While attending a Brethren assembly, he came in touch with an Apostolic church and was healed. On two occasions he saw visions—one (while travelling on a Glasgow tram) of sandy beaches, blue sea and surf, which he later identified as Manly, New South Wales; the other of two men in a sunlit country beckoning him, whom he believed represented Australia and New Zealand.[4]

Australian Apostolic Executive, c.1945 (Photo S.Cowling).

In 1929, there were in Perth, Western Australia, six small Pentecostal groups, disunited apparently because of disputes over leadership and a dearth of trained ministry.[5] A school teacher named Miss Flett, who had been a member of the Apostolic Church in the Orkney Islands, persuaded one of these groups to invite the Apostolic Church in Great Britain to send them a pastor.[6] They particularly wanted Andrew Turnbull, Apostolic patriarch and founder of the Apostolic Church in Scotland, to come, but at the 1929 convention in Penygroes, Wales, the church council unanimously settled on William Cathcart. In the light of his own prior sense of calling, he was more than willing.

Since 1923, Cathcart had been in full-time ministry and was currently involved in the Burning Bush Apostolic congregation in Glasgow. He was considered 'a prominent and successful apostle' with 'a profound expository ministry.'[7] On 1 February 1930, together with his wife and small son, he sailed for Perth. About 25 people met them on their arrival. It was Depression time and money was scarce. There was no support forthcoming from England, so Cathcart and two others devised a mixture of different brands of tea and sold it door to door under the name Triune Tea Company. Although there was much sacrifice, they were never in need. They conducted street meetings and gave food to the poor. Cathcart taught the 'Apostolic vision'. A small group of believers led by George Taylor joined the budding assembly and they began to grow. Discussions were held with a third group, who were having trouble paying the lease on their hall. Cathcart persuaded them of the validity of his teaching and they combined their resources under his leadership. Soon they were meeting in an imposing former Methodist church building in Brisbane Street, North Perth.

The Apostolic Church

The background to the Apostolic Church lay in the Welsh Revival of 1904–05, where there had been a strong emphasis on the fullness of the Holy Spirit.[8] It was plainly Pentecostal. But there were some clear differences. First, in contrast to the other Pentecostal groups in Australia who stressed local church autonomy, the Apostolic Church was centralised and tightly organised. By 1934, the British Church had a detailed constitution of over 200 typed pages which was accepted in Australia in 1939 with little change. Among other things, it set down that tithing was compulsory and that all offerings were to be paid to a central fund from which allocations were made to local assemblies. All pastors were salaried equally and appointed by the Commonwealth Council without consultation.[9]

Second, Cathcart was reserved and not given to shows of emotion. This approach won the confidence of some who were uneasy with the more flamboyant or expressive behaviour of some Pentecostals. Third, the most significant factor was the emphasis on the roles of apostles and prophets. Of the five ministry designations listed in Ephesians 4:11 (apostles, prophets, evangelists, pastors and teachers) historic churches tended to accept only the latter three. Pentecostal churches accepted all five, but generally used only two—pastor and evangelist—as titles. The Apostolics encouraged and recognised them all (see Table 9). The ninth tenet of the Apostolic Church reads—

> Church Government by Apostles, Prophets, Evangelists, Pastors, Teachers, Elders and Deacons.

In practice, there were clear lines of demarcation between the various offices. Apostles and prophets plainly stood well above the rest. Apostles exercised a 'governmental role.' Prophets provided guidance and direction. Once the

Church was established, there was a yearly Commonwealth Council, two thirds of which comprised apostles and one third prophets.[10] Prophets were urged to give the Word of the Lord in such meetings, including the calling of people to office. Based on the Lucan record of the commissioning of Saul and Barnabas, where prophets and teachers were involved, Apostolics argued that when the Holy Spirit spoke, he did so through a prophet (Acts 13:1ff). Hence, the concept of directive prophecy, in which prophets called people into various spheres of ministry.[11] Prophets were 'set' in place for this purpose.[12] All 'inquiries of the Lord' by Apostles were to be made only in the presence of a prophet.[13] 'The office of Prophet,' wrote W. A. C. Rowe, in his text book of Apostolic doctrine, 'is in vital union with the Apostolic office.' Indeed, ideally, they worked together as a single gift. They were so intimately linked that either one would be incomplete on its own.[14] Nevertheless—

> The determining and final power of The Apostolic Church in all matters spiritual, moral, governmental and financial, is invested in the body of Apostles of the Church, termed the General Council ...[15]

Table 9 Comparative table of recognition of ministry gifts.

	Recognised by Historic churches	Ordained or used as title	Recognised by Pentecostal churches	Ordained or used as title	Recognised by Apostolic Church	Ord use[d]
Apostle			X		X	X
Prophet			X		X	X
Evangelist	X		X	X	X	X
Pastor	X	X	X	X	X	X
Teacher	X		X		X	X

Constitutionally, apostolic duties were divided so that, where possible, one apostle was in charge of each district with a group of apostles governing each 'area' (i.e. a group of three to five districts). One of these apostles was to be in touch with Commonwealth Headquarters, and was 'generally responsible for all Governmental and Doctrinal matters in the Area.' Another was to be in active contact with the Missionary Advisory Board and a third with the Finance Board.[16]

There was also a clear distinction between the gift of prophecy which any believer might express and the office of prophet, although prophets, too, were categorised. Some were 'set apart by the authority of the General Council for

International work,' others were commissioned variously for Inter-Area, Area, District or local assembly work. While all prophets were expected to give the word of the Lord at any time to the Church, calling people to office was restricted to their sphere of ministry.[17]

Whereas prophecies in public worship services in other Pentecostal churches were usually brief, Apostolic prophecies could last for a quarter of an hour or more. Then an apostle might expound the prophecy in much the same way other preachers would explain the Scriptures.[18] Sometimes, preaching was abandoned altogether to give place to prophesying.[19] In practice, these prophecies, like most Pentecostal prophecies, were basically encouragements to God's people and were the first person format to have been changed to third person, would have seemed much like the kind of exhortation any believer might give to another. In 1942, for example, W. A. C. Rowe delivered the following message to the congregation in Adelaide—

> I have spoken to you of these facts in order that I might speak specifically to you—for you lack fear, holy fear... and not only you, but every member throughout the world. Living in days of great development and achievement, you lack a holy fear as My People. In order that you may not trespass upon the ground that you ought not to; in order that you will be kept free from such powers and forces (of evil) you need a holy fear. You require a greater and more august vision of Myself. It may be that your conception of My mercy has diminished your conception of My righteousness. Come to Me that I may give you a greater vision of Myself...[20]

The esteem with which such prophesyings were regarded is demonstrated by frequent quotations throughout the *Constitution* and *Guiding Principles* from prophetic statements endorsing or validating the rules or principles laid down. Often, they were profound. Sometimes, they were quite homely. For example, after a clause affirming that a public utterance in tongues should be divided into segments to allow for progressive interpretation, the following extract from a prophecy appears—

> When one speaketh in tongues, however long a time it is, it is one tongue; but it is best to be divided for the sake of convenience, and for the sake of interpretation. There is an advantage in this and I would have you remember that aspect. If what I have said is generally known in the assembly, it will save confusion and bring a general understanding so that I may be honoured and glorified.[21]

This entirely new emphasis on the ministry of apostles and prophets was an exciting revelation to many. Cathcart had little trouble gathering a band of people around him who believed the new church was yet a further development of the restoration of New Testament teaching and practice.

More than a few people were intrigued and enticed by what they saw and heard. 'To many it was a revelation of the way in which God is working in these last days,' wrote one newcomer, 'and we do esteem it a privilege to be in that place, where we can indeed know the Will of God.'[22]

William Cathcart

Nineteen thirty-one began with the news that the Commonwealth Arbitration Court ruled a reduction of wages by ten per cent, further increasing the hardships facing many people. In that year, two Australian icons passed away—Dame Nellie Melba on 23 February and artist Tom Roberts on 14 September. In England, cricketer Donald Bradman scored 334 runs, establishing a new test record; and the first England to Australia air mail was despatched from London on 14 April. And during that same year, William Cathcart was invited to Adelaide by Hines Retchford and J. E. Rieschiek who, evidently now disillusioned by Van Eyk, thought they would try again. Together with Jack and Emily Emes, they raised the money for his travel expenses.[23]

Cathcart arrived in Adelaide in January 1932.[24] Only eight people attended the first meeting in Wyatt House in Grenfell Street, but numbers quickly grew.[25] A series of six crowded Sunday night services in the Adelaide Town Hall resulted in a new church being born. People from the two existing Pentecostal congregations joined the Apostolic Church—including local leaders Hines Retchford, J. E. Rieschiek, Norman Priest and Robert Davis.[26]

In 1931, the Missionary Council in England appointed the warm-hearted and well-liked Joshua McCabe (b.1903) of Edinburgh as a prophet to Australia. Cathcart welcomed the new arrival in Perth in January 1932, and they preached together for several weeks. Soon 200 people were attending regularly and McCabe hired the Perth Town Hall for a special series of meetings. There were more converts and new members. Shortly after, yet another of the original Pentecostal groups joined the Apostolics. Before long new assemblies were opened in Victoria Park, Claremont and Fremantle.

Meanwhile Cathcart returned to Adelaide, where a garage in Pulteney Street, in the heart of the city, once used as a Bible Christian chapel, was purchased, renovated, renamed Zion Temple and opened on 30 October, 1932. Some 200 people were in regular attendance. People who were materially poor were 'rich in spiritual goods,' wrote Cathcart. 'People came in old vintage cars, bicycles galore, sometimes a horse and buggy or two, and some took the old way of walking to the services—some for miles—but who cares when revival comes!'[27] Local assemblies were also established in suburban and country areas.

Soon, bearing in mind a prophecy that Melbourne, Victoria, would be the headquarters of the Apostolic Church, Cathcart left for that city and McCabe moved to Adelaide where, in 1936, the Draper Memorial Church building in Gilbert Street was purchased and renamed Zion Tabernacle. It became the home of the Apostolics for over thirty years.[28] A. S. Dickson, an apostle from England, took over the work in Perth.

Cathcart's planned his strategy like a military campaign—an advance was made; ground taken; reinforcements brought in; the ground secured; another advance; and so on. To the Apostolics it was the result of a plan 'prophetically revealed' to McCabe and Cathcart while they were together in Perth. It was 'Divine in concept, prophetic in revelation, manifestly blessed and honoured by God and... scripturally sound in precedent and pattern.'[29]

Cathcart arrived in Melbourne knowing nobody except one Daniel Llewellyn, a solitary 'isolated member' from Wales.[30] 'I spent long hours in prayer,' he recalled later. 'My habit was to pray 6–8 hours a day. When I went out in ministry I would pray all morning.'[31] He hired the Protestant Hall and began to give Bible Studies. Claude Gadge (b.1907), an accomplished trumpeter and singer, became his associate minister and soon established an orchestra.[32] As it became obvious Cathcart was not just passing through, the numbers climbed to 100 on week nights and around 300 on Sundays. On Easter Sunday 1933, the first communion service was held, with 160 in attendance.[33]

Cathcart generally emphasised two themes—church government through apostles and prophets and the second coming of Christ. The Apostolic Church Tenets contained just eight words on the latter theme,[34] but it loomed large in Cathcart's preaching.[35] He was concerned about the Jews and their grip on world finances, and believed the Antichrist might already be alive on the earth.[36] He saw indications that 'so far as the signs of the times are concerned, the end of this age seems to be absolutely at the doors' but was careful to point out that God could extend the 'era of prosperity' and that He had 'veiled the exact moment'. However, he still thought the Second Coming was possible 'within the lifetime of most of us here.'[37]

A report on the opening of Zion Tabernacle in Adelaide, in August, 1936, states that 'two outstanding addresses... on the Second Coming of the Lord' were delivered by Cathcart who was 'well known as an able exponent of this truth' and the church, which seated several hundred people, was 'packed on each occasion, all listening with rapt attention as the speaker showed from the Scriptures how European affairs were dovetailing into the prophecies of the Word of God.'[38]

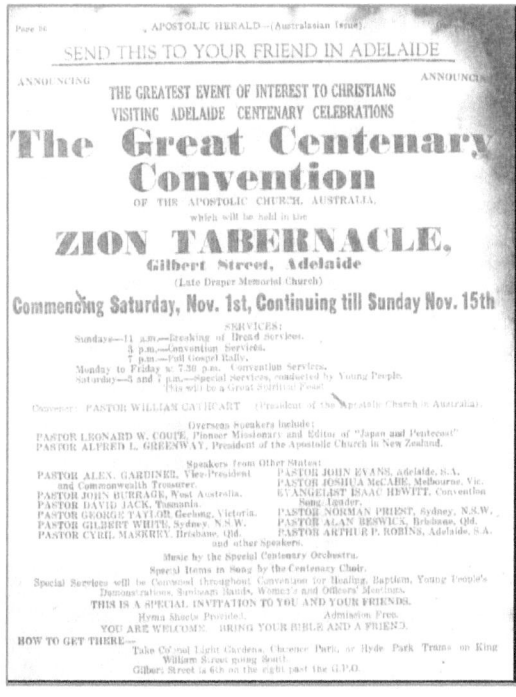

Fire-damaged promotion for opening of Zion Tabernacle in Adelaide, S.A., 1936.

Cathcart prepared a huge chart, said to be nearly twelve metres long, and 2.5 metres high, which outlined in graphic form the destiny of mankind from Creation to Culmination through five phases—Divine Intervention, Divine Intention, Divine Provision, Divine Possession and Divine Consummation.[39] 'To give a description of this chart,' continued the report, 'is out of the question, as to be appreciated, it must be seen.' In the chart, Cathcart suggested that the Return of

Christ might happen about the year AD 2120, but he was not dogmatic about it.[40]

John Henry Hewitt

John Hewitt.

In 1933, after his brief ministry experiences with Booth-Clibborn and Van Eyk, John Henry Hewitt (1900–1962), came to Melbourne. A huge, jovial Welshman, he was 'full of bounce and energy'. His preaching was lively and people responded readily to him.[41] In May 1933, Cathcart and Hewitt began a campaign in the Protestant Hall which they were soon forced to transfer to the 1,900-seat Collins Street Melbourne Auditorium for Sunday nights.[42] Thirty thousand flyers were printed and distributed; a team of volunteers was organised; three 15-metre red and blue banners bearing Scripture texts such as, 'Jesus Christ the same yesterday, today and forever' were hung in the hall. Over 1000 people attended the first meeting. The campaign was characterised by bright singing, led by the evangelist's younger brother Isaac (1911–1977), simple, direct preaching and prayer for the sick. On the opening night, 25 people responded to Hewitt's invitation to confess Christ and about 100 sought laying on of hands for healing. Within six weeks, there were no empty seats. Dozens of handkerchiefs were prayed over and sent to the absent suffering. As the campaign continued, there were impressive testimonies of healing. A sixteen-year-old girl claimed that sight had been restored in a blind eye. A lame man walked unaided. A little boy whose body was twisted and emaciated showed dramatic improvement. A woman deaf for eighteen years was able to hear. Others testified to healing from asthma, deafness, 'internal trouble', insomnia, blindness of 35 years standing and nervous disorder.

John Hewitt rally (Hewitt in centre).

The outstanding healing was that of Ensign H. Jenkins of the Salvation Army who for nine years had used a walking stick, crutches or a wheel chair. A week later she gave a public testimony and walked around the platform unaided to enthusiastic applause from the people. The Salvation Army's *War Cry* was careful not to give away too much, but commented, 'Ensign H. Jenkins who has been an invalid for some years, having to be wheeled everywhere in a chair, was miraculously cured recently, and is now walking about with comfort. Praise God!'[43] On 18 June, the final night, Jenkins again gave her testimony, 56 people responded to an invitation to become Christians and Hewitt personally prayed for 120 sick people. A number of clergymen endorsed the campaign. Hewitt was admired as an outstanding evangelist[44] whose preaching was simple and direct—

> It would be no good to show one that he is a sinner, if I could not show a way of escape; and be able to point to One Who is able to save: but Thank God we have One to whom to point... Oh, it is a glorious thing to know when you find yourself a lost, undone sinner, on your way to Hell, that there is One that tells you the way of escape... Where are we to go and wash? To the Fountain of Calvary. Oh, believe that Jesus Christ and his blood cleanseth us from all sin... Jesus... is the Divine Healer. I praise God that we believe, in the Apostolic Church, that he is the Healer... I believe that our Lord (as He is the very same Jesus) can do miracles of healing physically. And He can heal spiritual blindness! Because that is the biggest miracle—*to get you and I* [sic] *saved!*[45]

The first issue of the new Apostolic magazine *Revival Echoes* carried the excited if overstated two-page banner headline: 'Melbourne in the Grip of a Revival.' A month later it shouted, 'Melbourne Miraculously Moved—Revival Unabated,' with subheadings, '700 Decisions for Christ; 2,300 prayed for; Hundreds healed; Baptismal services conducted; Conclusive Proof the Day of Miracles is Not Yet Past'; and 'Church established in Bible Fashion'.[46]

This latter comment was significant. On Sunday 4 June, at a Breaking of Bread service, 107 people decided to join the new church, with another 40 following their lead over the next fortnight. And Joshua McCabe, who had come from Adelaide for the occasion, prophetically called a number of people into office as elders, evangelists and deacons. On 6 July, Cathcart and his wife and two sons were welcomed to Melbourne where they had now moved permanently.[47] After several months of frustration in finding a suitable meeting place, the Church secured a former Salvation Army building since converted into a theatre, with seating accommodation for 1,300 people. They renovated the premises and, on 12 August, opened the new Coventry Street Temple, the Headquarters of the Apostolic Church in Australia.[48] Having now refurbished three buildings, the Apostolics saw themselves fulfilling a prophecy which had been given in Adelaide that God would use them to rebuild broken altars.[49] Six years later, on Good Friday, 7 April 1939, they opened their own building in Punt Road, Richmond, a relatively short distance from C. L. Greenwood's Richmond Temple.[50] It was there, later that year, that fifteen-year-old Leo Hart was baptized in the Holy Spirit. 'I used to cycle (there) every Saturday afternoon... to attend a 'Tarry Meeting' as I was thirsty, desperately thirsty,' he wrote 47 years later. His thirst was satisfied and ultimately he was recognised as an apostle.[51] Among those who joined the Apostolics was a Brethren woman named Marion Hart who was baptized in the Holy Spirit in 1934 and who for more than 30 years, as 'Aunt Marion', wrote a regular children's column in the various church periodicals.[52]

Meanwhile, Hewitt had moved on to Adelaide where rallies were held in the Adelaide Town Hall and he preached to capacity crowds of 2,000 or so. There were some 500 conversions and two baptismal services were held in the Town Hall when 39 people were immersed.[53] Among them was Philip George Joyder Lovell (b.1914), who would later be the first Australian President of the Apostolic Church, and his wife Muriel.[54]

Hewitt prayed simply with people for healing, either with laying on of hands or anointing with oil—just a couple of drops on the forehead.[55] There were reports that cripples walked, the blind received their sight, the deaf heard, a lame girl was healed, cancers disappeared and bedfast people got up well. A woman who could not normally stay on a chair for more than a few minutes sat and listened to Hewitt for two hours and was cured.[56] Others recovered gradually.[57] Hewitt was asked to officiate at the funeral of a woman dying of cancer. He visited her in hospital, prayed for her and told the family she would not die. She did die—but not until thirty years later.[58] 'There was a consciousness of the presence of God I've never known since,' recalled Phil Lovell.[59] 'Adelaide Amazed, Critics Confounded,' declared *Revival Echoes*.[60]

Extra seating accommodation was found for the regular services at Zion Temple. On 30 July, the campaign concluded. About 175 people attended a communion service at the Temple and 30 people were accepted into membership. McCabe, now back from Melbourne, prophesied 29 people into office. Over succeeding weeks, there were more conversions and more baptisms in water and in the Spirit.[61] Hewitt moved to Perth where, as in Adelaide, hundreds of people attended his rallies in the Unity Theatre. There were some 650 converts. People testified to healing from cancer, deafness, lameness (a lad with leg irons no longer needed them) and blindness.[62]

Meanwhile, growth in Adelaide continued with new people being added almost daily to the church. Teenager Frank Elton and a friend, rode their motor cycles past the Apostolic Church one night in 1934, decided to investigate, and went in with no intention of staying. But Frank turned to the Lord.[63]

Like their Pentecostal brothers, the Apostolics eschewed the things of the world. The *Guiding Principles* of the Church noted that cleanliness, modest apparel and neatness were appropriate for witnesses to Christ.[64] Women were not permitted to attend meetings wearing makeup or jewellery and had to don hats in church. In Adelaide, if a woman didn't have a hat they would supply a handkerchief! Smoking, drinking, theatres and dances were all forbidden.[65]

The Adelaide Apostolic Church weekly calendar was full. Every day of the week was provided for—

> Sunday 11 am—Breaking of Bread
> Sunday 3 pm —Divine Healing
> Sunday 7 pm—Full Gospel Meeting
> First Monday of each month 7.45 pm—Missionary Meeting
> Tuesday 7.45 pm—United Meeting Apostolic Worship
> Wednesday 7.45 pm—Apostolic Witnesses
> Thursday 3 pm—Divine Healing

Friday—Open Air Meeting
Saturday 3 pm—Tarrying
Saturday 7.45 pm—Gospel Rally[66]

Such a program was normative for many early Apostolic churches.[67] One wonders how the people found time for anything else. But after the exciting launching of the church through the Cathcart and Hewitt campaigns, there was a tide of momentum that carried them along with it.

Overall, the numbers were still relatively small. More than 200 people attended the first Sunday morning worship service in the new Zion Tabernacle. There were probably, at this time, about the same number at the Pentecostal Church and between 50 and 100 regular attenders at the Apostolic Mission.[68] There were also a handful of people in branch assemblies in the suburbs and the country areas.[69] By contrast, in the 1933 Census, 164,531 South Australians called themselves Anglicans, 127, 978 claimed to be Methodists and there were 19,081 Baptists. Had the Pentecostals examined the Census figures, they might have been encouraged, however, to note that only 284 were recorded as Christian Brethren.[70]

Reaction

The aspect of Apostolic practice that proved to be most controversial, was the role of 'set' prophets. The official documents are careful to point out that no prophetic calling was to be pursued without apostolic confirmation.[71] Yet in practice, this seemed to be forgotten at times. In Melbourne in June 1933, in one service the following occurred—

The Lord called His servant Ellis to be Assistant Pastor in Melbourne, 10 elders, 4 Local Evangelists, 9 Deacons and 6 Deaconesses, and these were ordained to office. After Pastor Hewitt had expounded on the Prophetical ministry, he laid his hands upon several officers who were called, ordaining them to their part in the Lord's work. Many who had never been in an ordination service before were filled with amazement and wonder, and many were heard to exclaim, 'We never saw it in this fashion.'[72]

John Hewitt (centre) with elders in Hobart, Tasmanai.

Similarly, in Adelaide, two months later, 'the Lord proceeded to call a number of men and women into office' as McCabe named them as he prophesied. There were nine elders, eight deacons, one interpreter, ten deaconesses and one assistant pastor. Immediately, they knelt before Hewitt who laid hands on them and ordained them for their respective ministries.[73] Alan Geoffrey ('Dick') Bain (b.1910) recalled how he was called to be an evangelist in a meeting in Adelaide when he was resident in Port Pirie. The prophet, who did not know anything about him, began, 'I am calling my servant who is at present in Port Pirie...'[74]

No doubt Hewitt, as an apostle, felt he had the right to act promptly, but to others it seemed as if due consideration had not been given. Excited as many people were about it, some of those called were not in reality equipped for the allotted task. They might have been designated evangelists or elders but this did not make them so. Even worse, on occasion they were not even living consistent lives.[75]

Secondly, pastors of existing churches became understandably disturbed when members of their congregations were called into office in the Apostolic Church or were so attracted by the new ministry that they transferred their memberships. Years later an Apostolic historian claimed that by merging several congregations in Perth, the Church was actually promoting unity, not division.[76] Not everyone saw it that way. Charles Greenwood claimed that 65 of the 147 new Apostolics in Melbourne in 1933 had formerly been members at Richmond Temple.[77] The Foursquare church at Auburn lost most of their members.[78] About a third of the Pentecostals in Adelaide joined the new movement.[79]

Thirdly, some pastors left the Pentecostal Church of Australia or the Apostolic Faith Mission to become Apostolic. Norman Priest was a graduate of the Victorian Bible Institute. Robert Davis was a member at Good News Hall and an elder in the Pentecostal church in Adelaide. Cecil Harris and Len Jones had been Pentecostal pastors. George Dryden was formerly a Foursquare pastor, as was William Kay who then led an independent church in Sydney.

On the other hand, when Hewitt drew 2000 people to the Adelaide Town Hall only a few hundred of them at the most could have already been Pentecostal. The vast majority were either from traditional churches or no church. There is no doubt that the majority of people attracted by Hewitt's ministry had never attended a Pentecostal meeting before. Furthermore, the Apostolics did not see themselves as setting out to target other Pentecostals[80] and there is evidence that Cathcart went out of his way to avoid enticing people from existing churches, on at least one occasion closing a campaign early when it began to happen.[81]

The other Pentecostals were not convinced. For people who claimed to be filled with the Spirit, they responded with surprising acrimony. In Sydney, Philip Duncan, who also lost members to the new movement, wrote a tract entitled, *The Blasphemous Lie of the Set Prophet*, in which he raised all these issues.[82] He did not mince matters—

> A new sect has arisen in our city claiming apostolic blessing and introducing a new form of church government, which is unscriptural in its origin and evil in its effect, yet, incredible though it seems, there are those who are guiled and ensnared in the lure of the new altar.

> Preliminary meetings are held until the 'SET PROPHET' arrives. In the church he speaks as the oracle of God, and his word is claimed to be as 'INFALLIBLE AS THE WRITTEN WORD OF GOD.'
>
> This abominable and blasphemous assertion is received by many who allow themselves to be called into office as Apostles, Prophets, Evangelists, Pastors, etc., and are sent by the spoken 'Word of God' through the Prophet whither he demands...
>
> The spirits of Peter, Paul, Luther or Wesley shall rise in contemptuous judgement on these home-made apostles and pigmy [sic] prophets who presume to have divine right to establish from the unqualified—and often unsanctified—office in the Church, which call for dignity, experience and spiritual excellence.'

This pamphlet and another entitled *The Apostolic Church Error* were both published in the *Australian Evangel*.[83]

F.B. Van Eyk published a series of articles with the title, 'The Present Apostolic Church and Prophetic Delusion.' He began in plain terms—

> The Apostles of old always seemed especially anxious not to build on other men's foundations (Rom 15:20) not to boast in another man's line of things ready to hand (1 Cor 10:6) but the present Apostolic movement in Australia seems to delight in building on other men's labours; and indeed the whole of its work today in Australia stands upon the ruins of other Pentecostal churches.[84]

Van Eyk raised a succession of objections. Many prophecies which he had witnessed were nothing more than human invention. The use of the first person gave the prophecy divine authority yet the Apostolics taught that elders had a right to decide whether it was truly of God or not. Prophecies were being substituted for the Scriptures. It was God who appointed prophets (1 Corinthians 12:28), not man.[85] There was no single case in the whole of Scripture where anyone was called to office by prophecy. Indeed, if this was how people were called, why did Paul go to such lengths to detail the required characteristics of church leaders? In Acts 13:2 there was no indication of how the Holy Spirit spoke—it may or may not have been through prophets. When prophets tried to direct Paul he ignored their advice and proceeded according to his own leading (Acts 21:1ff). Much harm was called by recording prophecies—it lent them undue authority. The gift of prophecy was often displayed through inspired preaching where it was of greater significance. When elders were appointed in first century churches (Acts 14:23) it was by the raising of hands, as in voting. In the first Church Council in Jerusalem, where there was much discussion (Acts 15:1ff) why did no prophet simplify the process by telling them the mind of the Lord? And how could a prophet call someone to office who was brought home drunk a few days later? Van Eyk stressed that he firmly believed in both prophets and prophecies, but not in the regimented Apostolic way.[86]

Good News warned against listening to false prophets and assumed apostles.[87] Another person claimed the Apostolics would come 'as sure as crow to carcass' to take over an existing church.[88] A decade later Leo Harris published a booklet entitled, *Church Government—Babylonian or Biblical?* which was clearly directed at Apostolic teaching.[89]

Stung by the many criticisms, and hurt by the viciousness of some of them, the Apostolic Church's Commonwealth Council thoroughly examined the question of 'governmental prophecy'.[90] They expressed their unanimous belief that Paul and Barnabas had been called by prophecy to the work of apostleship (Acts 13:1ff) and that there had been prophetic input in the first Jerusalem Council (Acts 15:28); that Judas and Silas had exercised 'direct prophetical ministry' (Acts 15:32); that prophecies of directive nature were recorded elsewhere in Acts (20:23 and 21:4); and that the prophecies given to Timothy (1 Timothy 1:18; 4:14) were 'of a revealing, instructive and encouraging nature.' Nevertheless, they admitted that there was insufficient biblical evidence to assert that callings to the 'ascension gifts'[91] should be made only through prophecy.

On the other hand, despite the difficulties they had faced, they 'emphatically' reaffirmed their belief in 'prophetical ministry through ordained and approved channels', remembering that both Scripture and their own experience made it plain that no prophetic ministry and no prophet was infallible as there was always the possibility of the human element being present. Furthermore, there was ample evidence that New Testament apostles were sometimes led by direct revelation (e.g. Acts 27:22–26; 2 Corinthians 12:1–4; Galatians 2:1–2).[92]

They concluded by reaffirming their belief in the Tenets of the Apostolic Church but admitting that their dependence on prophecy had not had 'the fullest Scriptural support' and that in some cases results had not justified their expectations. They believed that it was 'essential to the welfare and progress of the Apostolic Church' that a sound biblical balance be maintained between the functioning of apostles and prophets and they insisted that all future prophetic ministry should conform to biblical standards.[93]

However, the controversy had done its work and there was a significant falling away. Len Jones, formerly of Richmond Temple, briefly joined the Apostolics, but later withdrew and for a time worked with F. B. Van Eyk.[94] Cyril Maskrey, an apostle who had come from Scotland in 1935, became disenchanted not only with Apostolic doctrines, but with Pentecostalism generally, and wrote a treatise against it.[95] Similarly, pastors Priest, Davis, Cameron, Harris, Taylor and, surprisingly, even Cathcart himself left the Church.[96]

Consolidation

Over the next decade, the Apostolics consolidated their work in Australia. At a conference in Adelaide, through the words of McCabe, one apostle, two State Prophets, four elders and one local evangelist were called to office. Then Cathcart prophesied that Hewitt was to go to New South Wales for a short time and McCabe was to be the State Pastor for Victoria. Cathcart and Hewitt were both called to 'Commonwealth ministry.' A week later, in Melbourne, three new apostles, a State Prophet for Victoria, two pastors and an evangelist were called through another McCabe prophecy. 'The Lord also spoke forming a Commonwealth Council composed of the seven Apostles and Prophets McCabe and Priest.'[97] In order to free Cathcart and Hewitt from administrative ties, it was also decided to ask the British Church to send a skilled administrator and as a result Alex Gardiner and his family arrived in October 1934 and he was appointed President of the Church.[98]

Cathcart now visited Wellington, New Zealand, where he had 'phenomenal success' and where he was later assisted by both Isaac and John Hewitt. After this, Hewitt visited New South Wales and before long seven separate congregations decided to join the Apostolic Church. Hewitt then pioneered an assembly in Brisbane and held campaigns in other cities. Davey Jack established new works in Tasmania. On one occasion, Hewitt was about to fly to Tasmania when there was a word of prophecy advising him to journey 'by way of the sea, and not by way of the air.' He cancelled his flight and sailed south. The plane crashed on which he was booked.[99] By the end of 1934, there were churches in every State of Australia and in New Zealand. All in all, some 40 congregations had come under the Apostolic banner in Australia.[100]

That year, their Centenary Convention celebrated the 100th anniversary of the founding of the State of Victoria. With orchestra, choir, apostles, prophets, evangelists pastors, teachers and people celebrating together, it was a momentous event.[101] While the populace generally were crowding the new and flourishing cinemas, where images of Rudolph Valentino, Charlie Chaplin, Boris Karloff and Mary Pickford filled the screen, or cheering their local Australian football team on Saturday afternoons in a year that would see Richmond win the Victorian premiership, the Apostolics found their joy in the Lord—

> What a sense of the immediate presence of God filled our hearts as we sat in His presence. His Word came forth in the power of the Holy Ghost... At the close of the service the Glory of the Lord came upon us and throughout the day we felt in the secret of His presence... The ministry of the Word was very edifying. Some accuse the Apostolic Church of having nothing but prophecy but any intelligent thinker... must have been impressed by the lucid, edifying and instructive messages...
>
> At times many were literally dancing with joy as the Glory of the Lord fell upon them; whilst at other times the Lord filled our mouths with laughter. The shouts of joy and praise resounded and re-echoed through the Temple from time to time... whilst at other times our spirits were hushed and mellowed as we realised the presence of Jesus.[102]

In 1935, Hewitt returned to England and two years later joined Cathcart and his brother Isaac in South Africa to pioneer there.[103]

At the memorial service to John Hewitt, 'Dick' Bain spoke prophetically—

> My servant could have taken a line of labour that would pay handsomely in the natural and many a time My servant could have had leisure hours but rather he chose to use his knowledge in the purposes of God.
>
> He would not accept deliverance from the wearisome demands of the every day experiences in My will but rather with delight he chose to go the way of the Cross...
>
> I am putting before the lives of the young at this time that they, too, will consider the path, and weigh it well, that they will take before the Lord.[104]

It was a fitting tribute.

The emergence of the Apostolic Church in Australia represented an interesting model of what may happen within a movement committed to an experiential model of spirituality. There are both advantages and disadvantages. There are many positive factors. People are excited and enthused about their faith. They are often dedicated and committed to a sacrificial life style. They are unashamed about their beliefs. They tend to adopt conservative values and to emphasise traditional mores of family and community life. On the other hand, they can become unhealthily dogmatic. The certainty infused by one's own experience can create an unhealthy rejection of the experiences of others.[105]

The excessive reaction of existing Pentecostal leaders to the Apostolic teaching was the clash of one set of certainties with another. Both sides saw their position as being vindicated by Scripture. There is no doubt that the effect of growing or declining memberships was also a primary factor. People who feel threatened usually are reactive. The real problem was not that each side had its own set of values but that they saw them as mutually exclusive and that they allowed them to become causes of bitterness and disaffection. As a result, for years the various Pentecostal groups generally refused to work together, which clearly hindered the development of the movement. While there were some mergers and transfers, they were usually at the expense of an existing group.

Time is a great healer and a generation later, through the actions of the next group of Apostolic leaders, including John Hewitt's son, also named John, the earlier practice of 'immediacy' in acting upon direction through prophets was dramatically modified, as was the centralized form of government.

Apostolic and Assemblies of God leaders were now sitting around the table together, engaging in united activities and accepting one another's ministers. The old issues were being resolved and forgotten.[106]

Ironically, by the turn of the century, some non-Apostolic groups were focusing as much, if not more, on prophesying than the Apostolics themselves! Perhaps something was learned from history after all. Or perhaps the spirit of Pentecost was now fluid enough to run between several sets of banks without diminishing the flow.

Notes

[1] An analogy used by Jesus in a slightly different context (John 3:8).

[2] J. McCabe, personal interview, 18 September, 1990; C. Gadge, personal interview, 2 March, 1992; K. Kirwan, personal interview, 11 September, 1991; L. and I. Wahlquist, interview, 19 November, 1991; M. Hurst, personal interview, 14 August, 1991; K. Kirwan, personal interview, 11 September, 1991.

[3] J. McCabe, personal interview, 18 September, 1990.

[4] P. Grant, 'William Cathcart: From Gloom to Glory,' in *Acts '88* January, 1988; A. Gardiner, 'A History of the Apostolic Church,' in *Acts '89*, November, 1989, 14f; 'Forward March in Australia,' in AH, 1:8, May, 1932, 2; 'Looking West: A Retrospect of the Work in WA,' in RE, 1:2, July 1933, 15ff. Further details of the beginnings of the Apostolic Church in Perth are from these sources unless otherwise stated.

[5] These included the original congregation affiliated with Good News Hall and a small Pentecostal Church of Australia group, together with a handful of splinter groups.

[6] McCabe claims that the woman's name was Marshall, but Gardiner's published history is probably a more reliable source.

[7] Gardiner, 1989, 14.

[8] For a useful introduction to the Welsh Revival see E. Evans, 1987; B. P. Jones, 1995.

[9] 'I never considered whether I was happy (about the system). I believed it was God's will and did it. That was it. Everybody was the same. It was the combined apostleship decision'—P. Lovell, personal interview, 6 September, 1991. Years later, one man was sent from Hobart, Tasmania, to Bunbury, Western Australia. The move would divide his family but if he did not accept the Council's decision he knew he would have to resign. He accepted.

[10] *Constitution*, Chapter 9, preamble.

[11] How this took place in practice was that a prophet would actually name people and tell them that God was calling them to a certain sphere of activity such as evangelism or eldership.

[12] 'We believe in set Prophets... we believe in set Apostles, too'—W. A. C. Rowe, *One Lord, One Faith* (Bradford: Puritan Press, n. d.), 250. The word 'set' was taken from the Authorised Version rendering of 1 Corinthians 12:28—'And God hath set some in the church, first apostles, secondarily prophets, thirdly teachers.'

[13] *Constitution*, Chapter 30, preamble and I–II.

[14] Rowe, n. d., 242f.

[15] *Constitution*, Chapter 12, preamble.

[16] *The Apostolic Church: its Principles and Practices*, 1939, 8:1–5.

[17] *Constitution*, Chapter 30.

[18] Personal knowledge. Prophecies were not always expounded. W. A. C. Rowe 'made a specialty of it.' See A. Turner, interview, 21 November, 1990.

[19] L. Wahlquist, interview, 19 November, 1991.

[20] HG, March, 1942, 32.

[21] *Guiding Principles*, 6:11. By the 1940s, prophecies were regularly being published in the Church periodicals.

[22] RE, 1:4, September, 1933, 57f.

[23] *Souvenir Exhibiting the Movement of God in the Apostolic Church;* W. Cathcart, *To Glory from Gloom* (Dallas: Christian Communications Trust, 1976), 123f; A.G. and F. Bain, personal interview, 20 August, 1990.

[24] AH, 1:8, May, 1932, 2.

[25] These were Hines Retchford, J. Rieschiek, 'Dad' and Dora Allen, Frederick and Elsie Fleming and their daughters Doreen and Marjorie. See Marjorie Hurst (nee Fleming), personal interview, 14 August, 1991. Note that Apostolic records generally quote ten as the number in attendance.

[26] One person claimed that 70 people left one of these churches. E.Watson, personal interview.

[27] Cathcart, 1976, 124.

[28] AH, 1:6, October, 1936, 88f. The Draper Memorial Church was named after the renowned Methodist evangelist Daniel Draper. See Hunt, 1984, 40.

[29] Gardiner, 1989, 15; *Acts '90*, March, 1990, 14.

[30] C. Gadge, personal interview, 2 March, 1992.

[31] Cathcart's devotion to prayer was recognised by others. One of his associates recalled, 'He would do all the praying—he would pray through the day'—A. G. and F.

Bain, personal interview, 20 August, 1990. Another said, 'He was a great prayer warrior... he would pray all day.' P. Grant, personal interview, 1988.

[32] Llewellyn knew Gadge and suggested Cathcart approach him. Gadge's father Stanley had been the first to welcome Valdez to Melbourne and the family had been involved in both Good News Hall and the Sunshine revival. Later he became a presiding elder of the Apostolic Church. C. Gadge, personal interview, 2 March, 1992; RE, 1:1, June, 1933, 8.

[33] Clearly many of these people had come from other congregations. The Apostolics made much of the fact that Cathcart had no existing organisation to initiate the work and that he had not engaged in evangelism but had undertaken the hard pioneering work of gathering a band of believers who would form the nucleus of a new church. See RE, 1:1, 1933, 4. Inevitably, this was to create disquiet in the existing churches.

[34] 'His (i.e. Christ's) Second Coming and Millennial reign on earth.'

[35] As Sarah Jane Lancaster had done before him, he tended to anchor his preaching in contemporary world events. In Adelaide on 23 September, 1934, he spoke on, 'The Coming Age-end Climax' and asked the question, 'Will the imperialistic war cloud in the West and the democratic war cloud in the East meet over Palestine before 1936?' He prophesied the hardening of Nazism and Fascism in the West and the awakening of China in the East.

[36] Most Pentecostals believed that just prior to the return of Christ, the Antichrist would appear as a world ruler who would oppose everything godly and institute a rule of terror. See GN, 18:9, September, 1927, 15; 19:9, September, 1928, 7; RE, 2:3, August, 1934, 43ff; RE, 2:12, May, 1935, 223ff..

[37] RE, 2:10, March, 1935, 189, 192ff.

[38] 'The Opening of Zion Tabernacle, Adelaide,' AH, 1:6, October, 1936, 89.

[39] F. Watson, interview, n. d.; K. Kirwan, interview, 11 September 1991. I have a photocopy of a smaller hand-copied version of Cathcart's chart, prepared by the late John Kirwan, a member of the Adelaide congregation.

[40] This date is given on the chart with a question mark.

[41] K. Kirwan, personal interview, 11 September, 1991. See Appendix B for Hewitt's background.

[42] RE, 1:1, June, 1933, 6ff. Further details of the Melbourne meetings are from this source unless otherwise stated.

[43] *War Cry,* 13 May, 1933 quoted in RE, 1:1, June, 1933, 9. Jenkins, later Mrs McFarlane, continued in good health for twenty years until she was killed in a road accident in New South Wales—A. Gardiner, 'A History of the Apostolic Church,' in *Acts '90,* October, 1990, 15.

[44] 'He was THE evangelist. He was fantastic,'—A. Turner, interview, 21 November, 1990.

[45] RE, 2:6–7, November–December, 1934, 130–131. See also Chant, 1984, 335ff.

[46] RE, 1:2, July, 1933, 22f. In May 1936, the name of the magazine changed to *Apostolic Herald* to bring it into line with the international Apostolic publication. In 1941 it became *Herald of Grace.* See RE, 3:10, March, 1936, 182.

[47] RE, 1:3, August, 1933, 39.

[48] RE, 1:4, September, 1933, 51f.

[49] RE, 1:4, September, 1933, 53.

[50] 'Apostolic Church Melbourne Opening Ceremony' brochure, 7 April, 1939.

[51] L. Hart, *Journey with Jesus,* published by the author, 1986, 5.

[52] M. Hart, *I Remember,* published by the author, 1983. The first column appeared in RE, 1:10, March, 1934, 172.

[53] RE, 1:4, September, 1933, 56ff.

[54] P. Lovell, personal interview, 6 September, 1991. Lovell had been searching for God for twelve months. One day his employer, a Seventh Day Adventist, told him how he had attended a 'strange sort of meeting' where a little deaf girl had been healed. He himself had tested her hearing. Lovell went to see for himself. It was a John Hewitt rally and there he found what he was looking for.

[55] A. G. Bain, personal interview, 20 August, 1990.
[56] F. Bain, personal interview, 20 August, 1990.
[57] RE, 1:3, August, 1933, 40f.
[58] A. G. Bain, personal interview, 20 August, 1990.
[59] P. Lovell, personal interview, 6 September, 1991.
[60] RE, 1:3, August, 1933, 40f.
[61] RE, 1:4, August, 1933, 58.
[62] RE, 1:5, October, 1933, 72f.
[63] F. Elton, interview, 11 September, 1991.
[64] *Principles and Practice*, 1939; *Guiding Principles,* 15:6.
[65] M. Hurst, personal interview, 14 August, 1991; K. Kirwan, personal interview, 11 September, 1991.
[66] From a photo of the notice board at Jubilee Temple, c.1934. See also S. Russell, interview, 17 September, 1991.
[67] The Ballarat congregation conducted a similar program in 1937. See C. Crawford, 'The first ten years of the Apostolic Church, Ballarat,' unpublished essay, Adelaide: Tabor College, 1983.
[68] AE, 8:3, July, 1935, 3. This report of a crowd at the Rechabite Chambers indicates a maximum attendance of about 300 at a special gathering, given the size of the building. See also the Apostolic Mission record book, November, 1929—July, 1940; photo copy in my possession.
[69] E.g. Kadina, Hope Forest, Strathalbyn. See AE, 8:2, May, 1935, 9; RE, 2:11, April, 1935, 210f.
[70] Vamplew, ed, 1987, 424.
[71] Turnbull, 1959, 178—'Many calls and changes have been made through the word received through the prophets, but it is not acted upon until it is first of all confirmed by the apostleship, who bear the final and first responsibility.' See also P. Lovell, personal interview, 6 September, 1991,'The word of a prophet was never just taken... The word had to come to the apostleship.'
[72] RE, 1:2, July, 1933, 24, 30.
[73] RE, 1:4 September 1933, 57.
[74] A. G. Bain, personal interview, 20 August, 1990.
[75] L. Harris, personal interview; GN, 24:4–5, April–May, 1933, 12f; S. Beaumont, 'Cyril Maskrey: former Apostolic pastor,' unpublished essay, Adelaide: Tabor College, 1986. On the other hand, according to Lovell, there were very few cases like this. P. Lovell, personal interview, 6 September, 1991.
[76] Gardiner, 1989, 15.
[77] Greenwood, *Life Story,* 65.
[78] T. A. Bentley, personal correspondence, August, 1994.
[79] L. Wahlquist, interview, 19 November, 1991.
[80] 'To my knowledge, there wasn't any attempt to persuade people to leave, but associated with this movement was this new doctrine ...' P. Lovell, personal interview, 6 September, 1991.
[81] P. Lovell, personal interview, 6 September, 1991.
[82] P. Duncan, 'The Blasphemous Lie of the Set Prophet,' pamphlet, n. d. but c.1934.
[83] AE, 7:3, June, 1934, 9.

[84] F. B. Van Eyk, 'The Present Apostolic Church and their Prophetic Delusion,' GC, 3:2, August, 1934, 20.
[85] 1 Corinthians 12:28—'And God hath set some in the church, first apostles, secondarily prophets, thirdly teachers...' (AV).
[86] Van Eyk,' GC, 3:2, August, 1934, 20ff; GC, 3:3, September–October, 1934, 45ff.
[87] GN, 24:4–5, April–May, 1933, 12f.
[88] Quoted by T. A. Bentley, personal communication, August, 1994.
[89] L. Harris, *Church Government—Babylonian or Biblical?* (published by the author, n. d.)
[90] *Minutes* of the Commonwealth Council of the Apostolic Church, 22 October, 1941 to 27 November, 1941, Items 38–40A. Although these minutes are dated 1941, they clearly reflect discussions which had been taking place for some time.
[91] i.e. apostles, prophets, evangelists, pastors and teachers—Ephesians 4:7–11.
[92] There were also allegations that there was collusion between apostles and prophets beforehand. Every Apostolic person I have interviewed has resolutely denied this e.g. A. Turner, personal interview, 21 November, 1990; A. G. Bain, personal interview, 20 August, 1990.
[93] In any case, there was no possibility of changing the tenets as the Constitution declared, 'The Confession of Faith as set out herein shall for ever be the doctrinal standard of the Apostolic Church, and shall not be subject to any change in any way whatsoever' —*Constitution,* Chapter 3:2.
[94] 'The Reason Why Len Jones Resigned from the Apostolic Church,' GC, 3:3, September–October, 1934, 43.
[95] C. Maskrey, *The Pentecostal Error* (Strathpine: Evangelistic Literature Enterprise, 1953, 1987).
[96] Chant, 1984, 187f; J. McCabe, 'A Man, sent from God, Whose name was John,' HG, 21:4, July–August, 1962, 74ff; D. Cathcart, personal interview, 13 September, 1993. Cathcart left because he was persuaded by Thomas Foster to accept British Israelism, not necessarily because he was disenchanted with Apostolic practice. He joined Leo Harris in his newly formed National Revival Crusade. Ultimately, Cathcart settled in the USA. T. Foster, personal interview; Chant, 1984, 187f.
[97] RE, 1:6, November, 1933, 88, 91.
[98] Gardiner, 1990, 15.
[99] Gardiner, 1990, 15.
[100] RE, 2:6–7, November–December, 1934, 132ff'; McCabe, personal interview, 1990; Gardiner, 1991, 14.
[101] RE, 2:6–7, November–December, 1934, 107, 118.
[102] RE, 1:12, May, 1934, 204f.
[103] Gardiner, 1990, 15; 1991, 14.
[104] A. G. Bain, 'On Being God's Ploughman,' HG, 21:4, July–August, 1962, 81f.
[105] 'I know the futility of trying to have a biblical discussion with those who are excited by some new experience and who resent any questioning of its validity'—C. Hill, 'Breaking the Mould,' *Renewal* No. 259, Crowborough, Sussex, December, 1997, 5.
[106] Personal knowledge. I was for many years a member of the Australian Pentecostal Ministers' Fellowship Steering Committee, formed in 1978, which at the time of writing, some thirty years later, was still meeting at least annually and representing all the major Pentecostal groups in the nation.

CHAPTER TEN

OBEYING THE SPIRIT

Pentecostal Ministry to the Aborigines (1905–1939)

From the earliest days, Pentecostals emphasised foreign missions. For them, the reason the Spirit had come was to empower them to be Christ's witnesses to 'the uttermost parts of the earth' (Acts 1:8). Less than five years after the opening of Good News Hall there were Australian Pentecostal missionaries in India; before long they were in Japan, Hong Kong, China and South Africa as well.[1]

Nor were the Australian Aborigines neglected.[2] From the earliest days, there were several remarkable pioneering efforts by a few bold individuals, although formal Aboriginal Missions were not established until the 1940s—in places like Jigalong, Western Australia, where the Apostolic Church worked for a quarter of a century (1945–1969) and Daintree, Queensland, a work established by the Assemblies of God.[3]

Isabella Hetherington and Ernest Kramer were immigrants who developed a profound love for their new country and who gave themselves sacrificially and courageously to Aboriginal communities. Both pioneered new works and proved to be innovative and self-reliant, often forging ahead with little or no support from either people or churches. Both were self-taught, having no formal missionary or theological training, but confident in their own knowledge of the Scriptures, their love for the people they served and the power of the Holy Spirit who had empowered them. Both worked in remote areas, well removed from obvious or easily accessible means of support.

Isabella Hetherington

The saintly Isabella Hetherington (c.1870–1946) devoted forty years of her life to ministry among Aborigines. Her compassion, dedication and determination won her respect and admiration from Christians and non-Christians alike. Initially in the southern States and in later years in Queensland, she exemplified biblical Christianity and courageous human endeavour.

A 33-year-old Irish nurse, Hetherington migrated to Australia on medical advice, after the death of both her parents. Her only brother had died through tuberculosis during her infancy. She arrived on 24 December 1903, and settled in Ballarat, Victoria.[4] Originally working as a governess for a doctor and his family,[5] she had a deep desire 'to go and succour others' who suffered as her family had suffered—especially the Australian Aborigines, about whose privations she had heard while still in Ireland. She had also been told that they were 'only Australian blacks' and virtually beyond redemption, a view held in the days of the early nineteenth century chaplain Samuel Marsden—who described the indigenous Australians as 'the most degraded of the human race' and who did not believe they were ready or able to receive the gospel[6]—and still being repeated by others a century later.[7] Indeed, this belief was seen to justify much of the abuse and slaughter of Aborigines in the nineteenth century. The compassionate Congregational missionary Lancelot Threlkeld wrote—

> It was maintained by many of the colony that the blacks had no language at all but were only a race of the monkey tribe. This was a convenient assumption, for if it could be proved that the Aborigines... were only a species of wild beasts, there could be no guilt attributed to those who shot them off or poisoned them.[8]

The growing popularity of Darwinian theories only served to consolidate this view: Aborigines were plainly lower down on the evolutionary scale. It was as simple as that.[9]

Hetherington was determined to prove this assessment wrong. In several ways, her life echoes that of her contemporary the renowned Daisy Bates (1859–1951). Like Bates, she was born in Ireland, migrated to Australia, initially worked as a governess, had a passion to relieve the sufferings of the Aborigines and was to spend much of her life living among them.[10]

From the beginning of European settlement, there were many generous and well-meaning attempts to relate positively to the Aborigines. Australia's first Christian clergyman, Richard Johnson, had worked hard in this area, even taking a teenage Aboriginal girl into his own home. In his address To All the Inhabitants of Port Jackson, he pleaded with his hearers to beware of laying stumbling blocks in the way of the 'poor, unenlightened savages' and to consider 'what may be the happy effects' of their observing godly behaviour among the Europeans and as a result seeking God's blessings for themselves.[11] Governor Arthur Phillip's instructions were to live 'in amity and kindness' with the Aborigines, which, initially, he attempted to do.[12] It was not long, however, before cultural misunderstanding, conflict of interests, the settlers' pastoral ambitions, Aboriginal attempts to protect their lands and families, sexual abuse, misplaced Darwinian theories of white superiority and the cruel effects of imported disease and drugs built impenetrable walls between the old and new inhabitants of the land. Inevitably, the uncertain face of ignorance became the ugly face of racism. And equally inevitably, it was the Whites, not the Blacks, who got the better of it. While there were always exceptions, it was the Aborigines who were excluded from the benefits of an increasingly comfortable lifestyle.[13]

After two years of working on her own in 'an Aboriginal camp on the banks of the Murray', in early 1906,[14] Hetherington was invited to join the Australian Aborigines Mission and served for the next three years in a community located 'beyond the rubbish tip', seven kilometres from Wellington, NSW.[15] Other Christian missions had been initiated years earlier under the leadership of such household names as Lancelot Threlkeld, Frederick Hagenauer, Carl Strehlow, Dom Rosendo Salvado, John Smithies and John Gribble.[16] While much faithful, persistent, compassionate work was undertaken by people like these, they often felt their efforts were being undermined by the ungodly lifestyle and open vices of many of the white community.[17] In the first decades of the twentieth century, further missions were founded at Roper River (Church Missionary Society, 1908), Mornington Island (Presbyterian, 1914), Croker Island (Methodist, 1915), Goulburn Island (Methodist, 1916), Groote Eylandt (CMS, 1921), Mount Margaret (United Aborigines Mission, 1921), Milingimbi (Methodist, 1921), Elcho Island (Methodist, 1922), Lockhardt River (Australian Board of Missions, 1924) and Oenpelli (CMS, 1925).[18] Hetherington was already actively serving Aboriginal people before most of these organisations were set in place. 'There were few missionaries in those days,' wrote Hetherington.[19]

A pleasant-faced, demure and 'extremely short-sighted' woman with small round glasses, Hetherington looked serious and caring.[20] During this period, she demonstrated qualities that were to characterise her life—compassion for the suffering, generosity, hard work (she cycled around the area), devotion to Christ and a willingness to serve with all denominations. Here, at the request of a dying Aboriginal 'princess', she adopted Nellie, her weakly three-year-old daughter, who was soon to be the only one of her family of ten still alive. Her father's drinking, their primitive living conditions and the rampant disease that decimated the Aboriginal population in Southern Australian had taken their toll. Alcoholism and illnesses such as smallpox, measles, influenza, tuberculosis, whooping cough and even the common cold, which were deadly enough among Whites, proved murderous among Blacks.[21] But young Nellie Hetherington survived and became a talented musician with both keyboard and guitar, with a gift for singing that softened many a heart. In later years, Hetherington and Nellie were to travel and minister together through many parts of Australia. Clearly, Hetherington loved children. Many of the few extant photos show her with at least one child.[22] In 1910, she took a six-year-old into her home to shield her from pneumonia.[23]

Nevertheless, while facing a constant battle with sickness and poverty, her first concern was always 'the spiritual side of the work'. She was delighted to tell of 'God's saving and keeping power' in the lives of some new converts and noted that the gospel was 'the only thing that can raise these dear people to that which is pure, lovely, and of good report'. She was also pleased to record that there were seven weddings in her first year at Wellington.[24] On the other hand, in her three years there, she 'stood by the death beds of thirteen of these dear people'. One of them, Maggie Bain, died with such a prayer on her lips that one who saw her observed, 'Kings might covet such a death as that of the poor Aboriginal girl.'[25] The strenuous work took a toll on Hetherington's own health and in 1910, she spent four weeks in hospital being treated for pleurisy. In late 1910, she left Wellington and went to Sydney, NSW, to rest. Given twelve months leave, accompanied by Nellie, she travelled through Victoria, partly to regain her health and partly to share the work of the Mission.[26]

In response to many requests to tell her story of the work 'amongst the dark people of our land', this work was extended well into 1912, until she settled for a term at Manunka near Point Macleay in South Australia. This was a small reserve of a few acres with some 50 inhabitants which had been established in 1859. The Government wanted to move the Aboriginal people into Point Macleay itself, but they were unwilling to go, an attitude which Hetherington supported.[27]

By this time, the violence and bloodshed that had marked much of the previous century's interaction with Aborigines was largely a thing of the past—although as late as 1926, there was a punitive expedition in Wyndham, WA, which resulted in at least twelve (probably many more) deaths.[28] However, Aborigines were by no means equal members of society. Australia's new Constitution of 1901 barely referred to them, their right to vote in federal elections was not granted until 1962 and they were not regarded or counted as citizens of the Commonwealth until 1967.[29] Malnutrition, epidemic, disease and bloodshed continued to take a terrible toll. An estimated 300,000 population in 1788 had declined to around 60,000 a century and a half later.[30] 'The evidence that Aboriginal people were dying out,' claims Harris, 'seemed irrefutable'.[31] Not till the 1920s did the birth rate begin to exceed the death rate, even among those of mixed blood. By the late 1930s, there were some 70,000.[32]

Australia's vacillation between what Reynolds calls 'the two great themes of confrontation and collaboration' picked its unsteady way into the twentieth century.[33] Although there were still nomadic, tribal Aborigines in the inland, many now lived in fringe camps around the cities while others were in Government reserves which had been first established in 1850 in New South Wales, in 1860 in Victoria, in 1897 in Queensland and in 1850 in South Australia, in an attempt to encourage Aborigines to settle down to agrarian pursuits, to provide basic education for their children and, often, to keep them separated from non-Aboriginals. There was also an expectation that full-blood Aborigines would remain in remote areas and eventually die out while those in the reserves or town camps would ultimately be assimilated into white culture.[34] Some were employed in rural industries as stock or harvest labourers. Frequently, wages were paid in kind—flour or clothing or blankets—rather than in coin. Discrimination was well-entrenched. Around 1915, a Presbyterian minister could still comment, 'It would be foolish to argue that all men are equal. The black-fellow [sic] is inferior and must necessarily remain so, but he is by no means so inferior as to be unable to rise above the level of a working animal.'[35] Not all Presbyterians were of like mind. The clergyman-anthropologist John Mathew, for example, would have strongly dissented.[36] But in greater or lesser degree, the opinion was still sufficiently widespread. Even the renowned 'Flynn of the Inland' generally ministered only to white people; the needs of Aborigines were left to others.[37] Basic rights such as full citizenship, equal education, equal job opportunities and social welfare were withheld. Insults or even physical attacks were common. White men frequently cohabited with black women, but few marriages ever resulted—and the reverse arrangement was almost unheard of.[38] By 1938, 30% of New South Wales' Aborigines lived in 71 reserves. Here, administrators had extensive powers and the residents' freedoms were limited. Housing was often below standard, health and dental services were inadequate, children could be separated from their parents, food and rations were often of poor quality.[39] It was to the people in or near the reserves that Hetherington gave the rest of her life. During her ministry in Victoria, she had met Sarah Jane Lancaster who initially proffered some financial support and then herself visited the Mission. Hetherington had been looking forward to her visit and 'for a mighty outpouring of the Holy Spirit'. As it happened, there was an outbreak of gastric illness and Lancaster joined her in ministering to the people, and then looked after her, as she, too, became ill. Hetherington recorded how 'dear Mrs Lancaster' personally purchased materials for a tent and dealt with government officials on her behalf.[40]

Just prior to this, in November 1911, at Good News Hall, a woman speaking 'in the Spirit' proclaimed, 'Kramer, the Aborigines'. Ernest Kramer (1889–1958), a flour miller, had arrived in Adelaide from Switzerland in 1889. Here he met J. E. Rieschiek who introduced him to faith in Christ.[41] Kramer was baptized in the Torrens River. Around 1910, he cycled to Melbourne where he worshiped at Good News Hall. A natural talent with sign writing soon emerged and he painted signs and texts around the new building. It was here he met and married the diminutive Euphemia (Effie) Buchanan, W. A. Buchanan's sister.[42] They were to spend many years in mission and evangelism among the Aborigines, a ministry to which the Kramer Memorial Church in Alice Springs still bears witness. To this point, Kramer had felt called to India, and actually had his passage booked. At the time, he and Effie were managing a home for aged men in Melbourne. Late in 1912, Hetherington left Manunka to go to Adelaide and then to Melbourne for the annual Mission Conference. The Kramers met her when Nellie Hetherington sang at the men's home. That same night, 'in a little cottage meeting', the Kramers offered to help in her service among the Aborigines. 'The Lord put a deep love and yearning in the writer's heart,' Kramer wrote years later, 'for the people in the bush and the aboriginals [sic].'[43] Hetherington soon reported to the Mission her delight that this young couple, who were 'both Spirit-filled', were prepared to take over the work.[44]

By January 1913, Hetherington, now in her early 40s, was stationed at the Mission's La Perouse base in New South Wales, where in earlier years the Baptist Retta Long (nee Dixon) had worked and there had been significant conversions.[45] She had been spending 'days and nights alone in prayer' that both the Aboriginal people and the missionaries would be filled with God's Holy Spirit.'[46] Early in March, there was an unusual expression of God's blessing. The resident missionary there, Miss H. Baker, reported—

> The first Sunday of March will be a day ever to be remembered here. The Christians gathered for prayer as usual at 9 o'clock, and while praying, the mighty power of God fell upon us. No church bell rang that day, but the building was filled with the sounds of praise, and this continued till 2 o'clock without a break. God has visited His people.[47]

A month later, Baker was still rejoicing in the dealings of God. The power of the Spirit was 'still manifest'. Soon after this, she was granted a month's leave, and Hetherington, who was clearly held in high esteem by the Mission, took her place.[48] It was not long before there were further evidences of God's presence—

> One of the dear native women was graciously baptized in the Spirit last Sunday morning. She was under the power of the Lord some five or six hours. I danced before the Lord one whole hour and so did she. She sang in the Spirit[49] for two or three hours and then the Holy Spirit gave the sign to unbelievers, speaking through her in other tongues... All church form was broken through. We started prayers in the morning about 8 o'clock and the meeting lasted until 11 at night. Several of the natives were under the power of God. It was a day long to be remembered...

There was also a revival with the girls who worked in the kitchen. After a reading from Acts 2, some of them asked if they could 'have the Spirit like that'. One girl, named Vera, with her face shining, spoke in tongues. Nellie herself 'longed and thirsted for God' and as the Spirit fell on her, she began to sing aloud and to laugh for joy. She felt that she was being healed of a long-standing chest complaint.[50]

Hetherington, in her own quaint fashion, recounted the astonishing story—

> After tea, we went to pray in the kitchen, and immediately the Spirit of the Lord began to pray through 'this clay'. Nellie and Vera fell down under the mighty power of God. How I wish you could have seen my Nellie. At first her little face looked as though she was undergoing crucifixion, then her arms went up to God one after the other. Her hands shook severely and her whole body was lifted off the floor several times. Then her little mouth was opened... a beautiful smile came over her face and she shouted, 'Praise Him!' and 'Yea Lord, I love Thee' and began to speak and sing in other tongues and to cast out demons. Both the girls were under God's power nearly three hours.[51]

At the end of May, Baker returned and the renewal continued. She herself had a Pentecostal experience of the Spirit. She collapsed to the floor and for some hours her whole being seemed 'to undergo crucifixion'. The next day she both spoke and sang in tongues.[52] 'The most cheering feature of the work at present,' she wrote, 'is the morning prayer meeting.' These were 'times of refreshing' and regularly lasted from nine in the morning till noon. [53] Inevitably, these expressions of glossolalia became too controversial for the Mission leaders.[54] Apparently, there had already been some emergence of the phenomenon at the Mission's January Conference. Its ongoing expression now proved to be a problem. Although there was clearly benefit to some people, overall, they admitted, the result was usually confusion. Recognised biblical scholars considered it to be unscriptural. Some who originally thought what they experienced was from God later understood it to have come from the devil. The consensus of experienced missionaries and Christian workers was that a warning should be sounded. They were sorry to introduce this controversial note to the columns of their magazine and freely admitted that some testified to genuine blessing through speaking in tongues. But the entry of the movement into the Mission's ranks had brought confusion and unrest. The result of the first six months of 1913 required them to sound a warning. Their duty was to proclaim salvation through the crucified and risen Saviour. Other teachings—and the people who promoted them—were not to be welcomed to the various stations.[55] It is not surprising that Isabella Hetherington's name appears no more in subsequent issues of *The Australian Aborigines' Advocate*. In 1916, she and Nellie conducted short missions around Victoria. They visited the small group of believers at Freeburgh, in the Ovens Valley, led by William Sloan.[56] A young woman named Ethel Vale had been converted through this ministry and was persecuted by her family as a result. In later years, she was to join Hetherington as a missionary to the Aborigines.[57]

Ernest and Euphemia Kramer

Meanwhile, Ernest and Effie Kramer had begun their own unique ministry.[58] Early in 1913, with their six-weeks-old baby son Colin, they journeyed from Melbourne to the Murray River, where they 'first found the Aboriginals', and then on to Port Augusta, 300 kilometres north of Adelaide.[59] They travelled a further 400 kilometres in a 'covered buggy' pulled by four donkeys beyond Tarcoola in South Australia's far West, following the line of the new East-West railway where they offered their services to the construction gangs and 'many doors' were opened to testify to their Lord. Later they turned north on the long 390 kilometre track to Oodnadatta. They did what they could for black and white alike, without prejudice. God 'does not look at the colour of the skin,' wrote Kramer. 'He is no respecter of persons, and the Blood of Jesus Christ, God's Son, alone can wash inbred sin from the heart.' They covered over 3,500 kilometres all told. From 1916 to 1921, they undertook two further missionary journeys, under the name 'Australian Caravan Mission'. With 21 pounds in hand, Kramer purchased a second-hand horse-drawn van, decorated it with biblical texts,[60] equipped it with harness, bedding and the like and set off from Adelaide. They were well received by the Methodist church at Port Wakefield and spent a week at Point Pearce mission where they baptized a number of Aborigines by immersion.

The Kramers were less aggressively Pentecostal than many of their associates. Their ecumenical spirit was displayed by their visiting churches of all persuasions on the journey north. On other occasions, they helped property owners with their harvesting. In the far north, they were forced to exchange their horses for donkeys, reducing their travel speed from seven miles an hour to two.[61] At this snail-pace, they arrived at Leigh Creek where they visited a nearby Aboriginal camp.[62] Here they taught the children and anointed a fevered woman with oil for healing (James 5:14–15). She recovered rapidly. They continued on, offering their services to any who were in need. Kramer recalled—

Kramer caravan.

> Thus sowing beside all waters, we have many opportunities of witnessing among pastoralists and others in the great bush, and among outstations, and many have received us gladly. We seek their spiritual welfare, in return they show their appreciation by attending to our comfort and temporal needs, and oftentimes giving us a change from camping on the road.[63]

In this way they continued their slow progress through the Outback. By September 1918, it was decided to return to Melbourne for a break to arrange for their son Colin's education. They stayed for a time with the Buchanans before returning by train in May 1919 to Quorn and thence to Oodnadatta to collect their van. They now had a small extra cart to carry their supplies. In Oodnadatta, Kramer was dismayed to see the terrible combined effects of poverty, neglect and an influenza epidemic among the Aborigines.[64] His compassion and deep concern for them was obviously a driving motivation for his work—

> Still by God's grace, the dear remaining few Aborigines were gathered together. In a nice building? No, in their rags and bags, often amongst the rubbish of tins and bottles, and any amount of dogs; still they sat attentively and heard the Word gladly. Then just at this time the natives fell sick with influenza.
>
> Oh, such sadness and such sights I shall never forget. They were so neglected and helplessly dying like animals, but with the doctor and policeman's help we rigged up an isolation camp outside the town, and then, with four donkeys in the van, the sick were gathered into camp and cared for.
>
> My heart was full of pain, for the sight was sad indeed. Many were carried in one

day in hope, and carried out later a corpse... Oh, how my heart cried out for help for these people in their darkness.[65]

They stayed for six weeks, trying to help the sufferers and 'losing not an opportunity to teach them of the great love of Jesus'.[66]

They recommenced their journey: it was fraught with difficulties. Heavy creeks, sand hills, rocks and stones, scant feed, waterless tracks, blistering heat, loneliness, a tiny van crammed with equipment, slow travel, struggling animals all combined to create enormous obstacles. 'At one time,' wrote Kramer—

> We had a terrible struggle to get over thirty-five miles of heavy, sandy country, with many creeks to cross. The donkeys were two days without water; the days were so hot we could only travel very early in the morning; and then after sundown for a few hours. One morning... a fierce north wind arose and continued for the whole day, just as though it were off a fire. We could not quench our thirst... The temperature remained at 107 degrees in the van.

Kramer's ministry was marked by a simple trust in God for every need, characteristic of the ministry of Good News Hall. After reaching Farina, in 40 degree heat, 'the Lord gave the word, Isaiah 33:16 ("water will not fail")'. Encouraged by this, Kramer dug in a creek and found a steady supply of fresh water which kept them for six months. Locals, meanwhile, were paying the large sum of two shillings and sixpence for a hundred gallons. When their first daughter Mary was born in a tent in Farina in temperatures up to 45 degrees, she was 'as healthy as a rosebud' and for ten months slept through each night. When repairs were needed for the wagon wheels, and they had only one penny to their names, the funds were provided. On another occasion, on a visit to town, money was wired to them just in time for them to buy food before the store closed. When the donkeys strayed during the night, Kramer found them after praying. Once a goat fell under the wheel of the van. 'We took our goat to Jesus in prayer, who has power over all flesh,' recalled Kramer. A week later, in fine health, she gave birth to two kids—to the Kramers this was simply another fulfilment of Scripture.[67] After struggling for two scorching days and nights without water to cover the final leg of the arduous, punishing trip to Alice Springs, 580 kilometres north of Oodnadatta, and then seeing rain pouring down flooding the Todd River, they thanked God it had not come sooner, and so cut them off from the town. Once when confronted with twelve tracks leading in different directions, they prayed for guidance and saw a rainbow over one of them, leading them to safety.

Ernie Kramer preaching in the Outback (Photo courtesy M.Kramer).

Kramer freely offered the gospel to any who would listen, but his major concern was for the Aborigines, who constituted a major part of the pastoral industry's work force in the Far North.[68] He had preached to them on his first journey and now on his return, he could report that they were glad to see him again. He was delighted to meet two boys who were still standing firm in the faith and another who had been a steadfast believer for four years. Others greeted them 'with beaming faces' and remembered what he had told them of the love of Jesus.

Using Bible pictures and Christian songs, he preached the gospel and many heard 'the sweet story' for the first time. They 'never grew tired' of his presentation. In Alice Springs, Kramer spent many hours teaching children of mixed blood and conducting open air services.[69] People came from as far as 130 kilometres away. Their daughter Mary, now five years old, would herself gather the children and teach them songs. In one place, an Aboriginal woman who had heard Kramer once before, walked fifteen kilometres carrying a three-year-old on her back to hear the gospel again. Kramer recalled these days with affection—

> When they would sight us driving along to this tree, with one donkey in our little cart, they would come running from all directions, old and young, men and women, with picannies [sic] on their backs. We have had over 50 in a gathering.

Again, it was Kramer's deep concern for the Aborigines which motivated him—

> To the south-east and west lay the McDonald [sic] Ranges, in their grandeur and possibilities of cultivation; but the cry of my heart went out to the benighted tribes of the aborigines [sic], unknown to me, but not to Him, who gave His life for them. Oh, how I longed that He would prosper and enable us to reach those yet some hundred miles further east, who have never been told of the love of Jesus...

Even those who worked on the stations were in constant need. They were rarely paid adequate wages and usually lived in squalid conditions, well removed from the more comfortable dwellings of the station owners. Usually, the only ones who saw the inside of the homesteads were women who worked as domestics or who provided sexual favours for the lonely men.[70]

How well Kramer was equipped with a knowledge of Aboriginal culture is questionable. He seems to have learned as he went. He understood the power of what he called the 'Black Fellows' Bone' and saw the love of Christ as an antidote for this. Furthermore, he did not make the mistake of many nineteenth century missionaries—and even some of his own day—who believed it was necessary to civilise the people before they could accept the gospel.[71] His aim, he said, was to encourage the people 'from a spiritual standpoint'. Whereas other missionaries had blamed the Aborigines for being incapable of understanding the Christian message,[72] Kramer prayed that he would have the ability to make it understandable—

> We do not profess to civilise them, but to show them 'the Light of Life' which is Jesus, the once crucified, and now risen Saviour, and soon coming King of Kings and Lord of Lords, whom we lift up, praying God to prepare the hearts of the Aborigines to receive Jesus. We seek for wisdom to make the Word plain and simple for these hearers.
>
> Civilisation is not congenial to them, yet before God they have souls to save, which are precious ...

Towards the end of the journey, they visited the 'Finke Mission Station', no doubt the Lutheran settlement at Hermannsburg, 100 kilometres south west of Alice Springs, where they were 'heartily welcomed' by the pastor and his wife, at that time the remarkable Carl Strehlow, whose ministry was to conclude with his death the following year.[73] Here, Kramer was delighted to hear Aborigines worshiping and singing in Aranda. From the earliest days, missionaries here had respected indigenous languages and had translated much of the Bible into the local dialect.[74] Kramer was overjoyed to see this willingness to reach out to the Aborigines. 'It was beautiful,' he recalled. 'It made our tears flow.'

Harris refers to the great trek of the Lutheran missionaries Heidenreich, Kempe and Schwartz from Adelaide to the Finke River, from October 1875 to June 1877, with their 2 400 sheep, 44 horses, 23 cattle, five dogs, four hens and one rooster, as a journey which 'stands alone' in the annals of missionary endeavour.[75] There seems little reason to challenge this claim. But Erny and Effie Kramer's much smaller, less publicised and more humble venture must also be seen as a remarkable example of pioneer missionary courage and enterprise. All in all, through extreme conditions and in the face of almost insurmountable difficulties, during 1913, 1916 and 1921, they covered well over 10,000 kilometres in their patient, plodding Outback ministry.

In 1921, Good News Hall urged the Kramers to return to Melbourne and assist in the work there, which, reluctantly, they did. But their hearts were still in the Outback, and they immediately began to make plans for establishing a 'Scriptural Knowledge Institution' in Alice Springs as a shelter for orphans and a base from which to reach the Aborigines.

Smith Wigglesworth's visit encouraged them to seek support for this venture and soon Robert Davis, who was baptized in the Spirit at that time, agreed to join them, although as it happened, this did not eventuate.[76]

In June 1924, *Good News* reported that Philip Adams was again building a caravan for 'a dear brother and his wife' who were, God willing, going 'to the back blocks with the full message for these last days'.[77] This was a more substantial wagon designed for horses. J. E. Rieschiek provided them with all the harnessing they needed.[78] They travelled by boat to Port Augusta and thence overland to Alice Springs.

Ernest Kramer and his second caravan, Melbourne, 1924.

1925 saw the beginnings of the Pentecostal Church of Australia, and the subsequent movement of people between the different groups, resulting in a loss of some financial support. Nevertheless, they set off, with young Colin, now eleven years old, looking after the horses, although Effie and the other children travelled by Dodge truck from Oodnadatta.[79] In Alice Springs, Kramer leased four blocks of land, where he displayed considerable ingenuity in getting established.[80]

He now began to use camels for his Outback travel, often being away for weeks at a time. Effie conducted services at Alice Springs for Aborigines. Around this time, Kramer became increasingly inter-denominational in his approach, and gave less emphasis to issues such as glossolalia. The Aborigines' Friends' Association offered some support for his ministry.[81] He was also learning greater flexibility—agreeing, for example, to the cooking of certain foods on Sundays because they would not keep in the hot weather if prepared the day before.

Kramer was able to purchase the land on which he had built, but a decade later, weary and suffering in health from his Outback travel, he sold the property and returned to Melbourne in 1934, where he became a representative for the Bible Society. He died in 1958 of leukemia. His wife continued to attend a Baptist church until her death in 1971. In April 1984, the Australian Missionary Society built an interdenominational building in Alice Springs and named it the Kramer Memorial Church, in honour of Ernest Kramer and his 21 years of ministry.[82]

Ernie Kramer's brother Fritz also had a heart for the Aborigines. He and his wife, who was a school teacher, worked with them at Redfern, Katoomba and Rolands Plains, NSW.[83]

North Queensland

Meanwhile, in the early 1920s, Isabella Hetherington attempted to purchase some land in Melbourne on which to erect bark huts for dwellings. This enterprise failed, but over a period of several years, a hundred Aborigines were 'instructed in the way of righteousness.'[84] By now, it was 1925, and Nellie found herself singing over a period of three months at the Sunshine Mission Hall and then in the Prahran Town Hall, during the ministry of A. C. Valdez.

Nellie suffered an attack of pneumonia, and on medical advice, Hetherington took her to the warmer climes of Brisbane, where they stayed for five months, and then on to Maryborough in 1928, where Nellie played and sang for Pastor George Burns of the newly-formed Christian Mission.

Not long afterwards, Hetherington was pioneering Pentecostal mission work among the Aborigines at Mossman, about 80 kilometres north of Cairns, in North Queensland.[85] Her long black dress particularly struck the scantily clothed northern Queenslanders.[86] Later Ethel Vale was to claim that there had never been a missionary at Mossman before.[87] She seems to have been misinformed here. In North Queensland, the non-denominational Queensland Kanaka Mission had been established in 1886 by the renowned evangelical missionary Florence Young.[88] Based in Bundaberg, the Mission soon established branches in other places, including Cairns and Mossman. In 1905, there was a revival of prayer during which people fell on their knees and variously cried and laughed for joy. The movement spread until in places as far removed as Bundaberg and Mossman, there were extensive prayer meetings being held during which missionaries and 'boys' alike cried out for an infilling of the Holy Spirit.[89] To what extent there were Pentecostal manifestations at these meetings is unclear, but one

Cairns inhabitant claimed that her grandfather, a South Sea Islander, attended 'Pentecostal' meetings at cane-cutters community camps in and around Cairns in 1904. George Malla Kulla was a recognised leader of these groups.[90] By the time Hetherington arrived 25 years later, most of the South Sea Islanders had been repatriated. But memories of the 1905 revival were still to be found.

In 1897, in an endeavour to counteract the continuing violence and exploitation of Aborigines and their ongoing decimation through alcoholism, opium addiction, poverty and disease, the Queensland Aborigines Protection and Restriction of the Sale of Opium Act had been passed requiring Aborigines to relocate to Government missions 'for their own protection'.[91] Although there were many restrictions—Aborigines on reserves were forbidden to take alcohol or opium, they could not vote and authorities had the right to search their dwellings and belongings at any time, to read their mail, to remove their children, to prohibit traditional practices, to confiscate their property—Hetherington believed the Act had been introduced for the Aborigines' benefit and that it would offer relief from their sorrows.[92] So she herself, now in her mid-fifties, moved to the Gorge Reserve to set up a 'Faith Mission' where she and Ethel Vale laboured together.[93] It was not easy. Initially, they lived in a humpy. The two women manually cleared dense jungle scrub and planted a variety of tropical fruits and shrubbery. They established a school and tried to provide medicine for the children. Hetherington personally milked the cow and attended to other menial tasks.[94] She was often without funds but trusted God to supply her needs.[95] She taught, conducted funerals, and cared for the children. She tended to the sick and washed the feet of Aboriginal brothers and sisters.[96] On occasion, she intervened to prevent spear fights between the men. 'She would run right out into the middle of the fight area and stop them,' recalled one woman. 'No one game to throw spear when she out there.'[97] Over one hundred new believers were baptized in water during the thirties, some of them in crocodile-infested streams. Hetherington was not afraid; she just trusted God.[98] She would often pray, 'Lord, send the fire down!' and, to those present, even the leaves on the big milk tree quivered.[99] Together with Nellie, she held meetings in the local Mossman 'sample shed.' Nellie played the piano and sang with 'a beautiful soprano voice' while Hetherington preached.[100] Ultimately, a house was built for her at Kubirri. Kathleen Bogle paid tribute to Hetherington—

> Sister Hetherington was just like a mother to the Aboriginal people. She'd get a dish of water and wash their feet and tend to them when they were sick. She ... would go to their camps, give them a wash and take care of them. Make soup and feed them. She was an angel in disguise.[101]

On 10 and 17 March, 1932, she was presented as 'our pioneer and veteran missionary' at the 'Canvas Cathedral' in Brisbane, where she spoke of her work at Mossman and Nellie sang among others a song entitled, 'The Hope of the Aboriginals.'[102] The journey would not have been easy. For a start, there was no road from Cairns, and either a boat trip or a train ride to Kurunda offered the only possibilities. At least one person was so challenged by her message he decided to become a Daintree missionary.[103] In that same year, she addressed the Queensland Assemblies of God conference, with the result that a year later she became recognised as their missionary to the Aborigines.[104] On occasion, Hetherington visited the Pentecostal church at Cairns. A photo taken around 1935, when Maxwell Armstrong was pastor, shows her standing with a group of the church people.[105] She was a slight, diminutive, white-haired woman. She was also said to be hard-working, set in her ways and on fire for God. Around this time, Hetherington declared that the Mayor of Mossman, who had assisted the work of the Mission in many ways, would not die before he turned to the Lord. Years later, after Hetherington's death, this came to pass.[106]

In 1938, the Aborigines' Progressive Association, under the leadership of William Ferguson, proclaimed 26 January as a Day of Mourning for Aborigines and campaigned widely for justice and equality, actions which resulted in the passing of the New South Wales Aborigines Welfare Act (1940).[107] In the same year, Albert Namatjira held his first exhibition in Melbourne.[108] Of much less import, but sufficient for those involved, after a decade of meetings in tents and sheds, was the opening, in 1938, by Isabella Hetherington, with the assistance of people from Brisbane, of a small building which served both as a Sunday meeting place and a school for the children. People came for miles around to the dedication service. The church was nicely filled, reported Charles Enticknap, and 'dedicated to the glory of God for the salvation of the native sons of Australia.'[109] For Hetherington, this was an achievement to be proud of; she was content to leave political activism to others.

On 27 July 1941, Henry Wiggins, the Chairman of the Assemblies of God in Australia, officially opened a new Mission at nearby Daintree, under the leadership of Hugh Davidson.[110] En route, he visited the Gorge at Mossman where, he wrote, 'nestles Sister Hetherington's Mission for Aboriginals.' The Gorge was 'more lovely than ever' but Hetherington was 'frailer than in past days.'[111]

Four years later, the new Assemblies of God National Chairman, Pastor Philip Duncan, described her as an 'aged worker of 76 summers, bent with age' who wept when they prayed together. 'She lives with the coloured folk,' he wrote, 'and she will die with them, for whom she left and gave her all.' She was devoted to God and 'passionately in love' with the people she served and on whose behalf she had invested so much.[112] When the Government policy of removing children with a non-Aboriginal father from their families accelerated in the 1930s, she opposed the idea.[113] Robert Missenden, a newly-ordained Methodist minister, conducted Hetherington's funeral. Before she died, he said—

> I was supposed to pray for her but she prayed for me … She sat up in bed and said, 'Lord Jesus, I am coming.' Then she lay back and was gone.[114]

One man, moved to tears as he spoke, claimed that the night Hetherington died people saw angels fly from her house to the church, where they heard them singing.[115]

Isabella Hetherington's love for God, her yearning, joyful mysticism and her commitment to His work come through strongly in these words—

> I am not worthy of the crumbs that drop from my Master's table, but I am finding out that it is not according to my merits or demerits that He blesses me but according to His riches in glory … My King has conferred his highest honour upon

me, even me, by pouring out His Holy Spirit upon me. I cannot understand this mystery of mysteries but oh! Who else but God could have produced such a rapturous height of holy delight as possessed my body ... Is it presumptuous to say that I was filled with the fullness of God? ... Oh that I could get entirely out of self and into God, indeed I hunger and thirst after the living God.[116]

The spirit of Pentecost could hardly be more finely expressed.

Hetherington's dedication to her calling is simply portrayed in a few lines she penned for Nellie to sing—

May I do it to Thy glory,
Whatsoe'er the work may be;
May each duty tell to others
That it is not I, but Thee.

And if Satan should applaud me
For the work that Thou dost do
In and through an empty vessel,
Thou canst hide me from his view.

In the secret of Thy presence
I am lost to all beside,
Knowing not of fame or glory,
But of Christ the Crucified

When the evening twilight cometh,
'Ere I lay this body down,
May my reckonings be found faithful,
So that no man take my crown.[117]

Compared with other Christian work among Aborigines, Pentecostal endeavours in the pre-war years were modest, to say the least. Nevertheless, given the small size of the fledgling movement and viewed in the light of the activities of older denominations in their first half-century of existence, the work was not insignificant. It reflected the passion ignited by their experience in the Spirit and their deep conviction that the Spirit was given to empower them for witness and evangelism.

A half-century later, beginning in the late 1970s, there was a widespread and significant charismatic revival among Aborigines at Arnhem Land and Elcho Island in the Northern Territory and at the Warburton Ranges in Central Australia, where hundreds were converted, many rescued from alcoholism and violence and Pentecostal manifestations common. Aboriginal preachers and musicians addressed crowded gatherings. Whole communities were changed.[118] Isabella Hetherington and Erny and Effie Kramer would have rejoiced to see this—it was the kind of growth of the faith they had dreamed of.

I am not aware of any direct connection between their work and this later revival. In some ways they were very different. The recent work has largely been led by Aborigines with comparatively little input from non-Aboriginal people. Nevertheless, in a general sense, the foundation of Christian faith and belief laid down by pioneers like Hetherington and the Kramers—and scores of other Christian missionaries—has plainly been a determining factor.

Isabella Hetherington and Erny and Effie Kramer provide fine models of Australian Pentecostal ministry. Hetherington and Erny Kramer were both immigrants who unreservedly made Australia their home. They were innovative and resourceful. They understood better than many the need to identify with the people they served. They did not try to impose an inflexible Anglo-Saxon 'civilised' model of Christianity on the Aborigines. They were prepared to work with or without denominational or organisational support. Their philosophy of ministry was defined by their understanding of God and the impartation of His Spirit. They clearly felt compassion for the Aborigines; they knew by personal experience the power of the Holy Spirit; they believed they were led by God to venture out as they did; they trusted God to meet their needs when no human aid was at hand. They worked hard; they sacrificed material comforts for the work of the ministry; they openly declared their love for God; they believed it was not unreasonable to ask God for the impossible They demonstrated, perhaps better than anyone, the spirit of Pentecost.

Isabella Hetherington and Nellie, c.1908.

Notes

1. GN 1:5, January, 1913, 8ff; GN, 1:6, October, 1913, 20; GN, 19:10, October, 1928, 16f; GN, 21:3, March, 1930, 16; GN, 21:5, May, 1930, 16; GN, 21:7, July, 1930, 15; GN, 21:11, November, 1930, 13; GN, 22:5, May, 1931, 14. I have restricted this study to Pentecostal activities in Australia; the subject of Pentecostal foreign missions is extensive and warrants separate treatment.

2. In contemporary usage, it is usual to employ the adjective *Aboriginal* as a singular noun and *Aborigines* as the plural noun. However, *Aboriginal Australian* and *Indigenous Australian* are also recommended, especially when Torres Strait Islander peoples are included. In South Eastern Australia, the term *Koori* has become common for Aboriginal people. See *Style Manual* (Canberra: Australian Government Printing Service, 1994), 40; T. Rowse, Áboriginal nomenclature,' in Davison et al, eds, 1999, 10.

3. In both of these cases, it took at least fifteen years from the founding of the

movement concerned to the establishing of a formal ministry to Aborigines. Given that it was 33 years after settlement before the first Christian missionary endeavour to Aborigines took place in Australia, that the Methodist Church, for example, had no denominational Aboriginal missionary program from 1855 until 1916 and that the Churches of Christ Federal Aborigines Mission Board was only formed in 1941, this was, by comparison, a reasonably prompt response to the need for ministry among Aborigines. See Harris, 1990, 181, 21, 801; R. Guy, *Baptized Among Crocodiles* (unpublished paper, 1998), 184, 254ff, 348f; J. Easton, personal communication, 6 February, 1995; interview, 24 February, 1995; S. Cowling, personal communication, 23 June, 1992, 6 October, 1992, 17 February, 1993, J. Turnbull, personal communication, June, 1991; Aborigine Rescue Mission News and Prayer Letter, 1:1, 10 April, 1946.

4. I. Hetherington, *Aboriginal Queen of Sacred Song* (Melbourne: Saxton and Buckie, 1929), 7. Further details are from this source unless otherwise stated. Generally, specific sources on Hetherington are limited. See also the *Australian Aborigines' Advocate*, 31 January, 1912, 5.

5. Myrtle Jackson, personal communication, 8 May, 1992.

6. AAA, 31 January, 1912, 5f; J. Harris, *One Blood* (Sutherland: Albatross, 1990), 22ff, 272, 488; Thompson, 1994, 28; Piggin, 1996, 46; 'Aborigines' in G. Davison, J. W. McCarty and A. McLeary, eds, *Australians 1888* (Broadway: Fairfax, Syme and Weldon, 1987), 130f; compare *Sunday at Home* (London: William Clarke, December 1877), 773— 'To save them from extinction, to reclaim them to any of the useful occupations of life, and even to implant in their minds the idea of a Supreme Being, is regarded as impossible.' The article goes on to refute this view.

7. Harris, 1990, 8092; Breward, 1993, 104; R. Broome, *Aboriginal Australians* (St Leonards, NSW: Allen and Unwin, 1994), 91. It is of interest that the *News and Prayer Letter* of the Aborigine Rescue Mission established by the Apostolic Church in 1945 noted that while 'the black man of Australia' had remained in the stone age, there was 'a growing conviction that the real character of the Aborigines' had never been properly understood 'nor their true merits appreciated' (1:1, 10 April, 1946, 1).

8. Quoted in Harris, 1990, 25.

9. H. Reynolds, *With the White People* (Ringwood: Penguin, 1990), 127; Broome, 1994, 92f.

10. For a concise overview of Bates' life and work see Annette Hamilton's entry in Davison et al, eds, 1999, 63f.

11. R. Johnson, *To All the Inhabitants and Especially to the Unhappy Prisoners and Convicts in the Colonies Established at Port Jackson and Norfolk Island* 30 October, 1792, 67ff.

12. Broome, 1994, 27.

13. Broome, 1994, 145.

14. Unfortunately, Hetherington is no more specific than this and so far I have been unable to ascertain the precise location of her early work.

15. Harris, 1990, 570. It was not uncommon for Aboriginal camps to be located 'a mile or two out of town— beyond the cemetery, the Chinese gardens or the rubbish dump or on the other side of the river'. See Henry Reynolds and Dawn May, 'Queensland,' in A. McGrath, ed, *Contested Ground* (St Leonards: Allen and Unwin, 1995), 181; Reynolds, 1990, 135. The Australian Aborigines Mission was originally called the Aborigines Protection Association. In 1894, its name changed to the La Perouse Aborigines Mission Committee; five years later it became the NSW Aborigines Mission and in 1907 the Australian Aborigines Mission. There was a breakaway group which took the name Aborigines Inland Mission. Finally, in 1929, the two reunited under the name United Aborigines Mission. In the 1970s, the church at La Perouse was transferred to the Aborigines

Evangelical Fellowship. See T. Mayne, 'La Perouse Celebrates 100 Years,' in *Indigenous Leadership*, No.14, February, 1998, 5ff. The CMS began their ministry to Aborigines at Wellington in 1832, but the work languished in 1843. See Harris, 1990, 56, 554f.

16. Harris, 1990, 255ff, 313ff, 381ff, 458ff; Piggin, 1996, 46; T. G. H. Strehlow, *Central Australian Religion* (Bedford Park, SA: Australian Association for the Study of Religions, 1978).

17. Piggin, 1996, 22; E. Kotlowski, *Southland of the Holy Spirit* (Orange: Christian History Research Institute, 1994), 113ff.

18. Harris, 1990, 689; Piggin 1996, 82f; Breward, 1993, 104. Bain Attwood comments, 'These dedicated men and women were exceptional in regarding Aborigines as fellow human beings... and at best their missions alleviated the suffering of fringe-dwellers and saved communities from extermination by protecting Aborigines from the worst ravages of colonisation.' See B. Attwood, 'Aboriginal missions,' in Davison et al, eds, 1999, 8.

19. Hetherington, 1929, 8, 26.

20. Hetherington, 1929, 7.

21. Reynolds, 1990, 154, 183f; Broome, 1994, 58ff. Broome claims that in the nineteenth century there was a death rate of 80% among Aborigines and that the major killers were alcoholism and disease. Around Port Phillip, for example, the original population prior to contact with Europeans was around 10,000 but by 1853 had dropped to just under 2,000.

22. For example, the first picture of her in AAA shows her with three small children—AAA, 31 August, 1908, 6.

23. AAA, 28 February, 1910, 8.

24. AAA, 31 March, 1909, 7; AAA, 31 May, 1920, 4, 6.

25. AAA, 30 September, 1910, 8.

26. AAA, 30 April, 1910, 3; AAA, 30 June, 1910, 8; AAA, 30 November, 1910, 1; AAA, 31 December, 1910, 7; AAA, 31 March, 1911, 1; AAA, 30 June, 1911, 1; AAA, 31 October, 1911, 4; AAA, 31 January, 1912, 5.

27. AAA, 30 July, 1912, 1; AAA, 30 September, 1912, 1; AAA, 31 December, 1912, 2f. The Point Macleay Mission was originally Presbyterian and became a government station in 1916. The Aborigines' Friends' Association continued to supply missionaries until 1923, after which the Parkin Trust accepted responsibility for missionary appointments there. In 1943, the Salvation Army took over this role. See Harris, 1990, 370ff. See also McGrath, ed, 1995, 223; AAA, 30 November, 1912, 5.

28. Harris, 1990, 514ff.

29. It should be noted that during the nineteenth century, in all colonies except Queensland and Western Australia, where they were specifically excluded, Aboriginal males, as British subjects, did have the right to vote. Only in South Australia was this right actually exercised. Although South Australians protested that the non-inclusion of Aborigines in the Commonwealth census would nullify the voting rights of Aborigines, the measure was passed. See P. Sretton and C. Finnimore, *How South Australian Aborigines Lost the Vote: some side effects of federation* (Adelaide: Old Parliament House, November 1991), 2ff. When female voting rights were approved in South Australia in 1894, Aboriginal women were included. For example, a polling booth was set up at Pt McLeay in 1896 where there were more than one hundred Aborigines on the rolls, of whom over 70% voted.

30. A. Markus, 'Under the Act', in Gammage and Spearritt, eds, 1987, 47ff. Breward, 1993, 105 suggests that 20,000 of Aboriginal deaths were the result of inter-racial violence. However, the greatest cause of death and declining population was probably introduced diseases such as smallpox. See McGrath, ed, 1995, 124ff, 141; Broome, 1994,

58ff.

31. Harris, 1990, 550.

32. Broome, 1994, 174.

33. Reynolds, 1990, 233ff.

34. McGrath, ed, 1995, 67f, 72, 135ff, 183, 223; P. Read, 'Aborigines', in Davison et al, eds, 1999, 14. That none of these options was acceptable to many Aborigines is indicated by the request from Nellie's mother to Isabella Hetherington, 'Don't let the Government get her, and don't send her to any home... and don't let her go alone to the camps. Take her now before she gets the cough.' See Hetherington, 1929, 10.

35. Quoted in Breward, 1993, 104.

36. See M. Prentis, *Science, Race and Faith* (Sydney: Centre for the Study of Australian Christianity, 1998), 151, 182. Prentis notes that although Mathew treated with the 'customary condescension' he had many Aboriginal friends whom he regarded with affection and respect, he gave an Aboriginal name to his youngest child and he appreciated Aboriginal religion.

37. Breward, 1993, 114ff.

38. Reynolds, 1990, 116ff, 179f, 204ff; Broome, 1994, 93, 132.

39. Broome, 1994, 143ff; Markus, 1987, 47ff; Reynolds, 1990, 154. Note that Broome claims there were only 22 reserves in New South Wales in 1936.

40. AAA, 30 July, 1912, 5; AAA, 31 August, 1912, 5; AAA, 30 September, 1912, 3; AAA, 30 November, 1912, 5; AAA, 31 December, 1912, 4.

41. C. Pope, *A Brief History of Ernest E. Kramer* (unpublished essay, Tabor College, 1986), 1; F. K. Metters and E. Schroeder, *Outback Evangelist: the Story of Ernest Kramer* (Norwood, S.A.: Peacock Publications, 2008). F. K. Metters was the Kramers' second daughter. Unfortunately, the book avoids references to their early Pentecostal connections.

42. It may have been Kramer who introduced the Buchanan family to Pentecostalism. See F. Lancaster, interview, 18 December, 1993. Effie Kramer may well have been the 'sister' referred to in the previous incident, but as few names are used in *Good News*, and in the absence to this point of further reliable sources, this cannot be assumed.

43. Hetherington, 1929, 17f; AAA 31 December, 1912, 4; E. Kramer, *Caravan Mission to Bush People and Aboriginals, Journeyings in the Far North and Centre of Australia*, n.d.; GN, October 1913, 10f; Chant, 1984, 61ff.

44. AAA, 31 December 1912, 4.

45. Retta Long founded the Aborigines Inland Mission (1905). See J. West, 'The Role of the Woman Missionary,' in *Lucas: an Evangelical History Review*, No. 21, 22, June and December, 1996, 50; Piggin, 1996, 67.

46. Hetherington, 1929, 3.

47. AAA, 31 March, 1913, page number obscured.

48. AAA, 31 May 1913, 4, 7.

49. In a Pentecostal context 'singing in the Spirit' usually means singing a spontaneous song which has not previously been learned, either in one's own language or in tongues, more commonly the latter. Here, it seems to mean singing a spontaneous song in English which later changed to tongues.

50. Hetherington, 1929, 3.

51. GN, No.6, October, 1913, 10; K. Smallcombe, personal correspondence, 1 September, 1994.

52. I. Hetherington, 'God's Work in and through a Missionary to the Australian Aboriginals,' GN, 1:6, October, 1913, 10.

53. AAA, 30 August, 1913, 6.

54. The idea of a separate experience in the Spirit was not unknown to the Mission.

Retta Dixon inscribed seven dates in the front of her Bible, which included: Born again— May 25 1884; Definitely received a clean heart— Nov 9 1888; Baptized— Nov 29 1891; Received into church fellowship— Dec 6 1891; Received the Holy Spirit— Jan 12 1893. See Mayne, 1998, 5ff. It was glossolalia which proved problematic.

55. 'The Tongue's [sic] Movement,' AAA, 30 August, 1913, page number obscured.
56. See Appendix B.
57. M. Jackson, personal communication, 8 May, 1992; Guy, 1998, 175, 187.
58. Kramer, *Caravan Mission*, n. d. Further details of Kramer's ministry are taken from this source unless otherwise stated. There are no page numbers in the original.
59. Daisy Bates moved to Ooldea in South Australia's far north in 1920.
60. The texts were: 'Thou shalt call his name Jesus for he shall save his people from their sins,'— Matthew 1:21 (which Kramer gives as 2:21); 'God is love'— 1 John 4:16; 'Prepare to meet thy God,'— Amos 4:12; 'Behold I come quickly and my reward is with me to give to every man as his work shall be'— Revelation 22:12.
61. A change which was viewed with wry amusement even by Kramer himself in the light of the text painted on the van, 'Behold I come quickly'; M. Kramer, personal communication, 1986.
62. Fifty years later, Aborigines were barred from actually living in the Leigh Creek township. See Peggy Brock, 'South Australia' in McGrath, ed, 1995, 212.
63. Kramer, *Caravan Mission*.
64. Aborigines were often refused treatment at public hospitals. See McGrath, ed, 1995, 94, 231.
65. Kramer, *Caravan Mission*.
66. Although many at Good News Hall eschewed the use of medicine, Kramer seems to have had no such scruples.
67 Proverbs 27:27— 'And thou shalt have goats' milk enough for thy food, for the food of thy household' (KJV).
68. 'A typical large station might employ half a dozen White people ... one or two Aborigines of mixed descent who took superior roles such as stock-camp boss, and twenty or more Aboriginal "ringers"— Peter Read, 'Northern Territory' in McGrath, ed, 1995, 273f. Reynolds notes that there were thousands of Aborigines in the rural workforce, including some 10,000 on sheep and cattle stations, and that on average there were about 25 Aboriginal workers, both male and female, per station who did 'practically all the work' (1990, 196ff). Broome argues that without Aboriginal labour, the stations could not have survived (1994, 127).
69. As was the custom at the time, he referred to them as 'half-caste' children. Legislation passed in South Australia in 1911 'for the better Protection and Control of the Aboriginal and Half-caste Inhabitants' actually enshrined this term and a subsequent (1913–1916) Royal Commission sought to distinguish between 'full-bloods' and 'half-castes'. See Brock in McGrath, ed, 1995, 225ff. A similar Act in Victoria in 1886 had used identical language. See Broome in McGrath, ed, 1995, 139.
70. Broome, 1994, 130ff.
71. This attitude was widespread. See Harris 1990, 260, 474, 802; Reynolds, 1990, 90f.
72. Harris, 1990, 271, 802. Of course, there were also many exceptions to this approach e.g. Harris, 1990, 479.
73. Harris, 1990, 405; Strehlow, 1978, 7ff; W. F. Veit, 'Strehlow, Carl Friedrich Theodor (1871–1922)' in *ADB, Vol 12, 1891–1939*, 121f. In later years, Strehlow's son, T. G. H. Strehlow and his wife Bertha developed a friendship with the Kramers and often stayed in their home in Alice Springs— Mary Kramer, quoted in the *Centralian Advocate*

23 July, 1991, 10.

74. Harris, 1990, 392ff.

75. Harris, 1990, 390.

76. Davis was converted as a result of the change in his wife when she spoke in tongues after attending Good News Hall. He attested that early one morning in 1919, he was smoking in bed when he saw a vision of Christ and the two thieves and he heard 'the sound of the drip-drip-drip of the blood of Jesus on the linoleum floor.' He was a builder and was responsible for much of the construction work at the Hall. In 1936, Davis was ordained to the ministry of the Apostolic Church. R. Davis, interview, n. d.; see also The Apostolic Church Certificate of Ordination dated 14 November, 1936.

77. This was obviously a reference to the Kramers and typical of the *Good News* practice— admittedly irregular and inconsistent— of avoiding the use of names in reports. See GN, 15:6, June, 1924, 7.

78. Pope, 1986, 6.

79. Pope, 1986, 7. Further details are from this paper unless otherwise stated.

80. According to his family, the house was built of pines from Pine Gap, which were termite-resistant, and bricks hand-made from lime and sand. Kramer designed a system of reticulated water to the house, reputedly the first in Alice Springs, and included netting-covered vents at both ground and ceiling level for air circulation. He also constructed a tennis court from crushed ant hills. In 1924, the Ebenezer Tabernacle was erected, the first concrete building in Alice Springs. See Pope 1986, 8ff. See also Jose Petrick, 'Spreading the Gospel,' *Centralian Advocate,* 8 October, 1986.

81. The Aborigines' Friends' Association was formed in South Australia in 1857 by a group of people concerned for the welfare of Aborigines. It continued to fulfil this aim for many decades. See Harris 1990, 356.

82. 'Four Children of Missionary Here for Opening,' *Centralian Advocate,* 1977 (specific date not recorded). Prior to the opening, Sir Douglas Nicholls, himself an Aborigine and then Governor of South Australia, wrote to Kramer's daughter Mary: 'Your father's name was widely respected for the great work he did as a missionary.' See Helen Innes, 'Ernest Kramer One of God's People in Oz,' *On Being,* August, 1978, 44. A photo taken of the church in 1991 shows a 'wayside pulpit' sign which reads, 'GROG is EVIL it will NOT make you happy; the HOLY SPIRIT will make you HAPPY indeed; JESUS CHRIST gives the HOLY SPIRIT to ALL who follow Him.' There may be some echoes of Kramer's teaching here.

83. F. Lancaster, interview, 18 December, 1993; E. Vale in Guy, 1998, 265f. In 1948, he visited Mossman and took over the mission for a time. Years later, a mural which he painted bore tribute to his work there.

84. Hetherington, 1929, 20.

85. AE, 7:11, October, 1941, 9. There was a significant Aboriginal population in this area. See the map in McGrath, ed, 1995, xxf.

86. W. Walker, quoted in Guy, 1998, 176

87. E. Vale, quoted in Guy, 1998, 188.

88. F. Young, *Pearls from the Pacific* (London and Edinburgh: Marshall Brothers, n. d.). See also relevant articles in ADEB, ADB. The Young family are still prominent in evangelical work today.

89. Young, *Pearls,* 160ff.

90. Esther Noble Frost, personal communication, 1 September, 1994.

91. This Act became the model for similar Acts in four other States.

92. Broome, 1994, 97ff.

93. Wilma Walker, quoted in Guy, 1998, 235. There was an understanding that missionaries could work on Government missions. See Harris, 1990, 765.

94. E. MacNamara quoted in Guy, 1998, 182. One of the few surviving photos shows Hetherington sitting on a stool milking a cow surrounded by dense thickets of tropical trees.
95. K. Bogle quoted in Guy, 1998, 187.
96. K. Bogle quoted in Guy, 1998, 191.
97. E. MacNamara quoted in Guy, 1998, 182.
98. AE, 5:8, July, 1939, 9; J. Done quoted in Guy, 1998, 180.
99. K. Bogle quoted in Guy, 1998, 187.
100. E. Jenkins quoted in Guy, 1998, 186.
101. Guy, 1998, 191.
102. *Cooee 6,* 13 March, 1932.
103. This was Jack Easton who was converted in a Salvation Army rally in Brisbane in November 1930 and began to attend Booth-Clibborn's Canvas Cathedral. After four years in the army, and a time of life-threatening illness, he became Superintendent of the Daintree Mission from 1945 to 1950, before going with his wife to Papua New Guinea as a missionary, where he was to serve for the next 26 years. See Guy, 1998, 184, 254ff; 348f; J. Easton, personal communication, 6 February, 1995; interview, 24 February, 1995.
104. S. Hunt, *The Assemblies of God Queensland Conference: A Story of its Formation and Mission* (Assemblies of God, n. d.), 21.
105. Broome, 1994, 166ff; Goodall, in McGrath, ed, 1995,.87; Davison et al, eds, 1998, 250.
106. Broome, 1994, 169.
107. This church at Cairns also conducted some outreach work with Aborigines in places such as Skeleton Creek, where there were, at times, significant changes in community life as a result. See GN, 18:2, February, 1927, 10; R. Dyer, Len Cook Jr, D. Parker, personal interviews, 28–31 January, 1994, and T. Hallop, personal interview, 15 April, 1993. In 1935, Charles Enticknap baptized some Aborigines in Innisfail, where he ministered to both Black and White people.
108. M. Jackson, personal communication, 8 May, 1992.
109. AE, 5:8, July, 1939, 9.
110. AE, October, 1941, quoted in Guy, 1998, 223ff. Davidson was Will Enticknap's son-in-law, having married Agnes Enticknap (b.4 September 1907) on 26 October, 1929. See A. Davidson, personal interview, 20 November, 1990. Hetherington spoke at the opening of the new Mission, recalling her early days of pioneering at Mossman.
111. AE, 5:8, July, 1939, 9; AE, 7:11, October, 1941, 2.
112. P. Duncan, 'Daintree Walkabout' in AE, 11:11, November, 1945, 3.
113. K. Bogle quoted in Guy, 1998, 234. The Queensland State Children's Act of 1911 was the third piece of legislation in Australia to give Government officials the right to remove Aboriginal children from their parents and place them in an institution. See Broome, 1994, 134. It became standard practice for children to be separated from their parents on Government settlements and missions. See Reynolds and May in McGrath, eds, 1995, 195.
114. Hunt, *Conference,* 21.
115. This was 31 August 1946. Hetherington was buried in an unmarked grave on which a stone was erected by Arthur Westbrook exactly 49 years to the day after her death. A. Westbrook, interview, 8 April, 1997; M. Jackson, personal communication, 8 May, 1992.
116. GN, No 6, October, 1913, 10.
117. Hetherington, 1929, 32. Hetherington seems to have written several poems. See A. Davidson quoted in Guy, 1998, 250. Most of these may now have perished. There is a

poem of some 40 lines entitled, 'In Loving Remembrance of Dear Little FORD,' a three-year-old who died prematurely. I have been told that this was written by Isabella Hetherington. The work itself is attributed to 'J. Hetherington'. It was given to me by Mrs Edna Faulkner, April 1992. Part of it eads—

> Then the Bridegroom embraced still one more of His bride,
> Who had braved death's dark river, so deep and wide,
> To sit at the banquet and be the King's guest.
> What felicitous joy! What a haven of rest!
> Yes, safe, oh, so safe, in that home of the blest,
> Where no evil thing cometh, and the weary find rest.
> He is waiting, dear parents, for you over there,
> When the Lord shall descend with his saints in the air.

118 The Aboriginal revival has been well documented in J. Blacket, *Fire in the Outback* (Sutherland, NSW: Albatross, 1997).

CHAPTER ELEVEN

WOMEN OF THE SPIRIT

The Role of Women in Evangelizing and Church Planting

According to Boswell, Samuel Johnson once said, 'Sir, a woman's preaching is like a dog's walking on its hinder legs. It is not done well; but you are surprised to find it done at all.'[1] Judging by the scope given to women to occupy Australia's pulpits in the late nineteenth and early twentieth centuries, many people agreed with him. It was all right to preach to Aborigines or to the heathen in other lands, but not to proclaim the Word at home.

In a memorial list of 297 ministers and probationers in Victorian Methodism published in 1935, there is not one woman.[2] It would have been surprising if there had been. In the late nineteenth and early twentieth centuries, with the exception of the Salvation Army, where women officers were active from its inception,[3] ordained women were unheard of. Not that this situation was universally approved. As early as 1893, one Methodist writer declared that it was 'in harmony with the spirit and practice of early Methodism that women should preach' and that the experience of the Salvation Army had made it plain that 'by closing the mouths of women' the church was depriving itself of 'one of the mightiest weapons of evangelization.'[4] However, this was clearly a minority view. Sabine Willis points out that in the nineteenth century, 'the Church, with its moral and social code, supported and promoted a strictly limited role for women.[5] Hilary Carey puts it even more strongly—

> Women—including clergy wives and religious—were excluded from almost all positions of clerical and administrative authority in the vast majority of Australian churches until very recently. Catholic, Lutheran, Orthodox and Islamic women have no official role in church governance, preaching or administration of the sacraments.[6]

In simple terms, ordination for women in both Catholic and Protestant churches, was not an option. Martha Turner occupied the pulpit of the small Unitarian church in Melbourne in the 1870s.[7] She was a rarity. The first woman member of the clergy in a recognized denomination, Reverend Winifred Kiek, a Congregationalist, was not ordained till 1927.[8] It was many years before any other established denomination followed suit. Among Catholics, there were opportunities for women to exercise highly effective and influential ministries through religious orders—Mary MacKillop and Mother Vincent Whitty being well-known examples. But their work was not without its struggles and there were significant clashes between the Sisters and the hierarchy on more than one occasion. Today, the great value of the work of these women is openly acknowledged, with Mary MacKillop's beatification now a matter of history. But as Janet West has pointed out, during the nineteenth and early twentieth centuries, many nuns and sisters faced strong opposition, criticism and victimization at the hands of church leaders. Their work was not always easy, and at times, they suffered painful restrictions or had to move elsewhere. According to West, the major problem was male prejudice and intransigence. In reality, while there was much the sisters could do, there were still very clear demarcations.[9]

For Protestants, there were some non-clerical roles of distinction which women could fulfil, especially in parachurch or lay movements such as the Woman's Christian Temperance Union (WCTU), where people like Mary Clement Leavitt and Frances Willard were internationally recognized. In arguing for universal suffrage, the WCTU asserted that 'woman must be acknowledged as the equal of man in reasoning, adjudicating and discharging business generally' and proved it by their highly effective work in temperance, prison welfare, philanthropic activity among the poor and unemployed, concern for children and work for women generally. Nevertheless, they did not believe it was appropriate for them to seek legislative office in either church or state. This was still the province of men.[10] For the WCTU, a woman's best place was the home, where her role in safeguarding family life and a strong social fabric was seen as primary.[11] Within most denominations, there were semi-clerical positions for women, or roles such as that of deaconess or missionary. And there was always the responsibility-without-privilege of being a clergy wife.[12]

From the earliest days of European settlement, many women served faithfully as missionaries. Protestants saw three roles for women in the great task of world evangelisation. Hilary Carey has summarised these as: money, marriage and mission. Women could raise money for missions; or they could be the wives of missionaries; or they could be missionaries in their own right. There were few in the latter category. Initially, most women on the field were married, although this was to change in the early years of the twentieth century.[13] Here they could perform a wide range of tasks—including running meetings in the absence of their husbands, teaching Sunday School or leading hymn singing. But they could not usually lead a Sunday service or preach, and they would not dare to administer the sacraments. If they were left widows, they were usually brought home. There was no place for them on their own.[14]

In the first Pentecostal churches, however, as in some of the other less recognized religious movements of the time, women preached regularly, and in spite of Johnson's reservations, by all accounts rather well. Sarah Jane Lancaster's pointed comments when Charles Anstis asked her to lay hands on him and pray for him, reflect her view of the contemporary status of women in ministry—

> What! In a conservative building where women might wash the cloth for the Lord's table, but were warned not to encroach on man's prerogative as their superior? Yes, for the Holy Spirit makes the bodies of women His temple, as well as those of men; He speaks and acts through either sex at His own sweet will, declaring that 'As many as have been baptized into Christ... have put on Christ ... there is, therefore, neither male or [sic] female, for ye are all ONE in Christ Jesus (Gal. 3:26, 27). The capitals are ours, to emphasize a truth which man, proud man, will rarely entertain, for just as Jewish Christians in the days of Paul found it hard to believe the glorious fact that the Christ of God had torn down the middle wall of partition between the Gentiles and themselves... so to-day the pride of man forbids his acceptance of the grace of God toward those women upon whom He has poured His Spirit, thus making men and women one in Christ.[15]

Evangelists

Women evangelists were not common, but they were recognized. Emilia Baeyertz, born in England of Jewish parentage, came to Australia around 1860, where she was converted after the death of her husband in 1871. She soon became involved in mission, especially with the YWCA in Melbourne. In the 1880's, she evangelized with the Baptists in South Australia, with considerable success, and with the Free Methodist Churches in Victoria. She was later to have a significant part to play in the spiritual development of T. C. Hammond.[16]

The Englishwoman Margaret Hampson held successful Australian meetings. In Melbourne, in May 1883, large crowds from all denominations attended her rallies in the Town Hall, the Bijou Theatre and various church venues. Over one thousand people attended mid-day services and hundreds were turned away from the evening rallies during the first week of her campaign.[17] There was 'not the slightest touch of hysterical excitement or... uncontrollable fervour,' noted the *Southern Cross,* yet the evangelist kept her audience 'spell-bound.' Her preaching was marked by 'force of eloquence, power, passion, and sweep of dramatic expression'. Her presentation was clear and forthright. The call to follow Christ was uncompromising. Over 700 people professed conversion, including 84 who nominated the Church of England as the church they wished to attend, 62 the Wesleyan; 53 the Baptist; 32 the Presbyterian and 29 the Congregational. Nevertheless, although Hampson was so well received and her name became 'a household word all over the Colony (of Victoria)' she was clearly the exception rather than the rule, both as an evangelist and a woman.[18]

In November 1914, the founder of the small Bethshan Holiness Mission at Wyee, NSW, Elliot John Rien (1866–1935) cheerfully acknowledged the work of several women—'Sister' Esther, 'Sister' Bruce, 'Sister' Rose and 'Sister' Elsie. Esther Wood ('Sister' Esther) was the matron. Rose Flaxman ('Sister' Rose) was an 'outstanding evangelist.'[19] Among South Australian Bible Christians, although there were no ordained women, there were some women evangelists.[20] When Aimee Semple McPherson visited Melbourne and Adelaide in 1922, one reporter wrote, 'Though women have taken up pretty well everything else and are not supposed to be at a loss for words in ordinary life, the idea of a woman as a minister, as a preacher, as leader of an evangelistic mission is decidedly startling.'[21] McPherson was not fazed. It was a woman who preached the first salvation message, she argued, namely the woman at the well. And as men were quick to point out that it was a woman who introduced sin into the world, why should not a woman do something to eradicate it? Not that she particularly liked to hear a woman preach. For that matter, she wasn't keen about men preachers. She liked to hear the Holy Spirit preach.[22]

A woman might preach and evangelize, but there were still limits to what else she could do. Stephen Judd summarizes the position among Sydney Anglicans—

> Laywomen were similarly restricted to an auxiliary role, such as parish visiting, mothers' union and the women's guild. They had little opportunity for participation in the making of decisions which affected Church life: they were denied participation in parish councils until 1922 and prior to 1978 could not be churchwardens. For those women who sought a more active church role in the extension of Christ's Kingdom there was only one option: missionary service, both overseas and in remote parts of Australia.[23]

Not that women were inactive. Anglican sisterhoods such as the Kilburn Sisters and Community of the Holy Name ran convalescent homes, cared for poor children and pursued other works of charity.[24] Orders of deaconesses were similarly busy with faith and good works. Although only a handful in number, the few women who passed through the Bethany Deaconess Institution in Sydney from 1891 achieved an enormous amount—visiting the sick, bringing food and clothing to struggling families, running Sunday Schools, opening schools and an employment agency for women, providing accommodation and training for women and children.[25] But these women 'never entered the administrative councils of the church, the parochial vestries, diocesan synods and boards, and particularly their finance committees.' For Anglicans, there were three categories for women: matron, maid or missionary.[26] Unitarians and Quakers gave more opportunity to women to exercise leadership and public ministry.[27] Not that women generally were looking for a more recognized role. When in 1866, Portland Methodists found the rules did allow for women to attend a local leaders' meeting, this fact was made known. Only two women braved it to the next meeting—a minister's wife and a minister's widow. On later occasions, the number did increase slightly.[28] When it came to joining the ranks of the clergy, or administering the sacraments or holding office in the denominational corridors of power, there was room only for men.[29]

Pentecostalism, while clearly different in other ways, was more akin in its approach to women's ministry to the newer nineteenth century radical religious movements where women were openly accepted in leadership in and some cases founded and led by women such as Ellen White (Seventh Day Adventism—1846), Mary Baker Eddy (Christian Science—1876) and Helena Blavatsky (Theosophy—1875). And at the World Parliament for Religions in Chicago in 1893, there were five papers presented by women.[30]

'... and daughters'

In the fledgling Pentecostal movement, as in its ante-Nicene precursor, Montanism, women openly expressed themselves as leaders, especially in the first two decades.[31] Fundamentally, this was a question of the nature of ordination as much as anything. Early Pentecostals believed they were living in the last days, that God was pouring out His Spirit on both men and women and that their 'sons *and* daughters' would prophesy (Acts 2:17–18), which they were doing in a new way through the prophetic gift of glossolalia. It was the coming of the Spirit that commissioned people for ministry—and He was coming not only to men, but to women, too. So ordination was no longer a gender issue. If God Himself had anointed someone with the Spirit, what further endorsement did they need? Rather than wait for official benediction, they simply went ahead. Recognition usually followed, rather than preceded, active ministry.

While this concept was held all round the world in Pentecostal churches, the ministry of women was a distinctive feature of the early Australian movement. The dominant leaders of American Pentecostalism, for example, were men. In spite of the incredible feats of an occasional woman preacher such as Maria Woodworth Etter, it was men like the pioneering Charles Parham, the black Holiness preacher William Seymour, Chicago's imposing William Durham, North Carolina's enterprising G. B. Cashwell and the widely-read A. J. Tomlinson who laid the foundations of the movement there.[32] True, six of twelve elders at Azusa Street were women, and there were several well-known women preachers in America such as Carrie Judd Montgomery and Aimee Semple McPherson, but they were clearly in the minority.[33] In the Church of God (Cleveland, Tennessee) in 1912, 12.2% of ministers were women. But although they were encouraged to preach and to evangelize, they were limited in the extent to which they could be involved in church government. From its earliest days, A. J. Tomlinson, the first General Overseer, taught that the Scriptures did not allow women to participate in governmental affairs. Nor did the Church approve the ordination of women.[34] The Assemblies of God, likewise, encouraged women to evangelize, prophesy and preach, but from the formation of the movement in 1914, they would not allow them to be elders, a condition that prevailed for the next twenty years.[35] Even for evangelists, there were different credentials for men and women. That women could evangelize very well was evident from the work of people like McPherson. But she was clearly seen to be the exception rather than the rule—and with her, there were still many who had reservations. In Sweden, the apostolic Lewi Pethrus's name towers above everyone else's. In Norway, Methodist preacher Alexander Boddy was the recognized pioneer. In England, the earliest leaders were men—such as William Oliver Hutchinson, Jones Williams, the remarkable Jeffreys brothers and the gentlemanly Donald Gee. In South Africa, it was John G. Lake's extraordinary evangelism that launched the movement. In Brazil, Swedish pioneer missionaries Daniel Berg and Gunnar Vingren laid the foundations.[36] The principal role of women was caring for the family and supporting the church through craft work and the like. There were women pastors, but they could only reach 'a certain pastoral level.'[37] In Fiji, the initial leadership was in the hands of men. Women were able assistants, but never in oversight.[38]

Mark Hutchinson points out that in the early days of Pentecostalism, its 'multi-ecclesial organization' and its 'ability to flex at the grassroots' enabled women to be more visible, but notes that 'gender rules' and 'advancing institutionalization' soon enough stifled their roles. Nevertheless, feminine sensitivity to the spiritual dimension continued to allow them to make a valuable contribution.[39]

In Australia, the earliest pioneers were women. And their role was not just that of active laywomen or ministers' wives. They not only preached, but were involved in decision-making, teaching, administering the sacraments and general leadership. This is not to say they worked harder than missionaries' wives or the women in organisations like the WCTU. But their role was different. As is usual in new religious movements, authority passed fairly quickly into the hands of men,[40] but it was not so at the beginning. Of the eighteen Pentecostal churches founded in this country up to and including 1925, eleven were planted by women. Of the 37 churches established by 1930, over half (20) were started by women.[41]

The first recorded meetings in Melbourne were held in the North Carlton home of Mrs J. H. Nickson in September 1906. Sarah Jane Lancaster attended Nickson's meetings and looked to her for guidance.[42] Lancaster's own extraordinary work has already been discussed. There seems little doubt that it was her prominence and success that opened the way for other women to exercise their gifts. Her ministry was clearly a model for others to follow.

Florence Mortomore (1890–1927)

Florrie Mortomore (1890–1927) showed daring and enterprise in exercising a ministry normally felt to be the province of men. She seems to have cared little about traditional concepts of ministry. For her, it was sufficient ordination to be anointed by the Spirit of God and to have the Good News to preach. Armed with her Bible, a deep sense of compassion for the lost and needy, a strong faith in the miracle-working power of God and an earnest desire to see Christians filled with the Holy Spirit, she travelled far and wide as an ambassador for Christ. In the 1920s, she established—or helped to establish—as many as seven congregations. Her ministry resulted in missionaries going overseas.

Born in 1890, she was the eldest child of Charles and Caroline Mortomore of Lilydale, Victoria.[43] Although she died at the young age of 37, Florrie achieved more for the kingdom of God than most people manage to do in twice the time. Charles and Caroline attended the Baptist church at Lilydale, where Charles was a lay preacher. Around 1909, Caroline visited Good News Hall and thirteen months later, with great joy and delight, she spoke in tongues.[44]

The Mission proudly advertised that Good News Hall was 'ALWAYS open to Christians, for waiting on God' and that hospitality was free (although friends coming would 'add to their comfort by bringing a cushion and rug'). Around 1910, the twenty-year-old Florrie availed herself of this invitation, and stayed for a weekend. During this time, she was baptized in the Spirit with 'such a mighty anointing' that Lancaster feared her family would not understand what had happened to her when she returned home. So she encouraged her to stay until the following Wednesday.[45] When she arrived home, she found a small prayer meeting in progress. Brimming with new-found zeal, she began to pray individually for those present. There were some dramatic results. A lady 'who had not walked without sticks for years, walked home without them.' The women in the group were enchanted. 'She is like an angel,' they said. Well might they think so, agreed Lancaster. 'With her delicate, ivory skin, surmounted by a wealth of flaxen hair, added to the deep spirituality of her words and actions,' she did seem out of this world. Later, her father was healed of an injury through her prayers.[46] In mid-1912, she volunteered for service in India.[47] As a missionary, she was both gifted and faithful, but reluctantly, for health reasons, she yielded to her parents' urging to return to Australia in 1914, where she settled in Brisbane, Queensland and was assisted in her work in the first twelve months by Emmy Field (later Close).[48] Mortomore now began a widespread work of evangelism in many parts of Queensland. 'She carried her Gospel torch,' said Lancaster, 'until many lights were kindled which shall never be put out.' At a time when travel was difficult and accommodation often spartan, Mortomore showed courage, persistence and strength in covering large distances in a large State 'now up the north coast, now down the south coast, or anon along the main railway line'. Testimonies of conversion, healing and baptism in the Holy Spirit followed her.[49]

In Mackay, one thousand kilometres north of Brisbane, she met Bessie Couldrey (1891–1958). Of Brethren background, Couldrey had been born in England, migrated to Canada and thence to Australia.[50] The two travelled together till the end of 1923, when Bessie married and settled in Cairns. In Mackay, Mortomore introduced Annie Dennis to the baptism in the Holy Spirit; she was also to become an effective minister.[51]

In Toowoomba, in 1921, Mortomore and Couldrey held weekly meetings in the O'Brien home where many spoke in tongues for the first time.[52] Some members of the Churches of Christ congregation at Meringandan, an outreach from the church in Toowoomba, had a charismatic experience, including George Burns, who was later to pioneer a new church in Mackay.[53] Initially, Burns had been disturbed about Mortomore's ministry, fearing that she was bringing division and harm. He was ultimately disarmed by a kindly letter from Mortomore telling him they were praying for him to be led into the fullness of the Spirit. Burns was 'half amused and half annoyed' at the suggestion that he was not already Spirit-filled, but ultimately humbled himself and cried out to God for an outpouring of the Spirit in his life.[54]

At Maryborough, Mortomore spent months in 'pioneering, visiting and giving out' until an assembly was formed. So many people responded that she had to call her parents from Melbourne to shepherd them. This they gladly did, later moving to Brisbane to help with the church there.[55]

When Aimee McPherson withdrew from her commitment to preach for Good News Hall,[56] Mortomore courageously undertook to be the campaign speaker in the Exhibition Building in Brisbane. Lancaster and Winnie Andrews, the church secretary, journeyed from Melbourne to assist her. Small numbers attended, but over a dozen people were converted to Christ.[57] A woman who had been 'stone-deaf' for six months received 'perfect hearing.' A lump immediately disappeared from another woman's side. A woman whose knees were bandaged because of injured cartilages walked normally the next day and burned the bandages. A young insomniac slept peacefully through the whole night and continued to do so thereafter. Others claimed healing from neuritis and rheumatism. One woman was converted from Christian Science and baptized in the local Church of Christ the following Sunday night. Three people were baptized in the sea at Sandgate and five more in a waterhole. In Brisbane, there was now a small but sound congregation of about fifty people, with three meetings every Sunday.[58] Shortly afterwards they visited Nambour and began meetings there. James Speer Conwell (1863–1943), a devout Presbyterian, was living with his family at Nambour when his son-in-law picked up a tract from Good News Hall at a railway siding. James read it and wrote to Melbourne for more information. As a result, Mortomore and Couldrey visited Nambour. Through their ministry, James was baptized in the Spirit, as was his son Thomas, together with a few neighbours. Tom Conwell's family left the Presbyterian church and he began home meetings This was the beginning of the Assembly of God work at Nambour.[59]

The dedication and passion of Florrie Mortomore's faith is indicated in an address she gave in Brisbane in 1922 at the Exhibition Buildings called 'The Dragon's Plot.' In this study on Revelation chapter 12, she argued that the 'woman' represented all believers and that the 'manchild' signified a small body of more dedicated saints. This company were those who had 'set their whole hearts on purifying themselves, and are calling others to do the same, that their Bridegroom may find them ready when He comes, and receive them with joy.' Was it against 'respectable churchgoers' that the Dragon was plotting? Or was it against those who were willing to go into the world to reach the lost and to stand for God's truth? She concluded with a plea that Christians would yield wholly to the Lord. While the validity of her exegesis might be questioned, the intensity of the application seems beyond question.[60]

In 1925, in an address on the 'Last Days', she drew heavily on the Bible, providing chapter and verse for every point—over 100 specific quotations in all! It is plain that there were several foundational beliefs to her philosophy of ministry. Firstly, she had a strong commitment to the authority and integrity of Scripture. Secondly, she clearly affirmed that salvation was secured on the basis of the atonement of Christ and that the Spirit of Jesus indwelt every believer. But to be in the body of Christ it was necessary to be baptized in the Holy Spirit for there was no other way into the body (1 Corinthians 12:13). First it was necessary to fulfill the conditions, especially repentance and baptism by immersion. It was important to obey God's Word in every respect, for God's 'true children' would 'rather die than dishonor [sic] God by denying Him.' The end of the age was fast approaching and the Lord would soon be returning for His Bride. There was no time for delay. It was important now to obey God's Word and ask for the 'latter rain' of the Spirit before it was too late.[61] Herb and Thera Smith were so challenged by Mortomore's message of total commitment, they journeyed in 1925 to Osaka, Japan, as missionaries,[62] as did the Neilsons of Townsville.[63]

In December 1923, Mortomore was back in Melbourne where she was one of several speakers at a special Christmas luncheon provided by the Mission for over a hundred 'poor and needy' people. In 1924, she was on the move again, travelling as far north as Cairns. In Maryborough she enjoyed 'sweet fellowship' with the believers there. One of the women of the church joined her[64] and they travelled on to Rockhampton, where she held tent meetings for most of June, with gatherings almost every night of the week. They unearthed some 'precious jewels' and three people 'followed the Lord in the waters of baptism,' one of them 'so mightily under the power of God' that he could hardly make it back to the tent. Florrie wrote, 'Oh! May I ever be an emptied, cleansed channel to be used as He wills.'[65]

In Townsville, they were able to share the Word with a number of Aboriginal people. The young Enticknap brothers, who had been called to the ministry through the work of Annie Dennis, were evangelizing there.[66] The two women continued to Mackay where they were greeted warmly and then went on to Cairns, where, on 9 December 1923, Bessie Couldrey married widower Carl Lewis (Charles) Kajewski (1891–1976).

Here Mortomore was glad to help in the quest of all those who longed for 'more of God and His righteousness'. There were both white and 'coloured folk', both old and young. Of particular joy was the fact that groups of 40 to 50 Aborigines were now meeting together in and around Cairns, evidently the fruit of the work of Isabella Hetherington.[67] A few short years previously, 'the glorious light of the Gospel with the accompanying baptism in the Holy Spirit had scarcely touched these places' but that now there were 'little companies of earnest Christians shining for Jesus, earnestly pressing on themselves and earnest for the blessing of others'.

In 1926, Lancaster visited Cairns. She reported that two Sunday services and an Apostolic Faith Sunday School were conducted regularly.[68]

All over Queensland and beyond, Florrie Mortomore won many hearts. Her simplicity of faith, her earnestness, her compassion, her dedication and her sweet disposition disarmed the most antagonistic. Only 36 years old, but again suffering ill health, she returned to Brisbane where in late 1926, Lancaster wrote of the 'hallowed joy' she experienced in being reunited with her and others there.[69]

By now there were two congregations in Brisbane—one at Wooloowin pastored by Harold Martin and one at the West End Mission House led by Mortomore, where sick and needy people were taken in and cared for.[70] Baptist layman F. W. W. Bates told how he had thought Pentecostal teaching was evil, but after meeting Mortomore, he was convinced of its truth. On 9 July he received the Spirit.[71] Mortomore was just as delighted with being able to give a New Testament to a small boy as she was when crowds came to her meetings.[72] Meanwhile, her health did not improve. Although Pentecostal ministers were later to recognize that divine healing may not apply when there has been bodily abuse, in those pioneering days, anything other than absolute trust in God for recovery could be seen as a lack of faith.[73] A call for increased prayer was issued. That year, although her work was openly honoured, she was not asked to serve on the Apostolic Faith Mission council. 'Our sister's health is too valuable,' wrote Lancaster, 'for the Conference to impose the strenuous duties of a Councillor upon her.'[74]

In 1927, in spite of the many prayers, she passed away. At the young age of 37, she had, to quote one member, 'burned out for God and precious souls.'[75] Winnie Andrews wrote—

> A few short weeks have sufficed to show the magnitude of her self-sacrificing labors for her beloved Lord, for all over Queensland we find rejoicing hearts, and lives sweetened, as the direct result of the life-giving word which she preached.[76]

A former neighbour in Lilydale wrote, 'I shall never forget the wonderful address (the last I heard her give) from Psalm 45: "The king's daughter is all glorious within"; the way this dear, weak sister held forth in a strong voice, her very being pulsating with love and joy, was indeed, an inspiration to all present.'[77] Her mother described her death in moving terms—

> Her end was sweet and peaceful; she did long for someone to continue in prayer most of the time. Saturday midday she asked for all to get down and pray for victory; it was a very busy day for most but God touched hearts and prayers ascended in real earnest. Father had a vision: 'all the cushions and carpet were sprinkled with earth.' I knew too well what that meant: 'Earth to earth.' During the evening she would have us sing hymns of victory and she joined in the singing...
>
> When we said, 'Jesus,' she would repeat it. We think she had a vision once; her face lit up, she smiled so sweetly and said: 'Blessed Jesus.' She died with 'Jesus' on her lips. Nurse Green said she never saw such a peaceful death— no struggling, just a simple falling asleep.[78]

A photo published at the time of her death shows her looking much older than her 37 years. But there is a serenity and an intensity in her gaze that reflects both her peace with God and her determination to serve Him unswervingly. After her death, Lancaster found a poem written in her handwriting which, as Lancaster put it, 'express(ed) her inmost feelings and desires'—

Laid on Thine altar, O my Lord divine,
Accept this gift to-day for Jesus' sake.
I have no jewels to adorn Thy shrine,
Nor any world-famed sacrifice to make;
But, here, I bring within my trembling hand
This will of mine—a thing that seemeth small,
And Thou, O Lord, alone canst understand
How, when I yield Thee this, I yield mine all.[79]

Pauline Heath (c.1889–1940)

Pauline Heath (c.1889–1940), like Sarah Jane Lancaster, pastored a Pentecostal congregation for many years. Having spent her childhood in India, where her father was a railwayman, and having been brought up as an Anglican, at the age of 21, she drifted away from the church.[80] Two years later, influenced by the writings of Thomas Paine, W. G. Foote and Robert Blatchford, she declared herself an agnostic, and became 'strong in her arguments for agnosticism,'[81] although she formed a set of rules by which she sought to direct her life. 'I was going to live ethically, be good, honest, truthful, helping and cheering others, to sacrifice myself, and help those I met into a happier frame of mind,' she said. She believed her philosophy was based on the teaching of Jesus and so felt reassured that all was well with her life.

However, for the next two decades, she felt increasingly despondent. Her motives were pure, but 'failure heaped on failure,' among them a divorce.[82] Since 1922, she had been the successful and popular proprietor of the Lone Hand Cafe in Rundle Street, Adelaide, but was still discontent.[83] Her parents continued to pray for her and to urge her to believe.

Then, having been depressed for months, she met Gustav Jansen, someone she felt she could trust, and stirred by his story, she attended the Apostolic Mission in Adelaide, a group that traced its origins to Good News Hall and to the visit of Smith Wigglesworth in 1922. On 13 November 1925, she made a public commitment there to Christ. It was a transforming experience.

As a result of her conversion, she was filled with joy and love. She gave up smoking, but began to be beset by doubts. How could she know what had happened to her was real? Then, two months later, she, received the Spirit—

> As I prayed, *something happened.* A softness of power fell upon me bringing with it a fragrance and soothing. How can I express the things of GOD in the words of man? Words fail. But there *was* an answer ... A voice, a vision, a message, yes, that would have been according to my idea, but this, *this soft, sweet power*. What was it? What could it be but the answer? Here then was the God I had been searching for... I was satisfied... But GOD, Who knew the hardness of my heart, knew also that I needed more. For even as I attempted to rise from my knees ... the POWER fell. This time, not sweet and fragrant, but like a stroke of lightning, like a swift electric current, like an overwhelming flood, it held me, I could not rise. It took possession, I could not kneel. Every muscle was visited, every nerve dealt with, till I lay on the floor, helpless under the POWER of GOD... I lay there for more than an hour.[84]

The spirit of Pentecost had done its work. She was never to look back again. Some thought her mad; others believed her testimony.[85]

By 1927, at the age of 38, she was the acknowledged leader of the work and known affectionately by the members of the Mission as 'Sister Joy'. Regular, although small, newspaper advertisements presented her as 'Sister P. A. Heath, the Ex-agnostic Gospel Preacher,'[86] with Hines Retchford as song leader. An undated flyer draws special attention to her being a woman, inviting people to 'Hear Adelaide's Ex-agnostic Lady Preacher.' No collections were taken and she received no salary. She was 'absolutely out on faith' trusting God for her needs to be met.[87] In 1930, the Mission launched an eight page quarterly called *The Apostolic News*.[88] Only original articles were published.

Sister Joy, Adelaide, 1930s.

The Mission did not grow significantly over the ensuing years. But Sister Joy was not overly concerned; she always counted a small dedicated group of people more valuable than a large group of indifferent ones.'[89] She spent a great deal of time in prayer—even to the point of wearing dark glasses to cover the redness in her eyes caused by weeping in intercession. 'We all knew when we were prayed for!' recalled Norm Fabian, the man who succeeded her as pastor.[90]

Heath's story illustrates very clearly the power of experience in affirming a religious conviction. A few lines evidently written by her appeared both in *Good News* and *The Apostolic News*. They reflect her spirit and heart for the faith she professed—

> Give me, my God, that upward look,
> That gazes but on Thee;
> That senses naught on earth, but grasps
> Thy matchless majesty...
> That realizes while on earth
> My life is lived with Thee,
> Hidden in Christ, and Thou alone,
> Life's grand Reality.[91]

For eight years—from December 1932 to her death in 1940—Heath published a series of short Bible studies on the Song of Solomon, some 32 in all. She got as far as chapter two verse 15. With tender tones, and a sense of longing and intimate love reminiscent of that of the mystic Teresa of Avila or the effusive Mother Julian of Norwich or the passionate Richard Rolle, she dwells lovingly on the Bride's relationship with the Bridegroom and her exquisite communion with Him. The spirit of Pentecost is hardly anywhere more intimately portrayed—

> Her beloved has called to her. She awakes. She hears. She moves. There is but one who could thus stir her heart, for there is only one who has won and now holds her love. 'Listen, listen,' she whispers, 'it is the voice of my beloved.'
>
> Hast thou a beloved, O soul of mine? Does the word of the Shulamite rouse an answering throb in thine heart? Is there *one* voice for whose tones thou art ever listening? Art thou waiting and longing to hear it?

Or,

> Earthly kisses lose their freshness ... But with the Bridegroom, Who loves with everlasting love, there is no weariness. Each new kiss comes with its own abiding joy, and a sweet promise of more yet to be...

Or,

> And knowing Him, seeing the banner of love floating overhead, the eyes of the Bride turn to Him Who has won her love, and the strength of that love overwhelms her. Her head drops on His bosom, she feels his Arm of strength around her, and she cries.

Or,

> My Beloved is mine... yea, all this and more, much more, O soul of mine. He is mine to speak to—mine to look to—mine to love—mine to care for me— mine to succour me—mine to understand my pain—mine to increase my joy—mine to walk with me all along my weary pilgrim path—mine to enfold me in His own love—mine to take me to be with Himself for ever.[92]

Yet in spite of this affective focus, there is a warning of the dangers of depending on experience alone. It was faith, not feeling, that pleased God. To seek emotional experiences was to allow feelings 'to usurp the place of the Word of God and of faith in that Word.'[93] The spirit of Pentecost was central to Heath's ministry, but never to the supplanting of Scripture. In all her published articles, Bible studies and sermons, the use of the biblical texts was paramount. She had no theological training but spoke 'by the inspiration of the Holy Ghost'. She regularly conducted open air meetings at the Kingston Statue, on Victoria Square, the city of Adelaide, and in Botanic Park, and occasionally organised special series of meetings.[94]

Prophesying was an integral part of worship in the Mission, and the texts of these prophecies were occasionally printed. Heath's interpretations of utterances in tongues, usually spoken in conjunction with a prepared sermon, were also published. One newspaper advertisement even quoted one. Like most Pentecostal interpretations it was largely a restatement of Scripture (in this case Psalm 45 and Revelation chapter 19) with a positive note of encouragement, proclamation and urgency.[95] Others of Heath's interpretations were disarmingly simple ('Behind the written word stands the living Word, the glorious invisible Saviour who reveals himself in secret to the loving heart'). Others were more profound—

> We revive the memory of His humiliation;
> we make a sacrament of His shame.
> Through centuries,
> His death is associated with His glory;

and when we preach,
it is the preaching of the Cross.

Or,

With His own hand
He lights the beacon fire
from hilltop to hilltop
till their wandering eyes
look back to the gates of Paradise
and there they see in glowing letters
the words God Omnipotent hath said,
'The woman's seed shall bruise the serpent's head.'[96]

These were not just ecstatic outbursts. They illustrate the subtle rhythms and striking imagery of a person with a natural feel for language and a deft balance between contemplation, inspiration and imagination. Heath's praying, too, was impressive. 'Sister Joy would lift you up to heaven when she was anointed by the Holy Spirit in prayer,' said Fabian.[97]

In spite of seven years of faithful ministry, inevitably, some disaffection arose about female leadership. So in 1934, Heath stepped down as pastor and took the title evangelist 'owing to the belief among our brethren in Christ that a woman is not permitted to be a pastor according to the Scriptures'.[98] However, Norm Fabian, the new pastor, later made the wry comment, 'We just carried on as usual.'[99] The titles had changed, but the roles had not.

Two years later, after preaching at the Bible Standard Church in Melbourne, Heath was offered a preacher's credential from them, which she accepted. She was pleased to find that she and the leader, Dr Mina Brawner, agreed on almost all points of doctrine.[100] In 1940, a building was erected in Compton Street, Adelaide, for the Mission. Sadly, Sister Joy never saw the fruition of this project. On 6 October, at the age of fifty, before the building was completed, she died of cancer and the key was first turned by her grand daughter.[101]

Ellen Caroline ('Nellie') Mather (b.1894)

Ellen Caroline ('Nellie') Mather (b.1894) was brought up on a farm in Gippsland, where she suffered with a gradual deterioration of the spinal cord and was bedfast much of the time. By the time she was 27, she was in so much pain she began to long for death. Any physical exertion would leave her exhausted for days. In September 1922, she heard of Aimee McPherson's meetings in Wirth's Olympia in Melbourne and arranged to be taken there. During this time, she felt something like an electric shock go through her body and

**Ellen Mather,
The Supreme Incentive.**

realized she was healed. Over the next few days, there was a struggle of faith as some of the symptoms reappeared, but she persisted in trusting God and soon was free of all pain and working hard on the farm without difficulty.[102]

Within a year, she preached for the first time in a Methodist church at Allandale, in South Australia. In 1924, she and her recently widowed mother established a boarding house in Geelong, Victoria. During that time, she began to hunger for a deeper spiritual experience and visited Robert Horne's Southern Evangelical Mission, where after praying for several days, she was baptized in the Holy Spirit—

> The hunger for the blessing intensified until I felt broken-hearted and almost despairing of ever receiving the gift as I wept and wept before the Lord.
>
> Suddenly it seemed as if liquid glory began flowing all over me and presently I began singing a beautiful melody in a language I had never learned. My tears of anguish and despair were turned to tears of joy and gladness. As I sang on and on a great joy was almost overwhelming me and my heart was overflowing with praises to the God of Heaven for hearing my prayer...[103]

She had imbibed the spirit of Pentecost. In 1926, she enrolled in the newly-established Victorian Bible Institute. She later described life at the College—

> The school was a two-storey building with a large lecture hall and many other rooms both upstairs and downstairs. My biggest difficulty was finding a place where I could get alone to pray. One morning... I made my way quietly down stairs, through the lecture hall and into the printing press enclosure. It was just what I needed...
>
> The young men students having apparently agreed together to try out the printing press, rose early and came bustling into the printing press enclosure to try their skill at printing. Needless to say that put an end to my sanctuary... One day I discovered an empty built-in wardrobe just a few doors away from our sleeping quarters, and I thought, 'I have found a place at last.' This one worked well for quite a time (apart from the stuffy feeling...) One morning, I was down on the floor in prayer in the wardrobe when suddenly the door flew open. I don't know who received the biggest fright, the young man or I.[104]

In October 1927, a 'tall, slim, dignified young woman,'[105], she launched out with a companion named Grace Greig in itinerant ministry.[106] Armed with a few hymn books, a collapsible chair and a small folding organ, they began by setting up in the street, just the two of them, and singing and preaching. After some rugged activities in Gippsland, they bought a second-hand car and ministered in Castlemaine. Then Mather was invited to pastor a Pentecostal church in Bendigo which she did for a few months until 'Daddy' Clarkson,' a former Salvation Army officer, took over. In June 1930, she and her mother were invited to serve in Ballarat for three months. The church, heavily in debt, was under the impression Mather had agreed to 'trust the Lord for her needs' and she laboured for several weeks in the cold of winter without any income. Finally, they gave her five pounds.[107] Not surprisingly, at the end of her term, Mather moved back to Bendigo, where she recuperated from a time of ill health, and then conducted meetings in many towns throughout country areas. In Echuca, over 50 people attended meetings—in spite of the town band playing right outside the hall.[108] In Wonthaggi, she slept in a tent for three months and suffered privation through lack of food and money. But there were rewards. Here, a young woman with a spinal injury was healed after anointing with oil, as was a woman with painful legs and a man with damage to his eye. One day, she prayed for a turnip to make soup: the next day she found one on the road. It was an encouraging sign of God's grace.

At the beginning of 1937, after a brief stay in Melbourne, Mather was back in Ballarat. The assembly's financial woes had not been alleviated. There were only a dozen people attending members' meetings and in May 1931, they still could not afford to pay a pastor. By 1937, they were able to offer a small stipend of around two pounds a week—a target they sometimes did not meet but which eventually was increased. Mather and her strong-minded assistant Gladys Williams were offered a twelve month term of office, which was renewed the following year. During this time, baptismal services were held in the City Baths, even in winter. After another six months, Mather declined a further invitation as she had 'other definite prospects'.[109] The congregation was grateful for her and her companion's efforts. The membership had doubled and many were baptized in the Holy Spirit.[110]

Assemblies of God conference, Maryborough, Qld, 1937.

In 1939, Mather moved to the warmer climes of Queensland and took over the Gympie Assembly of God church. She was not averse to hard work, and readily helped with milking a herd of 94 cows when the machines broke down. She also ministered in other towns in Queensland, before moving to Brisbane where she was to spend the next fourteen years, pastoring the Full Gospel Assembly at Woolloongabba, assisted still by Williams.[111] 'We had a visit from Sisters Mather and Williams,' wrote the pastor at Maryborough, 'and their ministry was greatly appreciated (and) enjoyed by all.'[112] She was willing to do anything—even sewing for Aboriginals at Daintree, in the Far North, 'from daylight to dark.'[113]

All through her ministry, Mather loved to conduct open air meetings, playing her portable organ or piano accordion as well as preaching.[114]

Ian Munro, in his foreword to Mather's autobiography, pays tribute to her ministry—

Her reputation as a spiritual and loving shepherd of the flock of God, was held in exceedingly high esteem, among the circles in which she moved. Her dedication to the call of Christ and obedience to the leading of the Holy Spirit, were at all times a direct inspiration... She was always a pioneer, and has never sought or asked an easy road.[115]

Mina Ross Brawner (b. c.1880)

Mina Ross Brawner was an American medical practitioner who, feeling called to Australia, arrived in Sydney in 1927.[116] She was welcomed into the Northbridge home of Jotham and Kate Metcalfe which she used as an operating base and where she had 'a deep-cushioned chair' where every morning she spent time in prayer.[117] Prior to her conversion in 1904, Kate Metcalfe had been constantly ill, and 'could not go two days without medicine.' She had not touched any since. She had also been baptized in the Holy Spirit, evidently through Lancaster's ministry.[118]

Brawner was a good speaker and made effective use of her medical training to illustrate her preaching of the gospel. She was dramatic in both dress and manner, her Aimee McPherson-styled gown and her white hair creating an impressive image. 'All the kids in Balmain and Rozelle thought she was an angel,' recalled one man.[119]

On 27 October 1928, she was accepted into the Apostolic Faith Mission as a Pastor-Evangelist.[120] She wrote a series of articles in *Good News* under the title, 'Woman in the Word', which later appeared as a book, published at Good News Hall. In this work, she unashamedly advocated the public ministry of women. As a doctor, she had served equally with men and been taxed equally with men. Why could she not preach equally? Both man and woman were named 'Adam' by God (Genesis 5:2). They were both given dominion over the earth. The 'female man' was the culprit in the Fall and thus her independence was lost. But through the Saviour, there was hope. As both male and female received the sentence of death, so in Christ, both receive life.

Jesus did not prevent the woman at the well from preaching. The Psalmist prophesied, 'The Lord gave the Word; great was the company of women that published it' (Psalm 68:11, RV). Joel foretold an outpouring of the Spirit on both men and women who would prophesy (Joel 2:28f). This passage, quoted by Peter at Pentecost, was the 'Magna Charta' [sic] of the Church. It gave men and women, slaves and servants, Jews and Gentiles, an 'absolute unalienable right, under the anointing of the Holy Spirit, to prophesy, or preach, in the Church.' Phoebe was not just a deacon, but the 'minister' or 'pastor' of the church at Cenchrea (Romans 15:1). Priscilla, Mary, Junia, Tryphena, Tryphosa—these and others were all preachers of the word. If the word *presbuteron* in 1 Timothy 5:1 could mean male elder, why could not *presbutera* mean female elder? The 'symbol of authority' on a woman's head (1 Corinthians 11:10) was not a hat but the anointing of the Holy Spirit. In Christ there was neither male nor female—we are all one. Finally, a challenge—

You may as well make room for us, brothers. We are here in the fulfillment of prophecy. The Lord gave the Word, that is, He has given us plentiful matter for speaking; we are never at a loss for a message.[121]

In arguing her case, she unashamedly touched the emotions —

> Ah! Blind, loving, hopeless women, your tear-dimmed eyes have missed a wondrous sight, for your Lord and Saviour went to His death holding in one hand the curse that rested upon all mankind because of sin, and in the other He held your special curse, while upon His brow He bore the curse of thorns. He lifted the curses up on the Cross where God and angels and men might see them, and when the thorns pierced His brow and the nails were driven through His dear hands, our curse was borne, our debt was cancelled...
>
> Every curse pronounced in Eden He bore in His own body on the tree... So weave the chaplet, thoughtless soldiers, entwine it about His holy brow; nothing becomes Him so much as the crown of thorns, for it is the *crown of suffering,* the *crown* of the curse, the *Crown of love.*[122]

Evangelist Norman Armstrong tells how Brawner came to his father's small church around this time and preached on Noah's ark, pointing out that the animals had more sense than the humans. 'I didn't want to be less sensible than a monkey,' he said, 'so I was converted.'[123]

At the end of 1928, Brawner organised a tent campaign in Mosman, New South Wales. Brawner herself assisted Jotham Metcalfe and some of the men as she 'pulled ropes, drove stakes, sawed boards, and did a man's work all week.' The holiday season was not the best time to open a campaign, but by mid-1929, she could report that she had preached 85 times in the tent, that there was a group of 25 to 30 people meeting regularly and that 24 adults had professed conversion in addition to many children. These figures could be trusted, she said, because she would 'never inflate a report'. She only counted those as converts who she had reason to believe had a 'real experience' of the Lord.[124] She had a regular program of preaching—

> Sunday afternoon—a message to Christians
> Sunday night—the gospel of salvation
> Tuesday night—divine healing
> Wednesday night—the Holy Spirit
> Thursday night—the second coming
> Friday night—open air gospel meeting
> Saturday afternoon—prayer and/or tarrying meeting[125]

The address given at the dedication of the tent mission clearly demonstrates both her Christocentric approach and her Pentecostal convictions. She spoke of Apostolic faith, of Apostolic preaching, of Apostolic signs. There was a strong emphasis on the need to be baptized in the Holy Spirit and on divine healing and speaking in tongues—

> *Lord send another Pentecost!* Another rushing mighty wind, another sound from heaven; the world is fed up on sounds from hell and is waiting now to hear from heaven. I am looking for such a mighty revival that the very atmosphere about

this tent will be charged with the breath of the Almighty, a spiritual cyclone! And it is coming, too. Bless God, 'I hear the sound of abundance of rain!'[126]

In 1929, Brawner spent the year in Ballarat, Victoria, where the assembly purchased a disused Lutheran Church building. During this time, some 50 people professed conversion, 17 were baptized in water and 19 in the Spirit.[127] The following year, she conducted a series of evangelistic campaigns in Victoria and Queensland, accompanied by Winnie Andrews. She had rewarding meetings in Good News Hall and then in Castlemaine.[128] For five weeks, through July and early August, she preached in Brisbane, often in the streets.[129] She held meetings for the unemployed and addressed a gathering of Methodist Lay Preachers, who urged her to address them again on her return. She and Andrews journeyed on to Rockhampton, Mackay and Townsville, ministering in each place. Finally, in August, eighteen months after Van Eyk's memorable visit, they arrived in Cairns.

That night, the first of the campaign, 'several hundreds' gathered and stood for half an hour at an open air meeting and some proceeded to the hall for the commencing rally, where there were four converts. On Sunday 17 August, her topic was 'The End in Sight.' Taking as her text 2 Peter 3:3–4, she challenged those who scoffed at the signs of the Coming of the Lord to consider the state of the world—the growth of population, the increasing shortage of food, the demands on energy resources, the escalating armament industry and the rising evidence of moral decadence. 'The outlook,' she declared, 'is bad, but the uplook is glorious.' God would one day lift His hand and bring an end to 'the mad rush of lawlessness' and when Christ returned the earth would be filled with the glory of the Lord.[130]

On the last Sunday night in August, a 'splendid open-air meeting' was held outside the Palace Theatre, where there were a thousand people 'listening attentively.' This was followed by a well-attended indoor service. During the campaign, there were twelve professions of faith and thirteen acknowledged cases of healing. Winnie Andrews reported that the local press gave favourable coverage and that almost the whole community heard the word of the Lord.[131]

In nearby Yungaburra, several people also claimed healing and spiritual blessing. On 26 September, a 'car-load of saints' travelled from Cairns and joined the group there in prayer. Several spoke in tongues including Beulah, a child of eleven, who had specifically come from Cairns to 'get under the showers of Latter Rain.' It was an occasion for both wonder and joy. Brawner reported her wonder at listening to 'the Heavenly Orchestra... playing the most heavenly music.' This phenomenon of an unseen symphony continued for half an hour, and several of them heard it. For a while, there seemed to be only stringed instruments; then it sounded like 'a supernatural full orchestra'. Others spoke of their joy in receiving the Spirit. 'Oh it was so sweet! She is just bubbling over with joy,' wrote Winnie Andrews of one lady. And of another, she said, 'Her mouth was filled with laughter' and she was 'full right up to the top.'[132]

After the meetings in Cairns, Brawner planned to spend a few days on the Coulters' farm on the Atherton Tablelands. Here, she held a few home meetings and 'the power and glory of God fell in a mighty way,' with the result that she stayed for twelve days and six people were baptized in the Spirit, including Mrs Coulters, who had been praying for ten years to be filled, and her daughter Gladys. Consequently, Brawner hired the Oddfellows Hall at Atherton and on 26 October, 1930, began another campaign.[133] For six weeks she persisted with regular meetings in the face of considerable opposition and little response. But there were encouraging features. One young man missed a ride but walked six miles to the meeting. Another determined to rid himself of his business of growing tobacco. Some were healed. A few were baptized in the Barron River. On 9 December, a small church was formed. The church was not an organization, Brawner declared, but an organism in which people could work together harmoniously. So those who joined, did so of their own free will. Nor was there any competition with others—

> We have no quarrel with any other body of Christians, but we are devoted to Apostolic Christianity. We have Apostolic aims, for we feel that the Church Jesus calls for must conform to the pattern of the Church He established; therefore, we preach Apostolic Doctrines, and look for Apostolic results. That is why we call ourselves 'Apostolic Faith', that the world and our fellow Christians may know just what we stand for—viz., all that the Apostles preached.[134]

In 1931, Brawner was ministering in Brisbane again. In March, a service of unity was held for the Pentecostal people in Brisbane—a gathering enhanced by the involvement of W. H. W. Lavers, who, together with his People's Evangelistic Mission, decided to link up with the Apostolic Faith Mission. Perhaps inspired by the not inconsiderable success of William Booth-Clibborn's tent mission, they launched a similar project. About 75 people were present as they dedicated their United Portable Tabernacle for evangelism at Spring Hill. That night several hundred people crowded in to hear the gospel and 20 people were converted. From then on, about 150 people attended nightly. In the first two weeks, some 112 conversions were recorded. After ten weeks, there were close to 300. It was Depression time, so offerings were small—about 15 shillings a week, mostly pennies. But they felt they had to go on. After ten weeks, and the conversion of several young people, Ernest Tooth, the church secretary, claimed that Spring Hill had been deeply stirred. Meanwhile, plans were going ahead to secure another hall on the opposite side of the valley from Lavers' church for the original AFM assembly and a small 'Bible and Theological Training College' was established.[135] 'I praise God that ever I came in contact with Doctor Brawner,' said Lavers, 'for she has been a tower of strength, and her life is a living testimony.'[136]

In July 1932, Brawner was in Gympie, Queensland, where there were twenty converts and people felt that a revival had begun.[137] In September she visited Toowoomba, setting up the Bible Standard People's Evangelistic Mission, a name which was also adopted by Lavers in Brisbane.[138] In the same month, she demonstrated another talent by designing the cover for *The Gathering Call*, published by F. B. Van Eyk.[139] In 1936, with Good News Hall's ministry now having languished since the death of its founder, Brawner took over the original building, renamed it the Lighthouse Temple and linked four congregations together under the name Bible Standard Churches in Australia, in Adelaide, Ballarat, Melbourne and Northcote.[140] At the end of that year, just 63 people attended a Sunday evening service in Melbourne, one third of them men. However, two years later, in a six-weeks' campaign, there were 108 conversions, 25 baptized in the Spirit and 69 in water.[141]

In 1939, Brawner planned a Bible Standard Training School which would offer a part-time Christian Workers' Course over a period of one year, covering such subjects as the Life of Christ, Genesis, Revelation, Church Organization, the Tabernacle, Soul Winning, Bibliology (presumably the authority and interpretation of Scripture) and 'Maranatha' (the Second Coming?). The rules were tough. 'Positively no talking, gum-chewing, eating or boisterous conduct' were allowed in class. Questions were to be in writing and signed. Single men and women had to sit separately. Students 'known to be guilty of smoking, drinking, movies, theatres, dance hall or card tables, lipstick, immodest dress or behaviour' would be 'positively refused admission'. Any student found unwilling to comply with the rules would be called before the Faculty. If 'after prayer and consultation' the offences did not cease, the offender would be dismissed. Nevertheless, the Faculty members were 'always glad to help and pray with any student' for, 'an Harmonious Bible School is carried on by love, prayer and co-operation.'[142] Perhaps not surprisingly, the numbers were small—still only six students in 1941—but apparently effective. 'Over the 53 years I have never found any fault in any single thing taught at the Lighthouse Temple, and still praise the Lord for... having been taught by that great little lady,' wrote one of them in 1993.[143] Among other things, Brawner tried hard to distance herself from some of Lancaster's unpopular beliefs, particularly Annihilation. To believe otherwise was to lower the value of Christ's sacrifice.[144]

With all her boldness, Brawner's heart was soft and she desired to live a life pleasing to God, not only in the spirit of Pentecost that comes with a mighty, rushing wind, but also with that of the gently settling dove. The following lines, written by her, are simply entitled, 'My Prayer.'

> If I have climbed o'er friend or foe to reach a greater height,
> If I have made a shadow fall where but for me 'twas light,
> If I have laid a stumbling block on any traveller's road,
> Forgive me, Lord, and let these arms help bear my brother's load.
>
> If I have failed to be as kind as Thou wouldst have me be,
> If malice in my heart abide, reveal it, Lord, to me.
> If I have held from any soul the tenderness he craved,
> By me let every pathway be with loving kindness paved.
>
> If I have caused one suffering heart to shed a needless tear,
> If I have filled one struggling soul with darkness or with fear,
> If I have ever dealt a blow that on my brother fell,
> Forgive, and let me evermore Thy wondrous mercy tell.[145]

Edith ('Edie') Anstis and Ruby Wiles

Sister Edie (L).

Edith Anstis and Ruby Wiles were two of six evangelists recognized by the Apostolic Faith Mission in 1927. They had both been involved with Good News Hall from the earliest days. Meetings had been held in the Anstis home in Ballarat, Victoria, in 1913. There Ruby experienced healing from abscesses on her neck when Grace Anstis prayed for her.[146] George Holroyd, later pastor of the work at Geelong, recalled how the two women had visited Geelong and challenged him to receive the Spirit. An hour later, he was baptized in the Spirit and the desire to smoke left him from that time.[147]

Known simply as 'Sister Edie' and 'Sister Ruby,' they left Ballarat in 1921, to establish a work in Perth, Western Australia.[148] Lancaster had previously visited that city, testified and preached on the street corners and distributed tracts.[149]

Returning to Melbourne, she sent her 'best' workers, Edie and Ruby, to continue the work. They began cottage meetings in several different homes.[150] Edie seems to have been the preacher; Ruby was 'always helping lame dogs over stiles' and loved to minister to the sick and needy.[151] On one occasion, when told of a woman suffering both from a nervous breakdown and 'internal trouble,' she had a vision of the woman sitting up and shouting, 'Hallelujah!' after being touched by God—which eventuated as she saw it.[152] Initially, they met a Salvationist named Mrs Palmer who had been praying for a long time that someone would come and help her raise up a Pentecostal church. For many years, the two women stayed at her home in Knebworth Avenue, North Perth.

The work was hard and slow. In 1923, while they were recuperating in Mildura, Victoria, there was plenty of pressure from family and friends to remain there. However, they returned to Perth and continued the work they had started. They did not lack courage. On Friday nights, they preached in the open air. In early 1924, they had the joy of seeing three young women kneel on the footpath in acts of penitence. A large crowd gathered and even the police came to investigate. Edie finished up preaching four times as the crowd would not disperse.[153] As they continued with home meetings in various places, a few people were baptized in the Spirit and some were healed. One of these was Edie herself, who recovered dramatically after suffering with rheumatoid arthritis for twelve months. Other testimonies included that of 'an aged saint' bed-ridden as the result of a stroke, who arose from her bed instantly after Edie and Ruby prayed for her. Others testified to healing from neuralgia, indigestion, influenza, boils, gallstones and skin disease.

However, by 1927, there was still just a 'little band' of people. Judging by the testimonies and reports, most of these seem to have been women. Among them were Ada Boaler, who was confined to a wheelchair, Mrs Hinson, Avis Kate Lucy, another Salvationist, and her daughter Avis, who was later to become a Pentecostal pastor's wife. Meetings were held in the homes of all these people.[154] Every week for nine years, Wednesday afternoon meetings were conducted in Ada Boaler's little weatherboard house in Charles Street, Maylands. Initially, the numbers were small—sometimes only seven or eight—and at one point, when Edie and Ruby were on furlough, just Avis Lucy and Ada Boaler. But Lucy had fond memories—

> Some meetings were very quiet, some full of manifested power, but always sweet...
>
> Prayer has been *wonderful* in that little place, and once we heard it rain on the iron roof, but when we looked outside everything was quite dry to the eye. Was it the 'latter rain'? We thought so.[155]

One by one, people were being immersed in water, or baptized in the Spirit and there were several visitors to the meetings, including a Baptist pastor.[156] Edie's preaching was simple and direct. She based it plainly on Scripture and took the promises at face value. At a women's Bible study, she spoke on healing, on praise and the baptism in the Holy Spirit. 'I was filled with wonder,' said one of her hearers, 'We women caught such a touch of the fire of the Holy Spirit from the sisters' ministry that... a revival began and the church enjoyed a season of spiritual blessing.' One night, while Edie was preaching, she felt something like an 'electric thrill.'[157] In a published message on tithing, Sister Edie told several stories of people who had refused to tithe and had suffered loss, while others who had been obedient, had prospered, just as God said they would. 'A sister owned a fig tree,' she related, 'that had never borne fruit.' She began to tithe and the fig tree had been 'loaded each year since'.[158]

She was delighted to report later that year that one elderly woman and three more young women had turned to the Lord and were all contemplating baptism. By mid-1927, they were using the name Apostolic Faith Mission, there were four regular meetings a week, and Ernest Jarvis, a printer who had received the Spirit at Good News Hall in 1923 and had opened his home for meetings and who was later to become a pastor, had been appointed as secretary.[159]

It was then that the South African evangelist Frederick Van Eyk arrived in Perth. He had made a brief stop there in March en route to Adelaide, and spoke on four occasions to a house jammed with people. Now he returned for a formal campaign. Large crowds attended his meetings, there was a significant number of converts and many claimed to have been healed. Much of the success of the Mission, ran one report, resulted from 'the devoted and faithful work' of the two women.[160] Again, Edie testified to healing. After being anointed with oil, the next day she helped push an invalid in a chair some six miles. Another woman claimed to have been delivered from evil spirits. More than 20 people were baptized in the Holy Spirit.[161]

Not long after Van Eyk's visit, trouble emerged and there was potential division. As elsewhere, there appears to have been some disaffection over women being in leadership. Edie and Ruby sent an urgent message to Good News Hall for help and John Adams, the president of the Apostolic Faith Mission, and J. Jones visited the Perth church. Jones excelled in the open air meetings and Adams encouraged the folk 'by his deep and powerful Bible lessons'. Ernest Jarvis now became pastor. Edie was able to report that the work was 'in good condition,' that the open air meetings were drawing good crowds, that numbers were increasing and that there were some good testimonies of healing, this time including Ruby, who had suffered a stroke. 'It was a miracle done all in a moment,' reported Edie.[162] A year later, *Good News* again referred to Edie as the pastor of the Perth assembly and reported that there were some 60 people now meeting on Sunday nights and that five people had been baptized in water and six filled with the Spirit.[163] They were now gathering in the Women's Service Guild Rooms in Murray Street. Numbers continued to grow steadily, partly as the result of the 121 open air meetings they held from August 1928 to April 1929.[164]

In November, 1928, M. A. Eather was attracted by one of these meetings. She went home 'with the message burning in... (her) heart.' Early next morning, as an undertaker's employee, she was called to attend to a corpse. The reality of death without Christ confronted her and she decided to yield to Him then and there. She shared her new faith with her seven brothers and sisters and they were all converted and baptized in water, with five of them speaking in tongues. 'Oh what peace and joy has come into our home,' she wrote eight months later. 'Our home stands among the happiest in Perth today.'[165]

In 1930, the two women were still 'keeping the Gospel flag flying... amid many trials and difficulties.'[166] In July 1934, Van Eyk returned to Perth and once again ministered with telling effect. Ernest Jarvis reported that although there was considerable criticism, especially from the churches, many who 'came somewhat prejudiced... remained till the end of the campaign.' Over 40 people were baptized in water. In one single meeting, 30 people made commitments to Christ. As ever, there were clear-cut testimonies of healing. The result was that with Lancaster having died earlier that year, the local church decided to join the Foursquare movement. So, too, did a small congregation at Fremantle.[167]

On 1 January 1936, Edie's health prevented her from continuing in leadership and Colonel John T. Bentley took over the pastorate and became superintendent of the Foursquare work in Western Australia. Not long after this, as Lancaster would have put it, Edie 'fell asleep'. Ruby continued for some years assisting in ministry, marrying late in life. She was around 80 when she died.[168]

Heather Burrows (1913–)

When the Apostolic Church came to Australia in 1930 with its more tightly developed structure, there was little place for recognized women's leadership.[169]

The *Constitution* allowed for Deaconesses, but there was no room for women to be apostles, prophets, pastors or teachers. They could pray, prophesy or speak publicly and engage in evangelism, but they could not be ordained.[170] How much opportunity was there for women to minister? 'You're joking,' was one woman's opinion. 'Only in Sunday School or Women's meetings or Open Air meetings.'[171]

One evangelist was Heather Isabel Burrows (b.7 March 1913) who was highly regarded as a speaker and travelled widely across Australia in the 1930s. Her family attended a Baptist church in North Sydney and at the age of eight, in a tent meeting, her 'childish eyes (were) opened to the precious reality of Jesus.' In June 1930, William Booth-Clibborn and his wife began an evangelistic crusade in the Railway Institute in Sydney which proved to be 'a time of revival.'[172] When Booth-Clibborn spoke on Joshua 24:15, the 17 year old Burrows made the 'instant, clear-cut choice' to follow Christ and was soon seeking to be baptized in the Holy Spirit. She attended tarrying meetings at the Foursquare Church in Australia Street, Newtown, where she had a 'tremendous experience' but did not speak in tongues. She felt as if she was being lifted out of her body and saw what she described as 'liquid fire' all over her. This filled her with a sense of awe and she held back from pressing in further.[173] After two months, Booth-Clibborn moved to Brisbane, but his wife Genevieve continued to conduct well-attended meetings in the Bourke Street Congregational Hall. She invited different people to speak and one night it was Heather Burrows' turn. To her astonishment, six people came to Christ. When, in October 1931, Genevieve Booth-Clibborn, joined her husband in Queensland, she invited Burrows to accompany her both as an evangelist and as her personal assistant.[174] The small, bright young woman stayed in Brisbane for three months, where she was baptized in water in the 'Canvas Cathedral.'[175] Not long after she arrived, she was advertised as 'Sydney's Girl Evangelist,' and preached for the first time in the large tent on Friday 30th October. She must have been reasonably successful, for she preached again on subsequent Fridays. Within a month, she was joined by the more renowned Mary Ayers. By the end of November, they were both occupying the platform on successive nights.[176] In December, when Booth-Clibborn came down with a 'high fever,' Burrows took two of the major midweek meetings. For a brief time she edited Booth-Clibborn's news letter.[177]

In January 1932, she was asked to conduct a three-weeks' tent mission in Toowoomba, deputising for Mrs Booth-Clibborn. In spite of having no training, she preached every night of the week. Her approach was a simple expression of the spirit of Pentecost—

> I just simply opened my mouth and the Lord filled it. I did not have at any time the privilege of a Bible School training or special teaching; the Holy Spirit

Heather Burrows. Photo from the *Apostolic Herald*, **June 1937.**

opened the Scriptures. He taught me and I did not even think it was strange or special.[178]

Her basic message was a simple gospel of salvation. 'Good news from Toowoomba,' reported a brief news item in the *Canvas Cathedral Cooee*. 'Crowded tent. Miss Burrows great form.'[179]

In 1934, Burrows joined the Apostolic Church in Sydney as a Young People's Deaconess. She was working as a secretary/stenographer, but it was not long before her speaking gifts came to the fore and within three years she was a full-time evangelist. Money was not plentiful—around one pound a week. But her travel expenses were covered and accommodation was provided, usually in private homes. Her ministry over the next few years would take her to every Australian State and to New Zealand. In 1934, she became the first Australian woman preacher to have her photo on the cover of the *Apostolic Herald*.[180] A leaflet advertising her meetings in Hobart, Tasmania, described her as 'Australia's Youngest Ordained Lady Evangelist.'[181] She was preaching every night except Fridays and twice on Sundays. Quoting from an un-named Victorian newspaper, the leaflet declared: 'Placed on the public platform as a speaker, she would shine. On the stage she would make her mark. Instead, she has chosen the path of duty and is proclaiming the way of salvation to an erring world.'[182] She held successful meetings in Brisbane and in the Prahran Town Hall, Victoria. Another undated news cutting from this period tells how the Tivoli Theatre in Brisbane was engaged to accommodate the crowds that came to hear her speak—

> This capable young preacher, still in her early twenties, has a power in oratory that holds the attention. Although the services have been in progress for more than five weeks, the interest has not waned, nor the speaker's grip on her audience decreased.

In Wellington, New Zealand, in the early 1940s, Heather Burrows was the main speaker at an Apostolic Convention where she was described as having been 'greatly used throughout every State in Australia.'[183] Although it was not the practice of the Apostolic Church to recognize women as church leaders, Burrows was an acknowledged evangelist and had 'no trouble at all' being accepted in the places she visited. There were other women preachers, but she was the only one who conducted authorised missions.

Burrows gave herself unstintingly to the work of evangelism. She not only preached the gospel but also prayed for the sick. She visited people in prison. She preached at open air meetings on Friday nights in the Sydney suburb of Rockdale where large numbers gathered to hear her.[184] Most of the time she went to places where there was no existing Apostolic church. Leila Higgs accompanied her as a pianist and violinist in Australia as did Margaret Smith in New Zealand. On one occasion, she travelled by troop train across the Nullabor, a journey which took several days, as she stopped to conduct services for Outback station people in Penong and Ceduna.

After a couple of years in Western Australia, she revisited New Zealand where her health broke down and she had to withdraw from ministry. She was years recovering. In 1956 she married Horace Thomson Hoskin (d.1989), a New Zealand Presbyterian. She did not preach again.

Winnie Andrews (1892?–1932)

When Winnie Andrews was still a baby in arms, Lancaster prayed for her— 'May she win many souls for Christ!'[185] Some fifteen years later, in November, 1907, Winnie appeared in a Bible Class and in early 1908 was converted and baptized in the Spirit.[186] Winnie had one leg four inches shorter than the other as the result of some childhood surgery. During an all night prayer meeting, she was partly healed. About that time, Lancaster was approached by Max Moorhead, later a member of the Springfield Council of the Assemblies of God in the USA, to be the 'Pentecostal secretary' in Australia. With characteristic self-effacement, she 'shrank from the publicity of such an office.' She felt encouraged by the Holy Spirit to offer the position to the teenage Winnie, who took it gladly.[187] While never a preacher, she was not afraid to confront difficult issues with courage and competence.[188] At her death, in 1932, Lancaster spoke of her 24 years' devoted labour for the Lord and of the way her face 'lit up with the glory of God' during her last days.[189]

Leila Buchanan (1895–1966)

Leila Buchanan.
Photo, Richmond Temple Souvenir, 1939.

Leila Buchanan (1895–1966), Lancaster's daughter, was from 1937 the editor of *The Australian Evangel* and an accomplished preacher as well.[190] Baptized in the Spirit at age thirteen, Buchanan gave herself to ministry to the derelicts of society, especially neglected children. After her marriage to W.A. ('Alex') Buchanan, she accompanied her husband in itinerant ministry and acted as secretary for visiting evangelists such as Smith Wigglesworth, whose sermons she took down in shorthand.[191] 'Through fear of man,' she hesitated to preach herself, but one night had a vision in which she saw a pulpit with a beautifully engraved open Bible on it, and behind it a gold crown against a stormy background. The vision was twice repeated and then 'a mighty hand' grasped the Bible and thrust it into her hands. She took this is a divine commission to preach the gospel in the light of the urgency of the hour and was later 'fully ordained' as an Assemblies of God minister.[192]

Other Women

The ministry at Good News Hall was commonly seen as a kind of sisterhood. A Queensland woman was grateful for letters from 'the dear sisters' at the Hall. H.

wrote, 'Much blessing has resulted, beloved sisters, from your visit in the precious Master's service.'[193] A young woman wrote a testimony addressed, 'Dear sisters'.[194] Regular reports were published in *Good News* of ministry by various 'Sisters'.[195]

Not all were preachers but they all carried out significant work. Annie Chamberlain and Annie Dennis both conducted services and founded churches. Mary Ayers was an itinerant preacher. As early as 1910, a woman was nominated as the first Pentecostal representative in South Australia. Readers of the first issue of *Good News* who were interested in 'the Outpouring of the Latter Rain and desiring to investigate' were advised to contact Miss Pight of Reynella, now an outer suburb, but then a country town. Some of the first Pentecostal meetings in Adelaide were held in the home of Fannie L. Collie (1867–1930), who lived on Magill Rd, Kensington Park North, an eastern suburb[196] and had evidently been introduced to Pentecostalism by Sarah Jane Lancaster around 1910.[197]

In the 1920s, 'Sister' Hotson and 'Sister' Turner devoted themselves to tract distribution and visitation in the Hornsby area of Sydney. 'Sister' Rowston did a similar work in Orange.[198] For many years, Alice MacCleary and Celia Casey who were honorary housekeepers at Good News Hall were especially busy during the Depression when they worked night and day to care for the needy. 'Only God Himself knows their years of faithful service,' said a report in *Good News*, 'and daily taking up of their cross in Jesus' Name.'[199]

In many ways the role of women in the early years of Australian Pentecostalism set the pattern for the future of the movement. Of sixteen women leaders, all but three were Australian-born. Two of these, Isabella Hetherington and Mina Brawner, lived most of their adult lives in this country. Only one, Aimee Semple McPherson, was a short-tem visitor. Seven had a Methodist or Evangelical background although it is probable that three more also came from that tradition. In this respect, women clearly reflect the overall religious heritage of the movement. All were prepared to travel and/or sacrifice for the sake of the ministry. Ten were unmarried, sacrificing security, home and family for the sake of the gospel. Most were self-educated: only two, Sarah Jane Lancaster and Mina Brawner, had tertiary qualifications (see Table 10).

After 1925, male leadership gradually gained the ascendancy, but the nature of this leadership was not dissimilar—those concerned were also mainly Australian-born although there was significant international input; the denominational roots tended to be Methodist or Evangelical; generally they were enterprising and capable, although not theologically trained; they were passionate in their desire to preach the gospel; and they saw the baptism and gifts of the Holy Spirit as of primary significance.

Table 10 Australian Pentecostal Women in Ministry Prior to 1939.

Name	Dates	Marital state	Place of birth	Tertiary training	Original denomination or religion	Affiliation	Main areas of activity
Andrews, Winnie	?1892–1932	Single	Australia	None	Baptist	Good News	Melb, Vic
Anstis, Edie	d.1936	Single	Australia	None	Not known	Good News	Perth, WA
Brawner, Mina	b.?1880	Married	America	Medicine	?Presbyterian; Methodist	Good News Hall (AFM); Bible Standard Church	NSW, Qld, Vic
Chamberain, Annie	b.?1868	Married	Australia	None (Salvation Army)	Salvation Army	Pent Church of Australia	Adelaide, SA
Heath, Pauline	?1889–1940	Divorced	Australia (childhood in India)	None	Agnostic	Apostolic Mission	Adelaide, SA
Hetherington, Isabella	?1869–1946	Single	Ireland	None	Evangelical	Good News Hall (AFM)	Vic, Qld
Lancaster, Sarah Jane	1858–1934	Married	Australia	Teacher	Methodist	Good News Hall (AFM)	Victoria and all Australian States
Mather, Ellen	1894–?1975	Single (married late)	Australia	None	Methodist	Pent Church of Australia	Vic, Qld
Mortomore, Florence	1890–1927	Single	Australia	None	Baptist	Good News Hall (AFM)	Qld
Wiles, Ruby	Not known	Single	Australia	None	Not known	Good News Hall	Perth, WA

Theoretically any office was still open to women. In spite of reservations being expressed at one point, the original Good News Hall congregation (and subsequently the Apostolic Faith Mission) together with the Pentecostal Church of Australia (later the Assemblies of God) and the Foursquare movement continued to affirm the right of women both to preach and to lead.[200] The prophet Joel promised that the Holy Spirit would be poured out on both men and women and that they would equally declare His Word (Joel 2:28f). At least in the early years, the Australian Pentecostal movement took this at face value. If God was not prejudiced, why should His people be? There was no gender discrimination in the spirit of Pentecost.

Notes

1. J. Boswell, *Life of Johnson* (Vol I, 31 July, 1763, 463), various publishers.
2. Benson, 1935, 505ff.
3. 'Father and I joined them because of their holiness teaching, and their opportunities for female ministry,' M. A. Alway, 'Jesus Christ the Same Yesterday, Today and Forever,' GN, 1:1, April, 1910, 14.
4. *Spectator*, 24 February, 1893, 148.
5. S. Willis, ed, *Women, Faith and Fetes* (Melbourne: Dove Communications, 1977), 12. It was not until 1908 that the last Australian State (Victoria) allowed women to vote in State elections.
6. Carey, 1996, 134.
7. Roe, JRH, December, 1968, 156.
8. R. McCutcheon, 'Margaret Holmes: Larger Than the Roles She Played', in Willis, ed, 1977, 97, 114.
9. Janet West, 'A Recipe for Confrontation: Female Religious Orders and the Male Hierarchy in Nineteenth Century Australia,' in M. Hutchinson and E. Campion, eds, *Long Patient Struggle: Studies in the Role of Women in Australian Christianity* (Sydney: Centre for the Study of Australian Christianity, 1994), 71ff.
10. A. Hyslop, 'Christian Temperance and Social Reform: The Woman's Christian Temperance Union of Victoria 1887–1912,' in Willis, 1977, 43ff.
11. J. Smart, 'The Panacea of Prohibition: the Reaction of the Woman's Christian Temperance Union of Victoria to the Great War,' in Willis, 1977, 179.
12. Carey, 1996, 111–139; Ruth Sturmey, 'Anglicanism and gender in Australian society,' in Black, ed, 1991, 39–51.
13. J. West, 'The Role of the Woman Missionary,' in *Lucas: an Evangelical History Review*, No. 21, 22, June and December, 1996, 46.
14. H. Carey, "Women's Peculiar Mission to the Heathen"—Protestant Missionary Wives in Australia, 1788–1900,' in Hutchinson and Campion, eds, 1994, 25ff.
15. GN, 17:10, October, 1926, 11.
16. Piggin, 1996, 57, 130; W. Nelson, *T. C. Hammond: Irish Christian* (Edinburgh: Banner of Truth, 1994), 37; J. Walker in B. Dickey, eds, *ADEB*, 1994, 18f. *The Observer and Free Methodist Chronicle*, Vol 1, No. 9, 26 November, 1886. Irish-born T. C. Hammond was the highly influential and strongly evangelical Principal of Moore College, Sydney, the recognized training institution for candidates for the Anglican priesthood, from 1936 to 1953.
17. SC, II:20, 19 May, 1883, 8; SC, II:25, 23 June, 1883, 5.

18. SC, II:21, 26 May, 1883, 7; SC, II:22, 2 June, 1883, 11f ; SC, II:26, 30 June, 1883, 5; SC, II:26, 30 June, 1883, 8.
19. Elliot T. Rien, *A Challenge to Holiness* (Wyee: Bethshan, 1975), 58, 89f.
20. Hunt, 1985, 129.
21. *Register*, 9 October, 1922.
22. *Register*, 2 October, 1922; *Advertiser*, 2 October, 1922.
23. Judd and Cable, 1987, 217.
24. Carey, 1996, 135f.
25. Judd and Cable, 1987, 153f.
26. R. Teale, 'Matron, Maid and Missionary: the Work of Anglican Women in Australia,' in Willis, ed, 1977, 117ff.
27. Thompson, 1994, 27.
28. Gribben, 1972, 70.
29. By 1917, there were women on the Council of the Australian Board of Missions. R. Teale, 'Matron, Maid and Missionary: the Work of Anglican Women in Australia,' in Willis, ed, 1977, 122.
30. Roe, 1986, 165. Roe points out that there were another fifty presented by men. But she also sees a limited, but rising, involvement of women in churches during the latter part of the nineteenth century (162ff).
31. For the role of the women Maximilla and Priscilla in Montanism, see Eusebius, *Historia Ecclesiastica*, xiv–xviii; Tertullian, *A Treatise on the Soul,* ix; *Against Praxeas,* i.
32. M. Woodworth-Etter, *A Diary of Signs and Wonders* (Tulsa: Harrison, 1916, 1980). For basic information on these men see Burgess et al, eds, 1988, relevant articles.
33. Richard Riss argues a case for the role of women in the early American Pentecostal movement, but struggles to find a substantial list of women in leadership. See Burgess et al, eds, 1988, 893ff. Mary Ruth Chamless recounts many examples of women preaching and evangelizing, most of whom were wives of pastors, but presents few of women in significant leadership. See Mary Ruth Chamless, *Behold God's Handmaid* (Belleville, Illinois: published by the author, 1988).
34. D. Roebuck, 'Perfect liberty to Preach the Gospel: Women Ministers in the Church of God,' *Pneuma,* 17:1, Spring, 1995, 25ff.
35. D.Gill, 'The Contemporary State of Women in Ministry in the Assemblies of God,' *Pneuma,* 17:1, Spring, 1995, 33. Note that the American Assemblies of God and the Assemblies of God in Queensland were formed independently of each other.
36. For basic information on these people, see relevant entries in Burgess et al, eds, 1988; Worsfold, 1991, 1ff; Hollenweger, 1988, 21ff, 75ff, 111ff, 176ff, 197ff, 206ff; E. Lawless, 'Not so Different After All: Pentecostal Women in the Pulpit' in C. Wessinger, ed, *Women's Leadership in Marginal Religions: Explorations Outside the Mainstream* (University of Illinois Press, 1993), 41—'Males founded Pentecostalism and males dominate the leadership ...' It is worth noting that the Brethren, who were in so many ways similar to Pentecostals, made no provision for women in leadership. Not one woman is given separate entry in a study of one hundred early Brethren leaders. Not surprisingly, the work is called *Chief Men Among the Brethren.* See Pickering, ed, 1918, 1961.
37. Gutierrez and Smith, eds, 1996, 152, 176.
38. Larson, 1997, 25ff.
39. Mark Hutchinson, 'The Contribution of Women to Pentecostalism' in Shane Clifton and Jacqueline Grey, eds, *Raising Women Leaders: Perspectives on Liberating Women in Pentecostal and Charismatic Contexts* (Chester Hill, NSW: Australian Pentecostal Studies, 2009), 200ff.
40. Weber, 1965, 104.

41. See GN, various issues from 1913–1926, in particular, 1:5, January, 1913, 32; 12:8, September, 1923, 21; 14:10, November, 1923, 18; 15:12, December, 1924, 22. There were also many home meetings led by women. For an overview see Chant, 1984, 34ff, 103ff, 125ff.

42. S. Muirhead, 'John Barclay,' 1988, 2; J. H. Nickson, 'Pentecost in Melbourne, Australia' in Moorhead, ed, 1908, 28. See also Chapter Five; J. Lancaster, 'Australia,' in *Confidence,* October, 1908, 18; J. Lancaster, GN, 17:9, September, 1996, 11; Chant, 1984, 34ff.

43. Mortomore had three younger brothers—Albert (b. 1892), Leonard (b. 1894) and Cyril (b. 1902). Her parents also adopted three children, Maizie, Dorothy and Mavis. Cyril became a Foursquare pastor, serving churches in several places in New South Wales, including Orange, Cessnock, Newcastle and Newtown. See John O'Connell, 'Cyril Ernest Mortomore, 1902–1974' (Unpublished essay, Sydney: Tabor College, 1993).

44. GN, 16:1, January, 1925, 10; Caroline already had some experience of divine power. On one occasion, one of the boys suffered from a painful knee, the result of an unnamed disease affecting the hip. His leg was strapped in irons and he could only walk with the aid of crutches. For many weeks, there was no sign of improvement. Finally, in desperation, Caroline sought help through prayer. Subsequent medical examination affirmed that the boy had recovered. See GN, 1:5, January, 1913, 12.

45. GN, 18:8, August, 1927, 14–15. Following details about Florrie Mortomore are from this source, unless otherwise stated.

46. GN, 1:6, October, 1913, 6

47. GN, 1:5, January, 1913, 9; 'Your Young Men Shall See Visions,' GN 1:5 January 1913, 17.

48. After this, the Closes itinerated through Victoria, New South Wales and Queensland , 'with a Gospel van' doing open air work. GN, 18:4, April, 1927, 11. They were later officially recognized as evangelists. GN, 18:6, June, 1927, 11.

49. For example, a woman who signed herself only as 'MD' reported a miraculous shower of rain in time of drought providing water for baptism by immersion, her own baptism in the Spirit and her own healing, all as a result of a visit from Florrie Mortomore. See 'Another Comforter,' GN, 9:1, February, 1923, 13. Little is known of Mortomore's preaching content. However, it was plainly Pentecostal. One of the few surviving written articles of hers is a brief Bible study on dreams and visions. See GN, 17:5, June, 1926, 17.

50. Leonard Cook, personal interview, 30 January, 1994; Ruth Dyer, personal interview, 28 January, 1994; N. Smallcombe, *Into the 21st Century* (Cairns: Cairns Christian Centre, n.d.), 6; GN, 18:2, February, 1927, 10.

51. *Richmond Temple Souvenir,* 1939, 42; see AE, 6:11, October, 1940, 9; AE, 13:1, December, 1946, 13f.

52. GN, 19:7, July, 1928, 12.

53. G. Burns, 'A Tribute to Sister F. Mortomore,' GN, 18:8, August, 1927, 15; for more on Burns see Chapter Eight.

54. 'Sister O'Brien', 'Pentecost in Toowoomba,' AE, 15:6, May, 1949, 18f; W. A. Buchanan, letter provided by Buchanan family. The first person in Toowoomba to experience the fullness of the Spirit was Edie Peters whose husband became one of the Pentecostal stalwarts in the district. Others to be affected were members of the Kajewski family. See H. Farnsworth, 'Pentecost in Toowoomba,' AE, 15:6, May, 1949, 18. In 1945, a Kajewski family reunion was held at Toowoomba, and according to a contemporary report, 'all but about half a dozen' of the 93 descendants of the original couple were present. An accompanying photo shows about 60 family members, AE, 11:11, October, 1945, 20f. It has already been mentioned that Florrie's brother Cyril married a Kajewski

girl. Mortomore also awakened the interest of an accountant named Cecil Swenson (b. 18 June, 1906) and his wife Pearl (b. 17 May, 1906), whose kinfolk are still in the church although it was actually under the ministry of W. A. Buchanan, Lancaster's son in law, that the Swensons were filled with the Spirit. Cecil Swenson's son was surprised that it was his father, not his mother, who first experienced the Spirit's anointing, as his mother was 'a good woman' but his father was 'not such a good man.' He concluded that his father needed God's blessing more than his mother! See C. B. Swenson, 'Pentecost in Toowoomba,' AE, 15:6, May, 1949, 16f; Pearl Swenson, personal interview, 16 April, 1993.

55. GN, 16:9, September, 1925, 17; J. Lancaster in GN, 18:8 August, 1927, 14.
56. See Chapter Six.
57. GN, 9:1, February, 1923, 18. Further details about Florrie Mortomore's Brisbane meetings are also from this source.
58. GN, 9:1, February, 1923, 23; H. Martin, 'Queensland report of Evangelist Van Eyk's Brisbane Visit,' GN, 18:4, April, 1927, 11.
59. Allan and Jean Conwell, personal interview, c.1991; M. Penny, personal interview, 23 March, 1992. Tom Conwell also initiated the work at Woombye—AE, 12:5, April, 1946, 20.
60. F. Mortomore, 'The Dragon's Plot,' GN, 14: 10, November, 1923, 3. It is of interest that a similar view of the 'Rapture' was presented in 1913 in Melbourne by John Coombe, who became the founder of the Australian Nepalese Mission. See J. Coombe, 'The Rapture of the Saints,' sermon transcript, 31 July, 1913. Van Eyk also drew a distinction between 'two classes of believers,' those who were in the kingdom and those who were in the Body of Christ—GN, 17:12, December, 1926, 5f.
61. F. Mortomore, 'In the Last Days,' GN, 16:1, January, 1925, 8–10.
62. 'First Australian Recruits for Japan,' GN, 17:3, March, 1926, 10f.
63. GN, 16:10, October, 1925, 10.
64. This woman is identified only as 'Sister B. D.' or 'Sister Bernice'. See GN, 15:6, June, 1924, 9; GN, 15:11, November, 1924, 11
65. GN, 15:6, June, 1924, 9; GN, 15:11, November, 1924, 11
66. GN, 16:9, September, 1925, 17. On Charles and Will Enticknap, see Appendix B.
67. See Chapter Ten.
68. GN, 18:2, February, 1927, 10.
69. J. Lancaster, 'The Editor Visits Queensland,' GN, 18:1, January, 1927, 10.
70. Roy Valentine, personal communication, 11 July, 1994; GN, 16:12, December, 1925, 19; GN, 18:7, July, 1927, 19; GN, 21:6, June, 1930, 7.
71. GN, 19:8, August, 1928, 7.
72. GN, 17:3, March, 1926, 12.
73. See B. Phillips, *The Life Story of Beryl Phillips* (Published by the author, 1985), 5. 'One time I was away with the pastor (C. L. Greenwood) and his family at Daylesford Springs for a rest. He was suffering from bad carbuncles on his neck, and when I asked why God didn't heal him, he said he hadn't the faith to ask for healing because he had worked too hard and needed rest.'
74. GN, 18:2, February, 1927, 19; GN, 18: 6, June, 1927, 11.
75. W. A. Buchanan, letter, quoted in Chant, 1984:45.
76. 'Secretary's Report of Brisbane Campaign,' GN, 18:11, November, 1927, 10.
77. F. W. Perrin, 'A Tribute of Christian Love,' GN, 18:8, August, 1927, 15.
78. GN, 18:8, August, 1927, 15.
79. GN, 18:8, August, 1927, 8. It is not clear whether Mortomore composed these verses herself or simply copied them.

80. GN, 17:6, June, 1926, 7; BSC, XII:2, December, 1940, 2ff; N. Fabian, personal interview, 15 August, 1991.
81. *News*, 30 November, 1927.
82. N. Fabian, personal interview, 15 August, 1991.
83. *News,* 31 March, 1927.
84. P. Heath, letter to the congregation at the Mission, 15 January, 1937, copy from Gus Jansen; 'Promoted to Glory,' BSC, XII:2, December, 1940, 4.
85. M. M. Fabian, AN, 3:2 December, 1931, page number deleted; GN, 16:12, December, 1925, 14. Reference is made here to a woman who was so filled with praise at her conversion that she was henceforth called 'Joy'. See also GN, 17:6, June, 1926, 7.
86. E.g. *News*, 31 March, 1927; 7 July, 1927; 30 September, 1927.
87. AN, 1:4, June, 1930, 2.
88. In 1937, the Mission became the Bible Standard Mission and the name was changed in December of that year to the *Bible Standard Call.* From a historian's viewpoint there is an annoying anonymity in the *News*. But this was a matter of policy: '...we do not print names in our paper except in very exceptional cases...'—BSC, 11:2, December, 1939, 4.
89. L. Hart, personal interview, n.d. but c. 1970.
90. L. Hart, interview; Norman Fabian, personal interview, 15 August, 1991.
91. GN, 17:9, September, 1926, 5; AN, 1:4, June, 1930, 4.
92. BSC, 9:3, March, 1938, 9; AN, 4:3, March, 1933, 6, 7; AN, 8:3, March, 1937, 12; BSC, XI:4, June, 1940, 10.
93. 'Faith or Feeling,' AN, 8:4, June, 1937, 2.
94. *News*, 30 November, 1927.
95. *Advertiser*, 1 October, 1927. The text of one advertisement reads—SUNDAY 7 p.m. SISTER HEATH CONDUCTS SERVICES. Being filled with the Holy Spirit, she often speaks with other tongues and interpretations as the Spirit gives her utterance. One message last Sunday night was, 'Arise, Oh Lord Jesus! Arise in Thy might and plead Thy Own cause. Thou Who art King of Kings and Lord of Lords, Whose vesture is dipped in blood. Ride gloriously forth in Thy might. Ride gloriously forth because of meekness, truth and righteousness. Arise and gird on Thy sword that all the earth be filled with Thy Presence and Salvation, his earth which Thou hast redeemed with Thy most precious blood.' Prove all things. Come and hear her who for 20 years was an agnostic and only converted two years ago. All welcome. No collection.
96. Pauline.Heath, 'Tongues and Interpretation.' This is a seven-page document provided by Norm Fabian and attributed by him to Heath
97. N. Fabian, personal interview, 15 August, 1991.
98. AN, 5:4, June, 1934.
99. N. Fabian, personal interview, 15 August, 1991.
100. P. Heath, letter to the congregation at the Mission, 15 January, 1937. See further on Brawner in this chapter.
101. For reports of the new building see BSC, XI:3, March, 1940, 1; BSC, XII:1, September, 1940, 1. See also N. Fabian, personal interview, 15 August, 1991.
102. GN, 15:12, December, 1924, 12f; Jordan, 1970, 14ff. Further details are from this source unless otherwise stated. Ellen (Nellie) Jordan's maiden name was Nellie Mather.
103. Jordan, 1970, 51.
104. Jordan, 1970, 56f. See also GN, December, 1924, 12f.
105. S. Douglas, personal interview, 21 November, 1989.
106. A. Davidson, personal interview, 20 November, 1990; RTS, 1939, 27.

107. *Minutes of Assembly of God Church (originally called Pentecostal Church), Ballarat Branch*, 16 June, 1930, 4 July, 1930 and 21 July, 1930.

108. AE, December, 1930, 10.

109. *Minutes* Ballarat, 31 December, 1936, 24 October, 1937 to 16 April, 1939.

110. *Minutes* Ballarat, 7 May, 1939.

111. AE, 7:7, June, 1941, 16.

112. AE, 7:1, December, 1940, 12.

113. F. Lancaster, personal interview, 18 December, 1993.

114. In 1949 in Brisbane Mather married, but within days of the wedding, her husband, a World War Two veteran, died. Six years later she married again, this time a widower named Jordan, who died in his sleep in 1961. In 1970, at the age of 76, she married Methodist minister Henry Lawson-Smith, at Pakenham East, Victoria, where they continued to minister together. See Jordan, 1970, 133ff.

115. Jordan, 1970, 'Foreword,' no page number.

116. GN, 19:12, December, 1928, 11. For background details on Brawner see Appendix B.

117. GN, 18:6, September, 1927, 19; 20:3, March, 1929, 5.

118. GN, 1:6, October, 1913, 11.

119. N. L. Armstrong, personal interview, October, 1993.

120. GN, 20:5, May, 1929, 12.

121. GN, 20:11, November, 1929, 13; GN, 20:12, December, 1929, 13; GN, 21:1, January, 1930, 12; GN, 21:3, March, 1930, 12.

122. GN, 20:7, July, 1929, 13.

123. N. L. Armstrong, personal interview, October, 1993. Note that Armstrong says this happened in 1927, but it could not have been before mid-1928. See M. Brawner, 'My Own Story,' GN, 19:12, December, 1928, 10f.

124. GN, 20:3, March, 1929, 15.

125. GN, 20:5, May, 1929, 14.

126. GN, 20:3, March, 1929, 5.

127. GN, 20:6, June, 1929, 11; GN, 20:9, September, 1929, 12f.

128. GN, 21:5, May, 1920, 20; GN, 21:7, July, 1930, 2.

129. GN, 21:10, October, 1930, 10. Following details about Brawner's work are from this source unless otherwise stated.

130. CP, 21, August, 1930.

131. Len Cook Jr does not remember large crowds attending or a significant number of conversions or new members to the church, but the description of these meetings is based on Winnie Andrews' report in *Good News* which is likely to be reliable. See GN, 21: 12, December, 1930, 10; Len Cook, personal interview, 30 January, 1994.

132. GN, 21:11, November, 1930, l2.

133. W. Andrews. 'Dr Brawner's Cairns Campaign,' GN, 21:12, December, 1930, 10.

134. GN, 22:2, February, 1931, 11.

135. GN, 22:5, May, 1931, 12; GN, 22:9, September, 1931, 17; GN, 22:7, July, 1931, 13; GN, 22:6, June, 1931, 12f; GN, 22:9, September, 1931, 17.

136. W. H. W. Lavers, 'Filled with His Spirit,' GN, 22:11, November, 1931, 12.

137. GN, 23:8, August, 1932, III.

138. GN, 23:10, October, 1932, 16,III.

139. GC, September, 1932, 8.

140. Len Outhred, 'Bible Standard Pentecostal Church,' *Minister's Bulletin,* March, 1998, 20; BSC, August, 1928, 7.

141. J. Heath, letter to the congregation at the Mission, 29 December, 1936. According to Len Outhred, around 50 people attended regular services; BSC, December, 1938, 10

142. 'Results of Examination' sheet for W. Larsen, June, 1941; 'Rules and Regulations,' The Bible Standard Training School for Christian Workers, Lighthouse Temple, North Melbourne, n. d. but c.1940; Christian Workers' Course Certificate, awarded to Walter Larsen, 13 December, 1941.

143. Wal Larsen, personal communication, 19 March, 1993.

144. 'Please tell Brother Gus,' wrote Heath, 'that Dr Brawner believes in eternal punishment, just as we do... and hates anything like annihilation.' P. Heath, letter to the congregation at the Mission, 15 January, 1937.

145. GN, 20:12, December, 1929, 13.

146. GN, 1:6, October, 1913, 31. Extraordinary stories of healing were not uncommon at that time—Harriet ('Grandma') Weldon, an 87-year-old woman, who had been 'an energetic church worker,' had a fall and cracked three ribs. Charles Anstis laid hands on her and there was a remarkable response. Four days later, she found herself speaking in tongues. Then her arms began to flail about until she felt one hand being applied to her side and massaging it 'like an iron' and she heard the sound of bones cracking. The next day, similar things happened, only now she laughed for joy. Two days later she spoke at great length in tongues. Then, she said, 'I got up and dressed, and I am well!' Three years later, she became ill with an enlarged liver, rheumatism in hands and feet, and distressing pains around the heart. One of the Anstis women visited and prayed for her. Two days later she was visiting people all around her parish, telling them how she was now totally well—GN, 1:6, October, 1913, 27f.

147. GN, 22:6, June, 1931, 10.

148. GN, 9:1, February, 1923, 21; GN, 18:6, June, 1927, 13. Their surnames do appear in a list of Apostolic Faith Mission officers in June 1927, but as the first names are not used, it is still not easy to identify them. See GN, 18:6, June, 1927, 11.

149. 'Brother Martin... told of the work of Sister Lancaster in the open air of every capital city in Australia,' GN, 22:5, May, 1931, 12.

150. A. Allday, quoted in J. Friend, *Pentecost in Western Australia* (Unpublished manuscript, c. 1991), 16; GN, 18:6, June, 1927, 19.

151. H. S. Kilpatrick, GN, 20:1, January, 1929, 14; GN, 22:7, July, 1931, 7.

152. GN, 24:11, November, 1933, 5.

153. GN, 15:6, June, 1924, 9.

154. A. Allday, 13 February, 1990, quoted in Friend, 1991, 16; GN, 15:11, November, 1924, 18; GN, 18:6, June, 1927, 13.

155. A. K. Lucy, 'One Little Room,' GN, 21:10, October, 1930, 16.

156. E. Anstis, 'God Blessing in Perth, WA,' GN, 18:1, January, 1927, 11.

157. C. Cousins, 'Ask and Ye Shall Receive,' GN, 17:2, February, 1926, 11.

158. Edie Anstis, 'Getting from God,' GN, 15:1, January, 1924, 8.

159. T. Bentley, personal interview, 23 April, 1997; GN, 24:4–5, April–May, 1933, III..

160. GN, 18:8, August, 1927, 11; 18:9, September, 1927, 12.

161. A. Allday, 13 February 1990, in Friend, 1991, 17; GN, 17:4, April, 1926, 19; GN, 17:5, May, 1926, 6; GN, 18:7, July, 1927, 11; GN, 19:6, June, 1928, 12.

162. A. Allday, 13 February 1990, in Friend, 1991, 18; GN, 18:11, November, 1927, 14; GN, 19:6, June, 1928, 10–12.

163. GN, 20:5, May, 1929, 16.

164. GN, 20:5, May, 1929, 10.

165. GN, 20:9, September, 1929, 13.

166. GN, 21:6, June 1930, 11.
167. S. F. Du Plessis, 'Western Australia's Mighty Visitation from on High,' and E. Jarvis, 'Some impressions of F. B. Van Eyk's Campaign in Perth, WA,' GC, 3:3, September–October, 1934, 40f.
168. T. Bentley, personal interview, 23 April, 1997; A. Allday, in Friend, 1991, 19.
169. J. McCabe, personal interview, 18 September, 1990; P. Lovell, personal interview, 6 September, 1991.
170. *The Apostolic Church—its Principles and Practices, Constitution* (Richmond: Apostolic Church, 1939), 6:3 and 4; 27:I and II. The question of whether a woman could be an apostle, for example, is not even raised here: it was taken for granted that only men qualified.
171. K. Kirwan, personal interview, 11 September, 1991.
172. AE, August, 1930, 9; H. Hoskin, personal interview, 21 November, 1997; personal communication, 10 February, 1998. Further details are from these sources unless otherwise stated.
173. AH, 2:2, June 1937, 31.
174. *Cooee*, 3:2, 13 March, 1932; *Cooee*, 2:6, 11 October, 1931.
175. L. Wahlquist, interview, 19 November, 1991. Burrows had been baptized earlier in a Baptist church but with 'little understanding' of what it meant.
176. *Cooee*, 2:8, 25 October, 1931; 2:9, 1 November, 1931; 2:11, 15 November, 1931; 2:12, 22 November, 1931; 2:14, 6 December, 1931; 2:16, 20 December, 1931. For more on Mary Ayers see Appendix B.'.
177. *Cooee*, 2:15, 13 December, 1931; 2:16, 20 December, 1931; 2:17, 27 December, 1931.
178. Personal communication, 10 February, 1998; see also H. Hoskin, personal interview, 21 November, 1997; 'Cooee,' Toowoomba, No. 7, 6 December, 1931; 'Cooee' 2:19, 10 January, 1932.
179. 'Cooee' 2:20, 17 January, 1932.
180. AH, 2:2, June, 1937, 1, 31. From the first issue of *Revival Echoes* in 1933, there was usually a cover picture of a pastor on each edition. With the exception of a missionary to India, Burrows was the first woman to have her photo appear there in the four years of the magazine's existence to that time.
181. Evidently Burrows's Hobart hosts overstated the case here. Although recognized as an evangelist, she was never formally ordained to the Apostolic ministry.
182. This leaflet is undated but evidently c.1940.
183. Undated leaflet, but c.1942.
184. 'You should have seen the people who came'—H. Hoskin, personal interview, 1997.
185. GN, 17:9, September, 1926, 11.
186. GN, 1:1, April, 1910, 6.
187. The matter was referred to Mrs Nickson and John Coombe who both felt uneasy about the younger woman's age. A week later, however, they both confirmed the decision, believing it to be the will of God.
188. See Chapter Six for her response to Aimee McPherson's withdrawal from her commitment to Good News Hall.
189. J. Lancaster, 'He Giveth His Beloved Sleep,' GN, 23:8, August, 1932, 16.
190. E.g. AE, 3:8, July, 1937, 6; AE, 4:5, April, 1938, 6; AE, 11:4, March, 1945, 2; F. Lancaster, personal interview, 18 December, 1993.
191. These were later incorporated in S. Wigglesworth, *Ever Increasing Faith* (Springfield: Gospel Publishing House, 1924).
192. *Richmond Temple Souvenir*, 1939, 45.

193. GN, 1:5, January, 1913, 23; GN, 1:6, October, 1913, 19; GN, 9:1, February, 1923, 15.

194. GN, 16:11, November, 1925, Supplement, 4; see also GN, 17:1, January, 1926, 15. This sisterhood was quite informal. Ultimately, the word 'sister' did tend to be used as a semi-formal title (e.g. 'Sister' Edie, 'Sister' Ruby), but initially it was simply an expression of Christian fraternity. There was no structured sisterhood as in the Catholic and Anglican churches.

195. E.g. GN, 24:4, 5, April–May, 1933, 7.

196. Chant, 1984, 135. Additional information on Fannie Collie is from V. Short and C. Coulthard-Clark, *A Genealogy of the Bonnet Family of Adelaide* (Canberra, 1983); Thea McKelliff, personal interview, November, 1992; Dorothy Reekie, personal interview, 14 August, 1991; Elaine Hulm, 'Fannie Collie,' unpublished essay, Tabor College, 14 December, 1990. Note that the name is sometimes spelt 'Fanny.'

197. 'By God's grace we had been the first to carry the "Latter Rain" message to Adelaide'—GN, 18:6, June, 1927, 10; 'For some seventeen years past, (we have) been in loving fellowship with the dear brethren there'—GN, 18:6, June, 1927, 10.

198. GN, 19:6, June, 1928, 15.

199. GN, 25:3, March, 1934, 20.

200. Women ministers are freely recognized in most Australian Pentecostal churches today, although the vast majority of ministers are men. And it appears there are ongoing reservations about women exercising ultimate leadership. Apart from Sarah Jane Lancaster holding office as President of the Apostolic Faith Mission, I am not aware to this point of any State or National Superintendent in any Australian movement having been a woman.

CHAPTER TWELVE

PREACHING IN THE SPIRIT

The Content and Focus of Pentecostal Preaching

As we have seen, preaching was the major dynamic in Pentecostal evangelism. The standard method of winning people to God's kingdom was to preach the gospel—on the streets, in the home, in hired halls, in tents—indeed wherever they could draw a crowd. Nothing else could compare with the proclamation of Christ in the power of the Spirit. The Spirit was given so that men and women could preach and it was by the hearing of the Word of God that people were saved. Most Pentecostal churches held at least two services on Sundays, with mid-week Bible studies, youth meetings, prayer meetings, tarry meetings and Sunday Schools as well. Even in the prayer meetings, there would be some preaching and teaching.[1] Preachers were expected to be inspirational. The common word for this was 'anointed', which meant that the Spirit came upon them and gave them convicting and convincing power which would result in healing and deliverance for the needy and oppressed (Luke 4:18). So when Pentecostals preached it was usually with fervour and enthusiasm.

It is not easy today to know specifically what was being proclaimed in the halls, tents and home groups by the many evangelists and preachers who scattered the country. With one exception, there are no extant sermon notes and, obviously, no electronic recordings. However, the printed page offers some idea, as hundreds of published sermons and teaching articles do survive.

These indicate that there were several common themes in the preaching and teaching of the early Pentecostals. As is to be expected, there was a significant emphasis on the baptism and gifts of the Holy Spirit. The most popular theme, however, was the second coming of Christ with Christian living also dominant.

I have catalogued 1028 teaching articles published in three Pentecostal journals from 1913 to 1939.[2] This survey is deficient in the sense that I do not have a complete collection of all the editions published over that period. However, there is sufficient material to form a useful overview of Pentecostal preaching in the 1920s and 1930s. In examining these data, I have selected only teaching articles occupying at least half a page, which, given the common font sizes, means at least 500 words in length. I have not attempted to catalogue church or missionary reports, testimonies, poems or special features such as children's and young people's pages.

I have also evaluated a rare collection of 177 sermon notes written by William Enticknap, a pioneer Pentecostal preacher. These offer a different perspective again, as they reflect what a local pastor found it needful to teach in a congregation of believers, rather than the more general issues a denominational paper might address.

Good News

In 116 extant issues of *Good News,* published during the ministry of Sarah Jane Lancaster, from January 1913 to June 1934, there were 633 teaching articles. In more than one instance, the same article appears two or three times. I have counted these as separate articles, given that there was often a space of several years between printings. While in some cases it is relatively easy to classify an article, in others it is quite difficult. Florrie Mortomore's 'The Dragon's Plot,' is a case in point. I have included it under 'consecration' but it also points out the need to be baptized in the Spirit and relates strongly to the return of Christ, and could easily be included in either of these categories.[3] There is inevitably a degree of subjectivity in classification.

There were several regular features in the pages of *Good News*. Firstly, there were hundreds of testimonies of salvation, divine healing, baptism in the Holy Spirit and the like. In fact, the first issue (April 1910) was almost exclusively devoted to testimonies. As time went on, there were less testimonies, proportionally, and more teaching, news reports and news comments. But the testimonies were always a significant part of the journal. Secondly, there were often up to four pages (approximately 20 per cent) of news from missionaries in India, China and Japan, and less often, from those working among Australian Aboriginals. Missionary work was clearly given a high priority and was seen as a major responsibility.[4]

Thirdly, there were regular reports from local churches or evangelistic campaigns. These are discussed elsewhere. Fourthly, for many years there was a four-page lift-out supplement for children and young people. Fifthly, there were always short items for reflection, poems, parables, pithy quotations and the like. *Good News* was relatively widely distributed, with a circulation of some 3,000 copies monthly.[5]

For all that, it is the teaching component which indicates the kind of themes local preachers were pursuing. In some cases, there is no doubt of this, as the articles were simply transcripts of messages preached. Often, they were reprints from overseas magazines, and again, usually sermons.[6] While these were not actually preached by Pentecostal ministers in Australia, it seems a fair assumption that, allowing for the usual editorial disclaimer, they were selected because their content was consistent with what was being presented, or, in the opinion of the editor, what should have been presented. In *Good News* the *Second Coming of Christ* was the most popular subject. Some 16.59% of all articles were devoted to this theme. Basically, the view adopted was dispensationalist, pre-tribulationist and pre-millennialist.[7]

Almost universally, world events were seen as pointing towards the time of the end. Over ten percent of published articles commented on what was happening in the world and related this to biblical prophecies and their fulfilment. If the features on the Second Coming and those on world events are combined, they represent over one quarter (27.27 per cent) of all articles. Developments in Italy, for example, pointed to the resurrection of the Holy Roman Empire under Mussolini, and events in the Middle East suggested that Turkey's Mustapha Kemal Pasha might well be the Antichrist. Furthermore, a study of the prophecies of Daniel and Revelation showed that time was almost running out and the year 1934 looked like being the beginning of the Tribulation.[8]

The second most popular theme was that of *the baptism and gifts of the Holy Spirit*. While only 12.16 per cent of articles were devoted specifically to the baptism of the Spirit, nearly one quarter of the total teaching content (23.37%) dealt with the baptism and gifts of the Spirit (2.21%), divine healing (8.21%) and the fullness of the Spirit (0.79%). No doubt, in a Pentecostal magazine, a high proportion of articles on these topics was to be expected. There was certainly no apology about it. The need to be filled with the Spirit and to speak in tongues was clearly presented. On the other hand, it is, perhaps, surprising that there were more articles on the return of Christ. Clearly, the second coming loomed very large in the thinking of the churches. It is of interest to note that premillennialism has been seen as one of the tributaries of Pentecostalism in the United States.[9] While it was a popular theme with early Australian Pentecostals, I have found no evidence that it was a significant factor in the emergence of the movement in this country. Pentecostal interest in the 'end times' was shared by many Christians of evangelical persuasion. Piggin describes it as an 'evangelical preoccupation' in the 1930s and 1940s.[10] The incidence of articles on this theme simply reflects the common heritage shared by Pentecostals and Evangelicals alike.

The third most popular theme was *Christian life*. Under this category are grouped topics such as coping with problems, good works, faith, love, trust, peace, hope, sacrifice and the like (12.30%). This estimate is fairly subjective and could be broken down into more specific topics. This is not as easy as it might appear, as often several aspects of Christian life are covered in the one article (such as prayer, faith, persistence and holiness). If we add in other subjects such as discipleship (4.8%), victorious living (2.69%), consecration (2.37%) and holiness (0.95%), the total represents over one fifth of all articles (22.89%). This category is a little diffuse, as additional themes such as prayer and unity might also be included. Nevertheless, it does indicate that in spite of a preoccupation with more dramatic doctrines such as that of the return of Christ and more inspirational themes such as life in the Spirit, there was still a recognition of the need to consider basic, everyday aspects of the faith.

Articles explaining *the gospel* were also common. There were 44 of these (6.95%). Some of the distinctive views and beliefs held by Lancaster on doctrines such as the Godhead, the Bride of Christ and the fate of the wicked, were also reflected in the pages of *Good News*. But as time went on, these issues usually proved so controversial that they tended to be dropped.

At times, particular issues were addressed—the role and ministry of women, for example. Articles also appeared on themes such as prayer, unity, revival, the authority of the Bible, the sacraments, evangelism and the like. Tithing warranted 13 treatments (2.05%), suggesting an ongoing need to jog people's consciences about giving. There were three positive articles about Christmas, although Lancaster did point out on one occasion that a simple repositioning of the letter 'n' would transform the word 'Satan' into 'Santa.'

The Australian Evangel

The *Australian Evangel* was the journal of the Pentecostal Church of Australia, and from 1937, the Assemblies of God. There was a circulation of less than 1000 in 1938.[11] A review of 215 major articles from 1930 to 1945 shows a similar focus to that of *Good News*. This is not, perhaps, surprising, given that the editor for many years was Leila Buchanan, Lancaster's daughter, who was well acquainted with the work at Good News Hall. Here, too, there was significant overseas content, although considerably less (23.25%) than in *Good News*. My collection of these magazines for this period is incomplete (only 40 copies) and some of these were severely damaged in an office fire in 1987, making the peripheries of many pages, including titles, difficult to read. Nevertheless, this summary is still sufficiently representative of the period concerned.

In 1936, the *Australian* Evangel was combined with a Queensland paper entitled *Glad Tidings Messenger*. For convenience's sake, I have treated the magazine as one unit over the period under examination. Again, the most popular subject was *the second coming of Christ*—some 37 (17.21%) articles were devoted to this theme—and the emphasis was on the significance of world events and on pre-tribulation premillennialism. The overall theme of *Christian living* was again dominant, covering a wide range of topics (13.95%). If subjects such as discipleship, holiness, consecration and victorious living are added, this area covers over one quarter of the total (26.98%). *The gospel* was also important (30 articles). The *baptism and gifts of the Spirit* also occupied a leading position, with a combined total of about 15 per cent.

The proportion of articles to testimonies was generally higher with the *Evangel*. There were not the large numbers of stories of healing, baptism in Spirit and other life-changing incidents as in the early issues of *Good News*. It is interesting to note that one of the few local, lengthy stories of divine healing in the *Evangel* was written by Harry Hultgren, whose testimonies often appeared in earlier years in *Good News*.[12]

The *Evangel* was more openly a denominational magazine, reflecting the greater degree of comfort with this concept than Lancaster experienced. For Lancaster, organisational structure was always to be treated with suspicion.

Apostolic Journals

Revival Echoes was the official organ of the Apostolic Church in Australia. In 1936, its name was changed to *Apostolic Herald,* to bring it in line with similar journals in other lands. For the purposes of this analysis, it is considered as one publication. An assessment of 180 articles in 50 issues from June 1933 to June 1939 yields a panorama slightly different from that of the other journals. For a start, there is a lower concentration of teaching articles per issue—only 3.6, compared with 5.38 for the *Evangel* and 5.46 for *Good News*. This is partly explained by the disproportionate amount of space devoted to reports of revival meetings and church planting in the first few years of the movement's existence. There was great excitement and enthusiasm in those years and this was reflected in both content and layout. Large headlines, photographs and detailed stories appeared highlighting the very effective missions being conducted by the Church. Also, there were no articles from overseas. All were written by Apostolic leaders in Australia.[13]

Revival Echoes **cover, 1934.**

Teaching articles were present from the beginning, however, and increased in number over the years. *Christian life* was clearly the favoured theme. Thirty-nine of 180 articles (21.7%) were specifically devoted to areas of faith, hope, love, Christian service and the like. If features on victorious living (3.3%), discipleship (2.78%), holiness (3.3%) and consecration (2.2%) are added, one third of all articles (33.33%) related to this area. Perhaps this is indicative of a later phase in the development of Pentecostalism. Although the Apostolic Church had its own particular emphases, it was recognised that with the development of the movement, it was necessary to address the day-by-day issues of simply living the life, a situation that all emerging groups necessarily confront at some point.

Here again, *the Second Coming* was a favoured theme. Some ten percent of articles were devoted to this. Ten percent were also dedicated to the various works of *the Holy Spirit*. Eleven pieces specifically explained *the gospel* (6.1%). The baptism in the Holy Spirit was emphasised (5%), as were other topics like baptism in water, the person of Christ, unity, the attributes of God and the authority of the Bible. It is surprising that only three articles in ten years were specifically devoted to divine healing. However, this is balanced by numerous reports and testimonies of recovery from illness and disease. In contrast to the other journals, two distinctive themes were evident. One was *church government and ministry*. Given that the Apostolic Church majored on its distinctive understanding of the role of apostles and prophets, this was to be expected. There were 16 articles on these topics (8.8%). The other distinctive area was that of *Bible Study*. Seventeen issues contained studies on the Bible itself (9.4%). There was clearly a strong commitment to teaching people to be biblically literate. In addition to these, there was also a series of studies for young people on the Pauline epistles.

General perspective

Overall, a study of the themes pursued in all three journals shows clearly the prominence of preaching on the second coming. Over one fifth of articles were devoted to this theme. Christian life was the second major area. The third was the work of the Holy Spirit (see Tables 11 and 12).

It is evident that Pentecostal writers covered a fairly wide range of topics, consistent with their basically Evangelical position. When it came to the practical realities of the Christian faith and practice, the crucial issues were still those of everyday living, commitment, discipleship, holiness and devotion to God. It is noteworthy that tithing was given reasonable attention in all three journals. No matter how spiritual a church, it still takes money to keep it going.

It is fair to ask what issues were not dealt with. Plainly, social questions received scant attention, apart from the regular reports in *Good News* during the Depression years on their welfare program. Neither was there any significant political comment, apart from interpreting world events as indicators of the fulfilment of biblical prophecies. Nor was there any serious criticism of the views of other churches. Where there were critical comments, they were usually reserved for those who doubted the veracity of Scripture. Otherwise, the views of others tended to be treated with respect.

Table 11 Topics of articles in Pentecostal journals 1913 to 1945.

Topic	No	%
Second coming, world events etc	227	22.08
Christian life	148	14.40
Baptism and gifts of HS	125	12.16
Discipleship, victorious living, consecration, holiness	116	11.28
The gospel	85	8.27
Divine healing	62	6.03

Table 12 Comparison of topics in Pentecostal journals.

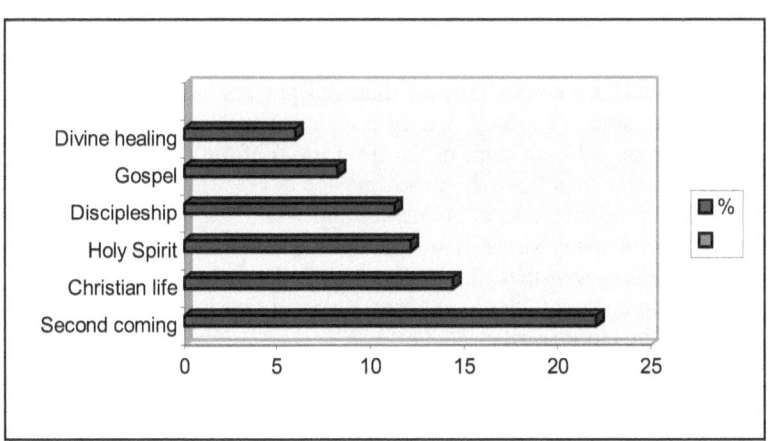

William John Enticknap

For over 40 years William John (Will) Enticknap was an Assembly of God pastor in several Australian States. Although he was State chairman for Queensland and also served on the Commonwealth Executive of the Assemblies of God, he never had a reputation as an outstanding minister or leader. In many ways, he represents the average Pentecostal pastor who plodded on week after week, faithfully fulfilling his ministry and doing his best to live and work in the spirit of Pentecost.

A collection of 177 of his sermon notes has survived roughly covering the period 1928–1956, although most are undated. These provide a fascinating insight into the kind of themes and topics Pentecostal ministers in small suburban and country churches might have been preaching, especially during the 1920s, 1930s and 1940s. They also show a man who was not, as might be suspected, preoccupied with narrow Pentecostal themes, but who ranged widely over many biblical topics and whose major concern was always to keep a central focus on the key issue of one's relationship with God.

Will's father, W. J. Enticknap Sr, was a self-taught man who, according to his daughter, 'could do anything.'[14] He eventually settled near Macknade in North Queensland, where he established a cane farm and his reputation as a handyman, amateur surveyor, repairman and even bush doctor soon spread. The rough track to the distant doctor's surgery was too difficult. 'If somebody broke their arm they'd come to him.'[15]

After his wife died of tuberculosis around 1900, when Will was the youngest of three children, W. J. remarried and another six children were born into the family, including Charles Golding (b.1905), who also became a Pentecostal pastor.[16]

For young Will, farm life provided many an illustration of Christian living. In later years, he remembered how as a boy, he had to plough straight furrows with five horses abreast and how the lads on the farm used to try to excel each other keeping the lines straight. It was a good pattern for life.[17] On another occasion, he observed the piles at Lucinda Point wharf absorbing the bumps of the boats docking, a lesson about resilience[18] and when a young man from England came to work on the farm he saw how his mother's prayers followed him around the world until he came to Christ.[19] A deep impression was made on him by the word 'Mizpah' engraved on a shell in the front room of the farm house. Later, he preached on that word at least 16 times.[20]

W. J. Enticknap became a local councillor and was a vice-president of a farmers' association for many years. It was in this capacity that, around 1920, he journeyed to Melbourne, at that time the seat of Federal Government. There it appears he came in contact with Good News Hall and first heard about a Pentecostal baptism in the Holy Spirit.

In 1923, Annie Dennis, leader of the Hebron assembly in Mackay, North Queensland,[21] visited the home and many of the family were baptized in the Holy Spirit.[22] The whole household was transformed. In the small hours of the morning, W. J. Enticknap would wake up and shout, 'Glory! Hallelujah!' And he would begin to pray in tongues. Soon others were awake and 'all over the house everybody was awake… praising the Lord.'[23]

Often 80 or 90 attended meetings in the large farmhouse dining room and within a few months 40 were baptized with the Spirit. Prior to this, the family had been reaching out to the Islanders, in the Halifax area in particular. Once valued as cheap labour, these people were now outcasts, unable or unwilling to return to their native lands but without basic rights to vote or to engage in significant occupations in Australia.[24] They were often wild and undisciplined in their behaviour and alcohol was a problem. The coming of the Holy Spirit made a huge difference. Previously, there had only been three or four conversions. Now there were 19 in five months including Charlie Coal, a notorious drinker. Another old man named Mundey could barely walk, but stumbled along with shuffling steps murmuring, 'Prayers Hin, prayers Hin.' He knew a handful of Bible passages and set a good example of steadfast faith.[25] For the Enticknaps, there was no difference between people. They were all welcome in their home. It was now known as the Beulah Mission House.[26]

At the end of the year, Enticknap wrote, 'A lovely year she (1924) proved to be. My life was crowned with liberty... right to His temple, Jesus came!' Thirty-one people had been baptized in the Spirit and a number in water. There were meetings being held at six different locations.[27] When floods threatened the district, 21 people, mainly Italians, sought refuge in the large Enticknap home—and found themselves in prayer meetings. After that they often came voluntarily.[28]

Ministry

Young Will now began to sense a calling from God to ministry. Early in 1925, he saw a vision of small companies of people rising up in several places and heard the voice of the Lord say, 'What have I healed you for?'[29] Shortly after this, he was asked by his brother Charles to assist with a tent campaign in Townsville. The tent was destroyed in a storm before they conducted even one service and Will was left to continue meetings in Townsville. It was a challenge for Will. Charles, not he, was the preacher. He had tried often, but found it well nigh impossible. Now, in Townsville, the words started to flow. Soon they had purchased another tent and they baptized 16 people in the Ross River.[30]

In that same year, the Townsville church followed the example of Good News Hall and adopted the name Apostolic Faith Mission, and Will, now married to Jean, was installed as pastor. After a visit by the evangelist F. B. Van Eyk earlier that year, some 40 people were attending tarry meetings and 70–80 were regularly attending Sunday morning services with over 100 turning up at night. One Sunday in July, Enticknap spoke on the fellowship of the Cross and many in the congregation were moved to tears. A year later, the attendances were holding. In October, 16 were immersed in a service held at the Baptist church, and 30 had been baptized in the Spirit. Open air meetings were, as with most Pentecostal assemblies, a strong part of the work. Every Saturday and Sunday night most of the believers testified on street corners. 'Great interest is shown by the public,' wrote Enticknap, 'and they stand around for the whole length of the service.' When Winnie Andrews visited, she reported that people were 'arrested by the power of God.' She also spoke highly of the 'faithful way' in which Will and Jean Enticknap were shepherding their flock.[31]

In 1932, Will launched out again with a tent, and although he had suffered with a bad throat for a long time, he was preaching every night except Monday without any trouble. He was gratified with the results. The meetings were 'fine' and God's presence was 'felt mightily.'[32] In 1934, they settled in Parkes, NSW, where Will's pronounced Queensland accent was a curiosity.[33] Three years later they moved to Maryborough, whence they journeyed to Scotland in 1939. From 1943 to February 1945, they served in Mackay. That same year, they returned to Townsville, where they stayed till 1948.[34] Around this time, Will became superintendent of the Queensland assemblies and in 1957, he was appointed to the Commonwealth Executive of the Assemblies of God.[35] The same year, he was ministering in Perth. By 1964, he was back in Queensland, pastoring in Bundaberg.[36]

Will and Jean were clearly much appreciated by the people they served. A letter from a woman named N. Parry reads—

Assemblies of God church, Parkes, NSW.

> Dear Brother and Sister,
>
> Sweet peace in the precious name of Jesus.
>
> Please except [sic] these H/kerchiefs as a keepsake. My dear brother, I thank you for your wonderful help in my spiritual life your gracious words have helped me to keep pussing [sic] on and trying to be a good christain [sic]. And my dear sister your actions and your holiness have been a lesson to me many times. I know my brother & sister I have grieved you many times in my own home by the foolish & fleshly things I have said but I wont [sic] you to know I have always been convicted after you left & asked Jesus to forgive me, I do love my Jesus and wish I could be better but I trust the next time we meet that I will have grown in grace & the knowledge of our Lord & Saviour Jesus Christ. I pray God will richly bless you both & that many souls shall be won through the ministry of my best beloved brother. God bless you sister & brother.[37]

Evidently, patience and gentleness were qualities of the Enticknaps' ministry. On the other hand, Will was neither articulate nor refined. One of his fellow-ministers observed—

He was a simple fellow. He loved the Lord. He was not dynamic, but he was faithful and loving and you could rely on him. His was a regular and constant faithfulness. The first three times I heard Will preach it was the same message, on the prodigal son. The major points, I can well remember. When the son left home, he said, 'Father, give me.' When he came back, he said, 'Father, make me.' He said that so often in the one sermon. I thought he must have only known the one sermon.[38]

Like many of his peers, Will Enticknap tended to equate simplicity of life style with saintliness. He always wore a cheap suit and travelled second class by train. To go first class in a sleeper—that would have been wasting God's money. When he travelled, even in his role as State chairman, he usually paid his own way. He and Jean 'gave themselves to the gospel'. They also held strong convictions about divine healing. He and his wife used to boast that they hadn't been to a doctor in 50 years.[39]

Will Enticknap.
Photo, Ricmond Temple Souvenir, 1939.

The Sermons

There are 177 sermons in the collection. They are nearly all hand written, in ink, in Enticknap's backward-sloping, thick-penned script on note paper. Some run into several pages; most occupy three or four. A few, evidently put together in haste, are single sheets. Unfortunately, there does not seem to be any clear order of arrangement. Only two of the addresses are dated (1928 and 1929), although dates can be deduced from the contents for seven of the others (1934, 1939, 1940, 1942, 1945, 1956 and 1959). There are still difficulties, as the 1956 sermon, for example, was preached in seven different places, obviously in other years, and the 1942 sermon was given in five places all told. There seem to be 399 preaching occasions all told. The extant notes are probably re-writes of earlier messages.

Generally, Enticknap wrote the names of the towns where he preached at the beginning of each set of notes. These make it possible to place most of the notes safely in the 1920s, 30s and 40s, at least in their earliest format. In a few cases, on the basis of his ministry career, it is also possible to assess the chronological order—although this is not as easy as it might seem, given that most were preached more than once. It is not even safe to try to link the kind of ink or paper used for the notes with the place-name, as it is clear that the notes were often revised and in some cases re-written, or partly re-written. Furthermore, often the names of the venues seem to have been added later. A few of the notes are written with ball point pen, which suggests they may be from the post-war period.

It is obvious that some were Enticknap's favourites. 'Mizpah' was preached at least 16 times. 'God's Dwelling Place' was delivered on nine occasions and 'World at the Crossroads', 'Baptism of Fire', 'Aeronautics' and 'Converted and Convicted' were used eight times each. 'Not Without Blood' was presented on seven occasions.

Table 13 Summary of topics in 177 sermons of William John Enticknap.

Topic	Number of times preached	Topic	Number of times preached
Discipleship	36	Word of God	7
The Gospel	32	Person etc of Jesus	6
Fellowship with God	28	Baptism in Water	5
Christian Living	27	Healing/deliverance etc	5
Second Coming	27	Encouragement	5
Fullness of Holy Spirit	25	The flesh and the Spirit	5
Christian Victory	24	Fruitfulness	4
Joy	24	Repentance	4
Christian character	15	Unity	4
Salvation/conversion	14	Will of God	4
Faith	11	Christmas/New Year etc	3
Love of God	11	The Cross	3
Prayer	9	Children's talks	2
Presence of God	9	Glory/greatness of God	2
Commitment	8	Church	1
Holiness	7	Sufficiency	1
Obedience	7	Trinity	1
Power of Praise	7	Truth	1
Trust in God	7		

In addition to the sermon notes, there are nine radio talks. These were all presented from April to August 1944 in Mackay and then, probably later, at Townsville. They follow a standard format of prayer, Scripture reading and message. Because they are written in full, they also provide examples of Enticknap's expression and style.

There are also several sets of notes. One is on 'Pastoralia'—a 40-page series of talks on ministerial conduct and ethics. Another is a study outline of the poetical books of the Bible. There are over 100 pages of studies on the book of Revelation, all but a few of which are handwritten. Finally, there is a note book dated 1 January 1927, in which there are 45 pages of Bible studies. Another note book, commenced 17 October 1927, has over 300 pages of comprehensive Bible Study material evidently compiled by Jean

While the note books are in excellent condition, most of the other papers are frayed at the edges, with corners turned and writing faded. Generally, the writing is legible, with only an occasional word indecipherable. Enticknap preferred to use shorthand notebook sheets, but at times he used anything from obviously high quality bond writing leaves to folded typing sheets, evidently to fit easily between the pages of his Bible.

Although there are regular spelling mistakes of some words (e.g. rememberance; Isreal; Dueteronomy), Will Enticknap could put words together well enough. This is reflected in some of his outlines. His notes are laid out artistically, with attention to sequences of ideas and sometimes alliteration.

In 'Passion Fruit', we read—

>Not a Fleshly Passion

>Not an Evil Passion

>But a Holy Passion

>But a Godly Passion

>After Christ, the Eternal Tree of Life.

>Say, Beloved, What Variety of Passion Fruit
>Are we producing? God grant it may be—

>a Holy one

>a Godly one

>a Passion for Him Who became to us

>a Tree of Life
>through the Death of the Cross

'God's Dwelling Place' follows a simple structure—

>At Eden (Gen 3:8), we find God in a Garden

>At Horeb (Ex 3:4), we find God in a Bush

>At Pi-Hahiroth (Ex 14:24), we find God in a Pillar

At Horeb (Ex 40:34–35), we find God in a Tabernacle

At Jerusalem (2 Chron 7:1–3), we find God in a Temple

Through Paul (2 Cor 5:19), we find God in Christ

Through Paul (1 Cor 3:16), we find God in You.

Enticknap's style is illustrated well in some of his radio talks. At times, his prayers, in particular, indicate his feeling for words. That he was well steeped in Scripture is also plain, as much of his imagery is biblical—

> Father, we thank Thee because we feel thy everlasting arms enfolding us and our souls following hard after thee. O God thou who art full of boundless compassion, when the pressure of evil lies heavy upon us, and we are prone to view the seething, struggling sea of humanity with hopeless eyes, be pleased to give us that touch of thine that will cause us to keep our hope in thee. And when the cruse of oil and the Barrel [sic] of meal seems to be about exhausted, open thou thy hand, and satisfy our souls, for no good thing wilt thou withhold from them that diligently seek thee (26 July 1944).

He demonstrates a tenderness in speaking of the bereaved—

> ...when it seems like the last earthly tie has been snapped. No one to turn to, no one to weep with you. Yet what a peace steals over the heart of such a one as they... realise that God is a very present help in time of trouble (3 May 1944).

Themes

Although Will Enticknap was a pioneer Pentecostal pastor, teaching about the baptism and gifts of the Holy Spirit occupied a relatively minor part of his public ministry. Only 25 of 399 messages were devoted to the former, only five to the latter, an average overall of 7.5%. It is true that when he does speak on this subject, he does so forcefully—

> Let us then allow God Who is a Consuming Fire to Melt away the Mountains of difficulties etc. Burn up the Brushwood of Vain thoughts etc.
>
> *Beloved*, By the Power of His Holy Presence your heart can get *warmed up*... can *Bubble up* like Boiling water.
>
> *The Presence* Makes our Affections warm up.
>
> We won't come to Church in a half hearted way
>
> We won't be waiting for another to Pray
>
> We won't be relying on another to exercise the gifts

> *Lukewarmness* will flit. It cannot exist where the fire burns.
>
> *Our hearts* will have Burning desires... Clothed with Burning Words.
>
> *Our tongues* Will become a flame of Fire to speak forth the glories of His Name. For He Makes His Ministers A Flame of Fire
>
> — from 'Revival'.

and,

> With God's mighty Spirit filled Influence,
>
> It's a Wonderful life to live.
>
> Privilege to enjoy.
>
> Power to possess
>
> — from 'Spirit Possessed Men'

and again,

> Say Beloved, Are you glad you Believe in Pentecost?
>
> Have you been Immersed In the Holy Ghost Since you Believed? If not, Claim the Promise now. Just where you are. You can be filled...
>
> — from 'Pentecost'.

Generally, he offers a wide catalogue of topics. Much of his preaching is standard evangelical fare. 'Mizpah' was a place of watchfulness, a place to meet God, a place of prayer and fasting, a place of setting things right, a place of fulfilling vows and a place of safety. This focus on fellowship with God was central to all his preaching. His most popular theme was *discipleship*, which he addressed in all manner of ways and from many different angles. But the message was the same: the need to be committed unswervingly to Christ. The combined themes of *discipleship*, fellowship with God, Christian living, Christian victory, Christian character, holiness and obedience represent 36% of his preaching. The proclamation of *the gospel* was also important, covering about 12.5% of topics, and implied in many others. *The second coming* was another significant theme, on a par with *fellowship with God* and *the fullness of the Holy Spirit* (6.75%). One of his favourite messages was, 'World at the Crossroads' which he preached at least eight times. While not directly teaching about the second coming, he made several references to political and international signs which indicated 'the rise of the Antichrist' and the subsequent coming of the Lord.

It is in his notes on Revelation, however, that his interest in end-times flourishes. He takes a pre-millennial, pre-tribulation-rapture perspective in his interpreting of the book. Consequently, wherever possible, he reads the text literalistically. The temple of Revelation 11 is an actual bricks-and-mortar structure. The two witnesses (John and Daniel?) prophesy for a literal three and a half years. The Millennium lasts a literal 1000 years. With usual pre-millennial inconsistency, however, he has no hesitation in seeing the 'great whore' of Revelation 17 as 'ecclesiastical Rome' or the seven-headed Beast of Revelation 13 as symbolic of human power.

It is interesting that Enticknap's views are clearly at odds with the approach taught by Dr Kelso Glover in the Pentecostal Church of Australia's Victorian Bible Institute in Melbourne in 1925. Jean Enticknap evidently attended the Institute and wrote detailed notes of Glover's lectures, which are included in the Enticknap papers. Clearly, Will did not adopt Glover's interpretation. Like most others in the Pentecostal movement, he was a dispensationalist.

Throughout, there is a passion for Christ and a genuine love for people. Enticknap's pastoral concerns are obvious. In 'God's Burying Ground,' he expounds Colossians 3. We have died, he explains, and our lives are hidden with Christ in God. Even more, we are buried. So we are dead to our own desires, yet nevertheless, we live an abundant life. We live in the secret place with God, under the shadow of the Almighty. The hidden life is a joyful life, where nothing can quench the faith or wound the heart.

There is an irenic spirit about Enticknap's preaching. There are no attacks on other churches. He is more concerned for the growth and development of his own church than with the failings of others. He does warn against the rising tides of Communism and Fascism. Islam, too, is a threat on the world scene. But the plans of Stalin and Mussolini might not work out as they expect— hitherto, all empires have been 'impeded by the Providence of God' ('World at the Crossroads'). He sees the world as the implacable foe of the church.

Apart from these references and the occasional lament about the state of society, there is no attempt to address social issues or to espouse a biblical philosophy of politics or social ethics. There is neither discussion of party politics nor comment on political affairs. It is impossible to learn anything about Government or Opposition from Enticknap's sermons. Some clergymen, like the Methodist John Lee, might have stood for parliament, but such activities might as well have been in another world, for all Enticknap apparently cared.[40] In spite of his family's early concern to reach out to Islanders and Aboriginals, there is no reference in his preaching to justice or to compensation in the wake of events such as the 1926 Forrest River massacre and the subsequent 1927 Royal Commission. In one sense, it would have been surprising if there had been, given that most churches had little to say on the subject.[41] But for Enticknap, the best answer for everyone, including Aborigines, was the gospel of Jesus Christ, and to present that in every possible way was his task.

Nor did the Great Depression extract any comment from him. While the first decade of his ministry covered the Depression period, his simple focus was still to preach the Word of God. When people sorted out their relationship with God, the rest would fall into place. He was equally unmoved by contemporary theological debates such as the so-called 'Angus affair,' if he was even aware of them.[42] To him, the Bible was God's Word, inspired by the same Holy Spirit who had so dramatically and so convincingly come upon him in 1924.

The notebook of Bible studies illustrates his simple and untroubled confidence in Scripture. It begins with the theme of 'The Original Condition of Man.' This is followed by a few pages on the Fall and ten pages outlining the condition of humanity and its future destiny outside of Christ. Other studies then follow on repentance, Levitical offerings, Joseph as a type of Christ, the tongue, life, 'The Alliterated Life of Christ,' salvation, an outline of Paul's epistles and a brief study on 2 Timothy. In the main, these are lists of Scripture references and quotations, with little or no comment. There is also a set of 26 memo pages of Bible Study notes on the Poetic books.

Jean Enticknap's notebook contains over 300 pages of neatly written studies on a wide range of subjects. Some of these appear to be Sunday School lessons ('Boys and girls'—p.16), but the majority are for adults. Some of the topics are: the Life of Christ, faith, Moses as a type of Christ, Joseph as a type of Christ, the attributes of God, salvation, the atonement, baptism, the Trinity, the life of Christ, the Holy Spirit—in fact, a fair outline of a course in basic introductory theology. There are some additional sets of notes on light (4 pp), justification (2 pp), the Word (2 pp), the life and divinity of Christ (4 pp), the Bride (4 pp), the Holy Spirit (3 pp) and Romans (7 pp). Like her husband's notes, these are mostly lists of relevant Scripture references and quotations, with some brief annotations.

Ethics

The 40 pages of Will Enticknap's notes on 'pastoralia' are evidently teaching notes prepared for ministerial trainees, probably delivered at an Assemblies of God Bible School. They reflect much sound, homespun common sense. 'Our own mistakes are often our best teachers,' he says. And, 'Don't fight with every fellow who comes around the corner with a chip on his shoulder.' He advises his students to listen both carefully and kindly to those with problems. And as for 'chronic trouble breeders,' there was only one cure: exclusion. Too many pastors had been dismissed from their pulpits through the efforts of one dissident.

There is a high view of ethics and integrity. These notes cover areas such as the calling of a pastor ('the noblest calling'), attitude to money and gifts ('It is better to do without than to be in debt'), resolving conflict, family responsibilities, character qualities ('living above reproach'), visitation and preaching. In ministry to the opposite sex, it was wise to have a 'trusted sister' present. Enticknap is not naive. Some older men were worse offenders than young men in this area. It was incumbent on a minister 'to be scrupulously honest'. It is interesting to observe that he draws on materials from Congregational, Presbyterian and even Unitarian codes. Prejudice was not a problem for Will Enticknap.

While the spirit of Pentecost was distinctively demonstrated through the charismata—it was something to be *experienced*—an examination of Pentecostal writing and preaching shows that this experience embraced more than the charismata. It ranged across the whole of life. Everything was different. It was not enough to use the gifts of the Holy Spirit; the fruits of the Spirit were to be cultivated too. The result was not only a more powerful lifestyle but a more gracious one.

One simple statement expresses the essence of Will Enticknap's philosophy of ministry—

> A gentleman may not be a Christian but a Christian must always endeavour to be a gentleman.

This may not be the popular caricature of a Pentecostal preacher, but popular caricatures are not always correct.

Overall, the major emphasis in Pentecostal preaching was on lifestyle and Christian character. While there was a keen interest in eschatology, the primary thrust here was still on the need to be ready for the return of Christ by living a holy life. Furthermore, when individual topics such as Christian life, discipleship and victorious living are combined, it is plain that there were far more sermons and articles on this general theme than anything else. There was a strong concern for integrity and uprightness.

Even the distinctive Pentecostal topic of baptism in the Holy Spirit was seen in the light of the holiness and separation from worldliness that would result.

The evangelical and sanctifying tributaries from which Pentecostalism grew, while now merged with the gifts and power of the Holy Spirit into a broader river, still largely directed the flow.

Notes

1. At Good News Hall, for example, there were seven weekly services plus three open air meetings. The Apostolic Church in Adelaide held ten services most weeks, not counting children's and youth meetings.

2. In the case of the *Australian Evangel*, I have gone to 1945. This is technically outside the period covered by this thesis, but it offers a more useable range of articles and a more comprehensive overview of topics and themes. There seems no reason to believe there was any significant change of emphasis from 1939–1945, with the exception of eschatology, which was clearly heightened by the incidence of war. There were over twice as many articles on this theme in the 1940–1945 issues as there were from 1930–1939.

3. F. Mortomore, 'The Dragon's Plot, GN, 14:11, November, 1923, 3f.

4. One particularly graphic article featured a sketch of several tombstones each representing the deaths of the heathen in various countries and each inscribed with the sentence, 'Will meet you at the judgement.' The article concluded, 'Are you doing your best? Are you giving until it hurts? Is your whole being so saturated with the love of God that, momentarily, there heaves that intercession for the heathen?'— GN, 18:7, July, 1927, 16.

5. GN, 19:6, June, 1928, 12.

6. It is not possible to identify the origins of all the teaching articles, but at least 340 (53.7%) of the 633 under consideration were of overseas origin.

7. This was the view that the end of the age would be marked by a time of intense tribulation, usually thought to be of seven years' duration, during which God's wrath would be poured out on the earth. However, those who formed the Bride of Christ would be caught up to meet the Lord in the air prior to the Tribulation, and while the inhabitants of the earth were suffering, they would enjoy the marriage supper of the Lamb. To be a member of the Bride, it was necessary to be baptized in the Holy Spirit, to live a consecrated life and to be an overcomer. Nominal believers would still be saved, but they would first have to endure the Tribulation. Then, Christ would return to the earth in great power, accompanied by the overcomers, bringing judgment on the wicked and rescuing the rest of the saints.

The parable of the virgins made it plain that it was important to be ready for His first coming. The rapture would occur simultaneously all over the world—some would be in bed and some in the fields. During the time of Tribulation, the Antichrist would appear. The Jewish nation was like the budding fig tree of which Jesus spoke, and there were now sure signs of the return of the Lord. The Jews were returning to Palestine and ere long the Temple would be rebuilt, in fact, 'operations were already in progress' to this end. At the end of the Tribulation, the nations would all gather around Jerusalem in battle, but then, at the blackest moment, Christ would come in power, like the lightning flashing across the sky, and destroy the nations at Armageddon. The Jews, so dramatically rescued from their hour of imminent destruction, would recognise Christ and believe in Him. See GN, 15:5, May, 1924, 2ff; GN, 15:6, June, 1924, 10; GN, 16:5, May, 1925, 3f; GN, 17:7, July, 1926, 12f; GN, 18:11, November, 1927, 6; GN, 19:9, September, 1928, 6f. The best overall summary is given in an article on the Second Coming by F. B. Van Eyk in GN, 18:10, October, 1927, 3–8. For a comprehensive more recent treatment of the pre-millennial view see Pentecost, 1981.

8. GN, 15:6, June, 1924, 11; GN, 15:8, August, 1924, 9; GN, 18:12, December, 1927, 8; H. Motherwell, 'An Emperor of the Latins?' GN, 21:7, July, 1930, 9ff; N. C. Beskin, 'The Mark of the Beast,' GN, 22:11, November, 1931, 4; GN, 25:6, June, 1934, 10–13; GN, 15:5, May, 1924, 3; GN, 16:11, November, 1925, 10; GN, 20:6, June, 1929, 9; GN, 23:6, June, 1932, 8; GN, 25:2, February, 1934, 7; GN, 22:11, November, 1931, 8.

9. Blumhofer, 1989, 17ff; Faupel, 1996.

10. Piggin, 1996, 80.

11. AE, 4:5, April, 1938, 6.

12. AE, 7:7, June, 1941, 14.

13. There is an interesting area for further investigation here. In Good News Hall and with the Assemblies of God, the leadership was primarily Australian-born. With the Apostolic Church, it was primarily of British origin. Perhaps the relative proportion of printed material from overseas reflects this. While the Australian leaders saw value in supplementing their teaching with useful material from elsewhere, those who had themselves come from overseas may have seen little need for further overseas input.

14. Agnes Davidson (nee Enticknap), personal interview, 20 November, 1990.

15. Agnes Davidson, personal interview, 20 November, 1990.

16. The other members of the family were Ambrosia, Helen, James, Charles, Agnes, Rebecca, Rhoda and Lawrie. Agnes married Hugh Davidson and served with him for many years in Papua New Guinea as a missionary; Rhoda married Les Crispe and continued as a faithful member of the Assemblies of God. P. Davidson, personal interview, 15 April, 1993; Chant, 1984, 46; GN, 15:6, June, 1924, 8. See Appendix B for more on the Enticknap family.

17. W. Enticknap, 'The Ploughman and the Plough,' sermon notes, n.d.

18. W. Enticknap, 'Taking the Bumps,' sermon notes, n.d.

19. W. Enticknap, 'The Value of a Soft Heart,' sermon notes, n.d.

20. W. Enticknap, 'A Wonderful Word,' sermon notes, n.d.

21. C. G. E(nticknap), 'They Shall Be Abundantly Satisfied,' GN, 15:9, September, 1924, 9; Agnes E(nticknap), letter dated June 25, 1924, 'Sister Dennis came here five months ago...'; GN, 15:8, August, 1924, 11; GN, 15:9, September, 1924, 11, 18. Annie Dennis was introduced to the Pentecostal message by Florrie Mortomore of Good news Hall and presumably, the Hebron congregation was connected with the Hall.

22. C. G. Enticknap, 'Address given at Calvary Temple, Townsville, Qld,' 13 May, 1984.

23. C. G. Enticknap, 'Address,' Rosewater, 17 October, 1965.

24. G. M. Clark, *A Short History of Australia* (Ringwood: Penguin, 1986), 175ff.

25. Agnes E(nticknap), GN 15:8 August 1924, p.11; Agnes Davidson, personal interview, 20 November, 1990.

26. GN, 15:6, June, 1924, 8; 15:12, December, 1924, 14.

27. GN, 16:1, January, 1925, 7; GN, 16:2, February, 1925, 9; GN, 16:3, March, 1925, 16.

28. GN, 18:7, July, 1927, 7; Agnes Davidson, personal interview, 20 November, 1990. One of these men occasionally used to hide a small whisky flask in his hip pocket, where Enticknap could not see it. One night, alone in the bush, he was accosted and threatened by an Islander. In fear and trembling, he took out the flask. His assailant thought it was a gun and fled.

29. *Richmond Temple Souvenir,* 1939, 48.

30. C. G. Enticknap, 'Address given at Calvary Temple,' Townsville, 13 May, 1984.

31. GN, 19:9, September, 1928, 11; GN, 19:9, September, 1928, 13; GN, 19:11, November, 1928, 11; GN, 19:12, December, 1928, 13; GN, 20:5, May, 1929, 14; GN, 21:10, October, 1930, 10.

32. GN, 23:7, July, 1932, 13.

33. C. and O. Tanswell, personal interview, 20 December, 1993.

34. AE, 5:8, July, 1939, 13; *Richmond Temple Souvenir,* 1939, 48; AE, 5:8, July, 1939, 13; *Richmond Temple Souvenir,* 1939, 48; AE, 7:3, June, 1934, 1,11; AE, 3:10, September, 1937, 8; AE, 11:5, April, 1945, 24; Minutes, Mackay Assembly of God, 28 October, 1943 and 15 February 1945; AE, 11:7, June, 1945, 24; AE, 12:10, September, 1946, 24; AE, 13:12, November, 1947, 24; AE, 14:10, September, 1948, 32.

35. AE, 14:5, April, 1957, 11

36. AE, 14:7, June, 1957, 32; AE, 16:3, February, 1959, 32; Norman Smallcombe, personal interview, 30 January, 1994; AE, 21:11, November, 1964, 22.

37. There is no information as to the date of this letter. I have a copy in my possession.

38. F. Lancaster, personal interview, 18 December, 1993.

39. F. Lancaster, personal interview, 18 December, 1993.

40. Thompson, 1994, 67.

41. Breward, 1993, 124f.

42. Emilson, 1991; Breward, 1993, 129; Piggin, 1996, 92ff.

APPENDIX A

Bibliographical Essay[1]

It is over twenty years since the first attempt at an historical overview of Australian Pentecostalism was produced, which was my own volume *Heart of Fire* (1973). Apart from a revision of this book in 1984, and a couple of loyal denominational chronicles,[2] nothing else substantial has been published. One looks in vain for credible histories of the Australian movement. However, encouraging developments are to be seen in the prolific work of Mark Hutchinson, former Director of Sydney's Centre for the Study of Australian Christianity, who is also researching aspects of Australian Pentecostal history and has written numerous journal articles on this subject[3]; and some recent publications on Australian Christian history do include chapters or segments on Pentecostalism. In 1982, D. Harris, D. Hynd, D. Millikan were among the first to do so in *The Shape of Belief*.[4] Tabernee and Gribben included chapters on Pentecostal practice in their series on Australian Churches (1984–1987)[5] as did Ian Gillman in his bicentennial *Many Faiths—One Nation*.[6]

In his *Evangelical Christianity in Australia: Spirit, word and world,* Australian historian and evangelical scholar Stuart Piggin makes frequent references to the Pentecostal movement and to its first-born heir, the charismatic renewal.[7] Ian Breward[8] and Hilary Carey both give serious consideration to it.[9] The Centre for the Study of Australian Christianity included chapters by or about Pentecostalism in some recent publications.[10] Humphreys and Ward also include valuable information on Pentecostal churches in their *Religious Bodies in Australia.*[11] Philip Hughes's recent volume *Pentecostals in Australia* is a valuable, comprehensive survey of the contemporary movement.[12]

The work of Australian sociologist Alan Black offers valuable insights which suggest lines of inquiry for the early movement.[13] The Christian Research Association, established in Melbourne in 1985, has provided a wealth of statistical and sociological data on many aspects of Australian Christian life, both in their published books and the regular newsletter *Pointers*. Among other works, the annual *A Yearbook of Australian Religious Organisations*, with its useful directories on all churches, including Pentecostal, has become a standard reference.[14] Similarly, the findings of the National Church Life Survey have provided a contextual framework for a study of Pentecostalism in the 1990s.[15]

Overseas movements have been better documented. Some of the early histories were basically just chronicles of people and events, with little attempt to evaluate their doctrines or practice or to relate them to the wider church. These include titles like Stanley Frodsham's *With Signs Following*[16], Gordon Atter's *The Third Force*[17], Donald Gee's *Upon All Flesh*[18] and Klaude Kendrick's *The Promise Fulfilled*[19]. Although serving a genuine need, in that they record information that might otherwise have been irretrievably lost, generally, these are patchy and uneven in content. Australia, in particular, is given scant and inadequate attention.

In more recent years, other general histories have been published which are more comprehensive. British charismatic leader Michael Harper's *As at the Beginning* (1966) is brief but thorough.[20] J. T. Nicholl's *The Pentecostals*, originally presented as a thesis, and published in America in 1970, showed more discipline than the earlier works.[21] *The Pentecostal Movement*, a revision of an earlier work in Norwegian (1956), by Nils Bloch-Hoell, theologian and one-time lecturer at the University of Oslo, and the first history written by a non-Pentecostal, was published in English in 1964.[22] It was also the first history presented from a more critical perspective. 'To Pentecostal readers unused at the time... to objective and critical scrutiny, the sociological and phenomenological analysis of their institutions, beliefs and worship was at first unsettling'.[23]

Since then, others outside the movement have also documented it. Best-known and, in spite of its lecture-note style, most authoritative is Walter Hollenweger's *The Pentecostals*.[24] First published in Switzerland in 1969, the book appeared in English in 1972, with several revisions since then. Hollenweger, a former Pentecostal pastor, writes from the perspective of one who has been both within and without the movement. However, there is little about Australia in the book and its value lies in its international perspective.[25] The same can be said of David Harrell's work on American Pentecostal evangelists.[26] Although restricted to North America, it is thoroughly documented and carefully presented. Harrell is himself not a Pentecostal, but his dispassionate approach is neither cynical nor sceptical.

American Pentecostal historian Vinson Synan's *The Holiness-Pentecostal Movement in the United States* (1971) and *Aspects of Pentecostal-Charismatic Origins* (1975)[27] are valuable and objective works.[28] So, too, are Donald Dayton's *Theological Roots of Pentecostalism* (1987) and William Faupel's *The*

Everlasting Gospel: The Significance of Eschatology in the Development of Pentecostal Thought.[29] The 1988 *Dictionary of Pentecostal and Charismatic Movements*[30] was an invaluable addition to the available literature, providing as it does for the first time, a readily accessible source for quick reference for people, places and events in American and European Pentecostalism.[31] Again, because of its confessed focus on the Northern Hemisphere, Australia was omitted, a fault that was rectified in the 2002 revised edition.[32]

A number of denominational histories are also now appearing, the best of which is probably Edith Blumhofer's two volume history of the American Assemblies of God.[33] This is a well-researched and thorough publication which, although written by a member of the Assemblies of God, retains a fair level of objectivity. There are many other such publications documenting the development of various overseas movements. Generally, although offering a rich lode of biographical and narrative sources, they tend to be propagandist in nature.[34]

Sociologists such as Bryan Wilson (1970), Malcolm Calley (1959, 1970) and Robert Anderson (1979) have attempted to explain the rise of Pentecostalism in socio-economic terms.[35] A more recent, and highly readable, assessment is Harvey Cox's *Fire From Heaven* (1994).[36] A 1997 collection of essays on Brazilian Pentecostalism offers interesting historical and sociological insights and theories which can be applied to Australia.[37] These works provide essential resource material and carefully documented analyses of the movement.[38] Here again, with the exception of Calley's study of the Bandjalang Aboriginal people, the research generally makes little reference to Australia.

Since the inception of the Pentecostal movement, there has been a plethora of Pentecostal journals, usually denominational papers or magazines promoting a particular ministry or organisation. Typically, they have followed the party line and been seen as evangelistic or public relations tools. It has been unusual in such periodicals for there to be critical reflection or discussion of controversial issues.

Over the last quarter of a century, however, several scholarly journals have emerged. In the autumn of 1967, the Assemblies of God in the United States launched *Paraclete*, a journal dedicated to 'the person and work of the Holy Spirit, covering such areas as Bible exposition, theology and history' and later, 'contemporary Pentecostal issues.'[39] The result is both a scholarly and a pragmatic approach. A decade later, in the Spring of 1979, the US-based Society for Pentecostal Studies (SPS) introduced *Pneuma*. As SPS is a non-denominational organisation, including members from mainline denominations as well as Pentecostals, *Pneuma* demonstrates greater breadth than *Paraclete,* dealing with a wide-ranging field of issues.[40] Again, there is virtually no reference to Australia in *Pneuma*, but many of the biblical and theological questions dealt with are relevant. The occasional historical piece offers useful comparison with the Australian setting.[41]

The Journal of Pentecostal Theology[42] appeared for the first time in late 1992. It is published by the Church of God School of Theology in Cleveland, Tennessee, and its editorial advisory board includes many international scholars. Its stated purpose is 'to facilitate constructive theological research from a Pentecostal perspective on an international scholarly level.' As its title suggests, the *Journal* contains little historical material, but its reflections on current Pentecostal movements provide useful stimuli for historical investigation.

As overseas, journals in Australia have tended to be mainly house magazines. Although there have been several attempts to publish a non-denominational journal,[43] most have languished, the latest of which was *New Day*, published by Tabor College. Originally formed in 1980 by a merger of Tabor College's *Impact* and Vision Ministries' *Vision*, *New Day* was committed to 'unity and revival.' Hence, it still tended to avoid controversial issues and to steer a middle path, in terms of Pentecostal/charismatic thought and tradition although from time to time, it launched into self-critical waters, boldly questioning common Pentecostal practices.[44]

In January 1993, the first issue of *Barsabbas* was published by the Centre for the Study of Australian Christianity. Describing itself as 'a newsletter for Pentecostal thought' it was fearless in its questioning of accepted theology and culture.[45] However, its life span proved to be very short and by 1994 it had failed. Later in 1993, *Renewal Journal* appeared for the first time. A half-yearly periodical, it declared its aim to be 'a resource in renewal ministries for the whole church,' and the editor's clear intent was to promote and encourage revival and church growth. Subsequent issues showed little indication of a willingness to engage in rigorous scholarly debate or to question popular attitudes.[46]

In 1997 the first issue appeared of *PCBC Journal*, published by the Association of Pentecostal and Charismatic Bible Colleges of Australasia. While modest in its beginnings (only eight A4 pages) this journal hoped to offer a forum for a wide range of academic issues, including history.[47] In 1998, the first editions of both *Australasian Pentecostal Studies* and *The Asian Journal of Pentecostal Studies* appeared. Both contained at least one article of a historical nature.[48]

For Australian scholars, in the area of secondary sources, there is little joy. In terms of general religious history, of course there is a great deal written—and being written—in this country. All the major denominations are well covered with substantial histories. This is also evidenced by the number of conferences on Christianity in Australia and the growing number of journals dealing with Christian history such as *The Journal of Religious History* (1960—) and *Lucas*. The latter, published by the Evangelical History Association, carries occasional articles on Pentecostal and charismatic issues and in some of the former, articles are now beginning to appear about Pentecostalism. Overall, however, historical study of the Pentecostal movement necessitates heavy reliance on primary sources and oral history.[49]

From 1991–1999, the Centre for the Study of Australian Christianity, based at Robert Menzies College, provided a valuable service through conferences and publications. In particular, the series *Studies in Australian Christianity* created a forum for many Australian historians, including those with an interest in things Pentecostal.[50] Naturally, the standard histories of other denominations offer valuable insights into the history of Christianity in this country, and provide the necessary background and setting for the study of Pentecostalism.[51]

Given the nature and topic of this thesis, many of the resources mentioned so far are useful primarily as background materials. It will be obvious from the following pages that the bulk of my research has been carried out with primary sources. There are simply no other resources available for gathering the foundational information required. To my knowledge, apart from my earlier book, this thesis contains the first serious attempt to narrate, document and appraise the beginnings of Australian Pentecostalism. In the following list, I have not attempted to detail all the primary sources: they have nearly all been noted at some stage in the body of the dissertation. What follows here is simply an overview.

Interviews

In researching both for my earlier book and for this thesis, I have conducted over 80 interviews. I did not know, 35 years ago, when I first became interested in the origins of Australian Pentecostalism, anything about the debate between written and oral history, or the fact that in recent years, oral history would hold its head much higher than it was once wont to do. It was simply a matter of locating information wherever I could. I was initially encouraged by hearing talks given by some Pentecostal pioneers. I found their narratives so fascinating, I began to interview other older people whom I knew about, and recording their responses. At that time, I did not always ask the right questions, but I still learned a great deal from those discussions for which I am now grateful and on which I have continued to draw.[52]

Most of the people I interviewed were personally involved in Pentecostalism. In many cases, their parents or grandparents had also been active. Often they were able to provide biographical or genealogical information. On occasion, information gained through interviews proved to be wrong, but this has been surprisingly uncommon. When attempting to verify data either through other interviews, or from reference to the available written sources, I have been gratified at the high level of reliability of the original information.

Transcripts of most of these interviews are in my possession, although some were either totally lost or partially destroyed in a fire which gutted my office in 1987.[53] These documents form a valuable source of biographical and personal information. I have learned a great deal about the people themselves—how they reacted to each other, how they viewed what happened in their meetings and in their fellowship, how they felt about their experience with God, how they saw the world and other churches and so on.[54] It is possible to gain the feel of things through oral history in a way that written history cannot provide. Sometimes in association with an interview and always where distance has made interviews impossible, I have used questionnaires of various kinds.

Journals and Magazines

I have been able to compile a comprehensive set of Pentecostal journals and magazines, the earliest one dating from 1910. The titles are all listed in the bibliography. These have proven to be an invaluable source, especially for hard evidence, and I have derived much of my foundational material from them, in particular *Good News*, the first Pentecostal journal to be published consistently in Australia.[55] Without access to these magazines, this work could never have been written.[56] Unhappily, many of my copies were completely or partially destroyed in the 1987 fire. However, I had already examined them in gathering data and I have photocopies which are about 90% readable.[57] In the last decade, I have been able to expand this collection to some extent, and occasionally, I still come across individual copies of such early publications, but they are now few and far between.

The data are usually reliable, and often quite detailed. On the other hand, there is also an annoying anonymity. On many occasions, especially in the early copies, articles and reports are either unsigned or acknowledged only with initials. Similarly, people mentioned in reports are often referred to only as 'Brother' or 'Sister'. It has sometimes been possible to deduce the names, but not always. In quoting stories and anecdotes, I have generally taken them at face value and reproduced them as they were given, even where there might be grounds for explaining them in some other way.

Private papers

Private papers are not easy to locate. It has been an ongoing frustration that documents which are priceless to a historian are often valueless to others and hence discarded. Of particular sadness was the loss of several cartons of letters, papers, documents and notes belonging to W. A. Buchanan, the son-in-law of Australia's first Pentecostal pastor, Sarah Jane Lancaster, which were all burned by his widow just a short time before I learned of them.

However, such papers do turn up from time to time, and I have been able to collect a useful number. These included exciting 'finds' such as an original letter written by Sarah Jane Lancaster; a complete set of sermon notes from the pen of W. J. Enticknap; ordination certificates for a couple of ministers; a letter from F. B. Van Eyk's widow to a close friend; and so on. I have been particularly fortunate with photographs, of which I have many. It seems that early Pentecostals were given to some sense of history, and did like to retain pictorial records of events.[58]

Institutional records

Institutional records appear to be almost non-existent. I have only been able to discover one membership list from one small church in the 1930s. I have copies of the marriage register from one congregation and minute books from four others. That is all. Were Pentecostalism a more centralised movement, institutional sources would be easier to locate. In its early, formative stages, however, churches were established as the result of personal initiative rather than centralised strategies, and leaders were basically either self-appointed or elected by local congregations. Furthermore, very few of the oldest churches had their own buildings; they commonly met in private homes or hired venues. It is more than likely that minutes and record books were simply mislaid or not passed on when there was a change of office holder.[59]

Given this fragmentary development, especially in the first two decades, there are virtually no statistical records. Hence, data such as lists of pastors and even of churches generally do not exist. They have to be compiled from other sources. This lack is partly compensated for by the magazines which do tend at least to name pastors and leaders and to include reports of conferences, annual meetings, pastoral appointments, property purchases and the like.

Biographies

Over the last two decades, there has been a spate of biographies and autobiographies by Pentecostal people. Many of these are amateurishly written and usually self-published. Often they omit crucial data such as dates and places of birth and full given names. Nevertheless, like the interviews, they offer intriguing firsthand glimpses of what the movement was like over half a century ago. Philip Duncan's handful of books has been helpful in this regard. His original volume, *Pentecost in Australia* is of particular value, as it is basically a compilation of articles published in the *Australian Evangel* documenting his visit to some 43 different Assemblies of God churches in 1946.[60] One of the best biographies is Lloyd Averill's *Go North Young Man*[61] which is thoughtful, personal and comprehensive. Several others are listed in the bibliography.

Newspapers, secular and denominational journals

Country and provincial newspapers often carried reports of early Pentecostal activities, given that church news was more likely to be reported half a century ago than it is today and given that in the country, any local news was of interest. Much of the data about the ministry of the controversial Frederick Van Eyk, for example, can be gathered from advertisements, letters and church news columns in the rural press. Similarly, obituaries and social news are sometimes helpful.

In the city press, however, apart from the churches' own advertisements, there is little helpful information. Occasionally, a charismatic personality such as John Alexander Dowie or F. B. Van Eyk or Aimee Semple McPherson attracted media attention, but these were rare events. Usually, one searches the pages of the secular media in vain for anything of significance. 'Why do the newspapers practically ignore evangelistic meetings?' asked the editor of *Good News*?[62] Well might a frustrated historian put the same question.

Denominational journals provide a rich source of background material for the origins of Pentecostalism. Methodist publications, in particular, have a mine of information on nineteenth century evangelism and revival. Similarly, Dowie's periodical *Leaves of Healing* provides an abundant source of pre-Pentecostal materials. After the turn of the century, however, denominational papers seem to have given little attention to specific groups such as Pentecostals. They normally focused only on their own interests, or, at best, on those where there was some perceived common ground between their denominational affairs and those of others. Usually, Pentecostalism did not fall into that category. Hence, articles or reports about Pentecostal activities are rare.

Australian Pentecostals have sometimes made much of the name 'Southland of the Holy Spirit,' alleging it to be prophetic of a great nation-wide revival. Given that this nomenclature was entrusted to the Portuguese explorer de Quiros in 1605 in the hope that the new southern continent would become a bastion of Catholicism, this is a questionable thesis, to say the least.[63] Nevertheless, Pentecostal revival has found a congenial home in this country and has developed its own distinctive personality.

Although sources vary greatly in both quantity and quality, it is nevertheless possible to set down a useful and comprehensive record of pre-war Australian Pentecostalism which will, I hope, offer valuable insights into the origins, distinctive qualities and significant contribution of this movement to contemporary Christian life and society.

Notes

1. Many additional books and papers have been written about Pentecostalism since this volume was first written, but it has been thought advisable only to include in this essay those that were available at that time. Further, for the sake of completeness, in the following footnotes, full publication details are given of all titles cited, even though they have been quoted previously in this work.

2. E.g. D. Cooper, *Flames of Revival* (Endeavour Hills, Vic: Christian Revival Crusade, 1995); D and G. Smith, *A River is Flowing* (St Agnes, SA: Assemblies of God, 1987).

3. E.g. M. Hutchinson, E. Campion and S. Piggin, *Reviving Australia, Essays on the History and Experience of Revival and Revivalism in Australian Christianity* (Sydney: Centre for the Study of Australian Christianity, 1994)

4. D. Harris, D. Hynd, D. Millikan, eds, *The Shape of Belief* (Homebush: Lancer, 1982).

5. W. Tabbernee (ed) *Initiation in Australian Churches* (Council of Churches, 1984); R. Gribben, ed, *Communion in Australian Churches* (Melbourne: JBCE, 1985); W. Tabbernee, ed, *Ministry in Australian Churches* (Melbourne: JBCE, 1987).

6. I. Gillman, ed, *Many Faiths—One Nation* (Sydney: William Collins, 1988).

7. S. Piggin, *Evangelical Christianity: Spirit, word and world* (Melbourne: Oxford University Press, 1996).

8. I. Breward, *A History of the Australian Churches* (St Leonards: Allen and Unwin, 1993).

9. H. Carey *Believing in Australia* (St Leonards: Allen and Unwin, 1996).

10. E.g. Hutchinson et al , 1994.

11. R. Humphreys and R Ward, *Religious Bodies in Australia* (Melbourne: published by the authors, 1986).

12. P. Hughes, *The Pentecostals in Australia* (Canberra: Australian Government Publishing Service, 1996).

13. For example, A. Black, ed, *Religion in Australia* (Sydney: Allen and Unwin, 1991).

14. P. Bentley, T. Blombery and P. Hughes, *A Yearbook of Australian Religious Organisations 1996* (Kew: Christian Research Association, 1995). Earlier volumes (1992–1996) were entitled *A Yearbook for Australian Churches.*

15. See P. Kaldor et al, 1994, 77.

16. S. Frodsham, *With Signs Following* (Springfield, Missouri: Gospel Publishing House, 1946).

17. G. Atter, *The Third Force* (College Press, 1962).

18. D. Gee, *Upon All Flesh* (Springfield, Missouri: Gospel Publishing House, 1947).

19. Klaude Kendrick *The Promise Fulfilled* (Springfield, Missouri: Gospel Publishing House, 1961).

20. M. Harper *As at the Beginning* (London: Hodder and Stoughton, 1966).

21. J. T. Nichol, *The Pentecostals* (Plainfield, NJ: Logos, 1971).

22. Nils Bloch-Hoell *The Pentecostal Movement* (Oslo, 1964).

23. C. E. Jones in Burgess et al, 1988, 90.

24. W. Hollenweger *The Pentecostals* (Peabody, Mass: Hendrickson, 1988).

25. There is a chapter on Australia in W. Hollenweger (ed) *Die Pfingstkirchen* Die Kirchen der Welt (Stuttgart: Evangelisches Verlagswerk, 1971), which I was asked to write. This is essentially a distillation of material from my *Heart of Fire*, 1984.

26. D. Harrell, *All Things Are Possible* (Indiana University Press, 1975).

27. V. Synan, ed, *Aspects of Pentecostal-Charismatic Origins* (Plainfield, NJ: Logos International, 1975); V. Synan, *The Holiness-Pentecostal Movement in the United States* (Grand Rapids, Michigan: Eerdmans, 1971, 1989); see also V. Synan, *In the Latter Days* (Ann Arbor: Servant Books, 1984).

28. Synan has since published V. Synan (ed), *The Century of the Holy Spirit: 100 Years of Pentecostal and Charismatic Renewal, 190–2001* (Nashville: Thomas Nelson, 2001), which was issued in commemoration of the end of the first century since the Pentecostal manifestations at Topeka, Kansas, under the leadership of Charles Parham, commonly seen as the beginning of the Pentecostal movement.

29. D. Dayton, *Theological Roots of Pentecostalism* (Metuchen, NJ: Scarecrow Press and ATLA, 1987); D. W. Faupel, *The Everlasting Gospel: The Significance of Eschatology in the Development of Pentecostal Thought* (Sheffield: Sheffield Academic Press, 1996).

30. Burgess et al, eds, 1988.

31. In some ways, the very existence of such a volume is a reflection on the growing sophistication and significance of the Pentecostal movement.

32. S. Burgess (ed) and E. M. Van Der Maas (Assoc Ed), *The New International Dictionary of Pentecostal and Charismatic Movements, Revised and Expanded Edition* (Grand Rapids: Zondervan, 2002).

33. E. Blumhofer, *The Assemblies of God: a Chapter in the Story of American Pentecostalism* (Springfield, Missouri: Gospel Publishing House, 1988).

34. E.g. F. Abeysekera, *The History of the Assemblies of God of Singapore* (Singapore: Assemblies of God, 1992); L. Larson, *The Spirit in Paradise: the History of the Assemblies of God of Fiji* (St Louis: Plus Communications, 1997); T. Turnbull, *What God Hath Wrought: a Short History of the Apostolic Church* (Bradford, England: Puritan,

1959); J. Worsfold, *The Origins of the Apostolic Church in Great Britain* (Wellington, NZ: Julian Literature Trust, 1991).

35. R. Anderson, *Vision of the Disinherited* (New York: Oxford, 1979); M. Calley, *Bandjalong Social Organisation*, (Unpublished thesis, University of Sydney, 1959); M. Calley, *God's People: West Indian Pentecostal Sects in England* (Oxford: Oxford, 1965); Wilson, *Religious Sects*, 1970.

36. H. Cox, *Fire From Heaven* Reading, (Mass: Addison-Wesley, 1994).

37. B. F .Gutierrez and D. Smith, eds, *In the Power of the Spirit* (Drexel Hill: AIPRAL and CELEP with Skipjack Press, 1996), 135ff.

38. Some of the theories offered in these writings are, in my opinion, arguable and have been discussed already in Chapter One.

39. *Paraclete*, 26:4, Fall 1992, inside cover; 28:3, Summer, 1994, 33.

40. For example, see *Pneuma: The Journal of the Society for Pentecostal Studies* 18:1 Spring, 1996. It is interesting that for several years the secretary of the Society was Fr Peter Hocken, a Catholic priest. See *Pneuma* 15:2, Fall, 1993.

41. For example, A. Cerillo, 'The Origins of American Pentecostalism,' *Pneuma*, 15:1, Spring, 1993

42. *Journal of Pentecostal Theology*, No.1, 1 October, 1992.

43. For example, *Charismatic Contact,* published by Faith Ministries,1972–1979?; *Renewing Australia,* published by Dan Armstrong, 1986–91.

44. See for example, *New Day* No. 145, March, 1995; ND, No.151, October, 1995, 5. Note that prior to 1979, *Impact* was published by the Christian Revival Crusade.

45. See *Barsabbas*, No. 1, January, 1993.

46. *Renewal Journal*, 1:1, Summer, 1993, 3.

47. *PCBC Journal*, 1:1, October, 1997.

48. *Australasian Pentecostal Studies* (Chester Hill, NSW, 1998—); *Asian Journal of Pentecostal Studies* (Baguio City, Philippines: the Faculty of the Asia Pacific Theological Seminary, 1998—).

49. *Lucas: An Evangelical History Review* Macquarie Centre: Evangelical History Association; *Journal of Religious History* (Association for the Journal of Religious History, Oxford: Blackwell, 1960—).

50. See for example Hutchinson et al (eds), 1994. Other titles in this series are listed in the bibliography.

51. For example, E. Campion, *Australian Catholics* (Ringwood, Vic: Penguin, 1988); A. Hunt, *This Side of Heaven* (Adelaide: Lutheran Publishing House, 1985); S. Judd and K. Cable, *Sydney Anglicans* (Sydney: Anglican Information Office, 1987); M. Newton, *Southern Cross Saints* (Laie, Hawaii: Institute for Polynesian Studies, 1991); P. O'Farrell, *The Catholic Church and Community* (Kensington, NSW: NSW University Press, 1985); Jill Roe, *Beyond Belief: Theosophy in Australia 1879–1939* (Kensington, NSW: New South Wales University Press, 1986); H. Taylor, *The History of the Churches of Christ in South Australia 1846–1959*.

52. I cannot help feeling wistful about this: there are so many questions I would like to ask now, but it is too late. Also, I did not always properly document my sources at the beginning, and as a result some references to interviews are undated or in other ways incomplete.

53. This is another reason why references to some interviews are undated or incomplete.

54. Sometimes, people told me things in confidence that they asked me not to repeat. To the best of my ability, I have honoured these requests.

55. *Good News* (North Melbourne: Good News Hall, 1910—). I have around 90% of all *Good News* magazines ever published. An earlier publication entitled *The Pentecostal Times* seems to have run only to a handful of issues.

56. I still lack a few of the very earliest copies. One wonders what crucial information might be in them! For instance, I only have three issues from 1910 to 1923. As the frequency of the magazine was irregular, I don't know how many are missing. Also, volume one covered at least 1910–1913. As the February 1923 edition is volume 9, number 1, it appears that from 1914 to 1922, a new volume was added annually. At this point, there was an attempt to regularise the numbering to bring it into line with the years of publication, and all 1924 editions are numbered Volume 15. Subsequent issues follow this pattern. The Mitchell Library in New South Wales, the Latrobe Library in Victoria and the Mortlock Library in South Australia also have some of these publications, but they do not have the early editions

57. The majority of these journals are in my possession. Dr Mark Hutchinson and I are considering ways in which a Pentecostal archive might be set up to enable wider use of these resources. On occasion, in quotations in this work, words are supplied where they have been obscured in the originals. I am confident that my suggested replacements are reliable.

58. In this regard, they were reflecting the growing popularity of photography, the result of the development of smaller, more readily available cameras and simpler processing. The papers and documents mentioned here are in my personal collection.

59. It is tantalising to wonder how many cardboard cartons or packages of minutes and financial records might still be hidden in people's wardrobes or linen presses, or how many have long since been turned to ashes or now lie rotting in rubbish dumps.

60. See P. Duncan, *Pentecost in Australia*, n. d. but c.1947; *The Charismatic Tide* (published by the author, 1978). Duncan was one of the first pastors in the Pentecostal Church of Australia. See Chapter Ten.

61. L. Averill, *Go North Young Man* (Springwood, Qld: published by the author, 1992). Averill was a pioneer pastor in the Assemblies of God.

62. GN, 18:7, July, 1927, 8. 'It seems next to impossible to get reports of real Gospel services into the papers any more, much less entire sermons,' lamented the editor, to whom it was a sign of the beginning of the end.

63. G. M. Clark, *A History of Australia* (Volume One, Brunswick, Vic: Melbourne University Press, 1985), 14ff.

APPENDIX B

BIOGRAPHICAL BACKGROUND MATERIAL

This section provides background material for some of the people who appear earlier in this study

AMES, Thomas James (1858–1928)

Thomas James Ames was the leader of the first Pentecostal assembly formed in Adelaide.[1] Born in South Australia on 30 October 1858, by 1882, he had established a printing business in the capital city of Adelaide which he also used as a medium for ministry.[2] His ABC Printing Works in Pirie Street were both an outlet for the biblical printed page and a venue for mid-week Bible studies.

In 1902, before there were any formal Pentecostal meetings in Australia, Ames published a little book called *A problem: Now and Then,*[3] a study on the nature of man. Its approach is philosophical, rather than theological, although there is frequent reference to Scripture. Some time later, he wrote a tract called *Concerning the Punishment of the Wicked.*[4]

How Ames became a Pentecostal and how he became associated with Good News Hall remains a mystery, although it was apparently a process of 'some years'.[5] Certainly, from the early days, his name is associated with Pentecostal ministry. Around 1909, he began to publish a 12-page periodical called *Pente-*

costal Times.[6] This was basically a collection of articles from overseas Pentecostal magazines, with one or two testimonies from local people and a couple of pieces by Ames himself. About the same time, meetings were held on Tuesday nights in the Willard Hall vestry in Wakefield Street, and on Saturdays in the Congregational Rooms at Hindmarsh Square. From around 1910 to 1926, there are published notices of him leading the Elim Assembly in Adelaide.[7] Numbers were not large, but Ames was not dissatisfied—

> We are glad to say that our little 'Elim Assembly' meetings continue to show marked concern for Apostolic blessings. There is manifested an earnest desire and fervency of spirit for the things of God, in His way. We are not concerned as to how the Lord carries on His work. But we have a right to expect that 'signs shall follow them that believe'.[8]

Meanwhile, they were trusting that their unity in the Spirit and their 'unwavering faith' would so glorify God that 'signs' and 'gifts' would occur. In fact, God's healing power was frequently being reported.

In 1924, Ames visited Tasmania and preached there. One who heard him reported, 'The Lord was with us in the power of the Spirit, and we were soon all bathed in its gentle, cooling streams.'[9]

Ames attended the Easter Convention at Good News Hall in 1926. 'We listened with much profit,' reported Lancaster, 'to several instructive and spiritual talks by Brother Ames'. What he taught was 'sound doctrine on the lines of the Apostles'.[10] But when Lancaster visited Adelaide later that year, it was to the Apostolic Faith Misson that she went. Although she clearly commended Ames for sticking to his convictions, and could be seen to be endorsing them, in fact his views were apparently too radical even for her. It is also clear that when Van Eyk first visited Adelaide, although he was glad to visit Ames in his office, the differences in doctrine were enough to make him prefer to use the Leavitt Hall assembly as a base for his mission.

At that time, Ames, now 68 years old, started Bible studies on Sunday nights at the Printing Works. In 1927, he published a 20-page pamphlet entitled *Christianity and Freemasonry: Can they go Together?* It is a strongly-worded attack on Freemasonry, in which he argues that it is fundamentally non-Christian and that it dishonours the Son of God. 'They have taken away my Lord,' he writes, 'and I know not where they have laid Him.' He draws heavily on Scripture and focuses strongly on the Lord Jesus Christ. There is a note of certainty about his faith here, not evident in his 1902 publication. It seems that his experience of the Spirit focused his faith and gave him a less philosophical and a more biblical understanding of Christianity.

He died on 31 August, 1928, after a short illness. Only a small notice appeared in *Good News*, but it was warm, noting that a large number of friends and relatives attended the funeral of 'our beloved and faithful friend'. There was some criticism of Lancaster for this description of Ames—enough for her to print an explanatory note two months later, pointing out that the words 'beloved and faithful friend' were 'purely the expression of the personal sentiments of the editor,' and noting that neither she nor the AFM were, or ever had been, associated with 'certain doctrines taught and published by Mr Ames'.[11] It is probably not without significance that of the many people I interviewed, not one made any reference to Ames's work. It seems that he was not considered as being in the mainstream of early Pentecostalism and that the movement generally chose to forget his contribution.

ARMSTRONG, Maxwell (1881–1959)

Maxwell Armstrong, affectionately known as 'Daddy Armstrong,' was a physically small man, although large in heart. Born and brought up in India, Armstrong became addicted to alcohol, ran away to sea at the age of 17 and was eventually converted in Lyttleton, New Zealand in 1903 at a Salvation Army citadel. He moved to Melbourne, underwent training to become an officer and moved to Sydney, NSW, where he met and married his diminutive wife May Beatrice Richards, who had been converted at the Chapman-Alexander mission of 1909.[12] Marrying a non-commissioned person, required Armstrong to resign his commission and the couple worshiped at Rozelle Methodist Mission.

A few years later, they encountered a couple named Braun who had been in John G.Lake's meetings in South Africa, and on 23 June 1918, they were baptized both in water and in the Holy Spirit.[13] Soon they were holding Pentecostal meetings in their home in Lilyfield and a number of 'Dowie-ites' joined them. In 1920, with their three sons Dalton, Norman and David, they moved to Cleveden, near Parkes, where they ministered for fifteen months. They returned to Sydney and led a group of about 70 people who, after a visit by Smith Wigglesworth, met in the Mechanics' Institute at Rozelle. In 1925, they met in Australia Street, Newtown.

In October 1929, they returned to Parkes, where they served for three years and four months. After working in several places in Queensland, they moved to Cairns. Armstrong and his wife May had a particular love for ministry to the derelicts of society. They often took needy people into their home. People, in turn, loved them.[14]

In 1944, Armstrong was appointed State Chairman of the Assemblies of God in New South Wales. A letter to his constituency reveals a great deal about his spirit, his enthusiasm, his intense, joyous love for his Saviour and his sense of urgency about the need to evangelise—

> Dear Brethren in our Glorious, Conquering Saviour, Again I take this opportunity to send forth loving greetings to you all, in the sweet name of Him Who loves us with an Everlasting Love, and Whom we are learning to love more and more as the glory of His comforting Presence becomes increasingly real to us...
>
> In the midst of the stupendous, and sometimes, bewildering happenings in the world today, it is very precious to know that this glorious work given to 'the fishers of the Lord' need never stop; and while ever there are Christians in the world who really love their Master, it shall never stop. We all realize that the fishers are

very few, and therefore the work of hauling in the nets is very heavy and difficult, but thank God for the faithfulness and perseverance of the few... May He call out many more fishers to launch into the great sea of humanity, which at the present time is so troubled and storm tossed.[15]

In later years, he became known as 'Daddy Armstrong' and was renowned for his exuberant shouts of 'Hallelujah!' at opportune moments.[16]

AYERS, Mary

Mary Ayers was well-known as a preacher in the Assemblies of God. Originally from Bundaberg, she journeyed to America when she was about 19. Apparently because she did not have permanent residency, she returned to Australia every few years and itinerated through the various Pentecostal assemblies. She also spent some time in North Queensland ministering with the Islander and Aboriginal people. She was heavily built, with an aggressive, overpowering personality.[17] She was not known as a great preacher, but she was bold and forthright and prophesied, prayed and preached with equal fervour.

'She preached with simple faith,' recalled one man. 'Those who were looking for intellectual content were often disappointed, but congregations generally loved her preaching.' Even children were touched by her ministry.[18]

BOOTH-CLIBBORN, William (b.1893)

Salvation Army records have little to say about Booth-Clibborn's father Arthur whom Wilson calls a 'wayward mystic'[19] and whom his mother Catherine described as 'a mighty man of God'. Young William labelled him a prophet who was 'a channel to bring all of us into the Pentecostal Blessing'. In 1902, the family resigned from the Army, to join Dowie's Zion movement and to preach 'a fuller gospel'.[20] Six years later, Arthur took fifteen-year-old William, one of ten children, to some London Pentecostal meetings where they heard glossolalia for the first time.[21] On 28 November 1908, William was the first in his family to be baptized in the Holy Spirit. Coming as he did from a musical family, he had a musical experience—

> My heart danced with bliss. My voice rose to new heights of song—and on and on came the streams of Glory and Power. Ah! It was an outpouring, a flood, yes! A glorious inundation! And all this time (about two hours) my eyes were steadily fixed on Jesus...

> Oh! How I sang and shouted His praises for restoring my soul... I had no thought about speaking in tongues—who would dream of thinking about such things when the Lord Jesus Himself was standing there!

But after praying initially in his native French and then in English, speak in tongues he did—

It was not very long until something let go and I was singing in a wonderful language words I had never learned, whose charm filled me with ravishing joy, and whose every sentence reached the throne of God. Then I sang with greater delight... I continued on my knees yet another hour intermittently singing and praying in this new, wonderful tongue... The Lord Jesus, in ineffable beauty, in an excellence of majesty indescribable, stood there before me and I knew He now possessed me body, spirit and soul.[22]

Young William was so 'hopelessly blessed' that he was unable to walk down the street unaided. His father told him to close his eyes and he would guide him. 'Not many fathers,' reminisced William, 'would be willing to lead their sons through the streets of London talking in tongues.' The Booth-Clibborns held regular meetings as a family, often into the small hours of the morning, and soon others also received the Spirit. When Catherine returned home, she acknowledged that this was the work of God.[23]

The spirit of Pentecost was to become the vital fluid of the trunk of William Booth-Clibborn's ministry. In 1930, now married, Booth-Clibborn arrived in Australia with his wife Genevieve and family. Genevieve had been converted at the age of twelve when she saw a vision of Jesus calling her to work for Him. At 19 she was filled with the Holy Spirit, began to preach and as a result was evicted from her home. Now she was travelling with Booth-Clibborn, assisting him in the ministry and 'taking full charge of the continuation of the campaigns'.[24]

Booth-Clibborn's brothers Eric and Theodore were also Pentecostal ministers. Eric lost his life in Africa where he had gone as a missionary.[25]

BRAWNER, Mina Ross (b.?1880)

Born in America, with five brothers and four sisters, Mina Ross Brawner grew up under the influence of a godly Scottish mother who prayed that one of her children would be a preacher of the gospel. Around 1906, as a young housewife, she decided to study medicine. She went into private practice both in America and New South Wales before returning to the United States for 16 years. She was baptized in the Holy Spirit at Angelus Temple in Los Angeles.[26] The circumstances were unusual. Although in a successful medical practice in Carson City, Nevada, she had suffered a breakdown in health and felt a personal emptiness. She cried out to God in desperation, 'O God, if You exist, will you reveal yourself to me?' The words, 'Go to church' were impressed on her mind and within the hour, she was chatting with a Methodist pastor's wife.

She attended services of worship and found to her astonishment that the minister was not so concerned about intellectual content 'so long as he reached the hearts'. He focused on the story of the cross and it did reach her heart. The pastor's wife also told her of her need to be baptized in the Holy Spirit. She read Pentecostal magazines on the subject—and also a medical journal which spoke of people 'dethroning' their reason and uttering unintelligible gibberish, which they supposed was the gift of tongues. As a physician, she had no intention of putting reason to one side, but she was still earnest in her desire for a deeper spiritual experience. She examined the Scriptures and prayed for guidance.

On 28 September 1924, she visited Angelus Temple, Aimee McPherson's church, in Los Angeles. There, she found herself kneeling in tears. She determined to be quiet and discreet, and began to whisper praises to God. But soon she found herself shouting, 'Glory!' her hands upraised. 'The doctor part of me was never more critically analytical,' she said later, as she considered what she was doing, but the presence of God was too real to draw back. Soon she sank gently to the floor and (as she discovered later) was healed from heart trouble. For an hour and a half, she spoke in tongues. She herself was the first person she had ever seen experience the coming of the Spirit like this. 'It was wonderful,' she wrote later, 'and like Peter on the Mount of Transfiguration, I wanted to stay forever.'

> During this time Jesus became so real to me that when the power lifted I sat up, and looking upon the faces of the saints about me, whom I had never seen before... I loved them. Then I turned my eyes heavenward and said, 'Lord, this pays for everything that has ever happened, and for every trial that can ever come; I've found the Pearl of great Price. And, bless God, it is still paying, I am drawing compound interest.[27]

Three years later she journeyed to Australia where she worked as a minister of the gospel for many years.

BUCHANAN, William Alexander (1893–1964)

William Alexander (Alex, sometimes Alick) Buchanan, as an eighteen-year-old farmer's son from Gippsland, Victoria, was baptized in the Spirit on 29 January 1912 through the ministry of Good News Hall. He soon began meetings in his parents' farmhouse and on 29 January 1915 he left home to engage in evangelism. One year later to the day, he married Leila Mary Lancaster (1895–1966), Sarah Jane Lancaster's daughter.[28] The young couple visited Queensland in 1917 for a three-months' preaching tour. Then Alex took over the printing of *Good News* but returned to Queensland in 1921.[29] Shortly after that, he itinerated with Smith Wigglesworth, for whom Leila acted as amanuensis, taking down his sermons in shorthand. For a time he accompanied Van Eyk until he became one of the prime movers in discrediting the evangelist's ministry. After a time in Victoria, the Buchanans returned to Queensland in 1931 and most of their subsequent ministry was undertaken there.[30]

Alex was fluent with the Scriptures and could quote large sections from memory. He regularly preached without notes. He was not forceful, but was inspirational and could keep people's interest. He also loved personal evangelism and shared his faith whenever he had an opportunity.[31] He was quick-witted and enjoyed a touch of humour.[32]

In June 1931, he and his wife ministered in Cooroy, on the Sunshine Coast, where there was a steady flow of converts and 'a whole crowd of hungry believers'. Leila was an accomplished speaker.[33] They visited a dozen other places in the vicinity, both ministering independently. In one street of Cooroy, there were seven neighbouring houses where the inhabitants of all but one were converted. 'We have christened the street "Hallelujah Lane",' commented Buchanan.[34] He reported 24 conversions and 23 baptized in water during November in Cooroy—a total of 105 commitments and 87 baptisms since he had begun the work. By mid-1932, the Buchanans were back in Brisbane and preaching regularly in the Canvas Cathedral. In later years, Alex established a wholesale book distribution and Leila was for many years editor of the *Australian Evangel*.[35]

CHAMBERLAIN, Annie (b? 1868)

Captain Annie Dainty (b.?1868) served full-time in the Salvation Army for a decade or so in the South Australian country areas of Renmark, Wallaroo and Moonta and the Adelaide suburb of Enfield. On her marriage to Albert Chamberlain, at the turn of the twentieth century, when she was 32 years old, she had of necessity to resign her captaincy and become an ensign. In 1918, four years after the death of her husband, in order to support her family, she went into business as proprietor of a produce store in O'Connell Street, North Adelaide. Three years later, for just over twelve months she managed a boarding house for blind people. In 1923, now in her mid-fifties, she moved to a large house in the inner middle class suburb of Hyde Park, where she was able to take in boarders—and where she was also able to conduct meetings.[36]

In March, 1922, through the agency of Good News Hall, Smith Wigglesworth (1859–1947) visited Adelaide. He conducted meetings in the Protestant Hall in Hindmarsh Square, which was crowded to capacity.[37]

Chamberlain was inspired by the Wigglesworth visit and one day, while praying alone, spoke in tongues. With her Salvation Army experience behind her, she began to organise others who were also enthused by Wigglesworth into a regular fellowship at her home and weekly 'tarry meetings' were held. Although Annie Chamberlain had been responsible for the initial gatherings, family responsibilities did not allow her to exercise continued leadership and others took over that role.[38]

Similar gatherings were held in the Pillifeant home in Parkside, another inner suburb. Mrs Martha (Mattie) Pillifeant's mother had been baptized in the Spirit in Joseph Marshall's meetings near Portland, Victoria, in 1889.[39] In 1921, she was suffering severely with gastric ulcers and made a vow that if she recovered through Wigglesworth's ministry she would seek the Spirit for herself. Both aims were accomplished. So the Pillifeant home was also opened for meetings, until Sunday services were conducted in the Leavitt Hall.[40]

CRIDGE, Dolly

Dolly Cridge was one of the first to be baptized in the Holy Spirit through the ministry of Good News Hall. She was almost blind and could not read the Bible or walk unaided. When she was baptized in the Spirit she expected her sight to be restored.[41] Physically, her vision remained the same; but spiritually, it was enhanced. Two years later, she saw a mental image of one of the women in the church surrounded by bare-headed black children. Soon, the woman concerned was working among Aboriginals. Four years prior to World War I, Dolly foretold conflict in the Balkans and war in Europe. 'It is the December of the age,' she cried. Some branded her a false prophet, but as Jeannie Lancaster later said, her words proved 'exactly true'.[42]

In 1913, she spoke repeatedly concerning coming war. Lancaster claimed that, given her meagre education and environment, she referred to names and places she could not have known otherwise. Lancaster claimed she foretold the siege of Ostend, over a year before it happened, giving particular reference to conscription, to men being flayed, to the requisition of a steeple and to a naval attack, and in oblique form, to Turkey's entry into the War. She also spoke of the return of the Jews to Palestine and of Australians bearing arms.[43]

In 1925, she made some further predictions which, in the light of the accuracy of her former perceptions, were published. She warned of impending war in the Middle East and of 'lamentable trouble coming to Australia' and urged the people at Good News Hall to pray that they might escape the tribulation to come, for there was to be judgement on the nation. 'If ever a prophetess spoke the truth, that woman did,' reflected one man forty years later. 'Blind Dolly,' as she came to be known, was also not averse to confronting people who had done wrong and urging them to put things right.[44]

DENNIS, Annie

At the age of nineteen, Annie Dennis, of Hawthorn, Victoria, 'having drunk of the world's pleasure-cup and found its contents unsatisfactory,' became a Christian and immediately resolved to preach the gospel. After working in country areas for a time, she engaged in mission work in Melbourne. In 1907, she moved to Queensland, where in 1923 she received the Spirit.

Probably now in her forties, she was large in build, and talked freely wherever she could of the gospel. She had a tendency to be forceful, but was a capable expositor of Scripture.[45] She was also sensitive to the Spirit. In January 1924, when she was pastoring a work called 'Hebron' in Mackay, North Queensland, she felt moved to return home by a different route. She encountered a man who had met her many years before and since turned away from the gospel, who told her that he had dreamed about her the previous night. As a result, he was restored to faith, healed and baptized in the Spirit.[46]

In January 1924, she was invited by W. J. Enticknap to visit his farm at Macknade, 500 kilometres north of Mackay. Although city streets were beginning to echo to the sound of motor vehicles, and radio sets were becoming common-place, travel and communication in outback areas were still rough and difficult. Dennis made the 500 kilometre trip the easiest way, by sea. She conducted several meetings there. Within a few months, 31 people were baptized in the Spirit. Former 'drunkards, gamblers and thieves' were preaching the gospel. There were nine meetings a week being conducted in six locations. She also worked in Bowen. Later that year, she moved from Mackay to Townsville and left the work in the care of Will Enticknap. In Townsville, she undertook door to door outreach and conducted open air meetings. There were encouraging signs. An 84-year-old man was healed of pleurisy and rheumatics. Among the Islanders, there were nineteen filled with the Spirit. Within a few months, a church had grown and she returned to 'Hebron'. By 1932, she was in Ayr, where again, she pioneered a church. Here, too, Aboriginal and Islander people were converted.[47] By now her work was well acknowledged—

> Her time and energy is completely absorbed in service for her Lord, both in evangelical and home-mission work. Portion of the outcome of that service can be seen in the halls and homes which have been built for the glory of God and for the salvation of souls.[48]

She was recognised as a woman of determination and faith.[49]

DOWIE, John Alexander (1847–1907)

John Alexander Dowie was born on 25 May 1847 in St Andrew's Parish, Edinburgh, Scotland just two months after the marriage of his parents John Murray Dowie and Anne Dowie (nee MacFarlane) in the Tron Church parish, in the same city. It was later alleged that Dowie denied this paternity and claimed that he came from nobler stock.[50]

In 1851, John Murray Dowie's brother Alexander migrated to South Australia and established the successful South Australian Boot Factory in Rundle Street, Adelaide. Nine years later, John Murray Dowie and his family followed his brother to South Australia where John continued his trade as a cutter.[51] The family were heavily involved in the activities of the Congregational Union. While Alexander's business 'took up all his attention', he still showed 'much practical interest in church work'.[52] John Murray was a member of the Congregational Union and Home Mission Committee. He was a fervent advocate of evangelism and urged the Union to promote house to house visitation. He considered that 'no work was more needed'. E. S. Kiek notes that John Murray Dowie was a respected deacon and lay-preacher.[53]

It is not surprising, then, that young John Alexander took an interest in things spiritual. Indeed, from a very early age, he showed godly aptitude. He is said to have read the whole Bible through at six years of age and to have had a definite conversion experience at the age of seven. Kiek describes him as 'amazingly precocious' and points out that he loved to attend Bible study classes and Christian meetings and asked questions which would normally be beyond those of a child of his age. Indeed, Kiek claims that 'few, if any, could rival his intimate knowledge of the sacred text' and refers to his 'amazing command of Scripture'.[54]

At the early age of six, Dowie pledged himself neither to drink nor smoke.[55] During his later ministry, he was to become a strong temperance campaigner and a fierce opponent of the use of tobacco in all its forms. When the family arrived in Australia, the young Dowie worked for the old established Adelaide firm of G and R. Wills.[56] He was not a robust youth, and suffered from chronic dyspepsia, but was divinely healed at the age of sixteen. During this period, he sat under the 'faithful and able ministry' of Rev William Francis Cox of Hindmarsh Square Congregational Church.

In 1867, after studying for the ministry in Adelaide, he returned to Edinburgh to continue his education where he studied New Testament Greek under John Stuart Blackie, attended lectures by Lindsay Alexander and became acquainted with the social reformer Thomas Guthrie (1803–1873). He also visited patients at the Edinburgh Infirmary and listened to medical lectures. This experience was to have a profound effect on him in later life, as the hopelessness of many of the patients undermined his faith in the medical profession.[57] By 1872, at the urging of his father, he was back in South Australia where, on 1 April, he accepted the call to become pastor of the Congregational church at the tiny settlement of Alma, some 80 kilometres north of Adelaide. On 16 April, he was duly ordained to the ministry of the Congregational Union.[58] Congregationalism was vigorous and active in nineteenth century South Australia, a colony of free settlers where the voice of non-conformism was heard more loudly than in other States.[59]

Just under 25 years old, Dowie struck a handsome figure, with his dark hair and flourishing moustache. He did not find the work easy. It was obviously a far cry from the busy streets of Edinburgh. He had four preaching stations requiring him to travel several times a week on horse back journeys of between six and twelve miles. He prepared four 'original sermons' every week and kept up his studies. His health was much better and at first he enjoyed his work.[60] By July the honeymoon was over. Dowie's comments on the situation are interesting, because they form a model of the kind of complaints he was going to raise more than once in other churches in years to come. In a letter to his parents, he wrote—

> My church here has been cruelly neglectful from the beginning, though I would not even to you say it, and now I fear there is something like open opposition impending, on account of the too searching character of my preaching. Dissimulation, wicked hypocrisy and Pharisaic formalism have been unmasked; and only Divinely given wisdom can help me through... My only fault is too great faithfulness and diligence—not sleepy half-heartedness in preaching or action.[61]

In November, just two members turned up for a monthly church meeting. Moreover, since he first arrived, the church had not been able to meet his stipend. So in December, he tendered his resignation, which was accepted 'with profound sorrow' by the members.[62] From Alma, he transferred to Sydney, where he was to begin what became an international ministry of divine healing.

ENTICKNAP, Charles (b.1905)

Charles Golding Enticknap (b.1905) was one of nine children born to W. J. Enticknap of McDade, North Queensland. In 1924, Charles, at the age of eighteen, was baptized in the Holy Spirit under the ministry of Annie Dennis. Years later he recalled—

> I was so hungry for God I felt I would die if God did not meet me. Consequently my heart was just an aching void. I wanted God. I didn't want blessing, I didn't want the baptism: I wanted God. My whole being was just like a vacuum that was crying out.[63]

At that point, his brother Will came and placed his hands on his head. The effect was like 'a bolt of glory from heaven'. Charles began to praise the Lord, which he had always found difficult before, and he felt as though 'liquid rays of glory' were being poured into him. Dennis had told him that when the Spirit came he would speak in tongues. Such was the intensity of what he was experiencing, he thought, 'Sister Dennis was wrong. I've received the baptism and I haven't spoken in tongues.'

> Then a remarkable thing happened. I was trying to say, 'Praise the Lord' but I couldn't say it. Then I felt a marvellous sense of God taking hold of all my vocal organs... and then came a flood of other tongues!

> Within 24 hours there were four of us baptized in the Holy Ghost and fire in the home. We got to bed some time during the night... I tell you heaven had come down into our home. God poured out his Spirit in an amazing fashion in that place...

Charles spoke in tongues for about an hour and a half. Beforehand, he could not stand up; afterwards, he could not sit down. He stood and danced and worshiped God.[64] Wp.J. Enticknap was ecstatic—

> As we praised the Lord for victory, Charlie got his baptism. I cannot describe it. It was SO lovely. He came right through and as he was dancing and praising the Lord... we all got together... Oh dear, I cannot describe it, it was so lovely—four of them filled with new wine at 2 a.m. Praise God![65]

Although only eighteen, Charles was a keen reader, especially of books on revival. Charles G.Finney was a favourite, for more reasons than one. Like other members of the family, he had been teaching Sunday School since he was fourteen and had been preaching both in the pulpit and in the open air for a year. On 2 March, 1924, Charles felt that God called him 'very personally and directly' to go and preach the gospel. He felt particularly led to Cairns. Previously he had dreamed that he and his brother Will were fishing when the Lord came walking towards them, his garments shining white. He called them to become 'fishers of men'.

'The Lord called Charlie,' said W. J., 'just as plainly as He called Samuel.' Charles felt this confirmed his dream. The parents were thrilled. Rebecca had already left home and now it was Charles's turn. 'We were bubbling over with joy... knowing the lad was fit,' wrote Enticknap.[66] As a result he moved to Cairns for a short time.

On 9 May, he returned home and then moved to Townsville where he took over the small group of believers there. It was not easy. He used a bicycle for transportation, sometimes with his partner Jim Hannah on the handlebars. At other times, he carried a portable organ on the bike! They preached everywhere, on street corners and in people's homes. They slept in primitive accommodation. There was opposition and abuse. But the work slowly grew. Charles's sisters Rhoda and Rebecca joined him for a time. Finally, he asked his brother Will to help. He, too, had felt a distinct call from God.

They planned to hold their first meetings in a tent. 'Sister' Howell donated 50 pounds and they bought a second hand tent. Their beginning was not auspicious. The tent was destroyed in a storm before they conducted even one meeting! Not discouraged, Charles visited Melbourne, where A. C. Valdez was preaching. They purchased another tent and a church was established. In 1927, Charles moved to Mackay, later pastored in Rockhampton, Maryborough, Toowoomba and Parkes and within a decade was Chairman of the Assemblies of God in Queensland and Vice-Chairman of the Commonwealth General Presbytery.[67]

In later years he engaged in itinerant work, teaching on personal evangelism.

GLOVER, Kelso

Kelso Glover had been training for ministry in the State University of California when he was introduced to Holy Spirit baptism by his mother who sent him an 'anointed handkerchief' when he was sick. His subsequent healing convinced him and he used the same method himself in later years. He had dreams of studying at Harvard, Oxford and Berlin Universities, but after attending a small unsophisticated Pentecostal assembly in a slum area and being challenged by the testimonial of a converted addict, he became increasingly convinced he should follow the path of full-time ministry. Even though offered 'the best church' in his denomination in California if he returned to seminary, he refused. After extended times of earnest prayer, he was baptized in the Holy Spirit, possibly at Azusa Street.[68]

> For several months I spent my time weeping. I was laying my all on the altar, and weeping because of the things He was taking away from me, instead of praising Him for what I was receiving from Him... Oh, something inside will move when you praise the Lord and sincerely tell Him you love Him. Friends, I did say 'Hallelujah'... and before I said it a half dozen times the fountains of the deep in my soul began to overflow, and it flowed up through my lips and tongue, until I began to sing with 'the tongues of men and of angels' ...Oh, since that time Jesus Christ... has been real to my soul.[69]

Glover came to Australia in 1926 to work for a time at Richmond Temple, Victoria.

HEWITT, John (1900–1962)

Baptized in the Holy Spirit in 1915, in South Wales,[70] he had also been encouraged by the exceptional Welsh revivalist Stephen Jeffreys in his early days to enter the ministry. However, opportunities had not arisen for this and he found himself laboring in the mines. He came to Australia in 1923 to work for a relative in a mine in Ipswich and then ministered in a Baptist church in New South Wales.[71] He left because of a reaction after he allowed incidences of glossolalia in the services, and in 1926 attended Philip Duncan's Pentecostal church at Newtown where he was soon made pastor.[72] On 19 January 1927, in the Silkstone Baptist church (Queensland), he married his fiancee Lily Newton (1904–1991) who had followed him from England. Their honeymoon was spent conducting revival and healing meetings in Sydney.

In 1929, Hewitt was invited to become the Dominion Evangelist in South Africa for the Apostolic Faith Mission. The Hewitts returned to Britain and it was there in 1932 that he received Booth-Clibborn's invitation to take over the work in Brisbane. After ten months there, he resigned to join F. B. Van Eyk's Foursquare movement. He was installed as pastor at Cessnock until he could assist Van Eyk in itinerant work. Initially, Hewitt was excited about the move—

> It is a great joy to me to be associated with the Principal and Executive Council of this movement. After having been in this country for more than ten months, working principally in Queensland, but being fully acquainted with all the Pentecostal movements and their respective leaders in Australia, I am convinced that the 'Elim Foursquare' movement of Australia has the real vision of Pentecost such as I desire to be associated with. I feel convinced that Brother Van Eyk is the called preacher of Australia, even as Brother George Jefferies [sic] is in England. I have... resigned my position... to identify myself with a movement which, I feel convinced, will sweep Australia in a very short time.[73]

His enthusiasm was short-lived. Within three months, he had accepted an invitation from William Cathcart to accompany him in Melbourne. Apostolic historian Alistair Gardiner relates that as the Hewitt family were passing through Adelaide, Cathcart was travelling in a tram, praying quietly about contacting Hewitt but did not know where he was. To his astonishment, he saw him walking along the street. He left the tram and the two men met and decided to join forces in Melbourne.[74]

HORNE, Robert (d.1950)

Robert Horne (d.1950), a married man with a wife 'whose patient, quiet and loving spirit endeared her to a multitude of friends', and seven children, was the founder of the Southern Evangelical Mission. Initially he was a Home Missionary in the South Melbourne Methodist circuit in 1910.[75] He also had associations with the Keswick movement. Early in his married life he had become very ill and was given only six months to live. Challenged to trust God for healing by the young United Gospel Mission preacher Anthony Lang, who majored on Second Coming and Revival themes,[76] he asked Lang to anoint him with oil. He was fully cured and lived for another four decades. Like Lang, and his Sydney counterpart, the Baptist William Lamb, he too preached often on the return of Christ.

In 1910, Horne heard of the baptism in the Holy Spirit, possibly through reading a tract containing William Durham's testimony.[77] He began to research this area, discovered people who had been at Eltham and heard of the 1905 visitation in Mukti, India. As a result, he resigned his position at the Methodist church, was baptized in water by immersion and was soon baptized in the Spirit. Young Charles Greenwood was present at the service where Horne announced his resignation and later recalled how Horne approached him, laid hands on his head and said, 'If you do what the Lord commands you, He shall baptize you with the Holy Ghost and fire.'

In 1911, Horne purchased St Aubin's, a large house in Caulfield, a Melbourne suburb, that served as a meeting place for many years. In 1927, they moved to Chevy Chase in Brighton, although main meetings were conducted in Collins Street in Melbourne.[78] In 1923, he launched a small magazine (*Southern Evangel*) and, taking advantage of the upsurge of the new medium of 'wireless', presented fifteen minute broadcasts several times a week, scripts of which were published and distributed.[79] While Horne did not establish branch congregations, he did travel interstate. In Adelaide, in 1924, he conducted meetings in the home of 'Dad' and Dora Allen.[80]

JANSEN, Gustav

Of German descent, Jansen was a school teacher who spent about ten years in South Australian country schools, initially at remote Elliston and then at the Lower North towns of Terowie and Watervale.[81]

Around 1911, troubled with rheumatism, he was led to Christ by a Pentecostal friend, probably J.E. ('Grandpa') Rieschiek.[82] Because of his belief in divine healing, some people, Rieschiek said, thought him mad, but to Jansen he had seemed a 'model Christian' who impressed him greatly.

A breakdown in health which left him a 'nervous wreck' forced Jansen to resign from the Education Department. For three years, he was basically unemployed. Then for a couple of years, he dabbled in land broking at Point Pass before returning to his home town of Eudunda where, with his brother, he managed a motor garage. He became a justice of the peace and moved between Adelaide and Eudunda, spending most of his time in Adelaide. Financially, he did well.

Then, again, he fell ill (a condition which Jansen saw as the result of his failure to cultivate his Christian life) and one night had a dream which frightened him into calling on Rieschiek for help. Spiritually he was refreshed, but in spite of repeated visits to a specialist, his physical condition did not improve. Finally, surgery was prescribed. Rieschiek prayed for him in the hospital and said, 'Who knows, Gus, whether the operation will be necessary?'

After a long night of emotional and spiritual struggle, Jansen decided to trust wholly in Christ. Immediately he felt strengthened. The next day, the elders of the Apostolic Faith Mission (Rieschiek's church) prayed for him and anointed him with oil. The results were dramatic—

> As soon as I had surrendered myself to the Lord Jesus Christ to be my Healer, there followed [flowed?] into my heart, the love of God, and I felt like running out into the streets, and shouting from the house tops the praises of our Lord and Redeemer... I could not refrain from singing out the praise of our Lord aloud, and absolutely had to suppress myself from continually shouting... because I knew in my heart that my dear mother would think I had gone out of my mind.[83]

It was 6 August, 1925. Warned against Pentecostal excesses by various ministers of religion, he was uncertain about becoming too involved with the new group. Then he read a copy of *Good News* from Good News Hall in Melbourne and decided to attend a convention there. On 26 December 1925, he was praying in a 'tarry meeting'—

> My heart longing for more of God. Well, dear reader, whilst praising God some power came over me, and I went down on the floor. I am of a rather reserved nature, often being nick-named 'sober-sides'. But here I was on the floor and a feeling of joy and merriment came over me, and I kicked my legs about in a state of ecstasy... Here was I like a drunken man, glorifying and praising God... and with that there broke forth from my lips unknown words to me... and with it such a love came into my heart which I had never known before... I said to my dear mother, 'Mother, I now know what it is to adore and praise our Saviour through all eternity and never tire of it.'[84]

For Jansen, the spirit of Pentecost was very real. Around this time, he took up a retail agency in Adelaide and eventually bought a house at Mile End that was devoted to the work of the Mission. It was called 'Bethcar'—taken to mean house of pasture.[85]

LANCASTER, Sarah Jane (1858–1934)

Born Sarah Jane Murrell, on 3 June, 1858, in Williamstown, Victoria, and known to her friends as 'Jeannie', Lancaster was the third child of Mary Anne (nee Hume) and William Lee Murrell, a master mariner who worked as a harbour pilot on Port Philip Bay from 1857 to 1894. On 23 December 1879, at the age of 21, she married Alfred Lancaster, who was to become Chief Inspector of Rolling Stock for the Victorian Railways.[86] She herself became the mother of seven children, five boys and two girls. Brought up to be an active Methodist, she was part of the York Street Mission Hall, in regional Ballarat, where she had many friends and was 'strengthened by studying the Word', but where people proved to be reticent about the things of the Spirit.[87] She and her husband used to hold open air meetings. Alfred had a strong bass voice and would sing old Methodist songs; a crowd would gather and Jeannie would preach.[88]

Some time prior to 1902, Alfred Lancaster was transferred to Melbourne by the Railways. Not long after this, when Jeannie Lancaster was 44 years of age, she was confronted with the question of divine healing. In 1902, an old man who had requested her to visit him asked that she read James 5:14–15, and then demanded, 'Where are the elders of the church? I have been lying here for 20 years waiting for them to come and raise me up!'[89] Promising to try to find some cooperative elders, Lancaster left him. She could not conceive of leaders from her own church handling the case. She knew Catholics gave anointing, but usually in preparation for death, and tried the Seventh Day Adventists, but without avail.

She studied the Scriptures, became convinced that divine healing was valid and began to preach and practise it. She herself was healed of a broken and disfigured arm. She showed rare determination in this matter, refusing for some months to have it treated or set, in spite of the nagging pain. When three of the girls in a Bible class she was teaching wanted to be baptized, she strapped her arm to her body, hoping to immerse them one-handed. In simplicity of faith, one of the girls asked if she thought the Lord would permit her to be hurt while she was doing His work. So she unstrapped the arm and baptized the girls in the waters of Port Philip Bay without aid. From that time, there was no more pain. However, her arm was still disfigured and short, having knit unevenly over the months. Challenged by a sceptic that any surgeon could do better than that, she prayed for complete healing, finally asking a prayer group to anoint her with oil. A week later, she found her arm swinging violently and then to her delight discovered it to be of normal length.

From that time on, divine healing was an important part of her witness for Christ. In 1904, the year that John Dowie last set foot in Australia, and two years before the renowned Azusa Street outpouring of the Spirit in the United States, in spite of her husband's and family's lack of interest, she began to put her new faith into practice. A number who were sick found healing through the prayer of faith. People early opposed her. Years later she wrote—

> 'Dowieite!' cried one. But we had never heard of Dowie. 'Christian Scientist!' cried another. But we knew little of Christian Science, save that it denied the blood of our Deliverer and was therefore 'un-Christian'...[90]

In October, 1906, she requested from England a pamphlet entitled, 'Back to Pentecost,' together with some other books. She studied these and became convinced that a Pentecostal baptism in the Spirit was valid for the twentieth century.[91] So she began to pray earnestly to be filled with the Spirit. Later she described her experience as such that God 'deepened her consecration even unto death' and she experienced some manifestations of the Spirit she did not fully understand.

Two years after this, on 2 April, 1908, at the age of fifty, she went through what she described as a 'Gethsemane'. Still on her knees at two a.m., she was baptized in the Spirit. She 'thought that the valves of her heart were giving way' and felt as though 'electric shocks went through her frame'. But then the Holy Spirit came. 'Strange and unwonted notes burst from her mouth, cleaving the air like living creatures.' She spoke four different languages and she burst into songs of praise to the Lord.[92]

Apparently her husband was less than enthusiastic about his wife's new experience and wondered if she had lost her reason. But their daughter Leila, who was about 15 at the time, saw God's hand in it and persuaded her father to accept it.[93] Lancaster learned about the Pentecostal meetings at the home of Mrs Nickson, and Nickson and young John Coombe were her mentors for a time.[94] Soon others received the Holy Spirit through her ministry. Within a month, she had written to the York Street Mission and offered to give them a week of revival services. She was delighted with what happened—

John Coombe (Photo, E.Faulkner).

> How richly God blessed these dear ones! We would love to dwell upon the way in which He laid hold upon them, gripping them with His Spirit, and forcing to confession and reconsecration ... 'Yes, Lord, I will—I will go and make it right with that woman; I will go and get baptized!' and so confession and restitution proceeded. One middle-aged man who had stolen money when a shop boy had to take it fourfold to his late master's daughter before he got the smile of God. Another had to return a hammer he had stolen when an apprentice, and so on. Oh, what joy they got out of these confessions and restorations![95]

The first to be filled with the Spirit was blacksmith Charles Anstis, who was both a lay preacher and an 'enthusiastic open-air worker'. He was to be a faithful supporter of the work for the rest of his life. Other members of the family were equally involved, especially Edie Anstis, who spent nearly twenty years ministering in Perth, Western Australia.

In 1908, Lancaster founded Australia's first Pentecostal church.

LENNON, Thomas Bingham

Lennon, a genial character, with wavy hair and a handlebar moustache, underwent a dramatic conversion in 1916 in a Presbyterian church in Belfast, Ireland ('Oh the love, the pure love of God!... My whole soul was filled and thrilled by that wonderful power. It was a night never to be forgotten.').[96] Early the next year, the English Pentecostal evangelist Smith Wigglesworth (1859–1947) laid hands on him and prayed for him to be baptized in the Holy Spirit. He was told he had received the Spirit but was still dissatisfied. At a subsequent gathering he heard people praying for the fire of God and left the hall in fear lest literal fire consume him. After months of frustration, on 17 December 1917, at the Hopton Street Full Gospel Mission Hall, he broke through. The Spirit came around 9.30 pm and Lennon did not leave the Hall till around two the next morning—

> I knelt down beside a Brother Finlay—one who lived in the presence of God and knew the secret of praise and victory. Each time he shouted 'glory' it went straight to my heart, and as I knelt down next to him, I said, 'Oh, how I would like to be able to praise the Lord like this man.' Again the dear brother at my side shouted. But this time I was not silent. I said, 'Lord, I will praise Thee, for Thou art worthy.' Just then the power fell, and the glory of the Lord filled this temple. I shook from head to foot, till at last my limbs were too weak to support me and I went to the floor in a heap. How long I was on the floor I know not. One thing I am sure of, and that is, I was with Jesus. 'Oh, hallelujah!' Sorrow was past. Joy came. At last something wonderful happened. I was in the act of shouting glory, but my tongue seemed tied. But I knew I was in the Lord's hands. I was baptized in the Holy Ghost, and did speak in other tongues as the Spirit gave me utterance.[97]

Lennon was a lively preacher with a good grasp of Scripture and a clear presentation. He was not pretentious, being able to laugh at himself (he told Irish jokes) and to open his heart readily to his hearers. *Good News* published a series of messages on Jacob as a type of Christ in which he demonstrated a clear understanding of the gospel and a passion for godly living.

> Christ brings heaven and earth together. He brings God to man and man to God, for He has bridged the gulf betwixt man and God. This is the only sure way: get on the ladder, it will not break ...
>
> We are blessed with all spiritual blessings in the heavenlies 'in Christ'. He is the chosen one, and we are blessed 'in Him'; but we must make these blessings ours. We will never get saved and healed and filled with the Holy Spirit if we don't accept them; they are offered free to all.[98]

Lennon and his wife, now probably in their forties, conducted a busy program at Elim Hall in Marrickville, in Sydney, with five meetings each week, including a Saturday night 'tarrying meeting'. They were uncompromising in their attitudes to worldliness. At a special youth service, 'no items of a worldly nature were given' and in the light of the imminence of the second coming, they could not 'waste their time in worldly pleasures'. There were no fancy-dress balls at Elim Hall and no cricket or tennis clubs could have any part in their program. Their meetings were 'interdenominational in spirit, evangelical in message and international in project'.[99]

However, in spite of encouraging attendances and a steady flow of conversions, Lennon found the going too tough in Sydney. In July he and his wife moved to Vancouver, Canada, to a large church where hundreds attended and there were overflow crowds. *Good News* took the opportunity to make a point—

> Bro.T. B. Lennon and wife [sic] have left for USA. This means loss, especially for Sydney, for his ministry has been owned of God, and the exercise of the gifts which the Spirit of God had bestowed on him brought untold blessing to his hearers. Brother Lennon made no secret of the fact that his efforts were not adequately seconded and his usefulness was curtailed by lack of funds. He considers that Australian Pentecostal Christians, with a few bright exceptions, are not awake to

their responsibilities as God's stewards and do not sufficiently value the privilege of denying themselves in order to further the establishment of Christ's Kingdom on earth.[100]

Three years later, the magazine was delighted to announce that Lennon had accepted an invitation to take over the Apostolic Mission in Adelaide. The church was to be congratulated on securing a minister who was 'so uncompromising, fearless and gifted'. Unhappily, the Lennons could not obtain an early passage and ultimately did not come.[101]

McPHERSON, Aimee Semple (1890–1944)

Aimee Semple, born on a farm in Ingersoll, Ontario, Canada, on 9 October 1890, was brought up in a Christian home, and underwent a personal experience of conversion at the age of 17 under the ministry of Pentecostal evangelist Robert Semple, whom she later married.[102] Together they went as missionaries to China, where Semple died of malaria.

After returning to America, Aimee Semple remarried and expected to settle down. However, her desire to preach and her enjoyment of the public arena prompted her to begin evangelistic meetings, which soon proved to be very successful. Large crowds flocked to hear her and stories of the sick being healed began to multiply. She undertook a transcontinental tour, from New York to Los Angeles, using a specially decorated latest model 'gospel car'. Although she was avowedly Pentecostal, her charm and poise won her friends in all denominations. The pressure of this activity made the marriage untenable and in August 1921, she was divorced.

By 1922, she had begun the construction of the 5,300 seat Angelus Temple in Los Angeles and had developed her concept of the Foursquare Gospel—Jesus the Saviour, Jesus the Healer, Jesus the Baptizer in the Holy Spirit and Jesus the soon coming King. She visited Australia in 1922.

NEWTON, Archibald

Arch Newton, who was baptized in the Spirit in England, was the Methodist minister at Wynyard, Tasmania, in 1929. As a result of his ministry, Gordon Chilcott, a farmer at Flowerdale, received a Pentecostal experience.[103] Chilcott's wife was concerned about his sanity and called Newton in to deal with the matter. To her surprise, Newton was delighted. Chilcott later offered part of his property for the building of a small Pentecostal meeting place.

A local preacher named Gordon Bowling, whose father William Bowling had attended Good News Hall, was also baptized in the Spirit.[104] Both he and Newton were asked by the Methodist Conference to withdraw their Pentecostal practices or withdraw from the ministry. Bowling chose to join the Apostolic Church; Newton remained a Methodist, but became more discreet in his expression of his convictions. In 1935, the Apostolic magazine *Revival Echoes* paid tribute to Newton—

About six years ago, in answer to the call of God, there came to the circuit... a little man who was a veritable giant in the things that belong to our God. It was under his ministry that many learned in this centre what it meant to have unalloyed love for the Lord Jesus...[105]

Others felt the same way. 'His face glowed,' recalled one woman, who was just a teenager at the time. 'I used to sit and watch him pray. The glory of the Lord was upon him for sure.'[106]

SLOAN, William Cunningham (1870–1922)

At the age of 38, William Cunningham Sloan of Freeburgh, Victoria, was baptized in the Holy Spirit at Good News Hall. When hands were first laid on him, he had a vision of a full cob of corn upon his head, and when, two months later, the Spirit came, he was struck dumb for several hours, during which he believed God told him he would experience a sudden death which would leave his wife Eliza widowed—as indeed it did.[107] Within the year, Sloan was travelling with a tent 'in remote districts' and preaching 'a full salvation'.[108] This charismatic encounter opened up a whole new dimension of possibilities for the Sloans—

> We have had a few cases of casting out of evil spirits of infirmity, causing torment. Very often, I notice, when this is done they attack others, and unless the person is pleading the Blood, the demons find an entrance...

> We have been tested in the cases of our children in sickness, and when we pray and lay hands on them in the Name of JESUS CHRIST, they recover without any medicine.

> Mrs. Sloan has suffered since our marriage with a bad back, that has now troubled her for six years. The doctors could do nothing for her. A little while ago we were impressed that it was not disease, but a spirit of infirmity, and ministered to her according to the Scriptures, successful results following.[109]

It was no wonder that wild reports began to spread the district. People were warned to keep away from the Sloans, 'because it was very catching'.[110] Eliza recalled—

> Sympathising neighbours came pitying my sad plight, for they thought, 'Truly, she is mad,' and one dear soul said, 'The worst feature in it is that her husband upholds her in her madness.' The policeman was notified, and made occasional visits, only to have the Gospel preached to him. The butcher, baker, grocer, and hawkers all had Christ preached to them as they came.[111]

People gathered from near and far and the large room in Sloans' house used for meetings became too small. Prayer meetings were held that often lasted most of the night. Some saw visions. Others were divinely healed or delivered from binding habits. Mrs Ellen, a teacher's wife, who had a prolapse of the uterus, was healed and had no further problem, although she lived to be an octogenarian. Joseph Roggiero used to cycle several miles to Bible studies. After he visited the Sloans, to seek the fullness of the Spirit, he renounced his Freemasonry. Eliza Jackson, at 45 years of age, with nine children, a sick husband and unable to work because of a weak heart, recovered her strength and lived to the age of 96. Many experienced glossolalia. On more than one occasion, it was claimed there were examples of xenolalia. An Indian hawker who happened to come knocking at the door was convinced there was one of his countrymen inside. A Chinese man reputedly declared, with his finger pointing to heaven, that it was 'velly good talk'. The Jackson family of six brothers and three sisters were all converted—as were other members of their families. A dredge hole near the Freeburgh hill was used for baptisms.[112]

Will Jeffrey (1862–1932), a 'tall thin, serene man' from Wangaratta,[113] who later became a Pentecostal pastor, testified how he had heard of the 'great commotion' at Bright and went there at once to find out what was going on. Eliza Sloan challenged him about wearing glasses. If he was going to trust the Lord for healing, he must remove them. When he returned in January 1909, again Eliza Sloan spoke to him about his spectacles. He removed them again and found he could read and write without them. He returned in August, and asked them to pray for the 'nicotine demon to be cast out', which they did. He was now assured he would receive the Spirit—a conviction reinforced by a vision of three golden ears of wheat. From this time on he lost the desire to smoke. Finally, at Williamstown in September, after waiting on the Lord for eight days, he spoke in tongues and interpreted. It was only when he was willing, he said, 'to become nothing, lay ALL upon the altar, and make a complete surrender' that the Spirit came.[114] In 1914, Jeffrey founded the first Pentecostal church outside of Melbourne at Cleveden, near Parkes, NSW.[115]

Sloan was of average build and well known in the community as a firm but fair and honest man who was 'charitable in the extreme,' renowned for his 'Christian spirit' and 'greatly esteemed' in the community.[116] On one occasion, while preaching in the open air, he was struck in the face with an egg. 'God bless you,' he responded.[117] In spite of early antagonism to his new beliefs, he continued to be highly regarded.

After years of faithful ministry as a Methodist local preacher and an upright and generous-hearted citizen, Will Sloan died suddenly, as for fourteen years he had known he would. Working on a new Buffalo River bridge on 16 May 1922, he was struck on the head when a large beam slipped from position. He died instantaneously. Many tributes were paid to him at his funeral. The officiating minister, Rev F.H.Metcalfe, spoke of his 'beautiful, sweet and winsome' life and described him as 'the best loved man in the whole district'.[118]

Jeannie Lancaster visited the Sloan household on occasion and knew the family well. At Will's death she wrote the following—

> It is no trouble to confess that, of all our Pentecostal brethren, Will Sloan was dearest to our hearts. It was the love of God shed abroad in his heart that drew men's hearts to him. His life was one beautiful expression of the Love of God.[119]

VALDEZ, Alfred (1896–1988)

Alfred Valdez was brought up a Roman Catholic. His family became involved with the Azusa Street revival in Los Angeles in 1906–1909. But Alfred left home at an early age and tried the ways of the world, often being drunk and riding the rods under railway trucks. Later he recalled—

> I was never satisfied, always desiring something new. A wholesale liquor dealer had a monthly income from my wages, and today... sits comfortably in a mansion I helped build for him with my hard earned money.[120]

Disillusioned, he tried to improve his lifestyle. Finally, one day while picking oranges in Tustin, California, he realized his need of divine help. That night he prayed for mercy. From that time, he changed. He attended night school to improve his education. In 1916, as a twenty-year-old, he was ordained an evangelist and in 1918, felt called to Australia, which was confirmed by a prophecy in 1924.

Notes

1. GN 17:5 May 1926, 18.
2. See *The Commercial and Trade Directory* (Adelaide: Morris, Hayter and Barry, 1882), 12;*Sands and McDougall Trade Directories* (Adelaide: 1911–1929).
3. T. J. Ames, *A Problem: Now and Then* Adelaide, published by the author, 1902.
4. Ames, *Punishment*, n. d.
5. *Pentecostal Times,* Adelaide, n. d., 1, 1.
6. Only two issues survive in the Mortlock Library, Adelaide, where they are classified as '1907?' This date seems too early, as there is an extract in the first issue from the *Latter Rain Evangel*, a journal first published in Chicago, Ill, in October 1908 and in the second issue from *Confidence*, an English magazine which also began in 1908. There is also a testimony from *The Apostolic Faith*. This would suggest a date of 1909 at the earliest for *Pentecostal Times*.
7. E.g. PT, 1, 8; PT, 2, 12; GN, 9:1, February, 1923, 23; GN, 17:10, October, 1926, 19.
8. PT, 2, 8.
9. GN, 15:6, June, 1924, 9.
10. GN, 17:5, May, 1926, 12.
11. GN, 19:10, October, 1928, 18; GN, 19:12, December, 1928, 18.
12. Brett, 'Maxwell Armstrong', 1996, 3; N. L. Armstrong, personal interview, 30 April, 1990. Further details of Maxwell Armstrong are from these sources unless otherwise stated.
13. AE, 6:2, January, 1940, 6; RTS, 1939, 42.
14. N. L. Armstrong, personal interview, 30 April, 1990; E. Michalk, personal interview, 18 December, 1993. In Parkes, if someone was absent from church, Armstrong would cycle to their home to anoint them with oil for healing. There was no other acceptable reason why they should not be present.
15. AE, 11:1, December, 1944, 17; AE, 11:9, August, 1945, 16.

16. Brett, 1996, 9.
17. AE, 6:11, April, 1933, 6, 11; AE, 13:10, September, 1947, 15; T. Bentley, personal interview, 23 April, 1997; M. Duncan, personal interview, 29 October, 1993; N. L. Armstrong, personal interview, 8 October, 1993.
18. T. Bentley, personal interview, 23 April, 1997; L. Manley-Breen, personal interview, July, 1990.
19. Wilson, 1948, 139; Booth-Clibborn, 1962, 55.
20. Wilson, 1948, 138; M. Troutt, *The General Was a Lady* (Nashville: Holman and Co),109, quoted in J. Owens, 'William Booth-Clibborn,' (unpublished essay, Sydney, Tabor College), 1994, 2.
21. Booth-Clibborn, 1962, 13, 17ff. Further details of Booth-Clibborn's early life are from this source unless otherwise stated.
22. W. Booth-Clibborn, 'How "The rest and the Refreshing" Came to Me,' GN, 20:7, July, 1929, 7.
23. E. Booth-Clibborn, 1989, 13.
24. *Cooee*, Toowoomba, No. 7, 6, December, 1931.
25. GN, 15:9, September, 1924, 18; AE, 10:8, July, 1937, 10.
26. GN, 19:12, December, 1928, 10; GN, 20:1, January, 1929, .9; GN, 23:11, November, 1932, 12f; GN, 24:3, March, 1933, 6f. Further details are from these sources unless otherwise stated.
27. M. Brawner, 'What the Printed Message Can Do', GN, 16:3, March, 1925, 13.
28. For brief background on Leila Buchanan see RTS, 1939, 45.
29. W. A. Buchanan, personal correspondence, n. d.; GN, January, 1913, 20ff. General details of W. A. Buchanan are from these sources unless otherwise stated.
30. L. Harris, personal interview, n. d.; GN, June, 1928, 14; GN, August, 1928, 10.
31. S. Douglas, personal interview, 21 November, 1989; F. Lancaster, personal interview, 18 December, 1993; A. Wilson, personal communication, n. d. but late 1994; Jean Conwell, personal interview, c.1991 ('He could quote half the Bible in one sermon').
32. Buchanan once said, 'If you marry a child of the devil don't be surprised if you have trouble with your father-in-law.' On another occasion, when accused of 'sheep stealing' (i.e. inviting members of other congregations to his church), he replied, 'The Bible says, My sheep hear my voice and a stranger they will not follow...' S. Douglas, personal interview, 21 November, 1989; F. Lancaster, personal interview, 18 December, 1993; R. Read, personal interview, 19 November, 1990.
33. M. Nugent, personal interview, November, 1990.
34. *Cooee*, 2:24, 21 February, 1932.
35. AE, 3:8, July, 1937, 6; AE, 4:5, April, 1938, 6; AE, 11.4, March, 1945, 2; F. Lancaster, personal interview, 18 December, 1993.
36. L. Priest, personal interview, 17 September, 1971; Salvation Army Records, Melbourne.
37. See Chant, 1984, 66ff; Frodsham, 1971; Hibbert, 1982, Hywel-Dvies, 1987; Chant, 1984, 70; D. Reekie, personal interview, 14 August 1991. Wigglesworth was a plumber by profession and poorly educated. At the age of 48 he had been baptized in the Holy Spirit and commenced an evangelistic ministry that was to take him around the world. He was forthright in manner and utterly fearless in ministry. He regularly prayed for the sick in his services. It was also not unusual for him to punctuate his preaching with glossolalic utterances, which he himself would interpret before resuming his message. Some of these interpretations are included in *Ever Increasing Faith*.
38. L. Priest, personal interview, 17 September, 1991.
39. D. Reekie, personal interview, 14 August, 1991; *The Christian Weekly and Methodist Journal*, 20 July, 1883; GN, 1:1, Apri,l 1910, 3, 5.

40. The hall was named after Mary Leavitt, whose prominence in the WCTU has already been noted.
41. GN, 1:1, April, 1910, 16.
42. 'Your young men shall see visions,' GN, 1:5, January, 1913, 17.
43. GN, 15:7, July, 1924, 10. Note that Dolly is not actually named in this article, but there seems little doubt she is the person being quoted.
44. Greenwood, *Life Story,* 1965, 50; GN, 16:9, September, 1925, 17.
45. A. Davidson (nee Enticknap), personal interview, 20 November, 1990.
46. 'H', 'By Ways that We Knew Not of,' GN, 15:7, July, 1924, 7.
47. GN, 15:8, August, 1924, 11; GN, 15:9, September, 1924, 11; Duncan, *Pentecost,* 50; GN, 16:1, January, 1925, 7; GN, 15:8, August, 1924, 11; GN, 15:9, September, 1924, 11; GN, 23:12, December 1932, 5.
48. RTS, 1939, 42.
49. Duncan, *Pentecost,* 50. There is some suggestion that Dennis married at one point but left her husband, which raised a question mark over her ministry in the minds of some people. See A. Davidson, personal interview, 20 November, 1990.
50. V. Chant, 'The Family Background of John Alexander Dowie,' unpublished essay, Tabor College, 1991; *Bulletin,* 3 March, 1904, 3; see also the *Advertiser,* 26 March, 1904, 10—'Referring to his name, he said he was known as John Alexander Dowie. That was not the name he ought to have. He was not going to talk on the subject in this city ... nothing would induce him to speak on the subject.' Hollenweger suggests that because Dowie knew he had been conceived out of wedlock, he may have come to the conclusion that John Murray was not really his father. Hollenweger, 1988, 117, 123.
51. *The Aldine Almanac and Directory for South Australia* (Adelaide: Isaiah Boothby, 1872), 115. This business was later acknowledged as 'admitted by experts in the trade to be one of the best, if not the best, boot factory in Australasia'. See W. F. Morrison, *The Aldine History of South Australia* (Sydney and Adelaide: The Aldine Publishing Company, 1890), 808; *Aldine Almanack*, 1868,7
52. Morrison, 807. David Hilliard notes that Congregationalists were particularly conscious of their 'special appeal to the commercial and trading classes' and that in the middle of the nineteenth century, 'the houses of Congregational businessmen dominated Rundle Street'. See Hilliard, 1980, 6.
53. *The South Australian Independent and Presbyterian,* Vol VI, January, 1878, 91; November 1878, 16; Kiek, 1927, 297.
54. Darms, 2; Kiek, 1927, 297f
55. Darms, 3–4; Sheldrake, ed, 1912, 13
56. *Register,* 11 March, 1907. Note that both Sheldrake (14) and Darms (4) claim that Dowie worked for his uncle Alexander in the boot factory.
57. Darms, 4; Kiek, 1927, 297; Carl Lee, 'God's Messenger', LH, Vol LXXXVIII, No 10, October, 1951, 77.
58. Sheldrake, 1912, 15. Note that Kiek suggests 1871 as the date for Dowie's appointment to Alma. See *Our First 100 Years, the Centenary Record of the South Australian Congregational Union* Adelaide: SA Congregational Union, n. d., 25. Cox, on the other hand claims he was ordained to the Alma pastorate on 21 May, 1872, a date which is quoted by Dowie himself in *Sin in the Camp*, which he wrote in 1883. See F. W. Cox, *Jubilee Record 1837–1887, The Congregational Churches of Australia (*Adelaide: Webb, Vardon and Pritchard, 1887). Cameron claims Dowie was called to Alma in May 1871. See J. Cameron, *In Stow's Footsteps* (Adelaide: SA Congregational History Project

Committee, 1987). This should probably read 1872. The dates in the text seem most likely as they are recorded in letters written at the time by Dowie.

59. Hilliard, 1980, 3ff.
60. Sheldrake, 1912, 15–16.
61. Sheldrake, 1912, 19.
62. Sheldrake, 1912, 26.
63. C. G. Enticknap, 'Address,' Rosewater, 17 October, 1965.
64. C. G. E(nticknap), 'They Shall Be Abundantly Satisfied,' GN, 15:9, September, 1924, 9; RTS, 1939, 44.
65. GN, April, 1924, 13; September, 1924, 9, 10.
66. GN, 15:6, June, 1924, 8; GN, 15:12, December, 1924, 14; GN, 16:2, February, 1925, 9. Note that Enticknap gives 29 January as the date, but in 1924 this was a Tuesday.
67. C. G. Enticknap, 'Address,' Townsville, 13 May, 1984; .RTS, 1939, 44; 'Cooee,' 2:24, 21 February, 1932.
68. K. Glover, AE, September, 1926, 4,5; AE, February, 1935, 4, 5, 10; AE, April, 1944, 6f.
69. K. Glover, 'Bethrothed to a Prince,' AE, April, 1944, 6f; K. Glover, 'The Overcomer,' lecture given on 29 April, 1926, at Richmond Temple, 26f.
70. J. Hewitt, 'How Pastor John Hewitt received the Baptism of the Holy Spirit,' HG, 21:4, July–August, 1962, 84.
71. L. Hewitt, personal interview, January, 1989.
72. SMH, 19 February, 1927, 7.
73. GC, 2:1, March, 1933, 90.
74. Gardiner, 1990, 15.
75. *Home Missionaries Card Records* (Uniting Church of Australia, Synod of Victoria Archives).
76. *Argus,* 11 March, 1922, 12.
77. William Durham received the Spirit in 1907 at Azusa Street, Los Angeles, and soon became a leader in the newly established Pentecostal movement in America, where his Stone Church at Chicago became a centre of Pentecostal preaching and practice— Durham, *Testimony,* 1911.
78. *Minute Book*, Southern Evangelical Mission, Brighton, Victoria.
79. The number of wireless licences in Australia rose from nil in 1920 to 300,000 in 1930. Several of Horne's scripts are extant.
80. M. Hurst, personal interview, 14 August, 1941; personal correspondence, 27 August, 1993; D. Harvey, personal interview, 24 September, 1991.
81. Terowie was made famous on 20 March 1942 as the place where General Douglas MacArthur made his historic vow, 'I shall return'.
82. Little is known of Rieschiek's background. He was involved in the beginnings of several Pentecostal congregations and meetings in Adelaide.
83. GN, 17:6, June, 1926, 13.
84. G. H. J (Gus Jansen) in AN, 3:2, December, 1931.
85. See the appropriate Trade Directories, 1912–1939; AN, 1:1, 1 September, 1929, 1; GN, 17:4, April, 1926, 13f; N. Fabian, interview, 15 August, 1991; D. McKenzie, interview, 25 September, 1991.
86. F. Lancaster, personal communication, 3 July, 1992.
87. GN, 17:10, October, 1926, 10f; GN, 1:1, April, 1910, 8.
88. F. Lancaster, personal interview, 18 December, 1993.
89. J. Lancaster, 'Can God Mend a Broken Arm?' GN, 1:1, April, 1910, 21ff.

90. GN, 19:11, November, 1928, 4f.

91. GN, 17:9, September, 1926, 10. Lancaster's grandson, Fred Lancaster, recalls his father saying that Lancaster first heard about Pentecostalism from a tract she found in a book purchased from Coles Book Arcade. This may have preceded her letter to England, but as this was not her own testimony, it cannot be verified. F. Lancaster, personal interview, 18 December 1993.

92. This description of Lancaster's baptism in the Spirit is based on her testimony in GN, 17:9, September, 1926, 10, the statement of faith in GN, 9:1, February, 1923, 23 and McPherson, 1923, 501.

93. F. Lancaster, personal interview, 18 December, 1993.

94. GN, 17:9, September, 1926, 11.

95. GN, 17:10, October, 1926, 11.

96. T. Lennon, 'A Wonderful Baptism,' GN, 15:2, February, 1924, .8ff; GN, 15:7, July, 1924, 13; T. Lennon, 'Jacob, a Type of Christ,' GN, 16:2, February, 1925, 11. Further details are from these sources unless otherwise stated.

97. This quotation is a blend of statements from the two records of Lennon's testimony in GN, 15:2, February, 1924, 9 and GN, 16:2, February, 1925, 11.

98. GN, 15:7, July, 1924, 12.

99. GN, 15:3, March, 1924, 18; GN, 15:6, June 1924, 8.

100. GN, 15:11, November, 1924, 16; GN, 18:11, November, 1927, 14; GN, 15:9, September, 1924, 11.

101. GN, 18:8, August, 1927, 20; GN, 18:11, November, 1927, 14.

102. See C. M. Robeck in Burgess et al, eds, 1988, 568ff; Blumhofer, 1993; Wilson, *Religious Sects,* 1970.

103. G. Chilcott, personal interview, n. d.

104. G. Bowling, personal interview, n .d.

105. RE, 2:12, May, 1935, 230.

106. Gladys Walters, personal interview, March, 1994. Apostolic meetings were held in her parents' home in the early 1930s. See RE, 2:12, May, 1935, 230.

107. J. Lancaster, 'Open Letter,' GN, 9:1, February, 1923, 6; *Alpine Observer,* 19 May, 1922.

108. *Confidence,* November, 1909, 260.

109. GN, 1:1, April, 1910, 20.

110. M. Jackson, personal communication, 8 May, 1992.

111. GN, 1:1, April, 1910, 10.

112. E. Faulkner, personal interview, 10 April, 1992; .M. Jackson, personal communication, 8 May, 1992. One of these brothers, Leigh Jackson, turned 100 years of age in April, 1982 and was 'still witnessing about his wonderful Saviour' in 1984, .E. Henshall, personal communication; M. Jackson, personal communication., 8 May, 1992.

113. M. Gozzard quoted in I. Aizstrauts, 'Will Jeffrey 1862–1932,' unpublished essay, Sydney: Tabor College, 1994, 7.

114. This was possibly at the home of Jeannie Lancaster or of Winnie Andrews, the first secretary of the Pentecostal churches in Australia. GN, 1:1, April, 1910, 6, 12ff.

115. AE, 30 November, 1930, 5; *The Western Champion,* 25 November, 1932.

116. 'Sad Fatality at Buffalo River,' AO, 19 May, 1922.

117. M. Jackson, personal communication, 8 May, 1992.

118. 'Sad Fatality at Buffalo River,' AO 19 May 1922. Sloan may have believed his death would be through persecution, but it turned out to be the result of an accident. E. Faulkner, personal interview, 10 April 1992.

119. J. Lancaster, 'Open Letter,' GN, 9:1, February, 1923,.6.

120. A. C. Valdez, 'My Chains Fell Off,' AE, August, 1928; Valdez, transcript, c.1964; A. C. Valdez, *Fire on Azusa Street, 1980;* Burgess et al, eds, 1988, 868.

APPENDIX C

THE PLACE OF EXPERIENCE

An essay on the significance in early Australian Pentecostalism of an experiential encounter with God

In the fledgling Pentecostal movement, the need for men and women to have a meaningful and identifiable encounter with God was a primary focus. From the earliest days, it was understood that 'true' Christianity was marked by an observable and biblically-justified manifestation of faith.

In 1925, *Good News* magazine published an article by English Pentecostal patriarch, Donald Gee entitled, 'A Plea for Experience', in which he argued that experience was essential to successful ministry. A man with an experience would never be intimidated by one who had only an argument. There were those who warned of the dangers of basing the Christian life on experiences, but through all the ages, revival had rested on the shoulders of just such people. Thousands of Pentecostal people were currently testifying of a 'mighty experience' of God that had changed their lives—including speaking in tongues—and were not ashamed of it. Then he concluded, 'We suggest that those who have no personal experience of these things might well speak more softly at times.'[1]

Gee is careful to stress that the Scriptures remain paramount, and that to ignore them is to court disaster, but his unapologetic stance here is illustrative of the widespread attitude of Pentecostals that, far from being embarrassed about charismatic phenomena, they see them as strengths. On another occasion, Gee suggested that just as it was impossible to be baptized in water on dry land, it was impossible to receive the Spirit on dry formality. Receiving the Spirit was a definite experience and you would know when it happened.[2] Christianity was a 'divine intoxication', wrote James Black.[3]

A 1923 testimonial at Good News Hall said, 'You can take many things from a man, but there is one thing you can never take, and that is his experience.'[4] Two years later, *Good News* included without comment the simple assertion, 'You cannot have a spiritual blessing without a material manifestation.'[5] Another writer asserted, 'An ideal Pentecostal Church is a demonstrative church.'[6] F. B. Van Eyk had no doubt of it—

> I tell you, 'Experiment is the test of truth'—no man can argue an experience away, and I know that, just as God baptized the Apostle Paul with the Holy Ghost, He has graciously and mercifully baptized me. Glory be to God!... My plea is for experience, and experience is the only test.[7]

Evangelist William Booth-Clibborn lamented, 'Many of us have too much of our religion in our heads and not enough in our hearts.'[8] AFM pastor Edwin Ridgway wrote, 'Let us press on and have a definite experience, one that measures up to the Word of God, so that we will not be among the foolish virgins when the Bridegroom comes.'[9] One evangelist affirmed that she would only count converts if she had reason to believe they had 'found the Lord in a real experience'.[10]

For Evangelicals, this emphasis on experience, far from being a strength, was a weakness. G. H. Morling, Principal of the Baptist Theological College of New South Wales from 1921 to 1960, wrote—

> The Pentecostal movement seriously disturbs scriptural balance and proportion. It exalts religious experience unduly, giving a place of improper prominence to the feelings as against the will which is ever primary. Not ecstasy, but action, best expresses loyalty to Christ.[11]

Notwithstanding Morling's reservations, there were experiences in abundance in the early Pentecostal meetings. Nellie Robson was sitting in Good News Hall with three other women. Three times she clearly heard her name called, but it was none of the others who spoke. A minister's wife lay for two hours, her arms outstretched in the form of a cross, groaning and crying as if she were being crucified. Walking home from a meeting one night, a Perth woman found herself laughing heartily and then nearly sank to the ground as she began speaking in tongues. Another man lay on the floor for hours and then was 'too helplessly drunk' to stand up. A Queensland woman testified to three and a half hours of 'shakings' before she received the Spirit. In Yungaburra, Queensland, in 1930, for over half an hour the group all listened to what they described as the sound of a full orchestra playing 'heavenly music'. F. B. Van Eyk spoke of singing in the Spirit, where the congregation all sang together in tongues, with neither leadership nor accompaniment. 'Its modulations, rhythm, harmony, expression and time are altogether beyond description,' he said. Singers were carried beyond their normal range and ordinary people sounded like trained vocalists. On another occasion, in Perth, for two minutes, 'the Holy Spirit blew so wonderfully that all felt the terrific force, violence, and awfulness of the wind.' This was followed by laughter and singing in the Spirit. One man related how an angel had hovered over his bed when he was nearly dying of diphtheria—he felt the wind over his face. After that, he recovered quickly. Lancaster related that on more than one occasion she had seen people lifted from one place to another 'as though they were feathers'. When Len Jones preached in Cessnock, 'like a mighty gale the Spirit of God swept over the audience' until scores of people were lying prostrate on the floor. When one family found themselves with no money even for food, a grey and white bird alighted in front of them with a piece of paper in its beak which it dropped. It was a ten shilling note. Other money was slipped under their door anonymously and by the end of the week the food shelves were full and there were seven pounds left over.[12]

On more than one occasion, Lancaster defended unusual physical behaviour by pointing out that actions such as 'travail,' trembling, lifting of hands, shaking, acting as a fool, behaving as though drunk, praying all night, sighing, speaking with stammering lips and other tongues and generally 'extraordinary' behaviour were all to be found in the Bible.[13] It was an exercise in proof texting rather than exegesis, but it was not entirely without validity.

Visions

The most common numinous experience was the seeing of visions. There were dozens of reports of these. One woman saw herself as ascending to meet Jesus but being dragged back by a relative. This was interpreted as a warning to those who would seek to frustrate the faith of others. William Sloan of Freeburgh, Victoria, saw a vision of a dove dropping a full cob of corn on his head when hands were laid on him. Doris Warburton appeared to grasp some unseen object. 'I've got it,' she exclaimed. 'The rain, the rain, the beautiful golden rain; enough for all; you can have a bucketful...'[14] When Tom Sharman's wife first came to Good News Hall in 1911, through laying on of hands, their daughter was healed of toothache and, although no one came near their son who was 'dying in hospital from typhoid and pneumonia', at the same hour that prayers were offered at the Hall, he recovered. All this made Tom Sharman angry rather than convinced. That night as he was lying smoking in bed, he saw a vision of two men struggling followed by an appearance of Christ. The message was plain—if he gave up the struggle, peace and blessing would be his. Finally, he yielded. He threw his pipe in the fire and, although largely illiterate, found he could read the Bible. Because he had no education, God 'taught (him) by visions'. Nearly a century later, there were five members of the Sharman family in Pentecostal ministry.[15]

In Melbourne, on 31 July 1914, K. Matthews predicted that the Japanese would overrun Australia, occupying the cities on the Eastern seaboard. The immediate future was to be enveloped in war and the great Day of Tribulation was near. On 30 September 1914, eight weeks after Great Britain declared war on Germany, she prophesied that the nations would be let loose at one another in punishment for rejecting His Son. She was so appalled by what she heard coming from her own lips, that she cried, 'Don't, Lord, don't! Dear Lord, spare them!' It would be nearly thirty years till the Japanese attacked Australia's shores, but there was sufficient evidence of distress among the nations for her to be taken seriously.[16]

One woman was worried about going through the Great Tribulation, but a voice woke her one night assuring her that at that time she would be 'enjoying herself with Jesus'. Another woman saw herself and her family walking on a narrow path surrounded by deep chasms. She was terrified the path was too narrow for them all, but she saw the words 'Cling to Me' before her in golden letters. 'Perhaps,' said her husband, 'we are on the broad path and thinking too much of this world.'[17]

William Lane of Maryborough saw a vision of Christ stretched on a cross midway between heaven and earth. Harriet Weldon saw a hand with its thumb severed—a warning against division in the church. A seven year old boy described a picture of crowds of angels descending upon him. Samuel Hack saw the people in his church walking through a door through a fountain of blood and being stripped and cleansed of everything that was of the world. Another saw horses as in Zechariah chapter one, and this was understood as a presage of troubled times. Another saw himself under a cloudburst but did not get wet—it was spiritual rain. To another, the word 'SOON' was written on the wall, an indication of the return of Christ. A woman beheld a man going off to get water while an outstretched hand, firm and soft, drew her upwards. The lesson was plain: not to leave it too late to gain the water of life.[18]

Dora Morris watched herself trying to climb a ladder, but needed help to reach the middle rung. Lancaster suggested this was the baptism in the Holy Spirit and that there were more rungs beyond that for which Dora should reach.[19] One of the sisters saw an angel hovering over her bed as a result of which she felt called to a ministry of visiting the sick.[20] Robert Davis beheld Christ being crucified between two thieves and could hear the drip-drip-drip of blood on the linoleum floor. The thieves faded and he saw only Jesus. This led to his conversion and to many years of service as an elder and pastor.[21]

A man had an extended vision of a group of his friends being burned in a terrible fire; then he was confronted by Christ who showed him the prints in His hands and feet. As a result he was baptized in water and filled with the Spirit. Later he also saw a bewitching woman but realized she was the seductive 'Babylon the Great'. On other occasions, he saw Italian and Russian troops marshalled and realized there was 'a terrible time coming'. During the opening prayer at a Sunday evening service, in Mackay in 1928, Annie Dennis could see war lords holding back straining dogs of war. The leading one for Australia was Japan. It was time to prepare our hearts to be overcomers.[22]

Being Baptized in the Holy Spirit

The primacy of the experiential is most obvious in early Pentecostalism through being baptized in the Holy Spirit. The earliest extant Australian published statement on this topic was written by Thomas James Ames, the leader of the first Pentecostal assembly formed in Adelaide (c.1909).[23] Around 1909, he began to publish a 12-page periodical called *Pentecostal Times*.[24] This was basically a collection of articles from overseas Pentecostal magazines, with one or two testimonies from local people and a couple of pieces by Ames himself. The Foreword to the first issue declared uncompromisingly that 'the power of the Apostolic Church was its Pentecost' and that the problem with the Church today was that overall it had relegated Pentecost to the past.

The *Times* found its way interstate and in 1924, was criticised in another journal for its belief in 'manifestations, signs and wonders'. There were excellent people connected with the Pentecostal movement, said the writer, and his sympathies lay with their desire for more spiritual power. Generally, Christians had given too little attention to the command to be filled with the Spirit. But these good people were making the mistake of looking for manifestations as an end in themselves. And anyone acquainted with history knew there was danger attendant on such phenomena.[25]

Ames had answered these objections from the beginning. Two full pages in the first issue were devoted to a study entitled, 'What is the Evidence of the Baptism of the Holy Ghost?' It was a challenging, but thoughtfully reasoned piece in which he asserted that baptism in the Holy Spirit with the sign of speaking in tongues was 'a pivotal doctrine in the Pentecostal movement'.[26] This teaching had drawn a great deal of criticism. Others had claimed various alternative experiences, but none satisfied the Scriptures. The Spirit had always worked in manifold ways, but there was 'no experience that could be compared with the glorious baptism'. The devil hated the doctrine of tongues because he knew that it was 'the evidence of the baptism', and when people believed in it, they would be filled with God's Spirit. Being filled with the Spirit should not be confused with feelings or the stirring of the emotions, although there might well be unusual manifestations. It was evident that in the days of the Apostles, people spoke in tongues when they were filled with the Spirit. If this was the case then, was it a mistake to believe it should be so today?

Ames then examined the record of Acts showing how in each of the significant passages detailing an effusion of the Spirit, glossolalia was present. So he threw out a challenge—

> Will someone be good enough to inform us why the Apostles in all these cases did not tell these converts simply to believe they had received the Holy Spirit and they would have Him? If the theories of today are right, these folks would have been taught that it was wrong for them to expect to feel anything or to expect any sign to follow; that the true way of faith was to simply take for granted that because God had promised a thing they had it, and that it was unbelief to expect to receive any tangible experience.

This early conviction that the experience of receiving the Spirit was a required part of Christian initiation was the cornerstone of Pentecostal theology. Ames concluded—

> We have set forth the Scriptural way of receiving the gift of the Holy Ghost—not, as the opposers accuse us of doing—of receiving the gift of tongues—but of receiving the gift of the Holy Spirit, which is evidenced in all cases by the speaking in other tongues as the Spirit gives utterance. Is it not sad that the one Scriptural

way of receiving the Holy Ghost is being criticised and condemned by the leading religious teachers?[27]

When they spoke in tongues, the early Pentecostals believed that the Spirit of God was speaking through them. It was not just an outburst of ecstasy. To them, they were uttering words given by God Himself. In the report of the first recorded Pentecostal baptism in the Spirit in Australia, Richard Beauglehole told how the Spirit took possession of his throat and tongue and spoke through him in other tongues. Pentecostal patriarch Alex Buchanan described his experience in the same way. Another thought it a miracle that God should take her tongue and make it speak a language she had never heard before.[28] Similar expressions occur regularly in published stories and testimonies.

Ames's approach was to become the standard for Pentecostal apologetics. Consistently, passages from the Acts of the Apostles were used as a basis for teaching and seen as precedents on which contemporary understanding and experience could be based.[29]

Edwin Ridgway, a prominent member at Good News Hall, followed a similar approach. It was possible to have the Holy Spirit within, he argued, yet not to have the full measure of the Spirit, as the parable of the Virgins clearly showed. Jesus promised not only a well of water, but also rivers of living water. He told His disciples to wait until the Spirit came on them in power. The Samaritans believed but did not initially receive the Spirit. The Ephesian believers had repented and then were baptized but still needed the Spirit. The sign of the coming of the Spirit in New Testament times was speaking in tongues, which occurred at Pentecost, at Caesarea, at Ephesus and at Corinth. God gave the Holy Spirit to those who obeyed him.[30]

Pioneer evangelist Florrie Mortomore taught that through the Old Testament prophets and the words of Jesus, God had promised to send His Spirit. When the Spirit came at Pentecost, marvellous phenomena were evident and there were astounding results—the sick were healed and the dead raised (Acts 3:8; 8:7; 9:37ff). And what was the effect of this? First, wonder, then mockery and finally persecution! But it was not strange that men should oppose God's work, for 'the natural man' usually did. It was clear that Christian believers already possessed the Spirit of Jesus (Romans 8:9) but it was also important to be baptized in the Spirit. In fact, although we became partakers of eternal life through the atonement of Christ, 'we would not be your friends if we did not tell you' that it was only by being baptized in the Spirit that you became a member of the body of Christ (1 Corinthians 12:13). In fact, it was impossible to become part of Christ's body in any other way.[31]

It was not enough to say you had experienced great joy or great power in prayer, she continued. The apostles experienced such things before they were baptized in the Spirit. It was necessary to repent and be baptized so that God could send His Spirit. How could we know when we were baptized in the Spirit? In the same way that Peter and Cornelius and Paul knew, through speaking in other tongues (Acts 2:4ff; 10:44ff; 19:6). God did not change (Malachi 3:6). Jesus promised that believers would speak in tongues (Mark 16:17).

We may have plenty of fruit trees and labourers, Mortomore pointed out, but without the rain they were useless. God was pouring out the 'latter rain' (Hosea 6:3) and it was now time to ask the Lord for it (Zechariah 10:1). God would not refuse to answer for He had promised to pour water on the thirsty (Isaiah 44:3). There were now some 200,000 believers around the world who spoke in tongues.

Then followed a personal testimony of Mortomore's own experience with an urgent exhortation to seek the Spirit in order to be ready for the Lord's coming again.[32]

The most lucid teaching on baptism in the Holy Spirit was given by John A. D. Adams, a former New Zealand barrister, now resident in Melbourne and at one time President of the Apostolic Faith Mission based at Good News Hall. From February 1928 to May 1928, *Good News* included a series of articles on the subject which were later published in book form, describing the Pentecostal position in the careful, plodding fashion of a legal document. First Adams examined biblical promises of the baptism in the Spirit; then he noted how they had been fulfilled in the early church. By cataloguing the signs and wonders they performed, he showed how the coming of the Spirit had transformed the first Christians. A brief study of spiritual gifts followed and then an argument for the baptism of the Spirit. Like others before him, he showed how there was a pattern in the book of Acts of the sign of glossolalia. The rest of the 71 pages were devoted to answering charges and summoning witnesses in support of his case.[33]

F. B. Van Eyk was also a strong advocate for the Pentecostal position. There was no doubt about his enthusiasm for his subject. Like Ames, Mortomore and Adams, Van Eyk used the record of the Acts of the Apostles as his foundation. Just as Jesus baptized various groups of early believers with the Spirit, so it was His prerogative still to do so today.[34] It was also plain that the usual sign of the Spirit's coming was speaking in tongues. There was a strong connection grammatically in Acts 19:6 between the phrases 'the Holy Ghost came on them' and 'they spoke with tongues'. It was quite clear that no one in Apostolic times ever thought of a baptism in the Spirit without tongues.

This being so, it was needful to note the infinite value of this sign of the sovereign grace of God. It served as a landmark locating both the honest man who thought he had the baptism and the dishonest man who posed as having the baptism when he did not possess it; and it acted as an impetus to the honest seeker, urging the uncertain soul to seek until he consciously and intelligently received it.

In one of her few signed articles, Lancaster addressed the question, 'What's the Use of Tongues?' Her answers were simple and straightforward and always undergirded by biblical texts. Firstly, tongues proved that Jesus spoke the truth, for He foretold that believers would speak in tongues (Mark 16:17). She did not mince matters. Those who had passed from death to life loved the brothers (1 John 3:14). If readers did not love those who spoke in tongues, they were still under condemnation of death! Secondly, tongues were a sign to unbelievers (1 Corinthians 14:21f). On the day of Pentecost, they demonstrated that the One they had crucified was alive again. Thirdly, tongues edified those who spoke (1 Corinthians 14:4). Fourthly, God was worshipped through tongues as they were worshiping 'in spirit' (John 4:23f). Next, tongues were for speaking 'mysteries' which God was revealing to the Church and used in exorcism and healing. Paul needed to speak in tongues (1 Corinthians 14:18) and expressed his desire that all believers should do so (1 Corinthians 14:5). Were tongues only for the establishing of the church? Well, in that case, they were still needed. The gifts that Christ gave after His ascension were to remain until we all came into unity and perfection (Ephesians 4:8, 13). Yes, there were counterfeit gifts, but this was no reason for avoiding the genuine. If we asked in faith, God would give us the Holy Spirit, not a counterfeit (Luke 11:11-13). Must it be written of the readers that they refused to receive God's Spirit? Tongue-speaking was the cry of the new-born babe in Christ. The Father loved to hear his children cry to Him. An objector might ask, Should not everything be done decently and in order? Certainly, but 'in God's order, not in man's'. There was disorder at Pentecost, but it was the work of God.[35]

It was common to refer to being baptized in the Spirit as being 'sealed' with the Spirit. Based on Ephesians 1:13, 14, this was the understanding that the fullness of the Spirit was a 'seal' or guarantee of true conversion. In Brisbane, two brothers who were 'very hungry' were both 'sealed' by the Lord. In Melbourne, several were guided to the meetings 'as though led by an invisible hand' and were 'sealed'. In Cairns, A. J. Deacon, who became one of the stalwarts of the church there, was 'sealed', after much prayer. In Maryborough, there were ten people 'sealed' at Easter 1928, with a total of 94 by the middle of the year. At the 1930 Christmas Convention at Good News Hall, on Christmas morning, a 'big six-foot-one unemployed convert—formerly a Roman Catholic communist' was 'sealed' with the Spirit, as was nine-year-old May Lancaster, and a group of her friends. A Salvation Army believer lamented that she was not 'truly sealed,' attended Good News Hall and was filled with the Spirit. The result was that she no longer had any doubts—she had received the guarantee of her faith and knew that Jesus was real. So the Lord knew those who were His through the 'seal' of the Holy Spirit. 'Brother' Barnes argued that without such a God-given utterance, believers would be tempted to stop short of being filled, mistaking 'a wealth of feeling' for the baptism in the Spirit. Emotion in itself was not enough.[36]

Demarcation

This concept was to become the point of demarcation between Pentecostalism and other revival movements. While there had been many revival movements over the years marked by varieties of emotional phenomena, none of them had enshrined such experiences in a biblical doctrine before. Wesleyanism had come closest to it, with its teaching of a climactic experience of Christian perfection. But as this concept was moved to the periphery of Methodist belief, so the experiential side of Methodism languished.

From the days of the second century Montanists, through the Middle Ages, with groups like the Cathars and the Templars, into the Reformation period, with the Anabaptists and later the so-called French Prophets, through the Wesleyan revival and the great Awakening, into the various nineteenth century revival movements such as the 1859 revivals and evangelical awakenings and on into early twentieth century phenomena like the 1904-1905 Welsh revival, religious experience and emotional responses to faith are common.[37] There are detailed records of every kind of emotional outburst one can imagine. Among the Anabaptists, for example, there were extremists whose behaviour included 'wild shouts and clamours,' dancing to the point of exhaustion, wild agitations, visions, falling to the ground, lying there as if dead, trembling and the like.[38] The French Prophets fell into states of ecstasy. They were said to collapse to the ground, to lie speechless, to shake and tremble, to foam at the mouth, to speak in unknown tongues, to make animal noises, to experience bodily convulsions.[39] During the Great Awakening in New England, there were times when whole congregations moaned and cried out to God with shrieking and weeping. People experienced visions and revelations.[40] In George Whitefield's meetings there were sometimes faintings, tears and cries of agony. With James Davenport, there were 'wild ungovernable efforts of enthusiastic zeal and fury,' with fainting, sobbing and weeping. Charles Chauncy accused the revivalists of 'vehement preaching,' unrestrained laughter and 'excesses and extravagances'.[41] Clearly, some of these descriptions depict the behaviour of extremists or reflect the prejudices of opponents. For most people, there were less dramatic responses such as those of Sarah Edwards, who was so overcome with a 'lively sense of the heavenly sweetness of Christ's excellent and transcendent love,' she was unable to stand on her feet, and had to sit for several hours, while she conversed with some friends about the glories of the gospel.[42]

John Wesley generally discouraged excesses of emotion, but nevertheless, they were not uncommon in his meetings. In the Welsh Revival, outbursts of emotion were frequent. Early in the ministry of Evan Roberts, he 'experienced that unique atmosphere created when an entire village was filled with uncontrollable excitement.' Strong men lay prostrate weeping over their sins; people variously fainted, climbed through the windows to get into crowded meetings, confessed their sins publicly and sang with fervour. There was crying, sobbing, weeping, shouting praises to God, agonising over sin and fervent prayer. There were also extremists who 'barked at the devil,' danced and prophesied.[43]

Because of the nature of things—that emotional expressions are usually tied very closely with either the ministry of a certain person or the gathering of people in certain places—such phenomena are usually short-lived. So Lambert writes of Catharism that its fall was as dramatic as its rise.[44] The Anabaptists survive today under names such as Mennonites, but the wild expressions of faith displayed in the sixteenth century are no longer to be observed. Today, tranquility and quiet simplicity of life are their hallmarks. Similarly, the Great Awakening was relatively brief. Its more overt expressions of fervour quickly died away. Within a decade of the height of the Awakening, Jonathan Edwards was dismissed by his Northampton congregation for requiring evidence of Christian conversion before admitting people to the sacrament of communion.[45] It seems incredible that there should have been such a turnaround in such a relatively short time. Gaustad writes—

> The suddenness with which the blessings of heaven fell on New England soil in 1741 is comparable only to the abruptness with which those showers were withdrawn. And the ending appeared as inexplicable as the beginning... in New England, that flood of religious anxieties, interests, reformations, excesses, exhortings, and conversions known as the Great Awakening lasted something less than two years. Its effects, to be sure, were felt in theology, denominational structure, education, and even politics into the nineteenth century... The 'great and extraordinary Work of God' itself, however, was powerfully and speedily accomplished... The dreadful concern, the traumatic awakenings, the accelerated devotion—these by their nature are of limited duration. The fever pitch must soon pass, else the patient dies.[46]

As Gaustad himself clearly shows, the reasons for the decline were more complex than this. But the fact remains that the emotional expressions of revival movements tend to be short-lived.[47]

In his classic work on the subject, Catholic scholar Ronald Knox concludes that religious enthusiasm cannot be sustained over a long period.[48]

Edwards early identified the causes of attrition as spiritual pride and a preoccupation with false experiences.[49] In his later writings, notably his *Treatise on the Religious Affections*, he probed more deeply, examining the whole question of the place of the will and the emotions in religious life.[50] While he strongly advocated the validity of the stirring of the affections, Edwards also made it plain that emotional expression was actually irrelevant to genuine faith and proved nothing. 'It is no sign,' he wrote, 'one way or the other, that religious affections are very great or raised very high.'

Although he considered many issues, for Edwards, there were three primary standards by which the genuineness of religious experience might be gauged. The first was the primacy of Christ. The only justification for any manifestations was great joy or overwhelming wonder at the excellence of the Person and work of Christ. Secondly, the text of Scripture. Only those experiences which were 'agreeable to the Word of God' were acceptable. Edwards's third test was consistent Christian living. It was not the level of experience, but the quality of upright life, that was important. Christian practice was 'the principle sign' by which we could assess both our own and others' genuineness as Christians.

Not that other evidences were of no value. There might be many indications, for example, that a fig tree was a fig tree, but the greatest was that it bore figs! So, no matter what revelations, divine encounters, emotional experiences and the like we might have, if they did not result in holy, upright, consistent living, they were to be disregarded.[51] Interestingly, Max Weber, a scholar of a very different kind, also points out that for early Christians it was their morality that validated their 'irrational charismatic gifts' and 'pneumatic achievements'.[52]

In Australia, non-Pentecostal Christians tended to be apprehensive about the validity of experience. It was too subjective, too susceptible to uncontrolled variables, too prone to deception or imitation. They were suspicious of experience which was not authenticated by doctrine. Although in the late nineteenth century, among Sydney Anglicans, there had been an openness both to revival and revivalism, there was a retreat from subjectivism in the early twentieth century, which resulted in later generations of Evangelicals remaining cautious about emphases on experientialism.[53] The Pentecostals, on the other hand, were suspicious of a sterile evangelical orthodoxy that left people's hearts untouched, of doctrine without authenticating experience. One frustrated Pentecostal believer referred to 'that type of modern refinement that abhors fever-heat of enthusiasm as if it were a plague' and to the 'modern thought virus' that lowered the spiritual pulse.[54] For Evangelicals, authenticity was judged by adherence to Scripture; for Pentecostals, it was experience that authenticated the Scripture.

Discerning the Genuine

Pentecostals knew from the earliest days that emotions in themselves could be deceptive. So experiences such as shaking, falling, trembling, weeping, laughing and the like were never seen as authoritative or determinative. There was no doubt that such manifestations were expected, and generally approved. But there were qualifications. Firstly, every manifestation had to be verified by Scripture. So attempts were early made to document what was acceptable. John Coombe, the first man in Melbourne to receive the Spirit, pointed out that silence was not necessarily more spiritual than noise—indeed, the reverse may well have been true. The Day of Pentecost was nothing if not noisy. In fact, shouting, crying aloud, speaking with other tongues, laughing, groaning and clapping hands—but not screaming—were all clearly described in Scripture as acceptable acts of worship. It was sad that more believers were not ready to shout, 'Glory to God'. Similarly, lifting of the hands, falling prostrate, dancing and kneeling were all biblical practices; but while falling on one's face in worship was proper, lying on the back was 'unseemly'. Laying on of hands also had biblical warrant, but striking or hitting people did not! It was the Spirit, not the flesh, that brought life. And it was essential to 'adhere closely to the Word.'[55] It is interesting that in the early Australian Pentecostal records, there are no known references to any of the bizarre behaviour of earlier revivals such as making animal noises or entering catatonic states. The leaders seemed well aware of the need to set up boundaries of acceptable behaviour.

As early as 1913, Lancaster was calling people to take a stand on the Bible. God had purified His Word and therefore they loved it and could love no other. If any brothers set up any strange Word demanding people either accept it or be cut off from fellowship, they would choose the latter with rejoicing.

Ten years later, in a series on Christian living, Lancaster was equally firm in her adherence to the canon of Scripture as the only rule of faith — 'Never believe what you feel if it contradicts God's Word,' she wrote. 'Ask yourself, "Can what I feel be true if God's Word is true?" and if both cannot be true, believe God.'[56]

Lancaster was accused of exercising inadequate restraints on people's behaviour.[57] However, there seems little evidence to justify this charge.

Adelaide's Pauline Heath, a sensitive soul who prized intimacy with God, also warned of the dangers of depending on experience alone. It was faith, not feeling, that pleases God, she said. To seek emotional experiences was 'allowing a feeling to usurp the place of the Word of God and of faith in that Word.'[58] John Adams noted the need to read all Scripture in the light of the context and warned against misusing or loosely handling the words of the Bible.[59] Queensland pioneer Will Enticknap told his hearers that it was a 'Pentecostal failure' to make experience an end in itself. Evangelism had to be our primary aim. 'If our roots are in Pentecost,' he said, 'our fruit should be to the ends of the earth.'[60] The precept, 'Fact before feeling', continued to be laid down in the years that followed.[61] In this regard, G. H. Morling seemed surprisingly ill-informed when he wrote—

> It (Pentecostalism) does not hold in true perspective the Fact of Christ and the Fact of the Spirit. The emphasis upon the word 'pentecostal' tends to alter the New Testament stress upon the pre-eminence of Christ Whom it is the 'loved and lovely' work of the Holy Spirit to glorify.
>
> It appears to regard the Holy Spirit unduly as an Impersonal External Power that comes upon us rather than as a Person of the Godhead Who dwells within us.[62]

Even a cursory examination of Pentecostal preaching and practice shows the inaccuracy of this allegation.

Secondly, as the many recorded testimonies show, people's experience of the Spirit consistently made them more devoted to Christ and more upright in their lifestyle. This was regarded as an essential outcome. These early Pentecostals may have had little knowledge of Jonathan Edwards, but their conclusions were very similar to his. Pentecostals also understood that it was not necessary to be in a crowd to experience the power of God. While numinous encounters commonly occurred in gatherings of believers, they could also occur in isolation. The primary focus was on an encounter with the Holy Spirit—which was not dependent on the presence of others. One woman described extravagant experiences when she was in her own home, quite alone, of sighing, groaning, stretching, gasping, twisting and prostration. Later she again fell on her face and shook violently in a home meeting. It was humiliating but she felt that God was dealing with her to make her pliable. The next morning again at home, she was filled with the Spirit and spoke in tongues, without the other phenomena. Another told how he had received the Spirit alone in bed at night, in the country, far from any meetings. Ruby Anstis of Perth recalled how she was sitting at the tea table when she was 'filled with Holy Laughter.' She tried to stop it by stuffing a handkerchief in her mouth. Eventually, she 'got down to prayer' and was soon speaking in tongues.[63]

The Significance of Glossolalia

Thirdly, there was the conviction that glossolalia was the distinctive sign of the Spirit's coming. They understood that tongue-speaking was divine in origin, and hence more durable and valuable than ecstatic phenomena. Unlike Knox, who put glossolalia in the same category as physical sensations and hysterical behaviour, the early Pentecostals believed that tongues were different. While it was an extraordinary privilege to speak in tongues, and it overwhelmed one with a sense of divine favour, it was in itself neither ecstatic nor emotional. It was a spiritual gift which was explained and advocated in Scripture. Every experience was secondary to the one great experience of being baptized in the Spirit. No matter how intense or exciting or fulfilling it might be, only the infilling of the Spirit accompanied by glossolalia was divinely sanctioned. Tongue-speaking was not an option. Everyone who was truly baptized in the Spirit was expected to do it. This lent an insistent element to the experience. It was not like laughter or tears or trembling or feelings of joy or love which might vary from person to person. It was a phenomenon which every believer was required to experience—especially if they wanted to be truly a member of the body of Christ and participate in the rapture. The evidence indicates that most believers did.

It is impossible to know now, decades later, what percentage of people actually spoke in tongues. My own observation of the post-war years is that glossolalia was almost universal among Pentecostals in the 1950s and 1960s. It seems fair to assume that this was also the position in the 1920s and 1930s. To my knowledge, all Australian Pentecostal denominations still require their pastors to speak in tongues as a condition of ordination.[64]

Because the 'evidence' of glossolalia was embedded in the movement as a non-negotiable practice, the place of religious experience was secured. As long as this doctrine remained, so would people go on being impelled into an experiential encounter with God. At the time of writing, the movement is just over a century old and so in historical terms, this thesis has yet to be tested by the passing of the years. Yet it has already outlasted most earlier revival movements. Knox asserts that 'there is no Christianity with a hundred years of history that does not become, to a more or less degree, institutional.'[65] So far, Pentecostalism in Australia has also been unable to resist this apparently inexorable pattern of all movements and is clearly institutionalised in a more sophisticated fashion than it was at the beginning. Nevertheless, the emphasis on religious experience remains dominant.

Early Pentecostal testimonies regularly highlight the transforming and renewing effect of Spirit-baptism. The earliest surviving testimony is of Richard Beauglehole (1870). 'Oh the heights and depths of the glory of God!' he said.[66] In 1910, Winnie Andrews, the first 'Pentecostal secretary' in Australia, told how the Spirit had come upon her in 1908 'in mighty power' and her heart was filled with love. It was not an experience just of the moment. Two years later, the sense of wonder was still present. She seemed hardly able to contain her joy—

> Oh, what love, joy and peace filled my soul! I had never experienced anything like it before. Praise the dear Lord! It is so lovely to feel the sweet spirit of Jesus moving within me. It has been a blessed life to me ever since. Praise Him!
>
> The dear Lord helps me and gives me victory over all my trials. Praise Him! And oh! He is working mightily in our midst. Glory to His name! He's the very same Jesus! The wonder-working Jesus! Our dear Heavenly Father and sweet Jesus are very dear to me. Glory![67]

In 1912, E. Jolly told how she had been warned that her tongues were one of the lying wonders to be performed by the Antichrist. But was the Antichrist going to point people to Jesus? Furthermore, since her baptism, she had been healed of a long-standing chest complaint, she had undergone a painless delivery of her baby and both her husband, who had spoken in Chinese at his baptism, and her children, had received 'instant deliverance' from influenza.[68]

Eliza Sloan, of Freeburgh, Victoria, was so thrilled with the Spirit's coming that her 'whole being was enraptured.' For days, she was rejoicing, praising God, preaching to her neighbours and witnessing about Christ. So exuberant was she that neighbours thought she had lost her reason.[69] William Booth-Clibborn told how he felt transported to heaven. Twenty years after the event, he was still speaking of the glory, the relish, the ecstasy, the laughter, the blessing, the transport, the refreshing and the bliss he experienced.[70]

Sometimes, the work of the Spirit and human, physical responses seemed to become rather tangled. A. F. Silcock reported that the Spirit caused 'all kinds of physical and facial exercises' and 'various inbreathings and exercises of the tongue.' But then came glossolalia—and in song, in which the tones ranged from baritone to falsetto, 'going through modulations more difficult than chromatics'. But after this, there were 'rich and varied experiences' and it was impossible to describe the joy and grace of it. M. A. Alway told how she received a sense of joy that was different from any other experience. Caroline Mortomore related how after she prayed for thirteen months, the Holy Spirit came upon her 'with the Bible evidence of speaking in tongues and magnifying God'—

> So wonderful an experience! The joy was indescribable, and the Lord was SO near. It was something beautiful! I cannot put all this precious experience into words... I now know more of my Lord and have a more intense love for Christ, with a greater desire to serve Him.

It was no flash in the pan. Since that time, members of the Mortomore family have served God faithfully in various parts of Australia. Alex Buchanan told how he was so full of joy that his shouts caused one woman to flee the room and then he was baptized in the Spirit, speaking, singing and praying in tongues. When the Buchanan family came to Good News Hall in 1925, 'Pa' Buchanan was singing the doxology with uplifted hands at the end of the service when he fell down 'full length at the feet of Jesus'. Within ten minutes he was speaking in tongues. Soon his six-year-old daughter also 'lay prostrate under that holy weight of Power' and she, too, was worshiping God in a new tongue. Beatrice Douglas spoke of indescribable joy when she received the Spirit and expressed her yearning to do the will of God all the days of her life.[71]

The stories seem to pile up one upon the other. E. Jenkins, who had been a member of the Churches of Christ for 35 years, after speaking in tongues for the first time in 1925, lay on the floor for over two hours worshiping and praising God. 'Oh!' he wrote, 'I can never forget the infilling. No pen can write, neither can the tongue tell the joy and happiness that filled me. It was glorious to be praising and blessing God.' A young widow with a five-year-old son came home to find her room flooded with light. The little boy cried, 'Oh, mamma!' and after 'a few moments' ecstatic wonder' she found herself praying in a new tongue.

Another man brought his wife and five children to a meeting and then found himself on his knees 'under the power of God'. His wife was very worried about what was happening to him, but when he finally 'came through, speaking in tongues', she realized God was with him. It was not always so dramatic. One woman received the Spirit as she sat quietly in her chair. In 1928, a report appeared in *Good News*, describing meetings in the North Queensland town of Rockhampton in which one woman had 'terrible shakings' in her body for three and a half hours and finally spoke in tongues.[72]

A Christadelphian testified gladly to being deeply convinced of the pre-existence of Christ. 'Experience has put an end to all (doubt) forever,' he wrote. Soon he was baptized in the Spirit and speaking in tongues.[73]

Some people's experiences stretched credulity. Charles Prickett claimed that he had been healed from leukaemia two years previously when Jesus personally visited him; that his conversion was the result of an angelic visitation; and that when he was baptized in the Spirit, the power of God was so 'heavy' it bent the legs of the bed on which he was lying and threw a cup and saucer across the room, while he felt himself engulfed in some kind of spiritual flame. Lancaster commented that the Bible spoke of 'diversities of operations' and that she did not doubt that Prickett's experiences, although 'in some cases unique,' were genuine.[74]

On occasion, there were claims of xenolalia. At Good News Hall in 1926, one man spoke in 'pure Zulu,' a claim confirmed by someone who had lived many years in South Africa. Another spoke 'fluently' in the Hebrew language. Dolly Cridge was told she was speaking Italian. In the Ovens Valley there were reports of both Indian and Chinese people understanding utterances in tongues. John Russell, whose father spoke Hindustani, believed he was speaking the same language. Another believed he spoke in Chinese, because he saw a vision of multitudes of Chinese people before him as he preached to them in their own tongue.[75] These claims were not easily verifiable, although attempts were sometimes made to check them.[76]

Laughter was often present when the Spirit came. One person told how the night before she received the Spirit she did nothing but 'laugh in the Spirit.' J. L. Wilson related that she was so full of joy her laughter actually hindered her from speaking in tongues. But then the new language just 'seemed to bubble over', she fell to the floor and was soon 'bathing in the sunshine of God's love, talking in tongues.' Owen French laughed in anticipation at what the Lord was about to do in his life, as did those around him. Three days later, he spoke in tongues.[77]

A 'lady preacher' struggled to find words to describe her joy and delight at being baptized in the Spirit—

> With my hands upraised, vainly did I try to utter words of praise and worship in my own language, but the Spirit took hold and my words were taken from me and a new tongue given (Is 28:11). I was upon my knees, still with hands upraised, the stammering rapidly becoming clearer and clearer, while I became most blessedly conscious of being in the most wondrous communion with my God that I had ever known in my life... In the afternoon, I was again before the Lord, this time standing with upraised hands; and now the Spirit was singing through me! Oh, the glory, the joy, the wonder of it all! It almost took my breath away... I

saw nothing; but oh, how much I felt! ...For days my joy was so great I could not refrain from speaking in tongues.[78]

Another woman told how words could not express the wonderful peace and joy that filled her and how three months later she was still 'filled to overflowing' with an indescribable peace. Struck with a sense of wonder, yet another was amazed that God should fill such a one as her with His own Spirit 'not for a moment or an hour, day, week, or month; but *forever.*'[79] Not everyone was enthused about such behaviour. 'If you want to see a good pantomime,' said one man, 'you should visit a Pentecostal church.'[80]

One of the most fascinating approaches to the baptism of the Spirit was an address by medical practitioner, Mina Brawner. She enumerated common objections to the baptism in the Holy Spirit—that those involved were mentally disturbed; that the experience was from Satan; that there was so much counterfeit behaviour that it was wise to reject it all.[81] But, she argued, Paul was called 'mad', Jesus was also told he 'had a devil', and it was plainly foolish to reject the whole because of one troubling part. When a farmer reaped a crop, there was much noise and dust and chaff, but the farmer did not reject the grain on this account. This was harvest time and the grain had to be secured.

Moreover, those who were baptized in the Spirit could hardly be demon-controlled, as they had a passion to win souls, a hunger for the Word of God, a rejection of the pursuits of this world and an ability to pray that plainly came from God.

Through the central nervous system, she continued, we could control bodily actions while the sympathetic nervous system had control over involuntary actions. So where was the human spirit to be found? God would not have put it where it could be controlled by the human will. Nor would it be located in a part of the body that could be lost, such as the hand. As a surgeon, Brawner had never understood where to find the spirit, but it was certainly there (Job 32:8). It was only after she had been baptized in the Holy Spirit that she found the answer— the solar plexus or 'abdominal brain'. This centre was not subject to the will but it was the seat of the emotions. This is why bodily changes sometimes occurred when the Spirit came—flushing, sweating and the like. Furthermore, Jesus said that when the Spirit came, rivers of living water would flow from the belly.

The last member to yield was the tongue. It sputtered and stammered and joined the disordered speech of the battlefield, but finally gave way to the Spirit. This was like raising the flag of victory. Then the speaker listened with as much interest as other hearers, for the words did not come from the intellect, but from 'the highest centre of man, the innermost being, or his heart'. Doctrines were held in the head; the Spirit occupied the heart. Doctrines divided, but the Holy Spirit united the people of God.[82]

Children and the Spirit

Children were often numbered among those who received the Spirit. This was further proof that an experience of God could be more wide-reaching in its impact than an understanding of doctrine. At the Easter convention at Good News Hall in 1926, a six-year-old boy lay on the floor for hours praising God and a girl of five years was also 'under the power of the Spirit'. On a trip to Queensland in 1927, Lancaster reported that a 'special feature' of her visit was 'the manner in which the Holy Ghost arrested the youths and children'. Hedley Ridgway told how at the age of six he and his brother had chosen to miss a school concert so they could have 'a little tarrying meeting' of their own. It was there he was baptized in the Spirit. At one of Mina Brawner's meetings, a dozen youngsters between the ages of nine and 15 were 'slain by the Spirit, crying to the Lord to humble them, cleanse them and give them power', and six of them were baptized in the Spirit. In Atherton, an eleven-year-old spoke in tongues. Jeannie Lancaster was especially delighted when her nine-year-old granddaughter Esther May was blessed—and even more so when the next day little May gathered some of her friends together and the Spirit came on them also. Not long after this, May was writing out passages from the Bible and dropping them in the street in the hope people would read them. Two years later, after a long illness, she passed away. During her last days, she asked people to help her lift her hands in prayer. 'Hold them up for me,' she pleaded. 'I must get the victory.' A ten-year-old wrote to Lancaster, 'Please, when may I come to the Hall to be baptized, I mean, first in water, second in the Holy Spirit.' Gladys Banks, aged fourteen, told how she and her friend had received the Spirit. It was, she said, 'the gate of heaven to our souls'. In Cairns, in 1927, a Sunday School picnic was taken as an opportunity to baptize four of the older children in Freshwater Creek. In Melbourne, a boy of nine was baptized in water. Was he too young? 'Any child who is old enough to know when he is doing wrong must be allowed the privilege of doing right,' said Lancaster.[83]

Tarry meetings

It was usual, but not mandatory, to be baptized in the Spirit at a 'tarry meeting', sometimes called a 'waiting meeting'. Based on the instructions of Jesus that His disciples should 'tarry' in Jerusalem until they were empowered by the Spirit (Luke 24:49), the concept was conveyed that it was still necessary today to spend time 'tarrying' or waiting for the Spirit to come. The exegesis might be questionable but the benefits were palpable. God had imposed a set of conditions to be satisfied, taught Florrie Mortomore, before the Spirit would come, namely repentance and baptism (Acts 2:38). This meant not only being sorry for sin but forsaking it as well. When these conditions were fulfilled, God would immediately pour out His Spirit. If, however, He delayed, this was to teach us patience. So it was necessary to tarry until we received, for God would keep His promise (Luke 11:13).[84] One man told how he had tarried for six days at Good News Hall and then remembered a disagreement with a neighbour. So he took a train journey to sort this matter out, was laughed at for his pains, but nevertheless felt at ease. That night he received the Spirit.[85] Tarrying allowed people to examine their hearts and prepare their lives for the infilling.

In an article apparently written by Jeannie Lancaster, seekers for the infilling of the Spirit were instructed to observe the following—

- Hand yourself over to the hands of the Lord
- Repent and confess all sin in heart and life
- Ask God to purify your motives
- Keep your eyes on Jesus
- Lay hold of the promise of Acts 1:5
- Spend all the time you can in prayer and praise
- Plead the blood of the Lamb over evil spirits
- Don't expect your experiences to be the same as those of others
- Tarry until you are endued with power from on high
- Yield to any manifestation of the Spirit (e.g. shaking of lips)
- Let the Holy Spirit do as He pleases with your body
- Then you will speak in an unknown tongue

Lancaster pointed out that it was not hard to receive the Spirit—when there was faith in the blood of Christ for cleansing it was really 'very easy'. Nevertheless, this did not mean there was no need to tarry. The biblical command still applied. It was true that some received almost immediately, but others waited a long time. The reason for this may have been that 'some of us die hard, and God has to use various ways to kill us to our own opinions.' Also, some did not 'get the full revelation of Jesus' they longed for straight away.[86]

Tarrying meetings were a priority. At the Hall, it was common practice to devote the Christmas holiday break to this end. On 24 December 1924, ten days of tarrying began, and even before it started 'the rain' was 'already falling'. One woman told how she had tarried for nine days before receiving the Holy Spirit. Tarrying could be hard work, but it was not always so. An anonymous report told how a young woman 'had a lovely time' sitting in the tarry room as she sang in tongues and how one Saturday night the congregation 'spent a happy time before the Lord, tarrying for the baptism of the Holy Ghost'. In Perth, in 1928, the secretary claimed that the house was literally shaken while they prayed. In Townsville, Leila Buchanan wrote to her mother, Jeannie Lancaster, that when she and her husband Alex conducted a tarry meeting, 'the power of God swept over the whole company shaking all like aspen leaves in the wind'. A former member of the Exclusive Brethren found it hard to accept Pentecostal teaching. But he was convinced by a young man in a tarry meeting whose face was full of light and joy and by others who laughed, sang and danced in the Spirit. Gus Jansen, who confessed to being of rather a reserved nature, experienced joy, merriment and love in a Boxing Day tarry meeting at Good News Hall. Heather Burrows 'really got to know the Lord' through tarry meetings. 'The tarry meetings had a tremendous significance,' said Stan Douglas. 'There was that touch of God that hallowed the atmosphere.'[87]

F. E. Emery of Rockhampton had thought that love was the 'seal' spoken of by the apostles, but now realized the seal was speaking in tongues, and 'how wonderfully the Scriptures opened up!' After a Van Eyk meeting in Rockhampton, she responded to the invitation to stay for a time of prayer. Van Eyk simply told people to 'get busy with God'. It was not easy—

> You can imagine the stiff, respectable, spoiled child of the Church letting go all pride and ceremony, and getting down humbly before God, pleading for His blessing.

After several days, involving putting things right and extended prayer, the Spirit filled her with 'wonderful love.'[88]

Different

The spirit of Pentecost was not just a matter of the heart. What people experienced internally was expected to show externally. Spirit-filled Christians were *different*. The Wesleyan quest for perfection and the evangelical emphasis on holiness remained at the core of Pentecostal piety. Naturally, sins such as murder, adultery, theft, drunkenness, assault and the like were eschewed. But equally to be avoided were practices like playing cards, ballroom dancing and smoking and bodily adornment such as cosmetics and jewellery. These were seen as signs of the imminent return of Christ. There had never been a time when people were more wickedly 'pleasure mad'. Would God allow feasting, drinking, dancing, theatre-going and smoking to go on forever? No, the 'cup of iniquity was full to overflowing. An anonymous testimony in *Good News* told how the young woman concerned used to indulge in worldly amusements 'such as dancing, theatre-going, unclean, suggestive picture shows, card-playing and many other attractive follies.' She saw no harm in such things, but now she had accepted Christ she had joy, peace and satisfaction in her soul. Beatrice Douglas testified that she had seen a vision of Christ on the cross and day by day tried to surrender everything to Him—even to the point of removing a ring from her finger and a gold bangle from her wrist. She had 'almost worshiped' the bangle but later discovered that 'God had forbidden His children to adorn themselves with gold.' While this girl's action was a spontaneous response to her own experience of faith, there was 'plenty of preaching' against such practices. Iris George recalled, 'We were all young and they were pulling us into line all the time. Separation [from the world] was the thing... No movies, no radio, no lipstick, no hair colour, no powder, no nothing.'[89]

In the Apostolic Church, a woman wearing makeup might be turned away at the door and instructed to come back when she had removed it.[90] C. L. Greenwood's son Les used to have a crystal set with the wire connected to the mattress under his bed so his father would not know about it. Given that his father preached against radio, the theatre, dancing, the use of cosmetics and the like, this seems to have been a wise move.[91]

There was no doubt about the evils of smoking. At one meeting, a young man dropped his cigarettes into the stove after quoting Revelation 21:27. If the cigarettes didn't go into the fire, those who smoked them would, said *Good News.*[92] In 1932, 'Brother Hills' told how he had been saved from smoking, drinking and violence: 'The Lord has done wonderful things for me—He has made a new man of me.'[93] When Gustav Bernhard ('Ben') Michalk (1884-1967) was converted at Parkes in 1916, he continued to smoke his pipe until one day, as he was lighting up, he heard the voice of God saying, 'You don't want that thing anymore.' He promptly nailed it to the fork of a pine tree where it remained visible for years until the tree grew over it.[94]

At Richmond Temple, people used to sing a song that ran, 'There'll be no smoking there, in my Father's house.' Other verses substituted 'dancing' or 'lipstick' for 'smoking'. The final stanza said, 'But Jesus will be there…'[95] Another song used in F. B. Van Eyk's meetings had these lyrics—

> Heaven is a clean place
> No tobacco there
> All the folks are holy
> Over there
> If you refuse to do God's will
> The Book says you'll be filthy still.
> There's a very noxious weed
> Filled with appetite and greed
> Chewed by goats and worms and foolish men;
> It discolours tooth and tongue
> In the aged and in the young
> It is time we put this poison under ban.
> Heaven is a clean place.[96]

In a stern editorial, Jeannie Lancaster denounced popular reading materials—

> We cannot speak too strongly in condemnation of the ordinary literature of the present day. It is truly appalling. Go to the nearest bookstall, pick up the first book you see and… you will almost certainly be shocked by its contents.

In Adelaide, too, novel-reading was frowned upon. It was questionable and therefore probably wrong.

This was not just blind fundamentalism. The main purpose in reading was 'to elevate, to foster a desire for nobler things.' A book that developed the intellect and satisfied the soul was fine. But if it did not, the remedy was simple—'Burn it!'

Cinemas were certainly inappropriate. There were at least 20 reasons why Christians should not attend them. In general, they resulted in lowered moral standards. But the major reason was that when Christ came again, He 'would not like to find you there.' Interestingly, the arguments supporting the case against children being exposed to moving pictures were very similar to those raised today against their exposure to television. Jazz music was also denounced. 'It will spoil your taste, will kill your prayer life, and undermine your spiritual life,' said a prominent Christian musician. In the early days, even school concerts or local community shows were forbidden and sport was frowned upon as a waste of valuable time and energy.[97] Florrie Mortomore saw such worldly pleasures as sufficient to disqualify believers from the rewards of overcomers.[98]

Sunday observance was strongly emphasised. Sunday work, shopping and entertainment were all frowned upon. In some cases, the use of public transport was disapproved and people were encouraged to cook their Sunday meals in advance on Saturday.[99]

Another expression of holiness was tithing, that is the giving of one tenth of one's income to the Lord. In Richmond Temple, there was a large 'tithe box' at the front of the auditorium. During the service, the people would walk to the front in joyful procession to place their offerings. For Apostolics, compulsory tithing was one of the unalterable tenets of the Church. Again, this was not just rigid legalism. The concept was that everything one owned now belonged to God. So tithing was simply returning to God a portion of what was his. Even threepence spent on a milk shake might be considered indulging the flesh.[100]

The fundamental issue was that of commitment. Spirit-filled Christians were expected to be totally dedicated to the work of God. Any flirtation with the world was considered immoral. But it was more than this. When the Spirit came, there was such joy, such wonder, such fulfilment, that people genuinely found little attraction in popular pleasures. For them it was literally more enjoyable to be at a prayer meeting than in a cinema or a dance hall. The spirit of Pentecost was more dynamic than the spirit of the world. Eileen Michalk remembers how it was during her childhood in Parkes, NSW—

> My parents had a real joy... They just prayed all the time. I remember wishing we could have someone in our house and it wouldn't turn into a prayer meeting! ... They'd say, 'Before you go...' and you'd know it would be two hours later before they would. You'd go to sleep on the floor. Goodness me, they seemed to be so hungry for more and more of God... There was an enthusiasm about those men that was wonderful... On the way home [from a prayer meeting] you'd be with a group of people and they'd always be talking about the Lord. And then you'd stand under a lamp post nearest the next person's home and they'd have another chat. I was often almost asleep sitting in the gutter... They just really talked so much of the Lord's coming and their love for God. Their commitment was incredible. I mean rain, hail or shine, you walked to meetings... There was always something happening—there was always an air of expectancy. I remember my mother walking so fast to a prayer meeting... 'I just want to get there,' she said, 'I really believe tonight's the night the Lord is going to baptize me.' And that was the night. It didn't matter if it rained. You never stayed home because it rained. You sat in church wet.[101]

Of course, there were those who found such a commitment too great a price to pay in spite of the blessings they received. But the eyes of those who persevered were so entranced by the beauties of the kingdom of God, the kingdoms of this world were but a passing blur. The spirit of Pentecost stole their hearts and dropped sweetness and honeycomb on their lips and many waters could not quench their love.

Notes

[1] GN, 16:11, November, 1925, 8f.

[2] AE, 7:2, January, 1941, 9.
[3] J Black, 'Tumultuous spirit,' AE, 7:7, June, 1941, 4.
[4] J. Russell, 'Saved to Serve,' GN, 14:10, November, 1923, 13; John Russell, 'A Testimony given at N. Melbourne March 8, 1924,' GN, 15:5, May, 1924, 7.
[5] GN, 17:7, July, 1926, 10.
[6] GN, 17:3, March, 1926, 14.
[7] F. B. Van Eyk, 'The far reaching results of the Baptism in the Holy Spirit,' GN, 17:12, December, 1926, 5; GN, 18:2, February, 1927, 12.
[8] GN, 20:7, July, 1929, 6.
[9] GN, 20:12, December, 1929, 6.
[10] GN, 20:3, March, 1929, 15.
[11] G. H. Morling, *Pentecostalism* (Baptist Department of Evangelism, n.d.), 15.
[12] N. Robson, 'Showing Mercy Unto Thousands of them that Love Me,' GN, 1:5, January, 1913, .24; J. Lancaster, 'Manifestations,' GN, 18:11, November, 1927, 7; C. Cousins, 'Ask and Ye shall Receive,' GN, 17:2, February, 1926, 11; GN, 9:1, February, 1923, 16; GN, 19:3, March, 1928, 12; GN, 21:11, November, 1930, 11; GN, 1:6, October, 1932, 21; E. Anstis, 'Revelation,' GN, 22:3, March, 1931, 16; GN, 22:11, November, 1931, 13; GC, 1:9, February, 1933, 71; GN, 18:4, April, 1927, 16.
[13] GN, 17:8, August, 1926, 15; GN, 18:11, November, 1927, 7; GN, 18:12, December, 1927, 15.
[14] GN, 19:2, February, 1928, 29; GN, 9:1, February, 1923, 16; GN, 16:9, September, 1925, 17; *Alpine Observer*, 19 May, 1922.
[15] H. T. Sharman, 'Unmerited Favour,' GN, 15:1, January 1924, 15; *Assemblies of God in Australia Directory 1995* (Mitcham: Assemblies of God in Australia, 1995), 32. Although no initials are given in this article, Sharman is probably the Harold T. Sharman referred to in GN, 19:6, June, 1928, 11 and GN, 16:4, April, 1925, 11.
[16] GN, 15:7, July, 1924, 10.
[17] GN, 18:10, October, 1927, 10.
[18] GN, 18:3, March, 1927, 14; GN, 18:7, July, 1927, 10; GN, 15:6, June, 1924, 7; GN, 15:8, August, 1924, 12; GN, 16:2, February, 1925, 9; GN, 16:5, May, 1925, 4.
[19] GN, 17:4, April, 1926, 12.
[20] GN, 22:10, October, 1931, 17. It is interesting that in this vision the angel was a female; only male angels are mentioned in Scripture.
[21] GN, 9:1, February, 1923, 17f; R. Davis, personal interview, n.d..
[22] GN, 22:3, March, 1931, 16; GN, 19:11, November, 1928, 14. There was general apprehension about Japan after the Sino-Japanese War of 1894-95 and the Russo-Japanese War of 1904-05. These utterances were set against this backdrop.
[23] GN, 17:5, May, 1926, 18. For background on Ames see Appendix B.
[24] *Pentecostal Times* Adelaide, n.d. Only two issues survive in the Mortlock Library, Adelaide, where they are dated '1907?' This date seems too early, as there is an extract in the first issue from the *Latter Rain Evangel*, a journal first

published in Chicago, Ill, in October 1908 and in the second issue from *Confidence*, an English magazine which first appeared in 1908. There is also a testimony from *The Apostolic Faith*. This would suggest a date of 1909 at the earliest for *Pentecostal Times*.

[25] A. S. Kentish, 'Manifestations,' GN, 15:11, November, 1924, 9ff.

[26] PT, No. 1, 11. Subsequent references are from this source.

[27] PT, No. 1, 12.

[28] R. Beauglehole, 'God Baptized in Portland, Victoria, nearly Fifty Years Ago!' GN, 1:1, April, 1910, 4; W. Alick [sic] Buchanan, 'God Blesses a Farmer's Son,' GN, 1:5, January, 1913, 20; GN, 18:6, June, 1927, 13.

[29] 'A Bible reading on Water and Spirit Baptism,' GN, 16:8, August, 1925, 16.

[30] E. Ridgway, 'The Baptism of the Holy Ghost,' GN, 17:6, June, 1926, 8f.

[31] It should be noted that contemporary Pentecostals do not take this position. All believers are freely recognised as being members of the Body of Christ (i.e. the Church). Baptism in the Holy Spirit is seen as an empowering experience, not a saving one. See B. Chant, *Creative Living* (South Plympton, SA: Tabor, 1986), 251ff; Chant, 2008, 76-85.

[32] F. Mortomore, 'In the Last Days,' GN, 16:1, January, 1925, 8-10.

[33] Adams, Scriptural Statement, n.d.

[34] F. B. Van Eyk, 'The Baptism of the Holy Spirit and Its Initial Evidence,' FGE, 1:1, May 1932, 3, 4.

[35] J. Lancaster, 'What's the Use of Tongues?' GN, 1:6, October, 1913, 7ff; GN, 24:7, July, 1933, 4f. The reprinting of this article 20 years after its first publication indicates that Lancaster had not shifted her position on this subject.

[36] GN, 18:4, April, 1927, 13; GN, 19:6, June, 1928, 13; GN, 22:3, March, 1931, 10 'Where there is No Vision the People Perish,' GN, 24:9, September, 1933, 9; J. Lancaster, 'What's the Use of Tongues?' GN, 24:7, July, 1933, 5; 'Brother' Barnes, 'The Promise of the Father,' GN, 19:7, July, 1928, 14.

[37] See Douglas, ed, 1978; M. Lambert, Medieval Heresy: Popular Movements from the Gregorian Reform to the Reformation (Oxford: Blackwell, 1992); Jones, 1995.

[38] Knox, 1987, 124.

[39] Knox, 1987, 360.

[40] Murray, 1987, 169, 217, 220.

[41] R. L. Bushman (ed), *The Great Awakening: Documents on the Revival of Religion, 1740-1745,* New York: Atheneum, 1970, 27, 49, 118. It should be noted that some of these descriptions come from enemies of the Awakening and may be exaggerated. See also Murray, 1987, 224ff.

[42] J. Edwards, A Faithful Narrative of the Surprising Work of God in The Works of Jonathan Edwards Edinburgh: Banner of Truth, (1834) 1984, Vol I, lxiiff.

[43] Jones, 1995, 50, 71f, 125, 158; Evans, 1987

[44] Lambert, 1992, 125.

[45] Murray, 1987, 326ff.

[46] E. S. Gaustad, *The Great Awakening in New England* Gloucester: Peter Smith, 1965, 1; see also Bushman (ed), 1970.
[47] K. Chant, *Better than Revival* Kingswood: Ken Chant Ministries, 1994, 67.
[48] Knox, 1987, 565.
[49] Edwards, Vol 1, 1984, lxxviii.
[50] Edwards, (1746), 1986. In my unpublished monograph entitled *Jonathan Edwards and Revival Phenomena*, 2007, www.barrychant.com, I have examined the writings of Edwards on this subject in more detail
[51] Edwards, (1746), 1986, 54, 71, 206, 363.
[52] Weber, 1965, 178.
[53] Lawton, 1990, 96ff; Piggin, 1996, 102.
[54] 'Brother' Barnes, 'The Promise of the Father,' GN, 19:7, July, 1928, 14f.
[55] J. Coombe, 'Waiting Meetings.'
[56] GN, 1:5, January 1913, 6; GN, 15:9, September, 1924, 20.
[57] C. and M. Gadge, personal interview, 2 March 1992—'Mrs Lancaster was very, very afraid of quenching the Holy Spirit—that was a weak spot as far as I was concerned ... Sometimes extravagant things took place.'
[58] 'Faith or Feeling,' AN 8:4 June 1937, 2.
[59] Adams, Scriptural Evidence, 3.
[60] W.Enticknap, 'Finding the Fruit,' sermon notes, n.d.
[61] RE May 1935, 231.
[62] Morling, *Pentecostalism*, 15.
[63] E. M. W., 'From a Lady Preacher,' GN, 18:12, December, 1927, 15; J. Jolly, 'He Shall Baptize,' GN, 12:8, September, 1923, 10; GN, 16:4, April, 1925, 20.
[64] In recent years, there has been less insistence among charismatic and 'Third Wave' movements on glossolalia and a broader acceptance of other 'manifestations' or gifts. This appears to have had an eroding effect on the Pentecostal position.
[65] Knox, 1987, 590.
[66] R. Beauglehole, GN, 1:1, April, 1910, 3f.
[67] W. Andrews, 'A Methodist Sunday School Scholar's Testimony,' GN, 1:1, April, 1910, 6.
[68] E. Jolly, 'He Shall Baptize You with the Holy Spirit,' GN, 1:5, January 1913, 3.
[69] GN, 1:1, April, 1910, 10.
[70] W. Booth-Clibborn, 'How "The Rest and the Refreshing" Came to Me,' GN, 20:7, July, 1929, 7.
[71] A. F. Silcock, 'I came not to call the Righteous, but Sinners to Repentance,' GN, 1:1, April, 1910, 11ff ; M. A. Alway, 'Jesus Christ the Same Yesterday, Today and Forever,' GN, 1:1, April, 1910, 14f ; GN, 1:5, January, 1913, 12, 20; GN, 16:9, September, 1925, 16; B. Douglas, 'Prove Me Now,' GN, 17:3, March, 1926, 16f.

[72] E. Jenkins, 'When Ye Seek Me with your Whole Heart You Shall Find Me,' GN, 17:5, May, 1926, 10f ; GN, 17:3, March, 1926, 12; GN, 19:3, March, 1928.

[73] F. Bryan, 'Baptism in the Holy Spirit,' GN, 18:2, February, 1927, 12f. Note that some words are obscured in this article through fire damage.

[74] C. Prickett, 'How I Was Healed,' GN, 17:12, December, 1926, 15.

[75] GN, 17:3, March, 1926, 12; GN, 1:1, April, 1910, 16; M. Jackson, personal communication, 8 May, 1992; J. Russell, 'Saved to Serve,' GN, 14:10, November, 1923, 13; P. H. Scarisbrick, 'Personal Testimony of P. H. Scarisbrick,' GN, 19:8, August, 1928, 15.

[76] George Burns, in his presidential address to the first Advisory Council Conference of the Apostolic Faith Mission in Brisbane in 1929, told how his wife spoke in tongues and interpreted— 'Neither of us had any knowledge of any part of it except the last word 'Yah,' which was rightly interpreted as Jehovah. This was the message: 'Touto! Touto! Touto! Helikos esti Yah!' And the interpretation given was: 'Sing! Sing! Sing! Great is Jehovah.' When I reached home I looked in *Young's Analytical Concordance* and to our joy we found that the message was perfect Greek with the last word in Hebrew.' Burns's enthusiasm o'erleapt itself here. While the latter part could be taken to mean, 'Great is Jehovah,' the first part is not an instruction to sing. It was hardly 'perfect' Greek. Nevertheless, for him it was a startling proof of the validity of glossolalia. As the printed version of this message was 'stenographically reported' by Leila Buchanan, it is conceivable, although unlikely, she may have got the words wrong, although none of the common Greek words for 'sing' seem to have any similarity to *touto* (which is the neuter singular demonstrative pronoun). See G. Burns, 'We Preach,' GN, 20:3, March, 1929, 15.

[77] GN, 18:1, January, 1927, 13; GN, 18:6, September, 1927, 17; O. French, 'The Spirit of Adoption,' GN, 23:3, March, 1932, 9.

[78] E. M. W., 'From a Lady Preacher,' GN, 18:12, December, 1927, 15.

[79] GN, 20:11, November, 1929, 12; GN, 18:6, June, 1927, 13.

[80] Quoted by C. Tanswell, interview, 20 December, 1993.

[81] e. g. J. Russell, 'A Straight Testimony,' GN, 17:7, July, 1926, 'I had been warned to keep away from them, and told it was all of the Devil. One Baptist minister especially warned me...'

[82] M. Brawner, 'The Baptism of the Holy Spirit from a Medical Standpoint,' GN, 24:3, March, 1933, 6f.

[83] GN, 17:5, May, 1926, 12; GN, 18:3, March, 1927, 10; GN, 18:7, July, 1927, 12; GN, 21:7, July, 1920, 2; GN, 21:11, November, 1930, 12; GN, 22:3, March, 1931, 10, 15, 17; GN, 24:4, 5, April-May 1933, 16; GN, 18:4, April, 1927, 13; GN, 23:1, January, 1932, 10.

[84] F. Mortomore, 'In the Last Days,' GN, 16:1, January, 1925, 9.

[85] J. Jolly, 'He Shall Baptize,' GN, 12:8, September, 1923, 10.

[86] S. J. Lancaster (?), 'Help to Seekers of the Baptism of the Holy Ghost,' GN, 21:10, October, 1930, 11.

[87] GN, 15:12, December, 1924, 22; GN, 17:3, March, 1926, 17; GN, 18:2, February, 1927, 11; A. Kilpatrick, 'A Cheering Report,' GN, 19:7, July, 1928,

13; GN, 19:9, September, 1928, 11; O. French, 'The Spirit of Adoption,' GN, 23:3, March, 1932, 9; H. Hoskin, personal interview, 21 November, 1997; S. Douglas, personal interview, 21 November, 1989.

[88] F. E. Emery, 'A Testimony to the Experimental Baptism of the Holy Spirit,' GN, 19:4, April 1928, 13.

[89] GN, 9:1, February 1923, 14f ; GN, 17:3, March, 1926, 15; E. Michalk, personal interview, 18 December, 1993; I. George, personal interview, 12 June, 1990.

[90] K. Kirwan, personal interview, 11 September, 1991.

[91] H. Dwight, personal interview, 12 June, 1990. Hazel Dwight is Greenwood's daughter.

[92] GN, 22:8, August, 1931, 12.

[93] GN, 23:5, May, 1932, 12. On one occasion, it was even suggested that insanity might be caused by smoking— GN, 24:7, July, 1933, 3.

[94] L. Michalk, personal interview, 18 December, 1993. To this day, 'Ben' Michalk's Bible carries the inscription in his own hand writing: 'Gustav Bernhard Michalk. Baptized in the Holy Spirit 18 October 1916. Glory to Jesus. Mark 1:8. Act 2:4.'

[95] K. Lowe, personal interview, 12 June, 1990; F. Lancaster, personal interview, 18 December, 1993.

[96] F. Lancaster, personal interview, 18 December, 1993.

[97] GN, 21:1, January, 1930, 19 ; 'The Sin-ema and Children,' GN, 23:12, December, 1932, Supplement, 3; GN, 23:6, June 1932, 11; C. Tanswell, personal interview, 20 December, 1993; L. Wahlquist, personal interview, 19 November, 1991.

[98] F. Mortomore, 'The Dragon's Plot,' GN, 14: 10, November, 1923, 3.

[99] K. Conner, personal interview, 6 June, 1991.

[100] K. A. Lowe, personal interview, 12 June, 1990; N. Fabian, personal interview, August, 1991.

[101] E. Michalk, personal interview, 18 December, 1993.

Bibliography

INTERVIEWS AND CORRESPONDENCE

Because of my interest in Pentecostal history, I began interviewing people on this subject in the 1960s. The original notes of many of these interviews were lost in a fire that destroyed my office in 1987, although I had by then drawn on them in compiling my earlier work *Heart of Fire*. As a result, it is not possible now to record all the relevant details. The notes, and in many cases cassette tapes, of all interviews after January 1987 are in my possession.

Armstrong, Dalton, 30 April, 1990.
Armstrong, Norman, 30 April, 1990, October 1993.
Averill, L., 28 March, 1992.
Averill, Lloyd, 20 November, 1990.
Bain, Alan Geoffrey and Florence, 20 August, 1990.
Banton, Bert.
Barclay, E., 30 December, 1987.
Baxter, W. J. E.
Bentley, T. A., 7 November, 1974; September, 1991; August, 1994; April, 1997.
Bowling, Gordon.
Brabham, D.
Brabham, Les.
Broadley, Harry.
Buchanan, Cyril James, 24 February, 1995.
Burger, Isak, 14 July, 1997.
Bushby, Doug.

Cathcart, D., 13 September, 1993.
Chant, Ken.
Chilcott, Gordon.
Conner, Kevin, 6 June, 1991.
Conwell, Alan and Jean, c.1991.
Cook, Leonard and Eileen, 31 January, 1994.
Coombe, S., 21 March, 1997.
Cowell, G., 22 March, 1997.
Cowling, Sheila, July, 1990 to February, 1993
Crisp, Rhoda, June, 1991.
Curtis, Tom.
Davidson, A. C.
Davidson, Agnes, 20 November, 1990.
Davidson, Pat, 15 April, 1993.
Davis, Robert.
Dawson, Don.
Douglas, Stan and Muriel, 21 November, 1989, 22 September, 1991.

Du Plessis, David.
Duncan, M, 29 October, 1993.
Dwight, Len and Hazel, 12 June, 1990.
Dyer, Ruth, 28 January, 1994.
Easton, Jack, 6, 24 February, 1995.
Elton, Frank and Mildred, 11 September, 1991.
Enticknap, Charles.
Evans, Andrew.
Evans, Carla, 1992.
Evans, Tom and Stella, 25 September, 1991.
Fabian, Norman, 15 August, 1991; 18 September, 1991.
Faulkner, Edna, 10 April, 1992.
Featherstone, Doris, 8 November, 1992.
Ferguson, Jessie.
Forrest, Phil, 24 September, 1991.
Foster, Thomas.
Freudenberg, Henry, 15 April, 1993; 21 August, 1993.
Frost, Esther, September, November, 1994.
Gadge, Claude and May, 30 March, 1992.
George, Gill and Iris, 12 June, 1990.
Goldshaw, Marjorie, June, 1991.
Gossling, P., 16 December, 1974.
Grant, Ann, Portland Family Advisory Group Inc, 1993.
Grant, Paul, 1988.
Greaves, Mabel, 1 August, 1994.
Greenwood, Elviss.
Greenwood, Les, 10 September, 1990.
Grey, Leonore, 13 November, 1983.
Hallop, Theo, 15 April, 1993; 30 April, 1993.
Harris, Leo and Belle, various times in 1970s.
Harrison, C. C. W.
Hart, L., c.1970.
Hart, Leo, 10 September, 1990.
Harvey, Doreen, 24 September, 1991.
Henderson, Mrs.
Henshall, E.
Hewitt, Joy, August, 1990.
Hewitt, Lily, January, 1989.
Hills, Philip, 10 September, 1990.
Hobbs, Phyllis, 1988.
Hood, Christine, 26 August, 1993; 20 August, 1996.
Hope, R, 1990.
Hoskin, Heather, 21 November, 1997, 10 February, 1998.
Houston, Frank.
Hurst, Marjorie, 14 August, 1991.
Jackson, M., 8 May, 1992;
Jones, Len.
Kirwan, Kathleen, 11 September, 1991.
Kramer, M.
Kuskoff, Murray, 15 April, 1993.
Lancaster, Fred and Doris, 18 December, 1993.
Larsen, Wal, 19 March, 1993, 9 August, 1993.
Laurens, Mavis, 12 June, 1990
Loft, Reginald, 12 September, 1991.
Lovell, Phil and Muriel, 6 September, 1991.
Lowe, K. A., 12 June, 1990.
Manley-Breen, Charles, July, 1990.
Manley-Breen, Lois, July, 1990.
Martin, I.
McCabe, J., 18 September, 1991.
McCabe, Joshua, 18 September, 1991.
McKelliff, Thea, February, 1992, November, 1992.
McKenzie, Dorothy, 25 September, 1991.
Michalk, L. L. ('Bill') and Eileen, 18 December, 1993.
Moeller, F. P.
Moulton, Norman..

Muir, George, 12 October, 1993.
Mullin, James.
Nugent, Wilbur and Merle, 19 November, 1990.
Painter, R.
Parker, Dawn, 28 January, 1994.
Penny, Marion, 23 March, 1992.
Phillips, Stella, 14 August, 1991.
Pocklington, Arthur.
Priest, Leila, 17 September, 1991.
Priest, Norman.
Rayner, Alice.
Rayner, E.
Read, Ralph, 19 November, 1990.
Reekie, Dorothy, 14 August, 1991.
Ridge, Mrs.
Ridgway, Ian, 4 June, 1998.
Russell, Shirley, 17 September, 1991.
Self, James.
Sharman, James.
Sheather, Pat, 1992.
Smallcombe, K., 1 September, 1994.
Smallcombe, Kendrie, March to October, 1994.
Smallcombe, N., 30 January, 1994.
Swenson, Pearl, 16 April, 1993.
Tanswell, Claude and Olive, 20 December, 1993.
Turnbull, Janet, 1990.
Turner, Adrian and Elsie, 21 November, 1990.
Tutt, Thelma, 20 November, 1990.
Valentine, R., 11 July, 1994.
Van Eyk, C. J.
Wahlquist, Laurie and Iris, 19 November, 1991.
Walters, Gladys, March, 1994
Warburton, Ivor
Watson, E.
Watson, Fred.
Weir, E.
Westbrook, A., 8 April, 1997.
Whitburn, Joyce, 22 March, 1997.
Wilson, Alan.
Wilson, F. C.
Wilson, Reginald.
Woodham, John and Ruth, 30 April 1990.

INSTITUTIONAL RECORDS

Annual Report of the Christian Revival Crusade in Australia, June 1994.
Assemblies of God in Australia Directory 1995 Mitcham: Assemblies of God in Australia, 1995.
Home Missionaries Card Records Uniting Church of Australia, Synod of Victoria Archives.
Membership list, Apostolic Mission, Adelaide, 1927.
Membership list, Glad Tidings Tabernacle, Brisbane, 1948-.
Minute Book, Southern Evangelical Mission, Brighton, Victoria.
Minutes of Annual Meetings, Glad Tidings Tabernacle, Brisbane, 1947-1951.
Minutes of Apostolic Mission, Adelaide, S.A., 1927-1940.
Minutes of Assembly of God Church, Ballarat branch, various meetings, 1929-1966.
Minutes of Board Meetings, Glad Tidings Tabernacle, Brisbane, 1944-1952.
Minutes of Board of Trustees, Richmond Temple, Victoria, 1934-1967.
Minutes of Deacons' meetings, Assembly of God church, Ballarat, 1939-1980.
Minutes of Deacons' meetings, Richmond Temple, Victoria, 1929-1967.
Minutes of General Assembly Meetings, Richmond Temple, Victoria, 1927-1943.

Minutes of Southern Evangelical Mission, 1913—.
Minutes of the Australian Pentecostal Ministers' Fellowship Steering Committee, 28 February 1995.
Minutes of the Commonwealth Council of the Apostolic Church, 22 October 1941 to 27 November 1941.
Minutes of the Eighth General Conference of the Methodist Church of Australasia, 1925.
Minutes of the Executive Committee, Melbourne Bible Institute, 2 June 1925.
Minutes of the Seventh General Conference of the Methodist Church of Australasia, Adelaide, 1923.
Minutes of weekly Bible Study meetings, Apostolic Mission, Adelaide, 1927-1940.
National Church Planting Department: Report to the 31st Biennial Conference of the Assemblies of God in Australia Chester Hill, NSW: Assemblies of God in Australia, 1997.
Students of the Bible College of Victoria (inc. Melbourne Bible Institute), Melbourne, 1989.
The Apostolic Church: its Principles and Practices Richmond: Apostolic Publications, 1939.

PAMPHLETS, LEAFLETS AND BULLETINS

'Apostolic Church Melbourne Opening Ceremony' brochure, 7 April, 1939.
'Our Pioneer Missionary: An appreciation of the late Rev J.H.Coombe by a Council Member,' RMBU News Bulletin cutting, n.d., but probably around 1957.
'Relevant Pentecostal Witness,' pamphlet, Chatsglen, R.S.A. n. d.
'Rules and Regulations,' The Bible Standard Training School for Christian Workers, Lighthouse Temple, North Melbourne, n. d. but c.1940.
'Results of Examination' sheet for W. Larsen, June, 1941.
'Christian Workers' Course Certificate,' awarded to Walter Larsen, 13 December, 1941.
'The Baptism of the Holy Ghost,' leaflet, n. d.
Aborigine Rescue Mission News and Prayer Letter, 1:1 10 April 1946.
Ames, T. J., *A Problem: Now and Then* Adelaide, published by the author, 1902.
Ames, T. J., *Concerning the Punishment of the Wicked,* Elim Pentecostal Assembly Tract No.23, Adelaide: ABC Printing Works, n. d.
Apostolic Church of Queensland and Hatton Vale Community Centenary, n.d.
Assemblies of God in Australia Directory 1995 Mitcham, Vic: Assemblies of God in Australia, 1995.
Beer, D., *Keswick Book Shop: its beginnings and now* n. d.
Bishop, A.E., *Tongues, Signs and Visions, not God's Order for Today* Chicago: The Bible Institute Colportage Association, 1920.
Booth-Clibborn, W. (ed), *Wings of Praise*, published by the author, Sydney, n. d.
Duncan, P., 'The Blasphemous Lie of the Set Prophet,' pamphlet, n. d. but

c.1934.
Durham, W., *A Testimony of the Power of God*, Adelaide: ABC Printing, 1911.
Richmond Temple Souvenir Richmond, Vic: Richmond Temple, 1939.
Jubilee Souvenir of the Municipality of Newtown, c.1912.
Mintern, E., ed, *This We Believe* Zion: Christian Catholic Church, n. d.
Morling, G.H., *Pentecostalism* Baptist Department of Evangelism, n. d.
Price, Alan, 'Pentecostalism,' Melbourne: Austral Printing and Publishing Co, n. d.
Rees, G., 'Eternity: the Unknown Man Who Wrote It,' pamphlet, n. d.
Richmond Temple Souvenir Richmond, Vic: Richmond Temple, 1939.
Ridley, J., *A Soldier's Testimony*, Melbourne: S.John Bacon, n. d.
Rivers of His Grace, Belgrave Heights Convention, Melbourne, 1959.
Seymour, William, 'The Apostolic Faith Movement,' Los Angeles: Apostolic Faith Mission, n. d.
Smallcombe, N., *Into the 21st Century* Cairns: Cairns Christian Centre, n. d.
Souvenir Exhibiting the Movement of God in the Apostolic Church, n. d.

JOURNALS AND NEWSPAPERS

Acts '88, Acts '89, Acts '90 Boronia, Vic, 1988, 1989, 1990.
Advertiser, Adelaide.
Age, Melbourne.
Argus, Melbourne.
Alpine Observer, Bright, Vic., 19 May, 1922.
Apostolic Faith, Los Angeles, September 1906-May, 1908.
Apostolic Herald, Melbourne: Apostolic Assemblies in Australia, May, 1936 to May, 1941.
Apostolic News, Adelaide: Apostolic Mission, September, 1929 to June, 1940. From December, 1937 to September, 1940 the name was changed to *Bible Standard Call*.
Asian Journal of Pentecostal Studies, Baguio City, Philippines: the Faculty of the Asia Pacific Theological Seminary, 1998—.
Australasian Pentecostal Studies, Chester Hill, NSW, 1998— .
Australian Aborigines' Advocate, Randwick, NSW, 1908-1913.
Australian Christian Commonwealth, 13 May, 1904.
Australian Christian World, 29 August, 1902.
Australian Evangel, the official organ of the Assemblies of God, 1928
Barsabbas, Sydney: Centre for the Study of Australian Christianity, 1993-1994.
Bulletin, Sydney, New South Wales.
Cairns Post, Cairns, Queensland.
Canvas Cathedral Cooee, Brisbane, 3 May, 1931 to 25 September, 1932.
Canvas Cathedral Cooee, Toowoomba, 17 October, 1931 to 22 November, 1931.
Centralian Advocate, Alice Springs, Northern Territory.
Cessnock Eagle, Cessnock, New South Wales.
Charismatic Contact, Aitkenvale, Qld, Faith Ministries, 1972—.

Christian Times and Australian Weekly News, 1858-62.
Christian Weekly and Methodist Journal, 20 July, 1883.
Christianity and History Newsletter, Leicester: Universities and Colleges Christian Fellowship for the Study Group on Christianity and History.
Church Growth, Yoido, Korea: Church Growth International.
Confidence, Sunderland, England, 1908-1926.
Contending Earnestly for the Faith, Blenheim, New Zealand, 1995—.
Daily Telegraph, Sydney, NSW.
Echoes of Grace, journal of the National (now Christian) Revival Crusade, 1942-1952.
Elim Foursquare Gospel Express, Newtown: Elim Foursquare Gospel Church, May, 1932-August, 1932.
Full Gospel Messenger, Caboolture, Queensland: the Full Gospel Churches of Australia.
Full Salvation, Salvation Army, 1 February, 1896, 2 March, 1896.
Gathering Call, Newtown: Elim Foursquare Gospel Church, September, 1932-August/September, 1935.
Good News, Melbourne: Pentecostal Mission (later, Apostolic Mission) 1910-1934. Some copies are held in the Latrobe Library, Melbourne, and the Mitchell Library, Sydney. I have copies of 116 issues from 1910 to 1934.
Harvest Grain, a quarterly published by Richmond Temple, first issued in 1944.
Herald of Grace, Replaced the Apostolic Church's *Apostolic Herald* in May, 1941.
Impact, Adelaide: Adelaide Crusade Centre, 1975-1978, and Unley Park: Tabor College, 1979-1980.
Indigenous Leadership, February, 1998.
Journal of Pentecostal Theology, Cleveland: Church of God School of Theology, 1992—.
Journal of Religious History, Association for the Journal of Religious History, Oxford: Blackwell, 1960—.
Journal of the Historical Society of South Australia, Adelaide, SA.
Keswick Quarterly, Melbourne, Victoria.
Korumburra Times, Korumburra, Victoria.
Latter Rain Evangel, Chicago: Evangel Publishing House, 1909—.
Leaves of Healing, Zion: Christian Catholic Church
Lucas: An Evangelical History Review, Macquarie Centre: Evangelical History Association.
Maryborough Chronicle, Maryborough, Queensland.
Minister's Bulletin, Mitcham, Vic: Assemblies of God in Australia, National Conference.
Ministries Today, Lake Mary, Florida: Strang Communications Company.
Ministry, International Journal of the Seventh-day Adventist Ministerial Association, Warburton, Vic: Signs Publishing Company.
Myrtleford Mail and Whorouly Witness, Myrtleford, 18 May, 1922.
New Day, Plympton, SA: Tabor College, 1980-1997.
New Life, Melbourne Vol 35, No.66, 21 September, 1972.

News and Prayer Letter, Aborigine Rescue Mission, Apostolic Church, 1945.
Observer and Free Methodist Chronicle, 31 March, 1886-1 April, 1890.
Paraclete, Springfield, USA: Assemblies of God, 1967—.
PCBC Journal, Sydney: Association of Pentecostal and Charismatic Bible Colleges of Australasia, 1997—.
Pentecostal Times, published by T. Ames, Adelaide, c.1909.
Pneuma: the Journal of the Society for Pentecostal Studies, Lexington, Kentucky.
Portland Guardian, Portland, Victoria, August-December, 1970.
Prayer Bell, July-August,1929 to September-October, 1936
Quiz, October, 1901.
R.M.B.U. News Bulletin, cutting, n. d. but probably around 1957.
Register, Adelaide, SA.
Renewal Journal, Strathpine, Queensland, 1993—.
Renewing Australia, Lyneham, ACT, 1986-1991.
Revival Echoes, Melbourne: The Apostolic Church, June, 1933 to April, 1936.
South Australian Bible Christian Magazine, Adelaide, South Australia.
South Australian Independent and Presbyterian, Vol VI, January and November, 1878.
Southern Cross, Melbourne, Victoria.
Southern Evangel, journal of the Southern Evangelical Mission, March 1923 –.
Spectator and Methodist Chronicle, official organ of the Methodist Church in Victoria and Tasmania.
Sun News Pictorial, Melbourne, Victoria.
Sunday at Home, London: William Clarke, December, 1877.
Sydney Morning Herald, Sydney, New South Wales.
The City Was Moved: Special Daily Edition of The Australian Christian World, Sydney, New South Wales, August, 1902.
The News, Adelaide, South Australia.
Torrey-Alexander Souvenir: Special Mission Number of the Southern Cross, Melbourne, Victoria, 10 September, 1902.
Truth, Sydney, New South Wales.
Victorian Banner, Victoria, 1881-84.
War Cry, Hawthorn: E. Burrows for the Salvation Army, 19 March, 1983 and various issues.
Warrnambool Independent, Warrnambool, Victoria, 2 July, 1883.
Wesleyan Chronicle, August, 1858 and subsequent issues.
Western Champion, 25 November, 1932.

ARTICLES

'Australia Gave Hot Reception to US Cultist,' *Daily Mirror* Sydney, 9 February, 1977.
'Chicago Suburb Has Curious Link Through Its Founder,' *Daily Mirror,* 25 January, 1950.
'The 40th Anniversary of the Yoido Full Gospel Church,' *Church Growth* 1998

Summer, Yoido, Korea: Church Growth International.
Blumhofer, E., 'Charles F.Parham's 1906 Invasion: a Pentecostal Branch Grows in Zion,' *Assemblies of God Heritage,* Fall, 1986.
Bowers, J., 'A Wesleyan-Pentecostal Approach to Christian Formation,' *JPT,* #6, April, 1995.
Camp, J. H., 'Rise and Fall of Zion City,' *The Australian Magazine,* 1 February, 1908.
Cerillo A., Jr, 'Interpretive Approaches to the History of American Pentecostal Origins,' *Pneuma,* 19:1, Spring, 1997.
_____. 'The Origins of American Pentecostalism,' *Pneuma*, 15:1, Spring, 1993.
Chant, B., 'Charismatic Spirituality,' *Lucas*, No. 16, December, 1993.
_____. 'Personally Speaking,' *New Day,* April, 1996.
Clines, D., 'The Postmodern adventure in Biblical Studies,' in *Australasian Pentecostal Studies*, No. 1, March, 1998.
Court, J., 'Discerning between the emotional, the psychotic and the spiritual,' *Renewal Journal*, No. 7, 1996.
Ditterich, E. K., 'Daniel James Draper—Master Builder,' in *Heritage* Melbourne: the Methodist Historical Society of Victoria and Tasmania, #26, October, 1874.
Gardiner, A., 'A History of the Apostolic Church,' in *Acts '89*, November, 1989; *Acts '90*, October, 1990; *Acts '91*, February, 1991.
Gill, Deborah, 'The Contemporary State of Women in Ministry in the Assemblies of God,' *Pneuma*, 17:1, Spring, 1995.
Grant, P., 'William Cathcart: From Gloom to Glory,' in *Acts '88*, January, 1988.
Grass, T. G., 'Edward Irving: Eschatology, Ecclesiology and Spiritual Gifts,' in *Christianity and History Newsletter*, No. 15, June, 1995.
Hedding, Bishop, 'What is Christian Perfection?' *Spectator,* 5:223, 8 August, 1879.
Hill, C., 'Breaking the Mould,' Crowborough, Sussex, *Renewal*, #259, December, 1997.
Hilliard, David, 'The City of Churches: Some Aspects of Religion in Adelaide about 1900,' in *Journal of the Historical Society of South Australia*, #8, 1980.
Horsley, J. F., 'Have Ye Received the Holy Ghost?' *Spectator*, 5:242, 19 December 1879.
Howe, R., 'Social Composition of the Wesleyan Church in Victoria During the Nineteenth Century,' *Journal of Religious History*, June, 1967.
Innes, H., 'Ernest Kramer One of God's People in Oz,' *On Being,* August, 1978.
Johns, C. B., 'Healing and Deliverance: a Pentecostal Perspective,' in *Concilium*, 1996, 3.
Johns, C. B., 'Pentecostals and the Praxis of Liberation: a Proposal for Subversive Theological Education,' *Transformation*, 11:1, January-March, 1994.
Johns, J., 'Pentecostalism and the Postmodern Worldview,' *Journal Of Pentecostal Theology*, 78, 1995.
Macchia, F., 'Sighs Too Deep For Words,' *Journal of Pentecostal Theology,*

No. 1, October, 1992.
_____. 'Tongues as a Sign: Towards a Sacramental Understanding of Pentecostal Experience,' *Pneuma*, 15:1, Spring, 1993.
Martin, D., 'Space for the Expansive Spirit,' in *Times Literary Supplement*, 28 March, 1997.
Mayne, T., 'La Perouse Celebrates 100 Years,' in *Indigenous Leadership*, #14, February, 1998.
Moulton, Dr, 'John Wesley's Doctrine of Christian Perfection,' in *Spectator*, 20 May, 1925.
Moorhead, M. W., *A Cloud of Witnesses to Pentecost in India*, Pamphlet #4, Bombay, 1908.
Outhred, Len, 'The Bible Standard Pentecostal Church,' *Minister's Bulletin*, Mitcham, Vic, Assemblies of God in Australia, March, 1998
Paproth, D., 'The Upwey Convention and C. H. Nash,' *Lucas*, #16, December, 1993.
Petrick, J., 'Spreading the Gospel,' *Centralian Advocate*, 8 October, 1986.
Piggin, S., 'God in History: Some Thoughts on the Recovery of a Useful Christian History,' in *Lucas*, #1, November, 1987.
Piggin, S., 'Historical Streams of Influence on Evangelical Piety,' *Lucas*, #18, December, 1994.
Pluss, Jean-Daniel, 'Azusa and Other Myths: The Long and Winding Road from Experience to Stated Belief and Back Again,' *Pneuma,* 15:1, No. 2, Fall, 1993.
Powell, P., 'Spiritual Drunks,' *Contending Earnestly for the Faith*, Blenheim, New Zealand, 1:4, May-July, 1995; 'Measuring False Prophets', 1:4, May-July, 1995.
Randall, I. M., 'Old Time Power: Relationships between Pentecostalism and Evangelical Spirituality in England,' in *Pneuma*, 19:1, Spring, 1997.
Roebuck, D., 'Perfect liberty to Preach the Gospel: Women Ministers in the Church of God,' *Pneuma*, 17:1, Spring, 1995.
Rosado, Caleb, 'Lessons from Waco,' *Ministry*, July, 1993.
Robins, J, 'The Rise and Fall of a Prophet,' *Advertiser*, Adelaide, 30 October, 1973.
Roe, J., 'Challenge and Response: Religious Life in Melbourne, 1876-86,' *Journal of Religious History*, 5:2, December, 1968.
Salter, O., 'What on Earth is God Doing?' *Renewal Journal*, No. 7, 1996:1.
Sewell, K., 'Christian Historiographical Methodology: Some Foundational Considerations,' in *Lucas,* No. 15, June, 1993.
Sollit, M., 'Australian Dictator in Zion,' *People*, 10 August, 1966.
Stibbe, Mark, 'Interpreting the Word in the Power of the Spirit,' in *Skepsis*, Autumn, 1996.
Supplement to *Anglicans for Renewal,* Derby, England: Anglican Renewal Ministries, 1996.
Walker, R. B., 'The Growth and Typology of the Wesleyan Methodist Church in NSW, 1812-1901,' *Journal of Religious History*, December, 1971.
Wessels, R., 'The Spirit Baptism, Nineteenth Century Roots,' *Pneuma*, 14:2,

Fall, 1992.
West, J., 'The Role of the Woman Missionary,' in *Lucas,* #21, #22, June and December, 1996.

BOOKS

A to Z of Who's Who in Australia's History (The). Brookvale: Child and Associates, 1987.
Aldine Almanac and Directory for South Australia (The). Adelaide: Isaiah Boothby, 1868, 1872.
Abeysekera, F. *The History of the Assemblies of God of Singapore.* Singapore: Assemblies of God, 1992.
Abrams, Minnie. *The Baptism of the Holy Ghost and Fire.* Kedgaon, India: Mukti Press, 1906.
Adams, John. *The Scriptural Statement concerning the baptism of (with or in) the Holy Spirit.* North Melbourne: Victory Press, n.d.
Aland, K. et al, eds. *The Greek New Testament* United Bible Societies, 1983.
Aldis, W. H., editor. *The Keswick Convention 1938: Notes of the Addresses Revised by the Speakers.* London: Paternoster, 1938.
Alford, H. *The Greek Testament.* Volume II, Chicago: Moody, 1968.
Allen, D. *The Unfailing Stream.* Tonbridge: Sovereign World, 1994.
Anderson, A. and W. Hollenweger, editors. *Pentecostals After a Century.* Sheffield: Sheffield Academic Press, 1999.
Anderson, R. *Vision of the Disinherited.* New York: Oxford, 1979.
Aplin, G., S. Foster and M. McKernan, editors. *Australians, A Historical Dictionary.* Broadway, NSW: Fairfax, Syme and Weldon Associates, 1987.
_____. *Australians, Events and Places.* Broadway, NSW: Fairfax, Syme and Weldon Associates, 1987.
Arthur, W. *The Tongue of Fire.* London: Wesleyan Conference Office, 1856.
Atter, G. *The Third Force.* College Press, Ontario, 1962.
Auclair, Marcelle. *St Teresa of Avila.* London: Burns Oates, 1953.
Augustine. *Confessions.* Various publishers.
Australian Dictionary of Biography. Vol 4, 1851-1890; Vol 6, 1851-1890; Vol 10, 1891-1939; Vol 12, 1891-1939; Melbourne: Melbourne University Press, 1972-1990.
Averill, Lloyd. *Go North Young Man.* Springwood, Qld: published by the author, 1992.
Banton, A. E. *Pentecostal Pioneering with the Foursquare Gospel in Australia.* Westmead, NSW: Essington Christian Academy, 1984.
Barclay, J. *Arise! The Story of Christian City Church.* Sydney: Covenant, 1987.
Barnard, M. *A History of Australia.* North Ryde: Angus and Robertson, 1962.
Barrett, D. *World Christian Encyclopaedia.* Oxford: Oxford University Press, 1982.
Bartleman, F. *Azusa Street.* Plainfield: Logos International, 1925, 1980.
Baxter, R. *The Reformed Pastor.* Edinburgh: Banner of Truth, 1656, 1983.
Behm, J. 'Παρακαλεω' in G. Friedrich, ed, *Theological Dictionary of the New*

Testament. Eerdmans, Volume V, 1975.
Benson, I. *A Century of Victorian Methodism.* Melbourne: Spectator, 1935.
Bentley, P. and P. Hughes. *Australian Life and the Christian Faith: Facts and Figures.* Kew, Vic: Christian Research Association, 1997.
Bentley, P. T. Blombery and P. Hughes, editors. *Faith Without the Church?* Kew: Christian Research Association, 1992.
_____. *A Yearbook for Australian Churches.* Hawthorn: Christian Research Association, 1990-1995.
Bittlinger, A. *Gifts and Graces.* London: Hodder and Stoughton, 1967.
Black, A.W., editor. *Religion in Australia: Sociological Perspectives.* Sydney: Allen and Unwin, 1991.
Blacket, J. *Fire in the Outback.* Sutherland, NSW: Albatross, 1997.
Bloch-Hoell, Nils. *The Pentecostal Movement.* Oslo, 1964.
Blumhofer, E. *Aimee Semple McPherson: Everybody's Sister.* Grand Rapids: Eerdmans, 1993.
_____. *The AOG: A Popular History.* Springfield: Radiant, Gospel Publishing House, 1985.
_____. *The Assemblies of God: A Chapter in the Story of American Pentecostalism,* Two volumes, Springfield: Gospel Publishing House, 1989.
Bollen, J. D. *Protestantism and Social Reform in NSW, 1890-1910.* Melbourne: Melbourne University Press, 1972.
Bolton, B. *Booth's Drum.* Lane Cove: Hodder and Stoughton, 1980.
Booth-Clibborn, E. *50 Years for Jesus.* Chichester: New Wine, 1989.
Booth-Clibborn, W. *The Baptism in the Holy Spirit.* Dallas: The Voice of Healing, 1962.
Boswell, James. *Life of Johnson*, Vol I, 31 July, 1763, various publishers.
Bouma, G. and B. Dixon. *The Religious Factor in Australian Life.* Melbourne: Marc, 1986.
Breward, I. *Australia 'The Most Godless Place Under Heaven'?* Melbourne: Beacon Hill, 1988.
_____. *A History of the Australian Churches.* St Leonards: Allen and Unwin, 1993.
Broome, R. *Aboriginal Australians.* St Leonards, NSW: Allen and Unwin, 1994.
_____. *Treasure in Earthen Vessels; Protestant Christianity in NSW Society, 1900-1915* Brisbane: University of Queensland Press, 1980.
Brown, R. editor. *Collins Milestones in Australian History 1788 to the Present.* Sydney: Collins, 1986.
Bruce, F. F. *In Retrospect: Remembrance of Things Past.* London: Marshall Pickering, 1993.
Brumback, C. *What Meaneth This?* Springfield: Gospel Publishing House, 1947.
Bruner, F.A. *A Theology of the Holy Spirit.* Grand Rapids: Eerdmans, 1970.
Budgen, V. *The Charismatics and the Word of God.* Welwyn: Evangelical Press, 1986.
Bunyan, J., *Grace Abounding to the Chief of Sinners.* Grand Rapids: Baker, 1986.
Burgess, S., G. McGee and P. Alexander, editors. *Dictionary of Pentecostal and*

Charismatic Movements. Grand Rapids: Regency, 1988.
Burgess, S. and E. M. Van Der Maas, editors. *The New International Dictionary of Pentecostal and Charismatic Movements, Revised and Expanded Edition.* Grand Rapids: Zondervan, 2002.
Bushman, R. L., editor. *The Great Awakening, Documents on the Revival of Religion, 1740-1745.* New York: Atheneum, 1970.
Butterfield, H. *Christianity and History.* London: G.Bell and Sons, 1949.
Calley, M. *God's People: West Indian Pentecostal Sects in England.* Oxford: Oxford, 1965.
Calvin, J. *Institutes of the Christian Religion.* Philadelphia: Westminster, 1559, 1960.
Cameron, J. *In Stow's Footsteps.* Adelaide: SA Congregational History Project Committee, 1987.
Campion, E. *Australian Catholics.* Ringwood: Penguin, 1988.
Capon, J. *John and Charles Wesley: the Preacher and the Poet.* London: Hodder and Stoughton, 1988.
Carey, H. *Believing in Australia.* St Leonards: Allen and Unwin, 1996.
Carruthers, J. E. *Memories of an Australian Ministry 1868-1921.* London: Epworth, n. d.
Carter, J. *Donald Gee—Pentecostal Statesman.* London: Assemblies of God, 1975.
Cartwright, D. *The Great Evangelists.* Basingstoke: Marshall Pickering, 1986.
Cathcart, W. *To Glory from Gloom.* Dallas: Christian Communications Trust, 1976.
Chamless, Mary Ruth. *Behold God's Handmaid.* Belleville, Illinois: published by the author, 1988.
Chant, B. *Breaking the Power of the Past.* Miranda: Tabor, 1995.
_____. *Creative Living.* South Plympton, SA: Tabor, 1996.
_____. *Empowered by the Spirit.* Miranda: Tabor, 2008.
_____. *Heart of Fire.* Unley Park, S.A.: Tabor, 1984.
_____. *Praying in the Spirit.* Miranda: Tabor, 2009.
_____. *Spiritual Gifts: a Reappraisal.* Miranda: Tabor, 1993.
_____. *The Return.* Chichester: Sovereign World, 1991.
_____. *Your Guide to God's Power.* Chichester: Sovereign World, 1986.
Chant, K. *Better than Revival.* Kingswood: Ken Chant Ministries, 1994.
_____. *Clothed with Power.* Kingswood, NSW: Ken Chant Ministries, 1993.
Chapman, W. *Power and Its Secret.* Melbourne: T. Shaw Fitchett, n. d.,
Chevreau, G. *Catch the Fire.* London: Marshall and Pickering, 1994.
Cho, P. Y. *The Fourth Dimension.* North Plainfield: Bridge, 1979.
Christenson, L. *Welcome, Holy Spirit.* Augsburg, 1987.
Clark, G. M. *A History of Australia.* Brunswick, Vic: Melbourne: Melbourne University Press, Vol I, 1985; Vol V, 1981; Vol VI, 1987.
_____. *A Short History of Australia.* Ringwood: Penguin, 1986.
Clark, M. *The History of Primitive Methodism in Victoria and Tasmania.* (n. p., n. d.).
Clifton, Shane, and Jacqueline Grey, editors. *Raising Women Leaders:*

Perspectives on Liberating Women in Pentecostal and Charismatic Contexts. Chester Hill, NSW: Australian Pentecostal Studies, 2009.
Commercial and Trade Directory. Adelaide: Morris, Hayter and Barry, 1882.
Cook, P. *Zion City, Illinois: John Alexander's Democracy.* Zion: Zion Historical Society, 1970.
Cooper, D. *Flames of Revival.* Endeavour Hills: Christian Revival Crusade, 1995.
Corum, F. T., editor. *Like As Of Fire: a Reprint of the Old Azusa Street Papers.* Wilmington, Mass, 1981.
Court, J. *Hypnosis, Healing and the Christian.* Carlisle: Paternoster, 1997.
Cox, F. W. *Jubilee Record 1837-1887, the Congregational Churches of Australia.* Adelaide: Webb, Vardon and Pritchard, 1887.
Cox, H. *Fire From Heaven.* Reading, Mass: Addison-Wesley, 1994.
Croucher, R. *Recent Trends Among Evangelicals.* Sutherland: Albatross, 1986.
Cumpston, J. H. L. *The History of Diphtheria, Scarlet Fever, Measles and Whooping Cough in Australia.* Canberra: Commonwealth of Australia Department of Health, 1927.
Dallimore, A. *Spurgeon.* Edinburgh: Banner of Truth, 1988.
_____. *The Life of Edward Irving.* Edinburgh: Banner of Truth, 1983.
Darms, A. *Life and Work of John Alexander Dowie, 1847-1907*, Zion: Christian Catholic Church, n. d.
Davison, G., J. Hirst and S. Macintyre, editors. *The Oxford Companion to Australian History.* South Melbourne: Oxford, 1999.
Davison, G., J. McCarty and A. McLeary, editors. *Australians, 1888.* Broadway, NSW: Fairfax, Syme and Weldon Associates, 1987.
Dayton, D. *Theological Roots of Pentecostalism.* Metuchen, NJ: Scarecrow Press and ATLA, 1987.
Denney, J. 'St Paul's Epistle to the Romans' in *The Expositor's Greek Testament.* Vol II, Grand Rapids: Eerdmans, 1967.
Dickey, B., editor. *The Australian Dictionary of Evangelical Biography.* Sydney: Evangelical History Association, 1994.
Dixon, P. *Signs of Revival.* Eastbourne: Kingsway, 1994.
Douglas, J. editor. *The New International Dictionary of the Christian Church.* Grand Rapids: Zondervan Regency, 1978.
Dowie Scrapbooks, collections of press cuttings, Zion: Zion Historical Society.
Dowie, J. *Doctors, Drugs and Devils.* Zion: Zion Printing and Publishing House, 1901.
_____. *Rome's Polluted Springs.* Melbourne: George Robertson, 1877.
_____. *Sin in the Camp.* Melbourne: Henry Cooke, 1883.
_____. *Spiritualism Unmasked.* Melbourne: George Robertson, 1882.
_____. *The Love of God in the Salvation of Man.* Chicago: Zion Publishing House, 1900.
Dowley, T., editor. *The History of Christianity.* Oxford: Lion, 1985.
Du Plessis, D. *The Spirit Bade Me Go.* Plainfield: Logos, 1970.
Duncan, P. *Great Things He Hath Done.* Published by the author, n. d.
_____. *Pentecost in Australia.* Published by the author, n. d.

_____. *The Charismatic Tide.* Published by the author, 1978.
Dunn, J. *Baptism in the Holy Spirit.* London: SCM, 1970.
Dyer, H. *Pandita Ramabai: the Story of Her Life.* London: Marshall, Morgan and Scott, 1914.
_____. *Revival in India.* London: Marshall, Morgan and Scott, 1907.
Edwards, J. *The Religious Affections.* Edinburgh: Banner of Truth, 1746, 1986.
_____. *The Works of Jonathan Edwards.* Edinburgh: Banner of Truth, 1834, 1984.
Elwell, W.A., editor. *Evangelical Dictionary of Theology.* Grand Rapids: Baker, 1984.
Emilsen, S. *A Whiff of Heresy.* Kensington: New South Wales University Press, 1991.
Eusebius,. *Historia Ecclesiastica.* xiv-xviii, various publishers.
Evans, E. *To Run With His Promises.* Slacks Creek, Qld: Assembly Press, 1988.
Evans, Efion. *The Welsh Revival of 1904.* Bryntirion, Wales: Evangelical Press of Wales, 1987.
Ewart, F. *The Phenomenon of Pentecost (a history of the 'Latter Rain').* St Louis: Pentecostal Publishing House, 1947.
Faupel, D. W. *The Everlasting Gospel: the Significance of Eschatology in the Development of Pentecostal Thought.* Sheffield: Sheffield Academic Press, 1996.
Fee, G. *God's Empowering Presence.* Peabody: Hendrickson, 1994.
_____. *The First Epistle to the Corinthians.* Grand Rapids: Eerdmans, 1987.
Fielding, H. *Tom Jones.* Ware: Wordsworth, 1994.
Findlay, G. G. *St Paul's First Epistle to the Corinthian* in *The Expositor's Greek Testament.* Volume II, Grand Rapids: Eerdmans, 1967.
Fison, L. *Methodist History of Victoria and Tasmania Special reprint from The Spectator.* 4 vols.
Fitchett, W. H. *Wesley and His Century.* London: George Bell, 1906.
Fletcher, Lionel. *Mighty Moments.* Manchester: Religious Tract Society, 1931.
Foulkes, R. *The Flame Shall Not be Quenched.* Devonport: Methodist Charismatic Fellowship, n. d.
Freud, S. *The Unconscious* in *Great Books of the Western World.* Volume 54, Encyclopaedia Britannica, 1952.
Friedrich, G., editor. *Theological Dictionary of the New Testament.* Volume VIII, Eerdmans, 1972.
Frodsham, S. *Smith Wigglesworth: Apostle of Faith.* Nottingham: Assemblies of God Publishing House, 1971.
_____. *With Signs Following.* Springfield: Gospel Publishing House, 1946.
Fullerton, W. *Charles H. Spurgeon.* Chicago: Moody, 1966.
Gammage, B. and P. Spearritt, editors. *Australians, 1938.* Broadway, NSW: Fairfax, Syme and Weldon Associates, 1987.
Garvin, M. *Us Aussies.* Sale: Hayzon, 1987.
Gaustad, E. S. *The Great Awakening in New England.* Gloucester, Mass: Peter Smith, 1965.
Gee, D. *Concerning Spiritual Gifts.* Springfield: Gospel Publishing House, n. d.

_____. *Spiritual Gifts in the Work of the Ministry Today.* Springfield: Gospel Publishing House, 1963.
_____. *Upon All Flesh.* Springfield: Gospel Publishing House, 1947.
Gibbney, H. J., 'Dowie, John Alexander (1847-1907),' in ADB, Vol 4, 1851-1890.
Gillman, Ian, editor. *Many Faiths One Nation.* Sydney: Collins, 1988.
Gribben, R. H., editor. *Communion in Australian Churches.* Melbourne: JBCE, 1985
_____. *The Portland Bay Methodists.* Portland: Wesley, 1972.
Grubb, G. *Notes of Sermons and Bible Readings.* Hobart: Mercury, 1893.
Gutierrez, B. F. and D. Smith, editors. *In the Power of the Spirit.* Drexel Hill: AIPRAL and CELEP with Skipjack Press, 1996.
Hancock, M., and F. Liebelt. *A Tangled We.,* Adelaide: Hancock and Martin Family Reunion Committee, 1986.
Harper, M. *As at the Beginning.* London: Hodder and Stoughton, 1966.
Harrell, D. *All Things Are Possible.* Indiana University Press, 1975.
_____. *Oral Roberts: An American Life.* Indiana University Press, 1985.
Harris, D., D. Hynd and D. Millikan, D., editors. *The Shape of Belief.* Homebush: Lancer, 1982.
Harris, J. *One Blood.* Sutherland: Albatross, 1990.
Harris, L. *Church Government —Babylonian or Biblical?* Published by the author, n. d.
_____. *Five Keys of Authority.* Fullarton, S.A.: Crusade, n. d.
Harrison, E., G. Bromiley and C. Henry, editors. *Baker's Dictionary of Theology.* Grand Rapids: Baker, 1985.
Hart, L. *Journey With Jesus.* Published by the author, 1986.
Hart, M. *I Remember.* Published by the author, 1983.
Hawthorne, G., R. Martin and D. Reid, editors. *Dictionary of Paul and His Letters* Downers Grove, Ill: InterVarsity Press, 1993.
Henry, M. *Matthew Henry's Commentary on the Whole Bible.* Vol VI, New York: Fleming H. Revell, n. d.
Hetherington, I. *Aboriginal Queen of Sacred Song.* Melbourne: Saxton and Buckie, 1929.
Hibbert, A. *Smith Wigglesworth—The Secret of his Power.* Chichester: Sovereign World, 1982.
Hilliard, David. *Popular Revivalism in South Australia from the 1870s to the 1920s.* Adelaide: 1982.
Hogan, M. *The Sectarian Strand.* Ringwood: Penguin, 1987.
Holden, J. S., editor. *The Keswick Convention 1938: Notes of the Addresses Revised by the Speakers.* London: Paternoster, 1929.
Hollenweger, W., editor. *Die Pfingstkirchen* Die Kirchen der Welt, Stuttgart: Evangelisches Verlagswerk, 1971.
_____. *The Pentecostals.* Peabody, Massachusetts: Hendrickson, 1988.
Horton, H. *The Gifts of the Spirit.* Springfield: Gospel Publishing House, 1934, 1975.
Houghton, S. M., editor. *Five Pioneer Missionaries.* Edinburgh: Banner of

Truth, 1987.
Houston, H. On *Being Frank*. London: Marshall Pickering, 1989.
Hughes, P., and T. Blombery. *Patterns of Faith in Australian Churches*. Kew: Christian Research Association, 1990.
Hughes, P. *Religion in Australia: Facts and Figures*. Kew, Vic: Christian Research Association, 1997.
_____. *The Pentecostals in Australia*. Canberra: Australian Government Publishing Service, 1996.
Hughes, P., C. Thompson, R. Pryor and G. Bouma. *Believe It or Not: Australian Spirituality and the Churches in the 90s*. Kew: Christian Research Association, 1995.
Hume, David. *An Enquiry Concerning Human Understanding* in *Great Books of the Western World*. Volume 35, Chicago: Encyclopaedia Britannica, 1952.
Hummel, C. *Fire in the Fireplace*. Downers Grove: Inter Varsity Press, 1978.
Humphreys, R., and R. Ward. *Religious Bodies in Australia*. Melbourne: published by the authors, 1986.
Hunt, Arnold. *This Side of Heaven*. Adelaide: Lutheran Publishing House, 1985.
Hunt, S. *The Assemblies of God Queensland Conference: A Story of its Formation and Missio*. Assemblies of God, n. d.
Hutchinson, M. and E. Campion, editor. *Long Patient Struggle: Studies in the Role of Women in Australian Christianity*. Sydney: Centre for the Study of Australian Christianity, 1994.
_____. *Re-visioning Australian Colonial Christianity: New Essays in the Australian Christian Experience 1788-1900* Sydney: Centre for the Study of Australian Christianity, 1994.
Hutchinson, M., E. Campion and S. Piggin, editors. *Reviving Australia: Essays on the History and Experience of Revival and Revivalism in Australian Christianity*. Sydney: Centre for the Study of Australian Christianity, 1994.
Hynd, D. *Australian Christianity in Outline*. Homebush: Lancer, 1984
Hywel-Davies, J. *Baptised by Fire —the Story of Smith Wigglesworth*. London: Hodder and Stoughton, 1987.
Isaacson, A. *Deeper Life*. London: Hodder and Stoughton, 1990.
Jackson, H. *Churches and People in Australia and New Zealand 1860-1930*. Wellington: Allen and Unwin, 1987.
James, William. *The Varieties of Religious Experience*. 1902, various publishers.
Johnstone, P. *Operation World*. Rydalmere: Crossroad Distributors, 1993.
Jones, B. P. *An Instrument of Revival: the Complete Life of Evan Roberts (1878-1951)*. South Plainfield: Bridge, 1995.
Jones, C. E. *A Guide to the Study of the Pentecostal Movement*. Metuchen, NJ: Scarecrow Press & American Theological Library Association, 1983.
Jones, L. *Confess It!* Hong Kong: World Outreach, 1974.
Jordan, E. *The Supreme Incentive*. published by the author, 1970.
Jubilee Souvenir of the History of Newtown. Newtown, 1912.
Judd, S. and K. Cable. *Sydney Anglicans*. Sydney: Anglican Information Office, 1987.

Julian of Norwich. *Revelations of Divine Love.* London: Hodder and Stoughton, 1987.
Kaldor, P and S. Kaldor. *Where the River Flows.* Homebush: Lancer, 1988.
Kaldor, P., J. Belamy, R. Powell, M. Correy, and K. Castle. *Winds of Change.* Homebush: Anzea, 1994.
Kaldor, P. *Who Goes Where? Who Doesn't Care?* Homebush: Lancer, 1987.
Kelsey, M. *Tongue Speaking: the History and Meaning of Charismatic Experience.* New York: Crossroad, 1981.
Kendrick, K. *The Promise Fulfilled.* Springfield: Gospel Publish House, 1961.
Kiek, E. S. *An Apostle in Australia.* London: Independent Press, 1927.
Kittel, G., editor. *Theological Dictionary of the New Testament.* Grand Rapids: Eerdmans, Volume I, 1964; Volume IV, 1967.
Klimionok, R. *God Sent His Angel.* Mt Gravatt: Vision Enterprises, 1983.
Knox, R. *Enthusiasm.* London: Collins, 1950, 1987.
Kotlowski, E. *Southland of the Holy Spirit,* Orange: Christian History Research Institute, 1994.
Kramer, E. *Caravan Mission to Bush People and Aboriginals, Journeyings in the Far North and Centre of Australia.* North Melbourne: Victory Press, 1921.
Lake, John. *Sermons.* Dallas: The Voice of Healing, 1949.
_____. *Spiritual Hunger: the God-men and Other Sermons.* Dallas: Christ for the Nations, 1984.
Lamb, W. *The Times of the Nations.* N. p., n. d.
Lambert, M. *Medieval Heresy: Popular Movements from the Gregorian Reform to the Reformation.* Oxford: Blackwell, 1992.
Larson, L. *The Spirit in Paradise.* St Louis: Plus Communications, 1997.
Latourette, K. *Christianity in a Revolutionary Age.* 5 volumes, Grand Rapids: Zondervan, 1969.
Lawton, W. *The Better Time to Be.* Kensington: New South Wales University Press, 1990.
Lederle, H. *Treasures Old and New.* Peabody, Mass: Hendrickson, 1988.
Lenski, R. C. H. *The Interpretation of St Paul's Epistle to the Romans.* Minneapolis: Augsburg, 1961.
Lewis, C. S. *Screwtape Proposes a Toast.* London: Collins Fontana, 1965.
Lewis, P. *The Genius of Puritanism.* Carey Publications, 1979.
Linder, Robert. 'Apostle to the Australians: The Rev Dr Samuel Angus in Australia, 1915-1943,' in G. Treloar, ed, *The Furtherance of Religious Beliefs: Essays on the History of Theological Education in Australia, Sydney.* Centre for the Study of Australian Christianity for the Evangelical History Association of Australia, 1997.
Lindsay, G. *The Life of John Alexander Dowie.* Dallas: The Voice of Healing, 1951.
_____. editor. *The Sermons of John Alexander Dowie.* Dallas: The Voice of Healing, 1951.
_____. *John G. Lake—Apostle to Africa.* Dallas: Christ for the Nations, 1980.
Lindsey, H. *The Late Great Planet Earth.* New York: Bantam, 1974.

Loane, M. *Hewn from the Rock: Origins and Traditions of the Church in Sydney.* Sydney: AIO, 1976.
Lovelace, R. *Dynamics of Spiritual Life.* Downers Grove: Inter Varsity Press, 1980.
MacArthur, J. *Charismatic Chaos.* Grand Rapids: Zondervan, 1991.
Maitland, S. *A Map of the New Country Women and Christianity.* Routledge, Kegan and Paul, 1983.
Marsden, G. *Reforming Fundamentalism: Fuller, the New Evangelicals.* Grand Rapids: Eerdmans, 1987.
Martin, D. and P. Mullen, P., editors. *Strange Gifts? A Guide to Charismatic Renewal.* Oxford: Blackwell, 1984.
Maskrey, C. *The Pentecostal Error.* Strathpine: Evangelistic Literature Enterprise, 1953, 1987.
McClung, L.S. (Jr). *Azusa Street and Beyond* Bridge. 1986.
McCullagh, J.S. and C. F. Hawkins. *The Downfall of Dowie.* Hawthorn: J. H. Edmonson, n.d.
McGrath, A., editor, *Contested Ground.* St Leonards: Allen and Unwin, 1995.
McLay, A., 'Writing Women's History: One Feminist Approach,' in M. Hutchinson and E. Campion, editors. *Long Patient Struggle: Studies in the Role of Women in Australian Christianity.* Sydney: Centre for the Study of Australian Christianity, 1994.
McPherson, A. J. *This Is That.* Los Angeles: Echo Park Evangelistic Association, 1923.
Menzies, W. *Anointed to Serve: The Story of The Assemblies of God.* Springfield: Gospel Publishing House, 1971.
Metters, F. K. and E. Schroeder. *Outback Evangelist: the Story of Ernest Kramer.* Norwood, S.A.: Peacock Publications, 2008.
Mikhaiel, N. *Slaying in the Spirit: The Telling Wonder.* Punchbowl: Bruised Reed, 1992.
Millard, E. C. *The Same Lord. An Account of the Rev. George C. Grubb M.A., in Australia, Tasmania and New Zealand from April 3rd 1891-July 7th, 1892.* London, E. Marlborough & Co., 1893.
_____. *What God Hath Wrought. An Account of the Mission Tour of the Rev G. C. Grubb, M.A., (1889-1890).* London: E. Marlborough and Co., 1891.
Miller, B. *William Carey.* Minneapolis: Bethany, 1980.
Millikan, W.A. *Divine Healing and Dowieism.* Adelaide, 1904.
Mills, W.E., editor. *Speaking in Tongues: A Guide to Research in Glossolalia.* Grand Rapids: Eerdmans, 1986.
Mintern, E., editor. *This We Believe.* Zion, Ill: Christian Catholic Church, n. d.
Mol, H. *The Faith of Australians.* North Sydney: Allen and Unwin, 1985.
Morrison, W. F. *The Aldine History of South Australia.* Sydney and Adelaide: the Aldine Publishing Company, 1890.
Moulton, J.H. and G. Milligan. *The Vocabulary of the Greek Testament.* Grand Rapids: Eerdmans, 1985.
Murray, A. *Waiting on God.* London: Oliphants, 1961.
Murray, I. *Australian Christian Life from 1788.* Edinburgh: Banner of Truth,

1988.
____. *Jonathan Edwards: A New Biography.* Edinburgh: Banner of Truth, 1987.
____. *Revival and Revivalism.* Edinburgh: Banner of Truth, 1994.
____.*The Puritan Hope.* Edinburgh: Banner of Truth, 1984.
____. *The Forgotten Spurgeon.* Edinburgh: Banner of Truth, 1973.
____. *The Epistle to the Romans.* Grand Rapids: Eerdmans, 1973.
Nash, C. H. *The Fourfold Interpretation of Jesus Christ in the New Testament.* Melbourne: S. John Bacon, n. d.
Neil, S. *A History of Christian Missions.* Harmondsworth: Pelican, 1982.
Nelson, W*., T. C. Hammond: His Life and Legacy in Ireland and Australia.* Ediburgh: Banner of Truth, 1994.
Newton, Marjorie *Southern Cross Saints.* Laie, Hawaii: Institute for Polynesian Studies, 1991.
Nichol, J. T. *The Pentecostals.* Plainfield: Logos, 1971.
Nicholl, W. R., editor. *The Expositor's Greek Testament.* Volume II, Grand Rapids: Eerdmans, 1967.
O'Farrell, P. *The Catholic Church and Community.* Kensington: New South Wales University Press, 1985.
Orr, J. E. *All Your Need.* London: Marshall, Morgan and Scott, 1936.
____. *Evangelical Awakenings in the South Seas.* Minneapolis: Bethany, 1976.
____. *The Light of the Nations.* London: Paternoster, 1965.
Otis, G. (Jr). *The Last of the Giants.* New York: Chosen, 1991.
Ottersen, R. *Peace to Thee!* Zion: Christian Catholic Church, 1986.
Our First 100 Years: The Centenary Record of the South Australian Congregational Union. Adelaide: SA Congregational Union, n. d.
Palamountain, W. J. *A.R. Edgar: A Methodist Greatheart.* Melbourne: Spectator, 1933.
Pearlman, M. *Knowing the Doctrines of the Bible.* Springfield: Gospel Publishing House, 1937.
Pentecost, J. D. *Things to Come.* Grand Rapids: Zondervan, 1981.
Perschbacher, W. J., editor. *The New Analytical Greek Lexicon.* Peabody: Hendrickson, 1990.
Pethrus, L. *A Spiritual Memoir.* Plainfield: Logos, 1973.
Phillips, W. W. *Defending 'a Christian Country': Churchmen and Society in New South Wales in the 1880's and After.* Brisbane: St Lucia, 1981.
Pickering, H., editor. *Chief Men Among the Brethren.* London: Pickering and Inglis, 1961.
Piggin, S. *Evangelical Christianity in Australia: Spirit, word and world.* Melbourne: Oxford University Press, 1996.
____. *Faith of Steel.* Wollongong: University of Wollongong, 1984.
Pollock, J. *George Whitefield and the Great Awakening.* Tring, Herts: Lion , 1986.
____. *John Wesley.* London: Hodder, 1989.
____. *Moody Without Sankey.* London: Hodder, 1983.
____. *The Keswick Story.* London: Hodder and Stoughton, 1964.

Portland Circuit History. Volume 2; Volume 4.
Pratney, W. *Revival*. Springdale: Whitaker, 1984.
Pratt, J. *The Religious Consciousness: a Psychological Study*. New York: Macmillan, 1928.
Prentis. *Science, Race and Faith*. Sydney: Centre for the Study of Australian Christianity, 1998.
Quebedeaux, R. T*he New Charismatics. II* San Francisco: Harper and Row, 1983.
Randles, B. *Weighed and Found Wanting: Putting the Toronto Blessing in Context*. Cedar Rapids, IA, n. d. but c.1996.
Record of the Fifth Annual Commemoration of the Rev John Alexander Dowie and Mrs Dowie's Ministry of Healing through Faith in Jesus held in the Free Christian Tabernacle, Fitzroy, Melbourne, on Lord's Day, December, 4th & Monday December 5th 1887. Containing Testimonies from those healed and Ebenezer Addresses. Melbourne: M. L. Hutchinson, 1887.
Renwick A. M. and A. M. Harman. *The Story of the Church*. Leicester: Inter Varsity Press, 1985.
Reports of Addresses at the Christian Convention Geelong September 15th, 16th, 17th, 1891. Ballarat: E. E. Campbell; Melbourne: Bible and Tract Depot; Melbourne: M. L. Hutchinson and Co; Adelaide: Wesleyan Book Depot, 1891.
Reynolds, H. *The Other Side of the Frontier: Aboriginal resistance to the European invasion of Australia*. Ringwood: Penguin, 1983.
_____. W*ith the White People*. Ringwood: Penguin, 1990.
Ridderbos, H. *The Epistle of Paul to the Churches of Galatia*. Grand Rapids: Eerdmans, 1972.
Ridgway, E. '*Ask for the Old Paths;' or Back to the Bible Way*. Foster, Victoria: published by the author, n.d. but c.1946.
Rien, E. T. *A Challenge to Holiness*. Wyee: Bethshan, 1975.
Rienecker, F. *Linguistic Key to the New Testament*. Grand Rapids: Zondervan Regency 1980.
Robeck, C. Jr., editor. *Readings in Pentecostal History*. Pasadena: Fuller Theological Seminary, 1987.
Roberts, A. and J. Donaldson, editors. *The Anti-Nicene Fathers*. Volume I, Grand Rapids: Eerdmans, 1979.
Roberts, D. *The Toronto Blessing*. Eastbourne: Kingsway, 1994.
Robinson, I., P. Kaldor and D. Drayton, editors. *Growing an Everyday Faith*. Homebush: Lancer, n. d.
Roe, Jill. *Beyond Belief: Theosophy in Australia 1879-1939* .Kensington: New South Wales University Press, 1986.
Rowe, W. A. C. *One Lord, One Faith*. Bradford: Puritan Press, n. d. but c.1963.
Russell, Bertram. *History of Western Philosophy*. London: George Allen and Unwin, 1955.
Ryle, J. C. *Christian Leaders of the 18th Century*. Edinburgh: Banner of Truth, 1885, 1978.
Samarin, W. *Tongues of Men and Angels*. Macmillan, 1972.

Sands and McDougall's Melbourne and Suburban Directory. Various years.
Schaff, P., editor. *The Nicene and Post-Nicene Fathers.* Volumes XI and XII, Grand Rapids: Eerdmans, 1979.
Shaw, G. B. *Plays Pleasant and Unpleasant: Volume II, Pleasant Plays.* London: Constable, 1898, 1947.
Sheldrake, E., editor. *The Personal Letters of John Alexander Dowie.* Zion City, W. G. Voliva, 1912.
Short, V. and C. Coulthard-Clark. *A Genealogy of the Bonnet Family of Adelaide.* Canberra, 1983.
Smith, D. and G. Smith. *A River is Flowing—A History of the Assemblies of God in Australia.* St Agnes, SA: Assemblies of God, 1987.
Snyder, H. *The Radical Wesley.* Downers Grove: Inter Varsity Press, 1980.
Spittler, R. *Perspectives on the New Pentecostalism.* Grand Rapids: Baker, 1976.
Spurgeon, C. H. *Autobiography.* Edinburgh: Banner of Truth, 1985.
Sretton, P. and C. Finnimore. *How South Australian Aborigines Lost the Vote: some side effects of federation.* Adelaide: Old Parliament House, November 1991.
Stagg, F., E. G. Hinson and W. Oates, editors. *Glossolalia: Tongue Speaking in Biblical, Historical and Psychological Perspective.* Abingdon, 1967.
Strachan, G. *The Pentecostal Theology of Edward Irving.* Peabody, Massachusetts: Hendrickson, 1973.
Strehlow, T. G. H. *Central Australian Religion.* Bedford Park, SA: Australian Association for the Study of Religions, 1978.
Sunday at Home. London: William Clarke, December 1877.
Symons, C. T. *Our Fathers' Faith and Ours.* Adelaide: Young Peoples' Department, Methodist Church of Australasia, South Australia Conference, n. d.
Synan, V., editor. *Aspects of Pentecostal-Charismatic Origins.* Plainfield: Logos International, 1975.
_____. *In the Latter Days.* Ann Arbor: Servant, 1984.
_____. *The Holiness-Pentecostal Movement in the United States.* Grand Rapids: Eerdmans, 1989.
_____. *The Century of the Holy Spirit: 100 Years of Pentecostal and Charismatic Renewal, 1900-2001.* Nashville: Thomas Nelson, 2001.
Tabbernee, W., editor. *Initiation in Australian Churches.* Melbourne: Council of Churches, 1984.
_____. *Ministry in Australian Churches.* JBCE, 1987.
Taylor, C. *Churches Aglow Down the Ages.* Published by the author, 1991.
Taylor, H. *The Biography of James Hudson Taylor.* London: Hodder, 1985.
Taylor, H. R. *The History of the Churches of Christ in South Australia 1846-1959.* Adelaide: Churches of Christ, n. d.
Taylor, J. *The Development of the City of Zion.* Zion, Ill; Christian Catholic Church, n. d.
_____. *Wilbur Glenn Voliva.* Zion: Zion Historical Society, n. d.
Taylor, W. G. *The Life-story of an Australian Evangelist.* London: Epworth,

1920.
Tertullian. *A Treatise on the Soul; Against Praxeas.* In A. Roberts and J. Donaldson, editors. *The Anti-Nicene Fathers* Vol III, Grand Rapids: Eerdmans, 1978.
The Downfall of Dowie! Hawthorn, Vic: J.H.Edmonson, n. d.
Thompson, R. C. *Religion in Australia.* Melbourne: Oxford University Press, 1994.
Torrey, R. A. *How to Receive the Holy Ghost.* Melbourne: Church Missionary Association, 1904.
_____. *The Baptism with the Holy Spirit.* Belfast: Revival Movement Association, n. d.
Treloar, G., editor. *The Furtherance of Religious Beliefs: Essays on the History of Theological Education in Australia.* Sydney: Centre for the Study of Australian Christianity for the Evangelical History Association, 1997.
Turnbull, T. N. *What God Hath Wrought.* Bradford: Puritan, 1959.
Tuttle, R. *John Wesley, His Life and Theology.* Grand Rapids: Francis Asbury, 1978.
Valdez, A. C. (Jr). *Fire on Azusa Street,* 1980.
Vamplew, W., editor. *Australians, Historical Statistics.* Broadway, NSW: Fairfax, Syme and Weldon Associates, 1987.
Vidler, A. R. *The Church in an Age of Revolution Harmondsworth.* Pelican, 1971.
Walker, A. *Coaltown.* Melbourne: Melbourne University Press, 1945.
Ward, R. *The Bush Still Burns—The Presbyterian & Reformed Faith in Australia, 1788-1988.* Wantirna: published by the author, 1989.
Warfield, Benjamin. *Counterfeit Miracles.* Edinburgh: Banner of Truth, 1918 1983.
Watsford, J. *Glorious Gospel Triumphs.* London: Charles Kelly, 1900.
Waugh, G., editor. *Church on Fire.* Melbourne: JBCE, 1991.
Weber, Max. *The Sociology of Religion.* London: Methuen, 1922, 1965.
Wesley, John. *The Works of John Wesley.* Albany: Sage Digital Library, 1996.
_____. *The Works of John Wesley.* Grand Rapids: Baker, 1996.
_____. *The Works of John Wesley.* Bicentennial Edition. Nashville: Abingdon Press, 1985.
Wessinger, C., editor. *Women's Leadership in Marginal Religions: Explorations Outside the Mainstream* University of Illinois Press, 1993.
Whitefield, G. *George Whitefield's Journals* Edinburgh: Banner of Truth, 1738-41, 1985.
_____. *Select Sermons of George Whitefield.* Edinburgh: Banner of Truth, 1985.
Whitehead, J. *Adelaide, City of Churches.* Magill, S.A.: M. C. Publishing, 1986.
Whittaker, C. *Great Revivals.* Springfield: Radiant, Gospel Publishing House 1984.
_____. *Seven Pentecostal Pioneers.* Springfield: Gospel Publishing House, 1983.
Wiebe, P. *Visions of Jesus: Direct Encounters from the New Testament to Today.* New York: Oxford University Press, 1997.

Wigglesworth, S. *Ever Increasing Faith.* Springfield: Gospel Publishing House, 1924.
Willis, S., editor. *Women, Faith and Fetes.* Melbourne: Australian Council of Churches, 1977.
Wilson, B. *Religious Sects.* London:World University Library, 1970.
Wilson, P. W. *General Evangeline Booth.* New York: Scribners, 1948.
Wimber, J. *Power Evangelism.* London: Hodder and Stoughton, 1985.
Wood, Laurence W., *The Meaning of Pentecost in Early Methodism, Rediscovering John Fletcher as John Wesley's Vindicator and Designated Successor.* Lanham, Maryland: Scarecrow Press, 2002.
Woodham, R. *Philip B.Duncan Pentecostal Pioneer.* Published by the author, 1997.
Woodworth-Etter, M. *A Diary of Signs and Wonders.* Tulsa: Harrison, 1916, 1980.
Woolmington, J. *Religion in early Australia.* Cassell, 1976.
Worsfold, J. *A History of the Charismatic Movements in New Zealand.* Bradford: Puritan, 1974.
_____. *The Origins of the Apostolic Church in Great Britain.* Wellington, N.Z., Julian Literature Trust, 1991.
Young, F. *Pearls from the Pacific.* London and Edinburgh: Marshall Brothers, n. d.

DISSERTATIONS AND THESES

Calley, M., *Bandjalong Social Organisation*, unpublished thesis, University of Sydney, 1959.
Hansen, D.E., 'Churches and Society in NSW, 1919-1939,' Ph.D. thesis, Macquarie University, 1978.
Hill, B., *The Southern Land of the Holy Spirit.* Springfield, Mo: AOG Theological Seminary, 1989.
Newton, Ken, *A History of the Brethren in Australia*, Ph.D. thesis, Pasadena: Fuller Theological Seminary, 1990.
Prosser, E., *Early Fire in Australia.* Springfield, Mo: AOG Theological Seminary, 1988.

UNPUBLISHED PAPERS, LEAFLETS AND DOCUMENTS

Australian Nepalese Mission (The),' typed transcript, no author, n. d.
'Michael Jonas Mintern,' unpublished notes, Zion, Ill.: n. d.
Aizstrauts, I., 'Will Jeffrey 1862-1932,' unpublished essay, Sydney: Tabor College, 1994.

Andrews, Winnie, 'Mrs McPherson's Open Letter Answered,' 24 October 1922.
Beaumont, S., 'Cyril Maskrey: former Apostolic pastor,' unpublished essay, Adelaide: Tabor College, 1986.
Brett, M., 'Maxwell Armstrong,' unpublished essay, Sydney: Tabor College, 1996.
Bruerton, E. R., letter to C. Hood, 13 December 1995.
Buchanan, W. A., personal correspondence, held by C. J. Buchanan, Wavell Heights, Queensland.
Chant, Barry, 'John Henry Coombe (1887-1957): a Dream Fulfilled,' unpublished paper.
_____. 'The Australian Career of John Alexander Dowie,' CSAC seminar paper, 1992.
_____. 'Jonathan Edwards and Revival Phenomena,' 2007, www.barrychant.com
Chant, Vanessa, 'The Family Background of John Alexander Dowie,' unpublished essay, Tabor College, 1991.
Coombe, A., 'Notes on the Coombe Family,' 1 February 1982.
Coombe, B., 'A Tribute to Dad,' handwritten note, n. d.
_____. 'Rev John Henry Coombe,' n. d.
Coombe, J. (?), 'Waiting Meetings,' typed sheet, n. d. Original supplied by E. Barclay.
Coombe, J., 'The Rapture of the Saints,' sermon transcript, 31 July 1913.
_____. 'The Second Coming of Our Lord,' typed transcripts of sermons in possession of Gwenda Cowell.
_____. 'The Vision of Nebuchadnezzar and its Interpretation,' sermon transcript, 19 June, 1913.
Coombe, J. A., 'Notes on the Coombe Family,' n. d.
Crawford, C., 'The First Ten Years of the Apostolic Church, Ballarat,' unpublished essay, Adelaide: Tabor College, 1983.
Deane, A. D., *The Contribution of the New Evangelical Movements of the Late Nineteenth Century to Evangelical Enterprise in Australia 1870-1920*, Sydney: unpublished MA thesis, 1983.
Dowie, J. A., letter to Willam Wright, approving his application for membership in the Christian Catholic Church, 22 January, 1904.
Duncan, P., 'Lecture to Students at Crusade Bible College,' Fullarton, SA: 1965.
East, Graham, 'The failure of F. B. Van Eyk to establish a continuing movement in Australia,' unpublished essay, Tabor College, 1984.
Enright, N., *A Comparative Review of Literature on Religious Experience P*aper presented at the Centre for the Study of Australian Christianity, July, 1993.
Enticknap, Charles, 'Address given at Calvary Temple, Townsville, Qld,' 13 May 1984.
_____. 'Address given at the Christian Revival Crusade, Rosewater, S.A.,' 17 October, 1965.
Enticknap, W. J., Sermon notes, 1928-1956.
Friend, J., *Pentecost in Western Australia*, unpublished manuscript, c.1991.
Glover, K., 'The Bride,' lecture given at Richmond Temple, n.d.

_____. 'The Overcomer,' lecture given on 29 April 1926, at Richmond Temple.
Grant, P., *Stones from the River Bed*,. unpublished paper, Pasadena: Fuller Seminary, 1986,
Greenwood, C. L., *Life Story* transcript of a series of addresses given at Richmond Temple, Vic., 1965.
_____. 'Address given at Australian Pentecostal Fellowship Convention,' Beulah Heights, Victoria, 1964.
Guy, R., *Baptised Among Crocodiles,* unpublished paper, 1998.
Heath, P., letters to the congregation at the Mission, 29 December 1936, 15 January, 1937.
_____. 'Tongues and Interpretation,' unpublished seven-page document attributed to Heath.
Hollenweger, W., 'The Five Roots of Pentecostalism,' a paper presented at the Conference on Pentecostal and Charismatic Research in Europe. Kappel, Switzerland, 3 July, 1991.
Hughes, Mrs *Notebook,* n. d. (now perished through fire).
Hulm, Elaine, 'Fannie Collie,' unpublished essay, Adelaide: Tabor College, 1990.
Hutchinson, M., 'Healing and Hurting: Mainline Relationships with Pentecostalism and the 1952 Valdez Crusade,' Sydney: Centre for the Study of Australian Christianity, 1992.
_____. 'This will be a Big Work: The Trans-oceanic Triangle in Planting Pentecostalism among Italian Migrants to Australia, 1958-1969,' paper presented at the Wheaton Conference, November, 1992.
Johns, C.B., 'Meeting God in the Margins: Preaching Among Modernity's Refugees,' and 'Presencing the Word: Preaching at the Carnival of Cruelty,' Jameson Jones Lectures in Preaching, Divinity School, Duke University, February 25-27, 1997.
Johnson, R., *To All the Inhabitants and Especially to the Unhappy Prisoners and Convicts in the Colonies Established at Port Jackson and Norfolk Island* 30 October, 1792.
Johnston, L., *Eternity,* documentary film, screened on ABC, 1994.
Johnstone, B., 'A biography of Joseph Marshall', unpublished essay, Tabor College, NSW, 2007.
Johnstone, H., letter to C. Hood, 22 January, 1996.
Jones, L., letters to C. H. Nash, 20 May, 1925; 8 January, 1926; 27 February, 1926; 30 July, 1927.
Keneally, C., *Other Tongues*, unpublished thesis, University of Melbourne, 1990.
Knight, N., *A Comparative Review of Literature on Religious Experience*, unpublished paper, Studying Australian Christianity Conference, Centre for the Study of Australian Christianity, Sydney, 14-16 July 1993.
Lancaster, J., letter to L. Mullin, 2 March 1931.
Muir, G and E., *Jubilee: a brief account of the Cessnock Evangelistic Campaign of 1929*, photo-copied booklet, Cessnock, n. d. but c.1979.
Muirhead, S., 'John Barclay,' unpublished essay, Tabor College, Adelaide,

1988.
Nash, C. H., letter to Len Jones, 23 March 1926
O'Connell, J., 'Cyril Ernest Mortomore (1902-1974)', unpublished essay, Tabor College, 1993.
Owens, J., 'William Booth-Clibborn,' unpublished essay, Sydney, Tabor College, 1994.
Pentecost, John, *William Booth and the Doctrine of Holiness* Sydney: Department of Studies in Religion, University of Sydney, 1997.
Phillips, B., *The Life Story of Beryl Phillips*, 1985, photo-copied reminiscences published by the author.
Piggin, Stuart, 'Billy Graham in Australia, 1959. Was it Revival?' Sydney: CSAC working paper, Series One, No.4, n. d. but c.1990.
_____.'Revivalism: the Holiness Movement and Millennialism, 1875-1899,' 1993.
_____. 'The History and Prospects for Religious Revival in Australia,' Heads of Churches seminar paper, Parramatta, 23 March, 1993.
Pittman, J., 'Frederick Duncan: his Significance and Contribution to the Pentecostal Movement,' unpublished essay, Tabor College, 1994.
Pope, C., 'A Brief History of Ernest E. Kramer,' unpublished essay, Tabor College, 1986.
Sewell, K., 'The Eclipse of History and the crisis in the humanities.' Unpublished paper, 1996.
Sjoberg, D., 'Testimony and Experience of Mrs Marjorie Hurst,' unpublished essay, Adelaide: Tabor College, 1989.
Valdez, A.C., 'The Call and Circumstances of A. C. Valdez coming to Australia and New Zealand in 1925,' transcript of taped address at Richmond Temple, Melbourne, n. d. but c.1964.
Van Eyk, Hilda, letter to Marie Allsopp, 14 February, 1940.
Wallis, J. K., *The Beginnings: an account of the 1929 Cessnock Revival*, Aberdare, 1989.
Wright, Arthur, letters to his brother Will from Zion City, 2 November, 1904, 26 January, 1907, 26 March, 1934.
Wright, J., 'Hervey Perceval Smith,' unpublished essay, Tabor College, Sydney, 1993.

Name Index

Abrahams, 'Grandma', 113
Abrams, Minnie, 93, 102-103
Adams, 'Sister', 116
Adams, John A. D., 14, 77, 122, 135, 138, 286, 367
Adams, Philip, 116-17, 139, 145, 250
Alexander, Charles, 4, 27, 90, 94
Allen, Dora, 235, 346
Allen, Ethan O., 62
Alway, M. A., 47, 374
Ames, Thomas James, 333–35
Andrews, Winnie, 118, 129–30, 145, 270, 272, 281, 289
Anstis, Charles, 13
Anstis, Edith, 145
Anstis, J., 145
Anstis, M., 145
Armstrong, Max ('Daddy'), 99, 203, 335–36
Armstrong, May, 203, 335
Armstrong, Norman, 280
Arthur, William, 39
Averill, Lloyd, 147
Ayers, Mary, 210, 287, 290, 336

Baeyertz, Emilia, 27, 265
Bailey, 'Colonel', 46
Bailey, Mrs., 46
Bain, Alan Geoffrey ('Dick'), 230, 233
Bain, Maggie, 242
Baker, H., 244
Banton, A. E. ('Bert'), 168
Banton, Edith, 180

Barclay, Elizabeth, 96
Barclay, John, 94–97
Beauglehole, Richard, 17, 42–44
Begbie, Harold, 120
Bennett, Gordon, 108, 146
Benson, Joseph, 33
Bentley, John T., 286
Bentley, T. J., 174
Berg, Daniel, 268
Beruldsen, John, 198
Blavatsky, Helena, 267
Blumhardt, Johann, 62
Boaler, Ada, 116
Boardman, William, 62
Boddy, Alexander, 268
Bogle, Kathleen, 252
Booth, Bramwell, 47
Booth, Catherine, 46, 336
Booth, Herbert, 27, 47
Booth, William, 45–46, 169, 205
Booth-Clibborn, Genevieve, 206, 210, 287, 337
Bowers, James 33
Booth-Clibborn, William, 4, 13, 47, 121, 126, 169, 205, 287
Bowling, Gordon, 351
Bradley, William 'Cairo', 211
Braun, Lisle, 190
Brawner, Mina Ross, 4, 14, 108, 136, 145, 276, 282, 290
Bryan, Frank, 150
Buchanan, Leila, 210, 289, 304, 338, 349, 385

413

414   Name Index

Buchanan, W. A. (Alex), 4, 289, 326
Buchanan, Euphemia, 243
Buley, Claire, 45
Buley, Edith, 45
Burnett, Matthew, 27, 42
Burns, George, 137, 158
Burrows, Heather Isabel, 210, 286–87
Butler, Bishop, 31

Carroll, Lillian, 98
Carter, R. Kelso, 62
Casey, Celia, 141
Cashwell, G. B., 267
Cathcart, William, 4, 13, 23, 221, 224–32
Cavill John, 13, 117, 147
Cerillo, Augustus Jr., 9, 26
Cherbury, C. M., 66
Chilcott, Gordon, 351
Christian, George, 112
Clarke, George Joseph, 133
Clarkson, 'Daddy', 48
Close, Emmy, 116, 269
Close, R., 116
Coal, Charlie, 309
Cole, J. C., 99
Collie, Fannie L., 290
Collins, William, 29
Conwell, James Speer, 262
Conwell, Thomas, 270
Cook, Thomas, 27
Coombe, John Henry, 96, 98, 121
Couldrey, Bessie, 269–71
Coulters, Gladys, 281
Cridge, ('Blind') Dolly, 47, 339
Crispe, Les, 319
Crispe, Rhoda (nee. Enticknap), 319, 344
Cullis, Charles, 62

Darby, John Nelson, 197
Dalveen, T. D., 64
Darling, J., 74
Darwin, Charles, 83
David, V. D., 86
Davidson, Hugh, 253, 319
Davis, Robert, 224, 230, 250, 364
Deacon, Jesse, 165
Dennis, Annie, 269
Dickey, Brian, 29

Dickson, A. S., 224
Dixon, Retta, 243
Douglas, Stan, 56
Dowie, Gladstone, 81
Dowie, Jane, 72
Dowie, Jeanie, 61
Dowie, John Alexander, 3–4, 59–77, 90, 95, 204, 327, 341–42, 348
Dowie, John Murray, 341
Draper, D. J., 42
Dryden, George, 230
Duncan, Frederick, 210
Duncan, Philip, 4, 178, 198, 202–205, 230, 253
Durham, William, 34

Easton, Jack, 256
Eather, M. A., 286
Eddy, Mary Baker, 267
Edwards, Jonathan, 175
Egan-Lee, 45
Ellis, J. E., 48
Elton, Frank, 228
Emes, Emily, 224
Emes, Jack, 224
Enticknap, Charles, 17, 342
Enticknap, Jean, 311
Enticknap, Rebecca, 343
Enticknap, Rhoda, 344
Enticknap, Will, 4, 311
Etter, Maria Woodworth, 62
Everett, Ethel, 161

Fabian, Norman, 13, 274, 276
Ferguson, Jessie, 95
Finney, Charles, 26, 343
Fitchett, W. H., 14, 40
Fleming, Elsie, 235
Fleming, Frederick, 235
Fletcher, John, 33
Flett, Miss, 14, 220
Fockler, Cyrus, 135
Forlong, Gordon, 27
Foulkes, Ronald, 51
Francis, Tom, 44
Fraser, Miss, 95
Frodsham, Stanley, 129

Gadge, Claude, 225
Gardiner, 'Captain', 46

Name Index

Gardiner, Alex, 233
Gee, Donald, 268
Geil, Walter, 4, 90
Gibson, Ben, 98
Glover, Kelso R., 4, 15, 197, 199
Gordon, A. J., 33
Greenwood, Charles Lewis, 4, 15, 99, 122, 133, 168, 190, 202
Greenwood, Elviss, 193
Greig, Grace, 277
Gribble, John, 235
Grierson, Joseph , 68
Grubb, George Carleton , 28
Guinness, Harry Grattan, 28
Gunnar, Vingren, 260

Hagenauer, Frederick, 235
Hallop, T., 179, 254
Hammond, Frederick, 170
Hammond, T. C., 257, 284
Hampson, Margaret, 28
Hannah, Jim, 336
Harford-Battersby, Dundas, 85
Harris, Cecil, 160, 230
Harris, Don, 180
Harris, Edward, 89
Harris, Leo, 191, 231
Hart, Leo, 220, 224,
Hart, Marion, 229
Haslam, J., 39
Hawkins, C., 71
Heath, Pauline, 4, 12, 273–276, 291
Hedding, Bishop, 33
Henderson, Tom, 114
Henson, W. E., 148
Hetherington, Isabella, 210, 239, 251
Hetherington, Nellie, 241, 243
Hewitt, Isaac, 225
Hewitt, John Henry, 4, 13, 210–234, 344–45
Hickson, James Moore, 116
Hickson, Mrs., 148
Higgs, Leila, 288
Hinrichsen, Earnest, 194
Hobbs, Phyllis, 182, 208
Hocking, Richard, 146
Holman, Florence, 116
Holroyd, George, 145
Hooker, E., 172, 180

Horne, Robert, 4, 44, 99, 190
Horsley, J. F., 39
Hotson, 'Sister', 290
Hugo, Isaac, 118, 133
Hultgren, A., 112
Hultgren, Harold, 48, 289
Hurst, Marjorie, 234
Huston, Emily, 112
Hutchinson, Thomas, 65
Hutchinson, William Oliver, 268

Irving, Edward, 17, 50, 215

Jack, Davey, 139
Jackson, Eliza, 353
Jackson, Myrtle, 256
Jansen, Gustav, 12, 154, 346
Jarrett, Lillian, 113
Jarvie, William, 99, 105
Jarvis, Ernest, 135, 285
Jefferis, James, 61
Jeffrey, Will, 4, 353
Jeffreys, George, 268, 345
Jeffreys, Stephen, 344
Jenkins, Ensign H., 226
Johnson, Richard, 240
Jones, J., 286
Jones, Len, 180, 230, 232
Jones, Nathaniel, 86
Jones, W., 195
Joyce, A. S., 98

Kajewski, Bessie, 164, 183
Kajewski, Carl Lewis (Charles), 145, 163, 271
Kajewski, Hilda, 167
Kay, William, 179
Kelley, R., 41
Kiek, Winifred, 264
Kilpatrick, H. S., 48, 298
King, Ethel, 212
Kirwan, John, 13, 236
Kirwan, Kath, 23, 220
Kitchen, John James, 196
Knox, Ronald, 32
Kramer, Ernest (Erny), 132, 239, 243–51, 254–55
Kramer, Fritz, 251

Lake, John Graham, 211
Lancaster, Alfred, 139, 347
Lancaster, Esther May ('Blossom'), 116
Lancaster, Fred, 114, 358
Lancaster, Sarah Jane (Jeannie), 4, 13, 44, 47, 98–99, 107, 148, 157, 165, 243, 269–73, 284, 289, 291, 324, 326, 338, 340
Lane, William, 218
Lansing, I. J., 39
Lavers, W. H. W., 282, 297
Leavitt, Mary, 364
Lennon, Thomas Bingham, 140, 349
Lewis, Ruby, 112
Lindsay, Gordon, 66
Llewellyn, Daniel, 225
Long, Retta, 243, 258
Loutit, Irene, 151
Lovell, Muriel, 228
Lovell, Philip George Joyder, 228
Lowe, Albert, 191
Lucy, Avis Kate, 285

Macartney, Hussey Burgh, 86
MacCleary, Alice, 141, 290
MacColl, D. Stewart, 196
Mackenzie, Kenneth, 75
MacKillop, Mary, 264
MacNeil, John, 87–88, 101
Malla Kulla, George, 252
Manoramabai, 93
Mansell, May, 115
Marks, Richard, 45
Marshall, Ann, 42
Marshall, Joseph, 42, 54, 99
Martin, Harold, 4, 146–147
Maskrey, Cyril, 232,
Mather, Ellen Caroline ('Nellie'), 99, 198, 276, 291
Mathew, John, 243
McCabe, Joshua, 220, 224, 232
McCullagh, J.S., 73
McGregor, Joan, 94
McLennan, H., 112
McNeil, T., 40
McPherson, Aimee Semple, 4, 129–137
Metcalfe, Jotham, 145, 280
Metcalfe, Kate, 202, 279
Meyer, F. B., 33. 96, 132

Michalk, Eileen, 354
Michalk, Gustav Bernhard ('Ben'), 158
Millard, E. C., 86
Mintern, Earl, 76
Mintern, Michael, 76
Mintern, R. A., 76
Montgomery, Carrie Judd, 62m 267
Moody, D. L., 90
Moorhead, Max, 289
Morecombe, Kate, 41
Moreton, Mary, 46
Morgan, Campbell, 132
Mortomore, Caroline, 269
Mortomore, Charles, 114
Mortomore, Cyril, 285
Mortomore, Florrie, 4, 99, 121, 124
Mott, John R., 27
Muir, George, 180
Muller, George, 27
Mullin, Jim, 123–24, 151
Murray, Andrew, 26, 33, 86

Nankervois, W. J., 213
Nash, C. H., 194–95
Neale, F., 36
Newton, Archibald, 45, 351
Nickson, J. H., 97, 102, 293
Noble, William, 27
Nokes, Elder, 198

Orr, J. Edwin, 211

Painter, Ada, 95
Palmer, Phoebe, 33
Panton, D. M., 132
Parham Charles, 9, 17, 20–21, 34, 267
Parker, Lucy, 67
Parker, M. G., 112
Parry, N., 310
Penfold, F., 204
Peters, Edie, 294
Phillip, Arthur, 53, 240
Pight, Miss, 290
Pillifeant, Benjamin, 44
Pillifeant, Martha (Mattie), 44, 339
Plenderlieth, Rev., 31
Price, Reg, 48
Priest, Norman, 12, 230
Purvis, 'Brother', 116

Rabley, Maudy, 95
Ramabai, Pandita, 92–95, 103
Read, Ralph, 56
Reed, Frances Ella, 186
Reekie, David, 44
Reekie, Thomas, 44
Renwick, Arthur, 64
Retchford, Hines, 13, 163, 183, 224
Richards, May Beatrice, 335
Ridgway Edwin, 138, 145, 196
Ridley, John, 203
Rieschiek, J. E., 154, 224, 243, 250, 346
Roberts, Evan, 103
Roberts, J. M., 44, 194
Robson, Nellie, 113
Rooke, 'Sister', 136
Rose, 'Captain', 48
Rowe, W. A. C., 222–23, 235
Rowston, 'Sister', 277
Rowston, Joshua, 115
Ruffell, Elder, 198
Russell, John, 114

Salisbury, William, 147, 151
Salvado, Dom Rosando, 241
Sandlant, Annie, 45
Scott, D., 48
Self, James, 109, 124
Self, Mary, 141
Seymour, William, 6, 20, 33, 100, 267
Sharman, Harold T. ('Tom'), 137
Simmons, Langley, 162
Simpson, A. B., 33, 62, 132
Singleton, John, 45
Slade, H. S., 45
Sloan, Eliza, 353
Sloan, William Cunningham, 44, 132, 352
Smart, Jessie, 112
Smith, 'Gypsy', 27, 194
Smith, Hervey Perceval, 92
Smith, Robert Pearsall, 84
Smith, Rosa 96
Smithies, John, 241
Sommerville, Alexander, 27
South, W. F., 46, 56
Spurgeon, Charles Haddon, 62, 132
Spurgeon, Thomas, 26–27
Stace, Arthur, 143

Stanton, R. L., 62
Stephens, Chief Stoker, 155
Stephens, James, 41, 54
Stern, Carl, 73
Stockmayer, Otto, 62
Strehlow, Carl, 241, 249
Sutton, Elizabeth, 45
Swenson, Cyril B., 45, 294
Swenson, Pearl, 165, 295
Symmonds, Langley, 203–204

Taylor, William 'California', 27
Taylor, William George, 37, 90
Thornton, Dr., 43
Threlkeld, Lancelot, 241
Todd, H. Nathan, 132, 135, 166
Tomlinson, A. J., 267
Tooth, Ernest, 145
Tooth, Robert, 64
Torrey, Reuben A., 4, 26, 52, 90, 194
Trudel, Dorothea, 62
Tuck, Elder, 198
Turnbull, Andrew, 221
Turner 'Sister', 290
Turner, Martha, 264

Valdez, Alfred C., 4, 14, 45, 133, 137, 192–98, 354
Vale, Ethel, 245, 252
Van Eyk, Cecilia, 154, 166
Van Eyk, Frederick B., 4, 13–14, 121–22, 133–38, 153–80, 210, 224, 226, 231–32, 285, 309, 327, 334, 338, 345, 362, 367, 378–79
Van Eyk, Hilda (nee Kajewski), 174, 179, 181
Varley, Henry, 27
Vickery, Ebenezer, 41, 54
Voliva, Wilbur G., 71, 73

Wallington, John S., 69
Walsh, Thomas, 32
Warburton, Ivor, 108, 124, 145
Warburton, Tom, 145
Watsford, John, 3, 35
Watson, James, 43
Waugh, J. S., 42
Webb, Allan, 88–109
Weimer, H., 137

Wesley, John, 30–33, 38, 49, 231
White, Ellen, 120, 267
Whitty, Vincent, 264
Wiggins, Henry, 202, 253
Wigglesworth, Smith, 4, 117, 132, 198, 289, 335
Wiles, Ruby, 4, 132, 284
Willard, Frances, 264
Williams, Gladys, 278
Williams, Jones, 268
Wilson, Alan, 193
Wilson, J. L. H., 47
Wilson, May, 113
Wood, Esther, 266
Woodworth-Etter, Maria, 62
Wordsworth, Ethel, 149

General Index

Aborigines, 132, 239–240, 245–46, 248–63, 271, 316
Aborigines' Friends' Association, 251, 257, 260
Abrahams, 113
Adelaide, 4, 8, 12–13, 19, 21, 23, 27, 35, 39, 41, 44, 48, 51–52, 54–55, 57, 59, 61, 65–66, 72–73, 75, 78, 82, 94, 101, 104, 111, 120, 127, 133, 154, 157, 163, 168, 182, 199, 223–32, 236–37, 243, 245, 249, 257, 266, 273–76, 283, 285, 290–291, 300, 318, 330, 333–34, 339, 341–42, 345–47, 351, 354, 356–57
Africa, 16, 109, 168, 211, 337
Alice Springs, 243, 247–51, 259–60
American Methodist Episcopal Church, 33
Apostolic Church, 2–3, 5, 13–14, 26–27, 50, 59, 71, 139, 180, 199–200, 204, 211, 219–22, 224–25, 227–28, 230–39, 256, 260, 286, 288, 299, 305–306, 318–19, 329, 351
Apostolic Faith Mission, 14, 34, 48, 52, 119, 133, 135, 137–38, 147, 153, 154, 157, 165–68, 171, 186, 210–11, 230, 272, 279, 282, 284–86, 291, 298, 300, 309, 345,
Assemblies of God, 24, 34, 44, 98, 100, 101, 104, 129, 137, 167–68, 186, 202, 205, 211, 214, 215, 218, 234, 239, 252–53, 261, 267, 289, 291, 293, 304, 307, 310, 317, 319, 323, 327–29, 331, 335–36, 344
Athanasian Creed, 123
Auckland, 70, 72
Australasian Secular Association, 83
Azusa Street, 6, 19–20, 33, 99, 118, 267, 344, 348, 354, 357, 359

Ballarat, 6, 21, 42, 44, 48, 87, 90, 94, 101, 111–12, 137, 144, 148, 198–199, 237, 240, 277, 278, 281, 283–84, 296, 347
baptism by immersion, 155, 271, 294
baptism by triune immersion, 70
baptism in the Holy Spirit, 3, 16, 18, 25, 33–34, 39, 52, 54, 87, 95, 98, 110–11, 161, 164, 177–78, 195–96, 269, 271, 285, 302, 306, 308, 318, 346
Bavaria, 110
Bible Christians, 40–41, 54, 266
Bible Standard Church, 276, 291
Black America, 16
Body of Christ, 120, 122, 135, 136, 149, 295
Brazil, 7, 20, 26, 268
Brethren, 14, 23, 27, 50, 127, 179, 196, 197, 215, 220, 227, 229, 269, 293, 335
Bride of Christ, 120–21, 197, 304, 319
Bridgewater, 44
Brisbane, 4, 8, 13, 27, 48, 50, 54, 94, 00. 100, 111, 126, 132, 135, 145–46, 158, 160–61, 163, 167, 171, 173,

206, 208–10, 217–18, 221, 233, 251, 252, 261, 269–72, 278, 281–82, 287–88, 295, 297, 339, 345

Cairns, 3, 6, 8, 107, 111, 163–65, 183, 251–52, 261, 269, 271, 281, 294, 297, 335, 343
Calvinistic Methodism, 26
Canvas Cathedral, 182, 207–208, 210, 252, 261, 287–88, 339
Catholic Church, 16, 27, 70, 72, 75–76, 78–80, 90, 330
Cessnock, 168–72, 175–76, 179–81, 185–87, 294, 345
charismata, 33, 49, 97, 186, 317
Chicago, 34, 70, 73, 80–81, 102, 126, 267, 354, 357
children, 10, 28, 38, 42, 105, 108, 122, 140–41, 145, 154, 159, 166, 168, 172, 174, 190, 196, 200, 211, 227, 241, 245, 248, 250, 252–53, 257, 259, 261, 264, 266, 271, 280, 289, 294, 302, 308, 318, 336–37, 340, 342, 345, 347, 352–53
Chile, 7, 26
China, 89, 105, 110, 236, 239, 302, 351
China Inland Mission, 89
Christian and Missionary Alliance, 62
Christian Covenanters' Confederacy, 206
Christian living, 85–86, 110, 199, 302, 304, 308, 315
Christian perfection, 3, 19, 25, 29–33, 51, 62
Christian Science, 27, 49, 156, 196, 267, 270, 348
church government, 7, 195, 225, 230, 267, 306
Church Missionary Society, 241
Churches of Christ, 27, 131, 159, 174, 194–95, 255, 269, 330
Cleveden,, 203, 335, 353
Congregationalism, 26, 78, 95, 342

Daintree, 239, 252, 253, 261, 278
dancing, 43–44, 47, 93, 170, 176, 233,
deliverance, 20, 30, 156, 233, 301, 312
demons, 93, 114, 177, 212, 244, 352

Divine Healing, 56, 59, 61, 67, 69, 74, 111, 156, 163, 172, 177, 228
Divine Healing Mission, 69
dream, 63, 65–66, 104, 110, 132, 284, 336, 343–44, 346
Dutch Reformed Church, 85

Easter, 97, 115, 135, 137–38, 145, 157, 168, 173, 199, 202, 213, 225, 334
Echuca, 113, 277
Elijah Declaration, 71
Elim Foursquare Church, 13, 172
Eltham, 92, 95, 105, 191, 346
England, 3–4, 26, 28, 39, 42–43, 63, 65, 69, 75, 81, 88–89, 92–93, 96, 109–10, 202, 210, 221, 224, 233, 265, 268–69, 308, 345, 348, 351, 358
enthusiasm, 32, 138, 158, 164–65, 170–71, 175, 194, 200–201, 301, 305, 335, 345
Evangelicalism, 4, 19, 77, 99, 105, 194

Farina, 44, 247
Federation of Australian States, 84
Fetter Lane Society, 31
'finished work', 34, 101
First River, 42
Fitzroy, 66, 79, 98, 105
foot washing, 151
Footscray, 37, 90, 190
Free Christian Church, 63, 66, 75
Freeburgh, 99, 111, 245, 352, 353
Fremantle, 174, 224, 286
French Prophets, 177
Fullness of the Spirit, 92, 104

Glad Tidings Tabernacle, 13, 125, 211, 218
Glossolalia, 1, 20
Good News Hall, 4–6, 10, 13–14, 20, 44, 48, 52–53, 56, 77, 100, 108–109, 112–14, 117, 120, 124, 126, 129–48, 151, 157, 163, 168, 178, 192–98, 203, 213, 218, 230, 235–36, 239, 243, 247, 250, 259–60, 269–70, 273, 279, 281–91, 299, 304, 308–309, 318–19, 331, 333–34, 338–40, 347,

351–52
Good News Pentecostal Alliance, 118
Gospel Crusade, 92
Great Depression, 21, 140, 207, 218, 316
Gympie, 173, 278, 282

Haiti, 110
Harvey Cox's *Fire From Heaven*, 5, 323
healing, 4, 6, 16, 25–26, 31, 46–47, 49, 51, 61–63, 67–70, 72–73, 75–78, 80, 87, 93, 95, 100, 108, 110–17, 120, 123, 125, 126, 131, 132, 143, 154–56, 159–66, 169–70, 174, 177, 191, 194–96, 204, 206, 214, 226–28, 246, 269–70, 272, 280–81, 284–86, 294–95, 298, 301–311, 334, 342, 344–48, 353–54
heaven, 32, 72, 84, 97, 120, 122, 127, 130, 146, 158, 176, 181, 201, 276, 280, 343, 350, 353, 361
Hell, 91, 227
Hobart, Tasmania, 37, 235, 288
Holiness, 7, 19, 20, 25–26, 32–34, 37, 50, 52, 56, 83, 85, 87, 97, 197, 266, 267, 292, 312, 322, 329
Holiness movement, 33
Hot Springs, Arkansas, 34

Immanuel's Bride, 120
Indian Christians, 93
Indian Revival, 93
indigenous movements, 99
International Conference on Divine Healing, 63, 70
International Divine Healing Association, 67
Irvingite movement, 26, 54
Italy, 16, 110, 303

jewellery, 89, 228
Jigalong, 239

Kadina, 41, 199, 237
Kansas, 9, 33, 329
Keswick, 4, 26–27, 84–89, 92–93, 95–96, 99, 100–102, 104, 345

Keswick Conventions, 4, 85, 88, 101, 102
Korea, 16

Labor Party, 84
Lake Zurich, 62
Latin America, 7, 16
laying on of hands, 87, 101, 112, 150, 214, 226, 228
Lithgow, 173, 175
London, 45, 63, 70, 78, 224, 336–37
Los Angeles, 6, 33–34, 99, 105, 110, 148, 337–38, 351, 354, 357

Mackay, 6, 8, 111, 165, 167, 170, 206, 269, 271, 281, 308, 310, 312, 320, 340, 344
Manly, 60, 220
Manunka, 242
Maryborough, 6, 8, 20, 22, 47, 56, 116, 158, 160, 163, 166–67, 177, 182–86, 251, 270–71, 278, 310, 344
'Marshallites', 42
Melbourne, 4, 6, 8, 10, 12–15, 21, 22, 27–28, 39, 40, 44–45, 59, 65–66, 71–72, 75, 86, 88, 89–98, 101–11, 122, 129–37, 144–48, 155, 157, 167–68, 170, 178, 184, 190–355
Methodism, 19, 28, 31–32, 38–40, 44, 48, 49, 52–54, 263
millennium, 70, 127
Mormonism, 3, 105, 196
Mount Kembla Coal and Oil Company, 41
Mukti mission, 94
music, 14–15, 18, 23, 88, 97, 155, 166, 189, 206, 281

National Revival Crusade, 160, 182, 238
Nepalese Mission Band, 99
New Zealand, 14, 50, 70, 77, 80, 86, 90, 96, 100–101, 103, 109, 134, 135, 141, 157, 192, 195, 212, 220, 233, 288, 335
Newtown, 60, 62–63, 78, 173, 204, 287, 294, 335, 345
Nicaragua, 7

Northern Ireland, 97, 220

Oakleigh, 112, 199
Oneness, 17, 118, 126
Oodnadatta, 245–247, 250
ordination, 139, 150, 229, 264, 267, 268, 326
Oregon, 35, 113
Ovens Valley, 44, 245

Palmer Street Mission, 99, 148
Parkes, 6, 8, 111, 158, 168, 173, 198, 199, 203, 310, 335, 344, 353–54
Pentecostal Church of Australia, 4–5, 14–15, 76, 122, 133, 137, 146–49, 168, 180, 189, 195, 204, 230, 235, 250, 291, 304, 316, 331
Pentecostal Mission, 44, 108, 122
Pentecostal phenomena, 5, 20, 42, 48, 96, 99
Perth, 3–4, 8, 14, 22, 48, 107, 111, 132, 135, 138, 145, 154, 160–61, 174, 185, 191, 198, 220–21, 224, 228, 230, 234, 284, 285–86, 291, 298, 310, 349
Peru, 7
Petersham, 204
Point Macleay, 242, 257
Portland, 8, 10, 24, 35–36, 42–44, 54, 55, 136–37, 266, 339
power of the Spirit, 3, 49, 84, 86, 158, 244, 301, 334
premillennialism, 26, 127, 197, 303–304
Prophecy, 75
prophesying, 26, 32, 51, 87, 223, 234
Protestant League, 65
Protestantism, 50, 91

Queensland., 6, 26, 37, 78, 88, 160, 163, 168, 199, 206, 210, 251, 269, 342

Regeneration, 92, 189
Regions Beyond Missionary Union, 99
repentance, 17, 29, 34, 94, 143, 271, 317
restorationism, 26

revival, 6, 26, 28–29, 33–55, 87–88, 90, 93–95, 102–103, 108, 134, 162, 170, 189, 194–96, 200, 208, 210–211, 224, 236, 244, 251, 254, 262, 280, 282, 285, 287, 304–305, 324, 328, 343, 345, 349, 354, 361
Richmond Temple, 14, 23, 48, 55–56, 125, 137, 146, 168, 196–202, 212–16, 227, 230, 232, 294, 299, 320, 344, 357
Rockdale, 111, 203–204, 288
Rockhampton, 6, 8, 48, 111, 161–63, 177, 183, 206, 210, 271, 281, 344
Roman Catholicism, 63, 164

sabbatarianism, 84
sacraments, 264, 265, 267, 268, 304
Salvation Army, 12, 19, 27, 39, 43, 44, 45, 47–48, 56, 65–66, 77, 95, 169, 171, 205, 226, 227, 257, 261, 263, 277, 291, 335–36, 339, 355
sanctification, 16, 19, 25, 29, 32–36, 51, 69, 87, 89, 101
Scotland, 4, 54, 60, 77, 87, 221, 232, 310, 341
second blessing, 33–34
Second Coming of Christ, 99, 110, 127, 177, 197, 303
Simultaneous Mission of 1902, 4, 41
Singapore, 110, 329
'Sounders', 42
South Africa, 4, 82, 84–85, 100, 135, 137, 166, 168–69, 173–74, 180, 190, 211, 233, 239, 268, 335, 345
South African, 13, 26, 48, 62, 153–54, 157, 285
South Australia, 10, 12, 14, 19, 28, 36, 39, 41, 44, 46–47, 51, 54, 60, 77–78, 83, 105, 154, 157, 168, 199, 242, 245, 257, 259–260, 265, 277, 290,
Southern Evangelical Mission, 22, 44, 133, 148, 192, 212, 277, 345, 357
Spirit-filled life, 94, 108, 131
Spiritualism, 27, 63–64, 79
Sports, 13
Sunday observance, 84
Sunshine, 98, 133, 148, 191–94, 198, 204, 212–13, 236, 251, 338

Sunshine Gospel Mission, 133, 148
Switzerland, 49, 62, 243, 322
Sydney, 4, 8, 12, 19, 21–22, 27–28, 36–38, 45, 50–51, 54, 56, 59–60, 63–64, 65, 71–73, 78–79, 81–82, 86–91, 94, 100–101, 103, 126, 142–43, 167–70, 174, 192, 194, 198–217, 230, 242, 258, 266, 279, 287–88, 290, 292, 294, 321, 328–30, 335, 342, 345, 350, 355–56, 358

'tarry meetings', 38, 339
Tasmania, 45, 51, 86, 89, 101, 139, 233–34, 351
three-stage concept, 34
Tipperary, 86
tithing, 221, 285, 306
tongues, 6, 16–18, 24–25, 32–34, 39, 42, 44–45, 47–48, 50–51, 76–77, 88, 91, 94–103, 111, 130, 148, 161, 165, 178, 191–215, 223, 244, 258, 260, 269, 275, 280–81, 286–87, 296, 298, 303, 308, 315, 336–44, 350, 353, 360–61
Toowoomba, 6, 8, 37, 135, 165, 167, 171, 173, 182, 209–210, 217–18, 269, 282, 287–88, 294, 299, 344, 355
Townsville, 6, 8, 165, 206, 271, 281, 309–310, 312, 320, 341, 343, 357
tribulation, 197, 304, 315, 319, 340
tribulations, 121
trinitarian, 118–19
Trinity, 19, 23, 94, 130, 312, 317

unitarian, 118
United States, 3, 5, 7, 19, 25, 63, 70, 101, 109, 118, 120, 210, 303, 322, 323, 329, 337, 348
Upwey, 92

Victoria, 6, 10, 14, 22, 24, 28, 36, 37, 39–40, 42, 44–45, 48, 50–51, 54–55, 64, 68, 72, 76, 78, 81, 83, 86–89, 92, 96, 99, 101, 108, 112, 124, 131, 136, 137, 144–45, 147, 154–55, 190, 199, 202, 213–15, 224, 232–33, 240, 242, 245, 259, 265–66, 269, 275, 277, 281, 284, 288, 291–92, 294, 297, 331, 338–40, 344, 347, 352, 357
Victorian Bible Institute, 198, 230, 277, 316
victorious living, 48, 304, 306–307, 318
Virgin Mary, 119
visions, 6, 32, 47, 93, 111, 145, 220, 294, 352, 356

Wales, 3, 4, 6, 23, 26, 28, 36, 38, 41, 50–51, 53–54, 64, 72, 78, 83, 86, 89, 99–101, 103, 116, 173, 199, 220–221, 225, 232–33, 236, 242, 253, 258, 280, 294, 330–31, 335, 337, 344
Wallaroo, 199, 339
WCTU, 264, 268, 356
Wellington, 50, 85, 233, 241, 257, 288, 330
Welsh Revival, 26, 94, 99, 103, 221, 235
Wesleyan revivalism, 83
Wesleyan revivalists, 44
Wesleyanism, 3, 25, 95
Western Australia, 14, 83, 154, 160–161, 185, 220, 235, 239, 257, 284, 286, 288, 298, 349
Western Australian, 128, 174
Woman's Christian Temperance Union (WCTU), 264
women, 3, 10, 13–14, 29, 45, 47–48, 53, 60, 71, 97, 108–109, 112, 124, 140–41, 145, 162, 166, 170, 184, 230, 243, 244, 248–49, 252, 257, 263–64, 265–71, 279–80, 283–93, 298, 300–301, 304, 339, 361
Wonthaggi., 111
World War II., 2, 5
Wyndham, 242

xenolalia, 17, 353

YMCA, 90, 214

York St Methodist Mission, 44
Zion city, 70
Zion, Illinois, 17, 211

www.ingramcontent.com/pod-product-compliance
Lightning Source LLC
Chambersburg PA
CBHW021814300426
44114CB00009BA/165